新制學測英文
10回決勝
模擬試題 [試題+詳解]

詳解本

TEST 01 ································· 2

TEST 02 ································· 32

TEST 03 ································· 64

TEST 04 ································· 94

TEST 05 ································· 126

TEST 06 ································· 158

TEST 07 ································· 188

TEST 08 ································· 218

TEST 09 ································· 250

TEST 10 ································· 282

TEST 01

第壹部分、選擇題
- 一、詞彙題
- 二、綜合測驗
- 三、文意選填
- 四、篇章結構
- 五、閱讀測驗

第貳部分、混合題

第參部分、非選擇題
- 一、中譯英
- 二、英文作文

第壹部分、選擇題

一、詞彙題

| 1. B | 2. C | 3. D | 4. A | 5. C | 6. B | 7. B | 8. A | 9. A | 10. D |

二、綜合測驗

| 11. D | 12. C | 13. C | 14. A | 15. B | 16. B | 17. C | 18. C | 19. D | 20. A |

三、文意選填

| 21. E | 22. A | 23. I | 24. B | 25. J | 26. F | 27. H | 28. D | 29. C | 30. G |

四、篇章結構

| 31. D | 32. C | 33. E | 34. A |

五、閱讀測驗

| 35. C | 36. C | 37. B | 38. B | 39. A | 40. B | 41. C | 42. D | 43. C | 44. D |
| 45. B | 46. C |

第貳部分、混合題

47. (A) performance   (B) focus

48. waiting lists (for certain procedures)

49. ☑ Sandra

50. ☑ Neither

第壹部分、選擇題（占 62 分）

一、詞彙題（占 10 分）

__B__ 1. 目前，尚不清楚烏克蘭是否<u>最終</u>能在與俄羅斯的戰爭中取得勝利。

- ⓐ (A) **essentially** [ɪˋsɛnʃəlɪ] *adv.* 本質上，基本上
  Tim's got his flaws, but he is essentially a nice guy.
  提姆是有他的缺點，但他本質上是個好人。

  (B) **eventually** [ɪˋvɛntʃʊəlɪ] *adv.* 最終，終究
  The ship will have to be repainted eventually.
  這艘船終究還是要重新上漆。

  (C) **partly** [ˋpɑrtlɪ] *adv.* 部分地
  I didn't enjoy the trip very much partly because of the bad weather.
  我不太喜歡這次旅行，部分是因為壞天氣。

  (D) **namely** [ˋnemlɪ] *adv.* 換言之，就是
  One group of people in particular will benefit from the proposal, namely the elderly.
  這項提案特別會讓一群人受益，也就是老年人。

- ⓑ 根據語意及用法，(B) 項應為正選。

> **必考重點**
>
> a. **at the moment** 目前，此刻
> I am very busy at the moment, so I can't talk to you for very long.
> 我現在非常忙，所以無法跟你講話講太久。
>
> b. **triumph** [ˋtraɪəmf] *vi.* 勝利，獲得成功 & *n.* 勝利，成功
> After months of hard work, the team finally triumphed over their competitors and won the championship.
> 經過數月的努力，這支隊伍終於戰勝了競爭對手，贏得了冠軍。

__C__ 2. 這公司決定將錢花在發展電動車上，因為他們相信投資這項產業時機<u>成熟</u>。

- ⓐ (A) **regretful** [rɪˋgrɛtfəl] *a.* 後悔的
  I'm regretful that I made such a mistake.
  我很後悔犯了這樣的錯。

  (B) **criminal** [ˋkrɪmənḷ] *a.* 犯法的
  Stealing is a criminal act.
  偷竊是犯法的行為。

3

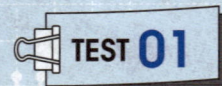

(C) **ripe** [raɪp] *a.* （農作物、時機）成熟的
The time is ripe for investing in this company.
現在正是投資這家公司的成熟時機。

(D) **swift** [swɪft] *a.* 迅速的，敏捷的，快的
A swift current carried the little boat down the river.
一道急流將小船順著河流沖走。

ⓑ 根據語意及用法，(C) 項應為正選。

必考重點

an electric vehicle　　電動車（縮寫為 EV）

D 3. 如果珊卓通過考試並取得駕照，她就能開車去上班而不用搭公車。

ⓐ (A) **reply** [rɪˋplaɪ] *n. & vi.* 回答，答覆
reply to / answer sb's question　　回答某人的問題
in reply to...　　回答……，答覆……
Many people called in reply to our ad for a job in the newspaper.
很多人打電話來回覆我們在報上登的徵人啟事。

(B) **signal** [ˋsɪgn̩l] *n.* 信號；標誌
You must obey the traffic signals.
你必須遵守交通號誌。

(C) **contract** [ˋkɑntrækt] *n.* 契約，合同
sign a contract　　簽約
After lengthy negotiations, we agreed to sign the contract.
在冗長的協商之後，我們同意簽訂這份契約。

(D) **license** [ˋlaɪsn̩s] *n.* 許可證，執照
a driver's license　　駕照
After checking my driver's license, the police officer told me to move on.
檢查過我的駕照後，那位警官叫我繼續上路。

ⓑ 根據語意及用法，(D) 項應為正選。

A 4. 我們應該捐一些食物和金錢幫助非洲的孩童，以免他們餓死。

ⓐ (A) **starve** [stɑrv] *vi. & vt.* （使）挨餓
starve (oneself) to death　　（把……某人）餓死
Those refugees will starve to death if the government does not lend a hand.
如果政府不伸出援手，那些難民就會餓死。

(B) **leak** [lik] *vi.* 漏，滲
We put some old towels on the floor to absorb the water leaking through the wall.
我們在地板上放了幾條舊毛巾來吸從牆壁滲出的水。

(C) **interfere** [ˌɪntɚˈfɪr] *vi.* 妨礙；干涉
interfere in... 干涉/干預……
interfere with... 妨礙……
Construction noise interfered with my afternoon nap.
工地建築的噪音妨礙了我的午睡。

(D) **negotiate** [nɪˈgoʃɪˌet] *vi.* 談判；協商
negotiate with... 與……談判/協商
Mary is negotiating with her boss for a raise.
瑪麗正和她老闆協商要求加薪。

ⓑ 根據語意及用法，(A) 項應為正選。

必考重點

a. **donate** [ˈdonet] *vt.* 捐獻，捐贈
Beth donated money to the charity to help people in need in Africa.
貝絲捐錢給該慈善機構以幫助非洲的窮困人民。

b. **prevent sb / sth from V-ing**
防止某人／某物……
You should put the meat into the fridge to prevent it from going bad.
你應該把肉放進冰箱以防它壞掉。

<u>C</u> 5. 傑克不是一個善於表達的人，所以你很難得知他的想法或感受。

ⓐ (A) **energetic** [ˌɛnɚˈdʒɛtɪk] *a.* 有活力的
Sabrina felt energetic after a good night's sleep.
莎賓娜在一夜好眠之後覺得活力充沛。

(B) **courageous** [kəˈredʒəs] *a.* 勇敢的
Winston Churchill was a courageous statesman.
溫斯頓・邱吉爾是個勇敢的政治家。

(C) **expressive** [ɪkˈsprɛsɪv] *a.* 善於表達的
be expressive of... 表達/流露出……
A baby's cry can be expressive of hunger.
嬰兒哭鬧可能表示他／她餓了。

(D) **carefree** [ˈkɛrˌfri] *a.* 無憂無慮的
Brenda has lived a carefree life since she was little.
布蘭達從小就過著無憂無慮的生活。

ⓑ 根據語意，(C) 項應為正選。

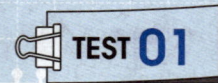

B 6. 雪莉昨天從腳踏車上摔下來，醫生說她的手腕有一點骨折。

ⓐ (A) **edge** [ɛdʒ] *n.* 邊緣
on the edge of... 在……的邊緣
Years of poor management have left the company on the edge of bankruptcy.
多年管理不善致使該公司瀕臨破產的邊緣。

(B) **fracture** [ˈfræktʃɚ] *n.* 骨折，斷裂
Vincent slipped in the bathroom while taking a shower and ended up with a fracture in his arm.
文森在浴室洗澡的時候滑倒，結果手臂骨折了。

(C) **ritual** [ˈrɪtʃuəl] *n.* 儀式，習俗
As this area was becoming increasingly civilized, many of the tribal rituals were lost.
這個地區日趨文明時，許多部落的習俗也跟著不見了。

(D) **hardship** [ˈhardʃɪp] *n.* 艱難，困苦
Despite his many hardships, Al finally succeeded in becoming an astronaut.
儘管困難重重，艾爾終於成為太空人。

ⓑ 根據語意，(B) 項應為正選。

B 7. 電影開始前請關掉你的手機，這樣鈴聲才不會打擾到其他觀眾。

ⓐ (A) **divide** [dəˈvaɪd] *vt.* 劃分
divide... into... 將……劃分為……
Let's divide the class into two groups.
我們來把全班分成兩組吧。

(B) **disturb** [dɪsˈtɝb] *vt.* 妨礙，打擾
Please don't disturb me while I'm working.
我在工作時請不要打擾我。

(C) **reveal** [rɪˈvil] *vt.* 透露；揭露
The agent was jailed for revealing secrets to the enemy.
該名探員因洩密給敵方而入獄。

(D) **satisfy** [ˈsætɪsˌfaɪ] *vt.* 使滿意
be satisfied with... 對……感到滿意
The teacher is not satisfied with your report.
老師對你的報告並不滿意。

ⓑ 根據語意，(B) 項應為正選。

必考重點

audience [ˈɔdɪəns] *n.* 觀眾；聽眾（集合名詞，不可數）
an audience of 500　　五百名觀眾（非 500 audiences）
The concert drew an audience of 20,000.
這場演唱會吸引了兩萬名觀眾。

A　8. 這場強烈地震對該地區造成嚴重的損害，並使得多棟建築物倒塌。

ⓐ (A) collapse [kəˈlæps] *vi.* 倒塌
　　Several people were trapped under the bridge when it collapsed.
　　那座橋梁倒塌時，有好幾個人被困在橋下。

(B) evolve [ɪˈvɑlv] *vi.* 進化，發展（與介詞 from 或 into 並用）
　　evolve from...　　由……演化／發展而來
　　evolve into...　　演化／發展為……
　　Most scientists believe that people evolved from apes.
　　大多數科學家認為人類是從猿猴演化過來的。
　　Though the company started very small, it evolved into a worldwide enterprise.
　　該公司雖然一開始規模很小，後來卻發展成一家全球企業。

(C) recover [rɪˈkʌvɚ] *vi.* 恢復（與介詞 from 並用）
　　recover from...　　自……中復原
　　It took Tim several years to recover from his serious illness.
　　提姆花了好幾年時間才從重病中復原。

(D) arise [əˈraɪz] *vi.* 升起；產生（三態為：arise, arose [əˈroz], arisen [əˈrɪzṇ]）
　　arise from...　　起因於……
　　The misunderstandings between Jack and Andy arose from a lack of communication.
　　傑克和安迪之間的誤會是由於缺乏溝通。

ⓑ 根據語意，(A) 項應為正選。

A　9. 在結婚典禮上，卡爾和妻子在親友面前承諾會對彼此忠貞。

ⓐ (A) faithful [ˈfeθfəl] *a.* 忠實的，忠貞的
　　be / stay faithful / true to...　　對……忠實／忠貞
　　Judy was always faithful to her word.
　　茱蒂總是言出必行。

(B) profitable [ˈprɑfɪtəbḷ] *a.* 有利可圖的
　　Buying and selling used cars is a highly profitable business.
　　買賣二手車是一項獲利很高的行業。

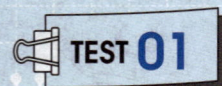

(C) **intelligent** [ɪnˈtɛlədʒənt] *a.* 聰明的，有才智的
Frank succeeded in his business because he was intelligent and diligent.
法蘭克的事業之所以成功是因為他既聰明又勤奮。

(D) **outgoing** [ˈaʊtˌɡoɪŋ] *a.* 外向的
David makes friends easily because of his outgoing personality.
大衛個性外向，因此很容易交上朋友。

ⓑ 根據語意及用法，(A) 項應為正選。

D **10.** 戴夫不知道怎麼清理他的傷口，所以弄髒了他的傷口並導致感染。

ⓐ (A) **imagination** [ɪˌmædʒəˈneʃən] *n.* 想像力
far beyond sb's imagination　　超出某人想像
exercise one's imagination　　發揮想像力
This story is made up and totally based on my imagination.
這故事完全是根據我的想像編造的。
The size of that building in Dubai is far beyond my imagination.
杜拜那棟建築物的規模遠遠超出我的想像。

(B) **distraction** [dɪˈstrækʃən] *n.* 使人分心的事物
Please hold all my calls. I don't want any distractions before the meeting.
請幫我接聽所有的電話。我不想在開會前分心處理其他的事。

(C) **attention** [əˈtɛnʃən] *n.* 注意
attract one's attention　　引起某人的注意
pay attention to N/V-ing　　注意……
The ants were attracted to the picnic table where someone had spilled some soda.
有人把汽水打翻在野餐桌上，吸引了螞蟻前來。
It is important that you pay attention to the expiration dates on food labels.
注意食物標籤上的有效日期是很重要的。

(D) **infection** [ɪnˈfɛkʃən] *n.* 感染
White blood cells help the body defend itself against infections.
白血球幫助我們的身體抵抗感染。

ⓑ 根據語意，(D) 項應為正選。

必考重點
a. **wound** [wund] *n.* 傷口 & *vt.* 使受傷
b. **result in...**　　造成……

二、綜合測驗（占 10 分）

第 11 至 15 題為題組

　　並非所有理想的島嶼觀光景點都在太平洋和印度洋上。當然，夏威夷、大溪地、帛琉以及馬爾地夫都是國際知名的「完美」度假勝地。地中海上的某些島嶼雖然沒有如此出名，但也絕對值得人們投入時間、金錢和心力來造訪。在這些島嶼之中，許多人都將希臘的聖托里尼島視為他們的首選。

　　聖托里尼位於希臘本土南方約兩百公里處，大約是去克里特島途中一半的位置。它提供給遊客的是異國風味的景觀及歷史地標。該島嶼是大約三千六百年前一場大型火山爆發所遺留下來的部分殘骸。此次事件徹底改變了聖托里尼的樣貌，創造了今日美麗的藍白建築群所在的著名懸崖。許多遊客就是衝著這些懸崖上奇佳的拍照景點和清澈透明的海水而來。

　　聖托里尼也擁有以該島在地食材所烹調的地方美食。有一種人氣選項是 *apochti*，是傳統的鹹豬肉菜餚，而 *chlorotyri* 則是聖托里尼獨有的山羊起司。若想要搭配飲料，遊客們可以試試當地釀製，曾獲得國際獎項的葡萄酒。

D 11. 理由

- (A) **shattered** [ˈʃætəd] *a.* 破滅的；破碎的
  Kenny's hopes of finding a better job were shattered.
  肯尼想要找到一份較好工作的希望破滅了。

- (B) **identical** [aɪˈdɛntɪkḷ] *a.* 完全相同的（與介詞 to 並用）
  be identical to...　和……完全相同
  To my surprise, Sam's answer is identical to yours.
  令我驚訝的是，山姆的答案跟你完全一樣。

- (C) **miserable** [ˈmɪzərəbḷ] *a.* 悲慘的
  Jasmine looked miserable after being scolded by her boss.
  潔絲敏被老闆罵過後看起來愁雲慘霧。

- (D) **renowned** [rɪˈnaʊnd] *a.* 有名的（= famous / noted / well known）
  be renowned as + 身分　以某身分而為人所知
  be renowned for...　以……而聞名
  George is renowned as a baseball player.
  喬治是知名棒球選手。
  This diplomat is renowned for his negotiation skills.
  這名外交官以談判技巧而聞名。

- 原題空格後有介詞 as，得知空格內應置形容詞 renowned，形成 be renowned as 的固定用法，故 (D) 項應為正選。

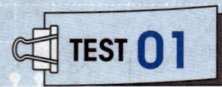

C 12. 理由

ⓐ 本句測試以否定副詞為首時，主詞與動詞應採倒裝的句構。空格前有否定副詞 Not 引導的片語 Not so well known but certainly worth the time, expense, and effort of getting there（雖然沒有如此出名，但也絕對值得人們投入時間、金錢和心力來造訪），空格後則有主詞 Some of the islands in the Mediterranean Sea（地中海上的某些島嶼），得知空格應置入 be 動詞複數形 are。原句實等於：<u>Some of the islands in the Mediterranean Sea are not so well known but are certainly worth the time, expense, and effort of getting there.</u>

ⓑ 根據上述，(C) 項應為正選。

C 13. 理由

ⓐ (A) religion [rɪˋlɪdʒən] *n.* 宗教
Many people believe that Buddhism is not just a religion, but a form of life.
許多人認為佛教不只是一種宗教，也是一種生活型態。

(B) routine [ruˋtin] *n.* 日常工作，例行公事
Linda learned to play tennis over time, and now it's part of her weekly routine.
琳達逐漸學會打網球，現在這已是她每星期的例行活動。

(C) explosion [ɪkˋsploʒən] *n.* 爆炸，爆破
= blast [blæst] *n.*
Incredibly, no one was killed in the horrible explosion.
不可思議的是，沒有人死於那場恐怖的爆炸事件。

(D) tribe [traɪb] *n.* 部落
Believe it or not, my grandfather was once the chief of that tribe.
信不信由你，我爺爺曾經是那個部落的酋長。

ⓑ 空格前有形容詞 volcanic（火山的），因此 (C) 項應為正選。

A 14. 理由

ⓐ 本題測試以下語意：(A) photo opportunities（拍照機會）、(B) purchasing experiences（購買經驗）、(C) life necessities（生活必需品）、(D) emergency kits（急救箱）。

ⓑ 根據語意，許多遊客為了欣賞這些懸崖美景而來，所以會想要拍照，故 (A) 項應為正選。

B 15. 理由

ⓐ (A) acute [əˋkjut] *a.* 敏銳的；急性的；嚴重的
Dogs have an acute sense of smell.
狗兒有敏銳的嗅覺。

(B) native [ˋnetɪv] *a.* 本地的，土生的
be native to + 地方　　為某地方所獨有

Kiwi birds are native to New Zealand.
鷸鴕是紐西蘭的原生種鳥類。

(C) **dreadful** [ˈdrɛdfəl] *a.* 可怕的
The dreadful explosion killed all the people on the spot.
這起可怕的爆炸事件使所有人當場喪生。

(D) **frank** [fræŋk] *a.* 坦白的
To be frank, ...　　坦白說，……
To be frank, I don't trust you.
坦白說，我不信任你。

ⓑ 根據語意及用法，(B) 項應為正選。

重要字詞片語

1. **destination** [ˌdɛstəˈneʃən] *n.* 目的地；終點
   a tourist destination　　觀光景點
2. **expense** [ɪkˈspɛns] *n.* 開銷，花費（常用複數）
   Ethan had to take a night job to cover his living expenses.
   伊森晚上也得兼差才夠付他的生活費。
3. **exotic** [ɪgˈzɑtɪk] *a.* 異國情調的
   Mary can transform a simple salad into an exotic dish.
   瑪麗能把一道簡單的沙拉變身成為充滿異國風味的佳餚。
4. **landmark** [ˈlændˌmɑrk] *n.* 地標
   The Statue of Liberty is one of America's most famous landmarks.
   自由女神像是美國最知名的地標之一。
5. **remains** [rɪˈmenz] *n.* 遺跡（恆用複數）
6. **massive** [ˈmæsɪv] *a.* 巨大的
   The massive earthquake caused extensive damage to the island.
   那場大地震對這座小島造成大規模的破壞。
7. **volcanic** [vɑlˈkænɪk] *a.* 火山的
8. **cuisine** [kwɪˈzin] *n.* 美食（不可數）
9. **be unique to + 地方**
   為某地方所獨有
10. **wash down sth**　　伴著飲料吃下……

<u>第 16 至 20 題為題組</u>

　　當我們想到十九、二十世紀的偉大畫家時，帕布羅·畢卡索、文森·梵谷和薩爾瓦多·達利便會浮現在腦海中。儘管上述幾個人作畫分處不同國家的不同時代，但他們有一項共通點：他們都是男性。女性畫家人數少得多也較不出名。但那並不代表她們的作品不值得欣賞。瑪麗·羅蘭珊就是明顯的例子。

　　二十世紀初是一段革命性的時期。就繪畫而言，以畢卡索、達利以及其他人為代表的立體派藝術家透過抽象而非寫實的畫作引發了視覺革命。身為立體派一員的羅蘭珊並不描繪女性在現實

TEST 01

生活中的樣貌，而是將她們描繪成為抽象女性特質的代表。然而立體派的畫風和羅蘭珊的畫存有相當大的差異。許多立體派畫家使用鮮豔甚至刺眼的色彩，羅蘭珊則偏好粉彩。立體派畫家傾向使用筆直而稜角尖銳的線條，而羅蘭珊則喜歡用曲線來描繪女性。

現在世界各地的博物館均可看到羅蘭珊的畫作，從她家鄉的巴黎到紐約與倫敦皆然。東京一度有一座專門展覽她作品的博物館。不過這間博物館已永久停業了。

B 16. 理由

ⓐ 本題測試以下固定用法：
have... in common　　有……共通點
As far as personality goes, Rachel has nothing in common with her twin sister.
就個性而言，瑞秋和她的雙胞胎妹妹完全不同。

ⓑ 根據上述，(B) 項應為正選。

C 17. 理由

ⓐ 空格後有比較級形容詞 fewer（較少的），得知空格應置副詞以修飾 fewer。

ⓑ 可用來修飾比較級形容詞或副詞的有下列副詞或副詞片語：
far, much, a lot, a great deal, still, even
In a word, practice is far more important than book knowledge.
簡言之，實踐遠比書本上的知識來得重要。
This question is a great deal more difficult than that one.
這個題目比那個題目要難得多。

ⓒ 根據上述，(C) 項應為正選。

C 18. 理由

ⓐ 空格前有否定副詞 not，得知空格應置連接詞 but，形成 not... but...（不是……而是……）對等連接詞的用法。
Ellen works not in Taiwan but in the Philippines.
　　　　　　　介詞片語　　　　介詞片語
艾倫工作的地方不在臺灣，而是在菲律賓。
Josh is not a professional golfer but an amateur.
　　　　　　名詞　　　　　　　名詞
喬許不是職業高爾夫選手，而是業餘玩家。

ⓑ 根據上述，由於本句 not 後面有 as，空格後也有 as，且 real life 與 abstract 為相反意思，可得知空格應置 but 以形成對等用法，故 (C) 項應為正選。

D 19. 理由

ⓐ 本題測試以下語意：(A) possible answers（可能的答案）、(B) ancient relics（古代的遺跡）、(C) various supporters（各種支持者）、(D) important differences（重大差異）。

ⓑ 根據後面幾句皆提及立體派藝術家與羅蘭珊創作的方式不同，可得知 (D) 項應為正選。

A 20. 理由

ⓐ 本題測試以下語意：(A) around the world（世界各地）、(B) in the public interest（對大眾有利）、(C) only in imagination（只在想像中）、(D) beyond description（難以描述）。

ⓑ 空格後提及從她的家鄉巴黎到紐約到倫敦的城市，可從語意中推知，(A) 項應為正選。

TEST 01

重要字詞片語

1. **come to mind**
   浮現腦海，湧上心頭
   When people think about the latest inventions for transportation, driverless cars come to mind.
   當人們想到交通方面的最新發明時，自駕車就會浮現在腦海。

2. **appreciate** [əˋprɪʃɪ͵et] *vt.* 欣賞；感激
   Only a few people could appreciate this beautiful poem.
   只有少數人懂得欣賞這首優美的詩。
   Eric never appreciates what his mother does for him.
   艾瑞克從不感激他媽媽為他所做的一切。

3. **a case in point**　明顯的例子
   Joyce is one of the greatest singers of all time, and her latest album is a case in point.
   喬伊絲是有史以來最偉大的歌手之一，她最新的專輯就是個明顯的例子。

4. **revolutionary** [͵rɛvəˋluʃən͵ɛrɪ] *a.* 革命性的
   revolution [͵rɛvəˋluʃən] *n.* 革命

5. **Cubist** [ˋkjubɪst] *n.* 立體派藝術家

6. **represent** [͵rɛprɪˋzɛnt] *vt.* 代表
   representative [͵rɛprɪˋzɛntətɪv] *n.* 代表 & *a.* 代表……的
   George represented his company at the press conference.
   喬治代表公司出席記者會。

7. **bring about...**　促成／導致……
   = lead to...
   = result in...
   The deforestation in the Amazon will bring about dramatic changes in the global climate.
   亞馬遜河流域的森林砍伐會導致全球氣候的巨大變化。

8. **abstract** [ˋæbstrækt] *a.* 抽象的
   I was able to grasp the artist's meaning even though his work was abstract.
   雖然這位藝術家的作品很抽象，我卻能理解他的含義。

9. **depict** [dɪˋpɪkt] *vt.* 描繪，形容
   = describe [dɪˋskraɪb] *vt.*
   depict A as B　把 A 描述／形容成 B
   = describe A as B
   Al depicted his ex-wife as an alcoholic.
   艾爾把他的前妻形容為酒鬼。

10. **femininity** [͵fɛməˋnɪnətɪ] *n.* 女性特質（不可數）

11. **glaring** [ˋglɛrɪŋ] *a.* 刺眼的，閃耀的

12. **pastel** [pæsˋtɛl] *n.* 粉彩；粉蠟筆

13. **angular** [ˋæŋgjələ] *a.* 有角的

14. **rejoice** [rɪˋdʒɔɪs] *vi.* 欣喜（常與介詞 in 並用）
    If we can learn to rejoice in others' success, our own happiness will increase.
    我們若能學習為他人的成功感到開心，自己也會更快樂。

13

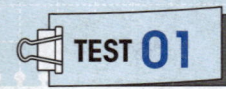

三、文意選填（占 10 分）

第 21 至 30 題為題組

　　polo 衫是現今最受歡迎的衣物之一。儘管名稱如此，穿 polo 衫並不代表需要在馬球比賽上騎著馬，揮舞著長長的木槌，打著小球。時至今日，這種襯衫被視為時髦的休閒裝扮，也是一種運動風格的象徵。

　　雖然這種襯衫經常與馬球有關，不過它其實源自網球運動。從十九世紀末至二十世紀初，網球員通常穿著筆挺的白色長袖鈕扣襯衫，並把袖子捲起，再搭配領帶和法蘭絨長褲。某些人認為這些衣服不適合這種移動迅速又劇烈的運動。值得慶幸的是，名叫何內・拉科斯特的法國人出現了。這位贏得七次網球大滿貫賽事冠軍的男子設計出寬鬆的白色短袖 T 恤以解決這個問題。他在 1926 年的美國網球公開賽上首度穿著這種比較實用且舒適的襯衫。然後拉科斯特為了認可媒體封給他的綽號「鱷魚」，他在作品上加了綠色鱷魚的標誌。他在 1930 年代初期退休之後，與商人安德烈・吉利耶合作成立一間公司並大量生產他的襯衫。襯衫大受歡迎，馬球選手很快就將他們自己既笨重又不舒適的服裝換成類似於拉科斯特所設計的襯衫。儘管網球運動比馬球運動還早採用這款襯衫，但在不久之後，網球選手便開始將其襯衫稱作 polo 衫。到了 1950 年代，所有人都這麼稱呼它。此外，職業高爾夫球選手也開始穿這種適合運動的襯衫來作為他們標準服裝的一部分。

　　如今，拉科斯特公司生產各式各樣的體育用品和服裝。現在不難在球場內外看到穿著繡有綠色鱷魚圖案、白色短袖運動衫的人。

E 21. 理由
- ⓐ 空格前有不定冠詞 a 及形容詞 sporty（愛好運動的），得知空格應置單數名詞。
- ⓑ 選項中符合上述的有 (B) fix（解決方案）、(C) standard（標準）、(E) attitude（態度；看法）及 (G) range（範圍），惟根據語意，(E) 項應為正選。

A 22. 理由
- ⓐ 空格前有對等連接詞 and，空格後有受格 them，且對等連接詞前有一過去式及物動詞 wore，得知空格亦應置入過去式及物動詞以形成對等。
- ⓑ 選項中符合上述的有 (A) paired（搭配）及 (D) adopted（採用），惟根據語意，且由空格後的 with 可知，(A) 項應為正選，以形成 pair A with B 的固定用法。

I 23. 理由
- ⓐ 空格前有形容詞 fast-moving（移動迅速的）及對等連接詞 and，空格後有名詞 sport（運動），得知空格亦應置入形容詞以形成對等。
- ⓑ 選項中符合上述的有 (C) standard（標準的）、(D) adopted（領養的）、(F) retiring（即將退休的）及 (I) vigorous（劇烈的；活力充沛的），惟根據語意，(I) 項應為正選。

B 24. 理由
ⓐ 空格前有引導不定詞片語的 to，空格後有名詞詞組 the problem（這個問題），得知空格應置入原形及物動詞。
ⓑ 選項中符合上述的有 (B) fix（解決）及 (J) acknowledge（認可），惟根據語意，且 fix a / the problem（解決問題）為固定用法，故 (B) 項應為正選。

J 25. 理由
ⓐ 空格前有引導不定詞片語的 to，空格後有名詞詞組 his press-given nickname（媒體封給他的綽號），得知空格應置入原形及物動詞。
ⓑ 選項中符合上述的僅剩 (J) acknowledge（認可），置入後亦符合語意，故為正選。

F 26. 理由
ⓐ 空格前有連接詞 After，空格後有時間介詞片語，而後則有主要子句，得知空格應置入現在分詞，且不及物，以形成副詞片語。原句實為：
After he retired in the early 1930s, he teamed up with businessman...
連接詞引導的副詞子句的主詞，若與主要子句的主詞相同，則此副詞子句可化簡為副詞片語，即：刪除副詞子句的主詞後，其後動詞化為現在分詞，若該動詞為 be 動詞時，變成現在分詞 being 之後通常予以省略。
ⓑ 選項中符合上述的僅剩 (F) retiring（退休），置入後亦符合語意，故為正選。

H 27. 理由
ⓐ 空格前有過去式 be 動詞 were，空格後有名詞詞組 their own heavy and uncomfortable attire（他們自己既笨重又不舒適的服裝），得知空格應置入及物動詞的現在分詞，以形成過去進行式。
ⓑ 選項中符合上述的僅剩 (H) replacing（替換），置入後亦符合語意，故為正選，並與空格後的 with 形成 replace A with B 的固定用法。

D 28. 理由
ⓐ 空格前有過去完成式助動詞 had，空格後有代名詞 it，得知空格應置入及物動詞的過去分詞。
ⓑ 選項中符合上述的僅剩 (D) adopted（採用），置入後亦符合語意，故為正選。

C 29. 理由
ⓐ 空格前有所有格 their（他們的），空格後有名詞 attire（服裝），得知空格應置入形容詞以修飾 attire。
ⓑ 選項中符合上述的僅剩 (C) standard（標準的），置入後亦符合語意，故為正選。

G 30. 理由
ⓐ 空格前有形容詞 wide（廣泛的），空格後有介詞 of，得知空格應置入名詞以被 wide 修飾。
ⓑ 選項中符合上述的僅剩 (G) range（範圍），置入後形成固定用法 a (wide) range of（各種的……，各式各樣的……），亦符合語意，故為正選。

TEST 01

重要字詞片語

1. **an article of clothing / furniture**
   一件衣服／傢俱
   clothing [ˈkloðɪŋ] *n.* 衣物（集合名詞，不可數）

2. **be associated with...**
   和……有關聯；和……聯想在一起

3. **stiff** [stɪf] *a.* 筆挺的，挺直的；僵硬的

4. **sleeve** [sliv] *n.* 袖子
   sleeveless [ˈslivləs] *a.* 無袖的

5. **flannel** [ˈflænl] *n.* 法蘭絨（不可數）

6. **unsuitable** [ʌnˈsutəbl̩] *a.* 不合適的
   suitable [ˈsutəbl̩] *a.* 合適的

7. **come along**   出現

8. **champion** [ˈtʃæmpɪən] *n.* 冠軍
   championship [ˈtʃæmpɪənˌʃɪp] *n.* 冠軍地位／頭銜

9. **practical** [ˈpræktɪkl̩] *a.* 實用的；實際的

10. **team up with sb**   與某人合作

11. **mass-produce** [ˌmæsprəˈd(j)us] *vt.* 大量生產

12. **attire** [əˈtaɪr] *n.*（正式的）服裝（不可數）

13. **refer to A as B**   把 A 稱作 B

14. **professional** [prəˈfɛʃnl̩] *n.* 職業選手；專家 & *a.* 專業的；職業的

15. **spot** [spɑt] *vt.* 看到，發現（三態為：spot, spotted [ˈspɑtɪd], spotted）

16. **athletic** [æθˈlɛtɪk] *a.* 運動的

四、篇章結構（占 8 分）

第 31 至 34 題為題組

　　米麗娜‧卡寧是一名蘇格蘭格拉斯哥附近一個大城鎮的女性。二十幾歲的時候健康出現一連串問題，她的醫生替她進行了人工昏迷治療。五十二天後，卡寧醒了過來，但卻沒了視力。她告訴 BBC：「當我醒來，我什麼也看不見。」31. 醫生告訴她，她因為罹患中風而失明。接著幾個月之後，奇怪的事情開始發生了。卡寧雖然眼盲，卻時常在腦中看見顏色。當她告訴醫生這件事時，醫生讓她與視覺科學教授戈登‧杜頓取得聯繫。杜頓決定進行一個實驗。32. 他在走廊上放了幾張椅子，叫卡寧走向它們。卡寧第一次嘗試時撞到了椅子。然後，教授叫她用快一點的速度再試一次。讓大家驚訝的是，她一張椅子都沒撞到。

　　杜頓告訴她，她有「盲視」，這是影響全球少數盲人的一種不尋常症狀。33. 他解釋說，我們的大腦有不同的路徑來幫助我們看見並感知物體。如果這些路徑全被破壞，我們就會「完全」失明。不過如果只有一些路徑受損，就可能出現盲視。雖然有盲視的人在生理上是看不見的，他們的潛意識卻保留了感知周遭環境的能力。這個神祕的能力似乎在當事者不專注或不太過於想看東西時最能發揮出來。34. 這樣能使他們的潛意識取得掌控來發揮這個能力。舉例來說，卡寧儘管失明，還是可以打掃家裡。她的大腦會自動促使她繞過地面上的東西，就算生理上她看不見它們。她不知怎地就是「知道」它們在那裡。卡寧告訴 BBC：「因為我是盲人，所以我應該看不到

東西，但卻看得見，這是一件很奇怪的事。」可是如果她試著專注，看東西這件事就會變得較為困難。盲視已讓科學家們知道，關於視覺方面和人類大腦仍有很多需要了解的地方。

D 31. 理由
- ⓐ 空格前提及，卡寧在接受人工昏迷治療後，醒來卻失去視力，空格後則提及，卡寧雖然眼盲卻能在腦中看見顏色，可推測空格應會提及造成卡寧失明的詳細原因。
- ⓑ 選項 (D) 表示，醫生告訴她，她因為罹患中風而失明，且選項中的 had gone blind（失明）與第三句的 without her eyesight（沒了視力）相呼應，填入後語意連貫，可知 (D) 項應為正選。

C 32. 理由
- ⓐ 空格前的句子提到，杜頓決定要做某實驗，而空格後的句子提到，卡寧在過程中撞到了椅子，可推測空格應置與椅子相關的句子。
- ⓑ 選項 (C) 表示，他在走廊上放了幾張椅子，叫卡寧走向它們，選項中的 asked Cunning to walk towards them（叫卡寧走向它們）與空格後的 Cunning crashed into the chairs（卡寧撞到了椅子）相呼應，填入後語意連貫，可知 (C) 項應為正選。

E 33. 理由
- ⓐ 空格前的句子提到，杜頓告訴卡寧她有「盲視」，而空格後的句子提到，如果它們全被破壞，我們就會「完全」失明，可推測空格應提及關於失明的一些資訊。
- ⓑ 選項 (E) 表示，他解釋說，我們的大腦有不同的路徑來幫助我們看見並感知物體，且空格後一句的代名詞 these（它們）即為選項中的 pathways（路徑），填入後語意連貫，可知 (E) 項應為正選。

A 34. 理由
- ⓐ 空格前提及，有盲視的人在潛意識中仍能感覺周遭，並說明最能發揮這個能力的情況，空格後則提及某項例子，可推測空格應置與潛意識有關，並符合空格後所舉例子情況的句子。
- ⓑ 選項 (A) 表示，這樣能使他們的潛意識取得掌控來發揮這個能力，填入後語意連貫，可知 (A) 項應為正選。

(B) 項中譯：幸好，卡寧的視力在意外發生六個月後恢復正常。

重要字詞片語

1. **coma** [ˈkomə] *n.* 昏迷
2. **stroke** [strok] *n.* 中風
   suffer / have a stroke　　中風
3. **crash into...**　　撞上……
4. **at a(n) + 形容詞 + pace**
   以……的速度/步調
   The army marched at a steady pace.
   部隊以穩定的步伐行軍。
5. **To one's amazement, ...**
   令某人吃驚的是，……
6. **bump into...**　　撞到……
7. **pathway** [ˈpæθˌwe] *n.* 路徑；道路
8. **unconscious** [ʌnˈkɑnʃəs] *a.* 潛意識的，無意識的；昏迷的 & *n.* 潛意識（不可數）
   an unconscious mind　　潛意識

TEST 01

9. **retain** [rɪˋten] *vt.* 保留
10. **mysterious** [mɪsˋtɪrɪəs] *a.* 神祕的
11. **subconscious** [sʌbˋkɑnʃəs] *a.* 潛意識的，下意識的 & *n.* 潛意識，下意識（不可數）
12. **take over (sth)**　　接管（某事物）
13. **manage to V**　　設法做成……
14. **automatically** [ˌɔtəˋmætɪkəlɪ] *adv.* 自動地；不自覺地
15. **nudge** [nʌdʒ] *vt.* 推進；以肘輕推
    I'm sorry. I didn't mean to nudge you when I got on the bus.
    很抱歉。上公車時我不是故意要推你的。

五、閱讀測驗（占 24 分）

第 35 至 38 題為題組

　　雪梨歌劇院是世界上最具指標性的建築之一。聳立於雪梨港，猶如層層堆疊貝殼的結構，其實是專為藝文活動建造的建築群。

Ecaterina Sciuchina / Shutterstock.com

　　在雪梨打造一座藝文中心這個想法，早在一九四○年代後期便開始萌芽。隨著澳洲逐漸成為更發達又富裕的國家，該國最大且成長最快的雪梨市的政府，認為有必要興建一座能提供各種藝術表演場地的中心。1955 年時為這座中心舉辦了一場國際設計競圖。兩年後，一位名叫約恩‧烏松的丹麥建築師獲選主導此建築群的施工，又再過了兩年後才開工。由於工程十分複雜，因此一開始就被分為三個階段。

　　歌劇院的施工過程遇到相當多困難。該建築的新穎設計造成諸多問題，花費了相當多時間試圖決定建造「貝殼」屋頂的方式。工期受到滂沱大雨和強風影響，幾乎從開工當天起進度就落後。還有就是約恩‧烏松在幾年後請辭。後面這個事件的原因是他和澳洲繼任的政府之間意見分歧，以及澳府不同程度上的干預。烏松最終在 1966 年退出計畫，由澳洲建築師彼得‧霍爾接替。霍爾監督剩餘工程直到 1973 年完工為止，完工時間晚了十年，且預算也嚇人地變成原來的十四倍。霍爾被視為替此案帶來了全新的明確目標。然而當講到這個舉世聞名建築的設計與建造時，人們總是會想到烏松的名字。

C 35. 本文的主要目的是什麼？
(A) 呼籲大眾支持藝術。
(B) 告知大眾即將舉行的藝術活動。
(C) 詳述某著名建築的歷史。
(D) 講述某知名建築師的生平故事。
理由
全文旨在介紹雪梨歌劇院的建造緣由及其過程，故 (C) 項應為正選。

C 36. 雪梨歌劇院的工程是什麼時候開始的？
(A) 1940 年代後期。
(B) 1955 年。
(C) 1959 年。
(D) 1973 年。

> 理由
>
> 根據本文第二段第三、四句，1955 年時為這座中心舉辦了一場國際設計競圖。兩年後，一位名叫約恩・烏松的丹麥建築師獲選主導此建築群的施工，又再過了兩年後才開工，故 (C) 項應為正選。

B 37. 誰是彼得・霍爾？
(A) 支持建造歌劇院的政府部長。 (B) 接替約恩・烏松的建築師。
(C) 在歌劇院表演的男演員。 (D) 啟發約恩・烏松創作的設計師。

> 理由
>
> 根據本文第三段第六句，烏松最終在 1966 年退出計畫，由澳洲建築師彼得・霍爾接替，故 (B) 項應為正選。

B 38. 建造歌劇院的過程中，本文未提及遇到哪項問題？
(A) 首席建築師請辭。 (B) 大眾對該建案興趣缺缺。
(C) 惡劣天候的出現。 (D) 特殊設計造成的困難。

> 理由
>
> 本文第三段依序提及建造歌劇院過程中遇到的問題，包含因建築新穎的設計遇到問題、工期受天氣影響，以及原本負責的建築師約恩・烏松請辭，全文未提及缺乏大眾的關注，故 (B) 項應為正選。

重要字詞片語

1. **iconic** [aɪˋkɑnɪk] *a.* 具代表性的
2. **harbour** [ˋhɑrbɚ] *n.* 海港，港口（此為英式拼法，美式拼法為 harbor）
3. **dedicate** [ˋdɛdə͵ket] *vt.* 獻給
   dedicate A to B　　把 A 獻給 B
   The generous man dedicated a large sum of money to the charity.
   這名慷慨的男子捐了一大筆錢給這間慈善機構。
4. **rapidly** [ˋræpɪdlɪ] *adv.* 迅速地
5. **venue** [ˋvɛnju] *n.* （舉辦）場所，地點
6. **sophisticated** [səˋfɪstə͵ketɪd] *a.* 精密複雜的
7. **divide** [dɪˋvaɪd] *vt. & vi.* （使）劃分
   divide (sth) into...　（把某物）分成……
   Darren divided the pizza into eight slices.
   達倫把披薩分成八塊。
8. **encounter** [ɪnˋkaʊntɚ] *vt.* 遭遇
9. **novel** [ˋnɑvl] *a.* 新奇的
10. **determine** [dɪˋtɝmɪn] *vt.* 決定，確定
11. **torrential** [təˋrɛnʃəl] *a.* 傾瀉的，急流般的
    torrential rain　　傾盆大雨
12. **resign** [rɪˋzaɪn] *vi.* 辭職
13. **successive** [səkˋsɛsɪv] *a.* 接續的；相繼的，連續的
14. **input** [ˋɪn͵pʊt] *n.* （提供的）建議，想法
15. **interference** [͵ɪntɚˋfɪrəns] *n.* 阻礙，干預（不可數）
16. **oversee** [͵ovɚˋsi] *vt.* 監督，監察
    （三態為：oversee, oversaw [͵ovɚˋsɔ], overseen [͵ovɚˋsin]）
17. **staggering** [ˋstægərɪŋ] *a.* 驚人的
18. **sb is credited with sth**
    某事要歸功於某人
    = sth is credited to sb

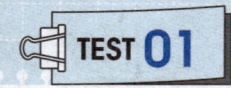

Emma is credited with the success of this project.
= The success of this project is credited to Emma.
這項計畫的成功是艾瑪的功勞。

19. **be associated with...** 與……有關
The manager believed the failure of the project was associated with poor teamwork.
經理認為該專案的失敗和團隊合作不良有關。

20. **renowned** [rɪˋnaund] *a.* 著名的
21. **take over (from sb)**
接管／接任（某人的職務）
Cole has taken over from the previous manager since she retired two months ago.
自前任經理兩個月前退休後，就由柯爾接管她的職務。
22. **inspire** [ɪnˋspaɪr] *vt.* 鼓舞，激勵，啟發

第 39 至 42 題為題組

　　想像有個國家面積是臺灣的三倍大，但人口卻只有三十六萬六千人。那個國家就是冰島，全世界最與眾不同的國家之一。

　　冰島位於北大西洋和北冰洋的交界處，一年大多處於天寒地凍的狀態。不過由於墨西哥灣的溫暖洋流流經此處，冰島有幸享有溫帶而非極地氣候。夏季溫度在攝氏十到二十度之間，十一月到三月之間的均溫會降到剛好低於零度。不過不意外地，冰島還是有相當的冰雪量。冰河覆蓋該國約 10% 的土地。苔原則占全島近三分之二面積，樹木無法在苔原上生長，因為地面下是永久的凍土。冰島有一百多座火山，堪稱全球地質最活躍的區域之一。因此當地的地震相當頻繁，但都不嚴重。

　　漁業向來是冰島經濟相當重要的一環，該產業如今仍占該國每年約 40% 的出口收入。不過不是所有漁產都用來出口，因為海產在冰島飲食中扮演不可或缺的角色，鱈魚和黑線鱈是最常見的兩種食材。冰島最臭名昭彰的海鮮大概就是 *hákarl*（發酵鯊魚肉）了。由於它會散發出阿摩尼亞的酸臭味，所以通常只會少量食用。毫無心理準備的遊客掙扎著將其吃下肚甚或吐出來的故事，可說不計其數。

　　觀光業每年吸引超過一百萬名遊客，大多數人前往當地觀賞冰河、火山，以及棲息於冰島海岸附近的多種鯨魚。儘管包含上述景點和瀑布、間歇泉的冰島之旅十分受歡迎，但大部分遊客會選擇住在首都雷克雅未克。冰島有三分之二的人居住在大雷克雅未克市區，該城市的發展遠超過其他地區，亦相當靠近另一處熱門旅遊景點 —— 名為藍湖的地熱溫泉。

A 39. 本文第二段的主旨為何？
(A) 描述冰島的地質與地理情況。 (B) 描述冰島的經濟風貌。
(C) 介紹某些棲息於冰島的稀有動物。 (D) 解釋為何冰島的人口如此稀少。

理由
本文第二段旨在介紹冰島的地理位置及地質狀況，故 (A) 項應為正選。

B 40. 下列哪一項最接近第二段中 temperate 的意思？
(A) 夏季特別熱。
(B) 不會太熱或太冷。
(C) 可能下很多雪。
(D) 會突然出現極端溫度。

> 理由
> 第二段的 temperate 前提及 warm ocean current（溫暖洋流），後文亦提及 rather than a polar climate（非極地氣候），可推測 temperate 為「溫帶的，溫和的」之意，故 (B) 項應為正選。

C 41. 根據本文，冰島的遊客最有可能如何形容 *hákarl*？
(A) 芬芳的。
(B) 令人食指大動的。
(C) 讓人反胃的。
(D) 吸引人的。

> 理由
> 根據本文第三段最後一句，毫無心理準備的遊客掙扎著將其吃下肚甚或吐出來的故事，可說不計其數，可推測 (C) 項應為正選。

D 42. 作者如何在最後一段下結論？
(A) 透過列出雷克雅未克區域的著名旅遊景點。
(B) 透過提供更多環島旅遊的細節資訊。
(C) 透過說明冰島的溫泉文化歷史。
(D) 透過提及駐足首都的另一個原因。

> 理由
> 本文最後一段提及前往冰島的遊客大多會選擇住在首都雷克雅未克，並說到該城市離另一個熱門景點藍湖很近，故 (D) 項應為正選。

重要字詞片語

1. **Atlantic** [ət`læntɪk] *n.* 大西洋（前須置定冠詞 the）& *a.* 大西洋的
   the Atlantic (Ocean)　大西洋
2. **Arctic** [`ɑrktɪk] *n.* 北極（海）（前須置定冠詞 the）& *a.* 北極的
   the Arctic (Ocean)　北冰洋，北極海
3. **current** [`kɝənt] *n.* 水流；氣流
   an ocean current　洋流
4. **gulf** [gʌlf] *n.* 海灣
5. **polar** [`polɚ] *a.* 極地的
6. **one's (fair) share of...**
   某人應得／應分擔的一份……
   Ed has done his fair share of the scientific research project.
   艾德已完成該科學研究專案中自己應做的部分。
7. **glacier** [`gleʃɚ] *n.* 冰河
8. **tundra** [`tʌndrə] *n.* 苔原
9. **severe** [sə`vɪr] *a.* （十分）嚴重的
10. **account for...**　占……
    Imports account for half of our economy.
    進口貿易占我們經濟規模的一半。
11. **integral** [`ɪntəgrəl] *a.* 不可或缺的
12. **ferment** [fɝ`mɛnt] *vt.* & *vi.* （使）發酵
    （文中為過去分詞作形容詞用）
13. **foul** [faʊl] *a.* 惡劣的
14. **ammonia** [ə`monjə] *n.* 阿摩尼亞；氨（不可數）
15. **abound** [ə`baʊnd] *vi.* 大量存在
16. **encompass** [ɪn`kʌmpəs] *vt.* 包含

TEST 01

17. **geyser** [ˈɡaɪzɚ] *n.* 間歇泉
18. **inhabitant** [ɪnˈhæbɪtənt] *n.* 居民
19. **reside** [rɪˈzaɪd] *vi.* 居住
    reside in + 地方　居住在某地
    Around 500 people reside in this small village.
    約有五百人住在這個小村落。
20. **geothermal** [ˌdʒioˈθɝml] *a.* 地熱的
21. **lagoon** [ləˈɡun] *n.* 潟湖
22. **geology** [dʒiˈɑlədʒɪ] *n.* 地質（學）（不可數）
23. **geography** [dʒɪˈɑɡrəfɪ] *n.* 地理（學）（不可數）

第 43 至 46 題為題組

　　捻角山羊是主要棲息在中亞、南亞的大型野生山羊，大多在巴基斯坦的山區，牠們亦是該國的國獸。捻角山羊出現在巴基斯坦情報局的標誌上，有段時間也曾是該國航空公司標誌的其中一部分。

　　關於捻角山羊的名字，有一說為源自波斯語的「食蛇者」。當地的傳說講述捻角山羊會用牠們的螺旋狀長角獵殺並吃掉蛇，然後吐一種泡沫狀的東西在地上。當地人會用此泡沫來做為據說可治療蛇咬的解藥。另一說是捻角山羊的名字取自牠們形狀如蛇般的羊角。還有一個說法指出其名譯自烏都語的「螺絲角山羊」，因為牠們的羊角也形似開瓶器。

　　除了獨特的羊角外，捻角山羊的其他身體特徵也很突出。牠們是山羊科中最高和最重的品種之一，高度可達一百五十五公分，體重可達一百一十公斤。冬天時牠們會長出又厚又長的毛來保暖。公羊和母羊都有鬍子，不過公羊的鬍子較長，會往下長至胸部。

　　這樣的毛能讓捻角山羊在山區不至於寒冷，在山區，牠們運用卓越的攀爬技巧，跟畜養山羊在夏季時爭奪綠草，冬季時爭食樹葉。冬天亦是交配季，在這段期間公羊彼此角鬥以吸引母羊的注意。不過一年之中大部分的時間，公羊會留下母羊和小羊，獨自出去覓食。

　　儘管牠們擁有在山崖間如履平地，讓人類望塵莫及的技能，捻角山羊仍面臨人類的持續威脅。獵人為了牠們珍貴且獨特的羊角追捕牠們。當地人則獵捕牠們為食。因此國際自然保護聯盟將捻角山羊列為「近危物種」。然而，有初步的跡象顯示捻角山羊的數量可能正在增加。

C 43. 下列哪一項並非「捻角山羊」名字起源的說法？
　　(A) 其名與吃掉某種爬蟲類動物有關。　　(B) 其名與紅酒開瓶器有關。
　　(C) 其名源自某飛機的外觀。　　(D) 其名與某動物的形狀有關。

> **理由**
> 根據本文第二段提及一些關於捻角山羊名字起源的說法，包含來自波斯語的「食蛇者」、和形狀如蛇般的羊角有關，以及羊角形狀類似開瓶器，全段落未提及與飛機外觀有關，故 (C) 項應為正選。

D 44. 第二段中的 this 指的是什麼？
　　(A) 捻角山羊的羊角。　　(B) 捻角山羊吃掉的動物。
　　(C) 捻角山羊居住的地方。　　(D) 捻角山羊留在地上的液體。

22

> 理由
>
> 根據本文第二段中 this 所在的句子前提及捻角山羊會吐一種泡沫狀的東西在地上，因此可推測 this 即指該泡沫，故 (D) 項應為正選。

B 45. 根據本文，下列哪一張圖片最接近捻角山羊的模樣？

(A)

(B)

(C)

(D)

> 理由
>
> 根據本文第二段最後兩句提及，捻角山羊的羊角形似蛇、開瓶器，再根據第三段最後一句，公羊和母羊都有鬍子，不過公羊的鬍子較長，會往下長至胸部，得知 (B) 項應為正選。

C 46. 根據本文，下列哪一項會對捻角山羊的未來造成威脅？
(A) 攀爬山嶺的能力退化。　　　　(B) 母羊拙劣的獵捕方式。
(C) 獵人覬覦牠們高價的身體部位。　(D) 較冷月份的食物匱乏。

> 理由
>
> 根據本文最後一段第二句，獵人為了牠們珍貴且獨特的羊角追捕牠們，故 (C) 項應為正選。

> 重要字詞片語
>
> 1. **feature** [ˈfitʃɚ] *vi. & vt.* 以……為特色 & *n.* 特徵，特色
> 2. **intelligence** [ɪnˈtɛlədʒəns] *n.* 情報；智慧（皆不可數）
> 3. **Persian** [ˈpɝʒən] *n.* 波斯語／人 & *a.* 波斯（語／人）的
> 4. **spiral** [ˈspaɪrḷ] *n.* 螺旋 & *a.* 螺旋的

TEST 01

5. **spit** [spɪt] *vt.* 吐出（三態為：spit, spat [spæt] / spit, spat / spit）
6. **foamy** [ˈfomɪ] *a.* 泡沫的
7. **substance** [ˈsʌbstəns] *n.* 物質
8. **supposed** [səˈpozd] *a.* 據說的；所謂的
9. **derive** [dɪˈraɪv] *vi.* 源自
    derive from...　　源自……
    The story derives from an old legend.
    這篇故事源自一則古老傳說。
10. **screw** [skru] *n.* 螺絲
11. **corkscrew** [ˈkɔrkˌskru] *n.* （拔軟木塞的）開瓶器，螺旋拔塞器
12. **aside from...**　　除了……
 = apart from...
 = except for...
    Aside from going hiking, Matt seldom takes part in outdoor activities.
    除了健行外，麥特很少從事戶外活動。
13. **appearance** [əˈpɪrəns] *n.* 外表
14. **remarkable** [rɪˈmɑrkəbḷ] *a.* 非凡的
15. **terrain** [təˈren] *n.* 地形，地勢
16. **domestic** [dəˈmɛstɪk] *a.* 馴養的；家庭的；國內的
17. **mate** [met] *vt. & vi.* （使）交配（文中為現在分詞作形容詞用）
18. **lock horns**
    以角互鬥；開始爭鬥／論
    The two men locked horns over whether to change the plan.
    這兩名男子為了是否要更改計畫而爭執不休。
19. **scavenge** [ˈskævəndʒ] *vi. & vt.* 尋覓（食物）
    scavenge for...　　尋覓……
    Some wild rabbits were scavenging for food in the woods.
    一些野兔在樹叢裡覓食。
20. **pursue** [pɚˈsu] *vt.* 追捕，追趕
21. **distinctive** [dɪˈstɪŋktɪv] *a.* 獨特的，特別的
22. **tentative** [ˈtɛntətɪv] *a.* 暫時性的
23. **reptile** [ˈrɛptaɪl] *n.* 爬蟲類
24. **ascend** [əˈsɛnd] *vt. & vi.* 攀登；上升

第貳部分、混合題（占 10 分）

第 47 至 50 題為題組

英國的醫療保健系統稱為國民保健署（NHS）。NHS 成立於 1948 年，基本理念是全民免費醫療，資金主要由一般稅收供應。以下是兩位民眾對 NHS 的看法。

珊卓

NHS 在我心中有特殊的地位。我以前是護理師，親眼見證過秉持著最高指導原則——不論貧與富，人人得照護——的 NHS 是如何救死扶傷的。富人繳比較多的稅，確保了貧困和弱勢族群能在需要時獲得照護。此外，我認為 NHS 為納稅人提供了超值的服務。如此大型的組織可以跟製藥公司協商出較低的藥品價格。NHS 在新冠疫情期間的表現也極為出色：首先做出疫苗，而大批鋪貨也是世界最快的國家之一。當然我也沒有對其缺點視而不見；沒有一個系統是完美的。例如某些醫療程序的等候名單太長了。不過我堅信 NHS 敬業又專業的員工是有能力把這等候名單縮短的。

克理斯

NHS 創立時的全民健保原則值得讚揚，而且運作順暢了許多年。其實我自己在年輕時也接受過 NHS 優質又及時的醫療。但有太多人覺得這些已經是過去式了。英國人口老化，許多年長者需要越來越貴的醫療程序。這些程序更貴而且導致住院時間更久，進而讓等候名單越來越長，其暴漲是因為疫情期間 NHS 過於專注在新冠肺炎患者身上，因而忽略了其他疾病的患者。這至今仍有後遺症。我覺得不是錢的問題，因為無論向 NHS 投入多少資金，等候人數也沒有明顯減少。這個組織實在過於龐大又官僚，其現狀已經跟目標脫節了，亟需進行改革。

47. 珊卓認為 NHS 在疫情期間的 (A) 表現很好，並舉推出疫苗為例，但克理斯則指出 NHS 過於 (B) 專注於治療新冠肺炎患者。
(A) <u>performance</u>　　(B) <u>focus</u>

理由
(A) 空格前有定冠詞 the，空格後有介詞 of，得知空格應置入名詞。根據珊卓看法的第六句 The NHS also performed extremely well...（NHS 的表現也極為出色……）得知，空格應置入 performed 的名詞 performance。
(B) 空格前有及物動詞 placed 和副詞 too much...，空格後有介詞 on，得知空格應置入名詞當作及物動詞 placed 的受詞。根據克理斯看法的第六句 ...the NHS focused excessively on COVID patients...（……NHS 過於專注在新冠肺炎患者身上……）得知，空格應置入 focused 的名詞 focus。

48. 珊卓的段落中「這些」指的是什麼？
（某些醫療程序的）等候名單
<u>waiting lists (for certain procedures)</u>

25

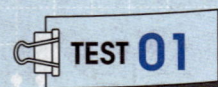

> **理由**
> 根據珊卓看法的倒數第二句提及 ...waiting lists for certain procedures are far too high（……某些醫療程序的等候名單太長了），故可推測 these 即指前句提及的 waiting lists (for certain procedures)（某些醫療程序的）等候名單。

49-50. 下列敘述適用於珊卓、克理斯，兩者皆是或兩者皆非？

49. 他們之前曾受僱於 NHS。
☑ 珊卓　　☐ 克理斯　　☐ 兩者皆是　　☐ 皆非

> **理由**
> 根據本文珊卓看法的第二句 As a former nurse, ...（我以前是護理師，……）得知，應勾選珊卓。

50. 他們認為所有英國公民需要支付更多的稅以供養 NHS。
☐ 珊卓　　☐ 克理斯　　☐ 兩者皆是　　☑ 皆非

> **理由**
> 根據珊卓看法的第三句 The wealthy contribute more in tax, ...（富人繳比較多的稅，……）得知，Sandra 是希望富人繳更多稅，而不是所有英國公民；Chris 則未提及，故應勾選皆非。

重要字詞片語

1. **taxation** [tæksˋeʃən] n. 稅收制度／行為（不可數）
2. **witness** [ˋwɪtnəs] vt. 目擊 & n. 證人
   The tourists witnessed the sunrise from the top of the mountain.
   遊客們在山頂上目睹日出的美景。
3. **access** [ˋæksɛs] n.（對人、地、物的）接近或使用的權利或門徑（與介詞 to 並用）& vt. 使用；（電腦）存取（資料）
   have access to...
   利用……；接觸到……
   Students in this school have access to a wide range of online resources.
   這所學校的學生可以利用各種線上資源。
4. **circumstance** [ˋsɝkəm͵stæns] n. 情況，環境（常用複數）
5. **contribute** [kənˋtrɪbjut] vt. 捐助，貢獻 & vi. 促成，導致（與介詞 to 並用）
   Many people contributed money to help rebuild the school after the earthquake.
   許多人捐錢資助地震後的學校重建工作。
6. **ensure** [ɪnˋʃʊr] vt. 確保
   Please double-check the report to ensure there are no mistakes.
   請再次檢查報告以確保沒有錯誤。
7. **vulnerable** [ˋvʌlnərəbl̩] a. 脆弱的；（生理或心理）易受傷的
8. **negotiate** [nɪˋgoʃɪ͵et] vt. & vi. 協商，交涉，談判
   The two companies are trying to negotiate a new contract.
   這兩家公司正在協商一份新合約。

26

9. **pharmaceutical** [ˌfɑrməˈsjutɪkḷ] *a.* 製藥的
   a pharmaceutical company
   製藥公司
10. **pandemic** [pænˈdɛmɪk] *n.* 大流行病
11. **vaccine** [vækˈsin] *n.* 疫苗
12. **rollout** [ˈrolˌaʊt] *n.* 大規模供應
13. **dedicated** [ˈdɛdəˌketɪd] *a.* 盡責的；專用的
14. **workforce** [ˈwɝkˌfɔrs] *n.* 勞動力／人口（常用單數）
15. **coverage** [ˈkʌvərɪdʒ] *n.* 保險（範圍）；涵蓋範圍；新聞報導（不可數）
16. **laudable** [ˈlɔdəbḷ] *a.* 值得讚賞的
17. **prompt** [prɑmpt] *a.* 及時的 & *vt.* 促使
18. **issue** [ˈɪʃju] *n.* 問題；議題；期刊
19. **bureaucratic** [ˌbjʊrəˈkrætɪk] *a.* 官僚的
20. **reform** [rɪˈfɔrm] *vt.* & *vi.* & *n.* 改革
    The company reformed its management structure to increase efficiency.
    這家公司進行管理架構的改革以提升效率。

TEST 01

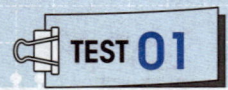

第參部分、非選擇題（占 28 分）

一、中譯英（占 8 分）

1. 最近，臺灣許多關於食品安全的負面新聞讓大家都很害怕吃外食。

   示範譯句
   Recently, a lot of negative news about food safety in Taiwan has made people afraid of eating out.

   或：Lately, a lot of bad news about food safety in Taiwan has made people scared of eating out.

   翻譯要點

   a. **negative** [ˈnɛɡətɪv] *a.* 負面的；消極的
      positive [ˈpɑzətɪv] *a.* 正面的；積極的
      People who have a negative attitude towards life are usually unhappy.
      對生命抱持消極態度的人通常不快樂。

   b. **safety** [ˈsefti] *n.* 安全（不可數）
      The scientists experimented on rats to test the safety of the product.
      科學家在老鼠身上做實驗，以測試該產品的安全性。

   c. **be afraid of...**　　害怕……
      = be scared of...
      = be frightened of...
      Bruce is afraid of flying, so he took a ship and then a train to Beijing.
      布魯斯害怕搭飛機，於是他搭船再轉火車去北京。

   d. **eat out**　　外食

2. 因此，許多人選擇自己在家作飯，因為那不但比較健康，也比較安全。

   示範譯句
   Therefore, many people choose to cook meals at home because it is not only healthier but also safer.

   或：Consequently, many people make a choice to cook meals at home since it is not only better for our health but also safer.

   翻譯要點

   a. **therefore** [ˈðɛrˌfɔr] *adv.* 因此，結果
      = consequently [ˈkɑnsəˌkwɛntlɪ] *adv.*
      = as a result
      Ian woke up with a terrible headache this morning and was therefore in a lot of pain.
      伊恩今天早上醒來時頭痛欲裂，因此十分痛苦。

   b. **make a choice**　　做選擇
      It's hard for Chris to make a choice between quitting and not quitting.
      克里斯在是否要辭職之間難以抉擇。

二、英文作文（占 20 分）

提示：你認為下面兩張圖中呈現的是什麼景象？你對這個景象有什麼感想？請根據圖片內容，寫一篇英文作文。文分兩段，第一段描述兩張圖片的內容，包括其中人、事、物以及發生的事情；第二段討論你認為未來應該採取什麼具體的措施，以避免相同的情況再次發生。

示範作文

  It is natural for people to want to go to bars or attend parties to drink alcohol and have a good time. People all over the world do it. The first picture shows one such occasion. A group of friends are drinking beer and enjoying themselves. However, some people in this situation make the huge mistake of driving after they have drunk alcohol. The second picture shows what can happen as a result: a car accident. One car has overturned, and firefighters are on the scene. They are helping the victims, who may be seriously injured or even dead.

  The simple way to avoid this is to not drive after you have drunk alcohol. There are plenty of other ways to get home after a party or a night out, such as calling a cab or using a designated driver. Some irresponsible and selfish people will always ignore this advice, though. That is why there should be severe punishments, from huge fines to long prison sentences, for those who drive while drunk. If this doesn't stop drunk driving, governments should increase the penalties further.

  人們想去酒吧或參加派對來喝點小酒，好好享受人生，是很自然的事。全世界的人都如此。第一張圖即顯示了一個這種場合。一群朋友正在喝啤酒，相當愉快。然而在這種情境中，有些人會犯下酒駕這種重大錯誤。第二張圖則顯示可能的後果：車禍。一輛車翻倒，而消防員在現場。他們正在幫助這場車禍中可能受重傷或甚至死亡的受害者。

  要防範這種情況，簡單的做法就是不要酒後開車。派對或夜晚狂歡後回家的方法很多，例如搭計程車或是使用指定代駕。然而有些不負責任和自私的人總是忽略這類勸導，所以對那些酒駕的人應該要有嚴厲的懲罰，從鉅額罰金到長期監禁不等。如果這還不能阻止酒駕，政府應該要更進一步加重刑罰。

TEST 01

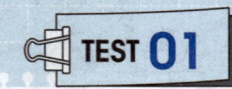

重要字詞片語

1. **overturn** [ˌovɚˈtɝn] *vi.* & *vt.* （使）翻倒；打翻
   During the burglary, many of the desks and shelves in the office had been overturned.
   小偷進來的時候，辦公室的許多桌子和架子都被翻倒了。

2. **be on the scene** 在現場
   The police were on the scene ten minutes after the accident.
   意外發生十分鐘後，警察就到現場了。

3. **designate** [ˈdɛzɪɡˌnet] *vt.* 指派（此處為過去分詞作形容詞用）
   a designated driver　　指定代駕

4. **fine** [faɪn] *n.* & *vt.* 罰款

5. **sentence** [ˈsɛntn̩s] *n.* & *vt.* 判刑

6. **penalty** [ˈpɛnl̩tɪ] *n.* 刑罰，懲罰

TEST 02

🌱 第壹部分、選擇題

一、詞彙題
二、綜合測驗
三、文意選填
四、篇章結構
五、閱讀測驗

🌱 第貳部分、混合題

🌱 第參部分、非選擇題

一、中譯英
二、英文作文

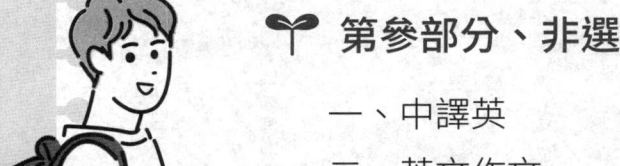

第壹部分、選擇題

一、詞彙題

| 1. B | 2. A | 3. C | 4. C | 5. C | 6. D | 7. D | 8. A | 9. D | 10. B |

二、綜合測驗

| 11. C | 12. A | 13. B | 14. B | 15. D | 16. B | 17. D | 18. C | 19. B | 20. A |

三、文意選填

| 21. E | 22. I | 23. D | 24. B | 25. F | 26. G | 27. A | 28. H | 29. J | 30. C |

四、篇章結構

| 31. E | 32. C | 33. D | 34. B |

五、閱讀測驗

| 35. C | 36. A | 37. B | 38. C | 39. B | 40. B | 41. C | 42. D | 43. C | 44. C |
| 45. B | 46. C |

第貳部分、混合題

47. B, E

48. pot

49. Tomatoes

50. roux

TEST 02

第壹部分、選擇題（占 62 分）

一、詞彙題（占 10 分）

B 1. 當傑夫抱怨餐廳的服務差時，店家給予他帳單折扣作為補償。

    ⓐ (A) **crash** [kræʃ] *n.* 墜毀；撞擊聲 & *vi.* 衝擊，撞擊
        At least 100 people were killed in the plane crash.
        這場空難中至少有一百人罹難。

       (B) **complaint** [kəmˋplent] *n.* 抱怨，投訴
        We've received a lot of customer complaints about our new products lately.
        最近我們收到許多客戶對我們新產品的投訴。

       (C) **interruption** [ˌɪntəˋrʌpʃən] *n.* 中斷；干擾
        I hate interruptions when I'm at work.
        我工作時很討厭被干擾。

       (D) **postponement** [pos(t)ˋponmənt] *n.* 延期，延緩
        The client seemed unsatisfied with the postponement of the delivery.
        該客戶似乎對於送貨時間延宕很不滿意。

    ⓑ 根據語意，(B) 項應為正選。

必考重點

give (sb) a discount　　給（某人）折扣／打折
If you buy more than three items, we can give you a discount on your total purchase.
如果您購買超過三件商品，我們可以給您總金額上的折扣。

A 2. 這名科學家描述近幾年夏天氣溫為異常，並表示氣溫都遠高於往常。

    ⓐ (A) **abnormal** [æbˋnɔrml̩] *a.* 不正常的，異乎尋常的
        John's abnormal behavior can be seen as a sign of mental stress.
        約翰異常的行為可視為心理壓力的徵兆。

       (B) **nutritious** [n(j)uˋtrɪʃəs] *a.* 有營養的
        Do you know that soy milk is actually as nutritious as milk?
        你知道其實豆漿和牛奶一樣有營養嗎？

(C) **informative** [ɪnˋfɔrmətɪv] *a.* 有內容的；能增進知識的
Tom found the television program quite informative.
湯姆發現這個電視節目蠻具教育性的。

(D) **apparent** [əˋpærənt] *a.* 明顯的；表面上的
It is apparent that... 很顯然，……
It is apparent that the fitness center has serious financial problems.
很顯然，該健身中心有嚴重的財務問題。

ⓑ 根據語意，(A) 項應為正選。

必考重點

state [stet] *vt.* 聲明；陳述
The driver stated the facts clearly.
該名駕駛人清楚地陳述了事實。

C **3.** 凱西切開牛排時發現它只有部分煮熟，於是便要求服務生拿回去換。

ⓐ (A) **readily** [ˋrɛdɪlɪ] *adv.* 容易地
The internet is readily accessible in most developed countries.
在大部分已開發國家，網路的取得相當容易。

(B) **necessarily** [ˋnɛsəsɛrɪlɪ / ˌnɛsəˋsɛrəlɪ] *adv.* 必要地；必定
The rich are not necessarily happy. Likewise, the poor are not necessarily sad.
有錢人未必快樂。同樣地，窮人也未必悲傷。

(C) **partially** [ˋpɑrʃəlɪ] *adv.* 部分地
Tom only partially answered the question.
湯姆只回答了這個問題的一部分。

(D) **equally** [ˋikwəlɪ] *adv.* 同樣地；平等地
Women and men should always be treated equally at work.
女性和男性在工作上應被平等對待。

ⓑ 根據語意，(C) 項應為正選。

必考重點

replace [rɪˋples] *vt.* 取代，以……代替
replace A with B   以 B 取代 A
Patrick replaced his old cellphone with a brand-new smartphone.
派翠克買了一支全新的智慧型手機來取代舊的那支手機。

C 4. 在地震來襲後，許多災民受困於山中，迫切需要醫療用品和水。

- ⓐ (A) **superior** [sə`pɪrɪɚ] *a.* 較優秀的，較好的
  be superior / inferior to... 比……好／差
  The lead singer believes that she's superior to the rest of the band.
  那位主唱相信自己比樂團裡其他的樂手都要優秀。

  (B) **accidental** [ˌæksə`dɛntḷ] *a.* 意外的，突發的
  I'm sorry, but the mistake was completely accidental.
  很抱歉，這個錯誤完全是無心之過。

  (C) **urgent** [`ɝdʒnt] *a.* 急迫的，緊急的
  be in urgent need of... 急需……
  The patient is in urgent need of a kidney transplant.
  這名病人急需腎臟移植。

  (D) **changeable** [`tʃendʒəbḷ] *a.* 善變的
  The manager's moods are changeable, so be careful around her.
  經理的心情非常善變，所以在她身邊要小心。

- ⓑ 根據語意及用法，(C) 項應為正選。

> **必考重點**
>
> a. **victim** [`vɪktɪm] *n.* 受害者，受災者
> b. **be trapped in...** 被困在……
>
> David was trapped in the elevator when the power went out.
> 停電時大衛被困在電梯裡。

C 5. 有隻大老鷹看見了一隻小兔子，於是便迅速俯衝去抓住那隻獵物。

- ⓐ (A) **authority** [ə`θɔrətɪ] *n.* 權威（人士）（與介詞 on 並用）
  My cousin is an authority on photography.
  我表哥在攝影方面是個權威。

  (B) **fluency** [`fluənsɪ] *n.* 流利
  The locals were charmed by the foreigner's fluency in their language.
  那些當地人聽到這個外國人能把當地的語言講得如此流利，都被他吸引住。

  (C) **prey** [pre] *n.* 獵物
  Rabbits and squirrels are often prey for larger animals.
  兔子和松鼠通常是大型動物的獵物。

  (D) **threat** [θrɛt] *n.* 威脅
  Never give in to his threat.
  千萬不要屈服於他的威脅。

- ⓑ 根據語意，(C) 項應為正選。

TEST 02

必考重點

a. **hawk** [hɔk] *n.* 老鷹
b. **catch sight of...** 看見……

Ian caught sight of his big belly in the mirror and decided to go on a diet.
伊恩看見鏡子裡自己的大肚子，便決定節食減肥。

D 6. 你要找的那件襯衫目前沒有，但下禮拜我們應該就會進一些貨。

ⓐ (A) **acceptable** [əkˋsɛptəbḷ] *a.* 可接受的
The plan we made should be acceptable to them.
我們擬的計畫對他們而言應該是可以接受的。

(B) **suitable** [ˋsutəbḷ] *a.* 適合的
I'm afraid this novel is not suitable for your children.
恐怕這本小說並不適合你的孩子閱讀。

(C) **tolerable** [ˋtɑlərəbḷ] *a.* 可容忍的；尚可的
The heat is high, but tolerable.
熱度雖高，但還可以忍受。

(D) **available** [əˋveləbḷ] *a.* 可買到的
This book is no longer available because it is out of print.
這本書已經買不到，因為它絕版了。

ⓑ 根據語意，(D) 項應為正選。

D 7. 經過多年的訓練，我達到空手道的黑帶，並有機會參加了一項國際性錦標賽。

ⓐ (A) **ignore** [ɪgˋnor] *vt.* 忽視，忽略
= **neglect** [nɪˋglɛkt] *vt.*
Vicky was disappointed when the manager ignored her hard work on the project.
經理忽視了薇琪在這項專案上所作的努力，讓她很失望。

(B) **calculate** [ˋkælkjə͵let] *vt.* 計算；估計
I have to calculate how much money I can spend next month.
我必須估算下個月所能花費的錢。

(C) **deliver** [dɪˋlɪvɚ] *vt.* 運送；發表
deliver a speech   發表演講
= **make a speech**
The package was delivered two days ahead of schedule.
包裹比預定的時間提早兩天送達。

36

Dr. Brown will deliver a speech covering topics of interest to high school teachers.
布朗博士將發表演講，內容涵蓋了中學老師感興趣的主題。

(D) **achieve** [ə`tʃiv] *vt.* 完成；達到
achieve / attain / accomplish one's goal(s)　實現某人的目標
If you work hard, you will eventually achieve your goals.
如果你努力，最後一定會達成目標。

ⓑ 根據語意，(D) 項應為正選。

必考重點

a. **karate** [kə`rɑtɪ] *n.* 空手道
b. **opportunity** [ˌɑpɚ`t(j)unətɪ] *n.* 機會
c. **compete in...**　參加……比賽

Tom can't compete in the swimming competition because his shoulder was injured.
湯姆無法參加游泳比賽，因為他的肩膀受傷了。

d. **tournament** [`tɝnəmənt] *n.* 錦標賽

A　8. 這項新產品的銷售量不如預期，所以公司必須想出新的行銷策略。

ⓐ (A) **expectation** [ˌɛkspɛk`teʃən] *n.* 預期，期望（常用複數）
live up to sb's expectations　達成某人的期望
= meet sb's expectations
Most children feel the pressure to live up to their parents' expectations.
大部分的孩子為達到父母期望而備感壓力。

(B) **nomination** [ˌnɑmə`neʃən] *n.* 提名；任命
win the nomination as...　贏得……的提名
After a fierce competition, John won the nomination as candidate for mayor.
經過激烈的競爭後，約翰贏得了市長候選人的提名。

(C) **combination** [ˌkɑmbə`neʃən] *n.* 結合
a combination of...　……的綜合
= a mixture of...
The accident was caused by a combination of errors.
許多錯誤的結合導致了這場意外。

(D) **imitation** [ˌɪmə`teʃən] *n.* 仿製品；模仿
This watch is not a real Rolex; it's an imitation.
這只錶不是真的勞力士錶；它是山寨品。

ⓑ 根據語意，(A) 項應為正選。

TEST 02

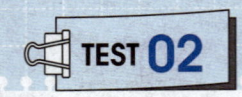

必考重點

a. **fall short of...**
未達到……（要求、期望等）
Peter is afraid that he will fall short of his father's expectations.
彼得怕他會達不到他爸爸的期望。

b. **figure out...** 想出……
We need to figure out a way to fix this problem.
我們得想出個方法來解決這個問題。

c. **strategy** [ˈstrætədʒɪ] *n.* 策略，對策

D 9. 士兵們不願向敵人投降，即使這意味著他們可能會在戰鬥中喪生。

ⓐ (A) **retreat** [rɪˈtrit] *vi.* 撤退
　= withdraw [wɪðˈdrɔ] *vi.*
　The troops retreated when they knew they couldn't win the battle.
　部隊明白打不贏這場戰役時，便撤退了。

(B) **transmit** [trænsˈmɪt] *vi. & vt.* 播送信號 & *vt.* 傳送；傳播
　（三態為：transmit, transmitted [trænsˈmɪtɪd], transmitted）
　transmit sth to... 將某物傳送到……
　The flu is transmitted from one person to another through the air.
　流行性感冒是藉由空氣在人與人之間互相傳播。

(C) **reunite** [ˌrijuˈnaɪt] *vi.* 再結合
　reunite with sb　與某人重逢
　The two brothers finally reunited with their father after 30 years apart.
　那對兄弟與父親分開了三十年之後終於重逢了。

(D) **surrender** [səˈrɛndɚ] *vi. & n.* 投降
　surrender to... 向……投降，屈服於……
　He who never surrenders to fate stands a better chance of achieving success.
　凡是不屈服於命運的人成功的機會都比較大。

ⓑ 根據語意及用法，(D) 項應為正選。

必考重點

a. **refuse to V**　拒絕做……
The actor refused to talk about his private life in the interview.
那位演員在訪談時拒絕談論他的私生活。

b. **combat** [ˈkɑmbæt] *n.* 戰鬥

B 10. 當地政府發起一項環保計畫，希望能提高大眾的環保意識。

ⓐ (A) **inhabit** [ɪnˈhæbɪt] *vt.* 居住於
　Only 500 people inhabit the small island.
　只有五百人居住在這座小島上。

38

(B) **initiate** [ɪˈnɪʃɪˌet] *vt.* 發起，開始
　　The government initiated a program of economic reform last year.
　　政府去年開始實施經濟改革方案。

(C) **assault** [əˈsɔlt] *vt.* 攻擊
＝ attack [əˈtæk] *vt.*
　　The criminal assaulted the owner of the store during the robbery.
　　該名罪犯在搶劫時襲擊商店老闆。

(D) **accuse** [əˈkjuz] *vt.* 指控
　　accuse sb of sth　　指控某人做了某事
　　be accused of...　　被指控……
　　I believe Tom is innocent of the crime he's been accused of.
　　我相信湯姆沒有犯下他所被指控的罪行。

ⓑ 根據語意，(B) 項應為正選。

必考重點
a. **eco-friendly** [ˈikoˌfrɛndlɪ] *a.* 環保的
b. **awareness** [əˈwɛrnɪs] *n.* 意識（不可數）
c. **protection** [prəˈtɛkʃən] *n.* 保護（不可數）

TEST 02

二、綜合測驗（占 10 分）

第 11 至 15 題為題組

　　裝冰淇淋的脆皮杯在我們的文化中相當重要，難以想像在吃冰淇淋時沒有它們會是什麼情況。然而，這種可食容器的起源卻是撲朔迷離且眾說紛紜。在美國，冰淇淋脆皮杯的發明有許多不同的傳說。最為人津津樂道的是有一個賣冰淇淋的人在小碗用完的情況下，把熱的威化餅拗彎了拿來盛冰淇淋給顧客。一般說法是這件事發生於 1904 年在密蘇里州聖路易市舉行的世界博覽會。但是有個叫伊塔洛・馬爾奇奧尼的義大利移民，早在一年前就已取得冰淇淋脆皮杯模具的專利。

　　儘管二十世紀剛開始時出現了這項專利紀錄，但有明顯證據顯示歐洲在更早就已經使用冰淇淋脆皮杯了。有幾本法國與英國的食譜都有提到，十九世紀時人們用可食用的威化餅來裝這種甜點。歷史學家羅伯特・J・威爾甚至寫過關於 1807 年冰淇淋脆皮杯圖片證據的事。我們或許永遠無法知道是誰最早想出冰淇淋脆皮杯的點子。不過每當夏天來臨，我們都會由衷感謝這項發明。

C 11. 理由
ⓐ (A) **recipe** [ˈrɛsəpɪ] *n.* 食譜
　　　a recipe for...　　料理……的食譜
　　　Can you give me the recipe for the onion soup?
　　　你能不能給我這道洋蔥湯的食譜？

39

(B) **chief** [tʃif] *n.* 負責人,首領
Mr. Wilson is the chief of our department.
威爾遜先生是我們部門的主管。

(C) **delight** [dɪˋlaɪt] *n.* 美食;樂事(可數);愉快(不可數)
take delight in...　　喜愛……
= take pleasure in...
Marvin takes delight in telling bedtime stories to his daughter.
馬文喜歡為他女兒講床邊故事。

(D) **fridge** [frɪdʒ] *n.* 冰箱(口語用法)
Remember to put all the food in the fridge, or it will go bad.
記得把所有食物放進冰箱,不然會壞掉。

ⓑ 根據語意及用法,(C) 項應為正選。

A 12. 理由

ⓐ (A) **run out of...**　　用光/用盡……
We are running out of gas, but the nearest gas station is fifty miles away.
我們的汽油快用光了,可是最近的加油站離這兒還有五十英里遠。

(B) **get used to...**　　逐漸習慣……
You should try to get used to living in the city.
你必須逐漸習慣都市生活。

(C) **get along with...**　　與……相處(很好)
John has been getting along very well with Peter.
約翰和彼得一直處得很好。

(D) **look up to...**　　尊敬……
I look up to my mother because she is so dedicated to our family.
我很尊敬我母親,因為她為這個家付出太多。

ⓑ 根據語意及用法,(A) 項應為正選。

B 13. 理由

ⓐ (A) **passion** [ˋpæʃən] *n.* 熱情
have a passion for...　　熱愛……
Robert has a passion for music and plays several instruments.
羅伯特熱愛音樂,還會彈奏好幾種樂器。

(B) **evidence** [ˋɛvədəns] *n.* 證據
The evidence showed that Gary was involved in the robbery.
證據顯示蓋瑞涉入這起搶案。

(C) **security** [səˋkjʊrətɪ] *n.* 安全(保障)
Our company has recently introduced a new security system.
我們公司最近引進一套新的保全系統。

40

(D) **adjustment** [əˋdʒʌstmənt] *n.* 調整，調節
make an adjustment to sth　調整某物
You can be healthier by making adjustments to your diet.
你可以藉由調整飲食來讓自己更健康。

ⓑ 根據語意，(B) 項應為正選。

B **14.** 理由
ⓐ 本題測試以下語意：(A) sealing the package（把包裹封起來）、(B) holding the treat（盛裝甜點）、(C) setting the table（布置餐桌）、(D) describing the taste（描述味道）。

ⓑ 前面已提及使用威化餅來盛裝冰淇淋，此句提及十九世紀時就已經在法式和英式的食譜上看到此種作法。根據語意，(B) 項應為正選。

D **15.** 理由
ⓐ (A) **relatively** [ˋrɛlətɪvlɪ] *adv.* 相對地
It's quite cold yesterday, but it's relatively warm today.
昨天很冷，不過今天天氣相對溫暖。

(B) **immediately** [ɪˋmidɪɪtlɪ] *adv.* 立即，馬上
= instantly [ˋɪnstəntlɪ] *adv.*
Alice raised her hand immediately when the professor asked for a volunteer.
教授徵求一位自願者時，艾莉絲馬上就舉起手。

(C) **mutually** [ˋmjutʃʊəlɪ] *adv.* 互相地
Let's meet in a mutually convenient place.
咱們找個對彼此都方便的地方碰面吧。

(D) **initially** [ɪˋnɪʃəlɪ] *adv.* 最初，起先
Einstein's research was initially ignored by other scientists.
其他科學家起初都不把愛因斯坦的研究當一回事。

ⓑ 根據語意，(D) 項應為正選。

重要字詞片語

1. **edible** [ˋɛdəbḷ] *a.* 可食用的
2. **shroud** [ʃraʊd] *vt.* 覆蓋；隱藏
be shrouded in...
覆蓋／籠罩在……中
The truth behind Atlantis is shrouded in mystery.
亞特蘭提斯背後的真相仍籠罩在一團迷霧中。
3. **disagreement** [ˏdɪsəˋgrimənt] *n.*
意見不同；爭論
4. **fold** [fold] *vt.* 摺疊
Please teach me how to fold these clothes.
請教我怎麼把這些衣服摺好。
5. **wafer** [ˋwefɚ] *n.* 威化餅；薄脆餅
6. **immigrant** [ˋɪməgrənt] *n.*（自外地移入的）移民
This area is populated by immigrants from India.
這一區居住著來自印度的移民。

7. **patent** [ˈpætənt] *n.* 專利權
8. **cookbook** [ˈkʊkˌbʊk] *n.* 烹飪書，食譜
9. **refer to...** 提及……
   Don't refer to that scandal again.
   別再提那件醜聞了。
10. **come up with...** 想出／提出……
    The manager came up with a way to solve the company's financial problems.
    經理想出一個解決公司財務問題的辦法。
11. **nevertheless** [ˌnɛvɚðəˈlɛs] *adv.*
  = **nonetheless** [ˌnʌnðəˈlɛs] *adv.*
    不過，儘管如此
12. **appreciate** [əˈpriʃɪˌet] *vt.* 感激；欣賞
    Sam never appreciates what his mother does for him.
    山姆從不感激他母親為他做的事情。
    Only a few students could appreciate this beautiful poem.
    只有少數幾名學生懂得欣賞這首優美的詩。

第 16 至 20 題為題組

幾乎世界各地所有的文化都會慶祝新年。新年在什麼時間點發生並不重要。大多數國家是在陽曆一月一日慶祝新年。在其他某些國家，新年落在早一點的十二月或稍晚的二月甚至四月。重點是大家可以放假並對即將到來的一年懷抱很高的期待。如果人們剛經歷難熬的十二個月，他們可能會把即將來臨的新年視為重新啟動他們人生和重設目標的機會。許多人喜歡立下新年的新志向。

在西班牙，十二月三十一日的午夜時分會有一項地方習俗叫做「十二顆葡萄」。在除夕的倒數十二秒，鄰里教堂與大教堂都會開始敲鐘，當地人會隨著每一次鐘響吃一顆葡萄。這項慶典的目的是迎來祥瑞又吉利的一年。

早在 1895 年，西班牙的葡萄果農就開始了這項習俗。到了 1909 年，它已擴散到整個西班牙帝國，包括現在的墨西哥與菲律賓等國。現在它已成為一種有趣又有味道的迎接新年方式。

B 16. 理由

ⓐ 空格前一句句首有副詞片語 In most countries（在大多數國家），並未指明是哪些國家，因此為非限定用法，得知空格應置 In others（在其他國家），others 在此也等於 other countries，故 (B) 項應為正選。

ⓑ 其他選項：
(A) other 可作形容詞用，例如：
   Kate has a talent for music. She can play the guitar, the piano, and several other instruments.
   凱蒂有音樂天賦。她會彈吉他、鋼琴和其他幾種樂器。
(D) the others 等於 the rest，用來描寫一個確知的數量。
   Only five students in our class passed the test, and the others failed.
   我們班只有五個學生通過考試，其餘的人都不及格。

D 17. 理由

ⓐ 本題測試以下語意：(A) night shifts（夜班）、(B) union members（工會會員）、(C) new records（新紀錄）、(D) high hopes（很高的期望）。

ⓑ 本句提及人們對於新的一年懷抱著何事，根據語意，(D) 項應為正選。

C 18. 理由

ⓐ (A) **exporter** [ɪksˋportɚ] *n.* 出口商；出口國
　　Giant started out as a bicycle parts manufacturer and exporter.
　　捷安特以自行車零件製造商和出口商起家。

(B) **copier** [ˋkɑpɪɚ] *n.* 影印機
　　Do you know how to fix the copier?
　　你知道如何修理這部影印機嗎？

(C) **local** [ˋlokl̩] *n.* 本地人 & *a.* 當地的
　　One of the locals showed me the way to the gas station.
　　有一個本地人告訴我前往加油站的路。

(D) **detective** [dɪˋtɛktɪv] *n.* 偵探；刑警
　　The detective found some chips of wood on the floor.
　　那名偵探在地板上找到了一些木屑。

ⓑ 根據語意及用法，(C) 項應為正選。

B 19. 理由

ⓐ (A) **probable** [ˋprɑbəbl̩] *a.* 很有可能的（用於下列句構）
　　It is probable that...　　很可能⋯⋯
　　It is highly probable that Andy will show up at the party tonight.
　　安迪今晚很可能會出席這場派對。

(B) **supposed** [səˋpozd] *a.* 認定的（用於下列句構）
　　be supposed to V　　應該（做）⋯⋯
　　Reporters are supposed to report first-hand information only.
　　記者應該只報導第一手訊息。

(C) **likely** [ˋlaɪklɪ] *a.* 很有可能的（用於下列句構）
　　be likely to V　　有可能⋯⋯
　 = It is likely that...
　 = It is probable that...
　　Joseph is likely to go to the movies with us tomorrow.
　 = It is likely that Joseph will go to the movies with us tomorrow.
　　喬瑟夫明天很可能會跟我們一起去看電影。

(D) **doomed** [dumd] *a.* 命中注定的（用於下列句構）
　　be doomed to V　　注定會⋯⋯（之後通常接有否定或消極意味的動詞）

TEST 02

43

TEST 02

Such a lazy man as Tom is doomed to fail.
像湯姆這麼懶惰的人注定會失敗。

ⓑ 根據語意及用法，(B) 項應為正選。

A 20. 理由

ⓐ 本題測試以下語意：(A) had spread throughout（已傳遍……）、(B) was invented by（被……發明）、(C) had been offered to（已提供給……）、(D) had endured for（已忍受了……）。

ⓑ 空格後提及西班牙帝國，包括墨西哥和菲律賓，故根據語意 (A) 項應為正選。

重要字詞片語

1. **solar** [ˋsolɚ] *a.* 太陽的
2. **upcoming** [ˋʌpˏkʌmɪŋ] *a.* 即將來臨的
3. **resolution** [ˏrɛzəˋluʃən] *n.* 志願，期望；決心
4. **achieve** [əˋtʃiv] *vt.* 達成，達到
   If you work hard, you will eventually achieve your goals.
   如果你努力，最後終將達成目標。
5. **cathedral** [kəˋθidrəl] *n.* 大教堂
6. **toll** [tol] *n.* 敲鐘
7. **prosperity** [prɑsˋpɛrətɪ] *n.* 興旺，繁盛（不可數）
   The prosperity of the company is due to the president's long-term policies.
   該公司的榮景乃由於總裁的長遠政策。
8. **vine** [vaɪn] *n.* 葡萄藤
9. **flavorful** [ˋflevɚfəl] *a.* 很有味道的；可口的
10. **bring in...** 帶來／迎接……
    All my family stayed up late to bring in the New Year.
    我們全家人都熬夜迎接新年。

三、文意選填（占 10 分）

第 21 至 30 題為題組

　　說到甜點，鮮少有像黑森林蛋糕一般美味的甜食。此蛋糕由數層以大量櫻桃和鮮奶油內餡分隔的巧克力海綿蛋糕所組成。之後，蛋糕再用額外的櫻桃、鮮奶油和巧克力碎片加以裝飾。內餡和糖霜之中很常加入櫻桃酒來提味，讓成果更上一層樓。

　　縱使人們品嚐黑森林蛋糕已有幾世紀之久，這道美食的起源卻有些爭議。據說這道甜食的起源可回溯至十六世紀末，歷史學家確信它最初是在德國的黑森林地區被製作出來。在那之後，事情就變得有些模糊不清。有些歷史學家認為此蛋糕得其名是因為食譜裡用的酒來自黑森林地區。其他學者則認為人們選擇這個名字是因為該蛋糕的外觀就像黑森林地區婦女過去的衣著樣式。十六世紀時，這些婦女的傳統服飾包含白襯衫、黑色連身裙和上面飾以紅色絨毛球的大帽子。

　　多年來，製作黑森林蛋糕的原始食譜已失傳，但是在德國西南部可能還有人持續在製作。一位名叫約瑟夫．克勒爾的糕點師聲稱他創造了這種蛋糕的現代版本。他說這是 1915 年的事了，

當時他在巴特戈德斯貝格小鎮的一家咖啡館工作。克勒爾之後將該蛋糕的食譜傳給他其中一位學徒奧古斯‧希伐。希伐將克勒爾的食譜保密，直到最後才將它傳給自己的兒子克勞斯。如今，克勞斯仍擁有這份手寫在一本老舊烹飪書上的食譜，而他持續遵循克勒爾的製作守則烘焙黑森林蛋糕。

E 21. 理由
- ⓐ 空格前有形容詞 several（數個的），而空格後有介詞 of，得知空格應置入複數名詞以被 several 修飾。
- ⓑ 選項中符合上述的名詞僅有 (E) layers（層），置入後亦符合語意，故為正選。

I 22. 理由
- ⓐ 空格前有介詞 with，而空格後有名詞 cherries（櫻桃），得知空格應置入形容詞以修飾 cherries。
- ⓑ 選項中符合上述的有 (B) disputed（有爭議的）、(C) secret（祕密的）及 (I) additional（額外的），惟根據語意，(I) 項應為正選。

D 23. 理由
- ⓐ 空格前有介詞 for 表目的，可譯為「為了得到……」，得知空格應置入名詞。
- ⓑ 選項中符合上述的名詞尚餘 (A) costume（服裝）、(C) secret（祕密）、(D) flavor（風味）及 (H) version（版本），惟根據語意，(D) 項應為正選。

B 24. 理由
- ⓐ 空格前有 be 動詞 are 及副詞 somewhat（有點），得知空格應置入形容詞或分詞。
- ⓑ 選項中符合上述的尚餘 (B) disputed（有爭議的）及 (C) secret（祕密的），惟根據語意，(B) 項應為正選。

F 25. 理由
- ⓐ 空格前有引導不定詞片語的 to，而空格後有介詞 to 及一時間點 the late 1500s（十六世紀末），得知空格應置入原形不及物動詞或片語動詞，且該空格與介詞 to 形成的片語須能和時間點並用。
- ⓑ 選項中符合上述的僅有 (F) date back（追溯），置入後亦符合語意，故為正選。

G 26. 理由
- ⓐ 空格前有一名詞詞組 the cake's appearance（蛋糕的外觀）作主詞，而空格後為另一名詞詞組 the way women in the Black Forest used to dress（黑森林地區婦女過去的衣著樣式），得知空格應置入第三人稱單數及物動詞或片語動詞。
- ⓑ 選項中符合上述的有 (G) resembles（像）及 (J) passed on（傳遞），惟根據語意，(G) 項應為正選。

A 27. 理由
- ⓐ 空格前有形容詞 traditional（傳統的），而空格後有動詞 included（包含），得知空格應置入名詞以被 traditional 修飾。

ⓑ 選項中符合上述的名詞尚有 (A) costume（服裝）、(C) secret（祕密）及 (H) version（版本），惟根據語意，(A) 項應為正選。

H 28. 理由
ⓐ 空格前有形容詞 modern（現代的），而空格後有介詞 of，得知空格應置入名詞以被 modern 修飾。
ⓑ 選項中符合上述的尚餘 (C) secret（祕密）及 (H) version（版本），惟根據語意，(H) 項應為正選。

J 29. 理由
ⓐ 空格前有名詞 Keller（克勒爾）作主詞及副詞 later（之後），而空格後有一名詞詞組 the cake's recipe（該蛋糕的食譜）及介詞 to，得知空格應置入第三人稱單數及物動詞或片語動詞。
ⓑ 選項中符合上述的僅有 (J) passed on（傳遞），置入後亦符合語意，故為正選。

C 30. 理由
ⓐ 空格前有動詞 kept（使處於）、作受詞的名詞詞組 Keller's recipe（克勒爾的食譜）及不定冠詞 a，而空格後有副詞連接詞 until（直到……為止），得知空格應置入單數可數名詞。
ⓑ 選項中符合上述的名詞僅剩 (C) secret（祕密），置入空格後形成固定片語 keep sth a secret（將某事保密）且符合語意，故為正選。

重要字詞片語

1. **When it comes to N/V-ing, S + V**
   談到／說到……，……
2. **a slice of...**　一片……
3. **consist** [kənˈsɪst] *vi.* 組成，包括
   consist of...　由……組成
4. **sponge** [spʌndʒ] *n.* 海綿蛋糕〔英〕
   (= sponge cake)
5. **generous** [ˈdʒɛnərəs] *a.* 大量的，豐富的
6. **amount** [əˈmaʊnt] *n.* 數量
   an amount of + 不可數名詞
   若干／一些……
   a number of + 複數名詞
   若干／一些……
7. **whip** [hwɪp] *vt.* 攪打（蛋／奶油）
   whipped cream　鮮奶油
8. **filling** [ˈfɪlɪŋ] *n.* 餡料
9. **be decorated with...**　以……裝飾
10. **alcohol** [ˈælkəˌhɔl] *n.* 酒；酒精（不可數）
11. **icing** [ˈaɪsɪŋ] *n.* （覆在糕餅上的）糖霜（不可數）
12. **notch** [nɑtʃ] *n.* 等級，檔次
    keep sth up a notch
    將某事物提升至更高等級
13. **origin** [ˈɔrədʒɪn] *n.* 起源
    original [əˈrɪdʒənḷ] *a.* 最初的，原先的
14. **somewhat** [ˈsʌmˌ(h)wɑt] *adv.* 有幾分，有點兒
15. **historian** [hɪsˈtɔrɪən] *n.* 歷史學家
16. **vague** [veg] *a.* 模糊的，不清的

17. **liquor** [ˈlɪkɚ] *n.* （烈）酒（尤指蒸餾酒）（不可數）
18. **recipe** [ˈrɛsəpɪ] *n.* 食譜；烹飪法
19. **be topped with...** 上面有……，被……覆蓋
20. **fluffy** [ˈflʌfɪ] *a.* 絨毛狀的；蓬鬆的，鬆軟的
21. **pompom** [ˈpɑmˌpɑm] *n.* （尤指裝飾帽子用的）小絨球
22. **pastry** [ˈpestrɪ] *n.* 糕點（複數為 pastries）
23. **chef** [ʃɛf] *n.* 廚師；主廚
24. **claim to V** 聲稱／宣稱……
25. **eventually** [ɪˈvɛntʃʊəlɪ] *adv.* 最後；終於
26. **instruction** [ɪnˈstrʌkʃən] *n.* 指示／命令（常用複數）

TEST 02

四、篇章結構（占 8 分）

第 31 至 34 題為題組

　　英文有句著名的諺語：「狗狗是人類最好的朋友。」對於被稱為偵測犬的一群菁英犬科動物而言，這句話尤其精確。為了協助防止和偵破犯罪，這些狗狗經常必須要冒著生命危險。作為回報，他們要求的不過就是個小小的禮物 —— 一個會吱吱作響的玩具。狗狗擁有比人類敏感數百倍的強大鼻子。31. 因此，他們甚至能夠偵測出少量在被訓練時作為標的的物質。他們運用絕佳的嗅覺，聞出與犯罪或走私有關的非法、危險物質，這包含毒品、炸彈和血跡。

　　偵測犬跟在引導他們到各種地方的執法人員或軍方人員身邊工作。32. 一個例子是在國際機場行李提領區巡邏的偵測犬。他們能從一段距離之外聞出行李箱內的物品是什麼。如果他們偵測到違禁品，就會向能處理這種問題的訓犬師發出警訊。在 2020 年代初期，諸如芬蘭赫爾辛基機場和美國邁阿密國際機場曾使用偵測犬來查明旅客是否感染了新冠肺炎病毒。烏克蘭戰爭期間，也曾使用偵測犬來偵測地雷和其他爆炸裝置。

　　大多數偵測犬在還只是幼犬時便接受專業訓練。雖然從德國牧羊犬到拉布拉多這幾種品種的狗能成為偵測犬，但大部分都是米格魯。與其他品種相較，這種小型獵犬的嗅覺特別敏銳。此外，米格魯也以生性沉著冷靜與渴望取悅人類而聞名。33. 因此，他們較能維持對任務的專注，被眾多人包圍時也不會變得有攻擊性。許多偵測犬都是在東歐受訓，而且每一隻狗的訓練花費可能高達將近新臺幣一百萬元。34. 因此，研究人員正試著開發能取代偵測犬的技術。然而，直到目前他們都尚未發明出任何可以和狗鼻子一樣精準的機器。

E 31. 理由

🅐 空格前一句提到，狗狗擁有比人類敏感數百倍的強大鼻子，而空格後一句提及，他們運用絕佳的嗅覺，聞出與犯罪或走私有關的非法、危險物質，可推測空格應與狗狗強大的嗅覺有關。

47

TEST 02

    ⓑ 選項 (E) 表示，因此，牠們甚至能夠偵測出少量在被訓練時作為標的的物質，填入後語意連貫，且選項中的 substances they are trained to target（牠們在被訓練時作為標的的物質）與後一句中的 illegal or dangerous substances（非法、危險物質）互相呼應，可知 (E) 項應為正選。

C 32. 理由

    ⓐ 空格前一句提到偵測犬在各種地方工作，空格後一句則提到行李箱內的物品，可推測空格應提及與行李箱有關的地方。

    ⓑ 選項 (C) 表示，一個例子是在國際機場行李提領區巡邏的偵測犬，填入後語意連貫，且選項中的 baggage claim areas（行李提領區）與空格後一句中的 suitcases（行李箱）互相呼應，可知 (C) 項應為正選。

D 33. 理由

    ⓐ 空格前一句提到，米格魯也以生性沉著冷靜與渴望取悅人類而聞名，可推測空格應反映出上述特質所帶來的優勢。

    ⓑ 選項 (D) 表示，因此，牠們較能維持對任務的專注，被眾多人包圍時也不會變得有攻擊性，填入後語意連貫，且該選項即在說明前一句中的 cool and calm temperament（生性沉著冷靜），可知 (D) 項應為正選。

B 34. 理由

    ⓐ 空格前一句提到偵測犬的訓練花費將近新臺幣一百萬元，而空格後一句提及直到目前他們都尚未發明出任何可以和狗鼻子一樣精準的機器，可推測空格應與研發能媲美偵測犬的機器有關。

    ⓑ 選項 (B) 表示，因此，研究人員正試著開發能取代偵測犬的技術，填入後語意連貫，可知 (B) 項應為正選。

(A) 項中譯：這隻狗在忠誠服役近十年後從警隊退休。

重要字詞片語

1. **elite** [ɪˈlit] *a.* 菁英的，最優秀的
2. **canine** [ˈkenaɪn] *n.* 犬科動物，狗
3. **detection** [dɪˈtɛkʃən] *n.* 偵查（不可數）
   detect [dɪˈtɛkt] *vt.* 偵測出
4. **put... at risk** 使……陷入險境
5. **prevention** [prɪˈvɛnʃən] *n.* 阻止；預防（不可數）
6. **resolution** [ˌrɛzəˈluʃən] *n.* 解決
7. **In return, S + V** ……作為回報
8. **insignificant** [ˌɪnsɪgˈnɪfəkənt] *a.* 微不足道的
9. **squeaky** [ˈskwiki] *a.* 嘎吱作響的
10. **extraordinary** [ɪkˈstrɔrdnˌɛrɪ] *a.* 非凡的
11. **sniff** [snɪf] *vi. & vt.* 嗅，聞
    sniff out... 嗅出……
12. **smuggling** [ˈsmʌglɪŋ] *n.* 走私（罪）（不可數）
    smuggle [ˈsmʌgl] *vt.* 走私
13. **explosive** [ɪkˈsplosɪv] *n.* 炸藥，爆炸物
14. **enforcement** [ɪnˈfɔrsmənt] *n.* （法律的）執行（不可數）

15. **patrol** [pə'trol] *vt.* 巡邏，巡查（三態為：patrol, patrolled [pə'trold], patrolled）
16. **contents** ['kɑntɛnts] *n.* 所容納之物（恆用複數）
17. **prohibit** [prə'hɪbɪt] *vt.* 禁止（本文為過去分詞作形容詞用）
18. **mine** [maɪn] *n.* 地雷；水雷
19. **specialized** ['spɛʃə͵laɪzd] *a.* 專業的，專門的
20. **breed** [brid] *n.* 品種
21. **retriever** [rɪ'trivɚ] *n.*（尋回射中獵物的）一種獵犬
22. **beagle** ['bigl̩] *n.* 米格魯
23. **hound** [haʊnd] *n.* 獵犬
24. **exceptional** [ɪk'sɛpʃən̩l] *a.* 卓越的，非凡的
25. **temperament** ['tɛmprəmənt] *n.* 性情
26. **aggressive** [ə'grɛsɪv] *a.* 具攻擊性的
27. **precise** [prɪ'saɪs] *a.* 精確的
28. **force** [fɔrs] *n.* 警察部門；武裝部隊

五、閱讀測驗（占 24 分）

第 35 至 38 題為題組

十個人當中有九個是右撇子，意味著只有 10% 的人類是左撇子。造成這種差異的可能原因是什麼？而多年來人們是如何看待慣用手這件事的？

對於為何大多數人是右撇子而非左撇子，有一種理論是說因為大腦中掌管說話和手工的部分在左腦。基於大腦的特性，結果就是人們慣用右手。另外一項理論則指出單純就是遺傳。由於大多數父母是右撇子，這種特徵就自然會遺傳給子女。就算父母都是左撇子，生下左撇子小孩的機率也只有 26%，但這已比一般大眾的比例高很多了。無論是單一原因或是多種原因所造成，人們有慣用手是不爭的事實。

但許多個世紀以來，左撇子一直不受右撇子歡迎。慣用左手這件事萌生了許多迷信與習俗。不僅是原始部落，就連基督徒、猶太教徒和穆斯林都曾鄙視左撇子，甚至視其為邪惡。歐洲學校裡的左撇子學童，曾面臨不用右手就得遭受體罰的待遇。即使在現代，中國小孩也是從小就被鼓勵用右手寫字和拿筷子。西方人在與人寒暄招呼時總是伸出右手來握手。語言也反映出這樣的差別待遇。舉例來說，英文字「右邊的」（right）亦指「正確的」或「恰當的」。左撇子使用日常物件時可能遇到困難，例如剪刀和衣服的拉鍊。簡言之，這個世界是為右撇子打造的。

但有些學者認為慣用左手具有某些優勢。左撇子經常跟創造力劃上等號，支持這種理論的人常舉出米開朗基羅及李奧納多·達文西這些知名藝術家也都是「左撇子」為例。然而並沒有確鑿的證據能將慣用左手與創造力聯結在一起。

TEST 02

C 35. 本文的主題是什麼？
(A) 世界上左撇子最普遍的地區。
(B) 左撇子如何象徵聰慧。
(C) 左撇子的起源以及人們對它的看法。
(D) 慣用左手的趨勢為何在未來可能上升。

理由
本文第二段提及慣用手現象的成因，第三、四段分別提及各國文化中對左撇子的歧視與左撇子具備的優勢，故 (C) 項應為正選。

A 36. 下列何者為本文第二段中 nature 一字的正確含意？
(A) 某事物的基本特質。
(B) 物質世界的現象。
(C) 人的特徵。
(D) 大多數人的態度。

理由
nature 為名詞，表「特點，性質」時，前面可加冠詞，若表「大自然」時，前面則不可加冠詞。根據本文第二段第一、二句上下文判斷，得知 (A) 項與此字定義最相符，故應為正選。

B 37. 根據本文，以前歐洲的左撇子學生有什麼遭遇？
(A) 他們被教導只能用右手吃飯。
(B) 如果他們用左手就會被打或甩巴掌。
(C) 他們被鼓勵雙手皆可用來寫字。
(D) 他們被迫就讀左撇子專門學校。

理由
根據本文第三段第四句，歐洲學校裡的左撇子孩童以前如果不用右手就得面臨體罰，故 (B) 項應為正選。

C 38. 本文為何提到李奧納多‧達文西？
(A) 他堅信慣用左手是一種罪。
(B) 他發現了慣用左手和創造力之間的關聯。
(C) 他是左撇子有藝術天分這種論點的佐證之一。
(D) 他引導了對慣用左手之優點的研究。

理由
根據本文第四段第一、二句，有些研究人員認為慣用左手具備優勢。慣用左手常和創造力有關聯，而支持這種關聯的人指出諸如米開朗基羅及李奧納多‧達文西等如此有名的藝術家也都是「左撇子」，故 (C) 項應為正選。

重要字詞片語

1. **disparity** [dɪsˋpærətɪ] *n.* 差異，懸殊
（複數為 disparities）
2. **handedness** [ˋhændɪdnɪs] *n.* 用手習慣
3. **handiwork** [ˋhændɪˏwɝk] *n.* 手工（不可數）
4. **given** [ˋɡɪvən] *prep.* 有鑒於／考慮到……
   = considering [kənˋsɪdərɪŋ] *prep.*
   Given his physical condition, John decided to retire from basketball.
   約翰考慮到自己的身體狀況，決定從籃壇退休。
5. **genetics** [dʒəˋnɛtɪks] *n.* 遺傳學（不可數）
6. **trait** [tret] *n.* 特點，特徵

7. **pass on sth / pass sth on (to sb)**
   傳遞某物（給某人）
   My aunt will pass on her pearl necklace to her granddaughter when she dies.
   我姑姑過世後會將她的珍珠項鍊留給她的孫女。

8. **offspring** [ˈɔfˌsprɪŋ] *n.* 子女，子孫，後代（單複數同形）

9. **superstition** [ˌsupɚˈstɪʃən] *n.* 迷信

10. **arise** [əˈraɪz] *vi.* 發生，產生（三態為：arise, arose [əˈroz], arisen [əˈrɪzṇ]）
    arise from...　起因於／引起……
    Our misunderstandings arose from a lack of communication.
    我們之間的誤會起因於缺乏溝通。

11. **look down on ...**　輕視／看不起……
    Don't look down on someone just because he or she is poor.
    別只因為一個人窮就看不起他／她。

12. **face** [fes] *vt.* 面臨，面對；朝向 & *n.* 臉；面子（不可數）
    Stay calm when you face a problem.
    面對問題時要保持冷靜。

13. **discrimination** [dɪˌskrɪməˈneʃən] *n.* 歧視，差別待遇（不可數）
    The women staged a demonstration in protest against sexual discrimination.
    這些婦女發動示威抗議性別歧視。

14. **proper** [ˈprɑpɚ] *a.* 合宜的，適當的；得體的

15. **Put simply, ...**　簡而言之，……
    = Simply put, ...
    = To put it simply, ...
    Put simply, we either accept their offer or go bankrupt.
    簡言之，我們要嘛接受他們的提議，要嘛就等著破產。

16. **creativity** [ˌkrieˈtɪvətɪ] *n.* 創造力；創意（不可數）

17. **proponent** [prəˈponənt] *n.* 擁護者，支持者

18. **conclusive** [kənˈklusɪv] *a.* 確鑿的；決定性的

19. **prevalent** [ˈprɛvələnt] *a.* 普遍的（= common）

20. **perceive** [pɚˈsiv] *vt.* 看待，視為；意識到
    perceive A as B　視 A 為 B
    This discovery was perceived as a major breakthrough in the medical field.
    這個發現在醫學界被視為一項重大突破。

21. **phenomena** [fəˈnɑmənə] *n.* 現象（複數，單數為 phenomenon [fəˈnɑməˌnɑn]）

22. **slap** [slæp] *vt.* 甩巴掌（三態為：slap, slapped [slæpt], slapped）
    Emily slapped her son in the face when he swore.
    艾蜜莉的兒子罵髒話時，她打了他一巴掌。

23. **sin** [sɪn] *n.* （宗教或道德上的）罪，罪過

TEST 02

TEST 02

第 39 至 42 題為題組

　　申請大學對於許多學生來說可能會是壓力很大的一段時間，他們做出的決定不僅會影響他們未來幾年的人生，可能還會決定他們一輩子的工作前途。

　　與那些採用統一辦理錄取流程的國家不同，美國的學生在申請學校的數量上並無限制。這就意味準備工作更加繁重，因為每所大學都必須個別申請。另一個不同點是申請時可使用「提前決定」方案。這對已經對特定學校心有所屬的學生而言是有利的。然而提前決定方案只能用於一所大學，如果錄取了你就非得去念不可。美國大學也採用與其他某些國家不同的篩選流程。好學校的招生委員要找的學生不能只是成績好。他們要找的是全方位發展的人選，即有多種興趣並參加各種課外活動的學生。教育界以外人士的推薦函以及個人論文，在優質美國大學決定錄取哪位申請人時，扮演相當吃重的角色。事實上，這些非學術因素常常具有決定性。

　　上大學對學生的職涯和未來收入有那麼大的影響嗎？簡單的回答就是「有」。諸多研究持續顯示大學畢業生賺的錢比沒大學學歷的人多。取得的學位越高，就讀的大學越有聲望，這種差異就越明顯。然而這種概念性的說法掩藏了許多差異。例如文科畢業生的工作收入往往低於理科畢業生。選擇不上大學而去學習一門技術如水管工的人，最終可能比許多就讀中等大學而且學非所愛的畢業生賺更多的錢。所以許多就業顧問會告訴學生，無論他們是在學術界還是其他地方，都該去追尋自己的興趣。

　　儘管如此，上大學 —— 雖然申請流程相當繁複 —— 對現今的學生來說依舊是壓倒性的人氣選項。

B 39. 本文第二段主要在講什麼？
(A) 世界各地不同大學的申請流程。
(B) 美國申請程序的特點。
(C) 優異成績對招生團隊來說的絕對重要性。
(D) 提前決定申請入學方案的簡史。

> 理由
> 第二段旨在介紹美國的大學申請流程及大學招生委員篩選學生的條件與某些其他國家不同的地方，故 (B) 項應為正選。

B 40. 根據本文，下列哪種學生最有可能被美國的頂尖大學錄取？
(A) 班上考試成績最好的學生。
(B) 有各種嗜好的聰明學生。
(C) 拿出老師盛讚信件的學生。
(D) 運動天賦強且把所有時間都花在運動上的學生。

> 理由
> 根據本文第二段第七、八句，好學校的招生委員找的學生不是只要成績好而已。他們要找的是全方位發展的人，即有多種興趣並參加各種課外活動的學生，故 (B) 項應為正選。

52

C 41. this generalization masks numerous differences 這句話有何暗示？
(A) 考慮出國留學獲得學位是明智之舉。
(B) 從長遠來看，學習一門手藝一定有更多好處。
(C) 你的收入不一定取決於你的教育程度。
(D) 選擇合適的高中就業顧問極為重要。

理由
本句粗體字表示，這種概念性的說法掩藏了許多差異。根據本句前提及大學畢業生賺的錢比沒大學學歷的人多，而本句後卻舉例出同是大學畢業生卻有不同的薪資待遇，以及非大學畢業生卻賺得比大學畢業生多的範例，故可推論該句表收入不一定取決於教育程度，得知 (C) 項應為正選。

D 42. 作者以何種方式結束本文？
(A) 提出建議。　　(B) 做出預測。　　(C) 舉例說明。　　(D) 承認現實。

理由
根據本文最後一段，儘管如此，上大學 —— 雖然申請流程相當繁複 —— 對現今的學生來說依舊是壓倒性的人氣選項，故 (D) 項應為正選。

重要字詞片語

1. **apply** [əˋplaɪ] vi. 申請；應徵
   apply to...　向……提出申請
   My sister applied to three universities but was only accepted by one.
   我姊姊申請三所大學，但只錄取一所。

2. **prospect** [ˋprɑspɛkt] n. 前途，前景（恆用複數）

3. **centralized** [ˋsɛntrə͵laɪzd] a. 集中化的

4. **admission** [ədˋmɪʃən] n. 錄取，招生（恆用複數）；入學（不可數）
   Are you familiar with the procedure for applying for admission to that college?
   你熟悉那所大學的入學申請程序嗎？

5. **involve** [ɪnˋvɑlv] vt. 涉及，需要
   I didn't know making a movie involved so much work.
   我不知道製作一部電影需要做這麼多的工作。

6. **institution** [͵ɪnstəˋtuʃən] n. 機構（此處指大學）

7. **application** [͵æpləˋkeʃən] n. 申請（書）

8. **be set on...**　決定要……
   My brother is set on becoming an astronaut.
   我哥哥決定要成為一名太空人。

9. **well-rounded** [ˋwɛlˋraʊndɪd] a. 全方位的，全面的

10. **individual** [͵ɪndəˋvɪdʒʊəl] n. 個人 & a. 個別的

11. **multitude** [ˋmʌltə͵tjud] n. 許多，大量
    a multitude of...　許多的……
    The singer received a multitude of requests to perform live.
    那位歌手接獲大量要他現場演出的要求。

12. **extracurricular** [͵ɛkstrəkəˋrɪkjələ] a. 課外的

13. **academic** [͵ækəˋdɛmɪk] a. 學術的；學業的

14. **decisive** [dɪˋsaɪsɪv] a. 決定性的

15. **consistently** [kənˋsɪstəntlɪ] adv. 一貫地，始終如一地

TEST 02

16. **graduate** [ˈgrædʒʊɪt] *n.* 畢業生 & [ˈgrædʒuˌet] *vi.* 畢業

17. **pronounced** [prəˈnaʊnst] *a.* 明顯的，顯著的

18. **prestigious** [prɛsˈtɪdʒəs] *a.* 有名望的，聲望高的

19. **generalization** [ˌdʒɛnərələˈzeʃən] *n.* （片面的）概括／泛論

20. **mask** [mæsk] *vt.* 掩飾，隱藏；掩蓋 & *n.* 面具；面罩
    John masked his sadness so no one could tell he was so depressed.
    約翰隱藏了他的哀傷，因此沒人能發現他其實非常沮喪。

21. **trade** [tred] *n.*（尤指需特殊技巧的）手藝；職業

22. **entail** [ɪnˈtel] *vt.* 需要
    Kate doesn't want to take a job that entails a lot of traveling.
    凱特不想接需要常出差的工作。

23. **procedure** [prəˈsidʒɚ] *n.* 程序，步驟

24. **in the long run** 從長遠來看，到頭來
    The job has short-term benefits but will not help your career progress in the long run.
    這份工作短期內有好處，但從長遠來看，它對你的職業進展沒什麼幫助。

25. **prediction** [prɪˈdɪkʃən] *n.* 預測

第 43 至 46 題為題組

　　在自己家裡舒舒服服地看電視是種非常風行的活動，而事實上它也有許多好處。它是一種容易取得的娛樂方式，可以一個人看，也可以成為多人共同享受的經驗。許多人喜歡一口氣看完一整季的電視影集，然而每個禮拜焦急地期待在下週看到你最愛影集中最愛角色的最新遭遇，也是一種樂趣。電視也具有教育意義。在好像無窮無盡的頻道選擇中，有許多主題多樣的優質紀錄片，從歷史、旅遊到烹飪一應俱全。電視還能提供陪伴，尤其是對於獨居老人，而且在新冠肺炎疫情封城的時候，它成為所有年齡層的人尋求逃避現實的來源。

　　不過看電視當然也有壞處。自從網飛等提供串流服務的媒體問世以來，一不小心就會看太多電視。這可能會迅速演變成一種成癮狀態，促使人們產生反社會行為，寧可接受電視而不是人際關係的刺激。它可能會導致久坐不動的生活方式，而在人們習於每天坐在桌子前上課或上班八小時的社會中，久坐已經是很嚴重的問題了。看電視確實會讓我們一直坐著而懶於四處走動。與之相關的健康問題包括肥胖、糖尿病和視力問題。

　　最起碼視力不良問題是有解的。例如看電視其實有合理的位置，從那裡看電視能減輕眼睛的負擔。以 1080p（1920×1080 像素）的高畫質電視而言，與電視的距離至少要達到螢幕尺寸的 1.5 倍。例如你的電視是四十英吋的 1080p 高畫質電視，你就應該坐在離螢幕至少六十英吋（約 1.5 公尺）的地方。不過如果你買的是 4K 超高畫質電視，就可以坐近一點而不會感覺眼睛疲勞。此外，無論你買的是哪種電視，你看螢幕的視角無論是俯視或仰視都不該超過十五度。

C 43. 下列哪個標題最適合本文？
(A) 超高畫質電視的優缺點　　(B) 為何電視紀錄片是一種教育工具
(C) 看電視的利與弊　　(D) 追劇如何成為全民嗜好

> 理由

根據本文前兩段提及看電視雖然給人們帶來許多好處，但其壞處是會衍生出視力不良等健康問題，故 (C) 項應為正選。

C 44. 文中並未列出下列哪一項支持看電視的論點？
(A) 它是一種相當方便的嗜好。
(B) 這是一項很有樂趣的團體活動。
(C) 它能防止人感到焦慮。
(D) 它能為老年人提供陪伴。

> 理由

根據本文第一段論述看電視的好處，分別提及看電視是一種容易取得的娛樂方式，可以一個人看，也可以成為多人共同享受的經驗，以及電視還能提供陪伴，尤其是對於獨居老人。本段並未提及看電視能防止人感到焦慮，故 (C) 項應為正選。

B 45. 第三段中的 sedentary lifestyle 最有可能是什麼意思？
(A) 一種工作和生活之間缺乏平衡的生活方式。
(B) 一種不常活動身體的生活方式。
(C) 一種過度享樂而鮮少學習的生活。
(D) 一種想花錢購買電視上打廣告產品的渴望。

> 理由

本文第三段第四句中的 sedentary 為形容詞，表「久坐不動的」，而 sedentary lifestyle 即表「久坐不動的生活方式」。根據本句後提及許多人習慣坐在桌子前八小時上課或上班，而且看電視確實會讓我們一直坐著而懶於四處走動，得知粗體字最有可能指的是一種不常活動身體的生活方式，故 (B) 項應為正選。

C 46. 下列哪一張圖顯示一個人坐著看五十英寸 1080p 高畫質電視時的最佳位置？

(A) ─五十英寸─

(B) ─七十英寸─

(C) ─七十五英寸─

(D) ─一百〇八英寸─

55

TEST 02

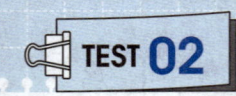

理由

根據本文第三段第三句，以 1080p（1920×1080 像素）的高畫質電視而言，與電視的距離至少要達電視螢幕尺寸的 1.5 倍。依此類推，看同畫質五十英寸電視則須保持七十五英寸（50×1.5=75）的距離，故 (C) 項應為正選。

重要字詞片語

1. **accessible** [əkˋsɛsəbl̩] *a.* 易接近的；易使用的
2. **entertainment** [ˌɛntɚˋtenmənt] *n.* 娛樂，樂趣（不可數）；娛樂節目（可數）
3. **collective** [kəˋlɛktɪv] *a.* 共同的，集體的
4. **binge** [bɪndʒ] *vi.* 暴食，狂吃（與介詞 on 並用）
   binge-watch [ˋbɪndʒˋwɑtʃ] *vt. & vi.* 連續看電視節目，追劇
   Sally likes to binge on popcorn when she's watching TV.
   莎莉看電視時喜歡狂吃爆米花。
   Jenny binge-watched the first season of *Emily in Paris* last night.
   珍妮昨晚一口氣看完了《艾蜜莉在巴黎》的第一季。
5. **in / at one go** 一口氣
   Jasmine couldn't finish the whole pizza in one go, so she saved some for later.
   潔思敏無法一口氣吃完整個披薩，所以她留了一些之後再吃。
6. **a wealth of...** 大量的……
   There used to be a wealth of job opportunities for people from all backgrounds.
   在以前，不論什麼背景的人都有很多工作機會。
7. **documentary** [ˌdɑkjəˋmɛntərɪ] *n.* 紀錄片（複數為 documentaries）
8. **manner** [ˋmænɚ] *n.* 種類，類型（不可數）
   all manner of... 各式各樣的……
   Humans come in all manner of shapes, sizes, and colors.
   人類的體型、高矮及膚色各有不同。
9. **escapism** [ɪsˋkepɪzəm] *n.* 逃避現實（的消遣活動）（不可數）
10. **advent** [ˋædvənt / ˋædvɛnt] *n.* 出現，到來（= coming）
    the advent of sth
    某事物的出現／到來
11. **streaming** [ˋstrimɪŋ] *n.*（影音的）串流，線上收看／聽（不可數）
12. **addiction** [əˋdɪkʃən] *n.* 成癮；入迷
13. **stimulation** [ˌstɪmjəˋleʃən] *n.* 刺激（不可數）
14. **sedentary** [ˋsɛdn̩ˌtɛrɪ] *a.* 坐著不動的；缺乏運動的
15. **obesity** [oˋbisətɪ] *n.* 肥胖（不可數）
16. **eyesight** [ˋaɪˌsaɪt] *n.* 視力（不可數）
17. **alleviate** [əˋlivɪˌet] *vt.* 減輕，緩和
    The doctor gave the patient some pills to alleviate the pain.
    醫生給那名病患一些減輕疼痛的藥丸。
18. **strain** [stren] *n.* 勞損；拉傷；扭傷
19. **pros and cons** 利與弊，優缺點
    You should analyze the pros and cons before quitting your current job.
    在辭掉現有工作前，你應先分析其利弊。
20. **companionship** [kəmˋpænjənˌʃɪp] *n.* 陪伴，友誼（不可數）

第貳部分、混合題（占 10 分）

第 47 至 50 題為題組

卡津和克里歐這兩種料理，基本上會讓人想到美國南部的路易斯安那州，特別是紐奧良市及其周邊地帶。它們有許多相似之處，但也有明顯的差異。

卡津料理的起源，可追溯到十八世紀被流放到路易斯安那州的法裔加拿大移民。最粗淺的做法可被稱作「鄉村料理」，以鄉村地區現有的食材為主，如米飯、豆類、雞肉和小龍蝦等。小龍蝦貌似龍蝦，棲息於河流和小溪中。簡單而飽足感強的卡津料理通常煮成一鍋，常包含所謂「大三元」的三樣蔬菜：洋蔥、芹菜和青椒／甜椒。儘管卡津菜的一鍋燉做法相對簡單，卻是味道十足，大量使用在地產的香草植物與香料。例如備受喜愛的燉小龍蝦，通常會煮很大一鍋，大家在戶外吃，裡面的料有小龍蝦、玉米、洋芋和香料。而小龍蝦燴飯是把甲殼類或雞肉跟蔬菜燉在一起，配米飯吃。卡津和克里歐料理中都有這道菜。卡津版通常比較辣，並用上深色的油麵糊打底。油麵糊是由動物油脂和麵粉混合而成。

一般認為克里歐料理比卡津料理精緻複雜，可稱其為「城市料理」。它源於紐奧良，融合法國、西班牙、加勒比海和非洲菜的遺風，有更廣泛的食材選擇。它跟卡津料理一樣也相當依賴蔬菜「大三元」，但不同的是它還會用大量番茄、牛油和鮮奶油。這些食材加上在地香草植物和香料，可創造更濃郁、奢華的風味。烹調克里歐料理比卡津料理複雜，步驟相當多。經典案例有：克里歐蝦是以番茄為基底的蝦料理，淋在米飯上；蔬菜白酒高湯是一種燉海鮮；紙包魚是把魚和蔬菜包在紙裡烘烤。許多克里歐菜餚會用中濃度的油麵糊當基底。

TEST 02

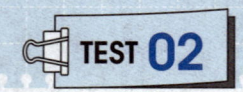

47. 哪三種蔬菜是卡津料理和克里歐料理中常使用的？

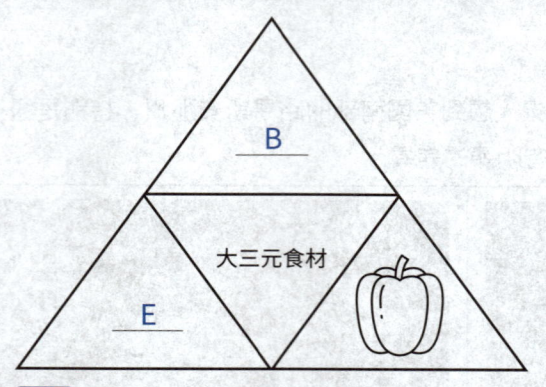

```
        ▲
       ╱ ╲
      ╱ B ╲
     ╱─────╲
    ╱╲ 大三╲╱╲
   ╱  ╲元食╱  ╲
  ╱ E  ╲材╱ 🫑 ╲
 ╱──────╳──────╲
```

理由

根據卡津料理第四句，…a "holy trinity" of vegetables: onion, celery, and bell peppers.（……「大三元」的三樣蔬菜：洋蔥、芹菜和青椒／甜椒。）及克里歐料理第三句也提及「大三元」的蔬菜，故得知 (B)、(E) 為正選。

48-50. 使用文章中的單詞，完成關於卡津和克里歐料理異同的圖表。

- 可被稱為來自鄉下的食物
- 菜餚通常在一個 48. 鍋 **pot** 中料理

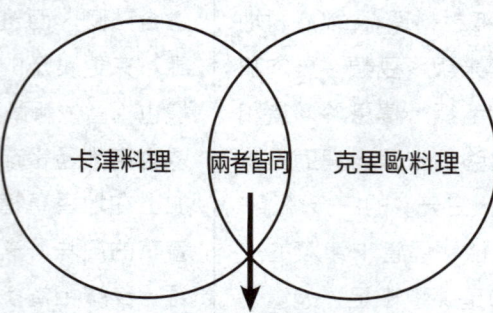

卡津料理　兩者皆同　克里歐料理

- 可被稱為來自城市的食物
- 49. 番茄 **Tomatoes** 為菜餚增添濃郁的風味

- 使用當地的香料和香草
- 使用 50. 油麵糊 **roux** 作為菜餚基底

理由

第 48 題，根據卡津料理第四句，… are often cooked in one pot…（……通常會煮很大一鍋……）得知，空格應置 pot（鍋）。

第 49 題，根據克里歐料理第三至四句 …includes a lot of tomatoes, butter, and cream.… result in richer, more luxurious flavors.（……用大量番茄、牛油和鮮奶油……創造更濃郁、奢華的風味。）且題目說到空格僅能填一個單詞，故得知空格應置 tomatoes（番茄）以符合空格後面動詞接 contribute（增添；有助於）的語法。

第 50 題，根據卡津料理和克里歐料理的最後一句，皆提及使用 roux（油麵糊）as a base（當基底），故得知空格應置 roux。

重要字詞片語

1. **cuisine** [kwɪˈzin] *n.* 菜餚
2. **fundamentally** [ˌfʌndəˈmɛntḷɪ] *adv.* 基本上
3. **settler** [ˈsɛtlɚ] *n.* 移居者，墾荒者

4. **exile** [ˈɛksaɪl / ˈɛgzaɪl] *vt.* 放逐 & *n.* 流放，流亡（不可數）；流亡者（可數）
The man was exiled from his country for treason.
那名男子因叛國被逐出國門。
* treason [ˈtrizn̩] *n.* 叛國（罪）

5. **describe sb/sth as + N/adj.**
把某人／某物描述成……
Sarah described the cake as the best dessert she had ever tasted.
莎拉形容這蛋糕是她吃過最好吃的甜點。

6. **ingredient** [ɪnˈgridɪənt] *n.*（食品）成分；（成功的）要素

7. **rural** [ˈrʊrəl] *a.* 鄉下的

8. **lobster** [ˈlɑbstɚ] *n.* 龍蝦

9. **hearty** [ˈhɑrtɪ] *a.*（食物）豐盛的；熱情的，興高采烈的

10. **trinity** [ˈtrɪnətɪ] *n.* 三位一體；三合一

11. **celery** [ˈsɛlərɪ] *n.* 芹菜（不可數）

12. **simplicity** [sɪmˈplɪsətɪ] *n.* 簡單；簡樸（皆不可數）

13. **herb** [(h)ɝb] *n.* 香草，藥草

14. **batch** [bætʃ] *n.* 一組，一批

15. **stew** [st(j)u] *n.* 燉的食物 & *vt.* & *vi.*（用小火）煮，燉

16. **version** [ˈvɝʒən] *n.* 版本；譯本；（文藝作品的）改編形式

17. **refined** [rɪˈfaɪnd] *a.* 精煉／製的

18. **arise** [əˈraɪz] *vi.* 產生，形成（三態為：arise, arose [əˈroz], arisen [əˈrɪzn̩]）
Conflicts often arise when people have different opinions.
衝突常出現在人們抱持不同意見時。

19. **embrace** [ɪmˈbres] *vt.* & *vi.* 樂意採納；擁抱；包含 & *n.* 擁抱
The company decided to embrace new technologies to improve efficiency.
這家公司決定採用新技術以提升效率。

20. **array** [əˈre] *n.* 一批，一系列
an array of... 一連串／一大堆……
The store offers an array of products, ranging from electronics to home appliances.
這家商店販售各色各樣的產品，從電子產品到家用電器應有盡有。

21. **rely on...** 依賴……；信賴……
Many people rely on public transportation to commute to work.
許多人依賴大眾交通工具通勤上班。

22. **supplement** [ˈsʌpləmɛnt] *vt.* 增加；補充 & [ˈsʌpləmənt] *n.* 補充物；（雜誌／報紙的）副刊
The company introduced new policies to supplement its existing employee benefits.
公司推出了新政策來增加現有的員工福利。

23. **result in...** 導致……
The heavy rainfall resulted in severe flooding in several areas.
大雨導致了多個地區嚴重積水。

24. **luxurious** [lʌgˈʒʊrɪəs] *a.* 豪華的，奢侈的

25. **involve** [ɪnˈvɑlv] *vt.* 涉及；包含，需要
The new project will involve a lot of research and data analysis.
這個新專案將包含大量的研究和資料分析。

26. **multiple** [ˈmʌltəpl] *a.* 眾多的，多重的

TEST 02

59

TEST 02

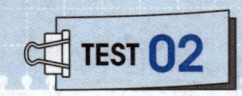

第參部分、非選擇題（占 28 分）

一、中譯英（占 8 分）

1. 許多學生在高中時都會參加社團，目的是為了讓他們的生活更多彩多姿。

   示範譯句

   Many students participate in clubs in high school to make their lives more colorful.

   或：In order to spice their lives up, many students take part in clubs in high school.

   翻譯要點

   a. **participate** [pɑrˋtɪsəˌpet] *vi.* 參加，參與
      participate in... 參加……
      = take part in...
      Due to the success of the last book fair, we'll participate in it again next year.
      由於上次書展辦得很成功，我們明年會再次參展。

   b. **club** [klʌb] *n.* 社團；俱樂部

   c. **colorful** [ˋkʌləfəl] *a.* 多彩多姿的
      colorful history / career / life
      多彩多姿的歷史／職涯／生活

   d. **spice** [spaɪs] *vt.* 使增添樂趣
      spice sth up 使某物變有趣
      We tried to spice the party up by playing some music.
      我們試圖播放音樂好讓派對變有趣。

2. 藉由參加社團，我們可以學到許多對自己的將來有所幫助的實用技能。

   示範譯句

   By joining clubs, we can learn many practical skills that are helpful for our future.

   或：By joining clubs, we can learn a lot of useful skills that can benefit our future.

   翻譯要點

   a. **practical** [ˋpræktɪkḷ] *a.* 實用的
   b. **helpful** [ˋhɛlpfəl] *a.* 有幫助的
   c. **useful** [ˋjusfəl] *a.* 有用的
   d. **benefit** [ˋbɛnəfɪt] *vt.* 有益於 & *vi.* 獲益（與介詞 from 並用）
      benefit from... 從……中獲益

   The doctor said a long rest would benefit the patient.
   醫生說長時間休息將會有益於該病患。
   Everyone living in the village will benefit from the new road.
   那條新路將會造福住在這個村子的每個人。

二、英文作文（占 20 分）

提示：下圖顯示某國青少年玩手機遊戲的習慣。請依據圖表內容寫一篇英文作文，文分二段，第一段描述圖表內容，指出該國青少年玩手機遊戲的習慣為何；第二段則說明自己屬於哪個類別，以及對於玩手機遊戲的看法。

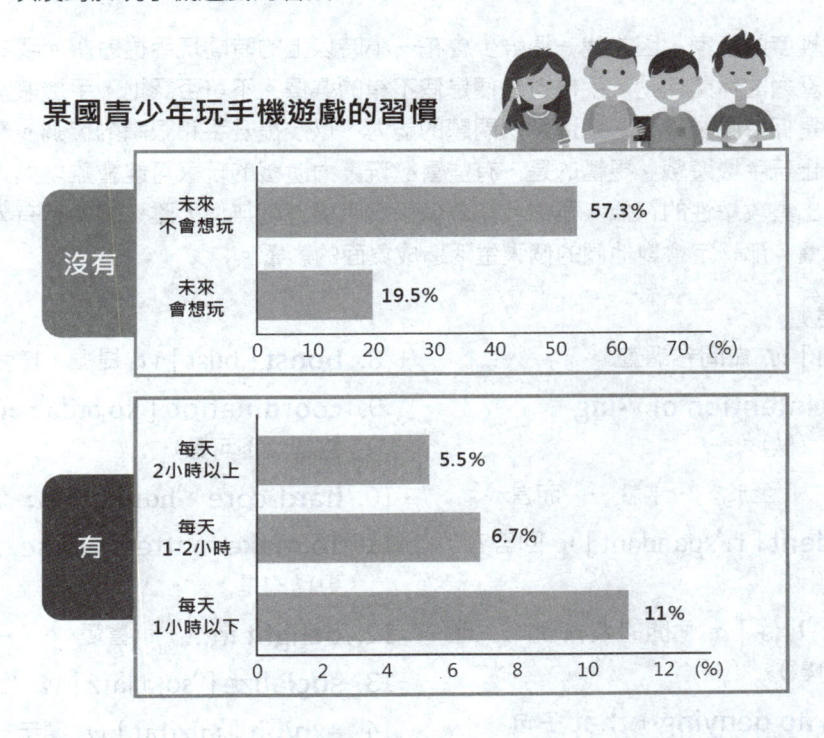

某國青少年玩手機遊戲的習慣

沒有：
- 未來不會想玩：57.3%
- 未來會想玩：19.5%

有：
- 每天 2 小時以上：5.5%
- 每天 1-2 小時：6.7%
- 每天 1 小時以下：11%

示範作文

  A recent survey on the game-playing habits of teenagers in a particular country found that nearly 77% of people polled have never played video games on their phones. Among those, 57.3% have no intention of playing games in the future, while 19.5% would like to try mobile games someday. As for respondents who are gamers, 11% of them spend less than one hour each day playing games, followed by 6.7% who play one to two hours and 5.5% who play more than two hours.

  I'm only a light gamer since I rarely spend more than one hour a week playing games. I think everyone needs leisure activities to relieve stress, and mobile games are a great option. There's no denying that mobile games offer benefits, like keeping our minds sharp, improving problem-solving skills, and boosting hand-eye coordination. However, many hard-core gamers are unable to stop playing. To make matters worse, some gamers who delight in violent games may have a hard time socializing or may even exhibit aggressive behavior. While I reckon it's harmless to play mobile games once in a while, if people can't control their gaming habit, it can definitely affect their personal life in a negative way.

TEST 02

　　近來一項關於某國青少年玩手機遊戲習慣的問卷調查發現，被調查的人當中有將近 **77%** 表示從來沒有玩過手機遊戲。在那些人當中，有 **57.3%** 的人在未來也沒有意願玩手機遊戲，而 **19.5%** 的人表示有朝一日會想玩玩看。至於回覆自己是玩家的人而言，其中有 **11%** 的人每天花不到一小時的時間玩手機遊戲，接著是玩一到兩小時的人有 **6.7%** 及玩兩小時以上的人有 **5.5%**。

　　我只是個輕度的玩家，因為我一週鮮少會花一小時以上的時間玩手機遊戲。我認為每個人都需要能夠紓解壓力的休閒活動，手機遊戲便是個不錯的選擇。不可否認地，手機遊戲為大家帶來許多益處，像是保持腦袋靈光、增進解決問題的能力，以及提升手和眼睛的協調。然而，許多重度玩家無法停止玩手機遊戲。更糟的是，有些喜歡玩暴力遊戲的玩家可能會難以與人交際，或者甚至可能顯露出具攻擊性的行為。雖然我認為偶爾玩手機遊戲無傷大雅，但倘若有人無法控制自己玩遊戲的習慣，那一定會對他們的個人生活造成負面的影響。

重要字詞片語

1. **poll** [pol] *vt.* 做問卷調查
2. **have no intention of V-ing** 沒有意圖（做）……
3. **as for...** 至於……；就……而言
4. **respondent** [rɪˋspɑndənt] *n.* 回答者，應答者
5. **leisure** [ˋliʒɚ] *a.* 休閒的 & *n.* 閒暇（時間）（不可數）
6. **There is no denying + that 子句** 不可否認，……
7. **keep one's mind sharp** 保持某人腦袋靈光
   My grandmother keeps her mind sharp by playing bridge with her friends.
   我外婆靠和朋友打橋牌來保持腦袋靈光。
8. **boost** [bust] *vt.* 提振，增強，促進
9. **coordination** [ko͵ɔrdəˋneʃən] *n.* 協調（不可數）
10. **hard-core** [ˋhɑrd͵kɔr] *a.* 信念堅定的
11. **To make matters worse, ...** 更糟的是，……
12. **delight in...** 喜愛……，以……為樂
13. **socialize** [ˋsoʃə͵laɪz] *vi.* 社交，交際
14. **exhibit** [ɪgˋzɪbɪt] *vt.* 顯示（特性、情感等）
15. **aggressive** [əˋgrɛsɪv] *a.* 具攻擊性的
16. **reckon** [ˋrɛkən] *vt.* 認為，想

TEST 03

第壹部分、選擇題
- 一、詞彙題
- 二、綜合測驗
- 三、文意選填
- 四、篇章結構
- 五、閱讀測驗

第貳部分、混合題

第參部分、非選擇題
- 一、中譯英
- 二、英文作文

第壹部分、選擇題

一、詞彙題

| 1. C | 2. B | 3. D | 4. A | 5. C | 6. A | 7. D | 8. D | 9. B | 10. A |

二、綜合測驗

| 11. D | 12. C | 13. A | 14. A | 15. B | 16. D | 17. A | 18. B | 19. D | 20. C |

三、文意選填

| 21. H | 22. J | 23. A | 24. G | 25. D | 26. B | 27. C | 28. E | 29. F | 30. I |

四、篇章結構

| 31. A | 32. D | 33. C | 34. B |

五、閱讀測驗

| 35. D | 36. C | 37. B | 38. D | 39. B | 40. C | 41. A | 42. B | 43. C | 44. C |
| 45. B | 46. B |

第貳部分、混合題

47. except

48. save time

49. kitchen

50. C, D

第壹部分、選擇題（占 62 分）

一、詞彙題（占 10 分）

<u>C</u> 1. 為了在瞬息萬變的世界中與時俱進，該公司決定拓展人工智慧領域。

❶ (A) rural [ˈrʊrəl] *a.* 鄉下的
Some people like to live in urban areas for convenience, while others prefer rural areas for a quiet environment.
有些人因為便利性而喜歡住都會區，有些人因為環境安靜而喜歡住鄉下。

(B) academic [ˌækəˈdɛmɪk] *a.* 學術的
Laziness may be responsible for Timmy's bad academic performance.
懶惰或許是提米學業成績不佳的原因。

(C) relevant [ˈrɛləvənt] *a.* 有關的
be relevant to...　　和……有關
Do you have any previous job experience relevant to this type of work?
你之前有沒有從事這種工作的相關經驗？

(D) cooperative [koˈɑpərətɪv] *a.* 合作的
Though Sandra didn't like the activity, she did her best to be cooperative.
雖然珊卓不喜歡這項活動，但她還是盡力去配合。

❷ 根據語意，(C) 項應為正選。

必考重點

a. **expand** [ɪkˈspænd] *vt. & vi.* （使）（尺寸或數量）擴大，增加
The company plans to expand its business into international markets next year.
這家公司計劃明年將業務擴展到國際市場。

b. **artificial** [ˌɑrtəˈfɪʃəl] **intelligence** [ɪnˈtɛlədʒəns]
人工智慧（縮寫為 AI）

<u>B</u> 2. 唐納‧川普第二次當選總統，令多數世人驚訝不已。

❶ (A) retirement [rɪˈtaɪrmənt] *n.* 退休
Ted became a volunteer after his retirement from business.
泰德自企業界退休後就成了一名義工。

(B) amazement [əˈmezmənt] *n.* 訝異，驚愕
in amazement　　驚奇地
To one's amazement, ...　　令某人吃驚的是，……

TEST 03

I thought my father would get angry, but to my amazement, he tried to comfort me.
我以為父親會生氣，但令我吃驚的是，他卻試著要安慰我。

(C) **announcement** [əˋnaʊnsmənt] *n.* 公告；宣布
The politician made a formal announcement that he would resign early next year.
這名政治人物正式宣告明年初他將辭職。

(D) **involvement** [ɪnˋvɑlvmənt] *n.* 參與；牽涉
Employee involvement is a big step for the company.
員工投入是這家公司的一大進展。

ⓑ 根據語意及用法，(B) 項應為正選。

D 3. 尼克的老師因為他英文考試作弊而責罵他，而且還因此給了他零分。

ⓐ (A) **advertise** [ˋædvɚˏtaɪz] *vt.* 將……登廣告 & *vi.* 登廣告
You should advertise your car in the local newspaper if you want to sell it quickly.
你如果想快點把車賣掉，應該在本地的報紙登廣告。

(B) **notify** [ˋnotəˏfaɪ] *vt.* 告知，通知
notify sb of sth　　通知某人某事
= inform sb of sth
The receptionist will notify you of the arrival of your guests.
有您的客人到達時，櫃檯人員會通知您。

(C) **endure** [ɪnˋdjʊr] *vt.* 忍耐，忍受
We must try to endure all pain in our quest for success.
在追求成功的過程中，我們必須設法忍受所有的痛苦。

(D) **scold** [skold] *vt.* 責罵，斥責
scold sb (for...)　　（因……）責罵某人
The person you scolded is the boss' son.
你罵的那個人是老闆的兒子。

ⓑ 根據語意及用法，(D) 項應為正選。

必考重點

a. **cheat on a test**　　考試作弊
b. **as a consequence**　　因此，結果
= as a result

Jane works late every day. As a consequence, she is always exhausted when she gets home.
珍每天都工作到很晚。因此，她回到家時總是精疲力盡。

A 4. 在這篇文章最後一頁的底部有本文的摘要，所以如果你沒時間讀完全部，你可以只看最後這幾行文字。

ⓐ (A) summarize [ˈsʌməˌraɪz] vt. 做摘要；總結
  Please summarize the story after you read it.
  讀完這個故事之後，請做摘要。

(B) memorize [ˈmɛməˌraɪz] vt. 記住，背熟
  Kevin loves this movie so much that he has memorized nearly every line in it.
  凱文非常喜愛這部電影，他幾乎記得裡面的每一句臺詞。

(C) motivate [ˈmotəˌvet] vt. 激發，刺激
  motivate sb to V　　促使/激發某人（做）……
  Scholarships often motivate students to study harder.
  獎學金經常能激發學生更用功學習。

(D) eliminate [ɪˈlɪməˌnet] vt. 消除；消滅
  The government has announced that it'll take action to eliminate corruption.
  政府宣布將採取行動肅清貪汙。

ⓑ 根據語意，(A) 項應為正選。

C 5. 人們往往會把寵物當成家人對待，因為這些動物總是陪伴著他們。

ⓐ (A) concrete [ˈkɑnkrit] n. 混凝土
  Most of the houses are built using concrete.
  大部分的房子是用混凝土蓋的。

(B) contrast [ˈkɑnˌtræst] n. 對照，對比
  in contrast to...　　與……成對比
  The puppy appears small in contrast to its mother.
  這隻小狗和母狗比起來模樣小多了。

(C) company [ˈkʌmpənɪ] n. 陪伴（不可數）；公司（可數）
  keep sb company　　陪伴某人
  Jason's girlfriend kept him company when he was in the hospital.
  傑森的女朋友在他住院時陪著他。

(D) commerce [ˈkɑmɝs] n. 商業
  Taipei is Taiwan's center of commerce.
  臺北是臺灣的商業中心。

ⓑ 根據語意及用法，(C) 項應為正選。

TEST 03

67

TEST 03

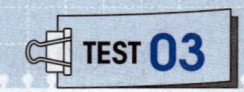

> 必考重點

treat A as B 把 A 當作 B 一樣對待
Mrs. Wang treats Jenny as her daughter.
王太太把珍妮當作女兒一樣對待。

A 6. 根據醫生表示，人們在流感或感冒症狀最嚴重時的傳染性是最高的。

ⓐ (A) **contagious** [kən`tedʒəs] *a.* 傳染性的
Chicken pox is a contagious disease, especially among children.
水痘是一種傳染性疾病，尤其好發於孩童之間。

(B) **convincing** [kən`vɪnsɪŋ] *a.* 令人信服的，有說服力的
= persuasive [pɚ`swesɪv] *a.*
John made a powerful and convincing speech at the meeting.
會議中約翰發表了一篇措詞有力且相當具有說服力的演講。

(C) **dependable** [dɪ`pɛndəbḷ] *a.* 可靠的
= reliable [rɪ`laɪəbḷ] *a.*
My car always breaks down. It is not dependable.
我的車子老是故障。它真是不可靠。

(D) **distinguished** [dɪ`stɪŋwɪʃt] *a.* 卓越的
= outstanding [`aʊt͵stændɪŋ] *a.*
The award went to a distinguished movie director.
該獎項頒給了一位傑出的電影導演。

ⓑ 根據語意，(A) 項應為正選。

> 必考重點

a. **flu** [flu] *n.* 流行性感冒　　　b. **symptom** [`sɪmptəm] *n.* 症狀

D 7. 我很難說服文森接受我對該計畫的建議，因為他是一個很固執的人。

ⓐ (A) **ambiguous** [æm`bɪgjʊəs] *a.* 模稜兩可的
The wording of this contract is ambiguous. Thus, we won't sign it.
這份合約的用字模稜兩可。因此，我們不會簽約。

(B) **admirable** [`ædmərəbḷ] *a.* 值得讚美的，令人欽佩的
The boy's heroic behavior is admirable.
那男孩英勇的行為令人欽佩。

(C) **occasional** [ə`keʒənḷ] *a.* 偶爾的
Except for an occasional headache, Jim is very healthy.
除了偶爾會頭痛外，吉姆非常健康。

(D) **obstinate** [`abstənɪt] *a.* 頑固的
= stubborn [`stʌbɚn] *a.*

be as obstinate as a mule　　像騾子一樣固執（喻「非常固執」）
Johnny was as obstinate as a mule on that point.
強尼在那個問題上非常固執。

ⓑ 根據語意，(D) 項應為正選。

必考重點

a. **have a hard time + V-ing**
= have difficulty / trouble + V-ing
= have problems + V-ing
（做）……有困難／麻煩

b. **convince** [kənˋvɪns] vt. 說服，使相信
convince sb to V　　說服某人……
Sherry convinced her husband to go to the dentist.
雪莉說服她的丈夫去看牙醫。

D　8. 泰德在一個偏遠的島嶼度假，因為他試圖逃離大城市的喧囂擾攘。

ⓐ (A) **reflect** [rɪˋflɛkt] vt. 反射，反映 & vi. 反省（與介詞 on 或 upon 並用）
reflect on / upon...　　反省……；仔細思考……
Luke's behavior reflects the changing attitudes of today's teenagers.
路克的行為反映了現今青少年態度的轉變。

(B) **assure** [əˋʃʊr] vt. 保證
assure sb of sth　　向某人保證某事
I can assure you of John's ability to handle the problem.
我能向你保證約翰具備處理這個問題的能力。

(C) **provide** [prəˋvaɪd] vt. 提供
provide sb with sth　　提供某人某物
= provide sth for sb
The school provides each student with two meals every day.
該校每天提供學生兩餐。

(D) **escape** [əˋskep] vi. & vt. 逃離
escape from...　　從……逃脫
The spider's prey was trying to escape from its web.
這隻蜘蛛的獵物想逃離蜘蛛網。

ⓑ 根據語意及用法，(D) 項應為正選。

必考重點

a. **remote** [rɪˋmot] a. 遙遠的

b. **the hustle and bustle**　　喧囂擾攘

B　9. 尚恩因為七年前的一場嚴重車禍造成永久殘障。自此之後便一直得坐輪椅。

ⓐ (A) **appropriately** [əˋproprɪətlɪ] adv. 適當地
The students were all appropriately dressed for the occasion.
參加那個盛會的學生們各個都穿著得體。

69

TEST 03

(B) **permanently** [ˈpɝmənəntlɪ] *adv.* 永久地
I'll be moving to Bangkok next month and live there permanently.
我下個月就要搬到曼谷永久定居了。

(C) **consistently** [kənˈsɪstəntlɪ] *adv.* 一致地；一向
Tom is consistently late for school.
湯姆上學一向遲到。

(D) **dynamically** [daɪˈnæmɪkəlɪ] *adv.* 不斷變化地；充滿活力地
The report predicts that the economy will continue to expand dynamically.
這份報導預測經濟將持續擴張。

ⓑ 根據語意，(B) 項應為正選。

必考重點

a. **disabled** [dɪsˈebəld] *a.* 殘障的   b. **wheelchair** [ˈwil,tʃɛr] *n.* 輪椅

A 10. 醫生叫護士將傷口縫合及綁上繃帶前，他仔細檢查了病患的傷口。

ⓐ (A) **wound** [wund] *n.* 傷口
Paul rubbed salt in Cindy's wound by telling everyone she was dumped yesterday.
保羅告訴大家辛蒂昨天被甩了，簡直是在她傷口上撒鹽。

(B) **temperature** [ˈtɛmprətʃɚ] *n.* 溫度
A greenhouse provides plants with constant temperatures.
溫室提供了植物穩定的溫度。

(C) **structure** [ˈstrʌktʃɚ] *n.* 結構；建築物
In terms of sentence structure, Chinese is very different from English.
就句子結構而言，中文和英文差異甚大。

(D) **deadline** [ˈdɛd,laɪn] *n.* 最後期限
Reporters always work under great pressure to meet the deadline.
記者總是在趕截稿時間的極大壓力下工作。

ⓑ 根據語意，(A) 項應為正選。

必考重點

a. **examine** [ɪgˈzæmɪn] *vt.* （仔細地）檢查，審查
b. **stitch** [stɪtʃ] *vt.* 縫 & *n.* 一針

A stitch in time saves nine.
及時一針省下了九針──亡羊補牢猶未晚矣。（諺語）

c. **bandage** [ˈbændɪdʒ] *vt.* （用繃帶）包紮 & *n.* 繃帶

二、綜合測驗（占 10 分）

第 11 至 15 題為題組

　　新生兒派對是一項從北美散播到世界上許多其他地方的傳統。習慣上新生兒派對就是為了慶祝嬰兒出生所舉行的派對。有些新生兒派對會在嬰兒快出生前舉辦，而有些則會在出生後才辦。以往的新生兒派對通常只有女性參加，不過情況已有所改變。現在男性也常參加新生兒派對，尤其是有邀請公司同事的那種。派對上常會玩遊戲，最受歡迎的遊戲之一是從超音波圖片上辨別寶寶的身體部位。

　　但新生兒派對的重點並不只是辦一場玩樂的派對，而是讓朋友和家人在育嬰成本上出點力。嬰兒出生後，突然間會增加許多新的開銷。新生兒派對的客人會帶禮物來給嬰兒，像是衣服、玩具和尿布等等。一場好的新生兒派對可以讓新手父母得到一些他們將會需要的東西，讓他們可以全心照顧嬰兒，而不必擔心預算超支。從這方面來說，新生兒派對是幫助夫妻準備為人父母的一項重要工具。

D 11. 理由

ⓐ 本題測試連接詞 while（而，= whereas）的用法：
some..., while others...　　有些人……，而有些人則……
When the fans saw the movie star, some yelled her name, while others wept on the spot.
粉絲看到那位電影明星時，有些人高呼她的名字，有些人則當場哭了出來。

ⓑ 本句句首有 Some baby showers（有些新生兒派對），空格後則有 others（另一些），得知空格應置 while 以形成上述固定用法，故 (D) 項應為正選。

C 12. 理由

ⓐ 本題測試以下語意：(A) aren't interested in（不感興趣）、(B) are no longer welcomed to（不再受歡迎）、(C) now often attend（現在很常參加）、(D) still dedicate themselves to（仍致力於）。

ⓑ 前一句說到以前新生兒派對通常只有女性參加，但情況已有所改變。故根據語意，(C) 項應為正選。

A 13. 理由

ⓐ 本題測試 have 作使役動詞的固定用法：
have + 受詞（通常為人）+ 原形動詞　　叫/使某人（做）……
= make + 受詞 + 原形動詞
= get + 受詞 + to + 原形動詞
Jenny had her husband wash her car.
= Jenny made her husband wash her car.
= Jenny got her husband to wash her car.
珍妮叫她老公幫她洗車。

ⓑ 空格前有使役動詞 have 及作受詞的名詞詞組 friends and family members（朋友和家人），得知空格內應置原形動詞，以形成上述固定用法，故 (A) 項應為正選。

A 14. 理由

ⓐ (A) **expense** [ɪkˋspɛns] *n.* 花費，支出
　　　at great expense　　所費不貲
　　　The stadium was constructed at great expense.
　　　這座體育場是花了很多錢建造的。

　　(B) **savings** [ˋsevɪŋz] *n.* 存款（恆用複數）
　　　I'd like to withdraw all my savings.
　　　我想要提出我全部的存款。

　　(C) **fund** [fʌnd] *n.* 基金
　　　raise funds for...　　為……募款
　　　They are raising funds for those orphans.
　　　他們正在為那些孤兒募款。

　　(D) **income** [ˋɪn͵kʌm] *n.* 收入，所得
　　　a high / low income　　高收入／低收入
　　= a large / small income
　　　People with high incomes usually have to pay more taxes.
　　　高收入的人通常都必須繳比較多的稅。

ⓑ 根據語意，(A) 項應為正選。

B 15. 理由

ⓐ 本題測試以下語意：(A) rushing to the hospital（趕往醫院）、(B) busting their budget（超出預算）、(C) taking maternity leave（請產假）、(D) consuming efficient nutrients（攝取有效的營養素）。

ⓑ 前句提及，新生兒派對會收到一些新手父母所需要的東西，這樣他們就不用另外花錢購買，故根據語意，(B) 項應為正選。

重要字詞片語

1. **a baby shower**　　新生兒派對
2. **involve** [ɪnˋvɑlv] *vt.* 包含；使涉入
   Kyle's plan involves some creative ideas.
   凱爾的計畫中包含一些有創意的點子。
3. **identify** [aɪˋdɛntə͵faɪ] *vt.* 指認，認定
   Tammy identified the purse as hers by telling what it contained.
   塔米說明手提包內有什麼物品，藉此指認這個手提包屬於她。
4. **anatomy** [əˋnætəmɪ] *n.* 身體
5. **sonogram** [ˋsɑnə͵græm] *n.*（尤指胎兒的）超音波照
6. **all at once**　　突然間
   = all of a sudden
   = suddenly
   Judy burst into tears for no reason all at once.
   茱蒂突然無緣無故就大哭了起來。

7. **diaper** [ˋdaɪpɚ] *n.* 尿布
8. **concentrate** [ˋkɑnsṇ͵tret] *vi.* & *vt.* 集中
   concentrate on... 專注於……
   = focus on...

You should concentrate on what the teacher says.
你應當專心聽老師所說的話。

9. **parenthood** [ˋpɛrənt͵hʊd] *n.* 為人父母

第 16 至 20 題為題組

你是個預算有限的學生。或者你喝得酩酊大醉，不敢回家面對家人的憤怒。又或者你是個趴趴走找生意做，想要撙節開支的個體戶。大多數飯店一個晚上的住房價大約都在一百美元以上。在日本，許多前面提到的人會選擇在膠囊旅館過夜。

膠囊旅館在 1979 年起源於日本大阪，現在已經變得相當熱門。對於那些要求一流服務、寬敞房間以及居家舒適感的人而言，千萬別去膠囊旅館。它提供每位顧客一間「房間」，只比太平間中用來存放屍體的格子大一點。基於這個原因，膠囊旅館顯然不適合有幽閉恐懼症的顧客。

每個膠囊裡面有一臺電視、空調設備以及閱讀燈。旅館也會提供公用廁所。可能還有一些其他的公共設施，像是點心吧、休閒室，甚至是三溫暖。膠囊旅館現在在世界各地都有，通常一晚要價大約二十至四十美元。對於那些手頭拮据的人，這個點子還不差。

D 16. 理由

ⓐ (A) **agency** [ˋedʒənsɪ] *n.* 代辦處，機關
   a news / travel agency　通訊社／旅行社
   My dad works at a travel agency.
   我爸爸在旅行社工作。

(B) **banquet** [ˋbæŋkwɪt] *n.* 盛宴
   Jessica was dressed in a gorgeous evening gown at the banquet.
   潔西卡在宴會上穿著一襲迷人的晚禮服。

(C) **document** [ˋdɑkjəmənt] *n.* 文件
   These confidential documents must be kept in a safe place instead of just lying on your desk.
   這些機密文件得放在安全的地方，而不是放你桌上。

(D) **trip** [trɪp] *n.* 旅行
   on a business trip　出差
   Jack is on a business trip and won't come back until this Friday.
   傑克去出差，要到這星期五才會回來。

ⓑ 根據語意，(D) 項應為正選。

TEST 03

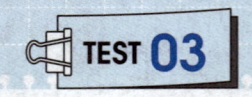

A 17. 理由

ⓐ (A) **cost** [kɔst] *vt.* 花費（三態同形）

cost 須以「物」或虛主詞 it 作主詞，而不可用「人」作主詞，且之後僅能接表「金錢」的名詞：

sth costs (sb) + 表金錢的名詞　　某物花了（某人）……（金錢）

it costs sb + 表金錢的名詞 + to V　　某人花……（金錢）做……

This new CD player cost me NT$5,000.
這臺新的 CD 播放器花了我新臺幣五千元。

It cost Rose three thousand NT dollars to buy the DVD burner.
蘿絲花了新臺幣三千元買這臺 DVD 燒錄機。

(B) **take** [tek] *vt.* 花費（三態為：take, took [tʊk], taken [ˋtekən]）

使用 take 時，可用虛主詞 it 或事物作主詞，與表時間的名詞並用，句型如下：

it takes sb + 時間 + to V　　某人從事……花費了若干時間

sth takes + (sb) + 時間　　某事物花（某人）若干時間

It took Polly a whole morning to clean up her bedroom.
波莉花了一整個早上才清理好她的臥室。

The job took me two hours to finish.
這工作花了我兩個小時才完成。

(C) **spend** [spɛnd] *vt.* 花費（時間、金錢）（三態為：spend, spent [spɛnt], spent）

spend 須以「人」作主詞，之後可接表「時間」或「金錢」的名詞。

sb spends + 表時間/金錢的名詞 + V-ing / on sth

某人花費……（時間/金錢）做……/在……上

Mary spends one-third of her salary buying clothes per month.
瑪麗每個月都會把她三分之一的薪水花在買衣服上面。

(D) **pay** [pe] *vt.* 付錢（三態為：pay, paid [ped], paid）

Thomas has already paid the bill.
湯瑪斯已經付帳了。

ⓑ 本句空格前有表「物」的主詞 Most hotels（大多數飯店），空格後有表「金錢」的名詞 around US$100 and up（大約在一百美元以上），得知空格應置 cost，故 (A) 項應為正選。

B 18. 理由

ⓐ 本題測試以下語意：(A) check in now（立即入住）、(B) look elsewhere（看看別處）、(C) renew your passport（更新你的護照）、(D) call for room service（打給客房服務）。

ⓑ 前面提及想要省錢的人可以選擇膠囊旅館，所以要求一流服務與品質的客人應該另尋別處，故根據語意，(B) 項應為正選。

D 19. 理由

ⓐ (A) **communicate** [kəˈmjunəˌket] *vi.* 溝通，交流（此選項以過去分詞作形容詞用）
communicate with... 與……溝通
The well-known scientist believes that he can communicate with life in outer space.
那位知名的科學家相信他能與外太空生物溝通。

(B) **communicable** [kəˈmjunəkəbl] *a.* 可傳達的（思想）；會傳染的（疾病）
Influenza is a communicable disease.
流行性感冒是會傳染的疾病。

(C) **communicative** [kəˈmjunəˌketɪv] *a.* 有表達能力的；善於言談的
A good leader is not only communicative but also willing to listen.
好的領導人不只要善於溝通也要願意傾聽。

(D) **communal** [ˈkɑmjʊnḷ] *a.* 公共的
There are five separate bedrooms and a communal kitchen in this apartment.
這間公寓裡有五間獨立臥室和一間公共廚房。

ⓑ 根據語意，(D) 項應為正選。

C 20. 理由

ⓐ (A) **via** [ˈvaɪə / ˈvɪə] *prep.* 經由（= through）
You can access our library's database via the internet.
你可以透過網路進入我們圖書館的資料庫。

(B) **among** [əˈmʌŋ] *prep.* 在……之中
Karen found a picture of her old boyfriend among her photos.
凱倫在她的照片中發現了她以前男友的照片。

(C) **per** [pɚ] *prep.* 每……（年、人、公里等）
The scenic spot attracts about three million visitors per year.
此旅遊景點每年吸引大約三百萬名觀光客。

(D) **since** [sɪns] *prep.* 自從
We haven't seen each other since last year.
我們從去年起就沒見過面了。

ⓑ 根據語意，(C) 項應為正選。

重要字詞片語

1. **budget** [ˈbʌdʒɪt] *n.* 預算
live / be on a tight budget
靠緊縮預算過活

Iris had to live on a tight budget after quitting her job.
辭職後，艾莉絲得緊縮荷包過活。

TEST 03

2. **capsule** [ˈkæpsḷ] *n.* 膠囊
3. **demand** [dɪˈmænd] *vt.* 要求
= require [rɪˈkwaɪr]
The teacher demanded that we (should) hand in our assignments by tomorrow.
老師要求我們明天前要交作業。
4. **first-class** [ˌfɜstˈklæs] *a.* 第一流的；極好的
= first-rate [ˌfɜstˈret] *a.*
5. **spacious** [ˈspeʃəs] *a.* 廣大的，寬敞的
6. **comfort** [ˈkʌmfɚt] *n.* 安慰，慰藉
7. **store** [stɔr] *vt.* 貯藏；保存
This flash drive stores a lot of information.
這個隨身碟儲存了許多資料。
8. **corpse** [kɔrps] *n.* 屍體
9. **morgue** [mɔrg] *n.* 太平間
10. **claustrophobia** [ˌklɔstrəˈfobɪə] *n.* 幽閉恐懼症（不可數）
11. **facility** [fəˈsɪlətɪ] *n.* 設施，設備（常用複數）
12. **a snack bar** 點心吧
13. **lounge** [laʊndʒ] *n.* 休息室
14. **sauna** [ˈsaʊnə] *n.* 三溫暖
15. **strapped** [stræpt] *a.* 手頭緊的
be strapped (for cash) 手頭緊的
Elaine is strapped for cash, so she won't go shopping with us today.
伊蓮手頭很緊，所以她今天不會和我們一起去逛街。

三、文意選填（占 10 分）

第 21 至 30 題為題組

　　色彩無所不在，並以不同的方式影響我們。比方說，黑色被視為嚴肅的色調，這就是為什麼在西方葬禮上常穿暗色衣服。另一方面，紅色是較為活潑的顏色。白色被視為純潔乾淨。那麼你可能會想，為何醫生替病人開刀時，身穿的是綠色或藍色而非白色的衣服。外科醫師確實曾經常穿白色的衣服。而這自二十世紀初期開始有所轉變。改變的原因和各種顏色以不同的方式影響我們的眼睛有關。

　　根據一篇 1998 年刊登在護理雜誌的文章，外科手術服裝，亦稱為 scrubs，會改為綠色是由於一名有影響力的醫生所致。顯然他認為白色對外科醫生來說過於刺眼。也就是說，醫生身上衣服的白色，以及手術房裡明亮的燈，會造成眼睛疲勞。綠色證實是個理想的選擇，因為在色環中它是紅色的對比色。那意味著，對在手術期間一直盯著紅色鮮血的外科醫生來說，綠色讓其眼睛得以放鬆。此外，偶爾看看綠色或藍色，讓醫生更容易察覺紅色色調上的差異，因為那些顏色比白色還更能和紅色形成鮮明的對比。

　　外科手術服為什麼更適合綠色或藍色還有另一個原因。假如有人看太多紅色後再看白色的表面，那個人就會看見綠色的影像。這些幻象可能會令人分心，顯然在手術房最好避免此狀況。因此，白色不再用於外科手術服是件好事。

H **21.** 理由
ⓐ 空格前有介詞 at，得知空格應置入名詞或動名詞。
ⓑ 選項中符合上述的有 (A) impact（影響）、(B) ideal（理想）、(C) staring（凝視）、(E) variations（變化）、(F) surface（表面）、(H) funerals（葬禮）及 (J) performing（施行），惟根據語意，(H) 項應為正選。

J **22.** 理由
ⓐ 空格前有 be 動詞 are，而空格後有名詞 operations（手術），得知空格應置入及物動詞的現在分詞形。
ⓑ 選項中符合上述的僅剩 (J) performing（施行），置入後亦符合語意，故為正選。

A **23.** 理由
ⓐ 空格前有作主詞的名詞詞組 various colors（各種顏色），而空格後有作受詞的名詞詞組 our eyes（我們的眼睛），得知空格應置入複數及物動詞，且根據本句時態，該動詞應為現在式。
ⓑ 選項中符合上述的有 (A) impact（影響）及 (F) surface（鋪上硬面），惟根據語意，(A) 項應為正選。

G **24.** 理由
ⓐ 空格前有作該形容詞子句主詞的名詞詞組 surgical clothing（外科手術服裝），而空格後有介詞 to，得知空格應置入不及物動詞，且根據本句時態，該動詞應為過去式。
ⓑ 選項中符合上述的僅 (G) switched（改變），置入後亦符合語意，故為正選。

D **25.** 理由
ⓐ 空格前有定冠詞 the，而空格後有名詞 lights（燈），得知空格應置入形容詞以修飾 lights。
ⓑ 選項中符合上述的有 (B) ideal（理想的）及 (D) bright（明亮的），惟根據語意，(D) 項應為正選。

B **26.** 理由
ⓐ 空格前有定冠詞 the，而空格後有名詞 choice（選擇），得知空格應置入形容詞以修飾 choice。
ⓑ 選項中符合上述的僅剩 (B) ideal（理想的），置入後亦符合語意，故為正選。

C **27.** 理由
ⓐ 空格前有 be 動詞 been，空格後有介詞 at，得知空格應置入不及物動詞的現在分詞形或及物動詞的過去分詞形。
ⓑ 選項中符合上述的有 (C) staring（凝視）及 (I) avoided（避開），惟根據語意，(C) 項應為正選。

E 28. 理由

ⓐ 空格前有及物動詞 see（看），而空格後有介詞 in，得知空格應置入複數名詞或不可數名詞以作 see 的受詞。

ⓑ 選項中符合上述的僅剩 (E) variations（變化），置入後亦符合語意，故為正選。

F 29. 理由

ⓐ 空格前有不定冠詞 a 及形容詞 white（白的），得知空格應置入單數可數名詞以被 white 修飾。

ⓑ 選項中符合上述的僅剩 (F) surface（表面），置入後亦符合語意，故為正選。

I 30. 理由

ⓐ 空格前有 be 動詞 is 及副詞 best（最好），而空格後有介詞 in，得知空格應置入不及物動詞的現在分詞形或及物動詞的過去分詞形。

ⓑ 選項中符合上述的僅剩 (I) avoided（避開），置入後亦符合語意，故為正選。

重要字詞片語

1. **affect** [ə`fɛkt] *vt.* 影響
2. **grim** [grɪm] *a.* 嚴肅的；令人沮喪的；嚴峻的
3. **vibrant** [`vaɪbrənt] *a.* 充滿活力的
4. **surgeon** [`sɝdʒən] *n.* 外科醫師
   surgical [`sɝdʒɪkl] *a.* 外科手術的
5. **shift** [ʃɪft] *vi.* 改變
6. **nursing** [`nɝsɪŋ] *n.* 護理；看護
7. **scrubs** [skrʌbs] *n.* 醫院工作服（恆用複數）
8. **influential** [͵ɪnflʊ`ɛnʃəl] *a.* 有影響力的
9. **apparently** [ə`pærəntlɪ] *adv.* 顯然地；似乎
10. **strain** [stren] *n.* 勞損；壓力
11. **opposite** [`ɑpəzɪt] *n.* 相反的人／事／物
12. **relief** [rɪ`lif] *n.* 舒緩；紓解
13. **occasionally** [ə`keʒənəlɪ] *adv.* 偶爾，有時候
14. **hue** [hju] *n.* 色調；顏色
15. **contrast** [kən`træst] *vi.* 形成對比
16. **illusion** [ɪ`luʒən] *n.* 錯覺；幻覺
17. **distracting** [dɪ`stræktɪŋ] *a.* 令人分心的

四、篇章結構（占 8 分）

第 31 至 34 題為題組

　　世界上某些最貧窮和最弱勢的人民居住在南亞、東南亞和非洲，當地的數億居民甚至連接受國小教育的機會都沒有。31. 大部分的農村村民能發展的天生才能大多受限。然而，從 1999 年開始，許多這樣的人開始在生活中看見另外一種可能性。

那一年，微軟公司的行銷主管約翰・伍德決定暫時遠離高壓的工作環境。32. 他選擇在喜馬拉雅山展開一趟為期三週的徒步旅行。當他在那裡時，他對當地人為孩童教育提供如此稀少的東西感到震驚。他發現除了從唯一一間教室窗戶照進來的光線外，這些孩子們沒有書籍、桌子或照明設備。伍德向一位男老師提及缺乏書本一事，他僅僅說：「先生，或許有朝一日你會帶著書本回到這裡。」那正是改變伍德以及四千多萬名孩童生活的催化劑。

不久之後，伍德和艾琳・甘祖與迪內什・什雷斯塔共同創立了「閱讀空間」，那是一個與當地村民合作以改善或提供設備與師資培訓的地方慈善機構。該機構設立識字計畫和圖書館，並協助改善學校基礎設施。並致力於改善性別平等，鼓勵女生完成中等教育並培養生活技能。33. 伍德想出了三條簡單的原則來指導他的新服務事業。第一條是大膽的目標會吸引大膽的人，且他們應試著與共享相同願景的人來往。第二條是把事情做完。34. 無論可行性為何，人們不該只談論要做什麼而是直接放手去做。第三條則是幫助人知道如何解決問題，而不只是施捨物品而已。「閱讀空間」期望當地居民可以竭盡所能來幫助他們的孩子建造學校。如今，數個發展中國家 —— 從巴基斯坦和柬埔寨到坦尚尼亞和尚比亞 —— 有四千萬名弱勢兒童有機會接受更多且更優質的教育。

A 31. 理由
- ⓐ 空格前的句子提到，當地有數億居民缺乏受教育的機會，而空格後的句子則提到，這些人開始看見另一種可能性。可推測空格應提及缺乏教育機會所面臨的問題。
- ⓑ 選項 (A) 表示，大部分的農村村民能發展的天生才能大多受限，且選項中 Most of these rural villagers（大部分的農村村民）與前句的 Some of the world's poorest and most underprivileged people（世界上某些最貧窮和最弱勢的人民）、後句的 many such people（許多這樣的人）互相呼應，填入後語意連貫，可知 (A) 項應為正選。

D 32. 理由
- ⓐ 空格前的句子提到，伍德暫時離開他的工作，而空格後的句子則提到，他發現當地人缺乏受教育的狀況。可推測空格應提及他離開工作後所做的事。
- ⓑ 選項 (D) 表示，他選擇在喜馬拉雅山展開一趟為期三週的徒步旅行，與前一句提及伍德離開他的工作形成關聯。空格後的 While there（當他在那裡時）亦與選項中的 in the Himalayas（在喜馬拉雅山）形成關聯，填入後語意連貫，可知 (D) 項應為正選。

C 33. 理由
- ⓐ 空格前提及，伍德創辦了「閱讀空間」，以及該機構致力做到的事情，空格後則依序提及三條原則，可推測空格應要提及創辦「閱讀空間」與三條原則之間的關聯。
- ⓑ 選項 (C) 表示，伍德想出了三條簡單的原則來指導他的新服務事業，與空格後提及三條原則的內容形成關聯，填入後語意連貫，可知 (C) 項應為正選。

TEST 03

B 34. 理由

ⓐ 空格前的句子提到，第二條原則為要把事情做完，而空格後的句子則開始說明第三條原則的內容，可推測空格應為第二條原則的說明及補充。

ⓑ 選項 (B) 表示，無論可行性為何，人們不該只談論要做什麼而是直接放手去做，與前句互相呼應，填入後形成關聯，可知 (B) 項應為正選。

(E) 項中譯：「閱讀空間」總部設於美國，在全球擁有超過 1,400 名員工。

重要字詞片語

1. **underprivileged** [ˌʌndɚˈprɪvəlɪdʒd] *a.* 弱勢的；貧困的
2. **rural** [ˈrʊrəl] *a.* 農村的，鄉村的
3. **innate** [ɪˈnet] *a.* 天生的
4. **marketing** [ˈmɑrkɪtɪŋ] *n.* 市場行銷（不可數）
5. **executive** [ɪgˈzɛkjutɪv] *n.* 主管 & *a.* 行政的；執行的
6. **opt** [ɑpt] *vi.* 選擇
   opt for... 選擇……
   Don't always opt for the easy option. Try something difficult.
   不要老是挑軟柿子吃。試著做點有難度的事情吧。
7. **trekking** [ˈtrɛkɪŋ] *n.* 長途行走／跋涉（不可數）
8. **appalled** [əˈpɔld] *a.* 感到震驚的
   be appalled at... 對……感到震驚
   The public was appalled at the brutality of the recent crime in their town.
   民眾對最近鎮上的一樁凶殘罪行感到驚駭萬分。
9. **in terms of...** 在……方面，就……來說
   Tammy is like her mother in terms of appearance.
   泰咪長得和她母親很像。
10. **other than...** 除了……
    Other than a sandwich, I haven't had anything to eat today.
    除了一份三明治，我今天還沒吃任何東西。
11. **catalyst** [ˈkætəlɪst] *n.* 促進改變的因素；催化劑
12. **literacy** [ˈlɪtərəsɪ] *n.* 識字（不可數）
13. **infrastructure** [ˈɪnfrəˌstrʌktʃɚ] *n.* 基礎建設
14. **equality** [ɪˈkwɑlətɪ] *n.* 平等，同等
15. **bold** [bold] *a.* 大膽的，英勇的；醒目的
16. **vision** [ˈvɪʒən] *n.* 遠見；視力
17. **odds** [ɑdz] *n.* 可能性，機會；困難（皆恆用複數）
    against all odds 克服重重困難
    Against all odds, the paralyzed man miraculously started walking again.
    那名癱瘓的男子克服重重困難，奇蹟似地再次開始走路。
18. **expect sb to V**
    期望／預料某人（做）……
    Betty's parents expected her to become a doctor.
    貝蒂的父母期望她能成為一名醫生。
19. **disadvantaged** [ˌdɪsədˈvæntɪdʒd] *a.* 弱勢的；貧困的
20. **headquarter** [ˈhɛdˈkwɔrtɚ] *vt.* 設置總部

五、閱讀測驗（占 24 分）

第 35 至 38 題為題組

在美國，說話帶東北部口音的人常被認為是知識分子，而講話帶南方口音則常被視為友善但教育程度較低的人。同時，使用紐約口音經常被評為沒有禮貌。在大西洋另一端，英國人對於地方性的口音也有他們自己並無根據的觀感或說偏見。他們看待伯明罕和利物浦人的方式類似美國人看待南方人。使用標準英國音 —— 也就是傳統上來自英國南部的中產階級口音 —— 的人，則給人有教養且值得信賴的感覺。

然而這些印象並沒有事實根據，而是隨著時間發展而來的刻板印象。我們在嬰兒時期就懂得信任某些口音。當我們誕生在世間的頭幾個月，就已能分辨語言與方言的不同。在那時我們就會表現出比較喜歡用我們熟悉方式說話的人。這種狀況稱之為「同口音偏見」，它在我們成長為孩童時仍延續著，讓我們比較不信任用陌生口音說話的人。除了懷疑與不信任之外，我們還更加意識到常與那些口音聯結在一起的社會地位和刻板印象。

好在此種情形不會是一成不變的。我們可以透過每天互動的人們來改變對口音的信任度。在人類歷史上的大部分時間，人們主要只跟同村或同社區的人往來。但在現今交流頻繁的世界裡，我們一直都在接觸來自多種地區、國家、國際的口音。我們有無數機會打破對口音的偏見，並且依據別人真實的模樣而非其口音的刻板印象來接納對方。

D 35. 美國南部人與來自伯明罕的英國人有什麼相同之處？
(A) 他們備受尊重。　　　　　　　　(B) 他們一點都不友善。
(C) 他們被視為沒禮貌。　　　　　　(D) 他們被認為教育程度較低。

理由
根據本文第一段第一句，講話帶南方口音則常被視為友善但教育程度較低的人，以及第一段第四句，他們看待伯明罕和利物浦人的方式類似美國人看待南方人，故 (D) 項應為正選。

C 36. 第二段中的 This 指的是什麼？
(A) 渴望聽到不同的說話口氣。　　　(B) 必須遵循固定每日例行公事。
(C) 喜歡和我們說話方式一樣的人。　(D) 喜歡聽到我們的父母說話。

理由
本文第二段第五句說明一種情況：在那時我們就會表現出比較喜歡用我們熟悉方式說話的人，可推測 This 即指該情況，故 (C) 項應為正選。

B 37. 人們可以如何擺脫對口音的偏見？
(A) 從小就學習說外語。　　　　　　(B) 花時間與許多不同的人相處。
(C) 訓練自己說話更加不帶口音。　　(D) 與家鄉的在地人往來。

理由
根據本文第三段第二句，我們可以透過每天互動的人們來改變對口音的信任度；以及第三段第四句中提到，我們一直都在接觸來自多種地區、國家、國際的口音，故 (B) 項應為正選。

D **38.** 作者對於口音抱持何種態度？
(A) 如今它們變得彼此更相似。
(B) 在他耳裡聽來都很好笑、陌生。
(C) 它們可以相當透露出某人的教養。
(D) 它們無法真正反映出一個人的性格。

理由
根據本文第三段最後一句，我們有無數機會打破對口音的偏見，並且依據別人真實的模樣而非其口音的刻板印象來接納對方，可推測作者對於口音的想法，故 (D) 項應為正選。

重要字詞片語

1. **accent** [ˈæksənt] n. 口音
   with a(n)... accent 帶著……的口音
2. **twang** [twæŋ] n.（某些方言的）鼻音
3. **uneducated** [ʌnˈɛdʒʊˌketɪd] a. 未受教育的
4. **across the pond** 大西洋彼岸，在大西洋的另一端
5. **unfounded** [ʌnˈfaʊndɪd] a. 無事實根據的
6. **bias** [ˈbaɪəs] n. 偏見
7. **regional** [ˈridʒənl̩] a. 地區的
8. **in the same light** 從相同的角度來看
9. **convey** [kənˈve] vt. 傳達，傳遞
   The artist's latest creation conveys his idea of time and space.
   這位藝術家最新的創作傳達了他對時間及空間的想法。
10. **worth** [wɝθ] prep. 有……的價值
11. **impression** [ɪmˈprɛʃən] n. 印象
12. **root** [rut] vt. & vi.（植物）生根
    be rooted in... 根植於……
    Chris believes that prejudice is rooted in ignorance and fear.
    克里斯認為偏見源自於無知和恐懼。
13. **stereotype** [ˈstɛrɪəˌtaɪp] n. 刻板印象
14. **dialect** [ˈdaɪəlɛkt] n. 方言
15. **manner** [ˈmænɚ] n. 方法
16. **suspicion** [səˈspɪʃən] n. 懷疑
17. **associate** [əˈsoʃɪˌet] vi. 往來
    associate with sb 與某人往來
    I don't like to associate with Jim because he is arrogant.
    我不喜歡和吉姆往來，因為他很自大。
18. **interconnected** [ˌɪntɚkəˈnɛktɪd] a. 互相連結的
19. **be exposed to...** 使接觸／暴露於……
    Most parents don't want their children to be exposed to violence on TV.
    大部分的父母都不想讓孩子接觸到電視上的暴力。
20. **prejudice** [ˈprɛdʒədɪs] n. 偏見
21. **fondness** [ˈfɑndnəs] n. 喜愛
22. **get rid of...** 擺脫……
23. **neutral** [ˈn(j)utrəl] a. 中立的
24. **reveal** [rɪˈvil] vt. 透露，揭露

第 39 至 42 題為題組

月亮在夜空中幾乎是永恆的存在，但它的外觀每天都會改變。最明顯、每晚都看得出來的改變，就是月球受日照面積的增減。當月亮最接近太陽且在地球上的我們看不見時，這個狀態稱為新月，而新月要達到表面完全受光照耀的滿月階段大約要兩週，這段期間稱為盈月。從滿月變回新月也要兩週左右的時間，而這段期間稱為虧月。

另一項與月亮相關的有趣事實是它的軌道。月亮繞著地球運轉，但它的軌道不是圓形，而是橢圓形。這意味著月亮有時候比較接近地球。當月亮離地球最近時（稱為「近地點」），距離大約是三十六萬三千公里。當月亮離地球最遠時（稱為「遠地點」），則大約是四十萬五千公里遠。這些差異導致月亮大小的變化多達 14%，而亮度差異高達 30%。當滿月落在或接近其近地點的時間時，被稱為超級月亮。

雖然以上各種術語都相當現代，但人們觀察月亮已有好幾千年了。由於月亮的可靠和規律性，許多古文明都用月亮來計算時間。一般相信西元前 4500 年至西元前 1900 年居住在美索不達米亞南部的古蘇美人，是第一個這麼做的民族。他們發明了共有十二個月的陰曆曆法，每月有二十九或三十天，從新月出現那天起算。每三年會多加一個月份來和太陽年保持一致。這類似每四年在二月底增加一天──由羅馬人發明的一種做法。

B 39. 什麼是盈月？
(A) 我們無法在空中看到月亮的期間。
(B) 新月到滿月之間的變化階段。
(C) 當月亮完全受光照耀時的兩週時間。
(D) 滿月變成新月的期間。

理由
根據本文第一段第三、四句，而新月要達到表面完全受光照耀的滿月階段大約要兩週，這段期間稱為盈月，故 (B) 項應為正選。

C 40. 根據本文，我們可對超級月亮作出何種推斷？
(A) 它每年會在空中出現一次。
(B) 它有時會在月亮位於遠地點時發生。
(C) 它比平時的月亮更亮更大。
(D) 它比過去更常出現。

理由
根據本文第二段最後兩句，這些差異導致月亮大小的變化多達 14%，而亮度差異高達 30%。當滿月落在或接近其近地點的時間時，被稱為超級月亮，故可推測 (C) 項應為正選。

A 41. 根據本文，古蘇美人做了什麼？
(A) 他們用月亮製作曆法。
(B) 他們撰寫有關月亮的神話和傳說。
(C) 他們根據月亮創造了許多新詞彙。
(D) 他們引進了月亮的概念給羅馬人。

理由
根據本文第三段第二、三句提及古蘇美人據信是第一個用月亮來計算時間的民族，以及第三段第四句提到，他們發明了陰曆曆法，故 (A) 項應為正選。

B 42. 第三段中的 a practice 指的是什麼？
(A) 把月份分成二十九或三十天。
(B) 每隔幾年就新增額外的一天。
(C) 三年後就加入一個新的月份。
(D) 陰曆和陽曆的實施。

理由

"a practice that was introduced..." 實為 "which is a practice that was introduced..."，為非限定形容詞子句，修飾前面的動名詞片語 "adding an extra day at the end of February every four years"，故 (B) 項應為正選。

重要字詞片語

1. **constant** [ˈkɑnstənt] *a.* 經常發生的
2. **visible** [ˈvɪzəbl̩] *a.* （肉眼）可見的
3. **sunlit** [ˈsʌnˌlɪt] *a.* 受陽光照射的；陽光充足的
4. **light** [laɪt] *vt.* 照亮（三態為：light, lighted / lit [lɪt], lighted / lit）
5. **waxing moon** 盈月（月亮從新月變成滿月的期間）
6. **transition** [trænˈzɪʃən] *n.* 轉變
   the transition from A to B 從 A 轉變為 B
7. **waning moon** 虧月（月亮從滿月變成新月的期間）
8. **orbit** [ˈɔrbɪt] *n.* （天體等的）運行軌道
9. **oval** [ˈovl̩] *n.* 橢圓形
10. **perigee** [ˈpɛrɪˌdʒi] *n.* 近地點
11. **apogee** [ˈæpəˌdʒi] *n.* 遠地點
12. **vary** [ˈvɛrɪ] *vi.* 變化
13. **terminology** [ˌtɝməˈnɑlədʒɪ] *n.* 術語，專門用語
14. **observe** [əbˈzɝv] *vt.* 觀察
15. **civilization** [ˌsɪvl̩aɪˈzeʃən] *n.* 文明
16. **reliability** [rɪˌlaɪəˈbɪlətɪ] *n.* 可靠性
17. **regularity** [ˌrɛgjəˈlærətɪ] *n.* 規律性
18. **Sumerian** [suˈmɪrɪən] *n.* 蘇美人 & *a.* 蘇美人的
19. **Mesopotamia** [ˌmɛsəpəˈtemɪə] *n.* 美索不達米亞
20. **lunar** [ˈlunɚ] *a.* 月亮的，與月亮有關的
    a lunar calendar 農／陰曆
21. **commence** [kəˈmɛns] *vi.* & *vt.* 開始
    commence with sth 以某事開始
    The celebration commenced with fireworks and a parade.
    慶典以煙火和遊行活動展開序幕。
22. **bring sb/sth into line (with...)**
    讓某人／某事物（與……）保持一致
    Our manager tried to bring our department into line with all the others.
    經理試圖讓我們部門跟所有其他部門同步。
23. **phase** [fez] *n.* 階段，時期
24. **interval** [ˈɪntɚvl̩] *n.* 間隔（的時間）
25. **concept** [ˈkɑnsɛpt] *n.* 觀念，想法
26. **implementation** [ˌɪmpləmɛnˈteʃən] *n.* 實施，執行

第 43 至 46 題為題組

多年以來，杜拜以其大膽的外海人工島、旋轉大樓、七星級飯店，甚至有空調的沙灘而屢次登上新聞頭條。不過要說讓杜拜最出名的，應該是它擁有全世界最高的建築物。哈里發塔高度將近 830 公尺 —— 竟然超過 0.5 英里 —— 輕易打破先前由臺灣的臺北 101 所保持的 508 公尺世界紀錄。事實上，就算在哈里發塔之後完工的諸多建築物，其高度仍不足以擊敗杜拜這棟摩天大樓。目前世界上第二高的大樓為 632 公尺的上海中心大廈。而吉隆坡的默迪卡 118 —— 預計於 2022 年年底完工 —— 高度將會逼近 679 公尺。

這棟最初名為杜拜塔的建築於 2004 年開工，工程耗時六年。完工時它已重新命名為哈里發塔，以向借錢給杜拜來協助大樓完工的阿拉伯聯合大公國總統致敬。雖然建築的整體設計模仿遍布阿拉伯聯合大公國的伊斯蘭建築風格，但許多細節是以安全為考量。例如樓層的 Y 字形設計可以降低風力對結構的影響，而混凝土的核心以及與主棟連接的側棟可以確保穩定性。

大樓其他各處也以安全為考量。儘管在建築物內供人活動的一百六十層樓當中，有五十七部電梯可以上下運送住戶、賓客、上班族、逛街的顧客以及用餐的人，但在面對緊急狀況時仍需要有替代方案。因此許多樓層有避難空間，可以在災難事件發生時提供庇護。

對於住在哈里發塔的大量穆斯林住戶而言，這棟摩天大樓的高度造成不一樣的問題。齋戒月期間，穆斯林必須從日出禁食至日落。但由於哈里發塔太高，太陽即使降至地平面仍可在高樓層看見。為了解決這個問題，住在高樓層的穆斯林被指示要比住在低樓層的住戶晚二至三分鐘開始進食。

C 43. 下列哪一項為各個建築物由高至低的正確高度順序？
(A) 哈里發塔 > 臺北 101 > 上海中心大廈 > 默迪卡 118
(B) 臺北 101 > 上海中心大廈 > 默迪卡 118 > 哈里發塔
(C) 哈里發塔 > 默迪卡 118 > 上海中心大廈 > 臺北 101
(D) 默迪卡 118 > 哈里發塔 > 臺北 101 > 上海中心大廈

理由
根據本文第一段提及哈里發塔高度將近 830 公尺、尚未完工的默迪卡 118 將會高達 679 公尺、上海中心大廈高度為 632 公尺，以及臺北 101 高度為 508 公尺，得知 (C) 項應為正選。

TEST 03

<u>C</u> 44. 本文暗示哈里發塔的哪件事情？
(A) 它在建造期間曾二度更名。
(B) 它的設計受到阿拉伯聯合大公國的總統影響。
(C) 它的建造工程已結束並在 2010 年啟用。
(D) 它的設計在阿拉伯聯合大公國是獨一無二的。

> 理由
> 根據本文第二段第一句，哈里發塔的建造於 2004 年開工，工程耗時六年，得知哈里發塔是於 2010 年完工，故 (C) 項應為正選。

<u>B</u> 45. 下列哪一項最接近第三段中 sanctuary 的意思？
(A) 壓力。　　(B) 安全。　　(C) 宗教。　　(D) 溝通。

> 理由
> 本粗體字表「保護，庇護」。根據本文第三段第一句提及大樓其他各處也以安全為考量，且提及 refuge areas（避難空間），可推測本粗體字最接近「安全」，故 (B) 項應為正選。

<u>B</u> 46. 根據本文，住在哈里發塔高樓層的穆斯林被要求做什麼？
(A) 齋戒月期間要搬到低樓層。
(B) 禁止飲食的時間要稍微久一點。
(C) 保護自己避免被明亮的陽光照到。
(D) 找尋與建築物高度相關的危險。

> 理由
> 根據本文最後一段第四句，住在高樓層的穆斯林受指示要比那些住在低樓層的穆斯林晚二至三分鐘才能進食，故 (B) 項應為正選。

重要字詞片語

1. **headlines** [ˈhɛd͵laɪnz] *n.* 新聞頭條（恆用複數）
   grab / make / hit the headlines 成為新聞頭條
   The scandal grabbed the headlines last week.
   這起醜聞在上星期登上了新聞頭條。
2. **audacious** [ɔˈdeʃəs] *a.* 大膽的
3. **skyscraper** [ˈskaɪ͵skrepɚ] *n.* 摩天大樓
4. **initially** [ɪˈnɪʃəlɪ] *adv.* 最初，起初
5. **emirate** [ˈɛmɪrət / ˈɛmərət] *n.* 酋長國
6. **facilitate** [fəˈsɪlə͵tet] *vt.* 促進，幫助
   The new policies are expected to facilitate employment.
   新政策預期會帶動就業率。
7. **mimic** [ˈmɪmɪk] *vt.* 模仿（三態為：mimic, mimicked [ˈmɪmɪkt], mimicked）& *n.* 善於模仿的人
   The audience roared with laughter when the comedians mimicked each other.
   這些喜劇演員模仿彼此時，觀眾全都大笑起來。
8. **Islamic** [ɪzˈlæmɪk / ɪzˈlɑmɪk] *a.* 伊斯蘭的；伊斯蘭教徒的
9. **architecture** [ˈɑrkə͵tɛktʃɚ] *n.* 建築風格；建築學（不可數）
10. **specifics** [spɪˈsɪfɪks] *n.* 細節（恆用複數）
11. **wing** [wɪŋ] *n.* 建築翼部；側廳；翅膀；派系

12. **habitable** [ˈhæbɪtəbl̩] *a.* 可居住的；適合居住的

13. **alternative** [ɔlˈtɝnətɪv] *n.* 替代方案，選擇 & *a.* 替代的

14. **refuge** [ˈrɛfjudʒ] *n.* 避難處（可數）；避難（不可數）

15. **disaster** [dɪˈzæstɚ] *n.* 災難，災害

16. **Muslim** [ˈmʌzləm / ˈmʊzlɪm] *n.* 穆斯林，回教徒 & *a.* 伊斯蘭教的，回教的

17. **fast** [fæst] *vi.* 禁食，齋戒 & *n.* 禁食期，齋戒期
    Rick fasts once a week for health reasons.
    由於健康因素，瑞克每週禁食一天。

18. **get around sth** 解決某事
    After hours of discussion, we still haven't found a way to get around the problem.
    經過數小時的討論，我們仍未找出解決這個問題的方法。

19. **refrain** [rɪˈfren] *vi.* 避免；忍住
    refrain from + N/V-ing
    避免……；忍住不……
    Please refrain from smoking in this area.
    請勿在此區抽菸。

TEST 03

TEST 03

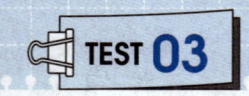

第貳部分、混合題（占 10 分）

第 47 至 50 題為題組

出租：

大安區一房公寓

這間位於臺北大安區小而美的一房公寓現在是待租狀態。客廳剛整修完畢，有現代化衛浴以及俯瞰美麗大安森林公園的小陽臺，此案一定很快就會成交下架。鄰近大安森林公園捷運站，前往臺北多處熱門地點均方便。所以如果您很重視生活機能又想省時間，這間公寓會是您的理想選擇。雖然沒有附廚房設備，但附近有許多平價餐館。各房間內傢俱齊全，電視除外。亦提供高速網路。

- 坪數：十五坪
- 租金：每月新臺幣三萬元
- 管理費：已含在租金內
- 最短租期：兩年
- 意者請洽：真臺北房屋租賃 02-1357-2468

A 君

我目前住在桃園的公寓，但這裡非常不適合我。我在臺北工作，所以我得非常早起以避開可怕的塞車，才能準時抵達公司。我每天也都很晚才回到家。每天的通勤時間已經開始影響我的生活。我幾乎沒有空閒時間來做我喜歡的事情，例如上健身房，或和朋友社交。感覺我的人生現在就是圍繞著工作打轉！

B 君

我目前住的公寓租約到下個月，所以我需要找個新的地方租屋。大安森林公園周邊充滿綠意和新鮮空氣，對我來說是絕佳的地點。此外，那裡離我父母住的地方很近。我需要有夠大的廚房讓我做飯。在家下廚不僅更健康，還能幫我省錢。我也喜歡邀一大群朋友來玩並且品嚐我的創新料理！

---

47. 除了電視之外，這間公寓傢俱齊全。

    except

    理由

    租屋廣告倒數第二句中的 exception（例外）為名詞，然因空格後仍有一名詞詞組 a TV（一臺電視），故空格無法直接置入 exception，須將其改為介詞的 except（除……之外）方符合該句文法、語意，故為正解。

48. 為什麼這間公寓適合 A 君？
    他去上班可以省時。

    save time

> 理由

租屋廣告第四句提到，這間公寓對想要省時（save time）的人來說是理想的選擇，再根據 A 君的訊息得知，A 君每天上下班都要花很多時間通勤，沒什麼時間做自己想做的事，故空格置入 save time 應為正解。

49. 為什麼 B 君不適合租這間公寓？
這間公寓沒有廚房。
kitchen

> 理由

根據租屋廣告倒數第三句，雖然沒有附廚房設備，以及 B 君的訊息第四句，我需要有夠大的廚房（kitchen）讓我做飯，故空格置入 kitchen 應為正解。

C D 50. 關於 A 君和 B 君，請從下列 (A) 項至 (F) 項中選出正確的敘述。
(A) A 君目前受僱在桃園。
(B) B 君目前與父母同住。
(C) A 君希望生活能有更多休閒時間。
(D) B 君喜歡在家辦派對。
(E) A 君利用通勤時間辦理公事。
(F) B 君較喜歡在室內運動。

> 理由

根據 A 君的訊息倒數第二句，我幾乎沒有空閒時間來做我喜歡的事情，以及 B 君的訊息最後一句，我也喜歡邀一大群朋友來玩並且品嚐我的創新料理，得知 (C)、(D) 項應為正選。

重要字詞片語

1. **compact** [kəmˈpækt] *a.* 小的，小型的
2. **stunning** [ˈstʌnɪŋ] *a.* 非常迷人的；令人吃驚的
3. **district** [ˈdɪstrɪkt] *n.* （行政）區
4. **refurbish** [rɪˈfɝbɪʃ] *vt.* 整修，翻新（文中為過去分詞作形容詞用）
5. **contemporary** [kənˈtɛmpəˌrɛrɪ] *a.* 現代的
6. **balcony** [ˈbælkənɪ] *n.* 陽臺
7. **abundance** [əˈbʌndəns] *n.* 豐富，充裕
   an abundance of... 充分的……
8. **furnished** [ˈfɝnɪʃt] *a.* 含有傢俱的
9. **tenant** [ˈtɛnənt] *n.* 房客
10. **horrendous** [həˈrɛndəs] *a.* 可怕的，驚駭的
11. **take a / its toll (on...)**
    （對……）造成損失／傷害
    Andrew's smoking habit took a toll on his health.
    安德魯抽菸的習慣危害到了他的健康。
12. **pursue** [pɚˈsu] *vt.* 追求
13. **revolve** [rɪˈvɑlv] *vi.* 旋轉
    revolve around... 繞著……轉
    Brian's whole life revolves around his family.
    布萊恩一生都以家人為中心。
14. **expire** [ɪkˈspaɪr] *vi.* 期滿，過期
15. **culinary** [ˈkʌləˌnɛrɪ] *a.* 烹飪的

TEST 03

第參部分、非選擇題（占 28 分）

一、中譯英（占 8 分）

1. 眾所周知，許多成功的人往往都很謙虛。

   示範譯句

   As we all know, many successful people tend to be humble.

   或：As we all know, a large number of successful people are prone to be modest.

   翻譯要點

   a. **As we all know, ...** 眾所周知，……
      As we all know, the singer was born into a poor family.
      眾所周知，那位歌手出身貧寒。

   b. **successful** [səkˋsɛsfəl] *a.* 成功的
      Keep working hard, and you'll be successful one day.
      繼續努力，那麼有朝一日你就會成功。

   c. **tend to V** 傾向……，往往會……
      = be prone to V
      If I stay out in the sun for too long, I tend to get serious sunburn.
      假如我在陽光下待太久，就很容易嚴重晒傷。

   d. **humble** [ˋhʌmbḷ] *a.* 謙虛的
      = modest [ˋmɑdɪst]

2. 這是因為他們知道自己所擁有的一切得來不易，因此總是心存感激。

   示範譯句

   This is because they know what they have is not easy to get, so they are always grateful.

   或：This is because they know it is not easy to get what they possess, so they are always thankful.

   翻譯要點

   a. **grateful** [ˋgretfəl] *a.* 感激的，感謝的
      = thankful [ˋθæŋkfəl]
      be grateful to sb for sth
      = be thankful to sb for sth
      因某事感激某人
      Robert is grateful to his wife for all of her love and support over the years.
      羅伯特感激他太太多年來付出的愛和支持。

   b. **possess** [pəˋzɛs] *vt.* 擁有
      Jack possesses a large number of baseball cards.
      傑克擁有許多棒球卡。

二、英文作文（占 20 分）

提示：臺灣的夜市文化是全世界數一數二的。除了逛街和玩樂外，夜市內的許多美食更被外國朋友譽為臺灣之光。假如你要向外國友人介紹臺灣的夜市文化，你要如何讓他留下深刻的印象呢？請以此為題，寫一篇英文作文，第一段請介紹臺灣的夜市文化，第二段則說明你會推薦哪一道夜市美食，並說明這道美食的特色及推薦原因。

示範作文

"Night market" is almost synonymous with Taiwan, so one cannot visit the island without dropping by one. As the sky darkens, night markets come alive with sounds and smells that will last late into the night. First and foremost, come with an empty stomach so you can eat to your heart's content. While munching your way from stall to stall, you'll hear vendors hawking a variety of merchandise. Don't hesitate to bargain for a good deal. Some intriguing games are worth a try, too. For example, nabbing a prize from a claw machine can be pretty challenging, yet it's extremely entertaining.

Not to be missed is stinky tofu. This pungent dish is to Taiwan what durian is to Southeast Asia; beneath the smell lies a divine taste. Don't be scared off by the stink and give this snack a try. After being deep-fried, stinky tofu is crispy on the outside and tender on the inside. It can be covered with a sweet and spicy sauce, and its juicy center gushes out with every bite. Stewed, grilled, or deep-fried, stinky tofu assaults your nostrils but delights your palate. In fact, it has won lots of converts among foreigners who wrinkled their noses at it initially and then found themselves pleasantly impressed. Next time you smell the distinctive odor in the night market, steel yourself to take a bite.

「夜市」幾乎是臺灣的同義詞，所以造訪臺灣的人一定都會去一趟夜市走走。當天色變暗，夜市便充滿了持續至深夜的聲音及香味。最重要的是，帶著空蕩蕩的胃過來盡情地吃。在你一攤接著一攤大快朵頤時，你將聽到小販叫賣各式各樣的商品。別猶豫，去討個好價錢吧。一些有趣的遊戲也值得一試。舉例來說，要在夾娃娃機內夾到一個獎品頗具挑戰性，但這非常好玩。

臭豆腐是你絕對不能錯過的。這道刺鼻的食物之於臺灣就如同榴槤之於東南亞，在這樣的氣味之下有著非常棒的滋味。千萬別被臭味嚇跑了，嚐嚐看這道小吃吧。臭豆腐經過油炸之後，便有著酥脆的外皮以及軟嫩的內餡。臭豆腐上頭可以淋上甜辣醬，而且臭豆腐多汁的中心在你咬下的每一口都會爆汁出來。被燉煮、烤製或是油炸過的臭豆腐雖然會刺激你的嗅覺，但能滿足你的味蕾。事實上，臭豆腐讓許多一開始看到它便皺起鼻子的外國人改變想法，他們後來發現自己對臭豆腐有著很好的印象。下次你在夜市聞到這個獨特的臭味時，下定決心嚐一口吧。

TEST 03

重要字詞片語

1. **synonymous** [sɪˋnɑnəməs] *a.* 同義的
   be synonymous with... 與……同義
2. **drop by...** 順道造訪……
   = stop by...
3. **to one's heart's content** 盡情地
4. **munch** [mʌntʃ] *vt.* & *vi.* 大聲咀嚼，用力咀嚼
   munch one's way 狼吞虎嚥／津津有味地吃
5. **hawk** [hɔk] *vt.* 叫賣；兜售
6. **intriguing** [ɪnˋtrigɪŋ] *a.* 有趣的，令人好奇的
7. **nab** [næb] *vt.* 獲得；搶獲
8. **a claw machine** 夾娃娃機
9. **stinky** [ˋstɪŋkɪ] *a.* 臭的
   stinky tofu 臭豆腐
10. **pungent** [ˋpʌndʒənt] *a.* (味道) 刺鼻的
11. **divine** [dəˋvaɪn] *a.* 極好的，極妙的
12. **gush** [gʌʃ] *vi.* 噴出；大量湧出
    gush out 噴出
13. **assault** [əˋsɔlt] *vt.* 襲擊
14. **nostril** [ˋnɑstrɪl] *n.* 鼻孔
15. **convert** [ˋkɑnvɜt] *n.* 改變信仰者
16. **wrinkle one's nose** 某人皺起鼻子（以示反感／反對）
17. **steel oneself to V** 下定決心做……

TEST 04

第壹部分、選擇題
一、詞彙題
二、綜合測驗
三、文意選填
四、篇章結構
五、閱讀測驗

第貳部分、混合題

第參部分、非選擇題
一、中譯英
二、英文作文

第壹部分、選擇題

一、詞彙題

| 1. B | 2. D | 3. A | 4. B | 5. C | 6. C | 7. D | 8. C | 9. A | 10. C |

二、綜合測驗

| 11. D | 12. B | 13. A | 14. C | 15. B | 16. A | 17. B | 18. C | 19. A | 20. D |

三、文意選填

| 21. H | 22. F | 23. D | 24. E | 25. I | 26. A | 27. G | 28. C | 29. J | 30. B |

四、篇章結構

| 31. E | 32. B | 33. A | 34. C |

五、閱讀測驗

| 35. B | 36. C | 37. D | 38. D | 39. C | 40. B | 41. C | 42. A | 43. C | 44. B |
| 45. D | 46. A |

第貳部分、混合題

47. A, D

48. B

49. A

50. C

第壹部分、選擇題（占 62 分）

一、詞彙題（占 10 分）

B 1. 艾瑪希望掃地機器人能幫助她年邁的父親，因為他現在彎不下腰。

- ⓐ (A) **criticism** [ˈkrɪtəˌsɪzəm] *n.* 批評，爭議；評論
  The new tax law has been the subject of criticism recently.
  這條新稅法最近成為爭議的話題。

  (B) **assistance** [əˈsɪstəns] *n.* 幫助，援助（不可數）
  The needy family was grateful for the assistance given by their neighbors.
  這個貧困的家庭對於鄰居給予的幫助感激不已。

  (C) **exposure** [ɪkˈspoʒɚ] *n.* 暴露，曝曬；接觸（與介詞 to 並用）
  Too much exposure to sunlight can cause skin problems.
  過度曝曬於陽光下可能引發皮膚問題。

  (D) **intelligence** [ɪnˈtɛlədʒəns] *n.* 聰明才智（不可數）
  Lily never ceases to amaze me with her intelligence.
  莉莉的聰明才智總會令我驚異連連。

- ⓑ 根據語意及用法，(B) 項應為正選。

【必考重點】
vacuum [ˈvækjuəm] *n.* 真空 & *vt.* 吸塵
a vacuum cleaner　　真空吸塵器

D 2. 太陽炙熱的強度促使葛瑞絲戴上帽子和她新的太陽眼鏡。

- ⓐ (A) **clarity** [ˈklærətɪ] *n.* 清楚，清晰（不可數）
  with clarity　　清楚地
  Some people can always assess a situation with great clarity.
  有些人總是能以清晰的思路來判斷情況。

  (B) **damp** [dæmp] *n.* 溼氣（不可數）& *a.* 潮溼的
  The clothes hadn't dried properly and still smelled of damp.
  這些衣服沒有全乾，仍聞得出溼氣的味道。

  (C) **scope** [skop] *n.* 範圍
  in scope　　範圍上來說

The problem is small in scope and won't take long to fix.
這個問題不算大，不用很長的時間就可以解決。

(D) **intensity** [ɪnˈtɛnsətɪ] *n.* 強度；熱切（不可數）
I can't stand the intensity of the heat.
我受不了高溫。

ⓑ 根據語意及用法，(D) 項應為正選。

必考重點

prompt [prɑmpt] *vt.* 促使
prompt sb to + V　　促使某人決定做……
The movie prompted Amy to read the book.
這部電影激發艾咪去讀這本書。

A 3. 愛麗絲試圖跟上那隻兔子，但當兔子從地洞中消失，她就找不到牠了。

ⓐ (A) **vanish** [ˈvænɪʃ] *vi.* 消失，突然不見
＝ disappear [ˌdɪsəˈpɪr] *vi.*
vanish from...　　從……消失
＝ disappear from...
Many ancient civilizations have vanished from history.
許多古文明已經從歷史中消失。

(B) **sparkle** [ˈspɑrkl̩] *vi.* 閃耀；發出光芒
＝ glitter [ˈglɪtɚ] *vi.*
When Nancy saw Mark, her eyes sparkled with love.
南希看見馬克時，她的眼神散發著愛意。

(C) **whisper** [ˈhwɪspɚ] *vi. & vt.* 低語，耳語
＝ murmur [ˈmɝmɚ] *vi.*
Seeing the men whispering suspiciously on the train aroused my curiosity.
看到火車上那些男子竊竊私語，激起了我的好奇心。

(D) **collide** [kəˈlaɪd] *vi.* 碰撞；抵觸
collide with...　　和……相撞；和……起衝突
That truck collided with a telephone pole.
那部卡車撞上了一根電線桿。

ⓑ 根據語意及用法，(A) 項應為正選。

必考重點

a. **keep pace with...**
跟上……；與……並駕齊驅

It is not easy for the elderly to keep pace with the young.
老年人要跟上年輕人的腳步並不容易。

b. **lose track of...**
　　失去……的蹤跡／線索

Amy has lost track of most of her college classmates.
愛咪和她大部分的大學同學都失聯了。

B 4. 當琳達的表弟告訴琳達他要結婚時，你可以從她真誠的笑容得知她是真的替他感到開心。

ⓐ (A) **ignorant** [ˈɪgnərənt] *a.* 無知的；不知道的
　　　be ignorant of...　　不知道……
　　　Larry is ignorant of how much his girlfriend loves him.
　　　賴瑞完全不知道他女朋友有多愛他。

(B) **genuine** [ˈdʒɛnjʊɪn] *a.* 真誠的；真的，非偽造的
　　John likes to flatter people, so his compliments do not necessarily seem genuine.
　　約翰很喜歡拍馬屁，所以他的恭維未必都是真誠的。
　　Most people can't tell the difference between a genuine painting and a fake.
　　大部分的人區分不出真畫和假畫。

(C) **critical** [ˈkrɪtɪkl̩] *a.* 挑剔的，吹毛求疵的；批評的
　　be critical of...　　對……很挑剔；批評……
　　You shouldn't be so critical of the men you date because you might just pass up Mr. Right.
　　妳不該對約會對象這麼挑剔，因為妳可能會錯過妳的真命天子。

(D) **distinctive** [dɪˈstɪŋktɪv] *a.* 獨特的，特別的
　　The policemen of this city wear a distinctive uniform, so they are easy to recognize.
　　該市的警察穿的制服很特別，因此很容易認出來。

ⓑ 根據語意，(B) 項應為正選。

C 5. 暴風雨接近的時候，風雨增強。因此，校長讓學生們立刻回家。

ⓐ (A) **react** [rɪˈækt] *vi.* 反應（與介詞 to 並用）
　　　Ted reacted calmly to the plaintiff's accusation.
　　　泰德對原告的指控反應冷靜。

(B) **shiver** [ˈʃɪvɚ] *vi.* 發抖
　　The princess shivered at the thought of kissing the frog.
　　公主一想到要親吻這隻青蛙就全身發抖。

(C) **approach** [əˋprotʃ] *vi.* & *vt.* 接近
People stocked up on food and water because a typhoon was approaching.
人們忙著囤積食物和水，因為有個颱風正接近中。

(D) **wander** [ˋwɑndɚ] *vi.* & *vt.* 徘徊
The security guard was suspicious of the man wandering around in front of the bank.
保全人員對那個在銀行前徘徊的男人起疑。

ⓑ 根據語意，(C) 項應為正選。

必考重點

principal [ˋprɪnsəpl̩] *n.* （中、小學）校長

C 6. 你應該事先打電話到那家日本餐廳訂位。否則，你可能要等上好幾個小時。

ⓐ (A) **originally** [əˋrɪdʒənəlɪ] *adv.* 起初
New York City was originally a Dutch colony.
紐約市原本是荷蘭的殖民地。

(B) **accordingly** [əˋkɔrdɪŋlɪ] *adv.* 因此，所以（= therefore）
Jerry didn't study for the test. Accordingly, he failed it.
傑瑞沒有準備這次考試。因此，他考不及格。

(C) **beforehand** [bɪˋfɔr͵hænd] *adv.* 事先
= in advance
You can change your mind anytime, but please tell me beforehand.
你隨時都可以改變心意，不過請事先讓我知道。

(D) **afterwards** [ˋæftɚwɚdz] *adv.* 之後
Nancy did the dishes and took a nap afterwards.
南希洗完碗後睡了個午覺。

ⓑ 根據語意，(C) 項應為正選。

必考重點

make a reservation 訂位，預約
Would you like me to make a reservation for dinner at that new restaurant?
你要我跟那家新餐廳預訂晚餐的位子嗎？

D 7. 該嫌犯回答問題時，這位刑警仔細地觀察他是否有任何說謊的徵兆。

ⓐ (A) **distribute** [dɪˋstrɪbjut] *vt.* 分發，分配
The volunteers distributed food and clothing to the refugees.
義工們將食物和衣物分發給難民。

(B) **criticize** [ˈkrɪtəˌsaɪz] *vt.* & *vi.* 批評，批判
Don't criticize others if you don't want to be criticized.
如果不想被人批評，就不要批評別人。

(C) **emphasize** [ˈɛmfəˌsaɪz] *vt.* 強調，著重
= stress [strɛs] *vt.*
The article aims to emphasize the importance of environmental protection.
這篇文章旨在強調環保的重要性。

(D) **observe** [əbˈzɝv] *vt.* & *vi.* 觀察
The doctor observed the child to see how he would react to the medicine.
醫生觀察那名孩子對該藥物有什麼反應。

ⓑ 根據語意，(D) 項應為正選。

> 必考重點
>
> a. **detective** [dɪˈtɛktɪv] *n.* 刑警；偵探
> b. **suspect** [ˈsʌspɛkt] *n.* 嫌疑犯
> c. **respond to...** 回答……，回應……
>
> Jane didn't respond to my question, which made me mad.
> 珍沒有回答我的問題，這讓我很生氣。

TEST 04

C 8. 如果你再這樣花錢不知節制，還有買一些你負擔不起的東西，最後將會沒有任何積蓄。

ⓐ (A) **passive** [ˈpæsɪv] *a.* 被動的，消極的
No teacher likes students who take a passive learning attitude.
沒有老師會喜歡學習態度被動的學生。

(B) **singular** [ˈsɪŋgjələ] *a.* 單數的；非凡的
a singular success　　無比的成功，非常成功
The play we saw last night was a singular success.
我們昨晚看的那齣戲非常成功。

(C) **reckless** [ˈrɛklɪs] *a.* 輕率的；不顧後果的；魯莽的
= careless [ˈkɛrlɪs] *a.*
The reckless driver was chased after by the police.
那名魯莽的駕駛遭到警方追捕。

(D) **moderate** [ˈmɑdərɪt] *a.* 適度的
Adding moderate amounts of olive oil to your diet can prevent heart disease.
在飲食中加入適量的橄欖油能預防心臟疾病。

ⓑ 根據語意，(C) 項應為正選。

TEST 04

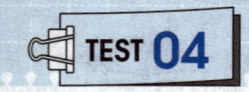

> **必考重點**

end up + 介詞片語　　結果……，以……收場
Andy's plan ended up in failure.
安迪的計畫結果以失敗收場。

<u>A</u> 9. 亨利今年獲得升遷時，他為了成為業務部經理所付出的努力終於有了收穫。

- ⓐ (A) **endeavor** [ɪnˋdɛvɚ] *n.* 努力
  make an endeavor / effort to V　　努力……
  The manager made an endeavor to get to the bottom of their poor sales performance.
  經理努力要釐清業績不佳的原因。
  ＊ get to the bottom of sth　　釐清真相

  (B) **reflection** [rɪˋflɛkʃən] *n.* 反射
  An echo is a reflection of sound.
  回音是聲音的反射。

  (C) **dilemma** [dəˋlɛmə] *n.* 困境，進退兩難
  in a dilemma　　陷入困境，左右為難
  Amy is in a dilemma about disobeying her father or losing the man she loves.
  愛咪在違抗父親與失去心愛的男人之間陷入兩難。

  (D) **qualification** [ˌkwɑləfəˋkeʃən] *n.* 資格
  What qualifications are required for this job?
  這份工作需要什麼樣的資格呢？

- ⓑ 根據語意，(A) 項應為正選。

> **必考重點**

pay off　　有代價，有收穫
Mark's hard work finally paid off when his book was published last week.
馬克的書上星期出版了，他的努力工作終於有了代價。

<u>C</u> 10. 琳達的嘴唇對乾燥天氣非常敏感並容易裂開，所以她總是隨身攜帶護唇膏在她的手提包裡。

- ⓐ (A) **satisfied** [ˋsætɪsˌfaɪd] *a.* 感到滿意的
  be satisfied with...　　對……感到滿意
  My mother is satisfied with the way her life has played out.
  我媽媽很滿意她目前的生活方式。

100

(B) **attractive** [əˋtræktɪv] *a.* 有吸引力的
　　be attractive to... 　　對……有吸引力
　　Girls that are smart and good-looking are very attractive to Rick.
　　聰明又漂亮的女孩對瑞克很有吸引力。

(C) **sensitive** [ˋsɛnsətɪv] *a.* 敏感的（與介詞 to 並用）
　　be sensitive to... 　　對……敏感
　　Allen is quite sensitive to loud noises and bright lights.
　　艾倫對大聲的噪音和明亮的光線相當敏感。

(D) **pleased** [plizd] *a.* 感到滿意的（與介詞 with 並用）
　　be pleased with... 　　對……很滿意
　= be satisfied with...
　　The boss was pleased with how Joe handled the project.
　　老闆對喬處理該專案的表現很滿意。

ⓑ 根據語意及 be sensitive to 的固定用法，(C) 項應為正選。

必考重點
a. **chap** [tʃæp] *vi.* 龜裂
b. **balm** [bɑm] *n.* 軟膏
　　lip balm 　　護唇膏

二、綜合測驗（占 10 分）

第 11 至 15 題為題組

　　準備超過你或你家人一餐能吃完的食物量，在已開發國家來說是很常見的。人們當然不希望把剩菜丟掉，浪費全然完好的食物。反之，他們會拿個密封保鮮袋，打開它然後把食物放進去，接著把袋口捏緊或把夾鍊拉起來。這樣他們就不需要用保鮮膜包住占據大量冰箱空間的碗盤。保鮮膜也會使食物變乾，讓後續碗盤的清洗更加困難。

　　裝剩菜的塑膠袋這類簡單的事物並非新點子。它已經有超過半個世紀的歷史。然而一直到八○年代，密封保鮮袋的生產方式有所改進使得價格更為便宜，它才真正成為一項消費性產品。現在幾乎每一個廚房或食品儲藏室都可以看得到它的蹤影，並且有針對不同用途的多種尺寸，從冷凍用的大袋子到裝零食的小袋子都有。當簡單的點子變得可行，便可能在某個產業掀起革命。密封保鮮袋如今已經成為一項家庭必需品。

D 11. 理由

ⓐ (A) **dominate** [ˋdɑməˌnet] *vt.* 統治，支配
　　That country seeks to dominate its neighbors.
　　那個國家設法要統治其鄰國。

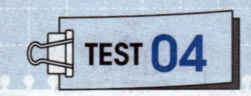

(B) **assemble** [əˋsɛmb!̣] *vt.* 組合 & *vi.* & *vt.* 集合
If you know how to assemble the computer yourself, you can save lots of money.
你若懂得自行組裝電腦，便可以省下很多錢。

(C) **sprinkle** [ˋsprɪŋk!̣] *vt.* 撒
I like to sprinkle pepper on my steak because it tastes better.
我喜歡在牛排上撒胡椒，因為那樣味道比較好。

(D) **waste** [west] *vt.* 浪費
Don't waste your time watching TV.
不要浪費時間看電視。

ⓑ 根據語意及用法，(D) 項應為正選。

B 12. 理由

ⓐ (A) **hold onto...** 堅守／緊抓……
= stick to...
You should hold onto your principles.
你應該堅守你的原則。

(B) **take up...** 占據……（空間或時間）
The project took up most of Bill's time.
那個專案占去比爾大部分的時間。

(C) **appeal to...** 吸引……
= attract...
Our products attempt to appeal to teens, especially teenage girls.
我們的產品主要想吸引青少年族群，尤其是少女。

(D) **stand for...** 代表……
= represent [ˌrɛprɪˋzɛnt] *vt.*
The poem stands for the pain everyone faces when they are under pressure.
那首詩代表了每個人在壓力之下所面臨的痛苦。

ⓑ 根據語意及用法，(B) 項應為正選。

A 13. 理由

ⓐ (A) **manufacture** [ˌmænjəˋfæktʃɚ] *vt.* & *n.* 生產，製造
Our company manufactures electronic devices.
我們公司生產電子產品。

(B) **volunteer** [ˌvɑlənˋtɪr] *vt.* & *vi.* 自願做 & *n.* 志願者，義工
The taxi driver volunteered to help.
這位計程車司機自告奮勇要幫忙。

(C) **vaporize** [ˈvepəˌraɪz] *vt. & vi.* （使）蒸發／汽化
The blazing sun quickly vaporized the drops of dew on the grass.
炙熱的太陽很快就蒸發掉了青草上的露珠。

(D) **season** [ˈsizn̩] *vt.* 調味 & *n.* 季節
Mother seasoned the soup with a bit of salt.
媽媽在湯裡加了點鹽巴調味。

ⓑ 根據語意及用法，(A) 項應為正選。

C 14. 理由

ⓐ 本題測試以下語意：(A) a range of flavors（各種口味）、(B) a list of competitors（競爭者名單）、(C) a multitude of sizes（各種尺寸）、(D) a series of commercials（一系列的廣告）。

ⓑ 根據空格後面提及從冷凍的大袋子到裝零食的小袋子都有，得知 (C) 項應為正選。

B 15. 理由

ⓐ (A) **anonymous** [əˈnɑnəməs] *a.* 匿名的
We never learned the identity of our school's anonymous benefactor.
我們一直不知道本校的匿名贊助者的身分。

(B) **practical** [ˈpræktɪkl] *a.* 實際的
We should abort this plan because it is not very practical.
我們應該中止這項計畫，因為太不實際了。

(C) **diligent** [ˈdɪlədʒənt] *a.* 努力工作的，勤奮的
= hard-working [ˌhɑrdˈwɜkɪŋ] *a.*
Every boss likes diligent employees.
每個老闆都喜歡勤奮的員工。

(D) **harmful** [ˈhɑrmfəl] *a.* 有害的
be harmful to... 對……有害
Excessive drinking is harmful to your health.
飲酒過量有害健康。

ⓑ 根據語意，(B) 項應為正選。

重要字詞片語

1. **occurrence** [əˈkɜəns] *n.* 事件，發生的事
2. **leftovers** [ˈlɛftˌovəz] *n.* 吃剩的食物，剩菜（恆用複數）
3. **grab** [græb] *vt.* 抓住，抓取（三態為：grab, grabbed [græbd], grabbed）
The thief grabbed my bag and ran away.
那個賊搶了我的皮包就跑走了。

103

TEST 04

4. **pinch** [pɪntʃ] *vt.* 捏，掐
   I pinched myself to make sure that I was not dreaming.
   我捏了自己一下，以確定自己不是在作夢。
5. **zipper** [ˈzɪpɚ] *n.* 拉鍊
6. **plastic wrap**　　保鮮膜
7. **pantry** [ˈpæntrɪ] *n.* 食品儲藏室
8. **revolutionize** [ˌrɛvəˈluʃəˌnaɪz]
   vt. （徹底）改革
   The techniques developed at this lab have revolutionized heart surgery.
   這個實驗室所研發出來的技術徹底改革了心臟手術。
9. **household** [ˈhaʊsˌhold] *a.* 家庭的 & *n.* 家庭
10. **necessity** [nəˈsɛsətɪ] *n.* 必需品
    There is no doubt that cellphones are a necessity nowadays.
    毫無疑問，手機是現代生活的一項必需品。

第 16 至 20 題為題組

　　如果你看到有人在啃咬他們的指尖，你也許會以為他們餓壞了，然後建議他們去買個三明治來吃。但這可能和飢餓沒有一點關係。許多人有咬指甲的習慣。幾乎有四成五的青少年會咬指甲，且對大多數人而言，這習慣很難戒掉。

　　啃手指除了給人不雅的印象以外，尚有其他因素讓人應該避開咬指甲的習慣。原因之一，尤其對重度咬指甲者來說是相當明顯的，就是會痛。這是由於皮膚和指甲交界的區域對疼痛極度敏感。指甲是細菌孳生的溫床，特別是當人們沒有徹底將手洗乾淨時。咬指甲也會因此造成腸胃不適和疾病。它也會導致牙齒問題和造成下顎疼痛。

　　這種習慣通常與焦慮有關，而治療方法也常包括消除壓力。此外還有幫咬指甲者換一個傷害較小的習慣的療法。然而更便宜的選擇就是在指甲塗上苦澀的指甲油來防止咬指甲。

A 16. 理由
ⓐ 本空格測試意志動詞的固定用法：
suggest + that 子句　　提議／建議……
suggest 作「建議」時，為意志動詞，其後的 that 子句中主詞之後須接助動詞 should + 原形動詞，但 should 可省略。意志動詞計有下列五大類：
1) 建議：suggest, recommend, advise, urge, propose, move
2) 要求：ask, desire, demand, insist, require, request
3) 命令：order, command
4) 規定：rule, regulate, stipulate
5) 主張：advocate, maintain
My mom suggested that I (should) participate in some extracurricular activities to meet more people.
我媽媽建議我參加一些課外活動以便多認識些人。

ⓑ 根據上述，空格前有意志動詞 suggested，得知空格內應置原形動詞 buy，故 (A) 項應為正選。

B 17. 理由

ⓐ (A) **come up with...**　　想出／提出……
John has to come up with a plan to finance his new business.
約翰必須提出一個計畫為他的新事業籌措資金。

(B) **get rid of...**　　免除／除去……
We can't seem to get rid of the mice in our apartment.
我們似乎沒法清除公寓裡的鼠患。

(C) **make up for...**　　補償……，彌補……
= compensate for...
Diligence can make up for one's deficiencies.
勤能補拙。

(D) **keep pace with...**　　跟上……的速度；與……齊步並進
Our company has been successful at keeping pace with our biggest competitor.
我們公司一直以來都能與最大的競爭對手並駕齊驅。

ⓑ 根據語意，空格內應置表「戒除」的片語動詞，故 (B) 項應為正選。

C 18. 理由

ⓐ (A) **pessimism** [ˈpɛsəmɪzəm] *n.* 悲觀（不可數）
A recent survey shows that pessimism about the economy continues to grow.
最新調查顯示對經濟的悲觀看法持續擴大。

(B) **recognition** [ˌrɛkəgˈnɪʃən] *n.* 認可；認識（不可數）
The scholar has won international recognition for his great findings.
這位學者的重大發現獲得國際認可。

(C) **impression** [ɪmˈprɛʃən] *n.* 印象
make a good / bad impression (on...)　　（給……）留下一個好／壞印象
It is easy to make a good impression on others. All you have to do is be yourself.
給人好印象是很簡單的。你只要做自己即可。

(D) **inspection** [ɪnˈspɛkʃən] *n.* 檢查
Those business establishments that have failed to pass safety inspections will lose their licenses.
凡是沒有通過安全檢查的營業場所將被吊銷執照。

ⓑ 根據語意，(C) 項應為正選。

A 19. 理由

ⓐ (A) **sensitive** [ˈsɛnsətɪv] *a.* 敏感的
be sensitive to...　　對……敏感

My lips are very sensitive to dry weather, and they chap easily.
我的嘴唇對乾燥的天氣很敏感，而且很容易就乾裂。

(B) **allergic** [ə'lɝdʒɪk] *a*. 過敏的（與介詞 to 並用）
be allergic to... 對……過敏
Some people are allergic to peanuts.
有些人對花生過敏。

(C) **critical** ['krɪtɪkl̩] *a*. 批評的；危及的
be critical of... 批評……；對……挑剔
That newspaper editorial is very critical of the government.
該報社論對政府大肆批評。

(D) **aware** [ə'wɛr] *a*. 知道的；察覺到的
be aware of... 意識到／明白／知道……
I'm not aware of any rules against singing in the office.
我不知道有任何禁止在辦公室內唱歌的規定。

ⓑ 根據語意，空格應置表「敏感」的形容詞，故 (A) 項應為正選。

D 20. 理由

ⓐ 本題測試以下語意：(A) paying for health insurance（付健保費）、(B) trimming off the fat（減肥）、(C) controlling the outbreak（控制爆發）、(D) dealing with stress（處理壓力）。

ⓑ 因空格前提及這習慣和焦慮相關，故根據語意，(D) 項應為正選。

重要字詞片語

1. **chew on...** 咀嚼／咬……
2. **be inclined to V** 有做……的傾向；容易做……
   John is inclined to lie, so I don't trust him.
   約翰容易說謊，所以我不信任他。
3. **have nothing / something / a lot to do with...**
   和……沒有關係／有關係／頗有關係
4. **have the habit of...** 有……的習慣
5. **Aside from N/V-ing, S + V** 除了……外，還……
   Aside from playing chess, Charlie also enjoys playing poker and other card games.
   除了下西洋棋外，查理還喜歡玩撲克牌和其他紙牌遊戲。
6. **a breeding ground** 繁殖地，滋生地
7. **bacteria** [bæk'tɪrɪə] *n*. 細菌（複數）
   （單數為：bacterium [bæk'tɪrɪəm]）
8. **lead to...** 導致……
   = result in...
   = bring about...
   = cause...
9. **discomfort** [dɪs'kʌmfɚt] *n*. 不舒適，不適（不可數）
10. **dental** ['dɛntl̩] *a*. 牙齒的
11. **jaw** [dʒɔ] *n*. 下顎
12. **be related to...** 與……有關；與……有親戚關係
    Evidence has shown that birds are related to dinosaurs.
    種種證據顯示鳥類和恐龍有親戚關係。

13. **involve** [ɪnˈvɑlv] *vt.* 包含
14. **therapy** [ˈθɛrəpɪ] *n.* 療法
15. **polish** [ˈpɑlɪʃ] *n.* 擦亮，磨光；上光劑 & *vt.* 擦亮

    nail polish　　指甲油

三、文意選填（占 10 分）

第 21 至 30 題為題組

　　現今，像是 Uber Eats 這樣的餐點外送服務在全球各地都能見到且都很受歡迎。它們仰賴數位資料庫與司機來將訂單準時送達。然而在印度，「達巴瓦拉」在不靠尖端科技的情況下這麼做，已經超過一百二十五年了。

　　在印度語中，「達巴瓦拉」這個字字面上指的是「帶著盒子的人」。達巴瓦拉就是快遞人員，他們利用腳踏車與公共鐵路系統，將午餐飯盒送到飢腸轆轆的印度民眾手上。達巴瓦拉的傳統始於 1890 年的孟買。在那個時候，速食並不存在，而上班族需要方便的餐點。該產業起步時只有一百位達巴瓦拉人員，但是這數字很快便增加了。如今，達巴瓦拉人員每天在印度各地運送大約二十萬份餐點。

　　多年下來，達巴瓦拉人員用來持續每日例行工作的方式，也變得越來越有效率。運送的流程一開始會由身著白色制服、傳統甘地帽的達巴瓦拉人員，騎腳踏車去上班族家裡收取當日的飯盒。因為許多達巴瓦拉人員的閱讀能力不好，所以午餐飯盒以不同的顏色編碼，以便傳達正確的運送資訊。達巴瓦拉人員接著就會把午餐飯盒運到一個中心集散地，在那裡將飯盒歸類分組。接著，一組組飯盒會被裝載到火車上。在每一個火車站裡，這些分好組的飯盒會被當地的達巴瓦拉人員領取，然後將飯盒送到客人手上。空的午餐飯盒在午餐後或隔天會被收集起來，送回它們各自的家。

　　雖然在印度已有現代快遞公司成立，達巴瓦拉產業卻不害怕競爭。事實上，達巴瓦拉產業每年以 5% 至 10% 的增長率繼續擴張。許多印度人偏好用達巴瓦拉人員，因為他們很可靠，服務也很便宜。這也有人文的因素在內，許多顧客與他們的達巴瓦拉人員多年下來每天見面，因此成了好朋友。

H 21. 理由

   ⓐ 空格前有介詞 without（沒有），而空格後有名詞 technology（科技），得知空格應置入形容詞或分詞以修飾 technology。

   ⓑ 選項中符合上述的有 (C) empty（空的）、(E) increased（增加的）、(F) hungry（飢餓的）、(H) advanced（先進的）及 (I) routine（例行公事的），惟根據語意，(H) 項應為正選。

107

TEST 04

F 22. 理由
- ⓐ 空格前有介詞 to，而空格後有名詞 Indians（印度人），得知空格應置入形容詞或分詞以修飾 Indians。
- ⓑ 選項中符合上述的有 (C) empty（空的）、(E) increased（增加的）、(F) hungry（飢餓的）及 (I) routine（例行公事的），惟根據語意，(F) 項應為正選。

D 23. 理由
- ⓐ 空格前有否定助動詞 didn't，而空格後有對等連接詞 and，且 and 後為一完整子句，得知空格應置入原形不及物動詞。
- ⓑ 選項中符合上述的有 (C) empty（變空）及 (D) exist（存在），惟根據語意，(D) 項應為正選。

E 24. 理由
- ⓐ 空格前有副詞 quickly（快速地），且根據本句時態，得知空格應置入過去式不及物動詞。
- ⓑ 選項中符合上述的僅剩 (E) increased（增加），置入後亦符合語意，故為正選。

I 25. 理由
- ⓐ 空格前有動詞片語 carry on（繼續）及形容詞詞組 their daily（他們每日的），得知空格應置入名詞以成為動詞片語的受詞。
- ⓑ 選項中符合上述的有 (G) location（地點）、(I) routine（例行公事）及 (J) competition（競爭），惟根據語意，(I) 項應為正選。

A 26. 理由
- ⓐ 空格前有引導不定詞片語的 to，而空格後有名詞詞組 the proper delivery information（正確的運送資訊），得知空格應置入原形及物動詞。
- ⓑ 選項中符合上述的有 (A) convey（傳達）、(B) prefer（偏好）及 (C) empty（使變空），惟根據語意，(A) 項應為正選。

G 27. 理由
- ⓐ 空格前有不定冠詞 a 及形容詞 central（中心的），得知空格應置入單數可數名詞以被 central 修飾。
- ⓑ 選項中符合上述的有 (G) location（地點）及 (J) competition（競爭），惟根據語意，(G) 項應為正選。

C 28. 理由
- ⓐ 空格前有定冠詞 The，而空格後有名詞 lunchboxes（午餐飯盒），得知空格應置入形容詞或分詞以修飾 lunchboxes。
- ⓑ 選項中符合上述的僅剩 (C) empty（空的），置入後亦符合語意，故為正選。

J 29. 理由
- ⓐ 空格前有定冠詞 the，得知空格應置入名詞。
- ⓑ 選項中符合上述的僅剩 (J) competition（競爭），置入後亦符合語意，故為正選。

B **30.** 理由

ⓐ 空格前有作主詞的複數名詞 Many Indians（許多印度人），而空格後有動名詞 using（使用），得知空格應置入複數及物動詞。

ⓑ 選項中符合上述的僅剩 (B) prefer（偏好），置入後亦符合語意，故為正選。

重要字詞片語

1. **rely on...** 依賴……
   = depend on...
   We can always rely on John for help.
   我們總是可以靠約翰幫忙。
2. **digital** [ˈdɪdʒətḷ] *a.* 數位的
3. **database** [ˈdetəˌbes] *n.* 資料庫
4. **literally** [ˈlɪtərəlɪ] *adv.* 照字面地
   When it comes to translation, don't translate articles literally.
   說到翻譯，千萬不要照字面翻譯文章。
5. **approximately** [əˈprɑksəmɪtlɪ] *adv.* 大約
6. **carry on...** 繼續……
   I'll carry on this project, even at the risk of losing my job.
   即使冒著丟掉飯碗的危險，我仍然要繼續這項計畫。
7. **efficient** [ɪˈfɪʃənt] *a.* 有效率的
8. **proper** [ˈprɑpɚ] *a.* 正確的；適當的
9. **transport** [trænsˈpɔrt] *vt.* 運輸／送
10. **organize** [ˈɔrgəˌnaɪz] *vt.* 安排，排列
11. **load** [lod] *vt.* 裝載
12. **launch** [lɔntʃ] *vt.* 推出；（首次）上市；發行
13. **expand** [ɪkˈspænd] *vi.* & *vt.* 擴大，拓展
14. **reliable** [rɪˈlaɪəbḷ] *a.* 可靠的
15. **element** [ˈɛləmənt] *n.* 因素
16. **on a daily basis** 每天

四、篇章結構（占 8 分）

第 31 至 34 題為題組

　　廣負盛名的聖家堂是巴塞隆納辨識度最高的地標之一，每年有超過四百五十萬人造訪這座建築。這座羅馬天主教教堂位於市內的擴展區，以其巨大的規模和雄偉而前衛的建築風格而出名。興建這座教堂的原始藍圖是在 1882 年起草的。**31.** 一開始，這個案子應當在建築師法蘭西斯柯・德・保拉・德爾・維拉的指導之下進行。他計劃要蓋一座傳統的哥德式教堂，類似於許多歐洲當時的其他教堂。然而，維拉在 1883 年辭去工作，然後一位三十一歲、名為安東尼・高第的年輕建築師接手了這項工程。當時，高第最為人所知的是設計維森斯之家，一座現代主義風格的私人建築，如今已成為博物館。

　　32. 高第將維拉為聖家堂設計的計畫徹底放棄，並提出了他自己的構想。他判定這座教堂應作為給基督徒祈求上帝赦免自身罪過的紀念館而矗立。因此，高第想要使用基督教所有的重要象

109

TEST 04

徵，以便給訪客真實的宗教體驗。高第的聖家堂計畫變得如此宏偉，他自己因而估計會需要好幾個世紀才能完工。當他於 1926 年被電車撞倒過世時，神殿只完成了 20%。不過，後代的人直到今日都在繼續他的大業。

　　33. 資金問題有時也拖慢了進度。聖家堂並不是政府資助的工程。所有募來支持這項工程的款項都是來自遊客與當地大部分居民的捐獻。聖家堂甚至在 2019 年以前都沒有建造許可證。雖然高第原本在 1885 年曾申請過一次，但從來沒有通過。所以根據當地法律，聖家堂是違章建築。34. 作為近期許可協議的一部分，聖家堂將支付大約五百萬美元以便取得新的許可證。它也需要另外支付四千萬美元作為過去一百三十多年來違法施工的罰款。目前，聖家堂將有望在 2026 年 —— 高第去世一百年後 —— 完工。

E 31. 理由
- ⓐ 空格前一句提到，興建聖家堂的原始藍圖是在 1882 年起草的，而空格後一句提及，他計劃要蓋一座傳統的哥德式教堂，可推測空格應與起草該原始藍圖的建築師是誰有關。
- ⓑ 選項 (E) 表示，一開始，這個案子應當在建築師法蘭西斯柯・德・保拉・德爾・維拉的指導之下進行，且本段倒數第二句提及，維拉在 1883 年辭去工作，得知空格後一句的代名詞 He（他）指的即是選項 (E) 中的 architect Francisco de Paula del Villar（建築師法蘭西斯柯・德・保拉・德爾・維拉），填入後語意連貫，可知 (E) 項應為正選。

B 32. 理由
- ⓐ 空格前一段倒數第二句提到高第這位年輕建築師接手這項工程，空格後的句子在說明高第會如何興建聖家堂，可推測空格應是帶出高第提出構想的引言。
- ⓑ 選項 (B) 表示，高第將維拉為聖家堂設計的計畫徹底放棄，並提出了自己的構想，且空格後提及他要如何興建該教堂，與前一段維拉計劃要蓋傳統的哥德式教堂背道而馳，填入後語意連貫，可知 (B) 項應為正選。

A 33. 理由
- ⓐ 空格後的句子提及聖家堂不是政府資助的工程，資金來源全靠遊客與當地居民的捐獻，可推測空格應是帶出興建聖家堂關於資金方面的引言。
- ⓑ 選項 (A) 表示，資金問題有時也拖慢了進度，且前一段倒數第二句提及高第過世時，神殿才完成了 20%，與進度問題相呼應，填入後語意連貫，可知 (A) 項應為正選。

C 34. 理由
- ⓐ 空格前提到聖家堂在 2019 年以前都沒有建造許可證，雖然有申請，但卻未曾通過，並且表示聖家堂是違章建築，而空格後一句則提及它需要支付一筆巨款做為長時間以來違法施工的罰款，可推測空格應與聖家堂的許可證有關。
- ⓑ 選項 (C) 表示，作為近期許可協議的一部分，聖家堂將支付大約五百萬美元以便取得新的許可證，填入後語意連貫，可知 (C) 項應為正選。

(D) 項中譯：聖家堂建築許可被拒的消息引起了承包商們的恐慌。

重要字詞片語

1. **recognizable** [ˈrɛkəɡˌnaɪzəbl̩] *a.* 可辨認的，認得出的
2. **landmark** [ˈlændˌmɑrk] *n.* 地標
3. **notable** [ˈnotəbl̩] *a.* 顯要的；顯著的
4. **immense** [ɪˈmɛns] *a.* 巨大的
5. **majestic** [məˈdʒɛstɪk] *a.* 雄偉的；壯麗的
6. **avant-garde** [ˌævɑŋˈɡɑrd] *a.* 前衛的
7. **blueprint** [ˈbluˌprɪnt] *n.* 藍圖
8. **initially** [ɪˈnɪʃəlɪ] *adv.* 開始時，最初
9. **be supposed to V** 應當（做）……
10. **take over...** 接手／接任／接管……
11. **modernist** [ˈmɑdɚnɪst] *a.* 現代主義的 & *n.* 現代主義者
12. **scrap** [skræp] *vt.* 放棄，拋棄；報廢（三態為：scrap, scrapped [skræpt], scrapped）& *n.* 碎片（可數）；廢品（不可數）
13. **estimate** [ˈɛstəˌmet] *vt.* & *n.* 估計，估算
14. **tram** [træm] *n.* 有軌電車（英式用法）
15. **financing** [ˈfaɪnænsɪŋ] *n.* 資金（不可數）
16. **permit** [ˈpɝmɪt] *n.* 許可證 & [pɚˈmɪt] *vt.* & *vi.* 准許，允許（三態為：permit, permitted [pɚˈmɪtɪd], permitted）permission [pɚˈmɪʃən] *n.* 允許，許可（不可數）
17. **apply for...** 申請……；應徵……
18. **roughly** [ˈrʌflɪ] *adv.* 大約
19. **penalty** [ˈpɛnəltɪ] *n.* 罰款；處罰，懲罰（複數為 penalties）

五、閱讀測驗（占 24 分）

第 35 至 38 題為題組

　　數千年來人類都會跟寵物 —— 最常見的就是狗 —— 一起睡覺。然而與寵物共眠的想法在現代卻引來兩極的反應。

　　由中央昆士蘭大學針對一萬三千多人所做的一項線上研究發現，許多與寵物同睡一張床的人睡得比和伴侶共眠還要香甜。這項研究顯示，伴侶 —— 尤其是會打鼾的人 —— 比寵物更容易擾人清夢。加州聖塔莫尼卡的知名獸醫羅傑．范倫汀表示，與狗共眠能夠減輕壓力，而且也會讓人們睡得更安穩。研究顯示，寵物主人的血壓比較低，且他們的心理幸福感也優於沒有寵物的人。的確，和寵物共眠可以幫助減輕焦慮和憂鬱，因為牠們扮演著安撫毯的角色。

　　某些醫生和公衛當局則以接觸過敏原、壁蝨和寄生蟲的風險增加為由，強烈反對與寵物一起睡覺的想法，而獸醫通常也不建議這麼做。狗很淺眠且對聲音和其他危險的徵兆會保持警覺，這表示牠們在床上會造成干擾，尤其在較小的床上。還有另一種危險是受驚的寵物可能會在晚上傷害主人，或主人可能在睡不安穩的夜晚傷到他們的寵物。

最終這還得由個人衡量利弊並自己做決定。那些想要和他們的狗共眠的人，還是有辦法確保彼此相安無事。一個是在睡前帶你的狗去散步讓牠們玩到累。另一個則是堅守狗在床上該睡哪裡的規矩。還有一個是定期更換寢具以確保清潔。

B 35. 第二段中的 they act as a kind of security blanket 是什麼意思？
(A) 看門狗可以嚇阻小偷闖入。
(B) 寵物對牠們的主人來說是獲得慰藉的來源。
(C) 狗和貓可能會破壞你的毯子和床單。
(D) 寵物可以幫助牠們的主人在冬天保持溫暖。

> 理由

本句粗體字表，牠們扮演著安撫毯的角色。根據本文第二段依序說明和寵物共眠可以降低血壓、減輕壓力和憂鬱，可推論寵物可讓主人感到慰藉，故 (B) 項應為正選。

C 36. 根據本文，為什麼與寵物共享一張床可能是不好的主意？
(A) 因為這種作法可能會讓你感到焦慮。　(B) 因為這種作法缺少其有益的證據。
(C) 因為這種作法有健康方面的隱憂。　　(D) 因為你的伴侶可能會吃醋。

> 理由

根據本文第三段第一句，有些醫生和公衛當局強烈反對這項作法，並指出此舉會增加與過敏原、壁蝨和寄生蟲接觸的種種危害，故 (C) 項應為正選。

D 37. 作者對和寵物共眠的看法是什麼？
(A) 這是一個不適合現代世界的作法。
(B) 因為有傷害寵物的風險，所以太危險了。
(C) 這肯定對所有的貓狗主人有益。
(D) 由每個人來評估其適用性。

> 理由

根據本文最後一段第一句，最終還是由個人衡量利弊並自己做決定，故 (D) 項應為正選。

D 38. 文中並未提及下列哪一項關於和狗共眠的建議？
(A) 確定你的狗知道哪裡可以睡哪裡不可以睡。
(B) 確定你的狗在睡前有運動。
(C) 確定你有定期更換床上的床單。
(D) 確定如果你的狗不乖，你會把牠趕下床。

> 理由

根據本文最後一段依序提及和狗共眠的建議，有睡前帶狗去散步、讓狗睡在確切的位置上以及定期更換寢具，全文未提及狗不乖，要把牠趕下床，故 (D) 項應為正選。

重要字詞片語

1. **snore** [snɔr] *vi.* 打鼾
2. **disruptive** [dɪsˈrʌptɪv] *a.* 擾亂的；破壞的
   James usually tells funny jokes, but sometimes he's disruptive in class.
   詹姆士通常會說好笑的笑話，但他有時候會擾亂上課。
3. **veterinarian** [ˌvɛtərəˈnɛrɪən] *n.* 獸醫
4. **psychological** [ˌsaɪkəˈlɑdʒɪkl̩] *a.* 心理（學）的
5. **well-being** [ˌwɛlˈbiɪŋ] *n.* 健全；福祉（不可數）
   Both parents should take responsibility for their children's emotional well-being.
   父母雙方都必須對孩子的心理健康負起責任。
6. **relieve** [rɪˈliv] *vt.* 減輕；緩和
   Aspirin will relieve your headache.
   阿斯匹靈會減輕你的頭痛。
7. **physician** [fɪˈzɪʃən] *n.* 醫生
8. **cite** [saɪt] *vt.* 以……為證；引用
9. **hazard** [ˈhæzɚd] *n.* 危險
10. **allergen** [ˈæləʊdʒən] *n.* 過敏原
11. **tick** [tɪk] *n.* 壁蝨
12. **parasite** [ˈpærəˌsaɪt] *n.* 寄生蟲
13. **opposed** [əˈpozd] *a.* 反對的
    be opposed to + N/V-ing
    反對……
    I'm opposed to adopting Tim's proposal because I don't think it is feasible.
    我反對採納提姆的方案，因為我認為那行不通。
14. **alert** [əˈlɜt] *a.* 警戒的 & *vt.* 提醒 & *n.* 警戒
15. **be up to sb...**　　有賴於某人……
16. **weigh** [we] *vt.* 衡量
    We weighed the options before we made a decision.
    我們先衡量了這些選擇，再做出決定。
17. **pros and cons**　　優缺點
18. **slumber** [ˈslʌmbɚ] *vi.* & *n.* 睡覺
19. **harmonious** [harˈmonɪəs] *a.* 和諧的
20. **pooch** [putʃ] *n.* 狗
21. **ruin** [ˈruɪn] *vt.* 破壞
22. **evaluate** [ɪˈvæljuˌet] *vt.* 評估
    We cannot make a final decision until the boss has evaluated the situation.
    直到老闆評估了這個情況後，我們才能做最後的決定。

第 39 至 42 題為題組

　　有些天災是如此地毀滅性以至於可以留名青史。其中一個令人無法忘懷的天災案例就是將近兩千年前義大利維蘇威火山的爆發。

　　西元 79 年維蘇威火山爆發時，約有兩萬名居民住在附近的龐貝城以及周邊地區。那年的八月二十四日 ── 長期以來都認為災難發生於這一天 ── 當地居民被一場讓天空瀰漫火山灰和煙霧的巨大火山爆發嚇壞

了。災難結束時，火山已經持續噴發將近兩天。災後並沒有任何救濟行動。救援完全無法到達那裡，因為龐貝城已被維蘇威火山噴出的大量火山灰掩埋。灰燼的量是如此龐大，整個龐貝城被埋在四到六公尺深處。當時著名的律師兼作家小普林尼寫道：「現在世界其他的地方是白天」但在龐貝城「黑暗比任何夜晚都還要更黑、更厚重」。據估計約有兩千人死亡。

　　這座被埋沒的城市被遺忘了許多個世紀，直到十六世紀末期被重新發現。考古學家在十八世紀開始挖掘這座城市。當時的結論是龐貝城居民死於火山灰及有毒氣體。世人長期以來都接受這樣的解釋，直到新的化驗結果認為真正的凶手是高溫而非火山灰和有毒氣體。火山噴發時的溫度極高，高達攝氏三百度，可以讓人當場喪命。這理論幫助解釋了為何許多罹難者的遺骸都以栩栩如生的姿勢被發現：他們在死前根本沒有時間去反應。

　　如今，龐貝城遺跡已被聯合國教科文組織列為世界遺產地點，並吸引許多觀光客。但是為了要保存這座被摧毀城鎮的殘留部分，旅遊被限制在某些區域。不管我們能不能去到某些遺跡，龐貝城毀滅的故事將永遠不會被遺忘。

C 39. 下列哪一項最接近第二段中 relief 的意思？
(A) 安心。　　(B) 減輕。　　(C) 援助。　　(D) 中斷。

> **理由**
> 根據本文第二段第四句，因為龐貝城已被火山灰掩埋，救援完全無法到達那裡，可推測 relief 為「救助，救援」的意思，故 (C) 項應為正選。

B 40. 為何在本文中提及小普林尼？
(A) 他在龐貝城的災難中身亡。　　(B) 他記錄對這起事件的觀感。
(C) 他發現龐貝城的遺跡。　　　　(D) 他警告火山的危險。

> **理由**
> 根據本文第二段倒數第二句，小普利尼寫下「現在世界其他的地方是白天」但在龐貝城「黑暗比任何夜晚都還要更黑、更厚重」。可知他是記錄了對這起事件的觀感，故 (B) 項應為正選。

C 41. 十八世紀時發生什麼事？
(A) 維蘇威火山發生另一起火山爆發。　　(B) 龐貝城開始吸引大量的觀光業。
(C) 專業人士開始挖掘龐貝城的遺址。　　(D) 危險氣體從火山噴發。

> **理由**
> 根據本文第三段第一句，十八世紀考古學家開始挖掘這座城市，可得知 (C) 項應為正選。

A 42. 後來的化驗證實這場火山爆發的什麼事情？
(A) 人們是如何喪命的。　　(B) 什麼原因造成了這場火山爆發。
(C) 火山什麼時候爆發的。　　(D) 多少人存活下來。

> **理由**
> 根據本文第三段第三句，直到新的化驗結果認為真正的凶手是高溫，而非火山灰和有毒氣體，得知 (A) 項應為正選。

重要字詞片語

1. **devastating** [ˈdɛvəˌstetɪŋ] *a.* 具毀滅性的
   Oil spills have a devastating effect on coral reefs in the ocean.
   漏油對海洋中的珊瑚礁有毀滅性的影響。
2. **eruption** [ɪˈrʌpʃən] *n.* (火山) 爆發
3. **volcano** [vɑlˈkeno] *n.* 火山
4. **resident** [ˈrɛzədənt] *n.* 居民
5. **tremendous** [trɪˈmɛndəs] *a.* 龐大的
6. **last** [læst] *vi.* 持續
7. **relief** [rɪˈlif] *n.* 救濟
   a relief effort 救災工作
8. **aftermath** [ˈæftɚˌmæθ] *n.* 餘波
   in the aftermath of...
   在（某件不好的事）發生之後
   Rescue work soon began in the aftermath of the earthquake.
   地震過後救援行動馬上展開。
9. **spew** [spju] *vi. & vt.* 噴出
   The volcano spewed a giant cloud of ashes into the air.
   那座火山將大量的火山灰噴入空中。
10. **volume** [ˈvɑljəm] *n.* 量（= amount）
    The new bridge was built to cope with the increasing volume of traffic.
    那座新橋建造的目的是要應付日漸增加的交通量。
11. **bury** [ˈbɛrɪ] *vt.* 埋葬（三態為：bury, buried [ˈbɛrɪd], buried）
    Because of the earthquake, hundreds of people were buried alive.
    數百人因為這場地震被活埋。
12. **daylight** [ˈdeˌlaɪt] *n.* 白天（不可數）
13. **estimate** [ˈɛstəˌmet] *vt.* 估計
    It is estimated that 20,000 people will participate in the demonstration.
    估計將有兩萬人參與這次的示威遊行。
14. **archeologist** [ˌɑrkɪˈɑlədʒɪst] *n.* 考古學家
15. **excavate** [ˈɛkskəˌvet] *vt.* 挖掘
16. **poisonous** [ˈpɔɪznəs] *a.* 有毒的
17. **blast** [blæst] *vt.* 噴出；炸開
    They had to blast a tunnel through the mountain.
    他們得炸出一條穿越這座山的隧道。
18. **instantly** [ˈɪnstəntlɪ] *adv.* 立刻地
    (= immediately)
19. **restrict** [rɪˈstrɪkt] *vt.* 限制
20. **preserve** [prɪˈzɝv] *vt.* 保存；維持
    The local residents want the ancient temple to be preserved for future generations.
    當地居民希望能為後代子孫保存這座古廟。
21. **emit** [ɪˈmɪt] *vt.* 發出（三態為：emit, emitted [ɪˈmɪtɪd], emitted）

第 43 至 46 題為題組

乍看之下，刺龍蝦和一般龍蝦無異：牠們有著長長的身體、上面覆蓋著堅硬的殼。然而，近看你會發現牠沒有傳統的龍蝦螯，而是背部有刺，頭上有長長的觸角用來嚇阻掠食者。從加勒比海到地中海再到紐西蘭，全球都可以找到不同的亞種。

TEST 04

　　刺龍蝦最有趣的一面或許是牠們的遷徙習慣。不像許多鳥類以 V 字隊形遷徙而著稱，刺龍蝦則排成又長又直的一條線，最多可達五十隻。然後牠們排成一路縱隊行進，從平常的棲息地 —— 珊瑚礁和礁石縫 —— 不間斷地行軍以尋找溫暖的海域過冬。大多數路程都是在漆黑的掩護下進行，就如同牠們也是在黑暗中覓食包括蛤蜊或螃蟹等食物。

　　研究指出，這些在黑暗中於陌生水域尋找新家的導航能力，歸功於牠們與地球磁場的連結。刺龍蝦能偵測地球的磁場，並用它來識別方向和制定路線。有兩支較小的觸角被牠們用來感應水流與水中的化學變化，藉此補強牠們不凡的導航技巧。

　　不過這種導航能力還是無法讓牠們不變成我們的盤中飧。如果你在餐廳吃過龍蝦尾，你吃的很可能是刺龍蝦。捕龍蝦是一個很大的產業。隨便舉個例子：它占巴哈馬群島出口經濟的一大部分。雖然許多國家都限制可捕捉刺龍蝦的數量、年齡以及體型大小，有些不肖漁夫完全無視這些限制。

　　諷刺的是，牠們的另一個威脅來自於前述的遷徙模式。當牠們成群結隊行走時，疾病會快速地一隻傳一隻。此外，牠們越來越容易感染疾病。這是因為牠們喜愛的珊瑚礁環境飽受氣候變遷之苦而改變所導致。

C **43.** 下列哪一項說明刺龍蝦遷徙的模式？

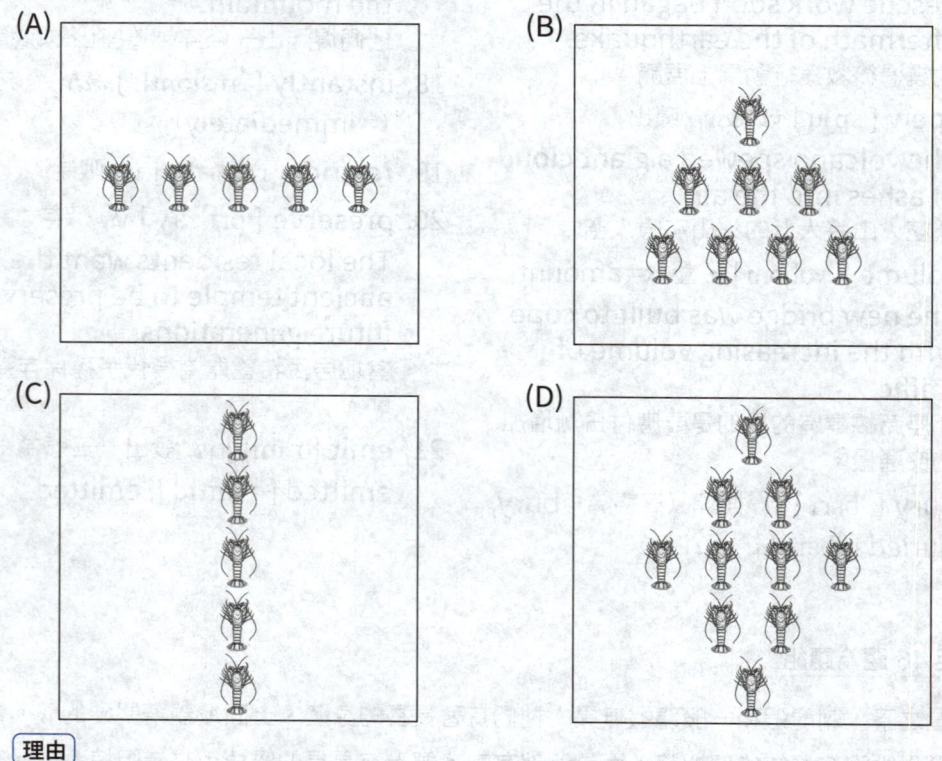

(A)　(B)　(C)　(D)

理由

根據本文第二段第二句，刺龍蝦排成又長又直的一條線，可得知 (C) 項應為正選。

B 44. 下列哪一項最接近第三段中 orient 的意思？
(A) 偽裝。
(B) 確定……位置。
(C) 集中。
(D) 保護。

理由
根據本文第三段第一句，這些在黑暗中於陌生水域尋找新家的能力取決於和地球磁場的連結，且從 navigate（確定……的方向）此字可推測 orient 為「尋找方向」的意思，故 (B) 項應為正選。

D 45. 根據本文，下列哪一項關於刺龍蝦的敘述是正確的？
(A) 牠們的外殼讓牠們和其他常見的龍蝦有所不同。
(B) 牠們在巴哈馬群島的數量現在少到令人擔憂。
(C) 牠們的刺幫助牠們在怪異的地形獵捕食物。
(D) 牠們的尾巴常在世界各地的餐廳裡被食用。

理由
根據本文第四段第二句，如果你在餐廳吃過龍蝦尾，你吃的很可能是刺龍蝦，故 (D) 項應為正選。

A 46. 為什麼在最後一段使用 ironically 這個字？
(A) 因為刺龍蝦遷徙的方式也是傷害牠們的原因。
(B) 因為刺龍蝦出乎意料地會感染疾病。
(C) 因為氣候變遷在現今的世界是很常見的問題。
(D) 因為龍蝦住在有珊瑚礁的地方是不尋常的。

理由
根據本文最後一段第一句，牠們的另一個威脅來自於前述的遷徙模式，後面則提及此種方式很容易傳播疾病，表示這種遷徙模式反而會危害牠們自己，故 (A) 項應為正選。

重要字詞片語

1. **spiny** [ˈspaɪnɪ] *a.* 帶刺的
   spine [spaɪn] *n.*（動、植物的）刺
2. **claw** [klɔ] *n.* 螯；爪
3. **possess** [pəˈzɛs] *vt.* 擁有，持有
   Peter's father possesses a good sense of humor.
   彼得的父親很有幽默感。
4. **antenna** [ænˈtɛnə] *n.* 觸角，觸鬚
   （複數為：antennae [ænˈtɛni]）
5. **predator** [ˈprɛdətɚ] *n.* 掠食者
6. **subspecies** [ˈsʌbˌspiʃɪz] *n.* 亞種
   （單複數同形）
7. **migratory** [ˈmaɪgrəˌtɔrɪ] *a.* 遷移的
   migrate [ˈmaɪɡret] *vi.* 遷移
8. **pattern** [ˈpætɚn] *n.* 模式，方式
9. **file** [faɪl] *n.* 排成一行的人或動物
10. **march** [mɑrtʃ] *n.* 行進 & *vi.* 前進
    Thousands of demonstrators marched toward City Hall at 2:00 yesterday afternoon.
    昨天下午兩點，數千名示威者往市政府方向前進。
11. **crevice** [ˈkrɛvəs] *n.*（岩石表面的）裂縫

TEST 04

12. **waters** [ˈwɑtɚz] *n.* 水域（恆用複數）
13. **navigate** [ˈnævəˌget] *vi.* & *vt.* 導航，航行
14. **magnetic** [mægˈnɛtɪk] *a.* 磁場的
15. **supplement** [ˈsʌpləmɛnt] *vt.* 補充
    Miranda likes to supplement her diet with vitamins.
    米蘭達喜歡吃維他命作為飲食補充。
16. **account for...**　　（在數量上）占……
17. **proportion** [prəˈpɔrʃən] *n.* 部分；比例
18. **restriction** [rɪˈstrɪkʃən] *n.* 限制
    have restrictions on...
    對……有限制

    That club has rigid restrictions on its membership.
    那家俱樂部對它的會員資格限制很嚴。
19. **unscrupulous** [ʌnˈskrupjələs] *n.* 無道德的；無恥的
20. **aforementioned** [əˈfɔrˌmɛnʃənd] *a.* 上述的
21. **vulnerable** [ˈvʌlnərəbl̩] *a.* 易受影響的；脆弱的
    Newborn infants are particularly vulnerable to the flu.
    初生的嬰兒特別容易被傳染流感。

第貳部分、混合題（占 10 分）

第 47 至 50 題為題組

這是一家新開張的無國界料理餐廳的廣告以及四位顧客對該餐廳的評論。

> *探索西班牙與臺灣的美味，盡在……*
>
> ***西灣小館！***
>
> *我們相信：西班牙人氣小吃塔帕斯與臺灣很普遍喜歡分食的方式是完美契合的。名廚胡安 - 佩德羅・巴拉托和廖雲芝二人共同打造了這家驚豔的全新無國界料理餐廳。請來品嚐結合兩國料理迷人風味的獨特菜餚，包括伊比利火腿餡小籠包、米酒蒜味蝦、臺灣香腸西班牙海鮮飯，族繁不及備載！*

(A) 麗塔

如果你在尋找全新的美食冒險，我由衷推薦西灣小館。我去過西班牙非常多次，對當地菜很熟，因此我知道應該要吃到什麼東西。我對臺灣菜就沒那麼習慣。不過這兩種料理的結合真是讓人開了眼界。我特別喜歡小籠包。當咬下包子皮爆漿的那一刻，裡面冒出來的是西班牙火腿，好神奇喔。更讚的是，這裡的價格相當實惠！

(B) 泰倫斯

在來這家餐廳用餐前，我擔心重口的臺灣味會蓋掉較低調的西班牙味。我很高興自己是多慮了。巴拉托與廖主廚巧妙地融合兩種料理的元素，讓兩種飲食文化同時得以凸顯。我自己也是主廚，知道這個任務有多麼艱鉅，所以要盛讚他們能做得這麼到位。我個人最愛的是西班牙洋芋配臺灣佐料。

(C) 艾比蓋兒

經過多年來多次的失望，我對無國界料理餐廳的評價是蠻低的。在西灣小館的開幕夜用餐後，很遺憾這看法並未改變。雖然價格實惠、氣氛佳，但我覺得食物和口味都不及格。既不夠西班牙，也不夠臺灣，這些菜落入一個模糊的中間地帶，無法讓我滿意。

(D) 布萊德利

起先我對這個概念抱持懷疑態度：幹嘛冒著破壞本就各有優點的兩種料理的風險，把它們搶婚送作堆呢？不過西灣小館讓我陶醉了。每道菜都出色，但最精彩的要算是米酒蒜味蝦。這道料理非常濃郁美味，讓我又點了一份。這麼好吃的料理又是這麼合理的價位，我當然要跟所有朋友推薦西灣小館囉。

TEST 04

47. 哪些評論者有提到廣告裡面提過的菜色？請寫下評論者的字母代號。

　　A, D

　理由
　根據麗塔評論的倒數第三句 I particularly loved the xiaolongbao.（我特別喜歡小籠包。）及布萊德利評論的第三句 …but the garlic shrimp in rice wine was the highlight.（……但最精彩的要算是米酒蒜味蝦。）與廣告最後一句所提到的料理小籠包和米酒蒜味蝦一致，故得知，(A)、(D) 項應為正選。

48-50. 請寫下與下列句子相關的評論者字母代號。

48. ___B___ 提到了自己的職業。

　理由
　泰倫斯評論的倒數第二句 As a chef myself, …（我自己也是主廚，……）得知 (B) 項應為正選。

49. ___A___ 提及自己旅行的經歷。

　理由
　麗塔評論的第二句 Having traveled to Spain on numerous occasions, …（我去過西班牙非常多次，……）得知 (A) 項應為正選。

50. ___C___ 曾在類似餐廳有過多次負面經驗。

　理由
　艾比蓋兒評論一開始就先說她對無國界料理餐廳的評價蠻低的，失望過很多次，結果到西灣小館用餐後依然沒有改變看法。中間又提及食物和口味都不及格。故得知 (C) 項應為正選。

重要字詞片語

1. **fusion** [ˋfjuʒən] *n.* 融合；結合（不可數）
2. **incredible** [ɪnˋkrɛdəbl] *a.* 難以置信的
3. **gel** [dʒɛl] *vi.* 膠化；使如膠似漆
   The new guy in the office gels well with the rest of the team.
   辦公室的新成員與團隊其他成員相處得很好。
4. **acclaimed** [əˋklemd] *a.* 受到好評的
5. **chef** [ʃɛf] *n.* 主廚
6. **launch** [lɔntʃ] *vt.* 發表（新書、新作品、新產品）；發動（活動）；發射（火箭、飛彈）
   The company launched the app to improve customer service.
   這間公司推出了這款應用程式來改善客戶服務。
7. **cuisine** [kwɪˋzin] *n.* 菜餚
8. **culinary** [ˋkʌlɪˌnɛrɪ] *a.* 烹飪的
9. **recommend** [ˌrɛkəˋmɛnd] *vt.* 推薦；建議
   I recommend this book to anyone who loves mystery novels.
   我推薦這本書給喜愛推理小說的人。
10. **in this / that regard**
    在這／那方面；在這／那點上
    The company makes a lot of money. It's successful in that regard. However, it has a huge pollution problem.
    該公司很賺錢，就那方面來講算成功的。但它有嚴重的汙染問題。

11. **accustomed** [əˈkʌstəmd] *a.* 習慣的
    be / get accustomed to + N/V-ing
    對……漸漸習慣
    Vince is accustomed to the fast pace of city life.
    文斯已習慣了都市的快節奏生活。

12. **revelation** [ˌrɛvḷˈeʃən] *n.* 被揭示的真相（可數）；揭露（不可數）
    be a revelation
    讓人大開眼界；令人耳目一新

13. **expose** [ɪkˈspoz] *vt.* 露出；暴露
    An investigative reporter exposed the mayor's bribery scandal.
    一位調查記者爆料市長的貪瀆醜聞。

14. **remarkably** [rɪˈmɑrkəblɪ] *adv.*
    非常地；引人注目地

15. **competitive** [kəmˈpɛtətɪv] *a.*
    （價格、服務等）具有競爭力的；競爭的

16. **overpower** [ˌovɚˈpauɚ] *vt.* （味道或感情）壓倒；征服
    The strong smell of garlic overpowered the other flavors in the dish.
    濃烈的蒜味壓過了菜餚中的其他風味。

17. **subtle** [ˈsʌtḷ] *a.* 細緻的；細微的

18. **ensure** [ɪnˈʃʊr] *vt.* 確保
    Please double-check the report to ensure there are no errors.
    請再次檢查報告，以確保沒有錯誤。

19. **shine through** （品質）顯而易見
    Eric's talent for music really shone through in his latest performance.
    艾瑞克的音樂才華在最近一次的表演當中展露無遺。

20. **commend** [kəˈmɛnd] *vt.* 讚揚，稱讚
    The manager commended Anita for her outstanding performance.
    經理讚賞艾妮塔的傑出表現。

21. **substandard** [sʌbˈstændɚd] *a.* 不合格的，低於標準的

22. **skeptical** [ˈskɛptɪkḷ] *a.* 懷疑的
    be skeptical about…
    對……表示質疑
    Many people are skeptical about the effectiveness of the new policy.
    許多人對新政策的效果表示質疑。

23. **highlight** [ˈhaɪˌlaɪt] *n.* 最精彩的部分

TEST 04

TEST 04

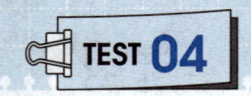

第參部分、非選擇題（占 28 分）

一、中譯英（占 8 分）

1. 隨著外送平臺的興起，越來越多顧客為了節省時間而選擇訂外送。

   示範譯句
   With the rise / emergence of food delivery platforms, more and more customers are choosing to get their food delivered (in order) to save time.

   或：As food delivery platforms rise / develop, more and more customers are ordering in with an eye to / with a view to saving time.

   翻譯要點
   a. **emergence** [ɪˋmɝdʒəns] *n.* 出現
   b. **delivery** [dɪˋlɪvərɪ] *n.* 遞送
      deliver [dɪˋlɪvɚ] *vt.* 遞送
      There is no postal delivery on Sundays.
      星期天郵差不送信。
   c. **platform** [ˋplæt͵fɔrm] *n.* 平臺
   d. **order in(...)** 叫（……）外賣
      We were too tired to cook after cleaning the apartment, so we ordered in pizza.
      我們打掃完公寓後累得不想煮飯，於是就叫了披薩外賣。
   e. **with an eye to N/V-ing**
      = with a view to N/V-ing
      為了（要）……
      Ron is saving money with an eye to buying a house.
      榮恩正在為了買房子而存錢。

2. 外送員滿街跑的現象引起許多爭議，其中一個大家最關注的議題就是外送員的安全。

   示範譯句
   The phenomenon of delivery people being all over the street / everywhere has caused / created / sparked / stirred a lot of controversy, and one issue that people are most concerned about is their safety.

   或：The rapid increase of delivery people all over the street / everywhere has provoked controversy, with the public expressing concern for their safety.

   翻譯要點
   a. **phenomenon** [fəˋnɑməˏnɑn] *n.* 現象（複數形為 phenomena [fəˋnɑmənə]）
      Lightning is an electrical phenomenon.
      閃電是一種電的現象。
   b. **a delivery person** 外送人員
   c. **controversy** [ˋkɑntrəˏvɝsɪ] *n.* 爭議
      cause / create / spark / stir / provoke / arouse controversy
      引發/引起爭議
      The new policy has caused controversy over the rights of employees.
      這項新政策引起關於員工權利的爭論。

d. **be concerned about...**
關切／擔憂……
The candidate was concerned about the state's water crisis.
該候選人很關注該州的水資源短缺問題。

e. **express concern for...**
表達對……的關切
Many parents expressed concern for the safety of schoolchildren after the attack.
這場攻擊事件過後，許多家長對學童的安全表示關切。

二、英文作文（占 20 分）

提示：你最好的朋友 Cindy 的生日即將來臨，因此你想安排一天請她看場電影來為她慶生。請寫一封信給 Cindy，根據以下的電影時刻表，告訴 Cindy 你打算帶她去看哪一部電影及時間，並告知她當天慶生活動的其他安排。文末請以 George 署名。

常春藤電影院 12 月 28 日，星期六	
星際大戰：天行者的崛起 類型｜科幻、動作	10:00 | 12:00 | 14:00 16:00 | 18:00 | 20:00 22:00
美女與野獸 類型｜動畫、奇幻	10:30 | 13:30 | 17:00 19:30 | 21:30
愛因斯坦的一生 類型｜自傳、劇情	11:30 | 15:30 | 19:30

示範作文

Hi Cindy,

　　How's it going? Are you getting excited about your birthday coming up? I am! I want to celebrate your birthday by taking you out to see a movie. I know you are a really big fan of *Star Wars*. So, I believe you'll want to see the latest movie in the series. I know you haven't seen it yet because it won't be released until next Friday, which happens to be your birthday. I've seen the trailer for it, and I'm sure it will be an amazing film!

　　I was thinking we could go to the show on your birthday. We could see the 4:00 p.m. showing. That way, we could grab a bite to eat somewhere after the show before we head to Star KTV. This will be my treat, of course, since it's your birthday. I've also invited Tammy and Howard to join us at the KTV. I think this will be a

TEST 04

fantastic way to celebrate such a special occasion. Please let me know. If you agree, we could meet at the Ivy Cinema around 3:30 p.m. I can reserve the tickets in advance online so we won't have to wait in line.

Cheers,
George

嗨，辛蒂：

　　近來如何？妳對即將到來的生日感到興奮嗎？我很興奮！我想帶妳出去看電影來慶祝妳的生日。我知道妳是《星際大戰》的忠實粉絲。因此，我認為妳會想看該系列的最新電影。我知道妳還沒看這部片，因為它要到下週五才會上映，那天剛好就是妳的生日。我已經看過預告片了，我相信它會是一部很棒的電影！

　　我想我們可以在妳生日那天去看這部片。我們可以看下午四點的電影。這樣一來，我們可以在電影結束後吃點東西，然後前往 Star KTV。當然，我請客，因為是妳生日。我還邀請了塔米及霍華一起來 KTV 加入我們。我想這是慶祝這種特殊場合的絕佳方式。請讓我知道妳怎麼想。若妳贊同的話，我們可以約下午三點半左右在常春藤電影院見面。我會先上網訂票，這樣我們就不必排隊等候。

喬治　敬上

重要字詞片語

1. **be coming up**　即將到來，即將來臨
   = be drawing near
   = be fast approaching
   When you know something important is coming up, make sure you are well prepared beforehand.
   當你知道有重要的事即將來臨時，要確保你已事先做好準備。
2. **celebrate** [ˈsɛləˌbret] *vt.* 慶祝
3. **series** [ˈsɪriz] *n.* 系列（單複數同形）
4. **release** [rɪˈlis] *vt.* 上映
5. **happen to V**　剛好……
   I happened to be in the neighborhood, so I decided to drop by.
   我碰巧在這附近，所以決定順道過來拜訪。
6. **trailer** [ˈtrelɚ] *n.* （電影或電視節目）預告片
7. **grab a bite to eat**　吃點東西
8. **my treat**　我請客
9. **occasion** [əˈkeʒən] *n.* 場合，時機
10. **reserve** [rɪˈzɝv] *vt.* 預訂

TEST 05

第壹部分、選擇題

一、詞彙題
二、綜合測驗
三、文意選填
四、篇章結構
五、閱讀測驗

第貳部分、混合題

第參部分、非選擇題

一、中譯英
二、英文作文

解答

第壹部分、選擇題

一、詞彙題

| 1. B | 2. A | 3. B | 4. D | 5. D | 6. C | 7. D | 8. D | 9. D | 10. C |

二、綜合測驗

| 11. C | 12. A | 13. B | 14. C | 15. D | 16. B | 17. C | 18. B | 19. D | 20. C |

三、文意選填

| 21. I | 22. E | 23. A | 24. G | 25. C | 26. J | 27. F | 28. D | 29. H | 30. B |

四、篇章結構

| 31. A | 32. E | 33. D | 34. B |

五、閱讀測驗

| 35. B | 36. D | 37. C | 38. B | 39. C | 40. B | 41. C | 42. B | 43. D | 44. B |
| 45. B | 46. C |

第貳部分、混合題

47. peeling

48. seasoning

49. cooling

50. nitrogen gas

51. B

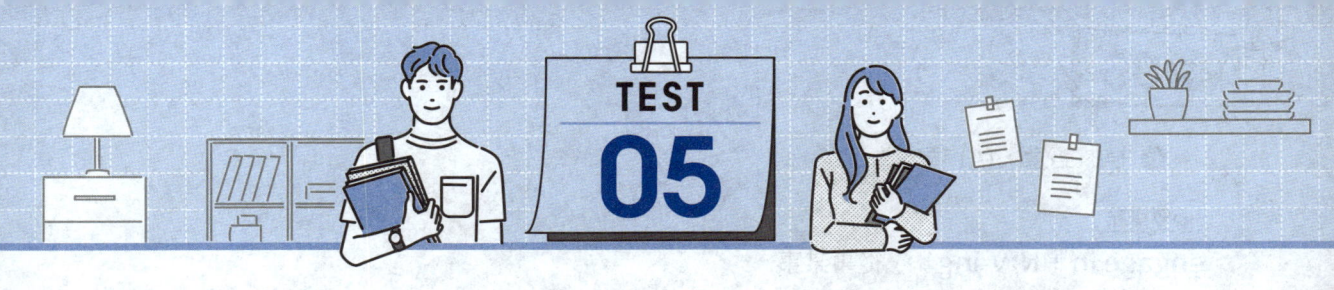

第壹部分、選擇題（占 62 分）

一、詞彙題（占 10 分）

B 1. 柯瑞前往印度前，需要等待該國核准他的簽證。

ⓐ (A) **strength** [strɛŋθ] *n.* 力量（不可數）；優點（可數）
  Operating this machine requires skill more than physical strength.
  操作這臺機器需要的技巧比體力還多。

(B) **approval** [əˋpruvl̩] *n.* 批准；同意（不可數）
  The board of directors gave Bill final approval of his plan.
  董事會最後批准了比爾的計畫。

(C) **volume** [ˋvɑljəm] *n.* 量；音量
  Would you mind turning the volume down? I'm studying.
  你介意把音量調小嗎？我正在念書。

(D) **property** [ˋprɑpɚtɪ] *n.* 財產（不可數）；特性（可數）
  They lost all their property in the fire.
  他們在這場大火中失去了所有財產。

ⓑ 根據語意，(B) 項應為正選。

必考重點

visa [ˋvizə] *n.* 簽證

A 2. 一些專家擔心，青少年花太多時間在智慧型手機上看短影片，而不是與人進行有意義的對話。

ⓐ (A) **meaningful** [ˋminɪŋfəl] *a.* 有意義的
  We had a meaningful and constructive meeting this afternoon.
  今天下午我們開了一場有意義且具建設性的會議。

(B) **sorrowful** [ˋsɔrəfəl] *a.* 悲傷的
  The sorrowful old man missed his wife, who recently passed away.
  那位悲傷的老先生很思念他最近過世的老伴。

(C) **grateful** [ˋgretfəl] *a.* 感激的
  I'm grateful to you for your help.
  對於你的幫助我非常感激。

(D) **truthful** [ˋtruθfəl] *a.* 誠實的；真實的
  You can trust Jim; he is a truthful and upright man.
  你可以信任吉姆，他為人誠實又正直。

127

TEST 05

ⓑ 根據語意，(A) 項應為正選。

> **必考重點**
>
> **engage in + N/V-ing**　　從事某事
> Kyle likes to engage in outdoor activities during the weekend.
> 凱爾喜歡在週末參加戶外活動。

B　3. 這種糖果含有過多的<u>人工</u>糖精和玉米糖漿，這兩樣都會導致體重增加和蛀牙。

- ⓐ (A) financial [faɪˋnænʃəl] *a.* 金融的，財務的
  The business closed due to financial problems.
  這個企業由於財務問題而關閉了。

  (B) artificial [ˌɑrtəˋfɪʃəl] *a.* 人工的，人造的
  Our herbal teas contain no artificial ingredients.
  我們的花草茶沒有添加人工成分。

  (C) reliable [rɪˋlaɪəb!] *a.* 可靠的，可信賴的
  The reporter got her information from a reliable source.
  該記者的消息出自可靠的來源。

  (D) honorable [ˋɑnərəb!] *a.* 可敬的；光榮的
  Scott wants to be a singer, but his father doesn't think it's an honorable profession.
  史考特想當歌手，可是他爸爸卻認為唱歌不是光榮的職業。

- ⓑ 根據語意，(B) 項應為正選。

> **必考重點**
>
> a. **sweetener** [ˋswitənɚ] *n.* 糖精　　　c. **decay** [dɪˋke] *n.* 腐爛
> b. **syrup** [ˋsɪrəp] *n.* 糖漿　　　　　　tooth decay　蛀牙

D　4. 我反對你的提議是因為它聽起來過於浪費，而且我們沒有足夠的資金來實行。

- ⓐ (A) assurance [əˋʃʊrəns] *n.* 保證
  Terry gave me his assurance that he would show up on time.
  泰瑞向我保證他會準時出現。

  (B) permission [pɚˋmɪʃən] *n.* 允許，同意
  Hannah went to the party without her parents' permission.
  漢娜沒有得到父母的允許就去參加派對。

  (C) conscience [ˋkɑnʃəns] *n.* 良心
  Don't press me to do anything against my conscience.
  不要強迫我做任何違反良心的事。

(D) **objection** [əbˋdʒɛkʃən] *n.* 反對，異議（與介詞 to 並用）
　　The lawyer made an objection to the witness' testimony.
　　律師對那名證人的證詞提出抗議。

ⓑ 根據語意，(D) 項應為正選。

【必考重點】

a. **proposal** [prəˋpozl] *n.* 提案；建議
b. **extravagant** [ɪkˋstrævəgənt] *a.* 奢侈的，浪費的
　　This novel depicts the extravagant life of the upper class.
　　這本小說描繪了上流社會奢侈浪費的生活。
c. **fund** [fʌnd] *n.* 資金（恆用複數）

D 5. 去年的紐約之旅激勵我更加用功，也更勤奮地研讀英文。

ⓐ (A) **extremely** [ɪkˋstrimlɪ] *adv.* 極端地；非常地
　　I was extremely happy upon hearing the good news.
　　我一聽到這個好消息便高興得不得了。

(B) **leisurely** [ˋliʒɚlɪ] *adv.* 悠閒地
　　John has been living leisurely in the country since he retired.
　　約翰退休後在鄉下一直過得很悠閒。

(C) **tightly** [ˋtaɪtlɪ] *adv.* 緊緊地
　　Please make sure the gas cap is tightly closed.
　　請確認油箱蓋要關緊。

(D) **diligently** [ˋdɪlədʒəntlɪ] *adv.* 勤奮地
　　Scientists are working diligently to find a cure for AIDS.
　　科學家正努力研究尋找治療愛滋病的方法。

ⓑ 根據語意，(D) 項應為正選。

【必考重點】

motivate sb to V　　激勵某人……
Scholarships often motivate students to study harder.
獎學金往往能激勵學生更用功學習。

C 6. 馬克昨晚回家時試圖悄悄溜進房間，但還是把他爸媽吵醒了。

ⓐ (A) **freeze** [friz] *vi.* 結冰，凝固（三態為：freeze, froze [froz], frozen [ˋfrozn̩]）
　　The water froze on the road, making it dangerous to drive.
　　水在馬路上結成冰，因此在上面開車很危險。

(B) **brake** [brek] *vi.* 煞車
　　Wendy braked to avoid hitting a stray dog.
　　溫蒂煞車以避免撞到一隻流浪狗。

TEST 05

129

(C) **sneak** [snik] *vi.* 鬼鬼祟祟而行，偷偷地走
（三態為：sneak, sneaked / snuck [snʌk], sneaked / snuck）
sneak into...　　悄悄溜進……
The burglar sneaked into the house and made away with everything valuable.
竊賊溜進屋內，把所有有價值的東西都偷走了。

(D) **peep** [pip] *vi.* 偷看
peep at...　　偷看……
Stop peeping at me like that. It embarrasses me.
不要那樣偷看我嘛。這令我怪難為情的。

ⓑ 根據語意及用法，(C) 項應為正選。

D　7. 雪倫是個好媽媽，因為她總是用讚美和擁抱來<u>獎勵</u>她的孩子，而不是用玩具或糖果。

ⓐ (A) **assign** [ə'saɪn] *vt.* 分配；指派
Our teacher will assign us tasks for the morning.
老師將會為我們分配早上的工作。

(B) **dodge** [dɑdʒ] *vt.* 閃躲，迴避（拳頭、子彈、問題等）
The actor dodged questions about his drug scandal.
這位演員迴避了有關他毒品醜聞的問題。

(C) **torture** ['tɔrtʃɚ] *vt.* 折磨
Ray was tortured by the thought of his ex-girlfriend dating someone else.
前女友和別人約會的這個想法折磨著雷。

(D) **reward** [rɪ'wɔrd] *vt.* 獎勵
reward sb with sth　　以某物獎賞某人
Rachel rewards her children with cookies when they do well at school.
瑞秋的孩子在學校表現良好時，她會給他們餅乾做為獎賞。

ⓑ 根據語意及用法，(D) 項應為正選。

D　8. 珍妮不善社交，所以她第一次和約會對象出去時，兩人之間並沒有太多<u>互動</u>。

ⓐ (A) **recreation** [ˌrɛkrɪ'eʃən] *n.* 消遣，娛樂
= pastime ['pæs͵taɪm] *n.*
Jim's favorite recreations are reading and watching movies.
吉姆最喜愛的消遣是閱讀和看電影。

(B) **confusion** [kən'fjuʒən] *n.* 困惑，混亂
be in confusion　　陷入混亂
The whole city was in confusion after the earthquake.
地震過後，整座城市陷入一片混亂。

(C) explosion [ɪkˋsploʒən] *n.* 爆炸
　= blast [blæst] *n.*
　Incredibly, no one was killed in the horrible explosion.
　不可思議的是，那場恐怖的爆炸事件中無人喪生。

(D) interaction [ˏɪntɚˋækʃən] *n.* 互動
　Sam rarely has any interaction with his co-workers.
　山姆和他的同事很少有互動。

❺ 根據語意，(D) 項應為正選。

必考重點

a. sociable [ˋsoʃəbḷ] *a.* 善於交際的
b. date [det] *n.* 約會對象

D 9. 我們認為吉米是一個<u>膚淺</u>的人，因為他只關心金錢、名聲和社會地位。

❶ (A) productive [prəˋdʌktɪv] *a.* 有生產力的
　All bosses like productive workers.
　所有的老闆都喜歡有生產力的員工。

(B) precise [prɪˋsaɪs] *a.* 精確的
　Barry checked and double-checked his measurements to make sure they were precise.
　貝瑞一次又一次地檢驗測量結果，以確保它們精確無誤。

(C) luxurious [lʌgˋʒʊrɪəs] *a.* 奢侈的
　Not all rich people live luxurious lives.
　並非所有的有錢人都過著奢侈的生活。

(D) superficial [ˏsupɚˋfɪʃəl] *a.* 膚淺的
　This kind of gossip magazine is often perceived as superficial.
　這種八卦雜誌經常被視為膚淺。

❺ 根據語意，(D) 項應為正選。

必考重點

a. be concerned with / about...
　關心……
　More and more youngsters are becoming concerned about the environment.
　越來越多的年輕人開始關心環境問題。

b. status [ˋstetəs / ˋstætəs] *n.* 地位

TEST 05

131

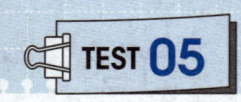

<u>C</u> 10. 傑克在簽約前沒有費心閱讀合約上的細小文字，這造成了他後來很大的麻煩。

ⓐ (A) **imply** [ɪmˋplaɪ] *vt.* 暗示（三態為：imply, implied [ɪmˋplaɪd], implied）
I am not implying anything about your cooking, but can we eat out tonight?
我不是在暗示你的廚藝有任何問題，但我們今晚可以出去吃嗎？

(B) **suggest** [sə(g)ˋdʒɛst] *vt.* 建議
The teacher suggested that Kevin keep a diary every day.
老師建議凱文每天寫日記。

(C) **bother** [ˋbɑðɚ] *vt. & vi.* 費心 & *vt.* 煩擾，打擾
bother to V 費心……
George didn't even bother to tell me he would be late.
喬治甚至連告知我他會遲到都懶。
I hate being bothered while studying.
我討厭讀書時被人打擾。

(D) **amuse** [əˋmjuz] *vt.* 為……提供娛樂
I amuse myself by listening to music.
我藉聽音樂自娛。

ⓑ 根據語意及用法，(C) 項應為正選。

必考重點

fine print 細小的印刷文字

二、綜合測驗（占 10 分）

第 11 至 15 題為題組

　　短暫的悲傷感覺與所謂重度或臨床的憂鬱症有很大差別。重度憂鬱症不是一兩天不快樂而已。它會影響人們在課業或工作上的表現、飲食與睡眠的方式，以及正常生活的能力。這種疾病的主要症狀是自卑以及對通常會感興趣的事物提不起勁。不過它有非常多其他的徵兆，常會被搞混成不同的疾病，這些徵兆包括活力降低、難以集中注意力以及消化方面的問題。

　　雖然人類對重度憂鬱症尚未有通盤了解，但已知它與大腦中不正常的化學物質含量有關。例如大腦中掌管行為、思考和情緒的區域可能出現某種化學失衡。醫師通常會開藥來調整化學物質的含量，幫助患者過正常生活。和受過訓練的治療師交談，了解如何找出你憂鬱症的其他原因並針對其作出因應，會有很大的幫助。治療重度憂鬱症通常是由藥物與治療師雙管齊下來進行。

C 11. 理由

ⓐ (A) **adopt** [ə`dɑpt] *vt.* 採取；吸收
The general manager adopted my proposal without hesitation.
總經理毫不猶豫地採用了我的提案。

(B) **attain** [ə`ten] *vt.* 達到；獲得
attain one's goal　　實現某人的目標
= accomplish one's goal
= achieve one's goal
You can attain your goals if you work hard and stay focused.
只要努力和專心，你就可以實現目標。

(C) **affect** [ə`fɛkt] *vt.* 影響
The lifespan of humans can be affected by the amount of pollution in the environment.
人的壽命會受環境汙染程度所影響。

(D) **abandon** [ə`bændən] *vt.* 丟棄，拋棄
The manager abandoned the plan to set up a new factory in Mexico.
經理放棄在墨西哥建立新廠的計畫。

ⓑ 根據語意，(C) 項應為正選。

A 12. 理由

ⓐ (A) **symptom** [`sɪmptəm] *n.* 症狀
Blood in your urine is a symptom of a serious problem.
血尿的症狀代表身體出了嚴重的毛病。

(B) **synonym** [`sɪnə,nɪm] *n.* 同義字
"Uprising" is a synonym for "revolution."
「起義」是「革命」的同義字。

(C) **symbol** [`sɪmbl̩] *n.* 象徵
as a symbol of...　　作為……的象徵
= as a token of...
= as a sign of...
I bought Mary a diamond ring as a symbol of my love.
我買了一枚鑽戒給瑪麗象徵我對她的愛。

(D) **symphony** [`sɪmfənɪ] *n.* 交響曲
My favorite piece of classical music is Beethoven's Ninth Symphony.
我最喜歡的古典樂是貝多芬的《第九號交響曲》。

ⓑ 根據語意，(A) 項應為正選。

TEST 05

TEST 05

B 13. 理由

(a) (A) **spare** [spɛr] *a.* 備用的
You really need a spare key. You're too forgetful.
你真的需要一把備用鑰匙。你太健忘了。

(B) **numerous** [ˈn(j)umərəs] *a.* 極多的（接複數可數名詞）
I have numerous problems to solve and will need your help.
我有許多問題要解決，需要您的協助。

(C) **obedient** [əˈbidɪənt] *a.* 服從的，遵守的
A good citizen is obedient to the law.
好國民都會守法。

(D) **fantastic** [fænˈtæstɪk] *a.* 極好的；幻想的
Bruce's latest novel is a fantastic story set in a futuristic background.
布魯斯最新的小說是在未來世界背景下的奇幻故事。

(b) 根據語意，(B) 項應為正選。

C 14. 理由

(a) (A) **admission** [ədˈmɪʃən] *n.* 入會；承認
We voted against the admission of new club members.
我們投票否決了俱樂部新會員的入會申請。

(B) **border** [ˈbɔrdɚ] *n.* 邊；國界
on the border of A and B　在 A 和 B 的交界處
My aunt and uncle live on the border of Germany and France.
我的嬸嬸和叔叔住在德法交界處。

(C) **imbalance** [ɪmˈbæləns] *n.* 不平衡，失調
Symptoms of hormonal imbalance in women may be early signs of many things, such as pregnancy or the onset of menopause.
女性體內荷爾蒙不均衡的症狀可能是許多事的前兆，像是懷孕或是更年期的開始。

(D) **meadow** [ˈmɛdo] *n.* 草地
Some sheep were grazing in the meadow.
有幾隻羊在草地上吃草。

(b) 根據語意，(C) 項應為正選。

D 15. 理由

(a) 本題測試以下語意：(A) become the norm（成為常態）、(B) have mixed emotions（有混雜的情緒）、(C) reach an agreement（達成共識）、(D) live normal lives（過正常的生活）。

(b) 空格前提及醫生會開藥調整大腦中化學物質的含量，根據語意，應該藉由此方式可大大幫助患者過正常生活，故 (D) 項應為正選。

重要字詞片語

1. **clinical** [ˈklɪnɪkl̩] *a.* 臨床的
2. **depression** [dɪˈprɛʃən] *n.* 憂鬱症；沮喪
3. **function** [ˈfʌŋkʃən] *vi.* 運行；起作用
4. **disorder** [dɪsˈɔrdɚ] *n.* 失調；混亂
5. **self-esteem** [ˌsɛlfəsˈtim] *n.* 自尊
6. **ailment** [ˈelmənt] *n.* 小病
7. **digestive** [dəˈdʒɛstɪv / daɪˈdʒɛstɪv] *a.* 消化的
8. **be connected to...** 與……相關
   Most people believe David is connected to the murder.
   大多數人認為大衛和這樁謀殺案有關。
9. **abnormal** [æbˈnɔrml̩] *a.* 不正常的
10. **prescribe** [prɪˈskraɪb] *vt.* 開（藥方）
    The doctor prescribed a stronger medicine for the pain.
    這位醫生開一種效力較強的藥來消除疼痛。
11. **sufferer** [ˈsʌfərɚ] *n.* 病患

第 16 至 20 題為題組

蜂鳥是美洲原生的小型、色彩鮮豔的鳥類。最小的蜂鳥品種之一體重僅達 1.8 公克。牠們的鳥喙有別於所有其他鳥類，因為它們的形狀特別適應用來吸取賴以為生花蜜的有溝槽舌頭。蜂鳥的飲食相當特定，所以無須與昆蟲爭奪花蜜，因為蜂鳥只吸取紅色、橙色和粉紅色花朵的花蜜。

牠們的飛行技巧也非常不尋常。牠們是唯一可以旋轉翅膀的鳥類，可以向前、向後、側飛或懸浮在半空中。牠們揮動翅膀非常快速，因此製造出人類可聽見的嗡嗡聲，並因此得名。這種聲音也用來和其他蜂鳥溝通，來警示牠們來者是友是敵。

雖然體型很小，但牠們可飛行非常長的距離。紅喉蜂鳥每年往返於加拿大及巴拿馬之間，距離長達兩千英里，當中包含連續不停飛行五百英里穿越墨西哥灣。這些蜂鳥在長途遷徙前通常會超量進食，以累積足夠的脂肪讓牠們足以成功飛越海洋。

B 16. 理由

    ⓐ (A) **bring up sth**   提起某事
      = raise sth
      bring up sb   養育某人
      = raise sb
      I hate to bring up business at lunch.
      我討厭在午餐時提起公事。
      Judy brought up five children on her own.
      茱蒂靠自己的力量把五個小孩拉拔大。

    (B) **live on sth**   （人、動物）以某物為食
      feed on sth   （動物）以某物為食
      People in southern China live on rice.
      中國南方人以米為食。

TEST 05

Small birds feed mainly on insects.
小型鳥類主要以昆蟲為食。

(C) **work out sth**　想出某事物
　　work out　進展
　　Sam has worked out a new way of solving the problem.
　　山姆想出這道題目的新解法。
　　Don't worry! Everything will work out all right.
　　不要擔心！一切都會進行得很順利。

(D) **pass down sth**　將某物傳承下去
　= hand down sth
　　These skills used to be passed down from a master to an apprentice.
　　這些技術過去曾是由師父傳承給徒弟的。

ⓑ 空格前 they 指 hummingbirds，之前有關係代名詞 which，代替逗點之前先行詞 flowers，形成非限定形容詞子句，根據語意，鳥應是以花為食，故 (B) 項應為正選。

C 17. 理由

ⓐ (A) **argue** [ˈɑrgjʊ] vi. 爭論
　　argue with sb over / about sth　為了某事與某人爭論
　　I argued with the waiter over the mistake on the bill.
　　我因為帳單上的錯誤和那位服務生理論。

(B) **bargain** [ˈbɑrgən] vi. 討價還價
　　bargain with sb over / about sth　與某人針對某物討價還價
　　My mother bargained with the vendor over the price of a clock.
　　我母親和攤販為了一個時鐘的價錢討價還價。

(C) **compete** [kəmˈpit] vi. 競爭
　　compete with / against sb for sth　與某人競爭爭奪某物
　　The brother and sister are competing with each other for their mother's attention.
　　那對兄妹爭著要得到母親的關注。

(D) **quarrel** [ˈkwɔrəl] vi. 爭吵，爭執
　　quarrel with sb over / about sth　為了某事與某人爭執
　　Henry quarreled with his brother over their father's will.
　　亨利為了父親的遺囑和他哥哥發生爭執。

ⓑ 根據語意，(C) 項應為正選。

B 18. 理由

ⓐ 本題測試以下語意：(A) kept them as a pet（把牠們當寵物養）、(B) led to their name（因而得名）、(C) caused hearing loss（導致聽覺喪失）、(D) misled the navigator（誤導領航員）。

ⓑ 根據語意，(B) 項應為正選。

D 19. 理由

  ⓐ (A) **disaster** [dɪˋzæstɚ] *n.* 災難
    a natural disaster　　天然災難
    Most families ran out of basic necessities during the natural disaster.
    在這場天災期間，多數家庭耗盡了他們的生活必需品。

  (B) **barrier** [ˋbærɪɚ] *n.* 障礙
    The river acts as a natural barrier to the northeast.
    那條河有作為東北方天然屏障的功用。

  (C) **anxiety** [æŋˋzaɪətɪ] *n.* 焦慮
    Some children may feel a lot of anxiety about their first day at school.
    一些小朋友可能會對第一天上學這件事感到非常焦慮。

  (D) **stretch** [strɛtʃ] *n.* (連綿地) 一塊土地、水域
    a stretch of coastline / road　　一段海岸／道路
    You rarely see boats on this stretch of the river.
    你在河流這一段很少會看到船隻經過。

  ⓑ 根據語意，(D) 項應為正選。

C 20. 理由

  ⓐ (A) **arrogant** [ˋærəɡənt] *a.* 傲慢的
    The arrogant young man shows no respect for the senior colleagues of the company.
    那名傲慢的年輕人對公司的資深同事不尊重。

  (B) **ethnic** [ˋɛθnɪk] *a.* 族群的
    The government launched a series of plans to protect the country's ethnic minorities.
    政府啟動了一系列保護該國少數民族的計畫。

  (C) **migratory** [ˋmaɪɡrəˌtɔrɪ] *a.* 遷徙的
    Swallows are migratory birds.
    燕子是候鳥。

  (D) **federal** [ˋfɛdərəl] *a.* 聯邦的
    This publishing company relies mainly upon federal funding.
    這家出版社主要依賴聯邦政府的資助。

  ⓑ 根據語意，(C) 項應為正選。

重要字詞片語

1. **hummingbird** [ˋhʌmɪŋˌbɝd] *n.* 蜂鳥
2. **species** [ˋspiʃiz] *n.* 物種（單複數同形）
   a species of...　　一個物種的……
   two species of...　　兩個物種的……
3. **beak** [bik] *n.* 鳥嘴，鳥喙
4. **set A apart from B**　　使 A 有別於 B
   Eric's creative style sets him apart from his co-workers.
   艾瑞克的創意風格使他有別於他的同事。

TEST 05

5. **adapted** [əˋdæptɪd] *a.* (因應環境等) 適應的，特化的
6. **grooved** [gruvd] *a.* 有溝槽的
   groove [gruv] *vt.* 在……上開出溝槽
7. **suck out...**　　吸出……
8. **nectar** [ˋnɛktɚ] *n.* 花蜜
9. **specialized** [ˋspɛʃə͵laɪzd] *a.* 專門的
10. **rotate** [ˋrotet] *vt.* & *vi.* 旋轉，轉動
    Stay well away from the helicopter when its blades start to rotate.
    當直升機的旋翼開始轉動時，離遠一些。
11. **sideways** [ˋsaɪd͵wez] *adv.* 朝向旁邊地
12. **hover** [ˋhʌvɚ] *vi.* 盤旋，停留在空中
13. **midair** [͵mɪdˋɛr] *n.* 半空中
    The bird caught the insects in midair.
    那隻鳥在半空中抓到那些昆蟲。
14. **foe** [fo] *n.* 敵人
15. **incredibly** [ɪnˋkrɛdəblɪ] *adv.* 很，極其；令人難以置信地
16. **annually** [ˋænjʊəlɪ] *adv.* 一年一度地
17. **non-stop** [͵nɑnˋstɑp] *a.* 不停的 & *adv.* 不停地
    a non-stop flight　　直飛班機
    We flew non-stop from Paris to Chicago.
    我們從巴黎直飛芝加哥。
18. **build up (...)**　　累積（……）
    Tension is building up between these two countries.
    這兩國之間的情勢正變得日漸緊張。

三、文意選填（占 10 分）

第 21 至 30 題為題組

　　就如同漢堡與薯條一樣，披薩流行於全球各地。世界各地的餐廳裡的人們都喜歡享用這道美食。人們經常將披薩的普及與發展歸功於義大利，因為古羅馬人過去曾食用某種上頭添加配料的扁平麵包。除此之外，拿坡里民眾用番茄發明了更加現代的種類。

　　表面的配料不僅讓披薩更具吸引力也更加美味。世界上許多地方都藉由添加他們當地的食材來發揮創意。對於某些人而言，鳳梨相當受歡迎，而對於其他人而言，這種熱帶水果顯然不適合任何地中海菜餚。雖然沒有人確定是誰首次將番茄醬用在拿坡里披薩中，歷史確實列有首次將鳳梨添加在披薩上的男子。

　　那名男子是移居至加拿大安大略省的希臘移民山姆‧潘諾普洛斯。1962 年，他想知道在披薩上頭撒著鳳梨嚐起來的味道。為了滿足自己的好奇心，他在披薩上撒上一些鳳梨以及些許火腿、培根。他非常喜歡這種甜甜多汁的水果與鹹香肉品之間的對比。他以自己使用的罐頭鳳梨名稱命名，將其稱為夏威夷披薩，而接下來的故事可說是家喻戶曉。

　　當冰島總統於 2017 年年初說，若可以的話他要禁止鳳梨當作披薩配料時，立刻遭到加拿大總理的質疑。幸好這場友善的爭執沒有帶來任何結果。即便如此，在披薩上使用任何非義大利配料的想法向來都備受爭議。持純粹派觀點的人堅持食物應該以保持原汁原味的傳統方式製作。其

他人則認為我們吃的所有東西都來自不同地方，因此可以針對菜餚進行實驗和改進。或許接受你若不喜歡某樣食物就不要吃下肚這一事實，所有這種爭論都可以煙消雲散。

I 21. 理由

ⓐ 空格前有 be 動詞 is 及副詞 often（經常），而空格後有介詞 with，得知空格應置入形容詞或分詞。

ⓑ 選項中符合上述的有 (B) different（不同的）、(F) canned（罐裝的）、(G) introduced（採用）、(H) traditional（傳統的）及 (I) credited（歸功），惟根據語意，(I) 項應為正選。

E 22. 理由

ⓐ 空格前有形容詞 modern（現代的），而空格後有分詞片語 using tomatoes（使用番茄），得知空格應置入名詞以被 modern 及 using tomatoes 修飾。

ⓑ 選項中符合上述的有 (C) immigrant（移民）、(D) ban（禁止）及 (E) variety（種類），惟根據語意，(E) 項應為正選。

A 23. 理由

ⓐ 空格前有助動詞 does 及否定詞 not，而空格後有介詞 in，得知空格應置入原形不及物動詞或片語動詞。

ⓑ 選項中符合上述的僅有 (A) belong（應在，適合），置入後亦符合語意，故為正選。

G 24. 理由

ⓐ 空格前有疑問代名詞 who 作主詞，而空格後為受詞 tomato sauce（番茄醬），得知空格應置入單數及物動詞或片語動詞，而根據語意應採過去式。

ⓑ 選項中符合上述的有 (F) canned（將……裝罐）及 (G) introduced（採用），惟根據語意，(G) 項應為正選。

C 25. 理由

ⓐ 空格前有不定冠詞 a 及形容詞 Greek（希臘的），而空格後有表「人」的關係代名詞 who 所引導的形容詞子句，得知空格應置入表「人」的單數可數名詞以被該形容詞子句修飾。

ⓑ 選項中符合上述的僅剩 (C) immigrant（移民），置入後亦符合語意，故為正選。

J 26. 理由

ⓐ 空格前有引導不定詞片語的 To，而空格後有受詞 his curiosity（他的好奇心），得知空格應置入原形及物動詞或片語動詞。

ⓑ 選項中符合上述的有 (D) ban（禁止）及 (J) satisfy（滿足），惟根據語意，(J) 項應為正選。

TEST 05

F 27. 理由
- ⓐ 空格前有定冠詞 the，而空格後有名詞 pineapples（鳳梨），得知空格應置入形容詞以修飾 pineapples。
- ⓑ 選項中符合上述的有 (B) different（不同的）、(F) canned（罐裝的）及 (H) traditional（傳統的），惟根據語意，(F) 項應為正選。

D 28. 理由
- ⓐ 空格前有助動詞 would，而空格後有受詞 pineapples（鳳梨），得知空格應置入原形及物動詞或片語動詞。
- ⓑ 選項中符合上述的僅剩 (D) ban（禁止），置入後亦符合語意，故為正選。

H 29. 理由
- ⓐ 空格前有介詞 in，而空格後有名詞 ways（方式），得知空格應置入形容詞以修飾 ways。
- ⓑ 選項中符合上述的有 (B) different（不同的）及 (H) traditional（傳統的），惟根據語意，(H) 項應為正選。

B 30. 理由
- ⓐ 空格前有介詞 from，而空格後有名詞 places（地方），得知空格應置入形容詞以修飾 places。
- ⓑ 選項中符合上述的僅剩 (B) different（不同的），置入後亦符合語意，故為正選。

重要字詞片語

1. **consume** [kənˈs(j)um] *vt.*（大量地）吃，喝；消費，消耗
 People consume a lot of fast food these days.
 現代人吃很多速食。
2. **spread** [sprɛd] *n.* 擴展
3. **development** [dɪˈvɛləpmənt] *n.* 發展
4. **ancient** [ˈenʃənt] *a.* 古老的
5. **topping** [ˈtɑpɪŋ] *n.*（加在食物上的）配料
6. **attractive** [əˈtræktɪv] *a.* 吸引人的
7. **creative** [krɪˈetɪv] *a.* 有創意的
8. **ingredient** [ɪnˈgridɪənt] *n.* 食材
9. **tropical** [ˈtrɑpɪkl] *a.* 熱帶的
10. **be certain of...** 確定……
 Ken was quite certain of his attacker's identity.
 肯對襲擊他的人的身分十分肯定。
11. **curiosity** [ˌkjʊrɪˈɑsətɪ] *n.* 好奇心（不可數）
12. **along with...** 以及……
13. **contrast** [ˈkɑn͵træst] *n.* 對比
14. **savory** [ˈsevərɪ] *a.* 鹹香的
15. **name A after B** 以 B 為 A 命名
16. **challenge** [ˈtʃælɪndʒ] *vt.* 質疑
17. **prime minister** 總理
18. **come of...** 由於……而產生，是……的結果
 I asked Joe a few questions about this matter, but nothing came of it.
 我針對這件事問了喬幾個問題，卻問不出任何結果。

19. **disagreement** [ˌdɪsəˈɡrimənt] *n.*
    爭執
20. **controversial** [ˌkɑntrəˈvɝʃəl] *a.*
    有爭議的
21. **purist** [ˈpjʊrɪst] *n.* 純粹主義者
22. **insist + that + S + (should) + 原形動詞**
    堅持……

注意：insist 表「堅持（主張/要求）」時為意志動詞，其後的 that 子句中須使用助動詞 should，但 should 可予以省略，而直接接原形動詞。

23. **experiment with sth**
    用某物做實驗
24. **improve upon / on sth**
    將某物加以改良

四、篇章結構（占 8 分）

第 31 至 34 題為題組

　　大家偶爾會飲食過量。也許是受到吃到飽自助餐廳裡一排又一排異國美饌的誘惑。或者你趁特別的節日大吃大喝一頓，接續吃著第二、三份美味多汁的感恩節火雞。<u>31. 不管是哪一種，你最後都會因為那些額外多吃的食物付出代價。</u>幾分鐘之內你的肚子就會鼓起來，腦袋也變得昏沉。如果你在家裡，你可能會走到離你最近的沙發，不一會兒就睡著了。有一個有趣的詞就用來描述這種因為大吃一頓而想睡覺的感覺：食物昏迷。

　　其背後發生的科學原理是，每當我們吃東西的時候，荷爾蒙會叫我們的身體製造胃液幫助胃消化食物。<u>32. 我們的胃因而需要更多血液來運送食物中的養分到其他地方。</u>當這發生時，身體其他地方就暫時擁有較少量的血液。當你吃了較大量的食物，胃便需要更多的血液。當我們腦部與肌肉的血液量較少時，就無法好好地運作。因此，身體的自然反應就是讓你覺得睏，並隱約地鼓勵你去休息。然後當你在做夢時，身體就專心地努力處理你剛大吃一頓的大餐。

　　<u>33. 決定你是否會陷入食物昏迷的不只是你吃下食物的量。</u>食物的品質也有關。攝取如烤雞佐時蔬或鮭魚配沙拉這類高蛋白質且無碳水化合物或過多脂肪的餐點通常不會導致食物昏迷，因為它們會刺激胺基酸的分泌。<u>34. 另一方面，吃大量加工過的碳水化合物會使胰島素攀升，讓你睡著的速度比想像中得更快。</u>在這種情況下，你應該要少吃點白飯、半成品加熱披薩和像甜甜圈這種高糖甜點。經常大吃大喝顯然不健康。這可能會導致體重增加，並提高罹患多種慢性疾病的風險，從高血壓到第二型糖尿病皆包含在內。但沒有證據指出食物昏迷本身長遠來看有何危險。

A 31. 理由

ⓐ 空格前提及人們會大吃大喝的兩種可能原因，而空格後的句子提到，大吃一頓後肚子會鼓起來，並會感到昏沉想睡，可推測空格應置能連接大吃大喝與其所造成該狀況的句子。

ⓑ 選項 (A) 表示，不管是哪一種，你最後都會因為那些額外多吃的食物付出代價，其中 **Either way**（不管是哪一種）呼應前句提及兩種大吃大喝的可能，**end up paying the price**（最後付出代價）則與後句大吃大喝後會造成的狀況形成關聯，填入後語意連貫，可知 (A) 項應為正選。

TEST 05

E 32. 理由
- ⓐ 空格前的句子提到，吃東西時，身體會製造胃液幫助胃消化食物，空格後的句子提到，此時身體其他地方暫時擁有較少量的血液，可推測空格應提及胃消化食物時與身體血液之間的關係。
- ⓑ 選項 (E) 表示，我們的胃因而需要更多血液來運送食物中的養分到其他地方，填入後語意連貫，可知 (E) 項應為正選。

D 33. 理由
- ⓐ 前一段旨在說明大量飲食如何造成食物昏迷，空格後一句提及食物品質也有關係，可推測空格應置能承接前一段，並引出食物品質與某狀況有關聯的句子。
- ⓑ 選項 (D) 表示，決定你是否會陷入食物昏迷的不只是你吃下食物的量，與後一句食物的品質也有關形成關連，填入後語意連貫，可知 (D) 項應為正選。

B 34. 理由
- ⓐ 空格前的句子提到，攝取高蛋白質且無碳水化合物或過多脂肪的餐點通常不會導致食物昏迷，而空格後的句子提到，要少吃白飯和半成品加熱披薩，可推測空格應提及與前句相反的情況。
- ⓑ 選項 (B) 表示，另一方面，吃大量加工過的碳水化合物會使胰島素攀升，讓你睡著的速度比想像中得更快，其中 processed carbohydrates（加工過的碳水化合物）與前句的 carbohydrates（碳水化合物）、後句的 white rice（白飯）、oven-ready pizzas（半成品加熱披薩）及 sugary desserts like donuts（像甜甜圈這種高糖甜點）相呼應，填入後語意連貫，可知 (B) 項應為正選。

(C) 項中譯：可以透過進行一些輕度運動來抵消食物昏迷的影響。

重要字詞片語

1. **at one time or another** 有時，偶爾，在某個時候
   Many people have trouble sleeping at one time or another.
   許多人不時會難以入眠。
2. **overeat** [ˌovɚˋit] vi. 吃得過多（三態為：overeat, overate [ˌovɚˋet], overeaten [ˌovɚˋitn̩]）
3. **temptation** [tɛmpˋteʃən] n. 誘惑，引誘
4. **stuff one's face** 大吃大喝
5. **succulent** [ˋsʌkjələnt] a. 多汁的
6. **consume** [kənˋs(j)um] vt. 攝取（食物）；消耗（時間、物品等）
7. **puff** [pʌf] vi. & vt. 噴出，冒出（煙、氣等）
   puff out (sth) （使某物）凸起，鼓起
8. **foggy** [ˋfɑgɪ] a. 朦朧的
9. **coma** [ˋkomə] n. 昏迷
10. **hormone** [ˋhɔrmon] n. 荷爾蒙，激素
11. **juice** [dʒus] n. 體液（常用複數）
    gastric / digestive juices
    胃液／消化液
12. **digest** [daɪˋdʒɛst] vt. 消化
13. **nutrient** [ˋn(j)utrɪənt] n. 養分
14. **portion** [ˋpɔrʃən] n. 一部分

15. **process** [ˈprɑsɛs] *vt.* 處理；加工
    processed [ˈprɑsɛst] *a.* 加工過的
16. **devour** [dɪˈvaʊr] *vt.* 吞食
17. **slip** [slɪp] *vi.* 陷入（另一種情況、狀態）（三態為：slip, slipped [slɪpt], slipped）
    slip into...　　陷入……
18. **protein** [ˈprotiɪn] *n.* 蛋白質
19. **carbohydrate** [ˌkɑrboˈhaɪdret] *n.* 碳水化合物
20. **salmon** [ˈsæmən] *n.* 鮭魚
21. **stimulate** [ˈstɪmjəˌlet] *vt.* 刺激
22. **an amino acid**　　胺基酸
23. **insulin** [ˈɪnsəlɪn] *n.* 胰島素（不可數）
24. **spike** [spaɪk] *vi.* 急速增加
25. **oven-ready** [ˌʌvənˈrɛdɪ] *a.* 半成品的，可直接放入烤箱的
26. **sugary** [ˈʃʊgərɪ] *a.* 含糖的
27. **chronic** [ˈkrɑnɪk] *a.* 慢性的
    a chronic disease　　慢性病
28. **diabetes** [ˌdaɪəˈbitɪz] *n.* 糖尿病（不可數）

五、閱讀測驗（占 24 分）

第 35 至 38 題為題組

　　一場專業簡報中，最常見的元素之一就是使用 PowerPoint。因為它的投影片簡報模式能創造影響力。它們可以聚焦聽眾的注意力並有效強調重點。事實上，有許多演講者若不使用 PowerPoint 就無法作出好的簡報。然而許多人在發表這類簡報時仍然會犯嚴重的錯誤。

　　人們所犯的最大錯誤可能就是在一張投影片裡放進過多資訊。有強大證據顯示人們只能記住有限的資訊。演講者常讓問題更嚴重的做法是用了超小的字體，想在一張投影片裡面塞進更多統計資料與分析。這些演講者都錯誤地相信簡報就應該要放超量的資料。其實聽眾難以閱讀及理解如此複雜的投影片。這些投影片會把聽眾的注意力從演講者及該傳達的訊息上面移開。

　　人們所犯的另一個錯誤就是演講者太依賴 PowerPoint 投影片以至於忽略了聽眾。換句話說，他們轉向通常位於身後的螢幕，將注意力從聽眾身上移到 PowerPoint 螢幕上。這類演講者可能以為自己作了一場好的簡報，但他們錯了。當演講者背對聽眾時，他們就會喪失原本面對聽眾時會有的影響力。

　　好在一旦演講者知道哪些事不該做，改善這些缺失是很簡單的。關於投影片放太多資訊的問題，毫不意外的解決方式就是簡化你的投影片。如果你一直看著你的投影片而忽略了聽眾，其解決之道應該也就擺在你眼前吧。

TEST 05

__B__ 35. 本文的主旨是什麼？
(A) PowerPoint 簡報好用的原因。
(B) 用 PowerPoint 作簡報時不該做哪些事。
(C) 許多演講者不再使用 PowerPoint 的原因。
(D) 有許多不同的 PowerPoint 簡報模式可以使用。

理由
本文自第一段最後一句起就開始說明用 PowerPoint 作簡報時常犯的錯誤。第二段及第三段詳細說明這些錯誤，最後一段則說明如何改善這些錯誤，故 (B) 項應為正選。

__D__ 36. 關於不該在一張投影片放入太多資訊的原因，原文未提及下列哪一項？
(A) 這麼做會吸走對你和你的簡報的注意力。
(B) 觀眾一次只能記住有限的細節。
(C) 這麼做得必須使用過小的字體。
(D) 製作投影片會很耗時。

理由
本文第二段皆在說明大家所犯的最大錯誤就是在一張投影片裡放入了太多的資訊，會讓聽眾難以閱讀與理解、且必須得使用小型字體以及會讓聽眾的注意力從演講者及要傳達的訊息上移開。文中並未提及製作投影片會很耗時一事，故 (D) 項應為正選。

__C__ 37. 根據本文，過於依賴 PowerPoint 的演講者會怎麼做？
(A) 使用難以閱讀的投影片。 (B) 進行一次難忘的簡報。
(C) 減少和聽眾目光接觸。 (D) 強烈關注聽眾。

理由
根據本文第三段第一到二句，演講者太依賴 PowerPoint 投影片，以至於忽略了聽眾，且將注意力從聽眾身上轉移到 PowerPoint 螢幕上，可得知此舉會減少和聽眾的目光接觸，故 (C) 項應為正選。

__B__ 38. 最後一段的目的為何？
(A) 舉出 PowerPoint 簡報的另一個錯誤。
(B) 提供解決簡報問題的建議。
(C) 討論讓你的投影片吸睛的方法。
(D) 略述為何需要觀眾的參與。

理由
根據最後一段，一旦演講者知道哪些事在演說時不要做，就蠻容易能改善這些缺失。因此最後一段的目的是在提供建議來解決簡報的問題，故 (B) 項應為正選。

重要字詞片語

1. **professional** [prəˋfɛʃən!] *a.* 專業的
Harry works very hard in the hopes of becoming a professional writer.
哈利很努力想成為專業作家。

2. **presentation** [ˌprɛzṇˋteʃən] *n.* 口頭報告

3. **lie in...** 在於……
 = consist in...
 The beauty of the city lies in its ancient buildings.
 該城市之美在於其古老建築。

4. **slide** [slaɪd] *n.* 投影片

5. **stress** [strɛs] *vt.* 強調
 My mother always stresses the importance of honesty.
 我母親總是強調誠實的重要性。

6. **deliver** [dɪˋlɪvɚ] *vt.* 發表（演說、課程）
 Dr. Brown will deliver a speech on educational reform.
 布朗博士將針對教育改革發表演說。

7. **compound** [kəmˋpaʊnd] *vt.* 使加重

8. **font** [fɑnt] *n.* 字體；字型

9. **cram** [kræm] *vt.* 填，塞（三態為：cram, crammed [kræmd], crammed）

10. **statistics** [stəˋtɪstɪks] *n.* 統計資料（恆用複數）；統計學（不可數）

11. **analysis** [əˋnæləsɪs] *n.* 分析（複數為：analyses [əˋnæləsiz]）

12. **overload** [͵ovɚˋlod] *vt.* 使超載
 be overloaded with...
 充滿了……
 Students in Taiwan are overloaded with schoolwork.
 臺灣學生的課業太沉重。

13. **complicated** [ˋkɑmpləˏketɪd] *a.* 複雜的

14. **rely on...** 依賴……
 It is time to rely on yourself instead of your parents.
 該是自立的時候，別再依賴父母親了。

15. **neglect** [nɪˋglɛkt] *vt.* 疏忽，忽略

16. **simplify** [ˋsɪmpləˏfaɪ] *vt.* 簡化，精簡
 （三態為：simplify, simplified [ˋsɪmpləˏfaɪd], simplified）
 You should simplify your explanation, or I won't understand what you are saying.
 你應該簡化你的說明，否則我不會了解你在說什麼。

17. **ignore** [ɪgˋnɔr] *vt.* 忽視

18. **stare sb in the face**
 對（某人）來說顯而易見

19. **detract from...** 搶走對……的注意力；對……產生不利影響

20. **entail** [ɪnˋtel] *vt.* 應有……
 entail + N/V-ing 必然會……

21. **time-consuming** [ˋtaɪmkənˏsumɪŋ]
 a. 耗時的

22. **outline** [ˋaʊtˏlaɪn] *vt.* 略述，重點說明
 At the interview, Nancy outlined the requirements for the position.
 面試的時候，南希就這個職位的必要條件做了重點說明。

TEST 05

第 39 至 42 題為題組

專家說大多數的成人每晚需要大約八小時的睡眠，不過確切的時間長度因人而異。然而一種稱作失眠的症狀讓有些人很難得到這麼多的睡眠時間。失眠症是人們難以入睡或保持入眠狀態的一種失調狀況。顯示一個人患有失眠的跡象包括眼睛下方難看的黑眼圈和眼袋，以及看起來昏昏欲睡的樣子。他們可能會易怒、很難記住事情以及難以專注。失眠症可能會引發更嚴重的健康問題，除了會增加人們罹患心臟疾病的風險外，也會增加中風或得糖尿病的機率。

TEST 05

　　造成失眠症的原因為何？重大人生事件，如失去親人或換工作等，可能會導致失眠，此外還有焦慮、憂鬱和其他心理健康問題等原因。使用某些處方藥、酗酒和吸食非法毒品也可能是元凶。這些原因中，有些可能只會造成短暫的失眠問題。舉例來說，轉職所感受到的壓力可能只會持續幾天而已。因此就算不靠外界的助力，失眠症也能自行復元。但長期心理健康問題導致的失眠症可能就會持續較久而需要治療。治療方式則包括服用安眠藥以及從受過訓練的專業人員那裡接受認知行為療法等等。

　　失眠症也可能會影響到動物。研究指出，老鼠被放置在充滿壓力的環境時也會經歷失眠的狀況。必須站著打盹的馬在這段期間沒辦法熟睡，牠們因此會表現出睡眠不足的跡象，有時還會昏倒。科學家也認為斑馬魚會受到睡眠失調的影響。這些研究結果可以幫助我們釐清與睡眠有關的謎題，也可能從中找到治療人們失眠問題的新療法。睡眠對人類和動物的健康、幸福極為重要，我們都要確保自己的睡眠充足。

C 39. 第一段的主旨為何？
(A) 睡眠失調的治療選項。　　　　　(B) 失眠症在人口中的盛行率。
(C) 失眠症的跡象和造成的後果。　　(D) 建議的每晚睡眠時數。

理由 本文第一段旨在介紹何謂失眠症，並說明失眠症的跡象及其可能引發的問題，故 (C) 項應為正選。

B 40. 第一段中的 They 指的是什麼？
(A) 失眠症的主要症狀。　　　　　　(B) 受失眠所苦的人們。
(C) 失眠症引發的健康問題。　　　　(D) 研究失眠症的專家。

理由 本文第一段第四句說明患有失眠症的人會有何種跡象，可推測其後的 They 即指前句所提及罹患失眠症的人，故 (B) 項應為正選。

C 41. 本文未提及失眠症的哪一種成因？
(A) 緊張和擔心的感覺。　　　　　　(B) 就業中斷。
(C) 長期的生理病痛。　　　　　　　(D) 食用非法毒品。

理由 本文第二段依序提及引發失眠症的原因為：換工作等重大人生事件、焦慮或憂鬱等心理健康問題，以及使用某些處方藥、酗酒和吸食非法毒品，全文未提及長期的生理病痛是原因之一，故 (C) 項應為正選。

B 42. 關於馬，我們可以從本文推知什麼事？
(A) 牠們比其他動物需要更多睡眠。　(B) 牠們躺著睡覺時較為熟睡。
(C) 牠們很少受重度失眠症所苦。　　(D) 牠們睡太久時會摔倒。

理由 根據本文第三段第三句，必須站著打盹的馬在這段期間沒辦法熟睡，牠們因此會表現出睡眠不足的跡象，有時還會昏倒，故 (B) 項應為正選。

重要字詞片語

1. **vary** [ˈvɛrɪ] vi. 變化
   The weather here varies between cool and very hot.
   這裡的天氣會在涼爽與酷熱之間變換。
2. **condition** [kənˈdɪʃən] n. 症狀，疾病
3. **insomnia** [ɪnˈsɑmnɪə] n. 失眠症
4. **disorder** [dɪsˈɔrdɚ] n.（身體或心理狀態）失調，不正常
5. **telltale** [ˈtɛl͵tel] a. 明顯的，遮掩不了的
   a telltale sign　明顯的跡象
6. **drowsy** [ˈdraʊzɪ] a. 昏昏欲睡的
7. **grumpiness** [ˈɡrʌmpɪnəs] n. 易怒（不可數）
8. **have difficulty (in) + V-ing**
   做……很難
   Some elders have difficulty using smartphones.
   有些年長者不太會使用智慧型手機。
9. **heighten** [ˈhaɪtn̩] vt. & vi. 增加，提高
10. **stroke** [strok] n. 中風
11. **prescription** [prɪˈskrɪpʃən] n. 處方，藥方
12. **culprit** [ˈkʌlprɪt] n. 起因；肇因
13. **transitory** [ˈtrænsə͵tɔrɪ] a. 短暫的
14. **intervention** [͵ɪntɚˈvɛnʃən] n. 干預
15. **linger** [ˈlɪŋɡɚ] vi. 持續，繼續存留
    The pleasant childhood memory has lingered in Kelly's mind for a long time.
    美好的童年記憶在凱莉的腦海中留存了很長一段時間。
16. **cognitive** [ˈkɑɡnətɪv] a. 認知的
17. **deprivation** [͵dɛprəˈveʃən] n. 缺乏，匱乏；剝奪
    sleep deprivation　睡眠不足
18. **collapse** [kəˈlæps] vi. & n. 昏倒；崩塌
19. **prevalence** [ˈprɛvələns] n.（疾病的）流行，盛行；普及
    the prevalence of...
    ……的盛行／流行／普及

TEST 05

第 43 至 46 題為題組

　　1789 年的法國大革命是歐洲與世界歷史中最關鍵的事件之一。儘管有些歷史學家對於大革命的起因有歧見，但沒有人會否認它長遠的影響。

　　1789 年前的數十年間，法國參加過許多戰爭。這些軍事行動造成大筆負債，而法國 —— 在國王路易十六奢侈又無效的統治下 —— 無法償還。火上加油的是，所有的稅都是平民在繳，而貴族與神職人員不用繳。1789 年中，對時局的挫敗感加上高失業率與大規模飢荒使得情勢失控。平民開始反擊。他們訴求更公平的賦稅制度、人人受到平等對待的社會，以及脫離君主政體控制的自由權。簡言之，他們想要民主。

　　革命黨的確達成某些成就：君主制度遭廢除，法國成為擁有新憲法與新稅收制度的共和國，且路易十六以叛國的罪名遭到處決。然而並非一切都如這個簡略版本般順利。革命運動的領導者之一馬克西米連·羅伯斯比展開恐怖統治，造成至少一萬八千名「反革命分子」死亡。這段政治混亂時期最終促使聲名狼藉的拿破崙·波拿巴崛起，他在法國實行了一段時間的軍事統治。

TEST 05

　　法國大革命的效應，在數十年甚至數百年後仍影響著歐洲各地。人們是國家公民而不僅是國王的臣民，這種思維演變成民族國家的信念，在歐洲大部分區域紮下了根基。處決路易十六對其他歐洲君主國形成壓力，逼迫他們適應變化中的世界並給予人民更多權利。革命黨的目的與手段成為其他在自己國家追求改變的人的榜樣。的確，1789 年的法國大革命與 1917 年的俄國革命之間，不難發現直接的關聯。

D 43. 作者可能會用下列哪一個單字形容路易十六？
(A) 有幫助的。　　(B) 缺乏幽默感的。　　(C) 英勇的。　　(D) 沒希望的。

理由
根據本文第二段第二句，路易十六以奢侈又無效的方式統治法國，可推論作者認為路易十六並非成功的君主，故 (D) 項應為正選。

B 44. 下列哪一項最有可能是法國革命黨的口號？
(A)「擁立法國新國王或女王！」　　(B)「公平稅收、平等社會！」
(C)「為貴族爭取更多機會！」　　　(D)「廢除民主；王權萬歲！」

理由
根據本文第二段第六句，平民百姓反擊時訴求的是公平的稅收制度、平等的社會，以及脫離君主制度，故 (B) 項應為正選。

B 45. 根據本文，馬克西米連・羅伯斯比做了什麼事？
(A) 殺死法國前任國王。　　　　　　(B) 殺害成千上萬的政敵。
(C) 除掉備受憎恨的拿破崙・波拿巴。　(D) 取代路易十六成為君主。

理由
根據本文第三段第三句，馬克西米連・羅伯斯比展開恐怖統治，造成至少一萬八千名反革命者死亡，故 (B) 項應為正選。

C 46. 本文並未提及下列哪一項法國大革命造成的結果？
(A) 對於自己國家的感情連結加深。　(B) 皇室對於臣民的態度轉變。
(C) 與全球宗教制度的關係疏遠。　　(D) 其他國家內追求類似改變的渴望增強。

理由
本文第四段提及人們開始認同自己是國家的國民、歐洲其他君主給予人民更多權利，以及其他國家追求改變時會以法國大革命做為榜樣，全段落未提及與全球宗教制度的關聯，故 (C) 項應為正選。

重要字詞片語

1. **revolution** [ˌrɛvəˈluʃən] *n.* 革命
   revolutionary [ˌrɛvəˈluʃənˌɛrɪ] *n.* 革命者 & *a.* 革命性的

2. **pivotal** [ˈpɪvət!] *a.* 關鍵的

3. **doubt** [daʊt] *n.* & *vt.* 懷疑
   be in doubt about sth
   對某事懷有疑慮
   No one is in any doubt about the severity of the situation.
   沒有人否認情況的嚴重性。

4. **consequence** [ˈkɑnsəkwəns] *n.* 結果（可數）；重要性（不可數）

5. **engage** [ɪnˈgedʒ] *vi.* 從事，忙於
   engage in + N/V-ing
   參與……；從事……
   Leaders of the two countries engaged in peace talks.
   兩個國家的領導人進行和平談判。

6. **debt** [dɛt] *n.* 負債

7. **reign** [ren] *n.* & *vi.* 統治

8. **extravagant** [ɪkˈstrævəgənt] *a.* 奢侈的；浪費的

9. **commoner** [ˈkɑmənɚ] *n.* 平民

10. **clergy** [ˈklɝdʒɪ] *n.* 神職人員（集合名詞，視為複數）
    clergyman [ˈklɝdʒɪmən] *n.* （男）神職人員；牧師；教士

11. **frustration** [frʌˈstreʃən] *n.* 挫折；沮喪

12. **famine** [ˈfæmɪn] *n.* 飢荒

13. **boil over**　（情勢）失控；（情緒）爆發
    Anger eventually boiled over when an innocent man was shot dead.
    一名無辜男子遭到槍殺時，憤怒的情緒終於爆發。

14. **just** [dʒʌst] *a.* 公平的，公正的 & *adv.* 正好；剛剛；只是

15. **monarchy** [ˈmɑnɚkɪ] *n.* 君主制，君主政體（不可數）；君主國（可數）
    monarch [ˈmɑnɚk] *n.* 君主

16. **democracy** [dɪˈmɑkrəsɪ] *n.* 民主（不可數）；民主國家（可數）

17. **abolish** [əˈbɑlɪʃ] *vt.* 廢除
    Slavery was abolished in the United States in the 19th century.
    美國的奴隸制度在十九世紀時廢除。

18. **constitution** [ˌkɑnstəˈt(j)uʃən] *n.* 憲法

19. **execute** [ˈɛksɪˌkjut] *vt.* 處決，處死；執行
    The soldier was executed for treason.
    這名士兵因叛國被處死。

20. **treason** [ˈtrizn̩] *n.* 叛國（罪）（不可數）

21. **counter-** [ˈkaʊntɚ] *prefix* 反，逆
    counter [ˈkaʊntɚ] *vi.* & *vt.* 反對；反擊 & *adv.* 相反地

22. **subject** [ˈsʌbdʒɪkt] *n.* 臣民，子民；主題；學科

23. **root** [rut] *n.* 根
    take root　　根植，紮根
    It takes time for democracy to take root in that country.
    民主制度要在那個國家紮根需要時間。

24. **adapt** [əˈdæpt] *vi.* & *vt.* （使）適應
    adapt to + N/V-ing　　適應……
    = adjust to + N/V-ing
    It's hard for Sally to adapt to city life.
    莎莉很不適應都市生活。

25. **tactic** [ˈtæktɪk] *n.* 手段，策略（常用複數）

TEST 05

TEST 05

第貳部分、混合題（占 10 分）

第 47 至 51 題為題組

洋芋片是經過油炸和調味的馬鈴薯薄片。它們的發明要不就是在 1817 年的英國，要不就是在 1853 年的美國，就看你相信誰。不管真相為何，洋芋片已發展成全世界最愛的零食之一，它們的製作方式也日趨完善。

馬鈴薯每日都會從農場送到製造工廠。一到那裡，它們會先接受檢查是否有黑斑、綠邊或是質地變軟等瑕疵。在淘汰劣質馬鈴薯後，開始進行削皮。這由削皮機自動完成，削皮機將皮分離後，將運回農場做為動物飼料。

切片是過程中下個重要的步驟。有兩種方式，一種是直刀直切，製作出一般的洋芋片，或是用鋸齒狀刀片，就會不意外地切出波浪形洋芋片。在過程中的這個部分，切好的洋芋片會經過水洗以去除多餘的澱粉。在高達攝氏 190 度的油槽中油炸是下一個重要的步驟 —— 不過現在有些製造商選擇用烘烤的方式，以生產較健康的產品。

另一個階段是冷卻，在金屬濾網上把油瀝乾。不過在此之前是調味階段，將鹽或其他調味粉如起司、酸奶油與洋蔥等撒到洋芋片上。當然，最後一個階段是包裝。將預先算好的洋芋片數量輕柔地放入每個袋子以降低破損的機會。此外還要打氮氣；不像氧氣，氮氣可維持內容物的新鮮度。

在整個過程中，品質控管是最重要的。洋芋片製造商依靠製造可靠、劃一而美味的產品來建立他們的商譽，因此會定期抽樣檢查產品的整體口味、調味程度，甚至是適當的色澤。這不起眼的洋芋片真的似乎需要大量的時間、精力和專注力來製造。

47-49. 根據文章，請將遺失的洋芋片生產步驟填入。

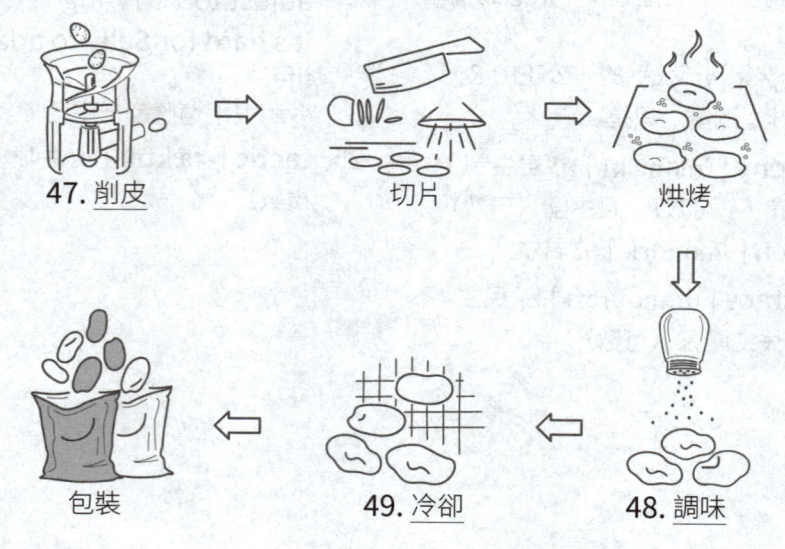

47. 削皮 ⇒ 切片 ⇒ 烘烤

包裝 ⇐ 49. 冷卻 ⇐ 48. 調味

47. **peeling**
48. **seasoning**
49. **cooling**

> 理由

根據本文第二、三、四段，依序說明洋芋片的生產步驟是削皮、切片、油炸或烘烤、調味、冷卻瀝油、包裝。且其餘的提示字皆為動詞加上 -ing 形成動名詞形式，故此三格答案也須一致。

50. 請從文章中選出一個單詞或詞組，使下列句子語意完整：
洋芋片袋中充滿氮氣以確保洋芋片維持新鮮。

nitrogen gas

> 理由

根據本文第四段最後一句，再加入氮氣，能夠維持內容物的新鮮度，可得知 nitrogen gas（氮氣）應為正解。

B 51. 選出本文中此句被挖空單詞的同義詞：
「在整個過程中，品質控管是 _____ 重要的」。
(A) 瑣碎的。
(B) 最高級別的。
(C) 昂貴的。
(D) 次要的。

> 理由

根據本文第五段第一句，在整個過程中，品質控管是最重要的。其使用到 paramount（首要的）這個字，可得知 supreme（最高級別的）最貼近此字，故 (B) 項應為正解。

> 重要字詞片語

1. **regardless** [rɪˋgɑrdləs] *adv.* 無論如何
   regardless of... 不論……
   Everyone is required to attend the meeting regardless of the typhoon.
   儘管有颱風，每個人還是被要求出席會議。

2. **plant** [plænt] *n.* 工廠

3. **flaw** [flɔ] *n.* 瑕疵；缺點

4. **texture** [ˋtɛkstʃɚ] *n.* 質地；口感

5. **weed out sth/sb**
   剔除某物/某人；淘汰某物/某人

6. **peel** [pil] *vt.* 剝／削（果皮）& *n.*（水果或蔬菜的）外皮
   I think it's rather troublesome to peel grapes.
   我認為剝葡萄皮很麻煩。

7. **feed** [fid] *n.* 飼料（不可數）

8. **ridged** [rɪdʒd] *a.* 鋸齒狀的

9. **excess** [ˋɛkˌsɛs] *a.* 過多的
   You can donate your excess food to the local food bank to help the homeless.
   你可以把多餘的食物捐給本地的食物銀行來幫助街友。

10. **starch** [stɑrtʃ] *n.* 澱粉

11. **vat** [væt] *n.* 大桶；缸

12. **mesh** [mɛʃ] *n.* 網；網狀物
    a wire mesh   金屬網篩

13. **drain** [dren] *vt.* & *n.* 排掉（液體）
The water in the bathtub should be drained first.
浴缸的水應該先放掉。

14. **season** [ˈsizn̩] *vt.* 調味
seasoning [ˈsizn̩ɪŋ] *a.* 調味的 & *n.* 調味品

15. **delicately** [ˈdɛləkətlɪ] *adv.* 小心地

16. **nitrogen** [ˈnaɪtrədʒən] *n.* 氮（氣）（不可數）

17. **contents** [ˈkɑntɛnts] *n.* 內容物（恆用複數）

18. **paramount** [ˈpærəˌmaʊnt] *a.* 首要的

19. **reputation** [ˌrɛpjəˈteʃən] *n.* 名譽，名聲

20. **consistent** [kənˈsɪstənt] *a.* 一貫的；前後一致的

21. **random** [ˈrændəm] *a.* 隨機的

22. **appropriate** [əˈproprɪət] *a.* 適當的；合適的
You should have taken more appropriate measures at that time.
當時你應該採取更合適的措施才是。

第參部分、非選擇題（占 28 分）

一、中譯英（占 8 分）

1. 網路詐騙層出不窮，而透過社群媒體所進行的金融犯罪有越來越普遍的趨勢。

   示範譯句
   Internet scams occur frequently, and financial crimes committed through social media show a tendency of becoming more prevalent.

   或：Online fraud is a common occurrence, and it appears that more and more financial crimes are being committed with the help of social media tools.

   翻譯要點

   a. **scam** [skæm] *n.* 詐騙
   b. **financial** [faɪˋnænʃəl] *a.* 金融的；財務的
   c. **commit** [kəˋmɪt] *vt.* 犯（罪）（三態為：commit, committed [kəˋmɪtɪd], committed）
      commit a crime　　犯罪
      If you commit the crime, you'd better be ready to do the time.
      你要是犯法，就要有坐牢服刑的準備。
   d. **social media**　　社群媒體
   e. **tendency** [ˋtɛndənsɪ] *n.* 趨勢，傾向
      There is a growing tendency of students taking time off before college.
      學生在上大學前會先休息一陣子的現象有逐漸上升的趨勢。

   f. **prevalent** [ˋprɛvələnt] *a.* 普遍的
   g. **fraud** [frɔd] *n.* 詐欺
   h. **occurrence** [əˋkɝəns] *n.* 事件（可數）；發生（不可數）
   i. **it appears + that** 子句
      看樣子／看來／好像……
      = it seems + that 子句
      It appears that someone has eaten all the cookies.
      看樣子有人把餅乾都吃光光了。
   j. **with the help of...**
      在……的幫助下

2. 因此，建議使用者每隔一段時間就更換密碼，密碼應包含大小寫字母、特殊符號和數字。

   示範譯句
   Therefore, users are advised to change their passwords at regular intervals, and the passwords should contain (both) uppercase and lowercase letters, special characters, and numbers / digits.

   或：Because of this, it is advisable that users (should) update their passwords regularly and select passwords that contain (both) uppercase and lowercase letters, special characters, and numbers / digits.

153

TEST 05

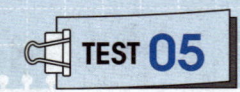

翻譯要點

a. **be advised to V**
   被建議／勸告做……
   You are advised to take a vacation to relieve anxiety.
   建議你去度假以消除焦慮。

b. **password** [ˈpæsˌwɝd] n. 密碼

c. **interval** [ˈɪntɚvḷ] n. 間隔時間
   at regular intervals
   每隔一段固定時間
   The trains leave at regular intervals.
   火車定時開出。

d. **uppercase** [ˌʌpɚˈkes] a. 大寫字母的

e. **lowercase** [ˌloɚˈkes] a. 小寫字母的

f. **digit** [ˈdɪdʒɪt] n.（從 0 到 9 的任何一個）數字

g. **advisable** [ədˈvaɪzəbḷ] a. 明智的；可取的
   it is advisable + that 子句
   最好／建議……

h. **update** [ʌpˈdet] vt. 更新 & [ˈʌpdet] n. 更新

二、英文作文（占 20 分）

提示：請仔細觀察以下三幅連環圖片的內容，並想像第四幅圖片可能的發展，然後寫出一篇涵蓋每張圖片內容且結局完整的故事。

> 示範作文

Erica and her younger brother were very excited because, after months of waiting, their summer vacation was finally starting. They wanted to go to a beautiful beach to enjoy themselves. After surfing the internet, they found Palm Beach. This was an ideal destination because it was not too far away from where they lived. They picked a Saturday morning to go and decided to take the train to avoid traffic jams. The night before they set out, they packed their swimwear, swimming caps, and goggles in their backpacks. The next morning they began their journey to the beach.

When they arrived, the beach was crowded with people as they had expected. Much to their disgust, however, they found the beach was littered with a lot of trash like plastic bottles and soda cans. Most of the people there seemed indifferent to the situation. After they took a dip in the water, they decided to help pick up the trash. They spent almost the entire afternoon doing this. In addition, to raise awareness about beach cleanup, they posted a few pictures on Facebook. A week later, they learned that some volunteer beach cleanup groups had promised to clean up the area on a regular basis. Hearing this news, they felt that their effort had paid off.

艾瑞卡和弟弟非常興奮，因為在等了幾個月後，他們的暑假終於開始了。他們想到美麗的海灘上好好享受一番。上網查了之後，他們找到了棕櫚灘。這個地點非常完美，因為距離他們住的地方不遠。他們選在一個週六早上出發，並決定搭火車以防塞車。出發的前一個晚上，他們將泳衣、泳帽和蛙鏡打包放進背包裡。隔天早上，他們踏上前往海灘的旅程。

當他們抵達時，海灘就如他們預期的一樣擠滿了人。不過，讓他們感到噁心的是，他們發現海灘上被丟滿了許多像是保特瓶和汽水罐等垃圾。大多數的人似乎對這樣的景象漠不關心。他們在水裡游了一下後，決定要幫忙撿垃圾。他們花了幾乎一整個下午做這件事。此外，為了提升大眾對於淨灘的意識，他們也將一些照片放上 Facebook。一週後，他們得知有些淨灘志工團體承諾會定期清理該區域。聽到這個消息後，他們覺得努力有了回報。

> 重要字詞片語

1. **palm** [pɑm] *n.* 棕櫚樹
2. **destination** [ˌdɛstəˈneʃən] *n.* 目的地
3. **a traffic jam** 塞車
4. **set out (for...)** 出發（前往……）
   We set out for the farm in the morning, hoping to make it there by lunchtime.
   我們早上出發前往農場，希望能在午餐時間前抵達。
5. **goggles** [ˈgɑglz] *n.* 護目鏡（因有兩個鏡片，故恆用複數）
6. **disgust** [dɪsˈgʌst] *n.* 作嘔；厭惡（不可數）
7. **be littered with...** 滿地遍布……
8. **indifferent** [ɪnˈdɪf(ə)rənt] *a.* 漠不關心的

155

TEST 05

9. **raise awareness about / of...**
   喚起關於……的意識
   The purpose of this ad is to raise awareness about the importance of environmental protection.
   這個廣告的目的是要喚起大眾對環保重要性的意識。

10. **on a regular basis** 定期
    = regularly [ˈrɛɡjələlɪ] *adv.*

11. **pay off** 取得成功，有收穫

TEST 06

第壹部分、選擇題

一、詞彙題
二、綜合測驗
三、文意選填
四、篇章結構
五、閱讀測驗

第貳部分、混合題

第參部分、非選擇題

一、中譯英
二、英文作文

第壹部分、選擇題

一、詞彙題

| 1. D | 2. C | 3. A | 4. A | 5. B | 6. B | 7. D | 8. B | 9. A | 10. C |

二、綜合測驗

| 11. C | 12. A | 13. C | 14. B | 15. D | 16. D | 17. B | 18. A | 19. D | 20. C |

三、文意選填

| 21. D | 22. H | 23. B | 24. F | 25. J | 26. E | 27. I | 28. A | 29. C | 30. G |

四、篇章結構

| 31. D | 32. A | 33. E | 34. B |

五、閱讀測驗

| 35. A | 36. D | 37. C | 38. C | 39. D | 40. C | 41. B | 42. D | 43. C | 44. C |
| 45. D | 46. D |

第貳部分、混合題

47. anxious

48. danger(s)

49. Armand

50. Gordon

51. Conrado

第壹部分、選擇題（占 62 分）

一、詞彙題（占 10 分）

D 1. 這家玩具店通常會在繁忙的聖誕節期間僱用額外的<u>臨時工</u>來協助正職員工。

ⓐ (A) **infinite** [ˈɪnfənət] *a.* 無限的
　　Life is finite, but knowledge is infinite.
　　生也有涯，知也無涯。── 諺語

(B) **authentic** [ɔˈθɛntɪk] *a.* （物品）真正的
　　This restaurant offers a wide variety of authentic Japanese cuisine ranging from sushi to sukiyaki.
　　這家餐廳提供各式各樣的正宗日本菜餚，從壽司到壽喜燒都有。

(C) **primitive** [ˈprɪmətɪv] *a.* 原始的
　　The tribespeople in the mountainous area still live a primitive life.
　　該山區的部落居民仍過著原始的生活。

(D) **temporary** [ˈtɛmpəˌrɛrɪ] *a.* 暫時的
　　The hunter made a temporary shelter out of branches.
　　獵人用樹枝做了一個臨時的避難小屋。

ⓑ 根據語意，(D) 項應為正選。

必考重點

permanent [ˈpɝmənənt] *a.* 固定的；常設的；永恆的

C 2. 威爾瑪正在廚房煮義大利麵；<u>與此同時</u>，她老公佛瑞德正在客廳看紀錄片。

ⓐ (A) **likewise** [ˈlaɪkˌwaɪz] *adv.* 同樣，也
　　I will respect your privacy. Likewise, I hope you will respect mine.
　　我會尊重你的隱私。同樣，我也希望你會尊重我的隱私。

(B) **besides** [bɪˈsaɪdz] *adv.* 此外
　　I've seen the movie before. Besides, it isn't that good.
　　我以前看過那部電影。而且，它也沒那麼棒。

(C) **meanwhile** [ˈminˌ(h)waɪl] *adv.* 同時
　　I'll do the cooking; meanwhile, you can do the laundry for me.
　　我來煮飯，同時，你可幫我洗衣服。

159

TEST 06

(D) thereby [ðɛrˈbaɪ] adv. 因此
Paul knocked over the red wine and thereby stained the tablecloth.
保羅打翻了紅酒,因此把桌布弄髒。

ⓑ 根據語意,(C) 項應為正選。

必考重點

documentary [ˌdɑkjəˈmɛntərɪ] n. 紀錄片 & a. 文件的;紀錄的

__A__ 3. 每個人的指紋都是<u>獨一無二</u>的,所以它們常被用來<u>確認</u>個人身分或破案。

ⓐ (A) **unique** [juˈnik] a. 獨一無二的,獨特的
be unique / indigenous / native to + 地方　　是某地所特有的
Kangaroos are unique to Australia.
袋鼠是澳洲特有的動物。

(B) **organic** [ɔrˈgænɪk] a. 有機的
The latest trend is to use organic fertilizers instead of artificial ones.
使用有機肥料代替人工肥料是最新的趨勢。

(C) **reluctant** [rɪˈlʌktənt] a. 不情願的,不願意的
be reluctant / unwilling to V　　不願……
Sam was reluctant to hand over his company to his youngest son.
山姆不願意把公司交給他最小的兒子管理。

(D) **brilliant** [ˈbrɪljənt] a. 出色的;明亮的
Newton was an absolutely brilliant scientist.
牛頓絕對是位傑出的科學家。

ⓑ 根據語意,(A) 項應為正選。

必考重點

a. **fingerprint** [ˈfɪŋgɚˌprɪnt] n. 指紋
b. **establish** [əˈstæblɪʃ] vt. 確定,證實;建立
c. **identity** [aɪˈdɛntətɪ] n. 身分

__A__ 4. 這家公司在新任執行長的帶領下<u>蒸蒸日上</u>。它甚至還被評選為亞洲最佳的企業之一。

ⓐ (A) **prosper** [ˈprɑspɚ] vi. 繁榮,昌盛
= thrive [θraɪv] vi.
= flourish [ˈflɝɪʃ] vi.
The store prospered under new management.
這家店在新的經營團隊下生意興隆。

(B) **persist** [pəˋsɪst] *vi.* 堅持；持續
persist in + N/V-ing　　堅持……
The defendant persisted in his innocence before the judge.
被告在法官面前堅稱自己的無辜。

(C) **rage** [redʒ] *vi.* 肆虐；發怒
The storm raged throughout the night, keeping us all awake.
暴風雨肆虐一整晚，讓我們無法入睡。

(D) **behave** [bɪˋhev] *vi.* 守規矩；表現
Mother told us to behave while she was away.
媽媽告訴我們她不在時我們要好好守規矩。

ⓑ 根據語意，(A) 項應為正選。

TEST 06

B　5. 我們懷疑約翰就是偷走機密文件的人，因為他是唯一擁有另一副保險箱鑰匙的人。

ⓐ (A) **define** [dɪˋfaɪn] *vt.* 給……下定義
define A as B　　將 A 定義為 B
Kelly defines happiness as spending time with her family.
凱莉將快樂定義為和家人共處。

(B) **suspect** [səˋspɛkt] *vt.* 懷疑
suspect sb of...　　懷疑某人……
We suspected Henry of stealing the jewels.
我們懷疑亨利偷了那些珠寶。

(C) **pledge** [plɛdʒ] *vt.* 保證，發誓
pledge to V　　保證/誓言要……
The government has pledged to clean up industrial emissions.
政府已保證要清除工業排放物。

(D) **command** [kəˋmænd] *vt. & n.* 命令
under sb's command　　在某人的指揮/統率之下
The general commanded the troops to fire on the enemy.
將軍下令部隊向敵軍開火。
The army did well under General Smith's command.
這支軍隊在史密斯將軍的指揮下戰績輝煌。

ⓑ 根據語意，(B) 項應為正選。

必考重點

a. **confidential** [ˌkɑnfəˋdɛnʃəl] *a.* 機密的

b. **document** [ˋdɑkjəmənt] *n.* 文件；紀錄

c. **safe** [sef] *n.* 保險箱

TEST 06

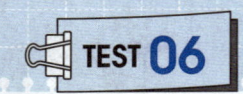

B 6. 是艾琳全心投入寫作，讓她的職涯在過去幾年來蓬勃發展。

ⓐ (A) browse [braʊz] vi. 瀏覽
browse through... 瀏覽……
I was browsing through a magazine at the bookstore when I noticed Sarah.
我在書店裡隨意翻閱一本雜誌時看到了莎拉。

(B) flourish [ˋflɝɪʃ] vi. 興盛，興旺
= thrive [θraɪv] vi.
Watercolors began to flourish in Britain around 1750.
水彩畫大約於 1750 年開始在英國興盛。

(C) vibrate [ˋvaɪbret] vi. & vt. 震動
The guitar string vibrates when it is plucked.
吉他的弦一撥就會震動。

(D) stutter [ˋstʌtɚ] vi. 結巴
As a child, Mary used to stutter but now she has grown out of it.
瑪麗年幼時常常口吃，但現在她已改掉了這個習慣。

ⓑ 根據語意，(B) 項應為正選。

必考重點
dedication [ˌdɛdəˋkeʃən] n. 奉獻，貢獻（不可數）（與介詞 to 並用）

D 7. 由於腳踝受傷，瓦特沒有選擇只好退出上個月的自行車比賽。

ⓐ (A) attraction [əˋtrækʃən] n. 吸引人的事物；吸引力
a tourist attraction 觀光勝地／景點
The prison was turned into a tourist attraction after the government shut it down.
政府關閉了這座監獄後，它就變成了一個觀光景點。

(B) realization [ˌrɪəlaɪˋzeʃən] n. 實現；了解
The realization of your dreams depends on whether you work hard.
夢想的實現取決於你是否努力。

(C) decoration [ˌdɛkəˋreʃən] n. 裝飾品（可數）& 裝飾（不可數）
As Christmas was drawing near, every store put up beautiful decorations for the holiday.
聖誕節快到時，每家商店都擺出漂亮的裝飾物以慶祝這個佳節。

(D) competition [ˌkɑmpəˋtɪʃən] n. 比賽；競爭
Connie is the youngest contestant in the swimming competition.
康妮是游泳比賽中最年輕的參賽者。

ⓑ 根據語意，(D) 項應為正選。

必考重點

a. **have no alternative / choice / option but to V**
除了……以外別無選擇

b. **drop out of...** 退出……

B 8. 媽媽在咳嗽糖漿藥瓶上貼上標籤，這樣我們就可以輕鬆地在櫥櫃內分辨它與其他瓶子的不同。

ⓐ (A) **constitute** [ˈkɑnstəˌtjut] *vt.* 組成，構成
Chinese people constitute the majority of the population in Singapore.
華人占了新加坡人口的大部分。

(B) **label** [ˈlebḷ] *vt.* 把……稱為；貼標籤，做標示 & *n.* 標籤
Lisa was labeled an oddball by her peers.
麗莎被同儕稱為怪咖。

(C) **plot** [plɑt] *vt.* & *vi.* 圖謀 & *n.* 陰謀
The rebels plotted to overthrow the government after the election.
反叛分子策劃在選舉之後要推翻政府。

(D) **invest** [ɪnˈvɛst] *vt.* & *vi.* 投資
invest in... 投資……
Oscar invested heavily in the property market in recent years.
近幾年來奧斯卡投資了很多錢在房市。

ⓑ 根據語意，(B) 項應為正選。

必考重點

a. **distinguish / tell A from B**
區分 A 與 B 的不同，辨別 A 與 B

b. **cabinet** [ˈkæbənɪt] *n.* 櫥，櫃

A 9. 在這起悲慘的高鐵意外後，政府官員對遇難者的家屬表達了哀悼和遺憾。

ⓐ (A) **regret** [rɪˈgrɛt] *n.* 後悔；遺憾
I have no regrets for what I have done.
我對我的所為並不感到後悔。

(B) **motivation** [ˌmotəˈveʃən] *n.* 動機
You should make sure that your motivation for losing weight is healthy.
你應確保自己想減肥的動機是健康的。

(C) **bargain** [ˈbɑrgən] *n.* 便宜貨，划算的東西
a real bargain   物超所值
The watch I bought yesterday was a real bargain.
我昨天買的那只錶真划算。

163

(D) **presentation** [ˌprɛznˈteʃən] *n.* 報告
Josh will give a presentation to the whole company tomorrow.
喬許明天將對全公司做簡報。

ⓑ 根據語意，(A) 項應為正選。

必考重點

a. **the high-speed rail**　　高鐵
b. **sorrow** [ˈsaro] *n.* 悲傷

C 10. 這位病患正在等她的健康評估，以確認她是否需要動心臟手術。

ⓐ (A) **evolution** [ˌɛvəˈluʃən] *n.* 進展；進化
the Theory of Evolution　　進化論

(B) **regulation** [ˌrɛgjəˈleʃən] *n.* 規則；規定
school / traffic regulations　　校規/交通規則

(C) **evaluation** [ɪˌvæljʊˈeʃən] *n.* 評估；估價
The architects will have to do a thorough evaluation of the land before the project begins.
在這項案子開始之前，這些建築師要對這塊土地做一次完整的評估。

(D) **revolution** [ˌrɛvəˈluʃən] *n.* 革命
launch a revolution　　發起革命
the Industrial Revolution　　工業革命

ⓑ 根據語意，(C) 項應為正選。

必考重點

surgery [ˈsɝdʒərɪ] *n.* 外科手術（不可數）
perform surgery on the patient　　對病人動手術
= perform an operation on the patient

二、綜合測驗（占 10 分）

第 11 至 15 題為題組

　　泰國這個以大象而出名的國家，以前稱作暹羅王國。雖然現在仍是君主國家，但以前它的國王擁有比現在大得多的權力與龐大的財富。正如同大部分皇室家族一樣，國王與那些試圖利用他或取代他的人之間會產生緊張關係。像這類的衝突造就了一個英文慣用語：**a white elephant**（昂貴而無用的東西）。

　　據傳說，某位泰國國王會送給他不喜歡的朝臣一頭白色的大象作為禮物。眾人都以為國王給了那位朝臣一件既珍貴又價昂的禮物。然而事實卻是，白象既難飼養又難照顧。每天都要給這頭巨大動物提供一百三十公斤的食物，這樣的經濟負擔足以將任何人推向破產的窘境。換句話說，它是件很麻煩的禮物，那位大臣就此毀了。所以現在 a white elephant 是個負面的詞彙，意指任何可能要花很多錢卻又被認為沒什麼用處的禮物或東西。

C 11. 理由

ⓐ 本題測試使役動詞 have 的用法：
have sb/sth + 過去分詞　　使某人／某物被……
I had my hair cut yesterday.
我昨天把頭髮剪了。

ⓑ 根據上述，(C) 項應為正選。

A 12. 理由

ⓐ (A) **dislike** [dɪsˋlaɪk] *vt.* 討厭
Albert dislikes keeping a low profile on the issue.
亞伯特討厭對此一問題保持低調。

(B) **discount** [dɪsˋkaʊnt] *vt.* 打折
Shops discount everything around holidays.
商店會在假日前後大減價。

(C) **discomfort** [dɪsˋkʌmfɚt] *vt.* 使不舒服
Ruby was slightly discomforted by her friend Emma's indifferent attitude toward the whole matter.
露比見她朋友艾瑪對這整件事一副事不關己的模樣，心裡有點不太舒服。

(D) **distinguish** [dɪˋstɪŋgwɪʃ] *vt.* 分辨，區別
It took me months to distinguish my girlfriend's voice from her sister's on the telephone.
我花了好幾個月才能在電話上分辨出我女友和她姊姊的聲音。

ⓑ 根據語意，(A) 項應為正選。

C 13. 理由

ⓐ (A) **decision** [dɪˋsɪʒən] *n.* 決定
make a decision　　做出決定
I'm sorry, but you'll have to make a decision quickly.
很抱歉，但你必須趕快做決定。

(B) **fortune** [ˋfɔrtʃən] *n.* 財富；幸運
Richard made a big fortune in real estate.
理查靠房地產賺了一大筆錢。
Frank always says it's his good fortune to work with so many brilliant and talented people here in this company.
法蘭克總是說他運氣好，能在這間公司跟這麼多優秀有才氣的人共事。

165

(C) **reality** [rɪˋælətɪ] *n.* 現實（情況）（不可數）；事實（可數）
In reality, ...　事實上，……
The suspect told the police he was out of town last night, but in reality, he stayed at home.
那位嫌犯告訴警方他昨晚出城去了，但事實上他卻待在家裡。

(D) **request** [rɪˋkwɛst] *n.* 請求
make a request for sth　請求獲得某物
The country made a request for international aid after the huge earthquake.
該國在那場大地震之後向國際社會求援。

ⓑ 根據上述用法，(C) 項應為正選。

B 14. 〔理由〕

ⓐ 本題測試以下語意：(A) is next to impossible（幾乎不可能）、(B) would be enough（就足夠）、(C) is more convenient than（比……更方便）、(D) could still be inefficient（仍然效率很差）。

ⓑ 根據語意，每天要給這頭巨大動物的食物，所花費的經濟負擔「足以」使任何人破產，故 (B) 項應為正選。

D 15. 〔理由〕

ⓐ 本題測試關係副詞 why 表「原因；理由」的用法。在表原因的關係子句中，先行詞是 the reason。the reason 在句中可以省略。故原句為 That is (the reason) why today, ...。

ⓑ 根據上述，(D) 項應為正選。

〔重要字詞片語〕

1. **monarchy** [ˋmɑnəkɪ] *n.* 君主國（可數）；君主政體（不可數）

2. **wield** [wild] *vt.* 運用；揮舞
wield power　行使權力

3. **as with...**　正如同……
Turtles, as with many other reptiles, can endure long fasts.
正如許多其他爬蟲類一樣，烏龜可以忍受長期不進食。
＊ fast [fæst] *n.* 禁食；齋戒

4. **royal** [ˋrɔɪəl] *a.* 皇家的

5. **arise** [əˋraɪz] *vi.* 發生；起因於（三態為：arise, arose [əˋroz], arisen [əˋrɪzn̩]）
arise from...　起因於……
Children should be disciplined when the need arises.
必要時孩童應該受到管教。
Tom's depression arose from his stress at work.
湯姆的憂鬱症起因於工作上的壓力。

6. **take advantage of...**　利用……
All students are invited to take advantage of our student discounts.
竭誠歡迎所有學生多加利用我們的學生折扣優待。

7. **conflict** [ˈkɑnflɪkt] *n.* 衝突
   come into conflict with...
   與……起衝突
   John was fired because he often came into conflict with his boss.
   約翰被炒魷魚了，因為他經常和老闆發生衝突。
8. **propel** [prəˈpɛl] *vt.* 推動，推進（三態為：propel, propelled [prəˈpɛld], propelled）
   This state-of-the-art sports car is propelled purely by solar energy.
   這輛最先進的跑車完全由太陽能所驅動。
9. **bankruptcy** [ˈbæŋkrʌptsɪ] *n.* 破產
10. **refer to...** 指的是……
    These figures refer to the money we've made this year.
    這些數據指的是我們今年的收益。

第 16 至 20 題為題組

對許多人來說，傘不是什麼珍貴的東西。最小的一陣驟風也可能導致它們開花壞掉，讓它們變成毫無用處。它們通常不值得花大錢購買，因為大多數的製造成本都很低廉。麥格里亞傘具公司的傘可不是這樣。

這間公司成立於 1854 年，目前由與該公司同名的第六代傳人弗朗切斯科·麥格里亞所擁有經營。他是義大利最高檔雨傘的製造業者之一，仍採用傳統的製作工法。他的傘是型式與功能的極品，全都經過八十道步驟手工製成。它們每把三百美元以上的售價，每一分錢都是物超所值。

無論晴雨天都非常實用的每把麥格里亞傘，由大約二十五個高品質配件組成。由當地木材製成中棒，再用堅韌卻時尚的布料製成傘布。同時還提供客製化服務，讓每位顧客親自挑選自己雨傘的每個細節。該公司最著名的傘在收合時看起來像支拐杖，產品製造以耐操為目標。它們夠堅固，能禁得起在街道上風雨的衝擊，也能抵擋幾乎任何來自大自然吹過來的東西。

D 16. 理由
- (A) **that** [ðæt] *conj.*（帶領從屬子句與主要子句連接）
  Alex told me that he came up with a good idea.
  艾力克斯跟我說他想到一個好點子。
- (B) **unless** [ʌnˈlɛs] *conj.* 除非，如果不
  Unless you make a reservation today, you won't get a table at that restaurant this weekend.
  除非今天去訂位，要不然這週末在那家餐廳你不會有位子坐的。
- (C) **although** [ɔlˈðo] *conj.* 雖然（= though）
  Although the family is poor, they lead a happy life.
  雖然這家人很窮，但他們過得很幸福。

(D) **because** [bɪˈkɔz] *conj.* 因為
I like Jeremy because he is polite.
我喜歡傑洛米，因為他很有禮貌。

ⓑ 根據語意，(D) 項應為正選。

B 17. 理由

ⓐ 本題測試以下語意：(A) dramatically declined（大幅減少）、(B) currently owned（目前擁有）、(C) heavily criticized（嚴厲批評）、(D) previously auctioned（先前拍賣過）。

ⓑ 根據語意，這間公司目前為弗朗切斯科·麥格里亞所有，故 (B) 項應為正選。

A 18. 理由

ⓐ (A) **process** [ˈprɑsɛs] *n.* 過程
It is healthy to steam food as no oil is used in the cooking process.
蒸食是健康的，因為在烹調過程中不放油。

(B) **structure** [ˈstrʌktʃɚ] *n.* 建築物
The government tore down the illegal structure.
政府拆除了那棟違章建築。

(C) **display** [dɪˈsple] *n.* 展示
The holiday ended with a stunning fireworks display.
該節日以施放令人極為驚豔的煙火落幕。

(D) **workload** [ˈwɝkˌlod] *n.* 工作量
Your help will certainly lighten my workload.
你的幫助肯定會減輕我的工作量。

ⓑ 根據語意，(A) 項應為正選。

D 19. 理由

ⓐ (A) **account for...**　　占……比例；說明……
That country accounts for more than one-fourth of the world's population.
該國占全球人口四分之一以上。

(B) **result from...**　　原因是／起因於……
Cancer can result from too much exposure to the sun.
在太陽底下曝晒過度可能會致癌。

(C) **engage in...**　　從事……，進行……
The two sides engaged in peace talks.
雙方進行和平談判。

(D) **consist of...** 由……組成／構成
A soccer team consists of eleven players.
一支足球隊由十一位球員組成。

ⓑ 根據語意，(D) 項應為正選。

C 20. 理由

ⓐ 本題測試以下語意：(A) act as a weapon（充當武器）、(B) provide political asylum（提供政治庇護）、(C) withstand the pounding（承受重擊）、(D) assist the needy（幫助需要的人）。

ⓑ 根據語意，空格前提及它們夠堅固，所以禁得起重擊，可得知 (C) 項應為正選。

重要字詞片語

1. **be a dime a dozen**
   不值錢的；隨處可見的
   Tablets are a dime a dozen nowadays.
   平板電腦現在很普遍。
2. **gust** [gʌst] *n.* 強風
   a gust of wind 　一陣強風
3. **inside out** 　裡外翻轉
4. **collapse** [kəˋlæps] *vi.* 瓦解
5. **invest** [ɪnˋvɛst] *vi.* 投資
   invest in... 　投資……
6. **descendant** [dɪˋsɛndənt] *n.* 後代，後裔
7. **namesake** [ˋnem͵sek] *n.* 同名的人或物
8. **exclusive** [ɪkˋsklusɪv] *a.* 高級的
9. **employ** [ɪmˋplɔɪ] *vt.* 採用
10. **masterpiece** [ˋmæstɚ͵pis] *n.* 傑作
11. **be worth every penny**
    = **be worth every cent**
    每一分錢都很值得
12. **shaft** [ʃæft] *n.* （工具或武器的）桿／柄
13. **stylish** [ˋstaɪlɪʃ] *a.* 時髦的，新潮的
14. **fabric** [ˋfæbrɪk] *n.* 布料
15. **canopy** [ˋkænəpɪ] *n.* 罩；頂篷

三、文意選填（占 10 分）

第 21 至 30 題為題組

　　南亞國家印度是世界第七大國，其教育體系也是競爭最激烈的國家之一。在一個人口超過十億的國家中，只有菁英中的菁英才能雀屏中選接受高等教育。相當常見的是，頂尖大學要求學生在國家考試中拿下超過九十八分的分數，才能得到入學許可。雖然這個體系培養了許多優異人才，並為全球提供了天賦異稟的員工，它也有其黑暗的一面。許多學生靠考試作弊或花大錢賄賂教授以取得更好的成績。更糟的是，研究顯示十三至十五歲的印度孩童中，有 **25%** 受憂鬱症所苦。

　　為了提升學生心理上與情緒上的健康，印度政府設計出一種特別的課程來教導學生快樂。上這堂課不需要任何書本，而且沒有回家作業。也沒有為了確認學生是否學到教材內容而舉行的考

TEST 06

　　試。取而代之的是，學生可以放輕鬆、聽故事與練習冥想。主要的目的是在教導學生如何有效地應付生活壓力。他們藉由給予學生如何管理自身壓力程度的訣竅與技巧來做到這一點。

　　在一個練習活動中，學生被要求閉上眼睛並專注聽自己呼吸的聲音。這個技巧聽起來也許很簡單，但它幫助學生暫停思考並回到當下的時刻。儘管現在要衡量這個課程的成功為時尚早，初期的回饋意見卻很不錯。快樂課程的概念似乎在其他地方流行起來。許多國家，包括墨西哥與秘魯，都計劃推出類似的課程，旨在提振學生的心情並處理他們的健康問題。

D 21. 理由
- ⓐ 空格前有 be 動詞 are，而空格後有介詞 for，故知空格應置入形容詞或分詞。
- ⓑ 選項中符合條件的有 (C) thinking（想）、(D) selected（被選中）、(F) emotional（情緒上的）及 (G) promising（有希望的），惟根據語意，(D) 項應為正選。

H 22. 理由
- ⓐ 空格前有及物動詞 gain（獲得），故知空格應置入名詞。
- ⓑ 選項中符合條件的有 (B) bribes（賄賂）、(C) thinking（思考）、(E) meditation（冥想）、(H) admittance（進入許可）及 (J) assignments（作業），惟根據語意，(H) 項應為正選。

B 23. 理由
- ⓐ 空格前有及物動詞的動名詞形 paying（付）及形容詞 large（大量的），而空格後有介詞 to，故知空格應置入名詞以被 large 修飾。
- ⓑ 選項中符合條件的尚有 (B) bribes（賄賂）、(C) thinking（思考）、(E) meditation（冥想）及 (J) assignments（作業），惟根據語意，(B) 項應為正選。

F 24. 理由
- ⓐ 空格前有形容詞 mental（心理的）及對等連接詞 and，而空格後有名詞 health（健康），故知空格應置入形容詞或分詞，以和 mental 形成對等並修飾 health。
- ⓑ 選項中符合條件的尚有 (C) thinking（想）、(F) emotional（情緒上的）及 (G) promising（有希望的），惟根據語意，(F) 項應為正選。

J 25. 理由
- ⓐ 空格前有 be 動詞 are 及單數名詞 homework（家庭作業），故知空格應置入複數名詞以和 homework 形成名詞詞組。
- ⓑ 選項中符合條件的僅剩 (J) assignments（作業），故為正選。

E 26. 理由
- ⓐ 空格前有及物動詞 practice（練習），故知空格應置入名詞。
- ⓑ 選項中符合條件的尚有 (C) thinking（思考）及 (E) meditation（冥想），惟根據語意，(E) 項應為正選。

TEST 06

I 27. 理由
ⓐ 空格前有引導不定詞片語的 to 及副詞 effectively（有效地），而空格後有作受詞的名詞詞組 the pressures of life（生活壓力），故知空格應置入原形及物動詞或片語動詞。
ⓑ 選項中符合條件的有 (A) focus on（專注在）及 (I) cope with（應付），惟根據語意，(I) 項應為正選。

A 28. 理由
ⓐ 空格前有引導不定詞片語的 to、原形動詞 shut（關上）及對等連接詞 and，而空格後有作受詞的名詞詞組 the sound of their breath（他們呼吸的聲音），故知空格應置入原形及物動詞或片語動詞。
ⓑ 選項中符合條件的僅剩 (A) focus on（專注在），且置入後符合語意，故為正選。

C 29. 理由
ⓐ 空格前有及物動詞 pause（暫停）及所有格 their，而空格後有對等連接詞 and，故知空格應置入名詞。
ⓑ 選項中符合條件的僅剩 (C) thinking（思考），故為正選。

G 30. 理由
ⓐ 空格前有主詞 the early feedback（初期的回饋意見）及 be 動詞 is，故知空格應置入名詞、形容詞或分詞。
ⓑ 選項中符合條件的僅剩 (G) promising（有希望的），故為正選。

重要字詞片語

1. **bribe** [braɪb] *n.* & *vt.* 賄賂
The politician appears to be incorruptible, but he actually accepts bribes.
那名政治人物看似清廉，實際上卻接受賄賂。
＊ incorruptible [ˌɪnkəˈrʌptəbḷ] *a.* 正直不阿的

2. **meditation** [ˌmɛdəˈteʃən] *n.* 冥想；打坐
Jane found inner peace by practicing yoga and meditation.
珍藉由練習瑜珈和冥想來得到內心的平靜。

3. **emotional** [ɪˈmoʃənḷ] *a.* 情緒上的

4. **promising** [ˈprɑmɪsɪŋ] *a.* 有希望的，有前途的

5. **admittance** [ədˈmɪtəns] *n.*（准許）進入（不可數）

6. **cope with...** 應付/處理……
I can cope with the situation on my own, so I don't need your help.
我自己就能應付這個情況，因此不需要你的幫助。

7. **assignment** [əˈsaɪnmənt] *n.* 作業；任務

8. **competitive** [kəmˈpɛtətɪv] *a.* 競爭激烈的

9. **score** [skɔr] *vt.* & *vi.* 得（分）& *n.* 得分

10. **talented** [ˈtæləntɪd] *a.* 有天賦的

11. **resort** [rɪˈzɔrt] *vi.* 訴諸
resort to... 訴諸/依靠……

TEST 06

12. **depression** [dɪˋprɛʃən] *n.* 憂鬱（症）
13. **in an effort to** V （努力）為了（要）……
14. **devise** [dɪˋvaɪz] *vt.* 設計；發明，想出
15. **ensure** [ɪnˋʃʊr] *vt.* 確保
16. **material** [məˋtɪrɪəl] *n.* 資料；材料
17. **instruct** [ɪnˋstrʌkt] *vt.* 教導
18. **effectively** [ɪˋfɛktɪvlɪ] *adv.* 有效地
19. **pressure** [ˋprɛʃɚ] *n.* 壓力
20. **breath** [brɛθ] *n.* 呼吸（不可數）
21. **pause** [pɔz] *vt.* & *vi.* 暫停
22. **it appears + that 子句** 似乎……
23. **catch on** 流行
24. **elevate** [ˋɛlə͵vet] *vt.* 提升；提振
25. **address** [əˋdrɛs] *vt.* 處理
26. **well-being** [͵wɛlˋbiɪŋ] *n.* 健康；幸福（不可數）

四、篇章結構（占 8 分）

第 31 至 34 題為題組

　　嚴格來說，她被稱為 AL 288-1，並由數百個骨化石所組成。**31.** 然而對那些非科學界的人士而言，這一堆古代的骨頭碎片被更親暱地稱作「露西」。露西為人族（早期現代人類）的化石，她在衣索比亞被美國研究員唐納德‧約翰森發現後很快就受到大眾喜愛。人們當時相信她是被發現的人類祖先最古老的樣本。她被取名為露西，因為約翰森和他的團隊在發現當晚聽了 1960 年代英國樂團披頭四的歌曲《鑽石天空下的露西》，並認為這個名字既迷人又有共鳴。

　　約翰森在 1974 年首先找到一根脛骨的一部分，它被判定存在了超過三百萬年。隔年，他和團隊重返當地，並找到一個頷骨、一截手臂骨頭和一個小型頭顱的後半部。他們持續搜尋並發現更多骨化石，其中包括骨盆和肋骨的碎塊。**32.** 他們一共找到露西約 40% 的骨架，這已足以好好了解她大致的樣貌。他們研判她的身高為一百一十公分、體重為二十九公斤，外表則長得像黑猩猩，且日常飲食以植物為主。透過腿骨和骨盆的檢測，研究員斷定露西已能直立行走。這項發現證實了早期人類在大腦增大之前就開始用腿走路的理論。

　　2016 年時，其他研究員在衣索比亞得到另一項驚人的發現。**33.** 他們找到一個幾近完整的人類祖先頭骨，其年代可追溯到比露西更早之前。這個化石被描述成極罕見的珍寶，能更清楚解釋人類的進化。這個新發現的頭顱被判定有大約三百八十萬年的歷史，比露西遺骸的時代更早。**34.** 然而，科學家認為這兩個種族同時存在了約十萬年的時間。雖然這給致力拼湊出人類進化歷史精確面貌的科學家增添複雜性，不過它也象徵著人類發展研究中一個更令人興奮的新階段。

D 31. 理由

- ❶ 空格前一句提到，嚴格來說，她被稱為 AL 288-1，並由數百個骨化石所組成，而空格後兩句提到露西為人族的化石，她在衣索比亞被美國研究員唐納德‧約翰森發現後很快就受到大眾喜愛，並提及露西的名字由來，可推測空格應提及這個化石的別稱為「露西」。
- ❷ 選項 (D) 表示，然而對那些非科學界的人士而言，這一堆古代的骨頭碎片被更親暱地稱作「露西」，填入後語意連貫，可知 (D) 項應為正選。

A 32. 理由

ⓐ 空格前提到約翰森團隊自 1974 年陸續發現了哪些露西的骨化石，而空格後一句提及了露西被研判的身高、體重、面貌及飲食習慣，可推測空格應提到約翰森研究團隊最終找到多少露西的骨化石來判定她的模樣。

ⓑ 選項 (A) 表示，他們一共找到露西約 40% 的骨架，這已足以好好了解她大致的樣貌，填入後語意連貫，可知 (A) 項應為正選。

E 33. 理由

ⓐ 空格前提到其他研究員得到另一項驚人的發現，空格後則提及該化石被視為珍寶，更能解釋人類的進化，可推測空格應提及發現一個更珍貴的化石。

ⓑ 選項 (E) 表示，他們找到一個幾近完整的人類祖先頭骨，其年代可追溯到比露西更早之前，填入後語意連貫，可知 (E) 項應為正選。

B 34. 理由

ⓐ 空格前提及新發現的頭顱有大約三百八十萬年的歷史，比露西遺骸的時代更早。又根據前文提到首先找到的露西脛骨判定超過三百萬年，可推測空格應提及這個頭顱和露西遺骸之間的時間關係。

ⓑ 選項 (B) 表示，然而，科學家認為這兩個種族同時存在了約十萬年的時間，填入後語意連貫，可知 (B) 項應為正選。

(C) 項中譯：儘管在衣索比亞有這些有趣的發現，露西的外貌仍然大多是個謎。

重要字詞片語

1. **technically** [ˈtɛknɪklɪ] adv. 嚴格說來
2. **consist of...** 由……組成
3. **community** [kəˈmjunətɪ] n. 界，群體
4. **affectionately** [əˈfɛkʃənɪtlɪ] adv. 親暱地，親切地
5. **hominin** [ˈhɑmɪnɪn] n. 人族
6. **species** [ˈspiʃiz] n. 物種（單複數同形）
7. **relatable** [rɪˈletəbḷ] a. 有關聯的；可理解的
8. **shinbone** [ˈʃɪnbon] n. 脛骨
9. **skull** [skʌl] n. 頭骨，顱骨
10. **pelvis** [ˈpɛlvɪs] n. 骨盆（複數為 pelvises）
11. **rib** [rɪb] n. 肋骨
12. **resemble** [rɪˈzɛmbḷ] vt. 和……相似
13. **chimpanzee** [ˌtʃɪmpænˈzi] n. 黑猩猩 (= chimp)
14. **upright** [ˈʌpˌraɪt] adv. 直立地
15. **shed light on...** 闡明／解釋清楚……
16. **evolution** [ˌɛvəˈluʃən] n. 進化，演化（不可數）
    evolutionary [ˌɛvəˈluʃənˌɛrɪ] a. 進化的，演化的
17. **predate** [priˈdet] vt. 在時間上早於……
18. **remains** [rɪˈmenz] n. 遺體；遺跡（恆用複數）
19. **piece together... / piece... together** 把……拼湊起來

TEST 06

五、閱讀測驗（占 24 分）

第 35 至 38 題為題組

我們居住的這個星球稱為地球，這真是一大諷刺。也許水球或海洋球是更適合的名稱。為什麼呢？那是因為這顆星球的表面有七成以上是被水覆蓋，而不是被陸地覆蓋。而這些水中，約有百分之九十七是鹹水。過去幾個世紀的地理學家已將鹹水水域中最大的幾個命名為「洋」：太平洋、大西洋、印度洋及北冰洋。雖然幾個世紀以來，只有四大洋被繪製在世界地圖上，但地理界已經逐漸接受承認第五個大洋 —— 南冰洋 —— 的存在。

這個新定義水域的邊界在地球最南端的大陸 —— 南極洲 —— 的四周，其範圍由向東流的南極環流來界定。在南極環流內圈的水域比其他大洋來得冷，也比較不鹹。它們是許多特殊物種的家園，像是南極冰魚和霍夫蟹。南冰洋在抑制氣候變遷所造成的破壞方面也發揮著作用，因為它的深水中儲存了大量的碳沉積物。然而，第五大洋並未受到普遍的承認。例如它得到國家地理學會的承認，卻沒有得到國際海道測量組織的承認。

撇開名字不談，我們應該記得要尊重我們的海洋。雖然海水的量體遠超過陸地，但也沒有逃過人類所帶來的危害。不管我們是否認為地球的大洋是獨立的個體，它們的溫度、構成及海洋生物都在承受環境汙染。生物學家說生物起源自海洋。假若地球上的所有生命都隨著海洋死去，那就實在太悲劇了。

A 35. 為什麼作者建議給我們的行星一個新名字？
(A) 因為我們這個星球大部分被水覆蓋。
(B) 因為古代的地理學家不了解我們的行星。
(C) 因為我們現在知道有多少海洋了。
(D) 因為淡水比鹹水更有用。

理由
根據本文第一段第四句，地球表面有七成以上是被水覆蓋，而不是被陸地覆蓋。所以作者認為原來的名字「地球」不適合，故 (A) 項應為正選。

D 36. 第二段中的 this newly defined body 指的是什麼？
(A) 南極環流。　　(B) 科學界。　　(C) 南極大陸。　　(D) 南冰洋。

理由
根據第一段最後一句，第五個稱作南冰洋正逐漸受到地理界的認可，承接下一段 this newly defined body（新定義的水域），故 (D) 項應為正選。

C 37. 根據本文，下列敘述何者正確？
(A) 南冰洋的名字來自國家地理學會。
(B) 霍夫蟹可以在全世界的許多海洋中發現。
(C) 南極環流的水域不如其他的水域溫暖。
(D) 南冰洋的碳沉積物可能會加速氣候變遷。

174

> 理由
> 根據本文第二段第三句，在南極環流內圈的水域比其他大洋來得冷，故 (C) 項應為正選。

C 38. 本文最後一段的主旨為何？
(A) 介紹南冰洋的更多細節。
(B) 宣稱大洋的數量已經改變。
(C) 強調環保的重要性。
(D) 不同意生物起源於海洋的觀點。

> 理由
> 本文最後一段先提醒大家要尊重海洋，並說因為環境汙染會對海洋生物造成影響等等，可得知應為告訴我們要環保，愛護我們的海洋，故 (C) 項應為正選。

重要字詞片語

1. **irony** [ˈaɪrənɪ] *n.* 諷刺
2. **appropriate** [əˈproprɪət] *a.* 適當的
3. **surface** [ˈsɝfəs] *n.* 表面
4. **geographer** [dʒɪˈɑgrəfɚ] *n.* 地理學家
5. **body** [ˈbɑdɪ] *n.* 大量；水域
   a body of... 大量的……
6. **the Pacific (Ocean)** 太平洋
7. **the Atlantic (Ocean)** 大西洋
8. **the Arctic Ocean** 北冰洋
9. **recognize** [ˈrɛkəɡˌnaɪz] *vt.* 認可，承認；認出
   Professor Rollins is recognized as one of the best educators in the country.
   羅林斯教授被公認為國內最傑出的教育工作者之一。
10. **border** [ˈbɔrdɚ] *n.* 邊界；國界
11. **continent** [ˈkɑntənənt] *n.* 大陸；洲
12. **Antarctica** [ænˈtɑrktɪkə] *n.* 南極
13. **current** [ˈkɝənt] *n.* 氣流；洋流
    Antarctic Circumpolar Current 南極環流
14. **be home to...** 為……的棲息地
15. **array** [əˈre] *n.* 一批，一系列
    an array of... 一連串，一大堆……
    I was attracted by a wide array of beautiful flowers in the garden.
    花園內種類繁多的美麗花朵吸引了我。
16. **store** [stɔr] *vt.* 儲存
    This flash drive stores a lot of information.
    這個隨身碟儲存了許多資料。
17. **deposit** [dɪˈpɑzɪt] *n.* 沉澱物，沉積物
18. **acknowledge** [əkˈnɑlɪdʒ] *vt.* 承認
19. **composition** [ˌkɑmpəˈzɪʃən] *n.* 成分
20. **marine** [məˈrin] *a.* 海洋的
    marine life 海洋生物
21. **be subject to...** 遭受……
    I am subject to headaches.
    我很容易頭痛。
22. **tragedy** [ˈtrædʒədɪ] *n.* 悲劇；慘劇
23. **highlight** [ˈhaɪˌlaɪt] *vt.* 強調
    You should highlight your work experience in the resume.
    你應該在履歷表中凸顯你的工作經驗。

TEST 06

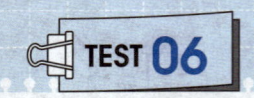

第 39 至 42 題為題組

　　路德維希・范・貝多芬是世界最知名且最受歡迎的作曲家之一。他的樂曲（其中有些以突破傳統的方式結合人聲和樂器）被視為天才之作。然而他的一生卻遭遇諸多艱困。

　　貝多芬於 1770 年出生於德國波昂。他的父親和祖父都是歌唱家，他的父親同時也教鋼琴和小提琴。但他父親是個暴力的酒鬼。上鋼琴課時，他會因為年幼的兒子一點些微的錯誤就毆打他，而且也很常為了練習而剝奪他的睡眠。儘管 —— 也可能是由於 —— 他父親這種變態的行為，年幼的貝多芬迅速發展出強大的音樂才能。在當今大部分孩子進小學的年紀，他已經開了第一場公開音樂會。十二歲時他發表了第一部作品，兩年後被任命為宮廷助理管風琴師。就像他同時期的沃夫岡・阿瑪迪斯・莫札特一樣，貝多芬確實是一位神童。

　　幸好除了他暴力的父親之外，貝多芬還有受到其他人的影響。雖然他是否真的曾和莫札特往來存在著爭議，但他確實曾跟當時另一位傑出音樂家約瑟夫・海頓學習。這名奧地利作曲家幫助貝多芬更加精進他已經相當傑出的才能。就在海頓的故鄉維也納，貝多芬以完美的演出及卓越的即興表演鞏固了他的名聲。儘管貝多芬的名氣很快就凌駕海頓之上，但他們兩人仍然維持良好的友誼，直到後者過世。

　　不過因為從未結婚，貝多芬的成年生活大部分都是一人度過。他甚至退出大部分的社交活動。這是因為他想要隱瞞他正在失聰這個令人心碎的真相。他寫過的信中透露他早在 1801 年就已經發生重聽的情形，而這情況日益嚴重一直到他 1827 年過世。不過這卻是他人生中最驚人的多產時期，正是這個時期創作出令人驚歎的交響曲、鋼琴奏鳴曲、序曲、歌曲，甚至是一齣歌劇。他在幾乎全聾的狀況下創作出這些舉世聞名的作品，實在令人難以置信。

D　39. 本文最適合的標題為何？
　　(A) 德國的音樂傳統如何發展
　　(B) 貝多芬最受認可的作品
　　(C) 酗酒是如何毀掉一個有前景的音樂生涯
　　(D) 路德維希・范・貝多芬的試煉與成功

> **理由**
> 根據本文第二段先提到貝多芬有一位酗酒的父親在幫他上鋼琴課的時候會毆打他甚至是剝奪他的睡眠。但也可能正因如此激發了他的音樂才能。第三段提及影響貝多芬的人，幫助他精進自己的才華。最後一段則提及他開始有失聰的現象，但這段時期卻又是他人生中最多產的時期。分別講到貝多芬所受到的苦難考驗以及他所獲得的成就，可得知 (D) 項應為正選。

C　40. 下列哪一項最接近第二段中 abhorrent 的意思？
　　(A) 防禦的。　　(B) 合作的。　　(C) 令人厭惡的。　　(D) 謹慎的。

> **理由**
> 根據本文第二段第四句，貝多芬的父親會因為一點些微的錯誤就毆打他，而且也常為了練習而剝奪他的睡眠，可知 abhorrent 的意思為「令人憎惡的」，與 disgusting（令人厭惡的）雷同，故 (C) 項應為正選。

B 41. 根據本文，下列哪一項敘述是正確的？
(A) 有很多證據顯示莫札特和貝多芬曾在一起學習。
(B) 路德維希・范・貝多芬比約瑟夫・海頓更受人讚賞。
(C) 莫札特和海頓相互較勁而影響了他們的音樂。
(D) 海頓和貝多芬的關係密切是因為他們都和自己的父親不和。

理由
根據本文第三段最後一句提到，儘管貝多芬的名氣很快就凌駕海頓之上，但他們兩人仍然維持良好的友誼，故 (B) 項應為正選。

D 42. 作者在最後一段暗示貝多芬何事？
(A) 他一生中其實創作了許多部歌劇。
(B) 他失聰這件事並未得到歷史學家證實。
(C) 他很有可能祕密結過婚。
(D) 他的失聰讓他的成就更顯偉大。

理由
根據本文最後一段倒數第一、第二句，他失聰後卻是他人生中最多產的時期，而這些舉世聞名的作品都是在幾乎全聾的狀況下製作出的，故 (D) 項應為正選。

重要字詞片語

1. **composer** [kəmˋpozɚ] *n.* 作曲家
2. **composition** [ˌkɑmpəˋzɪʃən] *n.* （音樂）作品
3. **groundbreaking** [ˋgraʊndˌbrekɪŋ] *a.* 創新的
4. **abusive** [əˋbjusɪv] *a.* 暴力的；辱罵的
5. **deprive** [dɪˋpraɪv] *vt.* 剝奪
   deprive sb of sth　剝奪某人的某物
   The court deprived the man of his civil rights for life.
   法庭判處該男子褫奪公權終身。
6. **prodigious** [prəˋdɪdʒəs] *a.* 強大的
7. **appoint** [əˋpɔɪnt] *vt.* 任命
8. **organist** [ˋɔrgənɪst] *n.* 管風琴手
9. **contemporary** [kənˋtɛmpəˌrɛrɪ] *n.* 同時期的人 & *a.* 當代的；現代的
10. **prodigy** [ˋprɑdədʒɪ] *n.* 天才，奇才
11. **distinguished** [dɪˋstɪŋgwɪʃt] *a.* 傑出的；著名的
12. **refine** [rɪˋfaɪn] *vt.* 改進；完善
    We refined our working process for better efficiency.
    為了更有效率，我們改善了工作流程。
13. **solidify** [səˋlɪdəˌfaɪ] *vt. & vi.* （使）穩固
14. **reputation** [ˌrɛpjəˋteʃən] *n.* 名聲，名譽
15. **flawless** [ˋflɔlɪs] *a.* 完美的
16. **improvisation** [ˌɪmprəvaɪˋzeʃən] *n.* 即興創作
17. **eclipse** [ɪˋklɪps] *vt.* 凌駕……之上；光芒蓋過……
18. **withdraw** [wɪðˋdrɔ] *vi. & vt.* 退出（三態為：withdraw, withdrew [wɪðˋdru], withdrawn [wɪðˋdrɔn]）
    The athlete's sore arm forced him to withdraw from the competition.
    這位運動員的手臂疼痛，迫使他退出比賽。

TEST 06

19. **conceal** [kənˋsil] *vt.* 隱藏
I sensed from Maureen's tone of voice that she was concealing something from me.
從茉琳的語調中，我感覺她有事瞞著我。

20. **deaf** [dɛf] *a.* 失聰的，耳聾的

21. **productive** [prəˋdʌktɪv] *a.* 多產的

22. **witness** [ˋwɪtnəs] *vt.* 是發生……的時間／地點；目擊 & *n.* 證人

23. **symphony** [ˋsɪmfənɪ] *n.* 交響曲

24. **verge** [vɝdʒ] *vi.* 接近；瀕臨
verge on sth　　接近；瀕臨

25. **admired** [ədˋmaɪrd] *a.* 讚賞的

26. **intense** [ɪnˋtɛns] *a.* 強烈的

27. **rivalry** [ˋraɪvḷrɪ] *n.* 競爭

28. **bond** [bɑnd] *vi. & vt.* 建立關係
bond with...　　與……建立關係
It's hard for Jim to bond with his co-workers.
吉姆很難和他同事打成一片。

第 43 至 46 題為題組

　　熱帶風暴──在世界不同的地區分別稱為颶風、氣旋和颱風──是風以環狀的方向快速移動的強烈風暴。它們在海上溫暖潮溼的空氣開始上升時成形，產生風暴和雲，接著開始旋轉。在北半球，它們以逆時針方向旋轉，而在南半球則是順時針方向。有時候兩個風暴會在近距離同時生成，彼此會逐漸貼近。這被稱為藤原效應。

　　這種現象的名稱來自日本氣象學家藤原咲平，曾被描述為兩個風暴在「共舞」。這支「舞」迴旋的方向同於風暴的旋轉方向，也分南北半球。基本上它們會圍繞著一個共同的質點轉動。雖然影響其發生的因素很多，但通常是在風暴彼此相距一千四百公里以內時發生。如果風暴的大小和強度都差不多，它們就會圍繞共同的中心點轉動。其中一個風暴可能會脫離原先的移動路線，如果它本來預計會侵襲陸地，這應該就是件好事。如果風暴的大小和強度不同，它們會互相繞圈圈，然後可能會開始合併。這並不會創造出超級風暴，而是較小的風暴會被較大的風暴吸收。

　　在過去二十年來，有許多藤原效應的案例。2005 年，威瑪颶風在侵襲佛羅里達州西南部時造成嚴重破壞，但到達大西洋時威力減弱。然而它一到那裡就吸納了熱帶風暴阿爾法而恢復強度。2008 年，熱帶氣旋費埃姆和古拉在印度洋西南部互動了一陣子，但仍然維持著兩個獨立的個體。四年後，珊迪颶風與一個冬季風暴合併，生成所謂的「超級風暴」。它侵襲美國、加勒比海和加拿大，造成兩百三十三人死亡以及將近七百億美元的財損。

(C) 43. 下列哪一項情況最有可能造成颶風生成？
(A) 陸地上溫暖潮溼的空氣。
(B) 冷空氣在海洋上升起。
(C) 海洋上炎熱潮溼的空氣。
(D) 陸地上低溫有雨的天氣。

理由
根據本文第一段第二句，它們在海上溫暖潮溼的空氣開始上升時成形，故 (C) 項應為正選。

C 44. 根據本文，如果 A 颱風（直徑一百一十公里）和 B 熱帶風暴（直徑六十五公里）在北太平洋上產生藤原效應，最有可能是下列哪一張照片？

(A)　　　　　　　　　　　　　　(B)

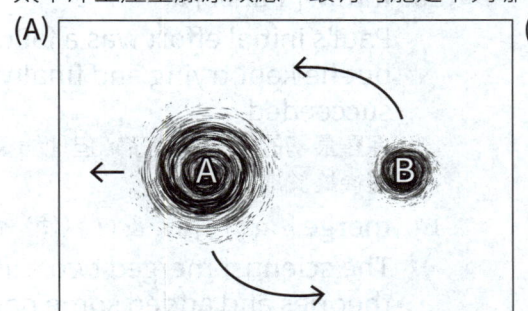

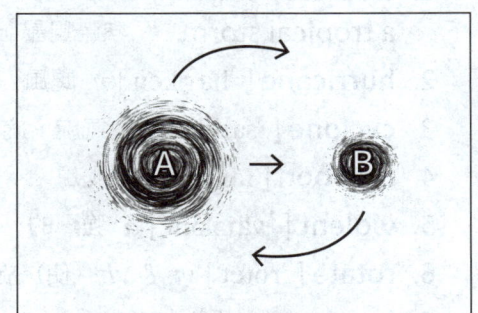

(C) 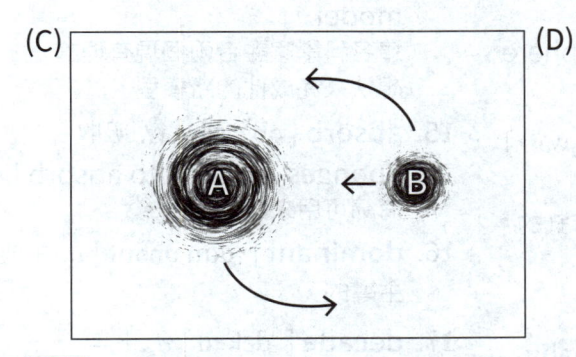　　　　　　　　　　　　　　(D)

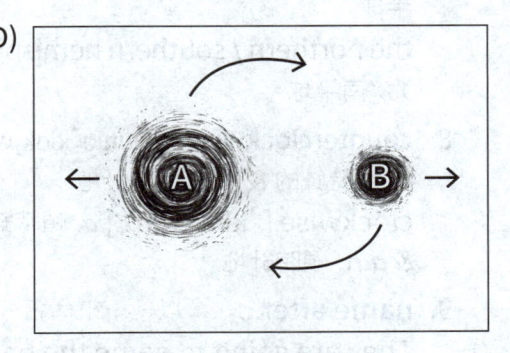

> 理由

根據本文第一段第三句，在北半球，它們以逆時針方向旋轉，可得知風暴的旋轉方向應為逆時針。另根據本文第二段倒數第一、二句，如果風暴的大小和強度不同，它們會互相繞圈圈，然後可能會開始合併。這並不會創造出超級風暴，而是較小的風暴會被較大的風暴吸收，可得知 (C) 項應為正選。

D 45. 下列哪一項最接近第二段中 trajectory 的意思？
(A) 力量。　　　(B) 結果。　　　(C) 後果。　　　(D) 路線。

> 理由

根據本文第二段第六句，其中一個風暴可能會脫離原先的移動路線，可得知 trajectory 為「軌跡」之意，故 (D) 項應為正選。

D 46. 根據本文，下列哪一項是正確的？
(A) 珊迪颶風在 2008 年造成破壞。
(B) 阿爾法熱帶風暴吸收了威瑪颶風。
(C) 2008 年費埃姆和古拉合併成一個氣旋。
(D) 當威瑪颶風遇到阿爾法時變得更強大。

> 理由

根據本文第三段第三句，然而它一到那裡就吸納了熱帶風暴阿爾法而恢復強度，故 (D) 項應為正選。

TEST 06

重要字詞片語

1. **tropical** [ˈtrɑpɪkl̩] *a.* 熱帶的
   a tropical storm　熱帶風暴
2. **hurricane** [ˈhɝɪˌken] *n.* 颶風
3. **cyclone** [ˈsaɪklon] *n.* 氣旋，旋風
4. **typhoon** [taɪˈfun] *n.* 颱風
5. **violent** [ˈvaɪələnt] *a.* 強烈的
6. **rotate** [ˈrotet] *vt. & vi.* (使)旋轉
7. **hemisphere** [ˈhɛməsˌfɪr] *n.* (地球)半球
   the northern / southern hemisphere 北/南半球
8. **counterclockwise** [ˌkaʊntɚˈklɑkˌwaɪz] *a.* 逆時針的 & *adv.* 逆時針地
   clockwise [ˈklɑkˌwaɪz] *a.* 順時針的 & *adv.* 順時針地
9. **name after...**　以……來命名
   They are going to name the baby boy after his grandfather.
   他們要用這名男嬰爺爺的名字來為他命名。
10. **meteorologist** [ˌmitɪəˈrɑlədʒɪst] *n.* 氣象學家
11. **mass** [mæs] *n.* 質量；團，塊；大量
12. **intensity** [ɪnˈtɛnsətɪ] *n.* 強度
13. **initial** [ɪˈnɪʃəl] *a.* 初期的
    Paul's initial effort was a failure, but he kept trying and finally succeeded.
    保羅最初的努力失敗了，但他繼續嘗試，最後終於成功。
14. **merge** [mɝdʒ] *vt. & vi.* (使)合併
    The scientist merged two existing theories and added some new ideas to come up with his new model.
    這名科學家融合兩個現有理論，並加入新想法來完成他的新模型。
15. **absorb** [əbˈsɔrb] *vt.* 吸收
    Sponges are used to absorb liquids.
    海綿可用來吸收液體。
16. **dominant** [ˈdɑmənənt] *a.* 主要的；主導的
17. **decade** [ˈdɛked] *n.* 十年
18. **immense** [ɪˈmɛns] *a.* 巨大的
19. **entity** [ˈɛntətɪ] *n.* 獨立存在體；實體
20. **dub** [dʌb] *vt.* 稱為……
    Roger Clemens is dubbed "The Rocket" because of his fastball.
    羅傑‧克萊門斯由於他的快速球，而有「火箭人」的封號。

第貳部分、混合題（占 10 分）

第 47 至 51 題為題組

電動車是以電力而非內燃機驅動的汽車。我們詢問了十位民眾對這種車的看法。

(A) 阿曼德

我搭 Uber 都會選電動車。電動車比起傳統汽車，對地球是更友善的，因為它們沒有排氣管排出的廢氣。不過我可能需要蠻久時間才能買得起電動車！

(B) 碧翠絲

我真後悔買了電動車。它充電好慢，而且充電站數量不足，造成我有里程焦慮。我必須仔細規劃旅程，才不會在到達目的地前就沒電。

(C) 康拉德

人們聲稱電動車對地球有益，但這並非事實。製造電動車時會排放有害氣體、電池很難回收，而且它們需要從燃燒化石燃料發電的供電網路來充電！

(D) 黛博拉

我最近買了臺電動車，覺得好極了。我可以在自己車庫裡趁夜間充電，而且每英里的動力成本遠低於汽油車。而且它非常靈敏，充滿駕駛的樂趣。

(E) 以諾

我有電動車里程焦慮，因為長途駕駛需要大量的事前規劃。但我能省下燃料費，還有開這麼節能的車的樂趣，彌補了這個缺點。

(F) 法蘭基

拜電動車之賜，在城市裡走路更加危險了。我總能聽到汽油車靠近我的聲音，但電動車太安靜了，它們過來時根本聽不見。不過我想它們應該是對環境有益吧。

(G) 戈登

我不能反駁電動車的理念。不過身為汽修師傅，我會擔心我的行業受到的衝擊。電動車的運轉零件比一般車少，所以它們維修需求也比較少。

(H) 亨麗埃塔

我開電動車的朋友抱怨充電速度太慢。但我有點嫉妒他的車。據我所知，電動車很好開：它們加速靈敏，而且不會熄火！

(I) 伊恩

電動車把我惹毛了！我們幹嘛被鼓勵去買這麼貴、充電慢得要死，而且一到冷天電池就會出問題的車？打死我也不會去買！

TEST 06

(J) 茱麗葉

我愛我的電動車！它非常環保，開起來還很過癮；充電便宜又方便；從不需要維修，而且還有許多智慧功能。好處三天三夜都講不完！

47-48. 有多人提及規劃開電動車的旅程會感到 **47.** 焦慮 **anxious**。同時另有一人提到電動車可能在市區道路上造成 **48.** 危險 **danger(s)**。

理由

第 47 題空格前有連綴動詞 feel（感到），得知空格應置形容詞。根據碧翠絲看法的第二至三句提及 ...leads to range anxiety（……造成里程焦慮）。以諾看法的第一句也提及 I suffer from range anxiety regarding my EV, ...（我有電動車里程焦慮，……）得知，空格應置入 anxiety 的形容詞 anxious。

第 48 題空格前有定冠詞 the，空格後為關係子句的主詞 EVs（電動車），得知空格應置名詞。根據法蘭基看法的第一句 Walking in the city is more dangerous thanks to electric vehicles.（拜電動車之賜，在城市裡走路更加危險了。）得知，空格應置入 dangerous 的名詞 danger(s)。

49-51. 根據回應內容從最正面到最負面排序，將缺少的名字填入下列清單中。
茱麗葉 > 黛博拉 > **49.** 阿曼德 **Armand** > 亨麗埃塔 > 以諾 > **50.** 戈登 **Gordon** > 法蘭基 > 碧翠絲 > **51.** 康拉德 **Conrado** > 伊恩

理由

根據以上十位民眾得知尚有阿曼德、康拉德和戈登三位尚未填入。阿曼德看法提到他搭 Uber 都會選電動車，且認為電動車對地球是更友善的，屬於正面評論。康拉德覺得製造電動車會排放有害氣體，且電池很難回收，並不環保，屬於負面評論。戈登則不排斥電動車，只擔心他的行業會受到衝擊。故可得知空格依序應置阿曼德、戈登、康拉德。

重要字詞片語

1. **combustion** [kəmˋbʌstʃən] *n.* 燃燒（不可數）
   internal combustion engine
   內燃機
2. **tailpipe** [ˋtelpaɪp] *n.* （汽車的）排氣管
3. **emission** [ɪˋmɪʃən] *n.* 排放；排放物
4. **anxiety** [æŋˋzaɪətɪ] *n.* 焦慮
5. **destination** [ˌdɛstəˋneʃən] *n.* 目的地
6. **manufacture** [ˌmænjəˋfæktʃɚ] *vt. & n.* （用機器大量）生產，製造

   Scientists are working to manufacture a vaccine that can combat the new virus.
   科學家們正在努力製造可以對抗新病毒的疫苗。

7. **emit** [ɪˋmɪt] *vt.* 散發，放射（三態為：emit, emitted [ɪˋmɪtɪd], emitted）
   Factories that emit large amounts of carbon dioxide contribute to global warming.
   工廠排放大量二氧化碳導致全球暖化。

8. **battery** [ˈbætərɪ] *n.* 電池
9. **recycle** [rɪˈsaɪkl̩] *vt.* 回收，重複利用
   Many companies now recycle old materials to create new products.
   許多公司現在將舊材料回收再利用以製造新產品。
10. **grid** [grɪd] *n.* 電力網；網格
11. **fossil** [ˈfɑsl̩] *n.* 化石
    fossil fuel [ˈfɑsl̩ ˈfjuəl]
    化石燃料（如石油、煤、天然氣等）
12. **purchase** [ˈpɝtʃəs] *vt. & n.* 購買
    Customers can purchase these products online or in-store.
    顧客可以在線上或實體店面購買這些產品。
13. **overnight** [ˌovɚˈnaɪt] *adv.* 整晚；一夕之間 & *a.* 在夜間的
14. **responsive** [rɪˈspɑnsɪv] *a.* 反應靈敏的
15. **make up for sth**　　彌補某事
    Andy bought flowers to make up for forgetting his wife's birthday.
    安迪買了花來彌補他忘記他老婆的生日。
16. **mechanic** [məˈkænɪk] *n.* 技工
17. **impact** [ˈɪmpækt] *n.* 影響，衝擊（常與介詞 on 並用）& [ɪmˈpækt] *vt.* 對⋯⋯產生影響
18. **maintenance** [ˈmentənəns] *n.* 維修，保養；維持（不可數）
19. **accelerate** [əkˈsɛləˌret] *vt. & vi.* （使）加速
    The car began to accelerate as it entered the highway.
    這輛車在進高速公路時開始加速。
20. **stall** [stɔl] *vi. & vt.* 熄火 & *n.* 攤位
    The car stalled in the middle of the intersection, causing a traffic jam.
    這輛車在十字路口熄火，導致交通堵塞。
21. **eternity** [ɪˈtɝnətɪ] *n.* 永恆
    an eternity　　極長的一段時間
22. **vulnerable** [ˈvʌlnərəbl̩] *a.* 脆弱的；（生理或心理）易受傷的
    be vulnerable to sth
    易受某事物的攻擊／傷害
    The flowers are vulnerable to cold weather.
    這些花不耐寒。
23. **adore** [əˈdor] *vt.* 喜愛；崇拜
    They adore spending time at the beach.
    他們非常喜歡去海灘玩。
24. **thrilling** [ˈθrɪlɪŋ] *a.* 令人興奮的

TEST 06

TEST 06

第參部分、非選擇題（占 28 分）

一、中譯英（占 8 分）

1. 從小，父母便教導我們要養成準時的好習慣。

   示範譯句

   Since we were little, our parents have been teaching us to develop the good habit of being on time.

   或：Our parents have been teaching us to get into the good habit of being punctual since we were very young.

   翻譯要點

   a. **develop the habit of V-ing**
   = cultivate the habit of V-ing
   = get into the habit of V-ing
   養成……的習慣
   Jenny has developed the habit of going to the movies every Sunday afternoon.
   珍妮已經養成了每週日下午看電影的習慣。

   b. **punctual** [ˋpʌŋktʃʊəl] *a.* 準時的
   My father always emphasizes the importance of being punctual.
   我父親總是強調準時的重要性。

2. 準時不僅可以表示尊重，同時也能給別人留下好印象。

   示範譯句

   Being on time not only shows respect but also makes a good impression on others.

   或：Being a punctual person not only signifies that you respect others, but it leaves a good impression on them.

   翻譯要點

   a. **respect** [rɪˋspɛkt] *n.* 尊重（不可數）& *vt.* 尊重
   Every individual should be treated equally and with respect.
   每個人都應該受到平等的對待和尊重。
   It is important to respect your parents and teachers.
   尊敬父母和師長是很重要的。

   b. **make / leave a good / bad impression (on...)**
   （給……）留下好／壞印象

   Mark dressed up trying to make a good impression on his girlfriend's parents.
   馬克盛裝打扮，試圖給女友的父母留下好印象。

   c. **signify** [ˋsɪgnəˌfaɪ] *vt.* 表示，象徵
   Andy's high blood pressure signifies that he is under a lot of stress at work.
   安迪的高血壓顯示他承受許多工作壓力。

二、英文作文（占 20 分）

提示：不同的游泳場所，可能樣貌不同，特色也不同。請以此為主題，並依據下列兩張圖片的內容，寫一篇英文作文，文分兩段。第一段描述圖 A 和圖 B 中的游泳場所各有何特色，第二段則說明你心目中理想游泳場所的樣貌與特色，並解釋你的理由。

A

B

示範作文

  Picture A shows an indoor swimming pool. Here, swimmers have their own individual lanes to swim in safely, and a lifeguard is on duty to rescue any swimmers who are in danger. The water in the pool should be a constant temperature, and the roof of the venue provides shade from the sun and protection against the elements. Picture B shows a sandy beach on a tropical island. Here, there is the opportunity to take part in water sports and swim in the ocean. Visitors to the beach can also soak up the sun, get a tan, and listen to the calming sound of the waves.

  Personally, I prefer to swim in a pool. I don't really like the saltwater in the sea, and it's almost impossible not to swallow some when swimming there! However, my ideal place to swim would be an outdoor pool near the beach. That way, I could do some exercise in the pool and then go down to the beach to sunbathe on the sand and enjoy the beautiful scenery. This would be the perfect combination.

  圖 A 是一座室內泳池。在這裡，泳者有自己的泳道可以游得安全，有值勤的救生員可以拯救任何發生危險的泳者。泳池的水應該是恆溫的，泳池的屋頂可遮陽及防禦惡劣天氣。圖 B 是一座熱帶島嶼的沙灘。在這裡，有參與水上運動和在海裡游泳的機會。遊客到沙灘也可以做日光浴並晒一身古銅色的皮膚，以及聆聽平靜的浪聲。

  就我個人而言，我比較喜歡在泳池游泳。我真的不喜歡海水，而在海裡游泳幾乎不可能不喝到一些海水！不過，我理想中游泳的地方會是靠近沙灘的戶外泳池。那樣，我可以在泳池運動，然後再到沙灘做日光浴並欣賞美麗的景色。這應該會是一個完美的組合。

TEST 06

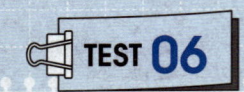

重要字詞片語

1. **lane** [len] *n.* 泳道
2. **rescue** [ˈrɛskju] *vt.* 拯救
   The fireman died trying to rescue a child from the blaze.
   那名消防員企圖拯救孩童時葬身火場。
3. **elements** [ˈɛləmənts] *n.* 天氣，(通常指) 惡劣天氣 (恆為複數)
4. **soak up the sun**　　晒太陽，做日光浴
5. **tan** [tæn] *n.* 晒成古銅膚色
6. **combination** [ˌkɑmbəˈneʃən] *n.* 組合；結合

TEST 07

第壹部分、選擇題

一、詞彙題
二、綜合測驗
三、文意選填
四、篇章結構
五、閱讀測驗

第貳部分、混合題

第參部分、非選擇題

一、中譯英
二、英文作文

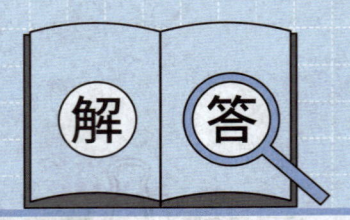

第壹部分、選擇題

一、詞彙題

| 1. B | 2. D | 3. B | 4. C | 5. C | 6. C | 7. A | 8. C | 9. A | 10. C |

二、綜合測驗

| 11. B | 12. D | 13. C | 14. A | 15. B | 16. B | 17. A | 18. C | 19. C | 20. D |

三、文意選填

| 21. D | 22. H | 23. F | 24. A | 25. J | 26. G | 27. I | 28. B | 29. C | 30. E |

四、篇章結構

| 31. C | 32. E | 33. D | 34. B |

五、閱讀測驗

| 35. D | 36. A | 37. B | 38. D | 39. B | 40. C | 41. B | 42. A | 43. D | 44. C |
| 45. C | 46. B |

第貳部分、混合題

47. behind closed doors

48. invaded

49. cancelation

50. postponement

51. C

第壹部分、選擇題（占 62 分）

一、詞彙題（占 10 分）

B 1. 在南極偏遠地區研究企鵝時，那位科學家感受到一種強烈的<u>孤立感</u>。

🅐 (A) **modesty** [ˈmɑdɪstɪ] *n.* 謙虛（不可數）
　　with modesty　　謙虛地
　　"I'm the chief of a small hospital," Dr. Walton said with modesty.
　　華頓醫師謙虛地說：「我是一家小醫院的主任。」

(B) **isolation** [ˌaɪslˈeʃən] *n.* 孤立，隔絕（不可數）
　　Clare lives in isolation like Robinson Crusoe.
　　克萊兒像魯賓遜‧克魯索一樣地離群索居。

(C) **tolerance** [ˈtɑlərəns] *n.* 容忍（不可數）
　　Try to show tolerance to your neighbors.
　　試著去包容你的鄰居們。

(D) **philosophy** [fəˈlɑsəfɪ] *n.* 哲學（不可數）
　　All the freshmen must take a course in philosophy.
　　所有的大一生都必須修一門哲學課。

🅑 根據語意，(B) 項應為正選。

必考重點

Antarctica [ænˈtɑrktɪkə] *n.* 南極洲

D 2. 科技業員工越來越嚮往以像是比特幣的數位貨幣支付薪資。

🅐 (A) **professional** [prəˈfɛʃənḷ] *a.* 職業的；專業的
　　Though Mr. Bagnell was once a professional TV comedian, he is now a politician in California.
　　巴格諾先生曾是職業的電視諧星，不過現在卻成了加州的政治人物。

(B) **economic** [ˌɛkəˈnɑmɪk] *a.* 與經濟有關的
　　Many shops have closed down because of economic depression.
　　因為經濟不景氣，很多商店都關門大吉。

TEST 07

(C) abrupt [ə'brʌpt] *a.* 突然的；唐突的
Many employees in that company felt confused about the abrupt change in policy.
那間公司許多員工對於政策突然轉變都感到很疑惑。

(D) desirable [dɪ'zaɪrəbl̩] *a.* 值得嚮往的；適合的
That busy corner is a desirable place for a restaurant.
那個車水馬龍的角落很適合開一家餐廳。

ⓑ 根據語意，(D) 項應為正選。

必考重點

a. digital ['dɪdʒɪtl̩] *a.* 數位的
b. currency ['kɝənsɪ] *n.* 貨幣
c. Bitcoin ['bɪtkɔɪn] *n.* 比特幣

B　3. 露西很怕待在水裡，因此她無法放鬆地漂浮在游泳池裡。

ⓐ (A) sweat [swɛt] *vi.* 流汗 & *n.* 汗水（不可數）
Teddy took extra clothes lest he (should) sweat too much and need to change.
泰迪多帶了些衣服以防流太多汗時需要更換。

(B) float [flot] *vi.* 漂浮
The fallen leaves floated on the still water.
落葉漂浮在平靜的水面上。

(C) tremble ['trɛmbl̩] *vi.* 發抖，顫抖
= shiver ['ʃɪvɚ] *vi.*
I could feel Judy tremble from the cold.
我可以感覺到茱蒂冷得發抖。

(D) drown [draʊn] *vi.* 淹死 & *vt.* 使溺斃；淹沒
The fisherman almost drowned when his little boat overturned.
小船翻覆，那位漁夫差點淹死。

ⓑ 根據語意，(B) 項應為正選。

C　4. 奧莉維亞非常沉迷於社交網站，時常每二十分鐘就要去查看一下她的臉書和推特網頁。

ⓐ (A) adequately ['ædəkwɪtlɪ] *adv.* 適當地
= properly ['prɑpɚlɪ] *adv.*
A spider can't adequately be called an insect.
把蜘蛛稱為昆蟲並不恰當。

(B) **spiritually** [ˈspɪrɪtʃʊəlɪ] *adv.* 精神上
Staying in high spirits is the best way to help you stay healthy physically and spiritually.
保持心情愉快是讓身體與心靈維持健康的最佳方法。

(C) **constantly** [ˈkɑnstəntlɪ] *adv.* 時常地
= **frequently** [ˈfrikwəntlɪ] *adv.*
Mr. and Mrs. Jones do not get along, so they quarrel constantly.
瓊斯夫婦處得不好，所以他們時常吵架。

(D) **mysteriously** [mɪsˈtɪrɪəslɪ] *adv.* 神祕地
She smiled mysteriously without saying anything.
她神祕地笑了笑，什麼也沒說。

ⓑ 根據語意，(C) 項應為正選。

必考重點

be / become addicted to + N/V-ing　　沉迷於……
The movie star became addicted to alcohol after her divorce and the death of her son.
這名影星自從離婚加上她兒子過世後，就沉迷於飲酒了。

C 5. 食物、空氣和水對生物而言都是<u>不可或缺的</u>，也就是說要在許多其他的星球上生活是不可能的事。

ⓐ (A) **favorable** [ˈfevərəbl̩] *a.* 有利的
Florida's weather is favorable to the growth of citrus fruit.
佛羅里達的氣候有利於柑橘類水果的生長。

(B) **accurate** [ˈækjərət] *a.* 準確的，精確的
We still don't have an accurate number on how many people perished in the bomb attacks.
我們尚無法得知此次炸彈攻擊的確切死亡人數。

(C) **essential** [ɪˈsɛnʃəl] *a.* 必要的，不可或缺的
be essential to / for...　　對……而言是不可或缺的
A diet high in fiber is essential to your health.
富含纖維的飲食對健康而言是不可或缺的。

(D) **immense** [ɪˈmɛns] *a.* 廣大的，無限的
= **enormous** [ɪˈnɔrməs] *a.*
The destruction caused by the earthquake was immense.
這次地震所引起的破壞很大。

ⓑ 根據語意及用法，(C) 項應為正選。

191

TEST 07

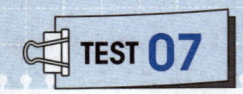

__C__ 6. 文森發現他再也無法忍受珍妮佛的壞脾氣，所以他決定訴請離婚。

ⓐ (A) **discard** [dɪsˋkɑrd] *vt.* 丟棄
Tina carelessly discarded a cigarette butt and caused a fire.
蒂娜亂丟菸蒂而引發火災。

(B) **allege** [əˋlɛdʒ] *vt.* 指控，宣稱
The politician is alleged to have accepted the bribes.
該政治人物遭指控收賄。

(C) **tolerate** [ˋtɑləˏret] *vt.* 忍受
= put up with...
How can you tolerate Jill's constant complaining?
你怎麼能忍受吉兒不停的抱怨？

(D) **compile** [kəmˋpaɪl] *vt.* 編纂，匯編
Bill compiled a lot of scientific data.
比爾匯集了許多科學資料。

ⓑ 根據語意，(C) 項應為正選。

必考重點

a. **temper** [ˋtɛmpɚ] *n.* 脾氣
lose one's temper　　發脾氣

b. **file for a divorce**　　提出／申請離婚

__A__ 7. 艾倫對日本的熟悉程度使得他與朋友很輕易到各城市觀光旅遊。

ⓐ (A) **familiarity** [fəˏmɪlɪˋærətɪ] *n.* 熟悉；通曉；親切感（不可數）
The familiarity of this restaurant made me feel at home.
這家餐廳的親切感，讓我有賓至如歸的感覺。

(B) **necessity** [nəˋsɛsətɪ] *n.* 需要（不可數）
Necessity is the mother of invention.
需要為發明之母。──諺語

(C) **possibility** [ˏpɑsəˋbɪlətɪ] *n.* 可能性
Our general manager hinted at the possibility of opening a new branch next summer.
總經理暗示了來年夏天開設新分公司的可能性。

(D) **quantity** [ˋkwɑntətɪ] *n.* 數量（與不可數名詞並用）
a large quantity of...　　大量的……
The farmer used a large quantity of water to irrigate his fields.
該農夫使用大量的水來灌溉他的農地。

ⓑ 根據語意，(A) 項應為正選。

C 8. 我們有一位同事月底要退休了，所以我們將為他計劃一場歡送會。

- (A) **potential** [pəˈtɛnʃəl] *a.* 潛在的
  We need to come up with new ways of attracting potential customers.
  我們需要想出能吸引潛在顧客的新方法。

- (B) **plentiful** [ˈplɛntɪfl] *a.* 充足的，大量的
  Rainfall is plentiful in the northern part of the country.
  該國的北部地區降雨量豐沛。

- (C) **farewell** [ˈfɛrˌwɛl] *a.* 送別的 & *n.* 告別
  The retiring teacher made a farewell speech.
  這位即將退休的老師發表了一場告別演說。

- (D) **furious** [ˈfjʊrɪəs] *a.* 憤怒的
  be furious at / with sb　　對某人生氣
  be furious at / about sth　　對某事感到憤怒
  Jerry was furious at himself for failing the test.
  傑瑞很氣自己沒考及格。
  Ted was furious at his son's bad manners.
  泰德對兒子的沒禮貌感到憤怒。

- 根據語意，(C) 項應為正選。

必考重點

a. **colleague** [ˈkɑlig] *n.* 同事　　b. **retire** [rɪˈtaɪr] *vi.* 退休

A 9. 一項研究發現，蜜蜂在日全蝕期間會停止飛行，因為牠們以為那是夜間。

- (A) **eclipse** [ɪˈklɪps] *n.* 蝕
  a total solar / lunar eclipse　　日／月全蝕
  a partial solar / lunar eclipse　　日／月偏蝕
  Legend has it that the god came to save the villagers during a solar eclipse.
  傳說該神在日蝕期間會降臨拯救那些村民。

- (B) **impact** [ˈɪmpækt] *n.* 衝擊／撞擊（力）
  on impact　　在衝擊／碰撞時
  The car burst into flames on impact.
  那輛車因衝撞而起火燃燒。

- (C) **horizon** [həˈraɪzn̩] *n.* 地平線（單數）；範圍，眼界（恆用複數）
  on the horizon　　在地平線上
  The visitors could see the sun setting on the horizon from their rooms.
  房客可以從房間看到地平線上的落日。

193

TEST 07

(D) **vacancy** [ˈvekənsɪ] *n.* 空缺;空位;空額
There are currently no vacancies at our company.
我們公司目前沒有職缺。

ⓑ 根據語意,(A) 項應為正選。

C 10. 書展有各式各樣的展區,包括漫畫、雜誌、小說,以及甚至電子出版品。

ⓐ (A) **skillful** [ˈskɪlfəl] *a.* 擅長的;高明的
be skillful in / at... 對……很在行
Terry is skillful in diving and has won several competitions.
泰瑞的跳水技術一流,他曾在許多比賽中獲勝。

(B) **influential** [ˌɪnfluˈɛnʃəl] *a.* 有影響力的
The non-profit organization is very influential in forming public opinion.
這個非營利組織對輿論的形成很有影響力。

(C) **various** [ˈvɛrɪəs] *a.* 各式各樣的,種種不同的
Society is composed of various kinds of people, and you should learn to deal with each and every one of them.
社會是由形形色色的人組成的,因此你應學習與每一個人的相處之道。

(D) **flexible** [ˈflɛksəbl̩] *a.* 有彈性的;可變通的
These pants are very flexible, so they fit people of all different sizes.
這條褲子很有彈性,所以各種身材的人都可以穿。
You have to be flexible to negotiate successfully.
你必須懂得變通才能協商成功。

ⓑ 根據語意,(C) 項應為正選。

必考重點

a. **a book fair** 書展
b. **electronic** [ɪˌlɛkˈtrɑnɪk] *a.* 電子的
c. **material** [məˈtɪrɪəl] *n.* 素材;材料

二、綜合測驗(占 10 分)

第 11 至 15 題為題組

據說眼睛是靈魂之窗。此說對貓來講尤其正確。牠們的眼睛會透露心情、情緒和更多訊息。貓眼的顏色也包含許多資訊。

所有貓的眼睛都會變色。其顏色由製造黑色素的黑色素細胞數量來決定。眼睛中這類細胞越多,顏色就越深。藍眼貓無此細胞,而綠眼貓有一些,金黃眼貓更多些,而紅銅眼貓最多。所有的幼貓都是藍眼睛,因為黑色素細胞尚未開始運作。它們在貓咪出生後四到六週之間開始運作。

四個月大時，幼貓便會擁有成貓後確定的眼睛色彩。有些貓的眼睛仍會維持藍色，但大多數都會變成綠色、金黃色、紅銅色和介於其間的各種色彩。

　　對貓來說，兩眼顏色不同也是正常的。然而顏色突然轉變則並非正常。這是患病的徵兆。健康的眼睛變成橘色或紅色代表它們正在發炎，而深黃色或褐色可能意味著貓白血病或貓愛滋病。貓眼的顏色確實不只是顏色那麼簡單喔。

B 11. 理由

    ⓐ (A) **preserve** [prɪˋzɝv] *vt.* 保存；維護
        Sausage is meat that has been preserved by the addition of salt and spices.
        香腸是藉由添加鹽及香料來保存的肉品。

      (B) **determine** [dɪˋtɝmɪn] *vt.* 決定
        Your overall health is partly determined by what you eat.
        你的整體健康有一部分取決於你的飲食。

      (C) **promote** [prəˋmot] *vt.* 晉升；促銷
        Joe performed so well that he was promoted by his boss.
        喬表現極佳，因此獲得老闆升遷。

      (D) **release** [rɪˋlis] *vt.* 發表／發行（書、唱片等）；透露（消息）
        Some of the writer's private papers were released by his grandson.
        那位作家的一些私人文件被他的孫子公諸於世。

    ⓑ 根據語意，(B) 項應為正選。

D 12. 理由

    ⓐ 本題測試以下語意：(A) most often（最常）、(B) the longest（最長）、(C) far inferior（遠不如）、(D) the most（最多）。

    ⓑ 根據語意，空格前面提及不同顏色眼睛的黑色素細胞多寡，故可得知 (D) 項應為正選。

C 13. 理由

    ⓐ (A) **check in** （在旅館）登記住宿；（在機場）辦理登機手續
        Let's check in before we have lunch at the hotel.
        咱們先在飯店辦好住宿手續再吃午餐吧。

      (B) **sign in** 簽到
        Please remember to sign in before taking your seats.
        各位在入座前請記得要先簽到。

      (C) **kick in** 開始，發生
        After 30 minutes the painkiller finally kicked in.
        止痛藥終於在三十分鐘後開始發揮效用。

TEST 07

(D) **fade in (...)** （使影片、廣播中的聲音）漸強；（使影片中畫面）漸顯
The words "The End" faded in at the end of the movie.
在電影結束時「劇終」二字慢慢浮現。

ⓑ 根據語意，(C) 項應為正選。

A **14.** 理由

ⓐ (A) **shade** [ʃed] *n.* 色調，色度
That shade of blue is perfect.
那種色調的藍恰到好處。

(B) **paint** [pent] *n.* 油漆（不可數）
Linda chose several kinds of paint for the house.
琳達為這房子選了好幾種油漆。

(C) **term** [tɝm] *n.* 用詞；術語
Mathematicians use the term "infinity" for a number that is limitless.
數學家用「無限大」這個詞來代表無限大的數字。

(D) **light** [laɪt] *n.* 光；燈
The sun radiates light and heat.
太陽會散發光與熱。

ⓑ 根據語意，(A) 項應為正選。

B **15.** 理由

ⓐ 本題測試以下語意：(A) happiness and joy（幸福快樂）、(B) sickness and disease（疾病）、(C) function and operation（功能操作）、(D) instinct and intension（本能和意圖）。

ⓑ 根據語意，前句說到貓眼突然變顏色是不正常的，後句則指出貓眼變成什麼顏色，代表可能罹患什麼疾病，故 (B) 項應為正選。

重要字詞片語

1. **when it comes to...** 說到……
= **in terms of...**
No one compares to Rachel when it comes to baking.
說到烘焙，沒人比得上瑞秋。
2. **feline** [ˈfilaɪn] *n.* 貓科動物 & *a.* 貓科的
3. **reveal** [rɪˈvil] *vt.* 透露；揭露
4. **emotion** [ɪˈmoʃən] *n.* 情緒
5. **melanocyte** [ˈmɛlənəˌsaɪt] *n.* 黑色素細胞
melanin [ˈmɛlənɪn] *n.* 黑色素（不可數）
6. **pigment** [ˈpɪgmənt] *n.* 色素；顏料
7. **inflamed** [ɪnˈflemd] *a.* 發炎的；紅腫的
8. **indicate** [ˈɪndəˌket] *vt.* 顯示；暗示
9. **leukemia** [luˈkimɪə] *n.* 白血症，血癌（不可數）

第 16 至 20 題為題組

　　任何待過臺灣的人，肯定都會注意到島上擁有數量龐大的便利商店。每個街角似乎都有 7-Eleven 和全家便利商店的身影，便利商店對臺灣人而言是一種生活方式。但這些無處不在的商店的起源為何？它們跟「一般」商店比起來又有何獨特之處呢？

　　1927 年，第一間「正港」便利商店突然出現在德州的達拉斯。它是由南方製冰公司員工約翰・傑佛遜・葛林所成立。他發覺人們常常在雜貨店打烊後還需要購買麵包、雞蛋和牛奶等商品。葛林的第一家商店門前有一根美國原住民的圖騰柱。它吸引了相當多的注目，最後造就了遍布達拉斯各處的「圖騰商店」連鎖。這些商店後來被一名達拉斯銀行家收購，他將其更名為 7-Eleven 以反映該商店新的營業時間：早上七點至晚上十一點。

　　現在全世界有超過七萬家 7-Eleven 便利商店，大部分都是全年無休。有些分店附有加油站、自動提款機和甜甜圈店面，其他則販賣幾乎能想像到的任何商品。毫無疑問，現代的便利商店的確名副其實。

B 16. 理由

- ⓐ (A) **accent** [ˈæksənt] *n.* 口音；腔調
  Jack spoke with such a heavy accent that I could barely understand him.
  傑克說話的口音很重，我幾乎聽不懂他在說什麼。

- (B) **origin** [ˈɔrədʒɪn] *n.* 起源
  Scientists are in disagreement over the origin of life.
  科學家對於生命起源的看法不一。

- (C) **charity** [ˈtʃærətɪ] *n.* 慈善
  Charity begins at home.
  為善從自家做起。── 英文諺語

- (D) **ground** [graʊnd] *n.* （興趣、知識或思想的）範圍/領域
  We've got a lot of ground to cover, so I suggest we do our best to stay on track.
  我們有很多事要討論，所以我建議我們盡可能不要偏離方向。

- ⓑ 根據語意，(B) 項應為正選。

A 17. 理由

- ⓐ (A) **spring up**　突然出現；（如雨後春筍般）湧現
  Fast food chain stores are springing up on nearly every corner in the city.
  速食連鎖店如雨後春筍般在這座城市的各處湧現。

- (B) **pass out**　昏過去，暈倒
  Jason passed out after eating nothing for three days.
  傑森三天沒吃東西，然後就昏了過去。

(C) **take part** 參加，參與
In the 1900 Olympic Games, women were allowed to take part for the first time.
在 1900 年的奧運中，女性首度被允許參加。

(D) **give birth** 生產
Ian couldn't bear watching his wife in pain when giving birth.
伊恩看著妻子生產時痛苦的模樣相當不捨。

ⓑ 根據語意，(A) 項應為正選。

C **18.** 理由

ⓐ 本題測試以下語意：(A) held an annual sale（舉辦年度拍賣）、(B) had a grand reopening（重新盛大開幕）、(C) had closed（打烊）、(D) carried little stock（有少量庫存）。

ⓑ 根據語意，人們會在雜貨店打烊後需要購物，可得知 (C) 項應為正選。

C **19.** 理由

ⓐ 空格前有先行詞 a Dallas banker（一名達拉斯銀行家），得知空格應置入可代替「人」的關係代名詞，以引導形容詞子句修飾先行詞 a Dallas banker。

ⓑ 選項中有 (C) who 及 (D) that 符合條件，但 that 前不可置逗點，故 (C) 項應為正選。

D **20.** 理由

ⓐ (A) **barely** [ˈbɛrlɪ] *adv.* 幾乎不；沒有
Hank can barely make ends meet every month.
漢克每個月的收支勉強打平。

(B) **namely** [ˈnemlɪ] *adv.* 換言之，即
The policy changes may lead to some problems, namely a recession and higher unemployment rates.
政策改變可能會造成一些問題，也就是不景氣以及失業率升高。

(C) **specifically** [spɪˈsɪfɪkəlɪ] *adv.* 特定地；明確地
Those seats are reserved specifically for the elderly and those in need.
那些座位是特別保留給年長者和需要的人使用。

(D) **practically** [ˈpræktɪkəlɪ] *adv.* 幾乎
Tom practically lost his mind when he found that his car had been stolen.
湯姆發現他的車子被偷時幾乎要瘋了。

ⓑ 根據語意，(D) 項應為正選。

重要字詞片語

1. **undoubtedly** [ʌnˋdaʊtɪdlɪ] *adv.*
   毫無疑問地
2. **vast** [væst] *a.* 廣大的，巨大的
3. **seemingly** [ˋsimɪŋlɪ] *adv.* 似乎
4. **local** [ˋlokl̩] *n.* 本地人，當地人 & *a.* 本地的，當地的
   One of the locals showed me the way to the gas station.
   有一位本地人告訴我去加油站的路。
5. **ever-present** [ˋɛvɚˋprɛzənt] *a.*
   無處不在的
6. **a totem pole** 圖騰柱
7. **majority** [məˋdʒɔrətɪ] *n.* 大部分
   The majority of residents on the island can only speak their own dialect.
   這島上大部分的居民只會說他們自己的方言。
8. **live up to...**
   符合……（期望、想法等）

三、文意選填（占 10 分）

第 21 至 30 題為題組

搭機旅客常有許多抱怨。不過，飛行中所供應的餐點無疑是他們一致抱怨的事項。有些網站上確實充斥著針對機上餐點品質的批評。許多航空公司做了很多研究來面對這些幾近全球性的抱怨，這些研究的結果既有助益也很有趣。

事實證明，當我們以平穩的速度航行於三萬英尺以上的平常高度時，傳達我們當下環境資訊的感覺會改變。然而，高度不是唯一因素。在一個加壓的飛機機艙內，溼度會大幅降低，使得我們的鼻道變得乾燥。由於我們不只是以口腔，也用鼻子來感受味道，我們的味覺必然受到影響。甜味與鹹味是在這種環境下最受影響的兩種味覺。因此，航空公司的廚師準備膳食時會添加更多甜味與鹹味，以彌補在高海拔用餐的體驗。苦、酸和辣的口味似乎並沒有受到太多影響。

出乎意料的是，研究人員還發現飛機引擎所發出一貫的噪音和我們在機上飲食的感覺有關聯。基本上，噪音會使我們在吃東西時分心。但戴著耳機收聽各種不同的音樂會減低我們正常味覺和嗅覺感官的損失。研究人員也正在思索料理、重新加熱食物的替代方式。基於安全考量，飛機上不允許使用天然瓦斯或是微波爐，因此送餐前，將食物放進塑膠袋裡慢慢加熱的新方法也被嘗試用來改善機上餐點的風味。希望飛機上的乘客很快就能嚐出在空中吃到的食物的不同之處。

D 21. 理由

ⓐ 本題測試以下固定用法：
in response to...　對……做出回應
Safety procedures were created in response to the accident.
意外發生後便建立了一套安全措施來作為防範。

ⓑ 根據上述，(D) 項應為正選。

199

TEST 07

H 22. 理由
ⓐ 空格前有所有格 our（我們的），空格後有名詞 environment（環境），得知空格應置形容詞，使其能修飾空格後的名詞。
ⓑ 選項中符合上述的有 (C) alternative（替代的）、(F) level（水平的）及 (H) immediate（當前的），惟根據語意，(H) 項應為正選。

F 23. 理由
ⓐ 空格前有定冠詞 the，空格後有介詞片語 of humidity（溼度的），得知空格應置名詞。
ⓑ 選項中符合上述的有 (C) alternative（替代方案）、(E) methods（方法）、(F) level（程度）、(G) ingredients（成分）、(I) connection（關聯）及 (J) sensations（感覺），惟根據語意，(F) 項應為正選。

A 24. 理由
ⓐ 空格前有此句主詞 we（我們），空格後有名詞 taste（味道）和介詞片語 with our nose（我們的鼻子），得知空格應置及物動詞，使其後的名詞、介詞片語能為該及物動詞的受詞。
ⓑ 選項中符合上述的有 (A) perceive（察覺）及 (B) reduce（降低），惟根據語意，(A) 項應為正選。

J 25. 理由
ⓐ 空格前有數量詞 two（兩個）、名詞 taste（味道），空格後有關係代名詞 that 引導的形容詞子句 that are impacted the most in this environment（在這種環境下最受影響的），得知空格應置複數可數名詞，使其能與 taste 形成名詞詞組，並能被其後的形容詞子句修飾。
ⓑ 選項中符合上述的有 (E) methods（方法）、(G) ingredients（成分）及 (J) sensations（感覺），惟根據語意，(J) 項應為正選。

G 26. 理由
ⓐ 空格前有形容詞詞組 sweet and salty（甜的與鹹的），得知空格應置複數可數名詞。
ⓑ 選項中為複數名詞的尚有 (E) methods（方法）及 (G) ingredients（成分），惟根據語意，(G) 項應為正選。

I 27. 理由
ⓐ 空格前有不定冠詞 a，空格後有介詞 between，得知空格應置以子音為首的單數可數名詞。
ⓑ 選項中符合上述的僅剩 (I) connection（關聯），置入後亦符合語意，故為正選。

B 28. 理由
ⓐ 空格前有助動詞 could，空格後有名詞詞組 the loss of our normal senses of taste and smell（正常味覺和嗅覺感官的損失）作受詞，得知空格應置原形及物動詞。
ⓑ 選項中為原形及物動詞的僅剩 (B) reduce（降低），置入後亦符合語意，故為正選。

C 29. 理由
ⓐ 空格前有現在進行式的片語動詞 are looking at（正在尋找），空格後有複數名詞 ways（方法），得知空格應置形容詞。
ⓑ 選項中為形容詞的僅剩 (C) alternative（替代的），置入後亦符合語意，故為正選。

E 30. 理由
ⓐ 空格前有形容詞 new（新的），空格後有介詞 of，得知空格應置名詞以被 new 修飾。
ⓑ 選項中為名詞的僅剩 (E) methods（方法），置入後亦符合語意，故為正選。

重要字詞片語

1. **grumble** [ˈgrʌmbl̩] vi. & vt. & n. 抱怨（常用複數）
   grumble about sth　抱怨某事
   Passengers often grumble about flight delays and lost luggage.
   乘客經常抱怨航班延誤和行李遺失。

2. **It goes without saying + that 子句**
   不用說……
   It goes without saying that you'll get nowhere without hard work.
   不認真努力你就不會成功，這是不用說的事實。

3. **unanimously** [juˈnænəməslɪ] adv. 全體一致地

4. **in-flight** [ˈɪnˈflaɪt] a. 飛行途中的

5. **universal** [ˌjunəˈvɝsl̩] a. 全世界的；普遍的

6. **conduct** [kənˈdʌkt] vt. 進行（調查、實驗等）

7. **It turns out + (that) 子句**
   結果／證明……
   It turns out Mother was right: Broccoli is good for me.
   結果媽媽是對的：青花菜對我有好處。

8. **alter** [ˈɔltɚ] vt. & vi. 改變

9. **cruise** [kruz] vi.（以穩定的速度）航行；巡邏

10. **altitude** [ˈæltəˌtud] n. 海拔高度
    at an altitude of...　在……的高度
    The airplane is now cruising at an altitude of 30,000 feet.
    這架飛機正在三萬英尺高空飛行。

11. **pressurized** [ˈprɛʃəˌraɪzd] a. 加壓的

12. **cabin** [ˈkæbɪn] n. 機艙，船艙；（在森林或山中搭建的）小木屋

13. **humidity** [hjuˈmɪdətɪ] n. 溼氣，溼度（不可數）

14. **nasal** [ˈnezl̩] a. 鼻子的
    nasal passages　鼻道

15. **impact** [ˈɪmpækt] vt. 對……產生影響

16. **make up for...**　補償／彌補……
    Michelle made up for her lack of talent with hard work.
    蜜雪兒以努力來彌補她天資的不足。

17. **perception** [pɚˈsɛpʃən] n. 感知，感覺（不可數）

18. **essentially** [ɪˈsɛnʃəlɪ] adv. 基本上；本質上

19. **distract** [dɪˈstrækt] vt. 使分心
    distract sb from sth
    使某人在某事上分心

TEST 07

TEST 07

四、篇章結構（占 8 分）

第 31 至 34 題為題組

　　你可能知道一些體操相關的事物。你可能甚至已經在學校的體育課練習過一些融合身體力量、特技和體操藝術的動作。<u>31. 但你可能不知道這項運動的起源可以追溯至古希臘。</u>

　　「體操（gymnastics）」一字源自於古希臘語，意思是「有紀律的運動」。早期的希臘人很重視身體健壯，所以在體育館（gymnasium，希臘語為 gymnazein）裡做劇烈運動一事備受鼓勵。他們確信，照顧身體健康對於改善心理和精神健康是必要的，而且身體健康有助於預防許多疾病。<u>32. 當羅馬人征服希臘後，他們將此運動正式化，並用訓練場所來為戰士打仗做準備。</u>然而當羅馬帝國走入歷史，體操亦漸趨沒落。這部分是因為當時一些基督徒認為強身健體不如靈性提升重要。

　　體操能再次活躍於現代，這點要歸功於另一個歐洲國家 —— 德國。<u>33. 十八世紀末，德國人弗里德里希・路德維希・楊恩發展出許多我們至今仍使用的器材。</u>他的發明包括平衡木、單槓和雙槓，這些都成了現代體操的標準器材。在 1880 年代移民美國熱潮之前，大家對體操的興趣便快速蔓延整個歐洲。而就在十九世紀結束前夕，男子體操成了第一屆現代奧運會的一部分。

　　體操至今仍是奧運會上受歡迎且不可或缺的項目。競技體操是由男女分開表演，包含在各式器材上進行為時短暫的表演動作。<u>34. 平衡木是女子競技賽事獨有的一項器材。</u>在這項女子比賽中，體操選手必須在一個有襯墊的彈簧柱上面進行一套跳躍和旋轉的動作來展現平衡與力量。鞍馬則是男子競技賽事特有的項目，體操選手須展示複雜的腿部動作。同時，韻律體操僅限女子選手參加。這項體操項目會用到如球、環、棍棒或彩帶等器具來一展柔軟度和音樂性。

C 31. 理由
- ⓐ 空格前提及一般大眾對體操的理解，以及實際上可能會接觸到的情況，空格後即為第二段的開頭，說明「體操」一字源自古希臘語，可推測空格應置與古希臘有關係的句子，使其能引導第二段。
- ⓑ 選項 (C) 表示，但你可能不知道這項運動的起源可以追溯至古希臘，選項中的 ancient Greece（古希臘）和第二段第一句的 ancient Greek（古希臘語）相呼應，填入後語意連貫，可知 (C) 項應為正選。

E 32. 理由
- ⓐ 空格前的句子提到，古希臘人對體操的重視，空格後的句子則提到體操亦隨著羅馬帝國沒落了，可推測空格應說明希臘與羅馬帝國之間的事情，及體操如何與兩國有關。
- ⓑ 選項 (E) 表示，當羅馬人征服希臘後，他們將此運動正式化，並用訓練場所來為戰士打仗做準備，選項中的 the Romans（羅馬人）與後一句的 the Roman Empire（羅馬帝國）相呼應，the sport（此運動）亦與前後文的 gymnastics（體操）形成關聯，填入後語意連貫，可知 (E) 項應為正選。

D 33. 理由

ⓐ 空格前的句子提到，德國使體操再度興盛，而空格後的句子提到，某人的發明成為現代體操的標準器材，可推測空格應提及與德國相關某人的資訊。

ⓑ 選項 (D) 表示，十八世紀末，德國人弗里德里希‧路德維希‧楊恩發展出許多我們至今仍使用的器材，選項中的 developed much of the equipment（發展出許多器材）和空格後的 his inventions（他的發明）相呼應，填入後語意連貫，可知 (D) 項應為正選。

B 34. 理由

ⓐ 空格前簡介現今體操在奧運會上的情形，而空格後的句子提到，在某項女子比賽中，體操選手必須如何進行的方式，可推測空格應提及該項女子比賽為何。

ⓑ 選項 (B) 表示，平衡木是女子競技賽事獨有的一項器材，選項中的 the women's artistic event（女子競技賽事）與空格後的 this women's competition（這項女子比賽）相呼應，填入後語意連貫，可知 (B) 項應為正選。

(A) 項中譯：正因如此，體操才在德國和希臘學校的體育課中如此普及。

TEST 07

重要字詞片語

1. **gymnastics** [dʒɪmˈnæstɪks] *n.* 體操（不可數）
   gymnast [ˈdʒɪmnæst] *n.* 體操選手
   artistic gymnastics　　競技體操
   rhythmic gymnastics　　韻律體操
2. **acrobatic** [ˌækrəˈbætɪk] *a.* 雜技的
3. **artistry** [ˈɑrtɪstrɪ] *n.* 藝術性（不可數）
4. **disciplinary** [ˈdɪsəplɪnˌɛrɪ] *a.* 紀律的
5. **physical fitness**　　身體強壯
6. **vigorous** [ˈvɪgərəs] *a.* 強而有力的
7. **ward** [wɔrd] *vt.* 避開 & *n.* 病房
   ward off...　　避開……
   Annie wore a scarf to ward off the cold wind.
   安妮圍上圍巾來抵禦寒風。
8. **conquer** [ˈkɑŋkɚ] *vt.* 征服
9. **formalize** [ˈfɔrmḷˌaɪz] *vt.* 正式化
10. **venue** [ˈvɛnju] *n.* 舉辦場所／地點
11. **partly** [ˈpɑrtlɪ] *adv.* 部分地
12. **credit** [ˈkrɛdɪt] *vt.* 將功勞歸因於……
13. **resurrect** [ˌrɛzəˈrɛkt] *vt.* 使再流行；使復甦
14. **era** [ˈɛrə] *n.* 年代，時代
15. **a balance beam**　　平衡木
16. **a horizontal bar**　　單槓
17. **parallel bars**　　雙槓
18. **integral** [ˈɪntəgrəl] *a.* 不可或缺的
19. **routine** [ruˈtin] *n.* 一套固定的動作／舞步
20. **padded** [ˈpædɪd] *a.* 裝有襯墊／護墊的
21. **pommel** [ˈpʌmḷ] *n.*（馬鞍的）鞍頭
    a pommel horse　　鞍馬
22. **showcase** [ˈʃoˌkes] *vt.* 展示，展現
23. **flexibility** [ˌflɛksəˈbɪlətɪ] *n.* 彈性，靈活性（不可數）
24. **musicality** [ˌmjuzɪˈkælətɪ] *n.* 音樂性（指對音樂的敏感性、知識或才能）（不可數）

TEST 07

五、閱讀測驗（占 24 分）

第 35 至 38 題為題組

　　吸菸的危害眾所周知。世界衛生組織估計，目前全世界大約有十三億人吸菸，他們當中每年大約有八百萬人因此喪命，比起瘧疾和愛滋病加起來的死亡人數還要高出六倍。由於菸草和吸菸有必然的關聯，減少菸草消耗量與吸菸者人數，每年就可以在醫療保健與生產損失方面省下數兆美元，更別說還有全世界無數的人命。

　　俄羅斯已加入大多數其他富裕國家的行列，正在採取步驟實現這個目標。2014 年，政府禁止大多數人買菸來源的路邊攤販售菸草產品。下一步則是禁止在學校和餐廳等公共場合吸菸，讓俄羅斯與許多其他國家同步。俄羅斯希望到 2025 年時可將吸菸率從 31% 降至 25%。最後但也很重要的一點，政府希望在 2033 年禁止所有年齡層的民眾以任何形式吸菸。

　　這些步驟將確認俄羅斯可以開始解決該國人口減少的問題。俄羅斯人口已從 1991 年的一億四千八百萬下降至如今的一億四千四百萬。由於每年有三十三萬名吸菸者喪命，人口減少很大一部分原因就是吸菸。目前俄羅斯的平均餘命只有七十三歲，而其他已開發國家則是七十九至八十二歲。

　　英國、日本以及美國的外商菸草公司想當然耳地反對這項新法案。這些公司占了俄羅斯大約 90% 的香菸銷售量，一年價值約一百九十億美元。當然，吸菸者也不意外地對新法規不滿，所以預期此新法很難落實。但是維護大眾健康的法律唯有在全體公民被要求遵守時才會奏效。

D 35. 本文的主旨是什麼？
(A) 世界各地不同的吸菸比率。
(B) 世界衛生組織對吸菸習慣所進行的研究。
(C) 俄羅斯傳染病帶來的挑戰。
(D) 某國試圖讓它的人民變得更健康。

> **理由**
> 本文第二到四段指出，俄羅斯造成大部分人口減少的主因是因為吸菸，並施行了幾項禁菸措施，最後一段的結論也說到維護大眾健康的法律只有在全體公民們遵守時才能奏效，可得知 (D) 項應為正選。

A 36. 關於俄羅斯政府處理該國菸草問題的做法，下列何者正確？
(A) 它逐步導入反菸作為。　　　　　(B) 它關閉了絕大部分的路邊攤。
(C) 它已經提高香菸價格以遏阻購買。(D) 它禁止販售外國香菸。

> **理由**
> 根據本文第二段，2014 年，俄羅斯政府禁止路邊攤販售菸草產品，下一步則是禁止在學校和餐廳等公共場合吸菸，他們希望到 2025 年時可將吸菸率從 31% 降至 25%，最後他們希望在 2033 年禁止所有年齡層的民眾以任何形式吸菸，故 (A) 項應為正選。

B 37. 根據本文，可以推論出關於俄羅斯人口的哪一點？
(A) 在菸草被列為非法之後，俄羅斯人口會更迅速地減少。
(B) 當吸菸的人口減少，俄羅斯人口會停止下降。
(C) 由於醫療設施改善，俄羅斯人口將急遽上升。
(D) 俄羅斯人口因為其他疾病仍繼續下降。

理由
根據本文第三段第一句，這些步驟將確認俄羅斯可以開始解決該國人口減少的問題，故 (B) 項應為正選。

D 38. 本文作者如何看待反菸草政策？
(A) 這些政策只有在全球都實施才會奏效。
(B) 這些政策將會增加而不是減少菸草消耗量。
(C) 這些政策會造成難以預料的問題。
(D) 如果民眾都必須遵守，這些政策才會成功。

理由
根據本文第四段最後一句，維護大眾健康的法律唯有在全體公民被要求遵守時才會奏效，故 (D) 項應為正選。

重要字詞片語

1. **cigarette** [ˌsɪgəˈrɛt] *n.* 香菸
2. **estimate** [ˈɛstəˌmet] *vt.* 估計 & [ˈɛstəmɪt] *n.* 估計
   It is estimated + that 子句
   據估計……
   It is estimated that 20,000 people will participate in the demonstration.
   估計將有兩萬人參與這次示威遊行。
3. **malaria** [məˈlɛrɪə] *n.* 瘧疾（不可數）
4. **tobacco** [təˈbæko] *n.* 菸草（不可數）
5. **consume** [kənˈs(j)um] *vt.* 攝取（食物）；消耗
   If you consume fast food on a daily basis, you will gain weight.
   如果每天吃速食，你就會發胖。
6. **step** [stɛp] *n.* 步驟；措施
   take steps to V
   採取步驟/措施（做）……
   The new manager decided to take steps to improve the company's efficiency.
   新上任的經理決定採取措施提高公司效率。
7. **ban** [bæn] *vt.* 禁止 & *n.* 禁令（三態為：ban, banned [bænd], banned）
   Having overstayed his visa, Tom was banned from re-entering Japan for two years.
   湯姆逾期居留，所以兩年內不得再入境日本。
8. **kiosk** [ˈkɪˌɑsk] *n.* 報攤，小亭商店
9. **keep... in line with...**
   使……與……一致
10. **last but not least**
    最後但也很重要的是
    We'll hear from the CEO and then, last but not least, the directors of our company.
    我們會聽取執行長的意見，最後也很重要的是，我們公司董事的意見。

11. **prohibit** [prəˋhɪbɪt] *vt.* 禁止
The law prohibits passengers from carrying sharp items on board an aircraft.
法令禁止乘客攜帶尖銳物品登機。

12. **ensure** [ɪnˋʃʊr] *vt.* 保證，確保
The company took many measures to ensure its product's success.
該公司採取了很多措施以確保其產品大賣。

13. **shrink** [ʃrɪŋk] *vt. & vi.* （使）減少（三態為：shrink, shrank [ʃræŋk], shrunk [ʃrʌŋk]）（本文為現在分詞作形容詞用）
The company had to shrink its staff from 30 to 20.
該公司必須將他們的員工從三十人縮減成二十人。

14. **population** [ˌpɑpjəˋleʃən] *n.* 全體人民；人口

15. **expectancy** [ɪkˋspɛktənsɪ] *n.* 預期（不可數）
life expectancy　平均／預期壽命

16. **legislation** [ˌlɛdʒəˋsleʃən] *n.* 法規；立法（不可數）

17. **enforce** [ɪnˋfɔrs] *vt.* 執行（法律）
There is no use having laws if nobody enforces them.
如果沒有人執法，法律又有何用。

18. **counter** [ˋkaʊntɚ] *vt. & vi.* 反對

19. **outlaw** [ˋaʊtˌlɔ] *vt.* 禁止；宣布……為非法

20. **consumption** [kənˋsʌmpʃən] *n.* 攝取量；消費（不可數）

第 39 至 42 題為題組

臺灣在日治時期（1895 年至 1945 年）使用的貨幣為臺灣銀行券。二戰結束後，大日本帝國戰敗，臺灣由中華民國統治。臺幣在一年後發行，並成為臺灣的貨幣。不過由於受到國共內戰的影響，臺灣和中國皆經歷惡性通膨，物價急遽上漲。為了對抗這個問題，政府必須發行面額越來越大的鈔票，最高曾發行面額一百萬元的紙鈔。終於，在 1949 年六月十五日，新臺幣取代了臺幣，兌換率為新臺幣一元抵舊臺幣四萬元。因此原來的臺幣常被稱為舊臺幣，以與現在的新臺幣有所區別。

不是只有臺灣以更換貨幣的方式來解決惡性通膨的問題。事實上，臺灣的狀況跟匈牙利相比，根本是小巫見大巫。二次大戰重創這個中歐國家的交通網絡和工業產能，使得該國經歷史上最慘的惡性通膨。為了刺激經濟，該國政府大量印製鈔票發給銀行、公司和消費者。不可思議的是，物價每十五小時就漲一倍！但事實上該政策證明是成功的，到了 1946 年八月（戰後一年），工業產能已恢復，政府也能以新的匈牙利貨幣福林來取代帕戈。

近期惡性通膨的例子則是委內瑞拉。此南美洲國家的社會主義政府對於經濟的管理失能，造成該國四分之三人口生活極度貧困的局面，在 2021 年，一條麵包要價七百萬玻利瓦。雖然玻利瓦尚未被全新貨幣取代，但自 2008 年以來，玻利瓦鈔票的面額已被陸陸續續減掉十四個零。許多專家預測減零的做法不會有什麼效用，經濟學家荷西・馬努・普恩迪說：「被拿掉的零……很快就會漲回來。」

B 39. 本文主旨為何？
　　(A) 歐洲與亞洲的知名貨幣。　　　　(B) 惡性通膨的不同經驗。
　　(C) 臺灣過去幾世紀以來的貨幣。　　(D) 通貨膨脹的相關術語。

> 理由
> 全文三段分別提及臺灣、匈牙利和委內瑞拉經歷惡性通膨的狀況，故 (B) 項應為正選。

C 40. 關於臺灣和匈牙利的惡性通膨，下列何者為非？
　　(A) 它們都因為戰爭而經歷惡性通膨。　　(B) 它們都透過更換貨幣來解決惡性通膨。
　　(C) 它們經歷惡性通膨的嚴重程度相當。　　(D) 它們大約在同一個時期經歷惡性通膨。

> 理由
> 根據本文第二段第二句，臺灣的狀況跟匈牙利相比，根本是小巫見大巫，故 (C) 項應為正選。

B 41. 本文第二段中的 doling it out 指的是什麼？
　　(A) 創造工作。　　(B) 發行錢幣。　　(C) 提供食物。　　(D) 降低價格。

> 理由
> 題目片語 dole sth out 有「分發某物」之意，亦可根據本文第二段第四句提及 printed reams and reams of money（大量印製錢幣）來推測題目片語中的 it 代指 reams and reams of money，故 (B) 項應為正選。

A 42. 根據本文，委內瑞拉未來很有可能發生什麼事？
　　(A) 惡性通膨會持續惡化。　　(B) 經濟狀況將會改善。
　　(C) 貧困程度將開始下降。　　(D) 麵包的價格將慢慢穩定。

> 理由
> 根據本文第三段最後一句，許多專家預測減零的做法不會有什麼效用，經濟學家荷西·馬努·普恩迪說：「被拿掉的零……很快就會漲回來。」故 (A) 項應為正選。

重要字詞片語

1. **occupation** [ˌɑkjəˈpeʃən] n. 占領（不可數）；職業（可數）
2. **currency** [ˈkɝənsɪ] n. 貨幣
3. **empire** [ˈɛmpaɪr] n. 帝國
4. **defeat** [dɪˈfit] vt. 擊敗 & n. 失敗
5. **republic** [rɪˈpʌblɪk] n. 共和國
6. **civil** [ˈsɪvl̩] a. 國內的；公民的
　a civil war　　內戰
7. **hyperinflation** [ˌhaɪpɚɪnˈfleʃən] n. 惡性通貨膨脹（不可數）

　inflation [ɪnˈfleʃən] n. 通貨膨脹，物價上漲（不可數）
　deflation [dɪˈfleʃən] n. 通貨緊縮，物價下跌（不可數）

8. **combat** [kəmˈbæt] vt. 制止；打擊
　combat inflation / crime
　對抗通貨膨脹／打擊犯罪
9. **issue** [ˈɪʃu] vt. 發行
10. **banknote** [ˈbæŋknot] n. 鈔票（= note）
11. **denomination** [dɪˌnɑməˈneʃən] n. （貨幣的）面額

207

TEST 07

12. **distinguish** [dɪˈstɪŋgwɪʃ] *vt.* 分辨，區別
    distinguish A from B
    區別 A 與 B 的不同
    Hailey couldn't distinguish a mule from a donkey.
    海莉分辨不出騾子和驢子的不同。

13. **incarnation** [ˌɪnkɑrˈneʃən] *n.* 化身

14. **pale** [pel] *vi.* 變得遜色；變得蒼白 & *a.* 蒼白的
    pale in comparison (to...)
    （與……相比）相形見絀，顯得遜色
    Emily thinks this movie pales in comparison to the one she watched yesterday.
    艾蜜莉覺得這部電影跟昨天她看的比起來遜色多了。

15. **decimate** [ˈdɛsəˌmet] *vt.* 重挫，大幅毀壞
    The country's tourism industry has been decimated by COVID-19.
    新冠肺炎重挫該國的觀光產業。

16. **stimulate** [ˈstɪmjəˌlet] *vt.* 刺激，促進
    The Congress is considering tax cuts in order to stimulate investment.
    國會正在考慮減稅方案以促進投資。

17. **ream** [rim] *n.* 大量（常用複數）
    reams of... 大量的……

18. **dole** [dol] *vt.* 發放
    dole sth out / dole out sth
    分發某物（如錢、食物、建議等）
    I'm sure Brian is willing to dole out advice on saving money.
    我確信布萊恩很樂意給予關於省錢的建議。

19. **colossal** [kəˈlɑsḷ] *a.* 巨大的，龐大的

20. **socialist** [ˈsoʃəlɪst] *a.* 支持社會主義的 & *n.* 社會主義者

21. **poverty** [ˈpɑvɚtɪ] *n.* 貧窮（不可數）

22. **as of + 時間點**
    截至……；自……開始
    Judy has saved NT$100,000 as of the end of January.
    茱蒂至一月底為止已存了新臺幣十萬元。
    As of next month, there will be tax increases on a wide range of goods.
    從下個月開始，許多種貨物的貨物稅將會增加。

23. **predict** [prɪˈdɪkt] *vt.* 預測

24. **terminology** [ˌtɝməˈnɑlədʒɪ] *n.* 術語

25. **severity** [səˈvɛrətɪ] *n.* 嚴重（不可數）

26. **endure** [ɪnˈd(j)ʊr] *vt.* 忍受，忍耐

第 43 至 46 題為題組

　　射水魚棲息於澳洲北部與南亞的淡水河流和紅樹林鹹水河流中。牠們體長為十二至四十公分，體型幾乎呈扁平狀。這使得牠們在接近獵物 —— 通常包含蒼蠅、蟋蟀這類在水面上生活的昆蟲 —— 時難以被察覺。不過牠們用來真正捕捉到獵物的方法，才是最神奇的。

　　射水魚的身體沉在水中，將嘴巴伸出水面，用舌頭頂住口腔上部，形成一個管道，然後從管道中噴射出最高可達三公尺的水柱。這條被完美控制的水柱其末速大於初速，意味當水柱快接近目標物時會擠成一坨水球。這顆水球便會將目標昆蟲擊落河中，被等待著的射水魚吞食。因此射水魚被比擬成水槍是毫不意外的。

　　射水魚捕食技巧的另一個層面也同樣卓越。射水魚必須學習如何調整牠們的準星，以彌補光線折射的誤差。也就是說，牠們得知道當光線從一種介質（如水）進入另一種介質（如空氣）時

會改變方向。射水魚會觀察年長的同類如何改變位置並調整噴射角度以成功擊中目標。研究證實射水魚偏好的位置並非是折射問題較小的獵物正下方，而是在斜前方或斜後方。

近期一篇發表在《動物行為》期刊並被《國家地理》雜誌報導的研究，披露了更多有關射水魚的有趣資訊。科學家用食物來訓練射水魚辨別不同人臉的 3D 立體圖像。即使臉部圖像被轉動，射水魚仍能把水噴至正確的圖像。這又再一次證明射水魚所擁有的非凡技巧。

D　43. 關於射水魚，下列敘述何者正確？
(A) 牠們只出現在鹹水中。
(B) 牠們有可以伸長達三公尺的舌頭。
(C) 牠們游泳的速度快過水槍中射出來的水。
(D) 牠們不容易被獵物察覺。

理由
根據本文第一段第三句，這使得牠們在接近獵物時難以被察覺，故 (D) 項應為正選。

C　44. 第二段中的 it 所指的對象最有可能是什麼？
(A) 射水魚自己。
(B) 射水魚的嘴巴。
(C) 射水魚噴出來的水。
(D) 射水魚捕捉到的獵物。

理由
根據本文第二段第三句主要子句的主詞為 This perfectly controlled jet（這條被完美控制的水柱），即為其後代名詞 it 所指的對象，故 (C) 項應為正選。

C　45. 哪一張圖片正確顯示射水魚尋找獵物時最偏好的位置？
(A) (B) (C) (D)

理由
根據本文第二段第一句，射水魚的身體沉在水中，將嘴巴伸出水面，以及第三段最後一句，射水魚偏好的位置並非是折射問題較小的獵物正下方，而是在斜前方或斜後方，得知 (C) 項應為正選。

B 46. 關於射水魚，最後一段暗示了什麼？
(A) 牠們的食物內容開始改變。
(B) 牠們能辨認出人臉。
(C) 牠們噴水的技巧變糟。
(D) 牠們無法在實驗室中被訓練。

> **理由**
> 根據本文第四段倒數第二句，即使臉部圖像被轉動，射水魚仍能把水噴至正確的圖像，可推測 (B) 項應為正選。

重要字詞片語

1. **freshwater** [ˈfrɛʃˌwɔtɚ] *a.* 淡水的
2. **mangrove** [ˈmæŋɡrov] *n.* 紅樹林
3. **flat** [flæt] *a.* 扁平的，平坦的
4. **approach** [əˈprotʃ] *vt. & vi.* 接近
   The dogcatchers approached the dangerous dog with caution.
   捕犬員小心翼翼地接近那隻危險的狗。
5. **prey** [pre] *n.* 獵物（集合名詞，不可數）
6. **consist of...** 包含……；由……組成
   A company's assets consist of buildings, equipment, cash, and specialist knowledge.
   一家公司的資產包含建築物、設備、現金和專業知識。
7. **submerged** [səbˈmɝdʒd] *a.* 在水中的；被水淹沒的
8. **poke** [pok] *vt. & vi.* （使）伸出來；戳
9. **jet** [dʒɛt] *n.* （從管口噴射出的）水/氣流
10. **blob** [blɑb] *n.* 一團/滴/點
11. **spit** [spɪt] *n.* （吐出的）口水（不可數）& *vt. & vi.* 吐出
12. **devour** [dɪˈvaʊr] *vt.* （尤指狼吞虎嚥地）吞食
    Feeling hungry, the boy devoured a whole pizza.
    小男孩肚子餓了，狼吞虎嚥地吃了整個披薩。
13. **pistol** [ˈpɪstl̩] *n.* 手槍
    a water pistol　　玩具水槍
14. **adjust** [əˈdʒʌst] *vt.* 調整，調節
15. **compensate** [ˈkɑmpənˌset] *vi.* 彌補
    compensate for...　　彌補……
    = make up for...
    Mark tried to work harder to compensate for the mistakes he had made.
    馬克嘗試更努力來彌補他之前犯下的錯。
16. **refraction** [rɪˈfrækʃən] *n.* 折射（不可數）
17. **medium** [ˈmidɪəm] *n.* 媒介（複數為 mediums 或 media）
18. **alter** [ˈɔltɚ] *vt. & vi.* 改變
    The internet has altered the way we seek information.
    網路已改變了我們尋找資訊的方式。
19. **reveal** [rɪˈvil] *vt.* 揭露
20. **distinguish** [dɪˈstɪŋɡwɪʃ] *vi. & vt.* 分辨，區別
21. **three-dimensional** [ˈθrɪdəˈmɛnʃənəl] *a.* 立體的
22. **extraordinary** [ɪkˈstrɔrdn̩ˌɛrɪ] *a.* 非凡的
23. **possess** [pəˈzɛs] *vt.* 擁有，持有
    The rich woman possesses a mansion and three sports cars.
    這名有錢女子擁有一棟豪宅和三輛跑車。

第貳部分、混合題（占 10 分）

第 47 至 51 題為題組

　　日本曾三度被選為夏季奧運會的主辦國。1936 年，國際奧委會宣布東京將主辦 1940 年夏季奧運，成為第一個獲此殊榮的非西方城市。準備工作隨即展開，包括規劃新建體育場和奧運村。然而日本在 1937 年大舉侵華，爆發第二次中日戰爭。–[1]– 在對外侵略遭到抨擊以及國內軍事支出增加的情況下，日本政府聲稱無法主辦奧運會。隨後國際奧委會將主辦權轉交給芬蘭的赫爾辛基，但最終因第二次世界大戰爆發而取消。–[2]–

　　不過國際衝突並未阻礙日本取得 1964 年夏季奧運的主辦權。此時日本已經以現代化、和平及工業化國家的形象重新登上國際舞臺，而奧運會則是此事實的體現。為避開溼熱的夏季，賽事到秋季方才展開。在籌備過程中，主辦城市東京脫胎換骨。–[3]– 地主國日本在熱情觀眾的加油聲中奪得 29 面獎牌，當時創下該國在奧運史上的最佳成績。這也是奧運首次透過衛星向全球直播，因此全世界共同見證了此種盛況。

　　半個多世紀後，東京再次主辦奧運會，而日本隊的獎牌數更是翻倍。–[4]– 然而 2020 年東京奧運的記憶點，與其說是運動員表現，倒不如說是當時的氛圍。原訂 2020 年 7 月舉行的奧運會因新冠肺炎疫情被延到 2021 年 7 月。然而當賽會真的開始後，大多以閉門方式進行比賽，生怕病毒像野火般傳播。體育場內沒了觀眾，不免影響比賽的氣氛，對選手的表現也有潛在的衝擊。話雖如此，此屆奧運仍見證了日本以及全球體育界在面對極度艱困的情況下所展現的韌性。

47. 本文中哪個片語表示「不允許民眾進入會場觀看」？
閉門比賽

behind closed doors

理由
根據本文第三段倒數第二句提及 The lack of spectators in the stadiums...（體育場內沒了觀眾……）解釋了前句 ...most events were held behind closed doors...（……大多以閉門方式進行比賽……），故得知空格應置 behind closed doors。

48-50.

年份	事件
1936	• 國際奧委會宣布東京將在四年後主辦奧運會。
1937	• 日本 **48.** 侵略 invaded 中國，引發第二次中日戰爭。
1940	• 第二次世界大戰導致奧運會被 **49.** 取消 cancelation。
1964	• 奧運會象徵日本重返國際舞臺。
2020	• 新冠肺炎疫情導致該年奧運會 **50.** 延期 postponement。
2021	• 2020 年東京奧運展現了日本能夠應對這種具挑戰性的情況。

TEST 07

> 理由

第 48 題空格前為名詞 Japan（日本），空格後也是名詞 China（中國），且為 1937 年所發生的事，得知空格應置過去式動詞。根據本文第一段倒數第三句提及 …in 1937, Japan launched a full-scale invasion of China, …（……日本在 1937 年大舉侵華，……）得知，空格應置入 invasion 的過去式動詞 invaded。

第 49 題空格前為定冠詞 the，空格後為介詞 of，得知空格應置名詞。根據本文第一段最後一句提及 …these were ultimately canceled due to the outbreak of World War II.（……最終因第二次世界大戰爆發而取消。）得知，空格應置入 canceled 的名詞 cancelation。

第 50 題空格前為定冠詞 the，空格後為介詞 of，得知空格應置名詞。根據本文第三段第三句 …in July 2020, the Games were postponed until July 2021 due to the COVID-19 pandemic.（……原訂 2020 年 7 月舉行的奧運會因新冠肺炎疫情被延到 2021 年 7 月。）得知，空格應置 postponed 的名詞 postponement。

C 51. 在標記 [1]、[2]、[3]、[4] 的四個位置當中，哪一項為下列句子的最佳位置？
「公路拓寬、新地鐵路線完工、連接東京和大阪的新幹線通車。」
(A) [1]　　　　(B) [2]　　　　(C) [3]　　　　(D) [4]

> 理由

根據本文第二段第三句提及 …the host city of Tokyo was transformed.（……主辦城市東京脫胎換骨。）得知，與本題句提到的 Highways were widened（公路拓寬）、new subway lines were completed（新地鐵路線完工）及 the bullet train between Tokyo and Osaka began operation（連接東京和大阪的新幹線通車）產生關聯，故 (C) 項應為正選。

> 重要字詞片語

1. **underway** [ˌʌndɚˈwe] *a.* & *adv.* 在進行中的（不用於修飾名詞）
2. **invasion** [ɪnˈveʒən] *n.* 入侵
3. **Sino-** [ˈsaɪno] *prefix* 中國的；與中國有關的
4. **amid** [əˈmɪd] *prep.* 在其中
5. **criticism** [ˈkrɪtəˌsɪzəm] *n.* 批評，爭議；評論（不可數）
6. **aggression** [əˈɡrɛʃən] *n.* 侵略，攻擊（不可數）
7. **expenditure** [ɪkˈspɛndətʃɚ] *n.* （政府或個人的）開支，開銷
8. **proceed** [prəˈsid] *vi.* 繼續；前進
   After the break, we will proceed to the next topic.
   休息後，我們將繼續進入下一個議題。
9. **ultimately** [ˈʌltəmɪtlɪ] *adv.* 最終；終究
10. **outbreak** [ˈaʊtˌbrek] *n.* 爆發
11. **get in the way** 妨礙；阻止；擋路
    I don't want my personal issues to get in the way of our work.
    我不希望我的私人問題妨礙到我們的工作。

12. **emerge** [ɪˋmɝdʒ] *vi.* 出現，冒出
 The sun began to emerge from behind the clouds.
 太陽開始從雲層後面露出來。

13. **industrialized** [ɪnˋdʌstrɪəlˌaɪzd] *a.* 工業化的
 industrialized nations / countries
 工業化國家

14. **symbolize** [ˋsɪmblˌaɪz] *vt.* 象徵，代表
 The dove is often used to symbolize peace.
 鴿子常常被用來象徵和平。

15. **muggy** [ˋmʌgɪ] *a.* 悶熱而潮溼的

16. **transform** [trænsˋfɔrm] *vt.* 變化，改變
 A good book can transform your thinking.
 一本好書能改變你的思維。

17. **enthusiastic** [ɪnˌθjuzɪˋæstɪk] *a.* 熱情的；熱心的

18. **witness** [ˋwɪtnəs] *vt.* 目擊；證明 & *n.* 證人
 Sandra witnessed the accident on her way to work.
 珊卓在上班途中目擊了那起事故。

19. **televise** [ˋtɛləˌvaɪz] *vt.* 電視轉播
 The football match was televised for the first time last year.
 去年這場足球比賽首次被轉播。

20. **satellite** [ˋsætlˌaɪt] *n.* 衛星

21. **tally** [ˋtælɪ] *n.* 計數；記錄

22. **circumstance** [ˋsɝkəmˌstæns] *n.* 情況，環境（常用複數）

23. **commence** [kəˋmɛns] *vi. & vt.* 開始
 The new semester will commence next Monday.
 新學期將於下週一開始。

24. **virus** [ˋvaɪrəs] *n.* 病毒

25. **spectator** [ˋspɛkˌtetɚ] *n.* （比賽、活動等的）觀眾

26. **inevitably** [ɪnˋɛvətəblɪ] *adv.* 不可避免地

27. **community** [kəˋmjunətɪ] *n.* 界；社區

28. **resilient** [rɪˋzɪlɪənt] *a.* 有復原力的；適應性強的；有彈性的

29. **exceptionally** [ɪkˋsɛpʃənlɪ] *adv.* 異常地

30. **prompt** [prɑmpt] *vt.* 促使 & *a.* 立刻的
 The teacher's question prompted a lively discussion among the students.
 老師的問題促使學生們進行了熱烈的討論。

31. **cope with...** 處理……
 Vicky had to cope with a lot of stress at work, but she managed it well.
 維琪必須應對工作中的大量壓力，但她應付得很好。

TEST 07

TEST 07

第參部分、非選擇題（占 28 分）

一、中譯英（占 8 分）

1. 按摩是一種減緩壓力、疼痛與肌肉緊繃的有效療法。

   示範譯句
   Massage is an effective treatment for reducing pressure, pain, and muscle tightness.

   或：Getting a massage has been proven to be effective in alleviating stress, soreness, and tight muscles.

   翻譯要點
   a. **massage** [mə'sɑʒ] *n.* & *vt.* 按摩
   b. **effective** [ɪ'fɛktɪv] *a.* 有效的
   c. **treatment** ['tritmənt] *n.* 治療，療法
   d. **reduce** [rɪ'djus] *vt.* 減少
      A low-sodium and low-fat diet can reduce the risk of high blood pressure.
      低鈉與低脂的飲食可以減少高血壓的風險。
   e. **tightness** ['taɪtnəs] *n.* 緊繃；緊密（不可數）
   f. **alleviate** [ə'livɪ,et] *vt.* 減輕，緩和
      This medicine will alleviate your flu symptoms.
      這種藥會減輕你的流感症狀。
   g. **soreness** ['sɔr,nəs] *n.* 疼痛（不可數）

2. 近年來，車站、醫院，甚至機場都有提供按摩的服務。

   示範譯句
   In recent years, massage services have become available in railroad stations, hospitals, and even airports.

   或：Over the past few years, massage parlors have been springing up in railway stations, hospitals, and even airports.

   翻譯要點
   a. 「近年來」可譯為 In recent years 或 Over the past few years。

      說明
      in recent years（近年來）和 over the past few years（過去幾年來）為時間副詞片語，在句中出現時，動詞時態多採現在完成式或現在完成進行式。表示到現在為止仍在繼續的動作或狀態時，使用現在完成式來表達；表示一直持續到現在且可能仍將繼續下去的動作，則使用現在完成進行式來表達。類似用法尚有：in recent months / over the past few months（近幾個月來）、in recent decades / over the past few decades（近數十年來）等。

   b. **available** [ə'veləbl] *a.* 可得到的，可用的
   c. **parlor** ['pɑrlɚ] *n.* 店（面）
   d. **spring up**　如雨後春筍般出現
      Lots of shops have sprung up all over the town.
      這小鎮有許多商店如雨後春筍般崛起。
   e. **railway** ['rel,we] *n.* 鐵路（英式用法）
   = railroad（美式用法）

二、英文作文（占 20 分）

提示：下圖顯示某個國家資源回收成果的狀況。請依據圖表內容寫一篇英文作文，文長至少 120 個單詞。文分二段，第一段描述圖表內容，指出該國垃圾回收的情形如何，第二段則說明你自家垃圾回收分類的比例與圖表上的異同，並解釋背後可能的原因。

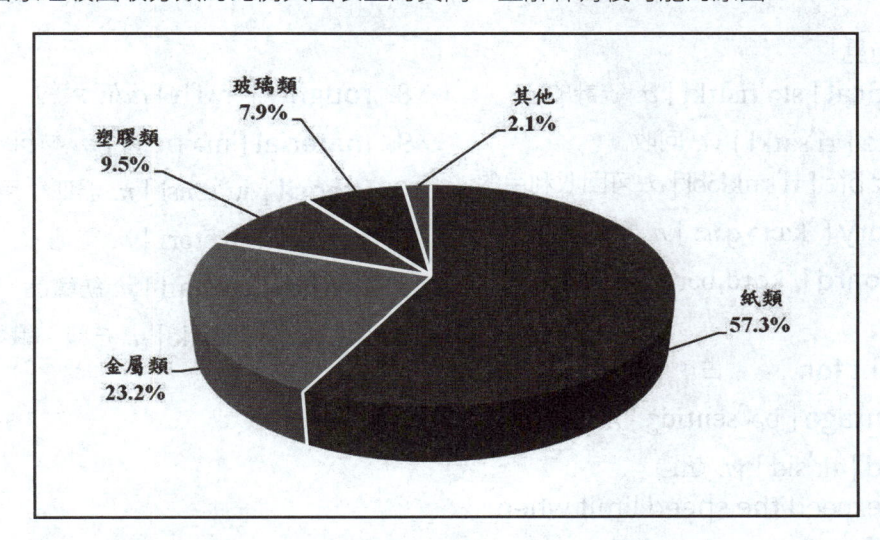

玻璃類 7.9%　其他 2.1%
塑膠類 9.5%
紙類 57.3%
金屬類 23.2%

示範作文

　　The pie chart shows the statistical results of what is recycled in a particular country. Among the five categories, paper and cardboard account for the highest percentage (57.3%), the only category to exceed 50%. The other four types are as follows: metal, plastic, glass, and others, all of which are far below 50%. Metal, making up 23.2%, is more than two times the percentage of plastic (9.5%), while it's roughly three times higher than glass products (7.9%). The lowest percentage in the pie chart goes to all other waste, which makes up about 2%.

　　There are similarities and differences between the pie chart and my family's recycling habits. Unlike the pie chart, my family produces more recyclable plastic material than any other type. This is because we use a lot of plastic utensils, bottles, and bags. Another difference is that my family recycles food waste, batteries, textiles, and fabrics, which would fall into the "others" category on the chart. Due to our eating habits, my family also recycles many paper products, followed by some glass and a little metal. We do recycle quite a lot overall, but I know that we could always do more.

　　這個圓餅圖顯示了某特定國家內回收物的統計數據。在這五個類別中，紙和紙板占最高比例（57.3%），是唯一一項超過 50% 的類別。其他四種類型如下：金屬、塑膠、玻璃和其他，這些全都遠低於 50%。金屬占 23.2%，是塑膠百分比（9.5%）的兩倍以上，而比玻璃產品（7.9%）高出約三倍以上。在圓餅圖中，百分比最低的是其他垃圾，約占 2%。

TEST 07

　　此圓餅圖與我家的回收習慣有一些異同之處。與這個圓餅圖不同的是，我家的可回收塑膠材料比其他任何類型都要多。這是因為我們使用很多塑膠器皿、塑膠瓶和塑膠袋。另一個不同之處是，我家會回收廚餘、電池、紡織品和布料，這些都被歸在圖表中的「其他」類別。由於我們家的飲食習慣，我家也回收了許多紙製品，緊接著是一些玻璃和少量金屬。總體而言，我們回收了不少東西，但我知道我們還是可以做得更多。

重要字詞片語

1. **statistical** [stəˈtɪstɪkḷ] *a.* 統計的
2. **recycle** [riˈsaɪkḷ] *vt.* 回收
   recyclable [riˈsaɪkləbḷ] *a.* 可回收利用的
3. **category** [ˈkætəˌɡɔrɪ] *n.* 類別，項目
4. **cardboard** [ˈkɑrdˌbɔrd] *n.* 硬紙板（不可數）
5. **account for...** 占……比例
6. **percentage** [pɚˈsɛntɪdʒ] *n.* 百分比
7. **exceed** [ɪkˈsid] *vt.* 超過
   Don't exceed the speed limit when driving.
   開車時千萬不要超速。
8. **roughly** [ˈrʌflɪ] *adv.* 大約
9. **material** [məˈtɪrɪəl] *n.* 材料，原料
10. **utensil** [juˈtɛnsḷ] *n.* 器皿；用具
11. **battery** [ˈbætərɪ] *n.* 電池
12. **textile** [ˈtɛkstaɪl] *n.* 紡織品
13. **fabric** [ˈfæbrɪk] *n.* 布料，織物

TEST 08

🌱 第壹部分、選擇題

一、詞彙題
二、綜合測驗
三、文意選填
四、篇章結構
五、閱讀測驗

🌱 第貳部分、混合題

🌱 第參部分、非選擇題

一、中譯英
二、英文作文

第壹部分、選擇題

一、詞彙題

| 1. D | 2. C | 3. D | 4. B | 5. B | 6. A | 7. B | 8. C | 9. A | 10. C |

二、綜合測驗

| 11. A | 12. D | 13. C | 14. B | 15. B | 16. C | 17. D | 18. C | 19. B | 20. A |

三、文意選填

| 21. J | 22. G | 23. D | 24. H | 25. A | 26. I | 27. B | 28. E | 29. F | 30. C |

四、篇章結構

| 31. B | 32. E | 33. A | 34. C |

五、閱讀測驗

| 35. D | 36. C | 37. B | 38. C | 39. C | 40. B | 41. B | 42. A | 43. B | 44. C |
| 45. C | 46. D |

第貳部分、混合題

47. turbines

48. finite

49. C, D

50. A

第壹部分、選擇題（占 62 分）

一、詞彙題（占 10 分）

<u>D</u> 1. 塔米的<u>路程</u>比平時更久，因為正值數千人從臺北大巨蛋的演唱會離場的時間。

    ❶ (A) **district** [ˋdɪstrɪkt] *n.* （行政）區
        Which district of the city do you live in?
        你住在這座城市的哪一區？

      (B) **council** [ˋkaʊnsḷ] *n.* 議會
        Rita sent an email to the council to complain about air pollution.
        麗塔寄了封電子郵件給議會，抱怨空氣汙染一事。

      (C) **budget** [ˋbʌdʒɪt] *n.* 預算
        We have to carry out the project on a tight budget.
        我們必須在有限的預算下完成案子。

      (D) **journey** [ˋdʒɝnɪ] *n.* 行程；旅行
        The journey will take approximately three and a half hours.
        這趟行程大約要花三個半小時。

    ❷ 根據語意及用法，(D) 項應為正選。

必考重點

dome [dom] *n.* 圓屋頂
Taipei Dome　　臺北大巨蛋

<u>C</u> 2. 這家新建的飯店位於<u>黃金地段</u>，靠近城裡最好的商店、酒吧和餐廳。

    ❶ (A) **guilty** [ˋgɪltɪ] *a.* 有罪的
        be guilty of...　　有……的罪
        The evidence shows that Peter is guilty of robbing the bank.
        證據顯示彼得搶劫銀行有罪。

      (B) **fragile** [ˋfrædʒəl] *a.* 脆弱的
        Please handle these glasses with care. They're fragile.
        請小心處理這些玻璃。它們很易碎。

      (C) **prime** [praɪm] *a.* 最好的；主要的
        The gallery features prime examples of modern art.
        這間畫廊展出了現代藝術的最佳範例。

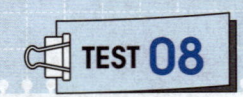

(D) **peculiar** [pɪˋkjuljɚ] *a.* 奇怪的；獨特的
Don't you think that Kelly is a little bit peculiar today?
你不覺得凱莉今天有點兒怪怪的嗎？

ⓑ 根據語意及用法，(C) 項應為正選。

必考重點

newly [ˋnjulɪ] *adv.* 新近；最近

D 3. 史帝夫・賈伯斯在電腦業界的成功激勵了世界上許多年輕學生去追求自己的夢想。

ⓐ (A) **entertain** [ˌɛntɚˋten] *vt.* 娛樂
entertain sb with sth　　用某物娛樂某人
Martha entertained all the kids with interesting stories.
瑪莎用有趣的故事把全部的小朋友都逗得很開心。

(B) **endanger** [ɪnˋdendʒɚ] *vt.* 危及，使遭到危險
Excessive drinking can endanger your health.
飲酒過量可能會危害你的健康。

(C) **witness** [ˋwɪtnɪs] *vt.* 目擊 & *n.* 目擊者
Chris witnessed two men running away from the scene of the crime.
克里斯目擊兩名男子逃離案發現場。
With the cooperation of the witness, we can solve this crime quickly.
有了目擊者的合作，我們很快就可以破案。

(D) **inspire** [ɪnˋspaɪr] *vt.* 鼓舞，激勵
inspire sb to V　　鼓舞某人做……
Adam's father inspired him to become a writer.
亞當的父親激勵他成為一名作家。

ⓑ 根據語意及用法，(D) 項應為正選。

必考重點

pursue [pɚˋsu] *vt.* 追求
We should do our best to pursue our goals.
我們應該盡力去追求我們的目標。

B 4. 我無法在兩小時內寫完考試的所有問題，真的覺得很沮喪。

ⓐ (A) **touched** [tʌtʃt] *a.* 受到感動的
= moved [muvd] *a.*
Everyone was touched by Joe's affectionate speech.
每個人都被喬真情流露的演講所感動。

220

(B) **frustrated** [ˈfrʌstretɪd] *a.* 沮喪的，挫敗的
be frustrated with... 因……而感到挫折／沮喪
All of us were frustrated with the outcome of the meeting.
我們所有人都對會議的結果感到很沮喪。

(C) **advanced** [ədˈvænst] *a.* 先進的
This digital camera is the most advanced model on the market.
這臺數位相機是市面上最先進的機種。

(D) **delighted** [dɪˈlaɪtɪd] *a.* 高興的，快樂的
be delighted with... 對……感到高興
The teacher was delighted with the surprise birthday party her students planned for her.
那位老師因為學生為她所安排的驚喜生日派對而感到很開心。

ⓑ 根據語意，(B) 項應為正選。

B 5. 不幸的是，我妹妹第一次開家裡的車出去時，就撞到圍欄並損壞了車子。

ⓐ (A) **accordingly** [əˈkɔrdɪŋlɪ] *adv.* 因此（= therefore）
John didn't study hard. Accordingly, he failed the test.
約翰不用功，因此他考試不及格。

(B) **unfortunately** [ʌnˈfɔrtʃənɪtlɪ] *adv.* 不幸地
Unfortunately, we have not accomplished our goal this year.
很不幸地，我們今年沒有達到目標。

(C) **undoubtedly** [ʌnˈdaʊtɪdlɪ] *adv.* 無疑地
= no doubt / without (a) doubt
This is undoubtedly the best sashimi that I have ever tasted.
這無疑是我嚐過最好吃的生魚片了。

(D) **genetically** [dʒəˈnɛtɪkəlɪ] *adv.* 基因上地
Most of the articles of the current issue of this magazine deal with genetically modified foods.
本雜誌最新一期的大多數文章在討論基因改造食品。

ⓑ 根據語意，(B) 項應為正選。

必考重點

crash [kræʃ] *vi.* 碰撞
crash into... 撞上……

TEST 08

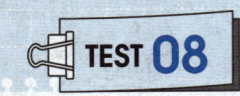

__A__ 6. 溫蒂一家人因為颱風的關係而必須離開山中的家。

  ⓐ (A) **abandon** [ə`bændən] *vt.* 離開；遺棄
     If the river floods, we'll have to abandon our home.
     如果河水氾濫，我們就得離家。

    (B) **revise** [rɪ`vaɪz] *vt.* 修改，修訂
  = modify [`mɑdə͵faɪ] *vt.*
     With a view to finding a new job, Julia revised her resume.
     為了找新工作，茱莉亞修改了她的履歷表。

    (C) **violate** [`vaɪə͵let] *vt.* 侵犯，違反
     violate the law   違法
     When you violate the law, you will be punished.
     你犯法就會遭受懲罰。

    (D) **console** [kən`sol] *vt.* 安慰，撫慰
  = comfort [`kʌmfɚt] *vt.*
     People tried to console the widow at the funeral.
     大家在葬禮上試著安慰那名寡婦。

  ⓑ 根據語意，(A) 項應為正選。

> **必考重點**
>
>   **as a result of...**   由於……
> = due to...
> = because of...
>   I got a cold as a result of going out in the rain without an umbrella.
>   我會感冒是因為在下雨天出門沒帶雨傘。

__B__ 7. 金門大橋是加州最獨特的指標，也是世界上最具辨識度的地標之一。

  ⓐ (A) **landlord** [`lænd͵lɔrd] *n.* 房東
     That rich landlord has five apartments to rent out.
     那名有錢的房東有五棟公寓要出租。

    (B) **landmark** [`lænd͵mɑrk] *n.* 地標
     The Eiffel Tower is an iconic cultural landmark in Paris.
     艾菲爾鐵塔是巴黎當地一個相當具指標性的文化地標。

    (C) **landscape** [`lænd͵skep] *n.* （陸上）風景，景觀
     Irene watched the landscape roll by as the train sped along.
     艾琳在火車疾駛時，看著窗外的景色一幕幕閃過。

(D) **landslide** [ˈlændˌslaɪd] *n.* 坍方，山崩；(選舉中) 一方選票占壓倒性多數
　　win in a landslide victory　　贏得壓倒性的勝利
= win by a landslide
　　The typhoon caused several landslides in mountain villages.
　　這次颱風造成山區村落多處坍方。
　　Most people believe that the mayor will win in a landslide victory again.
　　多數人相信現任市長會再度贏得壓倒性的勝利。

❺ 根據語意，(B) 項應為正選。

必考重點

a. **distinct** [dɪˈstɪŋkt] *a.* 獨特的；不同的；清楚的
b. **icon** [ˈaɪkɑn] *n.* 標誌，圖像
c. **recognizable** [ˈrɛkəɡˌnaɪzəb̩l] *a.* 為人熟知的

TEST 08

C　8. 雖然這名男子的聲音聽起來相當平靜，但他的臉部表情顯示他很焦慮。

❹ (A) **discussion** [dɪˈskʌʃən] *n.* 討論
　　under discussion　　在討論中
　　The plan is still under discussion.
　　這個計畫還在討論中。

(B) **formation** [fɔrˈmeʃən] *n.* 型態，形成
　　The army played a part in the formation of the young man's character.
　　這位年輕人性格的形成有一部分受軍中的影響。

(C) **expression** [ɪkˈsprɛʃən] *n.* 表達，表示
　　facial expression　　臉部表情
　　beyond expression　　筆墨難以形容
　　By Debbie's facial expression, I can tell that she's angry.
　　從黛比的臉部表情我可以看出她在生氣。

(D) **intonation** [ˌɪntoˈneʃən] *n.* 語調；聲調
　　Sara speaks with a delightful intonation.
　　莎拉說話語調輕快。

❺ 根據語意，(C) 項應為正選。

必考重點

a. **sound** [saʊnd] *vi.* 聽起來
　　Your idea sounds good to me.
　　我覺得你的想法聽起來很好。
b. **calm** [kɑm] *a.* 鎮定的
c. **indicate** [ˈɪndəˌket] *vt.* 顯示，表明
　　The survey of women in six Asian countries indicates that Korean women are the least satisfied with their looks.
　　那項針對亞洲六國女性的調查顯示，韓國女性對自己的外貌滿意度最低。

TEST 08

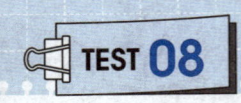

A 9. 這位作家有將平凡事件用幽默方式敘述的天分。她的書永遠會讓讀者開懷大笑。

- (A) **humorous** [ˈhjumərəs] *a.* 幽默的
 A good teacher should be able to lecture in a humorous and understandable way.
 一位優秀的老師應該要能以幽默易懂的方式來授課。

 (B) **defensive** [dɪˈfɛnsɪv] *a.* 防禦的
 We need both defensive and offensive weapons to face attacks from neighboring countries.
 我們需要防禦性及攻擊性的武器以對抗鄰國的攻擊。

 (C) **considerate** [kənˈsɪdərɪt] *a.* 體貼的
 be considerate / thoughtful of...　　體貼……
 The doctor is very considerate of his patients.
 那名醫生很體諒病人。

 (D) **pessimistic** [ˌpɛsəˈmɪstɪk] *a.* 悲觀的
 be pessimistic / optimistic about...　　對……很悲觀／樂觀
 Paul is always pessimistic about the future. He should learn to look on the bright side of life.
 保羅對未來總是抱持悲觀的態度。他應該學習看人生的光明面。

- 根據語意，(A) 項應為正選。

C 10. 餐廳裡的昏暗燈光增添其浪漫氛圍，但強尼幾乎無法閱讀菜單。

- (A) **tame** [tem] *a.* 溫馴的；被馴化的
 Camels are quite tame and only spit at people when they feel threatened.
 駱駝相當溫馴，只有在感受到威脅時會對人吐口水。

 (B) **frigid** [ˈfrɪdʒɪd] *a.* 寒冷的
 Paul prefers tropical weather to frigid weather.
 保羅喜歡熱帶天氣勝過寒帶天氣。

 (C) **dim** [dɪm] *a.* 昏暗的，陰暗的
 The dim lighting blended with the cozy setting to create a romantic atmosphere.
 微暗的燈光融入了舒適的環境，創造出一股浪漫的氛圍。

 (D) **vivid** [ˈvɪvɪd] *a.* 鮮明的；生動的
 Apply several coats of paint to the wall so that the color is more vivid.
 在牆上多塗幾層漆，這樣顏色會更鮮活些。

- 根據語意，(C) 項應為正選。

必考重點

a. **add to...** 增添……
b. **barely** [ˈbɛrlɪ] *adv.* 幾乎不

John could barely afford his health insurance while unemployed.
約翰在失業期間幾乎負擔不起自己的健保。

二、綜合測驗（占 10 分）

第 11 至 15 題為題組

　　就像美國的白頭海鵰、澳洲的袋鼠一樣，大象是象徵泰國的動物。牠們長久以來受到該國人民的珍惜。然而近年來為了幫助工業發展以及採收國內熱帶森林裡的貴重原木，大象被強迫勞動。不幸的是，許多大象因其被迫從事的工作而失明。更糟的是，當工作完成之後，大象就會被遺棄。基本上，牠們只能自生自滅。

　　為了要提供一個家給這些受虐的動物，「大象世界」因此成立。遊客們可以觀賞大象，還可以在關愛與管制的環境當中協助餵食大象和幫大象洗澡。當出生於英國的鋼琴家保羅・巴頓在網路上發現該庇護所時，被這些殘障動物的故事深深打動。他安排將自己的鋼琴搬運到園區內。在那裡他彈奏輕柔的古典樂。驚人的是，大象們的反應是站著不動並專注地聆聽。

　　大象與人類有許多共通點。牠們有長期記憶力，能以複雜的方式溝通，而且具有高度社交能力。牠們也有情緒反應。大象似乎也和人類一樣深受音樂感動。

A 11. 理由

(A) **harvest** [ˈhɑrvɪst] *vt.* 採收，收割
Eric and Laura meet once a year in France to harvest wild mushrooms together.
艾瑞克和蘿拉每年在法國碰面一次，一起去採收野菇。

(B) **release** [rɪˈlis] *vt.* 釋放
All the hostages were released after the police met the demands of the terrorists.
在警方滿足恐怖分子的要求後，所有的人質都被釋放了。

(C) **withdraw** [wɪðˈdrɔ] *vt.* 提領（金錢）(三態為：withdraw, withdrew [wɪðˈdru], withdrawn [wɪðˈdrɔn])
I withdrew US$3,000 from my bank account this morning.
我今天早上從銀行帳戶裡提領三千美元。

(D) **capture** [ˈkæptʃɚ] *vt.* 逮到；捕捉
The detective captured the criminal by using his wits.
那名警探利用機智逮捕了罪犯。

根據語意，(A) 項應為正選。

TEST 08

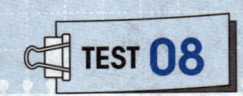

D 12. 理由

ⓐ (A) **in keeping with...** 符合……；與……一致
　= in line with...
　Molly's hair style is in keeping with the latest fashion.
　茉莉的髮型符合最新的潮流。

(B) **by means of...** 藉由……
　means [minz] *n.* 手段，方法；財富（單複數同形）
　We are determined to get the job done by means of working through the night.
　我們決定徹夜趕工來完成工作。

(C) **apart from...** 除了……
　= aside from...
　= except for...
　John occasionally goes hiking. Apart from that, he hardly has any hobbies.
　約翰偶爾會健行。除此之外，他幾乎沒有什麼嗜好。

(D) **due to...** 由於／因為……
　= because of...
　= on account of...
　= as a result of...
　= owing to...
　The bus was delayed for 30 minutes due to the heavy traffic.
　這班公車因為繁忙的交通狀況而延誤了半小時。

ⓑ 根據語意，(D) 項應為正選。

C 13. 理由

ⓐ (A) **yet** [jɛt] *adv.* 尚未 & *conj.* 然而（= but）
　Helen has not decided what to do yet.
　海倫尚未決定要做什麼。
　Ann is a little lazy, yet I still like her.
　安有一點懶，但我還是喜歡她。

(B) **instead** [ɪnˋstɛd] *adv.* 作為代替；反而
　Jones didn't go into the army. Instead, he chose to continue with his education.
　瓊斯並沒有去當兵，而是選擇繼續升學。

(C) **thus** [ðʌs] *adv.* 因此
　= therefore [ˋðɛr͵fɔr] *adv.*
　= hence [hɛns] *adv.*
　Larry sold confidential information and was thus terminated by the company.
　賴瑞盜賣機密資訊，因此遭公司解僱。

(D) **otherwise** [ˈʌðɚˌwaɪz] *adv.* 否則，要不然的話
You should listen to me; otherwise, you'll be sorry.
你應該聽我的話，否則你會後悔。

ⓑ 根據語意，(C) 項應為正選。

B 14. 理由
ⓐ 本題測試以下語意：(A) sports with his friends（和他的朋友一起運動）、(B) slow classical music（輕柔緩慢的古典樂）、(C) first chair in the band（樂隊裡的第一把交椅）、(D) in the entertainment business（在娛樂業）。
ⓑ 空格前一句提到他把鋼琴搬來公園，空格前又有 play（演奏）這個字，故根據語意，得知 (B) 項應為正選。

B 15. 理由
ⓐ (A) **on demand** 備索（「來取即付」或「一經要求就給」之意）
We can provide copies of past magazine issues on demand.
我們可以提供過期雜誌備索。

(B) **in common** 常與 have 並用，形成下列用法：
have... in common　　有……相同之處
have a lot in common　　有很多共同之處
I was surprised to find that Beth and I have a lot in common.
我很驚訝地發現我和貝絲有很多共通點。

(C) **within reach** 伸手可及
Low interest rates put owning a home within reach for everyone.
低利率讓每個人都能輕易的擁有房子。

(D) **under control** 在控制下
out of control 失控
The police took action and got the situation under control.
警方採取行動並控制了整個局面。

ⓑ 根據語意及用法，(B) 項應為正選。

重要字詞片語

1. **bald** [bɔld] *a.* 禿頭的
   a bald eagle　　白頭海鵰
2. **timber** [ˈtɪmbɚ] *n.* 木材（= lumber [ˈlʌmbɚ]，均不可數）
3. **be forced to V**　　被強迫從事……

4. **What's worse, S + V**
   = To make matters worse, S + V
   更糟的是，……
   My car broke down on the side of the road. What's worse, I didn't have my cellphone.
   我的車在路上拋錨了。更糟的是，我沒帶手機。

TEST 08

5. **discard** [dɪsˋkɑrd] *vt.* 丟棄
6. **fend for oneself**　　自謀生計；獨立生活
7. **provide A for B**　　把 A 提供給 B
   = provide B with A
   My boss provided a company car for me.
   老闆提供我一輛公司車。
9. **abuse** [əˋbjuz] *vt.* 虐待；傷害（本文為過去分詞作形容詞用）
10. **disabled** [dɪsˋebəld] *a.* 殘疾的
11. **shelter** [ˋʃɛltɚ] *n.* 庇護所；棲身處
12. **haul** [hɔl] *vt.*（用力）拖運，拖拉
13. **still** [stɪl] *a.* 靜止的，不動的
14. **intently** [ɪnˋtɛntlɪ] *adv.* 專注地，專心地

第 16 至 20 題為題組

　　你很可能對做菜時使用的刀子沒有太多想法。當然，有些刀比較好切，而對大多數人而言，對此切割用具的考量可能僅此而已。然而，也有像美國的鮑伯・克萊姆這種對刀具付出全副心力的人。

　　克萊姆是世界上最知名的製刀師傅之一。在 1990 年代初期，他去上一門製刀課程，之後便以製刀為業。成為製刀專家後，他決定販售自有產品。他使用一種特殊且耗時的製作工法，打造出品質超群的刀具。他的哲學是基於日本的「改善」理念，亦即不斷精進自己的技術。

　　剛開始他的一把刀售價約一百五十美元。但在一本烹飪雜誌報導克萊姆的刀，稱其是他們試用過最好的刀之後，需求量和價格便大幅提高。不久便出現了買刀的等候名單。現在他的刀在拍賣會上可以拍出天價。舉例來說，在 2015 年，一把克萊姆手工製的刀售價為三萬美元。要在廚房裡來這麼一把刀，可真是夠奢侈了！

C　16.　理由

- (A) **distribution** [ˌdɪstrəˋbjuʃən] *n.* 分配；分布
  That magazine enjoys a wide distribution.
  那本雜誌的發行遍及各地。

- (B) **motivation** [ˌmotəˋveʃən] *n.* 動機；幹勁
  You should make sure that your motivation for losing weight is health.
  你應該確認自己想減肥的動機是為了健康。

- (C) **consideration** [kənˌsɪdəˋreʃən] *n.* 考慮，斟酌
  Further consideration is necessary before we carry out this plan.
  在我們實施這項計畫前，必須再三考慮才行。

- (D) **prediction** [prɪˋdɪkʃən] *n.* 預測
  So far it's still very difficult for scientists to make accurate predictions about earthquakes.
  到目前為止，科學家要對地震做出準確的預測仍然很困難。

ⓑ 根據語意，(C) 項應為正選。

228

D 17. 理由

ⓐ 本題測試以下語意：(A) hired a kitchen hand（僱用一名廚房幫手）、(B) polished the silverware（擦亮銀器）、(C) struck the heated iron（敲打灼熱的鐵）、(D) made that his career（將其作為職業）。

ⓑ 空格前句提及，克萊姆是世界最知名的刀匠之一。空格前提到他上了一門製刀課程，根據語意，之後便以製刀作為職業，故 (D) 項應為正選。

C 18. 理由

ⓐ (A) **convince** [kənˋvɪns] *vt.* 使確信；說服
　　convince sb of sth　　使某人確信某事
　　convince sb to + V　　說服某人做……
　　How can I convince Ted of the dangers of running a red light?
　　我要怎樣才能讓泰德相信闖紅燈的危險性呢？
　　It seems I can do nothing to convince my husband to quit smoking.
　　我似乎拿不出辦法說服我老公戒菸。

(B) **forbid** [fɚˋbɪd] *vt.* 禁止（三態為：forbid, forbade [fɚˋbæd] / [fɚˋbed], forbidden [fɚˋbɪdn̩]）
　　Smoking is forbidden in this building.
　　本大樓內禁止吸菸。

(C) **forge** [fɔrdʒ] *vt.* （打）鐵；製造
　　The company forges high-quality tools that are sold at expensive prices in hardware stores across the country.
　　這間公司打造高品質工具，並以高價販售於全國各地的五金行。

(D) **afford** [əˋfɔrd] *vt.* 買得起，負擔得起
　　I can't imagine how such a poor man could afford such an expensive car.
　　我無法想像那樣窮的人竟買得起那麼貴的車。

ⓑ 根據語意，(C) 項應為正選。

B 19. 理由

ⓐ 本題測試以下語意：(A) surprisingly plunged（出人意料地暴跌）、(B) greatly increased（大幅增加）、(C) mistakenly overcharged（錯誤地超收費用）、(D) unwillingly shrank（勉強縮減）。

ⓑ 空格前面提及，因為有烹飪雜誌提到克萊姆的刀子是他們試用過最好的刀子之後，刀子需求量和價格便大幅提高，可得知 (B) 項應為正選。

A 20. 理由

ⓐ (A) **steep** [stip] *a.* （價格）過高的
　　The rent for this apartment is a bit steep for this part of town.
　　這間公寓的租金以鎮上的這個地區來說有點過高了。

229

(B) **violent** [ˈvaɪələnt] *a.* 暴力的，粗暴的
This movie is not fit for children because of its violent content.
本片有暴力的內容，因此孩童不宜觀賞。

(C) **chilly** [ˈtʃɪlɪ] *a.* 寒冷的
It is getting chilly in here. Let's turn the heater on.
這裡頭越來越冷了。我們把暖氣打開吧。

(D) **massive** [ˈmæsɪv] *a.* 大規模的；強烈的；巨大的
The tsunami caused massive destruction to the resorts along the beach.
這起海嘯對沿岸的度假村造成大規模破壞。

ⓑ 根據語意，(A) 項應為正選。

重要字詞片語

1. **course** [kɔrs] *n.*（單一）課程
2. **construct** [kənˈstrʌkt] *vt.* 建造，構築
3. **time-consuming** [ˈtaɪmkənˌsjumɪŋ] *a.* 耗時的
4. **outstanding** [aʊtˈstændɪŋ] *a.* 傑出的
5. **demand** [dɪˈmænd] *n.* 需求，需要
6. **auction** [ˈɔkʃən] *n.* 拍賣
7. **handmade** [ˈhændˌmed] *a.* 手工製造的

三、文意選填（占 10 分）

第 21 至 30 題為題組

　　冰川不僅僅是十分巨大、流動緩慢的冰河。當冰川融化時，會產生大量的水，最終創造出陸地上的湖泊與河流以及海洋中的冰山。大多數的冰川都在坐落於極北緯度地區的山脈中形成。有一個這樣的地點是加拿大的育空地區，育空地區夾在美國阿拉斯加州與廣大荒涼的加拿大西北領地之間。卡斯卡沃許冰川原本是供給兩條中型河川的水源，分別是斯林姆斯河和艾爾賽克河。在該冰川於 2016 年融化的幾個月過後，斯林姆斯河幾乎都乾涸了，而艾爾賽克河則變成一條洶湧的河流。怎麼會這樣呢？

　　地質學家長久以來都知道，一條供水給湖泊或河流的冰川，在緩緩流下一座山脈時，可能會改變流向或遭遇阻礙。當冰川及其水流改變流向時，改道的水流可能會淹沒像是平原或草地等先前為乾燥的地面，或者它可能會加入已經存在的水源，例如湖泊或河流。科學家將這一現象稱為「河道襲奪」或「河川襲奪」。一般而言，這段過程可能需費時數百年之久。事實上，在現代並沒有河道襲奪的實例被記錄下來。當這種河道襲奪事件僅在短短幾天內發生時，它給地質學家帶來待解決的新難題。

　　就卡斯卡沃許冰川而言，它的前沿被峽谷末端的大塊冰岩和巨石阻擋。這造成溢流的水進入艾爾賽克河水源而不是供給兩條河流。基本上，斯林姆斯河的水源遭到斷絕並迅速地消失了。這

是冰川在塑造地面景觀方面所扮演角色的另一個實例。看看在不久的將來是否會有更多類似的情況，就很有意思了。

J 21. 理由
ⓐ 空格前有形容詞 enormous（龐大的），空格後有介詞 of，得知空格應置名詞以被 enormous 修飾。
ⓑ 選項中符合上述的有 (A) obstructions（阻礙）、(B) process（過程）、(G) latitudes（緯度地區）、(I) flood（洪水）及 (J) quantities（量），惟根據語意，(J) 項應為正選。

G 22. 理由
ⓐ 空格前有形容詞 northern（北方的），得知空格應置名詞以被 northern 修飾。
ⓑ 選項中符合上述的有 (A) obstructions（阻礙）、(B) process（過程）、(G) latitudes（緯度地區）及 (I) flood（洪水），惟根據語意，(G) 項應為正選。

D 23. 理由
ⓐ 空格前有一完整的子句以及逗號，空格後則有介詞 between 引導的片語，得知空格應置入分詞，以形成分詞片語，修飾前面的先行詞 the Yukon Territory。
ⓑ 選項中符合上述的有 (C) caused（被造成）、(D) sandwiched（被夾在）、(H) raging（憤怒），惟根據語意，(D) 項應為正選。填入後形成固定用法 be sandwiched between A and B（被夾在 A 與 B 之間）。

H 24. 理由
ⓐ 空格前為不定冠詞 a，空格後有名詞 river（河流），得知空格應置形容詞以修飾名詞 river。
ⓑ 選項中符合上述的有 (E) modern（現代的）及 (H) raging（洶湧的），惟根據語意，(H) 項應為正選。

A 25. 理由
ⓐ 空格前提到 ... change course or meet...（……改變流向或遭遇……），其中 or 為對等連接詞，得知空格應置名詞以和 change course 形成對等。
ⓑ 選項中符合上述的尚有 (A) obstructions（阻礙）、(B) process（過程）及 (I) flood（洪水），惟根據語意，(A) 項應為正選。

I 26. 理由
ⓐ 空格前有助動詞 can（會……），得知空格應置原形動詞。
ⓑ 選項中符合上述的有 (B) process（處理）、(F) solve（解開）及 (I) flood（淹沒），惟根據語意，(I) 項應為正選。

B 27. 理由
ⓐ 空格前有指示形容詞 this，空格後有助動詞 may，得知空格應置單數名詞以被 this 修飾。
ⓑ 選項中為單數名詞的僅剩 (B) process（過程），置入後亦符合語意，故為正選。

TEST 08

231

TEST 08

E 28. 理由
 ⓐ 空格前有介詞 in，空格後有名詞 times（時代），得知空格應置形容詞以修飾 times。
 ⓑ 選項中為形容詞的僅剩 (E) modern（現代的），置入後亦符合語意，故為正選。

F 29. 理由
 ⓐ 空格前有引導不定詞片語的 to，得知空格應置原形動詞。
 ⓑ 選項中符合上述的僅剩 (F) solve（解開），置入後亦符合語意，故為正選。

C 30. 理由
 ⓐ 空格前有指示代名詞 This，空格後有名詞詞組 runoff water（溢流的水），而上下文的時態為過去式，得知空格應置過去式動詞。
 ⓑ 選項中符合上述的僅剩 (C) caused（造成），置入後亦符合語意，故為正選。

重要字詞片語

1. **glacier** [ˈgleʃɚ] n. 冰川
2. **iceberg** [ˈaɪsˌbɝg] n. 冰山
3. **territory** [ˈtɛrəˌtɔrɪ] n. 領土（複數為 territories）
4. **desolate** [ˈdɛslət] a. 荒涼的，荒蕪的
5. **expanse** [ɪkˈspæns] n. 廣闊的區域
6. **dry up** 乾枯
 The reservoir dried up during the long drought.
 水庫在長期乾旱中乾枯了。
7. **geologist** [dʒɪˈɑlədʒɪst] n. 地質學家
8. **course** [kɔrs] n. 河流流向；航向
9. **plain** [plen] n. 平原
10. **meadow** [ˈmɛdo] n. 草地，牧草地
11. **established** [ɪˈstæblɪʃt] a. 已建立的；已有良好基礎/名聲的
 There is an established electronics store on this block.
 在這個街區上有一家信譽良好的電子用品店。
12. **refer to A as B** 把 A 稱作 B
 Lily always refers to her dog as her best friend.
 莉莉總是把她的狗稱為自己最要好的朋友。
13. **piracy** [ˈpaɪrəsɪ] n. 海盜搶劫；盜版行為（不可數）
14. **capture** [ˈkæptʃɚ] n. & vt. 奪取；捕獲；占領
15. **block** [blɑk] vt. 阻擋
 The newly-built skyscraper blocked the view from the window.
 那棟新蓋的摩天大樓擋住了從窗戶看出去的景色。
16. **boulder** [ˈboldɚ] n. 巨石，巨礫
17. **canyon** [ˈkænjən] n. 峽谷
18. **runoff** [ˈrʌnˌɔf] n. 溢流（不可數）

四、篇章結構（占 8 分）

第 31 至 34 題為題組

　　過去幾十年來，「指甲彩繪文化」已經變成越來越普遍的現象。**31.** 這指的是將指甲油塗抹在手指甲或腳趾甲上的創意運用，又或兩者。在不久之前，指甲油被視為一種富家女用的高雅化妝品。當時，市面上大多只有紅色和粉紅色的指甲油款式。然而，幾個世紀以來，指甲油的發展和人們對其之認知實際上已發生了許多變化。

　　指甲油的歷史出奇地悠久。早在西元前 3000 年，所謂中華文化的初期，當時就不乏一些上流社會女子在她們的指甲上塗抹顏色。**32.** 到了西元前 600 年，周朝皇室成員偏愛金色和銀色的指甲油。兩千年後，明朝皇室則獨鍾紅色或黑色的色調。此外，不同階級和國家的人們偏好不同的顏色。舉例來說，在埃及，皇室成員與顯要曾將他們的指甲塗成紅色，而低下階層則使用較不起眼、淺的色調。

　　隨著中產階級因為工業革命而崛起，更多女性能夠負擔得起為她們的指甲上色。然而，傳統的風格是在手指甲或腳趾甲或兩者上使用單一色彩。這反映了當時人們嚮往的美學標準，偏好簡約與整潔。指甲上色被視為精緻與優雅的象徵，而這些特質在那個變遷的時代備受推崇。

　　現今似乎什麼指甲彩繪風格都有，而且有五彩繽紛的顏色及樣式任君挑選。**33.** 許多才華橫溢的美甲師在這個蓬勃發展的行業中嶄露頭角，有的甚至已經享譽國際。珍妮・布伊即為一位如此的美甲師。有「善用閃亮珠寶的美甲天后」之稱的布伊，在十幾歲時逃離了她的祖國柬埔寨，如今在紐約開了兩家美甲沙龍，旗下有二十名員工。**34.** 她的招牌彩繪圖案上都鑲滿了水晶，而且是美國饒舌歌手卡蒂・B 的最愛。藉由這一層與音樂圈的關係及擁有百萬粉絲的 IG 帳號經營成功之助，布伊在這一行的地位看來正要開始不斷攀升。

B 31. 理由
- ⓐ 空格前一句提及「指甲彩繪文化」已經變成越來越普遍的現象，可推測空格應接續說明其意義，以鋪陳接下來文章的發展。
- ⓑ 選項 (B) 表示，這指的是將指甲油塗抹在手指甲或腳趾甲上的創意運用，進一步說明了前一句的 nail art culture（指甲彩繪文化）為何，填入後語意連貫，可知 (B) 項應為正選。

E 32. 理由
- ⓐ 空格前一句提及指甲油的歷史悠久，早在西元前 3000 年的中華文化初期就有上流社會女子開始給指甲上色，而空格後提到兩千年後的明朝皇室則獨鍾紅色或黑色的色調，可推測空格應在舉例明朝前某朝代皇室偏好使用的指甲油。
- ⓑ 選項 (E) 表示，到了西元前 600 年，周朝皇室成員偏愛金色和銀色的指甲油，填入後語意連貫，可知 (E) 項應為正選。

TEST 08

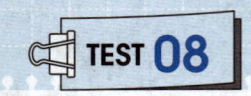

A 33. 理由

ⓐ 空格後一句提及珍妮‧布伊即為一位如此的美甲師，空格後兩句接著提到有「善用閃亮珠寶的美甲天后」之稱的布伊，在十幾歲時逃離了她的祖國柬埔寨，如今在紐約開了兩家美甲沙龍，可推測空格應在敘述某些美甲師在指甲彩繪界的發展情況，而珍妮‧布伊則是其中的舉例。

ⓑ 選項 (A) 表示，許多才華橫溢的美甲師在這個蓬勃發展的行業中嶄露頭角，有的甚至已經享譽國際，填入後語意連貫，可知 (A) 項應為正選。

C 34. 理由

ⓐ 空格前提及珍妮‧布伊有「善用閃亮珠寶的美甲天后」之稱，空格後提到藉由這一層與音樂圈的關係及擁有百萬粉絲的 IG 帳號經營成功之助，布伊在這一行的地位看來正要開始不斷攀升，可推測空格應在說明布伊的指甲彩繪風格及其與音樂圈的關係。

ⓑ 選項 (C) 表示，她的招牌彩繪圖案上都鑲嵌了水晶，而且是美國饒舌歌手卡蒂‧B 的最愛，填入後語意連貫，可知 (C) 項應為正選。

(D) 項中譯：然而，所有美甲沙龍都必須遵守嚴格的衛生規範。

重要字詞片語

1. **decade** [ˋdɛked] *n.* 十年
2. **phenomenon** [fəˋnɑməˏnɑn] *n.* 現象（單數）（複數為 phenomena [fəˋnɑmənə]）
3. **polish** [ˋpɑlɪʃ] *n.* 擦光油；亮光劑 & *vt.* 擦亮
   nail polish　　指甲油
4. **sophisticated** [səˋfɪstəˏketɪd] *a.* 高雅的；複雜的
   sophistication [səˏfɪstɪˋkeʃən] *n.* 精密；老練（不可數）
5. **makeup** [ˋmekʌp] *n.* 彩妝（不可數）
   比較
   cosmetics [kɑzˋmɛtɪks] *n.* 化妝品（恆用複數）
6. **means** [minz] *n.* 財富；金錢（恆用複數）
7. **perception** [pɚˋsɛpʃən] *n.* 認知，看法
8. **apply** [əˋplaɪ] *vt.* 塗；敷
   You can apply sunscreen to avoid sunburn.
   你可以塗抹防晒乳液，以免晒傷。

9. **hue** [hju] *n.* 顏色，色彩
10. **elite** [ɪˋlit] *n.* 菁英分子，顯要
11. **subtle** [ˋsʌtḷ] *a.* 不易察覺的
12. **pale** [pel] *a.* 淡色的；蒼白的
13. **shade** [ʃed] *n.* 色調，（顏色的）濃淡／深淺
14. **simplicity** [sɪmˋplɪsətɪ] *n.* 簡單；簡樸（皆不可數）
15. **elegance** [ˋɛləgəns] *n.* 優雅（不可數）
16. **trait** [tret] *n.* 特質，特點
17. **assortment** [əˋsɔrtmənt] *n.* 各式各樣；什錦
    an assortment of...
    各式各樣的……
    Mother bought an assortment of fish to put into the new tank.
    媽媽買了各式各樣的魚放進新的水族箱。
18. **emerge** [ɪˋmɝdʒ] *vi.* 出現，浮現
    Several new singers have emerged in recent months.
    最近這幾個月出現了幾位新歌手。

19. **flee** [fli] vt. 逃離，避開（三態為：flee、fled [flɛd]、fled）
The robbers fled from the crime scene as soon as they heard the police cars.
搶匪一聽到警車的警笛聲就逃離犯罪現場。

20. **signature** [ˈsɪɡnətʃɚ] a. 招牌的 & n. 簽名

21. **studded** [ˈstʌdɪd] a. 鑲滿珠寶／飾鈕的（與介詞 with 並用）

22. **association** [əˌsosɪˈeʃən] n. 關聯

五、閱讀測驗（占 24 分）

第 35 至 38 題為題組

航空公司經常遭到批評破壞環境。批評者一般的論點是飛行需要燃燒大量燃料而汙染空氣。不過人們往往忽略了乘客在飛機上製造的大量垃圾。

這些垃圾來自飛航過程中提供的餐飲而留下來的大量塑膠。想想你會用到的塑膠製或塑膠包裝的品項的驚人數量（尤其是長途航班）：餐盒、餐具、零食包裝紙、杯子和飲料瓶，更別提塑膠袋裝的耳機這類物品。根據國際航空運輸協會的數據，各航空公司在 2018 年總共製造了六百七十萬噸客艙垃圾，包括塑膠、食物和其他垃圾。這個數字肯定還會增加。儘管人們被告知塑膠可回收，但事實並非如此。大部分在飛機上產生的塑膠垃圾，最終都進了垃圾掩埋場，因為處理塑膠回收既昂貴又耗時。

有些航空公司已經採取行動來減少塑膠使用量，以因應此種憂心與違反永續的情況。在 2019 年世界地球日當天，阿提哈德航空公司進行了一趟不使用任何拋棄式塑膠的長途航班。同年，西班牙國家航空公司引進了更方便集中與分類垃圾以進行資源回收的新型送餐車。瑞安航空公司聲稱在 2023 年前要淘汰所有拋棄式塑膠用品。然而目前航空產業並沒有一個整體的策略來減少或消除飛機上塑膠的使用。儘管前述航空公司的具體努力值得稱讚，但路還很長。塑膠質輕又便宜，目前還沒有任何材料可以替代它。在科學界製造出這種新材料之前，大家很可能還會在三萬五千英尺的高空繼續使用某種形式的塑膠。

D 35. 本文第二段的主旨是什麼？
(A) 航空公司是如何消耗那麼多汽油的。
(B) 一家力求拯救環境的航空公司。
(C) 如何降低長途航班的成本。
(D) 航空公司及乘客造成汙染的一種途徑。

> 理由
> 本文第二段皆在敘述航空公司及乘客在飛機上會製造出哪些垃圾及這些垃圾最後並未被資源回收，故 (D) 項應為正選。

TEST 08

C 36. 根據本文，大部分的航空公司是如何處理塑膠垃圾的？
(A) 他們會花時間將其分類。
(B) 他們會將其送去資源回收廠。
(C) 他們會將其丟進垃圾桶。
(D) 他們會將其交給國際航空運輸協會處理。

> 理由
>
> 根據本文第二段最後一句，大部分在飛機上產生的塑膠垃圾，最終都進了垃圾掩埋場，因為處理塑膠回收既昂貴又耗時，故 (C) 項應為正選。

B 37. 本文第三段中的 lauded 最有可能是什麼意思？
(A) 批評。　　　(B) 讚美。　　　(C) 禁止。　　　(D) 懲罰。

> 理由
>
> laud 為及物動詞，表「稱讚，讚美」。本文第三段前文提及多家航空公司採取不同措施減塑做環保，且根據本句語意判斷他們付出的努力應被「稱讚」，故 (B) 項應為正選。

C 38. 作者覺得淘汰機上塑膠使用的機會有多大？
(A) 到 2020 年代中期肯定會實現。
(B) 某些特定航空公司可達成目標。
(C) 如果沒有更好的替代品，就不可能做到。
(D) 在長途航班上無法做到。

> 理由
>
> 根據本文第三段最後一句，在科學界製造出這種新材料之前，大家可能還會在三萬五千英尺的高空繼續使用某種形式的塑膠，故 (C) 項應為正選。

重要字詞片語

1. **criticize** [ˈkrɪtɪˌsaɪz] vt. 批評
   be criticized for N/V-ing
   因……受到批評
   The government was criticized for not taking immediate action to deal with the financial crisis.
   政府被批評並未採取立即行動處理那場金融危機。

2. **critic** [ˈkrɪtɪk] n. 批評者；評論家

3. **pollute** [pəˈlut] vt. 汙染
   That power plant has been polluting the environment for 15 years.
   那座發電廠已經汙染環境長達十五年之久。

4. **overlook** [ˌovɚˈluk] vt. 忽略，忽視
   Do not overlook the rules of grammar when writing an English essay.
   寫英文文章時，別忽略文法規則。

5. **plastic** [ˈplæstɪk] n. 塑膠（不可數）& a. 塑膠的

6. **sheer** [ʃɪr] a. 全然的，百分百的
   the sheer number / weight / size...
   （某事物）之多／之重／之大……

7. **haul** [hɔl] n. 旅程；一大批，大量 & vt. 拖，拉
   long-haul [ˈlɔŋˌhɔl] a.（尤指空運）長途的
   short-haul [ˈʃɔrtˌhɔl] a.（尤指空運）短途的

236

8. **cutlery** [ˈkʌtləri] *n.* 刀叉餐具（英）
（集合名詞，不可數）
= silverware [ˈsɪlvɚˌwɛr]（美）（集合名詞，不可數）

9. **cabin** [ˈkæbɪn] *n.* 機艙；船艙；小木屋

10. **case** [kes] *n.* 狀況，情形
It / This / That is not the case.
這不是真的。── 實情並非如此。
John thought he won, but it was not the case.
約翰以為自己贏了，但其實並沒有。

11. **wind** [waɪnd] up + 介詞片語/現在分詞
最後／到頭來……
If you don't work harder, you'll wind up getting fired.
如果工作不努力點，到頭來你會被炒魷魚。

12. **landfill** [ˈlændˌfɪl] *n.* 垃圾掩埋場

13. **sustainable** [səˈstenəbḷ] *a.* 永續的；能（長期）維持的
unsustainable [ˌʌnsəˈstenəbḷ] *a.*
無法永續的

14. **facilitate** [fəˈsɪləˌtet] *vt.* 有助於，促進
Kent's explanation facilitated my understanding of the situation.
肯特的解釋有助於我對情況的了解。

15. **vow** [vaʊ] *vt.* 發誓 & *n.* 誓言
vow to V　發誓……
All Peter's friends vowed to support him in the election.
彼得所有的朋友誓言在這次選舉中支持他。

16. **ditch** [dɪtʃ] *vt.* 丟棄；拋棄 & *n.* 溝渠
Amy finally ditched her old school uniform.
愛咪終於丟了她的舊學校制服。

17. **eliminate** [ɪˈlɪməˌnet] *vt.* 消弭，消除
I have no idea how he expects to eliminate his debt if he keeps spending like this.
我真不知道他再像這樣花錢下去，要如何才能消除債務。

18. **board** [bɔrd] *n.* 薄木板；牌子
on board
在（飛機、船等交通工具）上
There were 12 children on board the ship when the accident happened.
意外發生時船上有十二名小孩。

19. **sort** [sɔrt] *vt.* 分類 & *n.* 種類
sort out... / sort... out　把……分類
Linda sorted her documents out into two piles.
琳達將她的文件分成兩疊。

20. **alternative** [ɔlˈtɝnətɪv] *n.*（替代）選擇 & *a.* 替代的；另類的

TEST 08

第 39 至 42 題為題組

　　就像任何睡覺時曾作夢、說夢話或夢遊的人會告訴你的一樣，我們的大腦在我們睡著時絕對是還在運作著的。其實有一項研究證實大腦在我們睡眠時可以進行像是將字彙分類的複雜工作。

　　法、英兩國的研究人員進行了這項研究（後來在《當代生物學》期刊上發表），一群男女參與者被要求在一個黑暗的房間裡完成字彙分類的工作。此任務包括聆聽語音播出的字彙，然後按下右手的按鈕將之歸類為動物，或是按下左手的按鈕將之歸類為物品。受試者睡著後，他們仍可以像清醒時一樣準確辨識字彙。受試者睡著時不會真的用身體做出反應，但他們的左右腦半球裡展現的活動，跟醒著時會導致雙手按下按鈕的活動相同。唯一不同之處在於，他們分類字彙花的時間是醒著時的三倍，而且醒來後也不記得在睡著時所聽到的字彙。

TEST 08

　　研究員之一的西德・庫埃德爾解釋，這項研究也許能幫助理解：為何人類在睡著時會對他們的名字或特定的鬧鐘聲響有反應，卻又能對外面的噪音充耳不聞。這也可能有助於理解我們在睡眠期間的學習能力。我們長久以來已經知道睡眠可以幫助我們鞏固已經學過的東西，但它也能幫助我們學習新事物嗎？後面這個問題引出一個重要的議題：我們是否應該甘冒擾亂休養生息的睡眠時間的風險，來強迫我們的大腦進行學習。庫埃德爾說出他的關切：「對如何利用睡眠時間的專門研究，必須考慮此舉所付出的任何相關代價，以及這麼做是否值得。」

C 39. 第二段的主要目的是什麼？
　　(A) 辨識出某研究中的問題。　　　　(B) 討論一篇期刊的背景。
　　(C) 略述一項實驗的細節。　　　　　(D) 肯定睡眠的重要性。
　　理由
　　本文第二段主要在說明此一實驗的過程與結果，可得知 (C) 項應為正選。

B 40. 第二段中的 respond physically 指的是什麼？
　　(A) 開燈。　　　(B) 按按鈕。　　(C) 和研究人員談話。　　(D) 眨眼睛。
　　理由
　　第二段在說明實驗的細節，就是用手按按鈕來將字彙歸類。第四句提及睡著時不會真的用身體做出反應（respond physically），即指上面所提到的用手按按鈕將字彙歸類的實驗，故 (B) 項應為正選。

B 41. 受試者花三倍的時間做什麼？
　　(A) 在長時間睡眠後醒來。　　　　(B) 在睡眠期間對字彙做出反應。
　　(C) 在睡眠期間按按鈕。　　　　　(D) 背誦他們所學過的東西。
　　理由
　　根據本文第二段最後一句，他們分類字彙花的時間是醒著時的三倍，故 (B) 項應為正選。

A 42. 最後一段暗指什麼？
　　(A) 擾亂我們的睡眠來進行學習可能並不划算。
　　(B) 外界的聲響變得更難阻隔。
　　(C) 目前研究睡眠學習的成本太高。
　　(D) 在臥室裡適量的光線是很重要的。
　　理由
　　根據本文最後一段第四句，我們是否應該甘冒擾亂休養生息的睡眠時間的風險。最後一句話也提出質疑：whether it is worth it（是否值得），可得知 (A) 項應為正選。

重要字詞片語

1. **complex** [ˋkɑmplɛks] *a.* 複雜的
2. **classify** [ˋklæsə͵faɪ] *vt.* 分類
3. **asleep** [əˋslip] *a.* 睡著的
　　fall asleep　　睡著

The guard fell asleep while he was on duty last night.
守衛昨晚值班時睡著了。

4. **conduct** [kənˋdʌkt] *vt.* 進行

5. **object** [ˈɑbdʒɛkt] *n.* 物體
6. **subject** [ˈsʌbdʒɪkt] *n.* 實驗對象
7. **drift off (to sleep)**　　進入夢鄉
8. **identify** [aɪˈdɛntəˌfaɪ] *vt.* 辨別，認出
9. **accurately** [ˈækjərɪtlɪ] *adv.* 準確地
10. **exhibit** [ɪgˈzɪbɪt] *vt.* 顯示（特性、情感等）
11. **hemisphere** [ˈhɛməsˌfɪr] *n.*（大腦的）半球
12. **insight** [ˈɪnˌsaɪt] *n.* 洞悉，深刻的見解
13. **responsive** [rɪˈspɑnsɪv] *a.* 有反應的
    be responsive to...　　對……有反應
14. **block out... / block... out**
    阻擋……
15. **consolidate** [kənˈsɑləˌdet] *vt. & vi.*
    鞏固；加強
16. **disrupt** [dɪsˈrʌpt] *vt.* 使混亂
    A strike disrupted the train system.
    一場罷工使鐵路系統運作大亂。
17. **regenerative** [rɪˈdʒɛnəˌretɪv] *a.*
    再生的
18. **slumber** [ˈslʌmbɚ] *n.* 睡眠
19. **take advantage of...**　　利用……
    All students are invited to take advantage of our student discounts.
    竭誠歡迎所有學生多加利用我們的學生折扣優待。
20. **outline** [ˈaʊtˌlaɪn] *vt.* 略述，重點說明
21. **recite** [rɪˈsaɪt] *vt.* 背誦
    Emily has a photographic memory. She can recite an entire book after she finishes it.
    艾蜜莉有過目不忘的本領。她一本書看完後可以整本背出來。

TEST 08

第 43 至 46 題為題組

在很久以前，我們的祖先就注意到花草植物對他們有鎮靜效用。長久下來，他們便能從植物中萃取出香精來製作精油，並發展出我們現在所謂芳香療法的一種醫療形式。

古埃及人將精油用於烹調和沐浴，不過主要還是用於宗教儀式。例如神廟裡在晚上的時候會焚燒供奉神明的「奇斐」。古代中國人將芳香類植物和樹木的油用於宗教儀式和醫學。如檀香就會用於醫療功能，因為據信它能緩解呼吸問題和改善皮膚狀況。而古印度人將精油用於按摩，使用天竺葵和其他精油來促進深層舒緩。

現在精油的多種用途也與古代頗為類似。泡熱水澡時一次加幾滴精油；在薰香臺裡加水後一起加熱；或是加進按摩油中，以舒緩放鬆的方式為一天劃下句點。不過精油若沒有經過加入基礎油的稀釋，就絕不可直接擦抹在皮膚上。另一點重要提示是它們會對某些人產生副作用，所以在使用前應尋求專業的建議。

常見的精油不少，每種都有各自的功效。包括薰衣草和甘菊在內的鎮靜精油，往往帶有花香和甜香味。吸入前者有助於緩解頭痛，稀釋過後的精油抹在肌膚上可以緩解蚊蟲叮咬的腫脹和搔癢。後者可以經由蒸氣吸入來減輕焦慮並平靜翻騰的思緒。

TEST 08

　　提振精神的精油常是清新與果香的味道，包含檸檬草和薄荷。將前者稀釋後塗抹，有助於癒合傷口和預防感染，而吸入後者可促進消化系統健康，甚至可以減輕腸躁症的症狀。在皮膚擦上稀釋的薄荷油有助於舒緩晒傷和肌肉痠痛。

B 43. 第二段的主要目的是什麼？
(A) 論證古代文化使用芳香療法的目的是相同的。
(B) 詳細說明不同的文明是如何使用芳香療法。
(C) 探究芳香療法和精油起源的爭議。
(D) 討論按摩技巧的優缺點。

理由
本文第二段分別說明古埃及人、古中國人以及古印度人分別使用精油的方式，可得知 (B) 項應為正選。

C 44. 第三段中的 they 指的是什麼？
(A) 基礎油。　　(B) 按摩油。　　(C) 精油。　　(D) 薰香臺。

理由
根據本文第三段第三句的主詞為 essential oils（精油），後一句使用代名詞來做前句的補充說明，可得知這裡的 they 指的是前句的 essential oils，故 (C) 項應為正選。

C 45. 本文並未提及哪一項精油用法？
(A) 讓它們成為你每日按摩的一部分。　(B) 將它們納入你的沐浴習慣中。
(C) 將它們稀釋於飲料中來治療噁心感。　(D) 將它們與水一起燒熱後吸入。

理由
本文第三段第二句提及可以加幾滴精油在熱水澡裡，和水混合並在薰香臺裡加熱，或是加進按摩油中。並未提到可以將精油稀釋於飲料中，可得知 (C) 項應為正選。

D 46. 傑克因為吃了一頓大餐而且煩惱工作的事情而失眠。他應該使用哪兩種精油？
(A) 天竺葵和薰衣草。　　　　(B) 奇斐和甘菊。
(C) 檀香和檸檬草。　　　　　(D) 甘菊和薄荷。

理由
根據本文第五段第二句提及吸入薄荷可以促進消化系統健康；第四段最後一句提及甘菊可以減輕焦慮並平靜翻騰的思緒，可得知 (D) 項應為正選。

重要字詞片語

1. **ancestor** [ˈænsɛstɚ] n. 祖先
2. **extract** [ɪkˈstrækt] vt. 萃取，提煉
   extract A from B　從 B 提煉 A
   Our olive oil is extracted from fine olives and processed in our own factory.
   我們的橄欖油提煉自精選橄欖，並在我們自己的工廠內加工。
3. **fragrance** [ˈfregrəns] n. 香氣
4. **essential** [ɪˈsɛnʃəl] a. 必要的 & n. 不可或缺的
   essential oils　精油
5. **aromatherapy** [əˌreməˈθɛrəpɪ] n. 芳香療法（不可數）
6. **religious** [rɪˈlɪdʒəs] a. 宗教的

7. **ritual** [ˈrɪtʃuəl] *n.* 儀式
8. **utilize** [ˈjutḷˌaɪz] *vt.* 利用
Scientists utilize waterfalls to generate electricity.
科學家利用瀑布發電。
9. **aromatic** [ˌærəˈmætɪk] *a.* 芬芳的
10. **sandalwood** [ˈsændḷˌwʊd] *n.* 檀香油；檀香木（不可數）
11. **alleviate** [əˈlivɪˌet] *vt.* 減輕；緩和
The doctor gave the patient some pills to alleviate the pain.
醫生給那位病人一些減輕疼痛的藥丸。
12. **respiratory** [rɪˈspaɪrəˌtorɪ] *a.* 呼吸的
13. **incense** [ˈɪnsɛns] *n.* 香（不可數）
an incense burner　　香爐；薰香器具
14. **soothing** [ˈsuðɪŋ] *a.* 舒緩的
15. **dilute** [daɪˈlut] *vt.* 稀釋，沖淡
You should dilute the concentrated juice before drinking it.
在喝之前你應該先稀釋這濃縮果汁。
16. **lavender** [ˈlævəndɚ] *n.* 薰衣草（不可數）
17. **chamomile** [ˈkæməˌmaɪl] *n.* 甘菊（不可數）
18. **rub** [rʌb] *vt.* & *vi.* 搓揉，摩擦
19. **ease** [iz] *vt.* & *vi.* （使）減緩
After Rex took the medicine, his stomachache eased a little bit.
雷克斯吃了藥之後，胃痛稍微緩解了一些。

20. **swelling** [ˈswɛlɪŋ] *n.* 腫脹處；腫塊
21. **inhale** [ɪnˈhel] *vi.* & *vt.* 吸入
Experts argue that it is hazardous to inhale certain chemical fumes for a long period of time.
專家強烈認為長期吸入某些化學氣體是有害的。
22. **invigorate** [ɪnˈvɪgəˌret] *vt.* 使精力充沛，使活躍（本文為現在分詞作形容詞用）
23. **lemongrass** [ˈlɛmənˌgræs] *n.* 檸檬草（不可數）
24. **peppermint** [ˈpɛpɚˌmɪnt] *n.* 薄荷（不可數）
25. **digestive** [daɪˈdʒɛstɪv] *a.* 消化的
26. **irritable** [ˈɪrətəbḷ] *a.* 暴躁的
27. **bowel** [ˈbaʊəl] *n.* 大腸
28. **syndrome** [ˈsɪnˌdrom] *n.* 症候群（不可數）
irritable bowel syndrome
腸躁症候群
29. **probe** [prob] *vt.* & *vi.* 調查
30. **incorporate** [ɪnˈkɔrpəˌret] *vt.* 包含；整合
31. **nausea** [ˈnɔʃɪə] *n.* 噁心，嘔吐感（不可數）

TEST 08

241

第貳部分、混合題（占 10 分）

第 47 至 50 題為題組

化石燃料不但是有限資源，而且燃燒後會汙染我們的地球以及造成環境災害的威脅。所以許多國家投資替代能源，以下是其中四種：

太陽能

在地球上利用太陽能製造能源。小範圍的做法是在建築物屋頂裝設太陽能板，提供其暖氣與照明所用的能源。安裝太陽能板所費不貲，但它們可以迅速而明顯地降低電費開銷。大範圍的做法就是太陽能電場，可以供電給整個社區。太陽能顯然須仰賴天氣，所以多雲的地點 —— 像是沿海地區 —— 就不是那麼適合。

風力

就像太陽能一樣，風力可供應能源給單一住宅（透過小渦輪機）和廣大地區（透過風電場）。不過風力發電不甚可靠，因為風力太弱或太強對渦輪機來說都會產生問題，而且有人抱怨這些渦輪機破壞景觀，噪音又大。不過一旦開始運轉，維修和營運成本都很低廉，而且它們所在的土地還是可以用於農業。

水力

水力發電有多種方式，例如流過瀑布或水壩的水可以推動渦輪機葉片旋轉，因此為發電機提供動力。海浪的運動可以為位於水面上的發電機提供動力。可預期的潮汐運動也是利用同樣原理。不過這些都只能在特定地點發揮作用。

核能發電

核電廠使用核裂變 —— 也就是原子核分裂 —— 來製造能源。擁護核電的人聲稱其成本低廉且穩定，而它產生的能量可去除海水中的鹽分。反核者則指出核能意外的風險和處理核廢料的難度。此外，核能並非可再生能源，因為它所使用的燃料鈾無法永續。也就是說，它是有限的。

---

47. 風力和水力發電都包含使用渦輪機來產生能源。

    turbines

    理由

    風力發電的介紹中提及，風力可供應能源給單一住宅（透過小渦輪機）和廣大地區（透過風電場）。水力發電的介紹中則提及，流過瀑布或水壩的水可以推動渦輪機葉片旋轉，因此為發電機提供動力。兩則都有提到 **turbines**（渦輪機），故為正解。

48. 不像太陽能是取之不盡的，核能發電要靠鈾，而它是有限的。
  finite
  〔理由〕
  本句提及太陽能是 unlimited（無窮的），且從句首的 unlike（與……不同）可得知空格應填入與 unlimited 相反的字詞。核能發電介紹的最後一句提及它所使用的燃料鈾無法永續，是有限的，故空格置入 finite（有限的）應為正解。

C D 49. 有些人正在抗議在他們家附近建風電場。根據本文，他們可能會使用下列哪兩個口號？
  (A)「輻射不要靠近我們的家園！」
  (B)「維修它們的成本太高了！」
  (C)「有礙社區觀瞻！」
  (D)「它的聲音吵死人！」
  (E)「會增加我們的電費！」
  (F)「安裝很危險！」
  〔理由〕
  風力發電介紹的第二句提及風力發電的缺點是破壞景觀，噪音又大，(C) 與 (D) 項提到的皆為美觀與噪音方面，應為正選。

A 50. 西頓是一座臨海的大城鎮。根據本文，哪一種形式的替代能源最不適合這座城市？
  (A) 太陽能。 (B) 風力。 (C) 水力。 (D) 核能發電。
  〔理由〕
  太陽能介紹中的最後一句提及，多雲的地點 —— 像是沿海地區 —— 就不是那麼適合，可得知 (A) 項應為正選。

〔重要字詞片語〕

1. **finite** [ˈfaɪnaɪt] *a.* 有限的
2. **catastrophe** [kəˈtæstrəfɪ] *n.* 災難
   an environmental catastrophe
   環境劫難
3. **invest** [ɪnˈvɛst] *vi. & vt.* 投入；投資
4. **harness** [ˈhɑrnəs] *vt.* 利用
   This device can harness the power of the wind to generate electricity for this building.
   這個裝置能利用風力為這棟建築物提供電力。
5. **scale** [skel] *n.* 規模
   on a large scale   大規模，大幅
   on a small scale   小規模
6. **result in...**   導致……
   The car accident resulted in the death of five people.
   這起車禍造成五人死亡。
7. **utility** [juˈtɪlətɪ] *n.* 水／電／瓦斯等公共事業（常用複數）
   utility bills   水／電／瓦斯帳單
8. **reliant** [rɪˈlaɪənt] *a.* 依賴的
   A be reliant on B   A 依賴 B
   Most people nowadays are heavily reliant on computers.
   絕大多數的現代人都極度仰賴電腦。
9. **turbine** [ˈtɝbən] *n.* 渦輪機
10. **up and running**   運轉，運行

TEST 08

11. **agriculture** [ˈæɡrɪˌkʌltʃɚ] *n.* 農業（不可數）
12. **generate** [ˈdʒɛnəˌret] *vt.* 產生（光、電、熱）；造成，引起
    generator [ˈdʒɛnəˌretɚ] *n.* 發電機
    The dam generates electricity for the local community.
    該座水壩發電供當地社區使用。
13. **dam** [dæm] *n.* 水壩
14. **in turn** 因此，進而
15. **predictable** [prɪˈdɪktəbḷ] *a.* 可預測的
16. **fission** [ˈfɪʃən] *n.* （核）裂變，分裂（不可數）
17. **nucleus** [ˈn(j)uklɪəs] *n.* 原子核（複數為 nuclei [ˈn(j)uklɪˌaɪ] / nucleuses）
18. **atom** [ˈætəm] *n.* 原子
19. **proponent** [prəˈponənt] *n.* 提倡者
20. **detractor** [dɪˈtræktɚ] *n.* 惡意批評者
21. **dispose** [dɪˈspoz] *vi.* 處置
    dispose of... 處理掉……
    Most countries have difficulties in disposing of nuclear waste.
    大部分的國家都面臨處理核廢料的困境。
22. **renewable** [rɪˈnjuəbḷ] *a.* （能源）可再生的
23. **uranium** [juˈrenɪəm] *n.* 鈾（不可數）
24. **radiation** [ˌredɪˈeʃən] *n.* （核）輻射（不可數）
25. **eyesore** [ˈaɪˌsɔr] *n.* 難看的東西

第參部分、非選擇題（占 28 分）

一、中譯英（占 8 分）

1. 為了增加自己的競爭力，許多人會利用空閒時間學習第二語言。

   示範譯句
   To increase their competitiveness, many people use their free time to learn a second language.

   或：To be more competitive, many people devote their spare / leisure time to learning a foreign language.

   翻譯要點

   a. **competitiveness** [kəmˋpɛtətɪvnɪs]
      n. 競爭力（不可數）
      competitive [kəmˋpɛtətɪv] *a.* 競爭的
      Fiona was accepted to the private high school after passing the highly competitive entrance examination.
      費歐娜通過競爭激烈的入學考試後被私立高中錄取了。

   b. **free time** 空閒時間
      = spare / leisure time
      spare [spɛr] *a.* 空閒的；剩餘的
      in one's free / spare / leisure time
      在某人空閒的時候

      I like to go swimming and read novels in my spare time.
      我空閒時喜歡去游泳和看小說。

   c. **devote** [dɪˋvot] *vt.* 致力於；奉獻
      devote A to B　　將 A 投注在 B
      devote oneself to N/V-ing
      某人致力於……
      Angela devoted all of her time and passion to dancing.
      安琪拉在舞蹈上投注了她所有時間與熱情。
      Mr. Johnson has devoted himself to education for the past 50 years.
      強森先生過去五十年來都獻身於教育。

2. 他們深信擁有良好的外語能力是脫穎而出的方式之一。

   示範譯句
   They firmly believe that having a good command of a foreign language is a way of standing out.

   或：They firmly believe / are firmly convinced that being proficient in a foreign language serves as a way to stand out.

   翻譯要點

   a. **sb firmly believes + that 子句**
      某人深信……
      = sb is firmly convinced + that 子句
      firmly [ˋfɝmlɪ] *adv.* 堅定地
      convinced [kənˋvɪnst] *a.* 信服的；確信的

      I firmly believe that we will overcome all challenges.
      我堅信我們將會克服一切挑戰。

TEST 08

b. **command** [kəˋmænd] *n.* （語言）運用能力
have a good command of + 語言　精通某種語言
Those who wish to apply for this position must have a good command of Japanese.
想應徵這份工作的人必須精通日語。

c. **stand out**　脫穎而出；顯眼
stand out among / from one's peers　在某人的同儕中脫穎而出
Because of Andrea's excellent academic performance, she stood out among her peers.
安卓雅卓越的課業表現讓她在同儕中脫穎而出。
＊ peer [pɪr] *n.* 同儕，同輩

d. **proficient** [prəˋfɪʃənt] *a.* 精通的
be proficient in + 語言　精通某語言
It takes years of hard work to become proficient in English.
想精通英語得花上多年的努力才行。

二、英文作文（占 20 分）

提示：近來不知為何，你們教室突然開始出現很多垃圾，造成環境髒亂。請以衛生股長的身分（英文名字必須假設為 Paul 或 Rachel），寫一封信勸告亂丟垃圾的同學，請他們共同努力維持學習環境的舒適與整潔。

示範作文

Dear Classmates,

　　In recent weeks, I've discovered the floor of our classroom is often littered with trash such as tissues, empty plastic bottles, and even lunch leftovers. I don't know why, but I figure some of us must have thrown them away carelessly. In addition, the walls of our classroom have been marked with stains from coffee, tea, or juice. This is an eyesore not only for us but for our teachers as well! Our classroom is the place where we study and interact almost on a daily basis. We don't want to turn it into a pigsty!

　　As the leader of our class cleanup team, I would like all of you to help me keep our classroom clean and tidy. All you have to do is take care not to leave any trash or lunch leftovers on the floor and sort out your trash for recycling. If every one of us pitches in, I'm sure we will make our classroom a better place for us to focus on our studies. Incidentally, I need some volunteers to assist me in repainting the walls on the weekend. Contact me if any of you are interested. Let's work together to make our classroom the pride of the school.

Sincerely,
Rachel

親愛的同學們：

　　這幾個禮拜以來，我發現教室的地板常常滿地都是衛生紙、空寶特瓶，甚至是午餐廚餘等垃圾。我不知道為什麼，但我認為肯定是我們之中有些人不小心將那些垃圾亂丟。此外，教室牆上也常常沾上咖啡、茶或果汁的汙漬。這不只對我們來說很礙眼，對我們的老師來說也是！教室幾乎是我們每天讀書與互動的地方。我們不希望它變成豬窩！

　　身為班上的衛生股長，我希望你們所有人都能幫助我維持班上的整潔。你們只要小心不要將任何垃圾或午餐廚餘丟在地上，並且將自己的垃圾好好分類。如果我們每一個人都出一份力，我相信我們會讓教室成為更美好的地方，讓我們都能專心讀書。順帶一提，我需要一些自願者在週末時來幫我重新粉刷牆壁。如果有興趣的話請與我聯繫。讓我們一起合作，將我們的教室變成學校的驕傲。

瑞秋　敬上

重要字詞片語

1. **litter** [ˈlɪtɚ] *vi.* 亂丟垃圾 & *n.* 垃圾（不可數）
   be littered with... 滿地都是……
   It is a shame when parents don't teach their children not to litter.
   父母沒有教導孩子不可亂丟垃圾真是遺憾。
   That restaurant is always littered with empty cans.
   那家餐廳總是滿地的空罐子。
2. **leftovers** [ˈlɛftˌovɚz] *n.* 廚餘（恆用複數）
3. **figure** [ˈfɪɡjɚ] *vt.* 認為，想
4. **carelessly** [ˈkɛrlɪslɪ] *adv.* 不小心地
5. **stain** [sten] *n.* 汙漬
6. **eyesore** [ˈaɪˌsɔr] *n.* 礙眼的事物
7. **on a daily basis** 每天
8. **pigsty** [ˈpɪɡˌstaɪ] *n.* 豬窩／圈
9. **sort out...** 將……分類／整理
10. **pitch in** 出一份力
11. **incidentally** [ˌɪnsəˈdɛntəlɪ] *adv.* 順便一提（= by the way）；偶然地
12. **assist sb in V-ing** 協助某人做……

TEST 08

247

NOTE

TEST 09

第壹部分、選擇題
- 一、詞彙題
- 二、綜合測驗
- 三、文意選填
- 四、篇章結構
- 五、閱讀測驗

第貳部分、混合題

第參部分、非選擇題
- 一、中譯英
- 二、英文作文

第壹部分、選擇題

一、詞彙題

| 1. D | 2. B | 3. A | 4. C | 5. A | 6. C | 7. B | 8. C | 9. D | 10. C |

二、綜合測驗

| 11. B | 12. D | 13. B | 14. C | 15. A | 16. D | 17. C | 18. D | 19. A | 20. B |

三、文意選填

| 21. G | 22. C | 23. I | 24. D | 25. B | 26. E | 27. F | 28. A | 29. J | 30. H |

四、篇章結構

| 31. C | 32. D | 33. E | 34. B |

五、閱讀測驗

| 35. C | 36. B | 37. A | 38. B | 39. C | 40. D | 41. D | 42. A | 43. C | 44. D |
| 45. C | 46. C |

第貳部分、混合題

47. C

48. A

49. B

50. C

51. myriad

250

第壹部分、選擇題（占 62 分）

一、詞彙題（占 10 分）

D 1. 令人高度存疑的是，這兩國之間的貿易戰會對任一方造成任何正面的影響。

   ❶ (A) **racial** [ˈreʃəl] *a.* 種族的
       Racial discrimination is something that shouldn't be tolerated.
       種族歧視不應被容忍。

     (B) **prior** [ˈpraɪɚ] *a.* 在前的；優先的
       No prior knowledge of Spanish is required for the course.
       修這堂課你不必先具備任何關於西班牙語的知識。

     (C) **vain** [ven] *a.* 空虛的，徒勞的
       in vain　　白費工夫
       My father tried in vain to fix that broken fan.
       我父親試圖要修復那臺壞掉的電扇，卻白費功夫。

     (D) **doubtful** [ˈdaʊtfəl] *a.* 可疑的；起疑的
       be doubtful about...　　對……起疑
       I was doubtful about the old man's good intentions.
       這名老人的好意令我起疑。

   ❷ 根據語意，(D) 項應為正選。

> **必考重點**
>
> a. **result in...**　　導致……
> Tom's laziness resulted in his failure.
> 湯姆的懶惰導致了他的失敗。
>
> b. **positive** [ˈpɑzətɪv] *a.* 積極正面的

B 2. 如果地球持續變得更暖，合乎邏輯的結論是將會有更多的冰融化，而且海平面將會上升。

   ❶ (A) **visual** [ˈvɪʒuəl] *a.* 視覺的
       Japanese food is not only delicious, but it has visual appeal as well.
       日本食物不但好吃，視覺上也同樣誘人。

     (B) **logical** [ˈlɑdʒɪkl̩] *a.* 邏輯的
       The man has a clear and logical mind.
       這個人的思路清晰又合乎邏輯。

TEST 09

(C) **multiple** [ˈmʌltəpl̩] *a.* 多重的，眾多的
Darren's latest album consists of multiple versions of the same songs.
戴倫的最新專輯收錄了相同歌曲的許多版本。

(D) **messy** [ˈmɛsɪ] *a.* 雜亂的
How come your room is always messy?
你的房間為什麼老是很亂？

ⓑ 根據語意，(B) 項應為正選。

> **必考重點**
>
> a. **conclusion** [kənˈkluʒən] *n.* 結果；結論
> b. **melt** [mɛlt] *vi. & vt.* 融化；熔化
> The snow melted away soon after the sun rose.
> 太陽出來後不久雪就融化消失了。
> c. **rise** [raɪz] *vi.* 上升，升高（三態為：rise, rose [roz], risen [ˈrɪzn̩]）
> The sun rises in the east.
> 太陽從東方升起。

A 3. 有時候知名的電影明星和導演都無法保證他們的電影會是賣座強片。

ⓐ (A) **guarantee** [ˌgærənˈti] *n. & vt.* 保證
The guarantee from the manufacturer is valid for one year.
這家廠商的保證一年有效。
Stick to this diet and I guarantee that you'll lose 10 pounds by next month.
只要遵循這套減肥餐，我保證你下個月前就能瘦十磅。

(B) **chemistry** [ˈkɛmɪstrɪ] *n.* 化學（不可數）
Chemistry is my favorite subject at school.
化學是我在學校裡最喜歡的科目。

(C) **insurance** [ɪnˈʃʊrəns] *n.* 保險（不可數）
Alice filled out the questionnaire she received from her insurance company.
愛麗絲填妥保險公司寄來的問卷。

(D) **blossom** [ˈblɑsəm] *n. & vi.* 開花
in full blossom （花朵）盛開
The flowers in our garden are in full blossom now.
我們院子裡的花現在全都盛開了。

ⓑ 根據語意，(A) 項應為正選。

> **必考重點**
>
> a. **big-name** [ˈbɪɡˌnem] *a.* 知名的
> b. **blockbuster** [ˈblɑkˌbʌstɚ] *n.* 賣座強片

252

__C__ 4. 你到外國旅遊時應該當心扒手。如果不小心的話，你的錢和護照就可能被偷走。

- (A) **gesture** [ˈdʒɛstʃɚ] *vi.* 做手勢 & *n.* 手勢；表示
  When asked who she was talking about, Anna gestured at the handsome man sitting alone in the corner.
  當安娜被問到她在談論的人是誰時，她用手勢表示是那位獨坐角落的帥哥。

- (B) **frown** [fraʊn] *vi.* & *n.* 皺眉頭
  frown at sb　　對某人皺眉頭，表示不悅
  Mr. Roberts frowned at me for turning down his request.
  羅伯茲先生因我拒絕他的請求而對我皺眉表示不悅。

- (C) **beware** [bɪˈwɛr] *vi.* 當心，小心
  beware of...　　小心……
  Beware of that dog because it might bite you.
  小心那隻狗，因為牠可能會咬你。

- (D) **inquire** [ɪnˈkwaɪr] *vi.* & *vt.* 詢問
  inquire about...　　詢問有關……
  I'm calling to inquire about the job openings you advertised in the newspaper.
  我打電話來是想詢問貴公司在報上徵人的廣告。

- 根據語意及用法，(C) 項應為正選。

必考重點

a. **pickpocket** [ˈpɪkˌpɑkɪt] *n.* 扒手　　b. **passport** [ˈpæsˌpɔrt] *n.* 護照

__A__ 5. 凡妮莎克服了可怕的膝傷，將會在今年的網球錦標賽來臨時重返賽場。

- (A) **overcome** [ˌovɚˈkʌm] *vt.* 克服（三態為：overcome, overcame [ˌovɚˈkem], overcome）
  To overcome obstacles, you must work hard.
  你必須努力才能克服阻礙。

- (B) **control** [kənˈtrol] *vt.* 控制；克制
  Britney took a deep breath to control her urge to cry.
  布蘭妮深吸一口氣以克制住她想大哭的衝動。

- (C) **pursue** [pɚˈsu] *vt.* 追求
  With my father's support, I have been able to pursue my dreams.
  有了我爸的支持，我才能夠去追尋我的夢想。

- (D) **await** [əˈwet] *vt.* 等候，等待
  Gail was awaiting the call from the vet regarding the condition of her cat.
  蓋兒正在等待獸醫打電話來告訴她貓咪的情況。

- 根據語意，(A) 項應為正選。

253

TEST 09

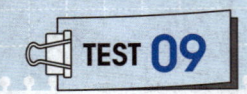

> **必考重點**
> a. **horrific** [hɔˋrɪfɪk] *a.* 可怕的
> b. **roll around** 來臨（= come around）

C 6. 空服員在起飛前客氣地指導大家繫上自己的安全帶並聆聽安全解說。

- ⓐ (A) **calculate** [ˋkælkjə͵let] *vt.* 計算
  calculate the costs　　計算費用
  We need to calculate the overall costs before we make any decisions.
  在做任何決定前，我們需要先計算一下全部的花費。

  (B) **withdraw** [wɪðˋdrɔ] *vt.* 提（款）；撤銷
  （三態為：withdraw, withdrew [wɪðˋdru], withdrawn [wɪðˋdrɔn]）
  withdraw / deposit money　　提／存款
  I used up all my spare money, so I'm going to withdraw some money from the bank this afternoon.
  我身上已沒多餘的錢了，所以今天下午我要到銀行提款。

  (C) **instruct** [ɪnˋstrʌkt] *vt.* 指示；指導
  instruct sb to V　　教導／指示某人（做）……
  The pilot instructed his co-pilot to prepare for take-off.
  主駕駛指導副駕駛準備起飛。

  (D) **assign** [əˋsaɪn] *vt.* 分配；指派
  Our teacher will assign us tasks for the morning.
  老師將會為我們分配早上的工作。

- ⓑ 根據語意，(C) 項應為正選。

> **必考重點**
> a. **a flight attendant**　　空服員
> b. **fasten** [ˋfæsn̩] *vt.* 繫緊
> c. **seat belt** [ˋsit ͵bɛlt] *n.* 安全帶
> d. **take-off** [ˋtek͵ɔf] *n.* 起飛

B 7. 珍妮絲得了重感冒，不過在休息數天後，她漸漸好轉並回去工作。

- ⓐ (A) **precisely** [prɪˋsaɪslɪ] *adv.* 精確地，確切地
  All the chemicals used in this experiment must be measured precisely.
  在這個實驗中用到的化學藥品都要經過精確測量。

  (B) **gradually** [ˋgrædʒʊlɪ] *adv.* 逐漸地
  = little by little
  Vincent is gradually recovering from his illness.
  文森正逐漸從病中康復。

(C) **regularly** [ˈrɛɡjələlɪ] *adv.* 定期地，規律地
= on a regular basis
Kelly has her hair cut regularly.
凱莉會定期剪頭髮。

(D) **practically** [ˈpræktɪklɪ] *adv.* 實際地
Practically speaking, ...　說得實際一點，……
Practically speaking, Jason isn't cut out for the job.
講得實際一點，這份工作傑森不能勝任。

ⓑ 根據語意，(B) 項應為正選。

必考重點

suffer from...　罹患／感染……（疾病）

C 8. 大多數的大學生偏愛穿休閒的服裝，像是牛仔褲、有圖案的 T 恤，以及連帽衫等。

ⓐ (A) **formal** [ˈfɔrml̩] *a.* 正式的
It is a formal occasion, so we all need to dress up.
那是個正式場合，所以我們都必須盛裝打扮。

(B) **splendid** [ˈsplɛndɪd] *a.* 富麗堂皇的；華麗的
The emperor built several splendid palaces to show off his wealth to the world.
這位皇帝建了幾座富麗堂皇的宮殿來向世界誇耀他的財富。

(C) **casual** [ˈkæʒʊəl] *a.* （衣服）休閒的；非正式的
You'll be overdressed if you wear a suit to a casual party.
如果你穿西裝去參加非正式的派對，那你就太過於盛裝了。

(D) **naughty** [ˈnɔtɪ] *a.* 頑皮的；搗蛋的
Henry was considered a naughty boy because he enjoyed playing pranks on his classmates.
亨利被認為是個調皮的男孩，因為他喜歡對同學惡作劇。

ⓑ 根據語意，(C) 項應為正選。

必考重點

a. **prefer** [prɪˈfɚ] *vt.* 較喜歡；寧可
prefer to V rather than V
= prefer V-ing to V-ing
喜歡……勝過……；寧願……而不願……

I prefer to listen to music rather than watch TV.
我喜歡聽音樂勝於看電視。

b. **graphic** [ˈɡræfɪk] *a.* 圖像的

c. **hoodie** [ˈhʊdɪ] *n.* 連帽上衣

TEST 09

255

TEST 09

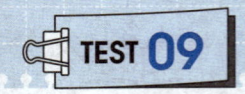

D 9. 安娜在畢業典禮上獻給老師一束花以示**感謝**。

ⓐ (A) **privilege** [ˈprɪvl̩ɪdʒ] *n.* 榮幸；特權
  privilege of N / to V　……的特權/榮幸
  Joseph Campbell once said, "The privilege of a lifetime is being who you are."
  約瑟夫・坎伯曾說過：「人一生的特權就在於做自己。」

(B) **dominance** [ˈdɑmənəns] *n.* 優勢；支配（地位）（不可數）
  The country's military dominance in the region ensured that its interests were protected.
  該國在該地區的軍事優勢確保其利益受到保護。

(C) **curiosity** [ˌkjʊrɪˈɑsətɪ] *n.* 好奇心（不可數）
  out of curiosity　出於好奇心
  Ann peeked inside the box out of curiosity.
  安出於好奇心而偷瞄了盒子裡的東西。

(D) **gratitude** [ˈgrætəˌtjud] *n.* 感激（不可數）
  I'd like to express my gratitude for your help.
  我想對你的協助表達感激之情。

ⓑ 根據語意，(D) 項應為正選。

必考重點

a. **present** [prɪˈzɛnt] **sb with sth**
  將某物獻給某人

b. **graduation** [ˌgrædʒʊˈeʃən] *n.* 畢業

C 10. 這個網站上的所有歌曲都受到**版權**保護。未經許可下載或分享都是違法的。

ⓐ (A) **privacy** [ˈpraɪvəsɪ] *n.* 隱私（權）；私生活（不可數）
  No one has the right to invade another person's privacy.
  沒人有權利侵犯他人的隱私。

(B) **discipline** [ˈdɪsəplɪn] *n.* 紀律（不可數）& *vt.* 管教
  Without discipline, these troops can't fight.
  這些部隊若無紀律就無法打仗。

(C) **copyright** [ˈkɑpɪˌraɪt] *n.* 版權，著作權
  When you see this symbol © on something, it means that thing is protected by copyright.
  當你看到某樣東西有 © 這個符號時，就表示那樣東西有受到版權保護。

(D) **moral** [ˈmɔrəl] *n.* 寓意
  The moral of the story is that crime doesn't pay.
  這個故事的寓意就是犯罪是不值得的。

ⓑ 根據語意，(C) 項應為正選。

二、綜合測驗（占 10 分）

第 11 至 15 題為題組

提到葡萄酒時，你常會聽到人們使用 aroma（芳香）及 bouquet（醇香）等字。這兩個術語都是用來形容葡萄酒的氣味。具體地說，它們意指氣味的來源。

葡萄酒的氣味有三種類別。第一種又稱作一級香氣，來自於釀造葡萄酒用的葡萄種類。這些酒的香氣通常帶有像是水果、花卉和香草植物的味道，各自的代表如水蜜桃、玫瑰和薄荷等。二級香氣源自於發酵過程。由於在釀酒這個階段中所添加的酵母影響，葡萄酒聞起來會類似啤酒或陳年起司的氣味。第三種稱作三級香氣，是葡萄酒經歷陳年的過程所產生。陳年過程通常於橡木桶中進行，替葡萄酒增添木香及堅果的氣味。類似焦糖和菸草的甜香，在這個種類中相當常見。

說到葡萄酒的芳香和醇香時，其實很簡單分辨。芳香指的是酒的一級香氣，而醇香則涵蓋了所有二級及三級中的香氣。雖然聞酒香並非精準的科學，但它確實對於釀造葡萄酒這種深受喜愛酒精飲品的過程提供了有趣的見解。

B 11. 理由

ⓐ (A) **scarcely** [ˈskɛrslɪ] *adv.* 幾乎不
   I can scarcely believe that the firm went bankrupt.
   我幾乎不敢相信這家公司破產了。

(B) **specifically** [spəˈsɪfɪkəlɪ] *adv.* 具體地，明確地
   I enjoy sports. Specifically, I like swimming and basketball.
   我喜愛運動。更明確地說，我喜歡游泳和打籃球。

(C) **relatively** [ˈrɛlətɪvlɪ] *adv.* 相對地；相當地
   Nowadays, the birthrate in Taiwan is relatively low.
   現在臺灣的出生率相當低。

(D) **accordingly** [əˈkɔrdɪŋlɪ] *adv.* 因此（= therefore）；照著
   Bill couldn't meet the job's requirements. Accordingly, he was fired.
   比爾沒能達到這份工作的要求，因此被炒魷魚。

ⓑ 根據語意，(B) 項應為正選。

D 12. 理由

ⓐ 本句省略了關係代名詞 which 及 be 動詞 is，原句實為：The first, or primary, aromas come from the type of grape <u>which is</u> used to make the wine.

ⓑ 在形容詞子句中，若關係代名詞作主詞且其前無逗點時（即限定修飾），可將該形容詞子句簡化成分詞片語。首先將關係代名詞刪除，之後的動詞變成現在分詞，若動詞為 be 動詞，變成現在分詞 being 後，可將 being 省略。

ⓒ 根據上述，將關係代名詞 which 刪除並將 be 動詞 is 變成現在分詞 being 後再予以省略，省略後即成本句，故 (D) 項應為正選。

TEST 09

B 13. 理由
- ⓐ 本題測試以下語意：(A) across the vineyard（在葡萄園對面）、(B) during this stage（在這個階段）、(C) on the shelves（在架子上）、(D) beside the storage（在倉庫旁）。
- ⓑ 根據空格上下文的語意，應該是指在釀酒的階段所添加酵母的影響，可得知 (B) 項應為正選。

C 14. 理由
- ⓐ (A) bring along... / bring... along　帶著……，帶……一起來
  You are welcome to bring your friends along to my wedding banquet.
  歡迎帶朋友一起來參加我的婚宴。

  (B) come across...　偶然發現／遇見……
  Kevin came across a lost child while he was at the mall.
  凱文在購物中心時碰到一個走丟的孩子。

  (C) go through...　經歷……
  Jim went through a series of interviews before being offered the job.
  吉姆經過一連串的面試才得到那份工作。

  (D) take over... / take... over　接管／占據……
  Who's going to take over the department after Mr. Johnson resigns?
  強森先生辭職後誰將接管該部門？

- ⓑ 根據語意，(C) 項應為正選。

A 15. 理由
- ⓐ (A) insight [ˈɪnˌsaɪt] n. 深入理解，深刻見解
  Amy Tan's novels give an insight into the lives of Chinese Americans living in the US.
  譚艾美的小說帶我們深入了解華裔美國人在美國的生活。

  (B) agency [ˈedʒənsɪ] n. 代辦處，機關
  a news / travel agency　通訊社／旅行社
  My dad works at a travel agency.
  我爸爸在旅行社工作。

  (C) emission [ɪˈmɪʃən] n. （氣體、光線等）排放
  The emissions of carbon dioxide by vehicles pollute the air.
  汽車排放的二氧化碳汙染空氣。

  (D) legend [ˈlɛdʒənd] n. 傳說
  Legend has it that...　傳說……
  Legend has it that there lived seven dwarfs in the mountains.
  傳說山裡頭住著七個小矮人。

- ⓑ 根據語意，(A) 項應為正選。

重要字詞片語

1. **aroma** [ə`romə] *n.* 芳香，香氣，香味
2. **bouquet** [buˋke] *n.* 醇香
3. **be tossed around**
   （想法、建議或說法）被提出來
4. **category** [ˋkætə͵gɔrɪ] *n.* 類別
5. **floral** [ˋflɔrəl] *a.* 與花有關的；用花製成的
6. **herbal** [ˋ(h)ɝbḷ] *a.* 草本的
7. **respectively** [rɪˋspɛktɪvlɪ] *adv.* 分別地，個別地
8. **fermentation** [͵fɝmɛnˋteʃən] *n.* 發酵（不可數）
9. **reminiscent** [͵rɛməˋnɪsn̩t] *a.* 使人想起的
   A be reminiscent of B　　A 讓人想到 B
10. **tertiary** [ˋtɝʃɪ͵ɛrɪ] *a.* 第三級的
11. **barrel** [ˋbærəl] *n.* 桶
12. **infuse** [ɪnˋfjuz] *vt.* 注入
    infuse A with B　　將 B 注入於 A
13. **nutty** [ˋnʌtɪ] *a.* 有堅果味的
14. **caramel** [ˋkærəml] *n.* 焦糖（不可數）
15. **tobacco** [təˋbæko] *n.* 菸草（不可數）
16. **scent** [sɛnt] *n.* 香味

TEST 09

第 16 至 20 題為題組

在距離俄羅斯遠東地區的最大城海參崴不遠之處，是一個叫做烏蘇里灣的寧靜小區域。它最近引起了全球人們的注意，但並非是因為它的黑沙海灘，而是因為它海岸邊不尋常的垃圾。

事情的始末是這樣的，過去當俄羅斯還是蘇聯的一部分時，一輛接一輛的卡車滿載垃圾將其傾倒至海灣中。它們運送的廢棄物是由破罐子、當地一家瓷器工廠的瓷器碎片，以及空的啤酒瓶、葡萄酒瓶與伏特加酒瓶所組成。不過這裡沒有單純地變成一座醜陋的垃圾場，而是發生了超乎尋常的事情。久而久之，海浪來回沖刷海灘，磨平了碎玻璃與碎瓷器的尖銳邊角，而且還將它們磨亮成為色彩斑斕的小石子，現在它們看起來與其說是石頭更像是珠寶。

它在當地被稱為玻璃海灘，幾十年來已吸引了大批觀光客前往它的彩虹海岸。不過由於遊客偷偷撿走小石子以及大海的持續侵蝕，這雙重因素讓這座海灘可能不會維持現狀太久。

D　16.　理由

(A) **lifeguard** [ˋlaɪf͵gɑrd] *n.* 救生員
　　Three lifeguards are on duty at the pool at all times.
　　泳池邊隨時都有三名救生員執勤。

(B) **perfume** [ˋpɝfjum] *n.* 香水
　　Are you wearing the perfume I bought for you the other day?
　　你是擦我前幾天買給你的香水嗎？

(C) **reptile** [ˋrɛptaɪl] *n.* 爬蟲類
　　Lena has an encyclopedic knowledge of reptiles.
　　莉娜擁有極為豐富的爬蟲類相關知識。

(D) **garbage** [ˈɡɑrbɪdʒ] *n.* 垃圾（不可數）
Sort out your garbage before dumping it.
倒垃圾前要先將垃圾分類。

ⓑ 根據語意，(D) 項應為正選。

C 17. 理由

ⓐ (A) **be fed up with...** 受夠了……
= be sick and tired of...
I am fed up with my brother always using my computer without asking.
我受夠了弟弟老是沒問我就用我的電腦。

(B) **be used as...** 被用來（當作）……
My old vehicle is now used as a delivery truck.
我的老爺車現在被用來當成送貨車。

(C) **be made up of...** 由……組成
= be composed of...
= consist of...
This class is made up of 20 boys and five girls.
這個班級是由二十個男生和五個女生組成。

(D) **be worn out by...** 被……弄得筋疲力盡
I was worn out by all this hard work.
這些辛苦的工作已經把我弄得精疲力竭了。

ⓑ 根據語意，(C) 項應為正選。

D 18. 理由

ⓐ (A) **edible** [ˈɛdəbḷ] *a.* 可食用的
Not all mushrooms are edible. Many are poisonous.
並非所有的菇類都可食用。許多是有毒的。

(B) **innocent** [ˈɪnəsṇt] *a.* 清白的，無罪的；純真的
be innocent of... 無……的罪
The suspect claimed to be innocent of the robbery, but no one believed him.
該嫌犯聲稱這起搶案他是清白的，但沒人相信他。

(C) **optimistic** [ˌɑptəˈmɪstɪk] *a.* 樂觀的
be optimistic about... 對……表示樂觀
Investors are still relatively optimistic about the company's prospects.
投資人仍對該公司的前景相對樂觀。

(D) **unsightly** [ʌnˈsaɪtlɪ] *a.* 難看的，不雅觀的
There's an unsightly garbage collection dump across from my house.
我家對面有處很醜的垃圾收集場。

ⓑ 根據語意，(D) 項應為正選。

<u>A</u> 19. 理由

    ⓐ (A) **smooth** [smuð] *vt.* 使平坦
          smooth out...   將（皺褶）燙平
          You need an iron to smooth out those wrinkles on your shirt.
          你需要用熨斗來燙平你襯衫上的那些皺褶。

       (B) **squeeze** [skwiz] *vt.* 擠，榨
          Don't squeeze your pimples unless you want scars on your face.
          不要擠你的青春痘，除非你希望臉上留下疤痕。

       (C) **tease** [tiz] *vt.* 揶揄
          I couldn't help getting angry when I found out John was teasing me.
          我發現約翰在揶揄我時，就忍不住生氣了。

       (D) **deliver** [dɪˋlɪvɚ] *vt.* 遞送，運送
          That pizza shop delivers pizzas in less than 30 minutes.
          那間披薩店會在三十分鐘內將披薩送達。

    ⓑ 根據語意，(A) 項應為正選。

<u>B</u> 20. 理由

    ⓐ 本題測試以下語意：(A) on a daily basis（每天）、(B) for much longer（更久）、(C) in the peak season（在旺季）、(D) from time to time（偶爾）。

    ⓑ 根據空格前提及維持現狀，應該是接續維持現狀的時間有多久，故根據語意，(B) 項應為正選。

重要字詞片語

1. **a stone's throw away**
（喻）相距不遠，投石可及的距離
2. **as the story goes**　據說
3. **dump** [dʌmp] *vt.* 傾倒；丟棄，扔掉
At present, most of the garbage people create is dumped in landfills.
目前，大部分人們製造的垃圾都傾倒在掩埋場中。
4. **crack** [kræk] *vt.* 使破裂（本文為過去分詞作形容詞用）
5. **porcelain** [ˋpɔrslɪn] *n.* 瓷器（集合名詞，不可數）
6. **extraordinary** [ɪkˋstrɔrdn͵ɛrɪ] *a.* 非凡的
7. **pounding** [ˋpaʊndɪŋ] *n.* 連續的撞擊（聲）
8. **edge** [ɛdʒ] *n.* 邊緣
on the edge of...
在……的邊緣；瀕臨……
9. **ceramics** [səˋræmɪks] *n.* 陶瓷器（恆用複數）
10. **pebble** [ˋpɛbl̩] *n.* 鵝卵石

TEST 09

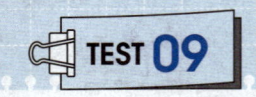

三、文意選填（占 10 分）

第 21 至 30 題為題組

　　已故英國理論物理學家史蒂芬·霍金有時被尊稱為現代愛因斯坦。他針對黑洞及其他天文現象所提出的理論和數學成就為他贏得了這項美名。霍金是理論宇宙學中心的研究主任，並獲頒總統自由勳章，他亦是暢銷書《時間簡史》的作者。簡而言之，霍金一發表談話，不僅是全科學界，而是全世界都會聆聽。他針對人類未來所發表的言論仍值得大家密切關注。

　　霍金很擔心人類今日面臨的許多問題。諸如戰爭、饑荒和經濟蕭條等社會問題，以及包括臭氧層破洞、酸雨和全球暖化等環境威脅，這些使得霍金提出唯一的解決辦法就是人類在未來要移居其他星球。換句話說，人類的生存可能要仰賴我們是否具備居住在月球、火星或其他天體的能力。人類總人口數目前已超過七十億，而且預計在二十一世紀中達到九十億。地球根本就沒有足夠的資源讓大家過安全且繁榮的生活。唯有藉著至少移居地球部分人口至外太空的其他世界，人類才得以生存。

　　當然，當霍金提出該想法時，他也知道要居住在地球以外的地方有費用及技術上的困難。他也警告萬一我們真的在外太空遇見外星人，我們應該要對這些外星人有所警覺，因為他們可能不太友善。人類最終命運的前景黯淡，然而卻也不全然毫無道理可言。也許霍金是藉由描繪出最糟的景況，來鼓舞我們全人類更加注意周遭常見的問題，並且共同努力解決這些問題。

G 21. 理由

ⓐ 空格前有本句主詞 His work in the theory and mathematics of black holes and other astronomical phenomena（他針對黑洞及其他天文現象所提出的理論和數學成就），空格後有間接受詞 him 和直接受詞 this recognition（讚賞），再根據前後文時態皆為過去式，得知空格內應置過去式動詞或過去式片語動詞。

ⓑ 選項中符合上述的有 (C) was concerned about（擔憂）、(G) earned（贏得）、(I) led（引導），惟根據語意，(G) 項應為正選。

C 22. 理由

ⓐ 空格前有主詞 Hawking（霍金），空格後有受詞 the many problems facing the human race today（人類今日面臨的許多問題），得知空格內應置動詞或片語動詞，然此句承接前文，故動詞時態應為過去式。

ⓑ 選項中符合上述的尚有 (C) was concerned about（擔憂）及 (I) led（引導），惟根據語意，(C) 項應為正選。

ⓒ 本題測試的固定結構：
be concerned / worried about...　　擔憂……
To tell you the truth, the manager is deeply concerned about this issue.
老實跟你說，經理很擔心這項議題。

I 23. 理由

ⓐ 空格前有本句主詞 Social problems...（社會問題……），空格後有受詞 Hawking，並根據前文時態，得知空格應置過去式動詞。

ⓑ 選項中符合上述的僅剩 (I) led（引導），置入空格後亦符合語意，且可與由空格後的不定詞 to 形成 lead sb to V 的固定用法，故 (I) 項應為正選。

lead sb to V　　引導／促使某人從事……
This evidence has led scientists to speculate on the existence of other galaxies.
這則證據促使科學家推測其他星系的存在。

D 24. 理由

ⓐ 空格前有形容詞 human（人類的），空格後有助動詞 may 及片語動詞 depend on（仰賴），得知空格內應置名詞，使其能被其前的形容詞修飾。

ⓑ 選項中符合上述的有 (D) survival（生存）、(E) resources（資源）及 (H) painting（繪畫），惟根據語意，(D) 項應為正選。

B 25. 理由

ⓐ 空格前有對等連接詞 and，空格後有原形動詞 reach（達到），得知空格應置入複數可數名詞作該子句的主詞，或是能讓 reach 作原形動詞的字詞，以形成對等。

ⓑ 選項中為複數可數名詞的僅剩 (E) resources（資源），但置入空格後不符合語意，故不可選；而 (B) is expected to（預期）的 to 為不定詞，其後可接原形動詞，且置入後亦符合語意，故為正選。

ⓒ 本題測試的固定結構：
be expected to V　　預期會……
House prices are expected to rise sharply.
房價預期會大幅上漲。

E 26. 理由

ⓐ 空格前有 There aren't（沒有）、形容詞 enough（足夠的），得知空格應置複數可數名詞。

ⓑ 選項中為複數可數名詞的僅剩 (E) resources（資源），置入空格後亦符合語意，故為正選。

F 27. 理由

ⓐ 空格前有介詞 by，得知空格應置動名詞作其受詞。

ⓑ 選項中為動名詞的有 (F) removing（移動）及 (H) painting（畫），惟根據語意，(F) 項應為正選。

TEST 09

A 28. 理由

ⓐ 空格前有 be 動詞，得知空格可置名詞或形容詞，但空格後又有介詞 of，得知空格內應置形容詞 wary（謹防的），以形成下列固定用法：
be wary of + N/V-ing　　小心提防……
You should always be wary of strangers who offer you a ride.
你應時刻提防讓你搭便車的陌生人。
I'm wary of giving people my address when I don't know them very well.
我對於要給那些我不太熟的人我家地址時會很小心謹慎。

ⓑ 根據上述，(A) 項應為正選。

J 29. 理由

ⓐ 空格前有所有格 man's（人類的），空格後有名詞 fate（命運），得知空格應置形容詞。

ⓑ 選項中為形容詞的僅剩 (J) ultimate（最終的），置入空格後亦符合語意，故為正選。

H 30. 理由

ⓐ 空格前有介詞 by，得知空格應置動名詞作其受詞。

ⓑ 選項中為動名詞的僅剩 (H) painting（畫），置入空格後亦符合語意，故為正選。

重要字詞片語

1. **theoretical** [θiəˋrɛtɪkl̩] *a.* 理論的
2. **physicist** [ˋfɪzɪsɪst] *n.* 物理學家
3. **astronomical** [ˌæstrəˋnɑmɪkl̩] *a.* 天文學的
   astronomy [əsˋtrɑnəmɪ] *n.* 天文學（不可數）
4. **phenomenon** [fəˋnɑməˌnɑn] *n.* 現象（複數為 phenomena [fəˋnɑmənə]）
5. **recognition** [ˌrɛkəgˋnɪʃən] *n.* 認可
6. **cosmology** [kɑzˋmɑlədʒɪ] *n.* 宇宙學（不可數）
7. **comment** [ˋkɑmɛnt] *n.* 評論
   make a comment on / about...
   針對……做出評論
   The manager made helpful comments on my work.
   經理針對我的工作做出了有幫助的評論。
8. **mankind** [mænˋkaɪnd] *n.* 全體人類（集合名詞，不可數）
   = humankind [ˌhjumənˋkaɪnd]
9. **deserve** [dɪˋzɝv] *vt.* 應得
   One player on our team in particular deserves a mention.
   我們隊上一位球員尤其值得一提。
10. **the human race**　　人類
11. **famine** [ˋfæmɪn] *n.* 饑荒
12. **depression** [dɪˋprɛʃən] *n.* 衰退，蕭條
    economic depression　　經濟蕭條
13. **threat** [θrɛt] *n.* 威脅
    pose a threat to...　　對……構成威脅
    Drugs pose a major threat to our society.
    毒品對我們的社會造成了重大威脅。
14. **ozone** [ˋozon] *n.* 臭氧（不可數）
    the ozone layer　　臭氧層

15. **acid rain**　酸雨
16. **prosperous** [ˈprɑspərəs] *a.* 繁榮的
17. **technical** [ˈtɛknɪkḷ] *a.* 技術上的
18. **unreasonable** [ʌnˈriznəbḷ] *a.* 不合理的
19. **scenario** [sɪˈnɛrɪˌo] *n.* 事態；情景
    the worst-case scenario
    最糟的情況
20. **encourage** [ɪnˈkɝɪdʒ] *vt.* 鼓勵
    encourage sb to V
    鼓勵某人從事⋯⋯

四、篇章結構（占 8 分）

第 31 至 34 題為題組

　　瑪雅是一個相對先進的文明，占據現今墨西哥及中美洲的領土長達三千多年。追溯至西元前九百年左右，提卡爾曾是馬雅文明的中心。提卡爾起初只是個小村莊，後來逐漸發展成一座人口估計略低於十萬的大城市。到了西元十世紀，該地已被廢棄，但在其全盛時期，它曾是重要的貿易與商業中心。

　　提卡爾坐落於現今瓜地馬拉北部的叢林中，以其宏偉建築最為人所知。**31.** 過去單在市中心就有三千多座建築林立，占地約十六平方公里。同樣引人注目的是稱為衛城的三座大型複合建築，由廟宇和宮殿所組成，推測是為上流階級而建。然而最壯觀的建築是六座主神廟，人們在那裡向先王致敬。**32.** 馬雅人就是在這些祭拜場所追蹤行星與恆星的運動。

　　這些觀星廟宇中，有兩座尤為突出。大美洲虎神廟高達四十五公尺，由九層階梯構成。**33.** 每一層都與馬雅文明的九層地獄一一呼應。面具神廟位於大美洲虎神廟的西邊，有四十二公尺高。這兩座建築作為大廣場盡頭的標記。該廣場是被宮殿、露天平臺以及球場包圍的廣闊公共空間。

　　這些宏偉建築的遺址是提卡爾國家公園的主要景點。該國家公園建於五〇年代，並在 1979 年被列為聯合國教科文組織世界遺產，現在每年約有二十萬遊客參觀。提卡爾國家公園由將近六萬公頃的溼地、大草原及雨林所組成。**34.** 它是各種動植物的棲息地。五種大型貓科動物、數種猴子和食蟻獸，以及超過三百種的鳥類都是一些較引人注目的野生動物。這座森林共有超過兩百種不同的樹木和兩千多種已被記載的植物。該公園和提卡爾已經成為瓜地馬拉的驕傲與國家象徵。

C 31. 理由
ⓐ 空格前的句子提到，提卡爾以其宏偉建築為人熟知，空格後的句子則提到，提卡爾亦有三座引人注目的複合建築，可推測空格應置與提卡爾建築相關的句子。

ⓑ 選項 (C) 表示，過去單在市中心就有三千多座建築林立，占地約十六平方公里，選項中的 More than 3,000 buildings（三千多座建築）可承接前句的 **its grand architecture**（其宏偉建築），亦可引出後句的 **three large complexes**（三座大型複合建築），填入後語意連貫，可知 (C) 項應為正選。

265

TEST 09

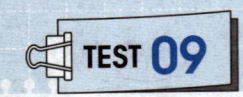

D 32. 理由
- ⓐ 空格前的句子提到，提卡爾最壯觀的建築是六座主神廟，空格後即為第三段的開頭，並介紹說明兩座廟宇，可推測空格應置與提卡爾神廟相關的句子。
- ⓑ 選項 (D) 表示，馬雅人就是在這些祭拜場所追蹤行星與恆星的運動，與後句的 these star-gazing temples（這些觀星廟宇）形成關聯，而選項中的 these places of worship（這些祭拜場所）亦與前句的 major temples（主神廟）相呼應，填入後語意連貫，可知 (D) 項應為正選。

E 33. 理由
- ⓐ 空格前的句子提到，大美洲虎神廟由九層階梯構成，空格後的句子則轉為提到面具神廟的資訊，可推測空格應提及與大美洲虎神廟相關的補充資訊。
- ⓑ 選項 (E) 表示，每一層都與馬雅文明的九層地獄一一呼應，選項中的 these 即為前句中的 nine tiers（九層階梯），而 nine levels（九層）亦與 nine tiers 相呼應，填入後語意連貫，可知 (E) 項應為正選。

B 34. 理由
- ⓐ 空格前的句子提到，提卡爾國家公園由將近六萬公頃的溼地、大草原及雨林所組成，空格後則提及該國家公園不同的野生動物、樹木和植物，可推測空格應置與該國家公園相關的句子。
- ⓑ 選項 (B) 表示，它是各種動植物的棲息地，選項中的 It 即指前句的 The park（該公園），a wide variety of plants and animals（各種動植物）亦與後文提及的各式野生動物、樹木和植物形成關聯，填入後語意連貫，可知 (B) 項應為正選。

(A) 項中譯：正是這場自然災害導致許多寺廟倒塌。

重要字詞片語

1. **civilization** [ˌsɪvələˈzeʃən] *n.* 文明
2. **occupy** [ˈɑkjəˌpaɪ] *vt.* 占據，占領
（三態為：occupy, occupied [ˈɑkjəˌpaɪd], occupied）
Those copy machines occupy most of that small room.
那些影印機占據了那個小房間的大半空間。
3. **estimated** [ˈɛstəˌmetɪd] *a.* 估計的，估算的
4. **population** [ˌpɑpjəˈleʃən] *n.* 人口
5. **abandon** [əˈbændən] *vt.* 放棄；離棄
The sailors were ordered to abandon ship.
船員們被命令棄船。
6. **prime** [praɪm] *n.* 全盛時期 & *a.* 主要的；最好的
7. **commerce** [ˈkɑmɝs] *n.* 商業（不可數）
8. **grand** [grænd] *a.* 雄偉的，壯麗的
9. **impressive** [ɪmˈprɛsɪv] *a.* 令人印象深刻的
10. **complex** [ˈkɑmplɛks] *n.* 綜合大樓，建築群大樓
11. **imposing** [ɪmˈpozɪŋ] *a.* 壯觀的，宏偉的
12. **worship** [ˈwɝʃɪp] *n.* & *vt.* 敬拜
13. **tier** [tɪr] *n.* （一）層

14. **correspond** [ˌkɔrəˈspɑnd] *vi.* 符合
    correspond to / with...
    和……相符
    The numbers on the keys correspond to the mailboxes on the first floor.
    這些鑰匙上的號碼跟一樓的信箱號碼相符。
15. **vast** [væst] *a.* 廣闊的
16. **terrace** [ˈtɛrəs] *n.* 陽臺（尤指露天大陽臺）
17. **ruin** [ˈruɪn] *n.* 廢墟（常用複數）
18. **declare** [dɪˈklɛr] *vt.* 宣布，宣告
    This area was declared a wildlife refuge by the government.
    這地區被政府公告為野生動物保護區。
19. **heritage** [ˈhɛrətɪdʒ] *n.* （歷史所留下的傳統、文化、語言等）遺產（不可數）
20. **comprise** [kəmˈpraɪz] *vt.* 包括；組成
    be comprised of...   由……組成
    = be made up of...
    = consist of...
    Our company's product line comprises 30 different items.
    我們公司的產品系列含有三十種不同的產品。
    This class is comprised of 50 students.
    = This class is made up of 50 students.
    = This class consists of 50 students.
    這個班級由五十位學生所組成。
21. **savannah** [səˈvænə] *n.* 大草原
    (= savanna)

TEST 09

五、閱讀測驗（占 24 分）

第 35 至 38 題為題組

　　亞馬遜王蓮是一種睡蓮，生長於南美洲亞馬遜河流域的平靜淺水域。幾乎像是從科幻電影裡走出來的這種植物，是世界上最大型的睡蓮。它在 1801 年被一名來自於現今捷克地區的植物學家兼探險家塔德烏斯・漢克發現，於十九世紀中葉引進歐洲，不過它的自然棲息地一直都圍繞著亞馬遜流域。

　　亞馬遜王蓮最主要的特徵就是其巨大的葉子和特殊的花朵。這些圓形的綠葉可以長到直徑三公尺，且據說它們強韌到足以托起重達三十公斤的人或動物。它們的圓周邊緣翹起，並有缺口便於排水，底部有稜紋，可以截留空氣並幫助它們漂浮。該植物亦開出外觀嬌柔的白色花朵，能長到直徑四十公分，但開花期僅能維持四十八小時。在這段時間內，它們用甜美類似鳳梨的香氣吸引飛行的甲蟲來為它們授粉。甲蟲落在花朵上後，它會暫時閉合並失去香氣。不過花朵不會吃掉昆蟲，隔天晚上就會放牠們飛走，讓牠們攜帶花粉至其他睡蓮。此時花會從白色變成粉紅色，並由雌花變成雄花。

　　亞馬遜王蓮值得注意的另一個地方是它看不到的部分。該植物的莖在水面下方可往下延展至八公尺長並將自己固定在河床。它們具有能保護自己免遭魚類啃食的尖刺。亞馬遜王蓮真正是一大奇觀。

TEST 09

C 35. 本文的主旨為何？
(A) 南美洲的植物多樣性。
(B) 針對特殊植物進行的研究。
(C) 一種獨特植物有趣的特徵。
(D) 全世界所發現不同種類的睡蓮。

> **理由**
> 全文主要講述亞馬遜王蓮這種獨特的植物，故 (C) 項應為正選。

B 36. 為何捷克會在本文中被提及？
(A) 它是第一個發現這種植物的地方。
(B) 發現這種植物的科學家來自於此。
(C) 這種植物現在大部分都生長於此處。
(D) 它是對這種植物做詳細研究的地方。

> **理由**
> 根據本文第一段第三句，它在 1801 年被一名來自於現今捷克地區的植物學家兼探險家塔德烏斯‧漢克發現，故 (B) 項應為正選。

A 37. 關於亞馬遜王蓮的花朵，下列哪一項陳述是正確的？
(A) 它們在第二天改變顏色。
(B) 它們吸引甲蟲以吃掉牠們。
(C) 它們會從雄性轉變為雌性。
(D) 它們大得足以支撐一個人。

> **理由**
> 根據本文第二段最後一句，此時花會從白色變成粉紅色……，故 (A) 項應為正選。

B 38. 最後一段中的 its unseen portion 指的是什麼？
(A) 葉子的底部。
(B) 該植物的莖。
(C) 河床。
(D) 該花的花粉。

> **理由**
> 根據最後一段，在「看不到的部分」下一句即緊接著提到，該植物的莖在水面下方可往下延展至八公尺長，故 (B) 項應為正選。

重要字詞片語

1. **lily** [ˈlɪlɪ] *n.* 百合
   a water lily　　睡蓮
2. **shallow** [ˈʃælo] *a.* 淺的
3. **basin** [ˈbesn̩] *n.* 流域；盆地
4. **botanist** [ˈbɑtənɪst] *n.* 植物學家
5. **habitat** [ˈhæbə͵tæt] *n.* 棲息地
   a natural habitat　　天然棲息地
6. **diameter** [daɪˈæmətɚ] *n.* 直徑
   be... in diameter　　直徑是……
   This circle is 5 cm in diameter.
   這個圓的直徑是五公分。
7. **weigh** [we] *vt.* 重達……；秤重量
8. **lip** [lɪp] *n.* (容器的) 嘴；嘴唇
9. **notched** [nɑtʃt] *a.* 有缺口的
10. **facilitate** [fəˈsɪlə͵tet] *vt.* 幫助，促進
    The new policies are expected to facilitate economic growth.
    這些新的政策預期會帶動經濟成長。
11. **drainage** [ˈdrenɪdʒ] *n.* 排水 (不可數)
12. **ribbed** [rɪbd] *a.* 有稜紋的，有羅紋的
13. **trap** [træp] *vt.* 保存 (熱量、水)，收集；捕捉 (三態為：trap, trapped [træpt], trapped)
14. **afloat** [əˈflot] *a.* 漂浮的
15. **scent** [sɛnt] *n.* 香味
16. **pollinate** [ˈpɑlə͵net] *vt.* 為 (植物) 授粉
    pollen [ˈpɑlən] *n.* 花粉 (不可數)

17. **temporarily** [ˈtɛmpəˌrɛrəlɪ] *adv.*
    暫時地
18. **release** [rɪˈlis] *vt.* 釋放，釋出
    After ten years in prison, the prisoner was released this morning.
    坐了十年牢後，那名囚犯今早獲釋。
19. **stalk** [stɔk] *n.* 莖
20. **embed** [ɪmˈbɛd] *vt.* 把……埋入／插入（三態為：embed, embedded [ɪmˈbɛdɪd], embedded）
21. **behold** [bɪˈhold] *vt.* 看見；注視
    （三態為：behold, beheld [bɪˈhɛld], beheld）
    The trip may have been expensive, but the opportunity to behold such a spectacular view was priceless.
    這趟旅行或許很貴，但能目睹這片美景的機會是無價的。
22. **vegetation** [ˌvɛdʒəˈteʃən] *n.* （總稱）植物（不可數）

第 39 至 42 題為題組

《平安夜》這首不凡的歌曲一直以來都受到慶祝聖誕季節的人們喜愛。事實上，它是史上最受人喜愛的聖誕歌曲，已被翻譯成三百多種語言。

在 2018 年，奧地利慶祝《平安夜》的創作兩百週年紀念，因為它的詞曲作者都是奧地利人。《平安夜》的首演就是由譜曲寫詞的兩人所帶來的：音樂老師弗朗茨・克薩維爾・格魯伯以及牧師約瑟夫・莫爾。他們在 1818 年的聖誕夜獻唱這首歌，不過莫爾在兩年前擔任助理牧師的時候，其實是將它寫成一首詩。咸信格魯伯本來將其寫成吉他伴奏曲，並以吉他演奏，因為他們要演唱的那座教堂的風琴故障了。事實上，這間在薩爾茲堡的歐本多夫的聖尼古拉教堂，之後也歷經了幾場洪水造成無法修復的損害，最終被平安夜禮拜堂取代，現在是這首歌曲的紀念館。

不久之後，其他人注意到《平安夜》的優美，於是在其他地區開始有人演唱它。有兩組家族歌手 —— 雷納家族和斯特拉瑟兄弟姊妹 —— 非常喜歡這首歌並將它納入巡迴表演的曲目。這首歌透過他們在英國、德國與瑞典都曾演出過，最後演變出與原曲略有出入但為我們現在所熟悉的旋律。當這首歌被收錄在某本書中後變得廣為人知。然而，直到美國歌手平・克勞斯貝於 1935 年錄製了他的《平安夜》版本後，這首歌才成為全世界的流行歌曲。

在那個時候，莫爾已被遺忘是這首歌的創作者之一。人們普遍認為應該是如莫札特或貝多芬等知名人物的作品。不過，莫爾的詩作手稿在 1995 年被發現，證明了他就是《平安夜》的歌曲創作者之一。因此，他重新成為這首全球最受喜愛聖誕歌曲之一的共同創作者。

TEST 09

C 39. 本文最適合的標題是什麼？
(A) 最受歡迎的奧地利聖誕歌曲
(B) 歌曲翻譯簡史
(C) 一首名曲的起源與演變
(D) 平安夜禮拜堂介紹

> 理由

本文先介紹《平安夜》歌曲的由來與創作者，後面介紹它被樂團在好幾個國家演奏，最後有與現今略為不同的旋律。之後再到它被發表在書中、被美國歌手錄製之後在全世界受到歡迎的過程。故 (C) 項應為正選。

D 40. 第二段中的 clergyman 最有可能是什麼意思？
(A) 學校校長。　(B) 導遊。　(C) 管風琴演奏家。　(D) 宗教領導。

> 理由

本文第二段第二句中 clergyman 的下一句緊接著提到 while working as an assistant priest（擔任助理牧師的時候），可推測 clergyman 為「牧師」之意，故 (D) 項應為正選。

D 41. 是什麼讓《平安夜》這首歌受到全世界的歡迎？
(A) 一名德國的遊客寫了它的新版本。
(B) 一名英國歌手將它介紹給他的家人。
(C) 一名瑞典作家寫了一本關於它的書。
(D) 一名美國歌手發行了他的演唱版本。

> 理由

根據本文第三段最後一句，然而，直到美國歌手平·克勞斯貝於 1935 年錄製了他的《平安夜》版本後，這首歌才成為全世界的流行歌曲，故 (D) 項應為正選。

A 42. 本文最後一段暗示約瑟夫·莫爾和《平安夜》的什麼事情？
(A) 多年來他對這首歌曲的參與被不公平的忽略。
(B) 他從一位知名的作曲家那裡偷來這首歌的構思。
(C) 他對這首歌曲的貢獻一直以來被誇大。
(D) 他糟糕的字跡使這首歌詞被誤讀。

> 理由

根據第四段表示，在那個時候，莫爾已被遺忘是這首歌的創作者之一，隨後並說明這首歌普遍被認為是他人的作品，直到發現莫爾的手稿才得到正名。故 (A) 項應為正選。

> 重要字詞片語

1. **adore** [ə'dɔr] *vt.* 喜愛，寵愛
Aria has 10 grandchildren, and she adores all of them very much.
艾瑞亞有十個孫子，每個她都很疼愛。

2. **beloved** [bɪ'lʌvɪd] *a.* 心愛的，受鍾愛的

3. **translate** [træns'let] *vi.* & *vt.* 翻譯（尤指筆譯）
be translated into...
被翻譯成……（語言）
I translated the sentence into English.
我把這個句子翻譯成英文。

4. **anniversary** [ˌænə'vɝsərɪ] *n.* 週年（紀念）

5. **owing to...**　由於……
Owing to a couple of holidays, we delayed answering your fax inquiry.
由於放了數天假，我們延遲回覆您傳真來的提問。

6. **pen** [pɛn] *vt.* 寫（三態為：pen, penned [pɛnd], penned）
   pen a letter / novel / poem
   寫信/小說/詩
   It had been a long time since Jim penned a letter.
   吉姆已好久沒寫信了。

7. **lyrics** [ˈlɪrɪks] *n.* 歌詞（恆用複數）

8. **eve** [iv] *n.* 前夕
   Christmas Eve　　聖誕前夕，平安夜

9. **priest** [prist] *n.* 牧師，神父

10. **operational** [ˌɑpəˈreʃən!] *a.* 運作中的

11. **beyond repair**　　無法修復
    The car is beyond repair. You should buy a new one.
    那輛車不能修理了。你該買新車了。

12. **chapel** [ˈtʃæp!] *n.* 小禮拜堂

13. **monument** [ˈmɑnjəmənt] *n.* 紀念碑

14. **perceive** [pəˈsiv] *vt.* 察覺；認為
    The mother perceived a subtle change in her daughter's behavior.
    這位母親察覺到女兒的行為有微妙的變化。

15. **melody** [ˈmɛlədɪ] *n.* 曲調，旋律

16. **assume** [əˈsum] *vt.* 認為（以 that...作為受詞）
    Paul assumed that his girlfriend was joking when she said he was ugly.
    保羅的女友說他很醜時，他認定她一定是在開玩笑。

17. **figure** [ˈfɪgjɚ] *n.* 人物

18. **tune** [tjun] *n.* 曲子；旋律

19. **release** [rɪˈlis] *vt.* 發行，發布
    After Phoebe released that song, she became an overnight star.
    菲比發行了那首歌之後，一夕之間成了明星。

20. **overlook** [ˌovɚˈluk] *vt.* 忽略
    Do not overlook the rules of grammar when writing an English essay.
    寫英文文章時，不要忽略文法規則。

21. **overstate** [ˌovɚˈstet] *vt.* 過於誇大

TEST 09

第 43 至 46 題為題組

　　胸花是別在西裝外套或男士小禮服翻領上的花。所謂翻領就是外套胸前翻折的長條布料。雖然你可能會看到胸花被別在不同的位置 —— 例如外套右側或是上衣口袋 —— 但事實上只有一個適合的位置，那就是在翻領的扣眼上，在穿衣者外套的左側。花的莖通常會被扣眼後面的一個小環固定住。如果沒有環，則將花用別針別在外套上加以固定。

　　關於胸花的起源眾說紛紜。有些人主張它們可追溯至古埃及，另外有些人則指出這種裝飾品首先在英國內戰期間佩戴以識別敵我。然而是到了十八、十九世紀，我們現在所認知的胸花才流行起來。佩戴胸花作為衣著的一部分，被認為不但可以袪除不好的味道還能驅鬼避邪。此外，這樣的配件變成每日時尚宣言且被認為是文雅世故的象徵。這個想法延續到二十世紀。

　　如今，胸花專門留給正式場合使用，像是婚禮和正式舞會。在婚禮上，胸花的顏色很可能會搭配新娘捧花的顏色。婚禮中的男性 —— 新郎、伴郎和新娘與新郎的父親 —— 全都戴上胸花是標準慣例。不過新郎的胸花可能會比較大或比較特別。傳統上也規定使用花的品種，像紅色或白

色的康乃馨、藍色的矢車菊，或是白色的梔子花是最常見的。但其他種類的花也越來越常被採用，大多是以新娘與新郎的意願，以及婚禮的色彩主題，來決定選擇這重要的最後點綴。

C 43. 根據本文，哪裡是佩戴胸花的正確位置？
(A) 位置 A。
(B) 位置 B。
(C) 位置 C。
(D) 位置 D。

理由
根據本文第一段第三句，事實上只有一個適合的位置，那就是在翻領的扣眼上，在穿衣者外套的左側，故 (C) 項應為正選。

D 44. 下列哪些字用來意指文中的胸花？
a. 裝飾品　　b. 意願　　c. 配件　　d. 花　　e. 花束　　f. 點綴
(A) a, b, d, f
(B) b, c, d, e
(C) a, b, c, d
(D) a, c, d, f

理由
根據本文分別將胸花意指為花、這種裝飾品、這樣的配件、最後點綴，故 (D) 項應為正選。

C 45. 本文中並未提及下列哪一項是胸花可能的起源？
(A) 它們被某個古文明的人所佩戴。
(B) 它們在十九世紀時被用來當作日常穿著。
(C) 它們被創造用來識別不同的家庭。
(D) 它們被用來分辨在戰場上的人。

理由
根據本文第二段第二句，有些人主張胸花可追溯至古埃及，而有另一些人指出胸花首先在英國內戰期間佩戴以識別敵我。另外，第二段第三與六句提及在十八、十九世紀，胸花變得流行起來，且其變成每日時尚宣言到二十世紀仍持續下來。僅有 (C) 項未被提及，故為正選。

C 46. 根據本文，在現代的婚禮中，最有可能決定胸花的選擇是什麼？
(A) 新郎的身高與體型。
(B) 花店裡有賣什麼花。
(C) 準新人的意願。
(D) 所搭配花束的大小。

理由
根據本文第三段最後一句，大多是新娘與新郎的意願，以及婚禮的色彩主題，來決定選擇這重要的最後點綴，故 (C) 項應為正選。

重要字詞片語

1. **boutonnière** [ˌbutn̩ˋjɛr] *n.* 胸花
2. **lapel** [ləˋpɛl] *n.* （西服上的）翻領
3. **tuxedo** [tʌkˋsido] *n.* （男）小禮服
4. **breast** [brɛst] *n.* 上衣前部
   a breast pocket　　上衣口袋
5. **loop** [lup] *n.* 環，圈

6. **opposing** [ə`pozɪŋ] *a.* 對立的
7. **attire** [ə`taɪr] *n.* （正式的）服裝，衣著（不可數）
8. **refinement** [rɪ`faɪnmənt] *n.* 文雅；高雅（不可數）
9. **sophistication** [sə͵fɪstə`keʃən] *n.* 世故，老練（不可數）
10. **persist** [pɚ`sɪst] *vi.* 持續；堅持
    Go find a doctor if your headache persists.
    如果你頭痛一直持續，還是去找個醫生吧。
11. **prom** [prɑm] *n.* 正式舞會
12. **bouquet** [bu`ke] *n.* 花束
13. **dictate** [`dɪktet] *vt. & vi.* 規定
    The committee didn't dictate how the money should be spent.
    委員會並未規定這筆錢應該怎麼花。
14. **carnation** [kɑr`neʃən] *n.* 康乃馨
15. **gardenia** [gɑr`dɪnɪə] *n.* 梔子花
16. **scheme** [skim] *n.* 方案，計畫
17. **adopt** [ə`dɑpt] *vt.* 採用，採納
    The general manager adopted my proposal without hesitation.
    總經理毫不猶豫地採用了我的提案。
18. **build** [bɪld] *n.* 身材，體型

TEST 09

TEST 09

第貳部分、混合題（占 10 分）

第 47 至 51 題為題組

以下是一則新聞報導以及四位民眾對該報導帶出的話題的看法。

別忘了帶牙刷！

本報記者／亞當・德內希

臺灣的旅館現在被禁止向房客提供一次性盥洗用品。新法規於 1 月 1 日生效，規定旅館不得提供小於 180 毫升容量的用品，如沐浴乳和洗髮精等。此外也不得在房間內提供梳子、刮鬍刀和牙刷等個人衛生用品。房客可自行攜帶或向旅館櫃檯索取或購買。此政策旨在減少塑膠垃圾並推動永續觀念。

(A) 伊琳諾

我很清楚這項政策對環境是好的。過去我在打掃房間時，經常要丟掉用了一半的洗髮精和潤髮乳瓶子。現在我只要補滿房間內的大瓶裝就好了。我確信有些客人會為了不再提供小條牙膏去櫃檯抱怨，但為了更乾淨的地球，這只是小小的代價。

(B) 雷特

免費盥洗用品是住旅館的好處之一。我經常到臺灣出差，很喜歡從前房間裡會提供屬於我的一套小小盥洗用品組。如此我就可以在見客戶前好好梳洗一番，不必擔心行李裡頭少帶了什麼東西。現在我得自己帶上從刮鬍刀到梳子等拉拉雜雜的各種東西。

(C) 希薇亞

我可以理解減塑垃圾的必要性，但制定這些政策的政府官員不用面對發飆的旅館客人。儘管我們已在官網上公告新規定，但當我在客人辦理入住時告知這項政策後，他們還是震驚不已，然後就會抱怨不知道需要自備牙刷或刮鬍刀，還要額外付費購買。

(D) 查德

除了減少塑膠垃圾外，此政策還有其他數不清的優點，包括：每年減少約 2,500 公噸碳排放、鼓勵人們在生活其他層面養成更永續的習慣，以及展現臺灣在世界舞臺上的負責任形象等等。我就對自己在推行這項政策中扮演的角色深感自豪。

47-49. 在最有可能的職稱旁填入上述人名字母代號。

旅館櫃檯人員： 47. ___C___

旅館清潔人員： 48. ___A___

外勤業務： 49. ___B___

> 理由

第 47 題，根據希薇亞看法的第二句 ... when I remind them about the policy at check-in.（當我在客人辦理入住時告知這項政策後……）得知，空格應置 (C)。

第 48 題，根據伊琳諾看法的第二句 When I was cleaning rooms in the past, ...（過去我在打掃房間時，……）得知，空格應置 (A)。

第 49 題，根據雷特看法的第二句，I travel to Taiwan regularly for business, ...（我經常到臺灣出差，……）及第三句 ... I could freshen up properly before meeting clients...（……我就可以在見客戶前好好梳洗一番……）得知，空格應置 (B)。

___C___ 50. 哪一種一次性用品在新聞中有提到，並在至少兩個看法中也有提到？

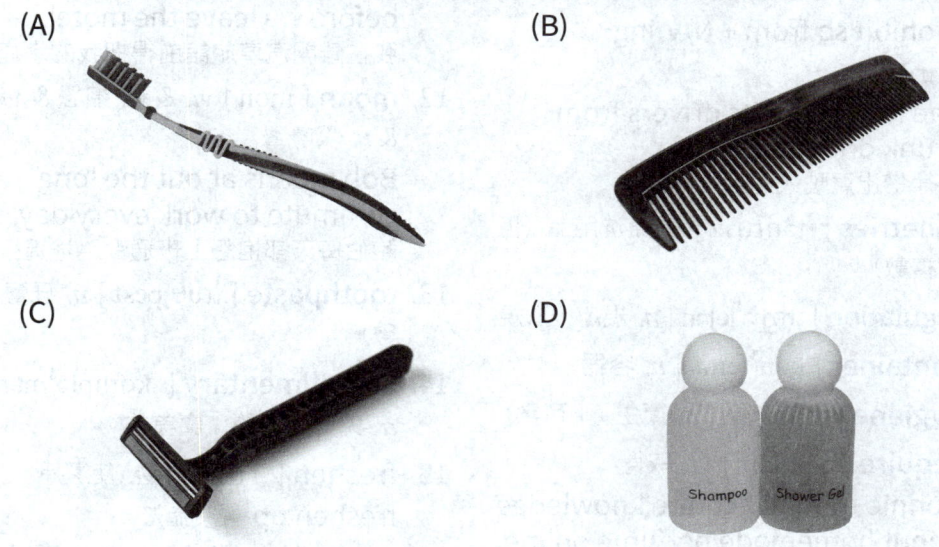

(A)

(B)

(C)

(D)

> 理由

根據新聞第三句提到 ...not allowed to provide personal hygiene products such as combs, razors, and toothbrushes in the rooms.（……不得在房間內提供梳子、刮鬍刀和牙刷等個人衛生用品。）且雷特看法的最後一句 ...I have to bring everything from a razor to a comb with me.（……我得自己帶上從刮鬍刀到梳子等拉拉雜雜的各種東西。）和希薇亞看法的最後一句 ...they complain about paying for a toothbrush or a razor...（……就會抱怨不知道需要自備牙刷或刮鬍刀，還要額外付費購買……），得知 (C) 項應為正選。

TEST 09

51. 回應中的哪一個字表示「數量非常多」的意思？

極大數量

myriad

理由

根據查德看法的第二句提到了 reducing carbon emissions（減少碳排放）、encouraging people to adopt more sustainable habits（鼓勵人們養成更永續的習慣）、showing that Taiwan is a responsible player（展現臺灣負責任形象），後面又講到 and many more（等等），解釋了前句 a myriad of other benefits（其他數不清的優點），得知空格應置 myriad。

重要字詞片語

1. **issue** [ˋɪʃjʊ] *n.* 重大議題；爭議；期刊 & *vt.* 發行

2. **prohibit** [prəˋhɪbɪt] *vt.* 禁止
   prohibit sb from + N/V-ing
   禁止某人……
   The law prohibits drivers from drunk driving.
   法律禁止駕駛人酒駕。

3. **toiletries** [ˋtɔɪlɪtriz] *n.* 盥洗用品（恆用複數）

4. **regulation** [ˏrɛgjəˋleʃən] *n.* 規定，法規

5. **container** [kənˋtenɚ] *n.* 容器

6. **hygiene** [ˋhaɪdʒin] *n.* 衛生（不可數）

7. **acquire** [əˋkwaɪr] *vt.* 取得
   Bonnie tried to acquire knowledge about homemade perfume online.
   邦妮試圖在網路上取得自製香水的知識。

8. **reception** [rɪˋsɛpʃən] *n.* 服務臺

9. **sustainability** [səˏstenəˋbɪlətɪ] *n.* 永續性；持續性（不可數）
   sustainable [səˋstenəbḷ] *a.* 可持續的，能長期維持的

10. **conditioner** [kənˋdɪʃənɚ] *n.* 護髮素

11. **refill** [riˋfɪl] *vt.* 填補；填充 & [ˋrifɪl] *n.* 填充物
    I need to refill my water bottle before we leave the motel.
    我在離開汽車旅館前得把我的水壺裝滿。

12. **moan** [mon] *vt.* & *vi.* 抱怨 & *vi.* 哀嚎 & *n.* 哀嚎聲
    Bob moans about the long commute to work every day.
    鮑伯每天都抱怨上班通勤路途遙遠。

13. **toothpaste** [ˋtuθˏpest] *n.* 牙膏（不可數）

14. **complimentary** [ˏkɑmpləˋmɛntərɪ] *a.* 免費贈送的；讚美的

15. **freshen** [ˋfrɛʃən] *vt.* 使潔淨
    freshen up　梳洗
    After a long flight, I always like to freshen up in the hotel.
    長途飛行後，我總要在旅館裡梳洗一番。

16. **annoyed** [əˋnɔɪd] *a.* 感到惱怒的

17. **publish** [ˋpʌblɪʃ] *vt.* 公布，發表；出版
    The news was published online.
    這則消息在網上公布了。

18. **slash** [slæʃ] *vt.* 削減 & *n.* 斜線（表有其他選擇）；（長又深的）砍痕
    The company decided to slash its advertising budget.
    公司決定削減其廣告預算。
19. **carbon** [ˈkɑrbən] *n.* 碳
    carbon emissions　碳排放
20. **estimated** [ˈɛstəˌmetɪd] *a.* 估算的，預計的
21. **metric** [ˈmɛtrɪk] *a.* 公制的
22. **annually** [ˈænjʊəlɪ] *adv.* 每年
23. **implement** [ˈɪmpləˌmɛnt] *vt.* 實施 & [ˈɪmpləmənt] *n.* 工具，用具
    The government plans to implement new regulations to reduce pollution.
    政府計劃實施新的法規來減少汙染。

TEST 09

第參部分、非選擇題（占 28 分）

一、中譯英（占 8 分）

1. 行動支付結合了消費者的錢包與手機而成為新的消費趨勢。

   示範譯句
   Mobile payments have become a new trend for spending money by combining the consumer's purse and mobile phone.

   或：Mobile payments are now a popular way of paying for things by integrating consumers' wallets with their smartphones.

   翻譯要點
   a. **mobile payment** 行動支付
   b. **trend** [trɛnd] *n.* 趨勢；潮流（常用複數）
   c. **combine** [kəmˋbaɪn] *vt.* & *vi.* 使結合，使組合
      combine A and / with B
      結合 A 與 B
      The artist combined red and blue paint to make purple.
      那位藝術家混合了紅藍兩色來調出紫色顏料。
   d. **consumer** [kənˋs(j)umɚ] *n.* 消費者
   e. **integrate** [ˋɪntəˌgret] *vt.* & *vi.* 使結合／合併
      integrate (A) with B
      （將 A）與 B 整合
      integrate A into B 使 A 併入／融入 B
      The art teacher was trying to integrate art with history in the lesson.
      那位美術老師試著在課堂上將美術與歷史做結合。
      The new computer software integrates last year's data into this year's.
      這款新電腦軟體可將去年的資料併入今年的。

2. 這讓人們就算沒有攜帶任何現金也可以在店家購物。

   示範譯句
   This enables people to make purchases at a shop even if they are not carrying any cash.

   或：This makes it possible for people to purchase items at a store without having to bring cash with them.

   翻譯要點
   a. **enable sb to V** 使某人能夠……
      The year-end bonus enabled Ethan to take a trip to Paris.
      這筆年終獎金讓伊森得以來趟巴黎之旅。
   b. **purchase** [ˋpɝtʃəs] *n.* & *vt.* 購買
      make a purchase (of…)
      購買（……）

When there's a big sale, I often have to wait in line to use the fitting room or make a purchase.
當有大特價時，我通常必須排隊使用試衣間或排隊購物。

You should have purchased the tickets for the concert two months ago.
你兩個月前就該買音樂會的票了。

c. **make it possible for sb to V**
使某人能夠做……
The bank loan will make it possible for us to start our own business.
這筆銀行貸款將讓我們能夠自己創業。

二、英文作文（占 20 分）

提示：你認為凡事都要事前規劃嗎？請寫一篇短文說明你的看法。文分兩段，第一段針對是否要事前規劃，說明你的看法及理由，第二段則舉例說明你曾事前規劃過什麼事情，並描述規劃後有什麼結果。

示範作文

　　The importance of planning ahead cannot be overemphasized, as leaving things until the last minute can cause some major problems. It can cost you time, money, and sometimes even your job. When you plan ahead, you feel more in control of your day-to-day life, which helps you achieve future success in almost anything. In other words, planning ahead can make it easier to complete new projects, reach your goals, and realize your dreams.

　　Several months ago, a few friends and I planned a one-day trip to Hualien in eastern Taiwan. We agreed on going to Farglory Ocean Park since none of us had been there. Despite the good weather in the early morning, it began to pour when we were about to reach Hualien. The heavy rain prevented us from enjoying the water rides in the park, so it was a good thing that we had a plan B: visiting Hualien Stone Sculpture Museum. Thanks to the plans we had made ahead of time, we still had a good trip to Hualien.

　　事前規劃的重要性再怎麼強調也不為過，因為把事情留到最後一刻才處理會導致一些重大問題。那樣會耗費你的時間、金錢，有時甚至會丟掉工作。當你提前計劃時，你可以更好掌控日常生活，這有助於在幾乎任何事情上取得未來的成功。換言之，事前規劃讓你更容易完成新的企劃、達成目標並實現夢想。

　　數個月前，我和幾個朋友計劃去東臺灣的花蓮一日遊。我們一致同意去遠雄海洋公園，因為我們都沒去過那裡。儘管清晨天氣很好，我們快抵達花蓮時就開始下起大雨。這場大雨使我們無法享受公園裡的水上設施，因此我們採取 B 計畫：參觀花蓮縣石雕博物館。由於提前制訂的計畫，我們仍然有一趟美好的花蓮之旅。

279

TEST 09

重要字詞片語

1. **overemphasize** [ˌovɚˈɛmfəˌsaɪz] *vt.* 過分強調
   Keeping the bathroom clean and tidy cannot be overemphasized.
   保持浴室的清潔與整齊再怎麼強調也不為過。

2. **in control of...** 掌控／控制……
   Don't worry. We're already in control of the whole situation.
   別擔心。我們已掌控全局。

3. **achieve** [əˈtʃiv] *vt.* 完成,實現

4. **reach one's goal(s)** 達成某人的目標

5. **realize one's dream(s)** 實現某人的夢想

6. **agree on...** 對……一致同意
   My roommate and I agreed on who is responsible for taking out the trash.
   室友和我一同決定好該由誰負責倒垃圾。

7. **pour** [pɔr] *vi.* 傾盆而下

8. **prevent sb from V-ing** 阻止某人從事……

9. **sculpture** [ˈskʌlptʃɚ] *n.* 雕刻品,雕塑品

10. **thanks to...** 由於／幸虧……

11. **ahead of time** (較預定時間或排程) 事先／提前

TEST 10

第壹部分、選擇題

一、詞彙題
二、綜合測驗
三、文意選填
四、篇章結構
五、閱讀測驗

第貳部分、混合題

第參部分、非選擇題

一、中譯英
二、英文作文

第壹部分、選擇題

一、詞彙題

| 1. D | 2. A | 3. C | 4. B | 5. C | 6. C | 7. B | 8. A | 9. D | 10. A |

二、綜合測驗

| 11. B | 12. D | 13. A | 14. D | 15. C | 16. B | 17. A | 18. C | 19. C | 20. D |

三、文意選填

| 21. C | 22. F | 23. A | 24. H | 25. E | 26. B | 27. J | 28. G | 29. D | 30. I |

四、篇章結構

| 31. B | 32. C | 33. A | 34. D |

五、閱讀測驗

| 35. A | 36. C | 37. C | 38. B | 39. A | 40. B | 41. D | 42. B | 43. C | 44. B |
| 45. B | 46. A |

第貳部分、混合題

47. repair tissue, regenerate cells, and strengthen our immune system

48. our eyes move rapidly

49. process our experiences and memories from the previous day

50. B, E

第壹部分、選擇題（占 62 分）

一、詞彙題（占 10 分）

D 1. 這兩位名人在 IG 上發布一份聯合聲明，宣布他們將於夏天結婚。

ⓐ (A) **cunning** [ˈkʌnɪŋ] *a.* 狡猾的
The fox is often portrayed as a cunning animal in fairy tales.
童話故事裡，狐狸通常被描述成狡猾的動物。

(B) **steady** [ˈstɛdɪ] *a.* 穩定的
It's hard to find a steady job these days.
這年頭要找一份穩定的工作很難。

(C) **satisfactory** [ˌsætɪsˈfæktərɪ] *a.* 令人滿意的
I couldn't get a satisfactory explanation for what had occurred.
對於所發生的事我找不到滿意的解釋。

(D) **joint** [dʒɔɪnt] *a.* 聯合的，共有的
The young couple opened a joint account for convenience's sake.
這對年輕夫婦為了方便起見開了個共同戶頭。

ⓑ 根據語意及用法，(D) 項應為正選。

【必考重點】
celebrity [səˈlɛbrətɪ] *n.* 名人（可數）；名聲，名氣（不可數）

A 2. 艾蜜莉亞對於無法買到泰勒絲演唱會的票感到失望，因為太快就賣光了。

ⓐ (A) **purchase** [ˈpɝtʃəs] *vt.* 購買
I purchased some face masks and hand sanitizer at the store.
我在店裡買了些口罩和乾洗手。

(B) **cite** [saɪt] *vt.* 引用
The author cited a passage from Lincoln's Gettysburg speech in her new book.
這位作者在她的新書中引用了林肯蓋茨堡演說中的一段。

(C) **compromise** [ˈkɑmprəˌmaɪz] *vt.* 違背（名譽、原則）；危及 & *n.* & *vi.* 妥協
Dylan would rather die than compromise his principles.
狄倫是寧死也不肯違背自己的原則。

TEST 10

　　(D) **sue** [su] *vt.* & *vi.* 控告，對……提起訴訟
　　　　They are going to sue the company for breaking the contract.
　　　　他們將控告那間公司毀約。

b 根據語意及用法，(A) 項應為正選。

必考重點

sell out　　銷售一空
Jane's book was so popular that it sold out on the first day of release.
珍的書非常受歡迎，發售當天就賣光了。

C 3. 該工廠的年度安全檢查將會著重在預防火災、緊急照明以及備用能源上。

a (A) **limitation** [ˌlɪməˋteʃən] *n.* 限制
　　　　That club has rigid limitations on its membership.
　　　　那家俱樂部對它的會員資格限制很嚴。

　　(B) **association** [əˌsosɪˋeʃən] *n.* 協會；聯合
　　　　We decided to set up an association of photography lovers.
　　　　我們決定成立一個攝影愛好者協會。

　　(C) **inspection** [ɪnˋspɛkʃən] *n.* 檢查，稽查
　　　　a safety inspection　　安全檢查
　　　　Business establishments that fail to pass safety inspections will lose their licenses.
　　　　未通過安全檢查的營業場所將被吊銷執照。

　　(D) **composition** [ˌkɑmpəˋzɪʃən] *n.* 作文；（樂曲、畫、詩等）作品；成分
　　　　The teacher said my composition on honesty was excellent.
　　　　老師說我那篇關於誠實的作文寫得很棒。

b 根據語意及用法，(C) 項應為正選。

必考重點

a. **annual** [ˋænjʊəl] *a.* 一年一度的，每年的
b. **prevention** [prɪˋvɛnʃən] *n.* 預防，防止（不可數）
c. **backup** [ˋbækˌʌp] *a.* 備用的

B 4. 這座游泳池淺到連我三歲的妹妹都能輕鬆站在裡面。

a (A) **dense** [dɛns] *a.* 密集的；濃密的
　　　　Taipei and Hong Kong have very dense populations.
　　　　臺北和香港的人口都很稠密。

(B) **shallow** [ˋʃælo] *a.* 淺的；膚淺的
No diving is allowed in the shallow end of the pool.
游泳池較淺的那一端不允許跳水。
I don't like to deal with shallow people.
我不喜歡和膚淺的人打交道。

(C) **narrow** [ˋnæro] *a.* 狹窄的 & *vt.* & *vi.* (使) 變窄/狹窄
There was only a narrow gap between the bed and the wall.
這張床和那道牆之間只有一條窄縫。

(D) **gigantic** [dʒaɪˋgæntɪk] *a.* 巨大的
Graceful and gigantic, ocean sunfish are one of the ocean's strangest and most wondrous sights.
體型龐大但姿態優雅的曼波魚是海洋中最奇特、最不可思議的奇觀之一。

ⓑ 根據語意及用法，(B) 項應為正選。

C 5. 這名芭蕾舞者跳得如此優雅，讓觀眾席的每個人都為她優雅的動作驚豔不已。

ⓐ (A) **awkward** [ˋɔkwəd] *a.* 笨拙的
Mary looked awkward trying to eat pizza with chopsticks.
瑪麗試著用筷子吃披薩的樣子看起來很笨拙。

(B) **tricky** [ˋtrɪkɪ] *a.* 複雜的，難處理的；狡猾的
Installing the equipment is a tricky business.
安裝這個設備很費事。

(C) **elegant** [ˋɛləgənt] *a.* 高雅的，有氣質的
Your aunt is one of the most elegant women I've ever met.
你阿姨是我見過最有氣質的女士之一。

(D) **solemn** [ˋsɑləm] *a.* 嚴肅的，莊嚴的
You're not supposed to laugh out loud on such a solemn occasion.
在這種嚴肅的場合你不該笑出聲來。

ⓑ 根據語意及用法，(C) 項應為正選。

必考重點

ballet [bæˋle / ˋbæle] *n.* 芭蕾舞

C 6. 在將新電腦連接到網際網路前，請確保安裝了防毒軟體程式。

ⓐ (A) **adapt** [əˋdæpt] *vt.* & *vi.* (使) 適應
adapt (oneself) to N/V-ing   使（自己）適應於……
It took my grandfather years to adapt to city life.
我爺爺花了好多年的時間才適應都市生活。

285

(B) **equip** [ɪˋkwɪp] *vt.* 配備（常用被動語態）（三態為：equip, equipped [ɪˋkwɪpt], equipped）

be equipped with...　有……的裝備

All the classrooms are equipped with state-of-the-art facilities.
所有的教室都配有最先進的設備。

(C) **install** [ɪnˋstɔl] *vt.* 安裝，設置

Several problems arose when we tried to install the new software.
我們試灌新軟體時，問題接二連三發生。

(D) **relate** [rɪˋlet] *vt.* 使相關；敘述 & *vi.* 和……有關；理解

relate A to B　找到 A 與 B 有關

= A is related to B

Spanish and French are related to Latin.
西班牙文及法文與拉丁文有淵源。

ⓑ 根據語意及用法，(C) 項應為正選。

必考重點

a. **anti-virus** [ˌæntɪˋvaɪrəs] *a.* 防毒的
b. **software** [ˋsɔftˌwɛr] *n.* 軟體（不可數）

B 7. 這位經驗豐富的老師使用很多教學技巧來滿足不同學生的學習需求。

ⓐ (A) **bulletin** [ˋbulətɪn] *n.* 告示公告；新聞快報

a bulletin board　布告欄

The city government just released a bulletin, asking all the residents to be wary of the flu.
市政府剛剛發布公告，要求所有居民謹防流感。

There's an hourly news bulletin on this radio station.
這家廣播電臺每小時都有新聞快報。

(B) **technique** [tɛkˋnik] *n.* 技巧；技術

Sheryl hoped to perfect her dancing technique.
雪柔希望她的舞技能臻於完美。

(C) **souvenir** [ˌsuvəˋnɪr] *n.* 紀念品

Anita brought back some souvenirs for us from her trip to Paris.
艾妮塔從她的巴黎之旅帶回了一些紀念品給我們。

(D) **invitation** [ˌɪnvəˋteʃən] *n.* 請帖，邀請卡；邀請

Have you received an invitation to the party?
你收到這次派對的邀請卡了嗎？

ⓑ 根據語意及用法，(B) 項應為正選。

> 必考重點

a. **employ** [ɪmˋplɔɪ] *vt.* 使用（工具、手段等），運用

b. **a variety of...** 各式各樣的……

A 8. 在萬聖夜，許多小朋友會穿上嚇人的服裝，試圖嚇唬鄰居要給他們糖果。

ⓐ (A) **costume** [ˋkɑstjum] *n.* （特殊裝扮用的）戲服，服裝
The woman made a Halloween costume for her son instead of buying one.
那位女士幫她兒子製作了一套萬聖節服裝，而不是用買的。

(B) **remark** [rɪˋmɑrk] *n.* 言論 & *vt.* 談到，說起
Mr. Lee's casual remark caused a political storm.
李先生無心的言論引發了一場政治風暴。

(C) **fabric** [ˋfæbrɪk] *n.* 布料，面料
I like silk fabric because it is smooth and natural.
我喜歡絲質面料，因為它滑順又天然。

(D) **wagon** [ˋwægən] *n.* 四輪馬車
Centuries ago, travel plans were determined by how long you could stand a wagon or horse ride.
數千年前，旅遊計畫的擬定取決於你能夠忍受坐馬車或騎馬的時間有多長。

ⓑ 根據語意及用法，(A) 項應為正選。

> 必考重點

frighten sb into V-ing 把某人嚇得（做）……
Tom frightened Jim into keeping quiet.
湯姆嚇唬吉姆要保持安靜。

D 9. 那家餐廳的魚料理是我吃過數一數二的。此外，它們新鮮又不貴。

ⓐ (A) **perhaps** [pɚˋhæps] *adv.* 也許，大概
Perhaps I'll call on you tonight.
我今晚也許會去看你。

(B) **somehow** [ˋsʌm͵haʊ] *adv.* 不知怎麼地；用某種方法
My blind date was dressed beautifully, but somehow I didn't find her attractive.
我的相親對象穿得很美，不過不知怎地我並不覺得她很有魅力。
We'll raise enough money to pay for the trip somehow.
我們總會有辦法籌到足夠的旅費。

(C) **nevertheless** [ˌnɛvəðəˈlɛs] adv. 然而，不過，儘管如此
Linda wants to buy the skirt. Nevertheless, she can't afford it.
琳達想買這件裙子。不過她買不起。

(D) **furthermore** [ˈfɝðəˌmɔr] adv. 而且，此外
The movie was very boring. Furthermore, I didn't even understand the ending.
這部電影很無聊。再者，我根本就看不懂結局。

ⓑ 根據語意及用法，(D) 項應為正選。

A 10. 傑佛瑞的工廠生產各種大小和顏色的拉鍊，並將它們外銷至世界各地。

ⓐ (A) **manufacture** [ˌmænjəˈfæktʃə] vt. & n. （大量）製造
Our company manufactures electronic devices.
我們公司生產電子設備。

(B) **demonstrate** [ˈdɛmənˌstret] vt. 示範 & vi. 示威
demonstrate against... 示威反抗……
The salesman demonstrated how to work the machine to us.
該業務員向我們示範說明如何操作這部機器。
Thousands of people demonstrated against the government's new policy this morning.
今天早上有好幾千人抗議政府的新政策。

(C) **construct** [kənˈstrʌkt] vt. 建造
The workers tore down the old building and constructed a parking garage.
工人拆掉舊大樓並蓋一座停車場。

(D) **harvest** [ˈhɑrvɪst] vt. & vi. & n. 收成
Watermelons are usually harvested in the summer.
西瓜通常是在夏季收成的。

ⓑ 根據語意及用法，(A) 項應為正選。

必考重點

a. **zipper** [ˈzɪpə] n. 拉鍊
b. **export** [ɪkˈspɔrt] vt. 出口
c. **globe** [glob] n. 世界

二、綜合測驗（占 10 分）

第 11 至 15 題為題組

　　從許多方面來看，印度西姆拉的「書香咖啡館」就是間單純的咖啡館。它有足以容納四十位顧客的座位區、多種美味點心與可口飲品，以及四百五十多本書籍供顧客閱讀。遊客可以放鬆並將山色的屏息之美納入眼簾。

　　不過書香咖啡館與其他咖啡館不同的地方，在於它的員工。它是由目前正在附近的凱圖監獄服無期徒刑的四名囚犯所經營的。在遠離獄警的監視情況下，他們每天從早上十點工作到晚上九點。然後，他們漫步回監獄過夜。

　　書香咖啡館由喜馬偕爾邦監獄部門創建以幫助囚犯洗心革面，是同類商店中的先驅。它給予受刑人機會成為社會中有貢獻的一分子，同時也能賺錢給家裡。在 2017 年四月開幕後，書香咖啡館給予囚犯新技能以及與外界再度建立連結的機會。更重要的是，它讓他們能夠過著有尊嚴的生活並感到自己真的具有價值。遺憾的是，書香咖啡館在 2019 年被一名商人接手且自此永久停業。

B 11. 理由

ⓐ (A) **abortion** [əˋbɔrʃən] *n.* 墮胎；失敗
When it comes to abortion laws, many people sit on the fence.
談到墮胎法，許多人都是騎牆派。

(B) **selection** [səˋlɛkʃən] *n.* 可供選購的同類商品
a selection of...　　各種的……
The department store carries a selection of perfumes from Italy.
這間百貨公司販售各種來自義大利的香水。

(C) **possession** [pəˋzɛʃən] *n.* 擁有
be in possession of...　　擁有……
Tim is in possession of many skills. He can build furniture and fix cars, to name just a few.
提姆擁有許多技能。隨便舉幾個來說，他會做家俱及修車。

(D) **description** [dɪˋskrɪpʃən] *n.* 描述，形容
The witness provided the police officer with a detailed description of the robber.
目擊者向警方提供了那名搶劫犯的詳細描述。

ⓑ 根據語意，(B) 項應為正選。

TEST 10

289

TEST 10

D 12. 理由

ⓐ 本題測試疑問詞引導名詞子句的用法：

疑問詞（how, what, when, where, why 等）可引導名詞子句，在主要子句中作主詞、受詞或置於 be 動詞後作主詞補語。

ⓑ 空格後有一子句，且本句中已有動詞 was，得知空格應置疑問詞以引導該名詞子句，作本句的主詞。選項中為疑問詞的僅有 (C) Where 及 (D) What，根據語意，(D) 項應為正選。

A 13. 理由

ⓐ (A) serve [sɝv] vt. & vi. 服（役／刑）；任（職）
Israeli males have to serve at least three years in the military.
以色列男性公民都須在軍中服役至少三年。

(B) appoint [əˋpɔɪnt] vt. 選定；指定；指派
Dave and I appointed our favorite restaurant as the place for the meeting.
我和戴夫選定在我們最喜歡的那家餐館碰面。

(C) deceive [dɪˋsiv] vt. 欺騙
The blind woman was deceived by the young man who claimed to be her son.
這名盲眼的婦人被一名自稱是她兒子的年輕男子給欺騙了。

(D) exhibit [ɪgˋzɪbɪt] vt. 顯示；展示
The artists exhibited their paintings in the gallery.
這些藝術家在畫廊展示他們的畫作。

ⓑ 根據語意，(A) 項應為正選。

D 14. 理由

ⓐ (A) fluent [ˋfluənt] a. 流利的
I can express myself in fluent English.
我可以用流利的英文表達自己的意思。

(B) delicate [ˋdɛləkət] a. 精緻的；脆弱的
Jonathan gave me a set of delicate china teacups for my birthday.
喬納森送了我一組精緻的瓷器茶杯作為生日禮物。

(C) negative [ˋnɛgətɪv] a. 負面的，消極的
Plastic waste has a negative impact on the environment.
塑膠廢棄物對環境有負面的影響。

(D) productive [prəˋdʌktɪv] a. 有生產力的
A factory needs to be highly productive, or it will soon close.
工廠必須有高生產力，否則很快就會倒閉。

ⓑ 根據語意，(D) 項應為正選。

C 15. 理由

ⓐ 本題測試以下語意：(A) the annual coffee trade fair（年度咖啡貿易展）、(B) the information center there（那裡的服務臺）、(C) the outside world again（再度與外面的世界）、(D) the security guard now（現在的警衛）。

ⓑ 空格前面提及書香咖啡館給予囚犯和某事物連結的機會，根據語意應該是與外面的世界再度接觸，故 (C) 項應為正選。

重要字詞片語

1. **tasty** [ˈtestɪ] *a.* 美味的，可口的
2. **take in...** 欣賞……，觀看……
   I have to get closer to take in the full beauty of the ocean.
   我必須再靠近一點，才能欣賞到海洋美麗的全貌。
3. **breathtaking** [ˈbrɛθˌtekɪŋ] *a.* 令人驚歎的
4. **convict** [kənˈvɪkt] *vt.* 判……有罪（本文為過去分詞作形容詞用）&
   [ˈkɑnvɪkt] *n.* 囚犯
   Even though John has been convicted of murder, he insists that he didn't do it.
   儘管約翰已被判謀殺罪，他仍堅持說自己沒有行兇。
5. **criminal** [ˈkrɪmənl] *n.* 罪犯
6. **a life sentence** 無期徒刑
7. **watchful** [ˈwɑtʃfəl] *a.* 警惕的；注意的
8. **stroll** [strol] *vi. & n.* 散步
9. **change one's ways** 改過自新
   I hope you've learned the lesson and start to change your ways.
   我希望你學到教訓並改過自新。
10. **dignity** [ˈdɪgnətɪ] *n.* 尊嚴（不可數）

TEST 10

第 16 至 20 題為題組

　　一項新的研究讓配戴隱形眼鏡者看見了自己的錯誤。由亞利桑那州立大學的研究人員進行的這項研究顯示，許多隱形眼鏡消費者在不知不覺中汙染了環境。當他們將隱形眼鏡用排水管或馬桶沖走時，就造成了傷害。

　　就像一次性的吸管、雜貨袋以及餐具一樣，隱形眼鏡是由塑膠製成，屬於拋棄式產品，使用也很普遍。事實上，光在美國就有四千五百萬人使用隱形眼鏡來矯正視力。他們每年要戴上大約一百五十億片隱形眼鏡。不幸的是，其中有百分之二十最終進入了下水道。

　　接下來，這些小塑膠片會在汙水處理廠被進一步分解成塑膠微粒。由於塑膠微粒幾乎不可能被濾除，它們流入地下成為廢水的一部分。此外，它們還會流入河中，最終進入大海。到那時傷害就已造成，因為鳥類、魚類以及其他動物會錯將看似美食的塑膠微粒吃下肚。接下來汙染物就會進入延伸更廣的食物鏈中。

　　配戴隱形眼鏡者不應將隱形眼鏡沖入馬桶，而是應該將它們和其他家庭垃圾一起丟進垃圾桶。

TEST 10

B 16. 理由

- (A) **reserve** [rɪˈzɝv] *vt.* 預約，預訂（座位等）
  I'd like to reserve a room for three nights.
  我要訂房住三晚。

- (B) **conduct** [kənˈdʌkt] *vt.* 進行（研究、調查等）
  The experiment conducted by experts in marine biology went smoothly.
  由海洋生物專家進行的這項實驗相當順利。

- (C) **suspend** [səˈspɛnd] *vt.* 暫停，使中止
  All activities were suspended due to the snowstorm.
  所有活動都因這場暴風雪而暫停。

- (D) **maintain** [menˈten] *vt.* 保持，維持
  Laura maintains her figure by exercising daily.
  蘿拉靠每天運動來保持身材。

- 根據語意，(B) 項應為正選。

A 17. 理由

- (A) **utensil** [juˈtɛnsḷ] *n.* 用具，器皿
  a kitchen utensil　廚房器具
  A whisk is a kitchen utensil for beating eggs and cream.
  攪拌器是一種用來打蛋和奶油的廚房用具。

- (B) **outfit** [ˈaʊt͵fɪt] *n.* （尤指整套的）服裝（可數）
  Patrick looks stylish in that outfit.
  派翠克穿那套衣服看起來很時髦。

- (C) **facility** [fəˈsɪlətɪ] *n.* 設備，設施（常用複數）
  After paying your membership fee, you will have access to all the gym's facilities.
  繳了會費後，你就可以使用該健身房的所有設施。

- (D) **appliance** [əˈplaɪəns] *n.* 用具（尤指家電用品）；裝置
  Mona bought several new appliances for her home.
  夢娜為家裡添購了數件新家電。

- 根據語意，(A) 項應為正選。

C 18. 理由

- (A) **other than...**　除……之外
  = except (for)...
  Everyone other than Tina agreed to this proposal.
  除了蒂娜以外，所有人都同意這項提議。

(B) **as far as...** 達到……的程度

as far as sb knows, ... 就某人所知，……

As far as I know, that problem is highly unlikely to occur.
就我所知，那問題是不大可能發生的。

(C) **next to...** 幾乎……

= almost [ˈɔl,most] adv.

The company pay me next to nothing, but I really enjoy the work.
公司沒付給我多少錢，但我實在很喜歡那份工作。

(D) **by no means** 絕不

The job was by no means easy, but it was rewarding.
這份工作一點都不輕鬆，但卻很值得。

ⓑ 根據語意，(C) 項應為正選。

C 19. 理由

ⓐ 本題測試以下語意：(A) later have been recycled（之後被回收）、(B) then create huge waves（然後掀起巨浪）、(C) eventually out to sea（最終流入大海）、(D) finally improve the ecosystem（最終改善生態系統）。

ⓑ 空格前面提及微小塑膠一步一步地往地裡面流、流到河中，根據語意，最後應流往大海，故 (C) 項應為正選。

D 20. 理由

ⓐ (A) **cargo** [ˈkɑrgo] n.（船、飛機、車輛裝載的）貨物

The airline company makes most of its profit from its cargo planes.
這家航空公司的利潤大多來自貨機。

(B) **diploma** [dɪˈplomə] n.（有學位的）文憑

After receiving his diploma, Luke jumped for joy.
在接到文憑之後，路克高興得雀躍不已。

(C) **faucet** [ˈfɔsɪt] n. 水龍頭

I turned on the faucet, but no water came out.
我打開水龍頭，卻沒有水流出來。

(D) **pollutant** [pəˈlutənt] n. 汙染物

Air and water pollutants may cause some cancers.
空氣和水汙染物可能導致某些癌症。

ⓑ 根據語意，(D) 項應為正選。

重要字詞片語

1. **a contact lens** 隱形眼鏡鏡片
2. **consumer** [kənˈsumɚ] n. 消費者
   consume [kənˈsum] vt. 消費
3. **unknowingly** [ʌnˈnoɪŋlɪ] adv. 不知不覺地

TEST 10

4. **flush** [flʌʃ] *vt.* 把⋯⋯沖下馬桶
   flush sth down the toilet
   將⋯⋯從馬桶沖走

5. **disposable** [dɪˋspozəb!̣] *a.* 用完即丟的

6. **sewer** [ˋsuɚ] *n.* 下水道

7. **be broken down into...**
   被分解成⋯⋯

8. **microplastics** [ˋmaɪkrə͵plæstɪks] *n.*
   塑膠微粒（恆用複數）

9. **filter out... / filter... out**
   過濾／濾除⋯⋯

10. **food chain**　　食物鏈

三、文意選填（占 10 分）

第 21 至 30 題為題組

　　許多來到臺灣旅遊的觀光客只會走訪臺北市及其鄰近地區，例如淡水、基隆以及瑞芳。然而，臺灣其實還有更多可看之處。有太多遊客錯過了臺灣東海岸、墾丁國家公園以及位於離島的澎湖與蘭嶼的壯麗景觀。而另外一個許多遊客不知道的景點就是坐落於嘉義縣的阿里山森林鐵路。

　　這座鐵路系統建於 1912 年，當時臺灣被日本所佔領。它最初建造的目的是供伐木用。然而，到了 1918 年，這座全長八十六公里的鐵路系統增加了客車，讓遊客得以將臺灣中央山脈令人嘆為觀止的景觀盡收眼底，並在阿里山山頂劃下完美的句點。還有哪裡可以搭火車從海拔三十公尺處通往海拔兩千兩百一十六公尺處呢？隨著海拔上升，沿途的植被從熱帶轉變為溫帶，再轉變為高山植物。臺灣於 1945 年光復之後，阿里山森林鐵路持續作為商業用途使用。阿里山公路於八○年代開通後，這條鐵路主要變成了觀光景點。

　　不幸的是，阿里山地區容易發生地震，偶爾也會受到颱風侵襲。多年來，這些災害已對鐵道線造成損壞，也限制了鐵路系統的使用。這些問題再加上像是火車出軌等人為疏失已減少阿里山森林鐵路的吸引力。這實在相當可惜，因為像這樣的鐵路系統如今鮮少在世界其他地方使用。有趣的是，該鐵路系統的路線一點也不直。整段鐵路系統包括了五十條隧道、七十七座木橋和 Z 形的之字狀陡坡，保證讓搭乘的人會有一趟刺激的旅程。然而，這也意味著修復該鐵道可能會是一項複雜且耗時的任務。但願它們未來毋須經歷太多次修繕且阿里山森林鐵路也能繼續為國內外的觀光客服務。

C 21. 理由

  ⓐ 空格前為複數的主詞 Too many tourists（有太多遊客），空格後為名詞片語 the splendors of Taiwan's east coast...（臺灣東海岸⋯⋯的壯麗景觀）作受詞，而上下文為事實陳述，得知空格應置複數現在式動詞或片語動詞。

  ⓑ 選項中符合上述的僅有 (C) miss out on（錯失），故為正選。

  ⓒ 本題測試的固定用法：
　　miss out on...　　錯失⋯⋯（的機會）

Don't dwell on the past, or you will miss out on the present.
別老是想著過去，否則你將錯失現在。

F 22. 理由
- ⓐ 空格前有形容詞 Japanese（日本的），得知空格應置入名詞以被 Japanese 修飾。
- ⓑ 選項中符合上述的有 (F) occupation（占領）及 (H) elevation（高度），惟根據語意，(F) 項應為正選。

A 23. 理由
- ⓐ 空格前有定冠詞 the，空格後有名詞 views（景色），得知空格應置入形容詞以修飾 views。
- ⓑ 選項中符合上述的有 (A) breathtaking（令人嘆為觀止的）及 (J) restricted（受到限制的），惟根據語意，(A) 項應為正選。

H 24. 理由
- ⓐ 空格前有不定冠詞 an，空格後有介詞 of，得知空格應置入母音開頭的名詞。
- ⓑ 選項中符合上述的僅剩 (H) elevation（高度），置入後亦符合語意，故為正選。

E 25. 理由
- ⓐ 空格前有連綴動詞 became（變成），空格後有名詞詞組 a tourist attraction（觀光景點），得知空格應置入副詞以修飾 became。
- ⓑ 選項中符合上述的有 (D) rarely（很少）及 (E) primarily（主要地），惟根據語意，(E) 項應為正選。

B 26. 理由
- ⓐ 空格前為主詞 the Alishan district（阿里山地區），空格後為名詞詞組 earthquakes and sometimes typhoons（地震以及偶爾颱風）作受詞，而上下文為事實陳述，得知空格應置現在式動詞或片語動詞。
- ⓑ 選項中符合上述的僅剩 (B) is prone to（易於……），置入後亦符合語意，故為正選。
- ⓒ 本題測試的固定用法：
  be prone to N/V　　往往會／易於……
  We are prone to take natural resources for granted nowadays.
  現今，我們往往將自然資源視為理所當然。

J 27. 理由
- ⓐ 空格前有完成式助動詞 have 以及過去分詞與受詞 damaged the railway lines（對鐵道線造成損壞），另有對等連接詞 and，空格後有作受詞的名詞片語 the network's usage（鐵路系統的使用），得知空格應置及物動詞的過去分詞以形成對等。
- ⓑ 選項中符合上述的有 (I) repaired（修理）及 (J) restricted（限制），惟根據語意，(J) 項應為正選。

295

TEST 10

G 28. 理由

ⓐ 空格前有主詞 These problems 以及逗號，空格後則為一名詞詞組 man-made faults such as derailments（像是火車出軌等人為疏失）以及本句的動詞 have reduced（已減少），得知空格應置入分詞或介詞，以形成分詞片語或介詞片語修飾主詞。

ⓑ 選項中符合上述的有 (G) along with（連同）及 (I) repaired（修理），惟根據語意，(G) 項應為正選。

ⓒ 本題測試以下固定用法：
along / together with...　　連同……
Venice, along with Rome and Milan, is among the most popular tourist attractions in Italy.
威尼斯和羅馬及米蘭都是義大利最受歡迎的觀光景點之一。

D 29. 理由

ⓐ 空格後有過去分詞 used（被使用），得知空格應置副詞以修飾 used。

ⓑ 選項中符合上述的僅剩 (D) rarely（很少），置入後亦符合語意，故為正選。

I 30. 理由

ⓐ 空格前有動詞片語 need to be...（需要被……），得知空格應置過去分詞以形成被動語態。

ⓑ 選項中符合上述的僅剩 (I) repaired（修理），置入後亦符合語意，故為正選。

重要字詞片語

1. **surrounding** [səˋraʊndɪŋ] *a.* 附近的；周圍的
2. **splendors** [ˋsplɛndəz] *n.* 壯麗景色（恆用複數）
3. **offshore** [ˏɔfˋʃɔr] *a.* 離岸的，近海的
4. **logging** [ˋlɔgɪŋ] *n.* 伐木（不可數）
5. **take advantage of sth** （善加）利用某事物
   Many people took advantage of the holiday sales.
   許多人都利用假日大拍賣時去採購。
6. **culminate** [ˋkʌlməˏnet] *vi.* 達到高點
   culminate in / with...
   在……達到高潮；以……告終
   The concert culminated in a huge finale with all the singers on the stage.
   當所有歌手在臺上進行盛大的終場表演時，這場演唱會達到了最高潮。
7. **vegetation** [ˏvɛdʒəˋteʃən] *n.* 植被，植物群落（集合名詞，不可數）
8. **tropical** [ˋtrɑpɪkḷ] *a.* 熱帶的
9. **temperate** [ˋtɛmprɪt] *a.* 溫帶的
10. **alpine** [ˋælpaɪn] *a.* 高山的
11. **liberation** [ˏlɪbəˋreʃən] *n.* 解放（不可數）
12. **man-made** [ˋmænˋmed] *a.* 人為的；人造的
13. **derailment** [dɪˋrelmənt] *n.* （列車）出軌

14. **be anything but adj. / N**
  = be not adj. / N at all
  一點也不是……，絕不是……
  The puzzle was anything but difficult because it only took me 30 seconds to solve.
  = The puzzle was not difficult at all because it only took me 30 seconds to solve.
  這道謎題一點也不難，因為我只花三十秒就把它解開了。

  Jack is anything but a considerate person.
  = Jack is not a considerate person at all.
  傑克一點也不體貼。

15. **switchback** [ˈswɪtʃˌbæk] *n.* （公路或鐵路坡道上的）Z 字形路線

四、篇章結構（占 8 分）

第 31 至 34 題為題組

儘管費時許久，臺中國家歌劇院終於在 2016 年開張營業了。**31.** 它是由舉世聞名的日本建築師伊東豐雄所設計的，不過它實際上看起來彷彿是出自外星人的設計。這座充滿未來感的多媒體功能建築已使臺灣的中部城市臺中聲名大噪。

早在 1992 年，臺灣中央政府便提議興建一座國家歌劇院。十年過後，多虧了當時的臺中市長胡志強的努力，政府決定將這棟建築設立於他管轄的城市。伊東豐雄和其他來自十二個國家的三十二位建築師都投出他們的設計方案。**32.** 伊東在這場角逐中勝出，並於 2009 年簽下合約設計臺中國家歌劇院。同年，也是由伊東所設計的高雄國家體育場也落成啟用。

臺中國家歌劇院的建築簡直令人瞠目結舌。該劇院坐落於一座巨大的公園，四周被高科技摩天大樓環繞。此建築基本上是長方形的，但由波浪形設計覆蓋，打破許多單調現代建築的直線邊緣框架。劇院內的牆壁是彎曲的，為表演廳及現場演出帶來動態的氛圍。伊東也將環保特色納入設計。**33.** 其屋頂可收集雨水來為周圍的公園、花園以及廁所馬桶供給水源。該建築所使用的建材都可回收利用。甚至連建築的形狀都能減少能源消耗。

這座劇院的內部更加令人興奮。大劇院是該棟建築最具價值的瑰寶，每場表演可供兩千零七位藝術愛好者入座。除此之外，有七百九十四席座位的中劇院與兩百席座位的小劇場能為其他多數非音樂性質的藝術表演提供場地。在這些場地中，該劇院每年舉辦多項藝術節，包括臺灣國際藝術節、夏日放／FUN 時光以及遇見巨人。

臺中是設立國家歌劇院的最佳地點。**34.** 該市乾淨、高效能又充滿活力，集所有二十一世紀永續大都會的特質於一身。如今，隨著臺中國家歌劇院受到歡迎，這座城市也搖身一變成為了藝術中心。即便是在沒有舉辦表演時，到該劇院走一趟也會是一場視覺饗宴。

TEST 10

B 31. 理由
- ⓐ 空格前一句提及臺中國家歌劇院終於開張了，空格後一句提及這座建築充滿未來感並使臺中聲名大噪。可推測空格應連貫第一句，且與未來感相關。
- ⓑ 選項 (B) 表示，它是由舉世聞名的日本建築師所設計，不過看起來像是外星人的設計，即在進一步介紹臺中國家歌劇院，填入後語意連貫，可知 (B) 項應為正選。

C 32. 理由
- ⓐ 空格前一句提及伊東豊雄和其他國家的建築師都投出他們的設計方案，且第一段已說明此建築為伊東豊雄設計的，可推測空格應接續指出伊東豊雄從中勝出。
- ⓑ 選項 (C) 表示，伊東在這場角逐中勝出，並於 2009 年簽下合約設計臺中國家歌劇院，填入後語意連貫，可知 (C) 項應為正選。

A 33. 理由
- ⓐ 空格前一句提及建築師伊東也將環保特色納入設計，而空格後一句則提到該建築所使用的建材都可回收利用。可推測空格應具體說明其環保特色的設計。
- ⓑ 選項 (A) 表示，其屋頂可收集雨水來為周圍的公園、花園以及廁所馬桶供給水源，填入後語意連貫，可知 (A) 項應為正選。

D 34. 理由
- ⓐ 空格前一句提及臺中是設立國家歌劇院的最佳地點，空格後一句提及如今隨著臺中國家歌劇院受到歡迎，這座城市也搖身一變成為了藝術中心。可推測空格應提及臺中適合設立國家歌劇院的原因。
- ⓑ 選項 (D) 表示，該市乾淨、高效能又充滿活力，集所有二十一世紀永續大都會的特質於一身，填入後語意連貫，可知 (D) 項應為正選。

(E) 項中譯：這位音樂家在開幕之夜於該場地的演出獲得了樂評們大多正面的評價。

重要字詞片語

1. **futuristic** [ˌfjutʃəˈrɪstɪk] *a.* 未來（派）的
2. **put... on the map** 使……出名／為人所知
   Sky lanterns have put Pingxi on the map.
   天燈讓平溪出了名。
3. **be nothing short of...** 簡直是……
   Monica's success was nothing short of a miracle.
   莫妮卡的成功簡直就是個奇蹟。
4. **eye-popping** [ˈaɪˌpɑpɪŋ] *a.* 令人目瞪口呆的，令人驚奇的
5. **skyscraper** [ˈskaɪˌskrepɚ] *n.* 摩天大樓
6. **wavy** [ˈwevɪ] *a.* 波浪狀的
7. **tedious** [ˈtidɪəs] *a.* 單調乏味的
8. **fluidity** [fluˈɪdətɪ] *n.* 流動性；流暢（不可數）
9. **eco-friendly** [ˈikoˌfrɛndlɪ] *a.* 環保的
10. **recyclable** [rɪˈsaɪkləbl̩] *a.* 可回收再利用的
11. **consumption** [kənˈsʌmpʃən] *n.* 消耗（量）（不可數）

12. **the crown jewel**
    鑲在皇冠上的寶石，指「瑰寶」
13. **additionally** [əˋdɪʃənəlɪ] *adv.* 此外
    ＝ in addition
14. **accommodate** [əˋkɑməˌdet] *vt.*
    為……提供空間；提供住宿
15. **annual** [ˋænjʊəl] *a.* 每年的；年度的，一年的
16. **vibrant** [ˋvaɪbrənt] *a.* 充滿活力的
17. **have all the makings of...**
    有……的特質／特徵
18. **sustainable** [səˋstenəb!] *a.* 永續的
19. **metropolis** [məˋtrɑpəlɪs] *n.* 大都市，大都會

五、閱讀測驗（占 24 分）

第 35 至 38 題為題組

　　葡萄酒已經有數千年的歷史。已知最早的釀酒廠可追溯到六千多年前，是在亞美尼亞的一個洞穴群裡。由於涼爽的環境和固定的溼度，洞穴和地下酒窖是理想的藏酒地點。但現在有一種藏酒的新趨勢：海底藏酒。

　　西班牙的「克魯索寶藏」即是這種借助海洋來陳酒的酒廠。當葡萄酒裝瓶後，他們不會把酒瓶存放在架子上或貯藏在控溫的房間裡，而是把它們放進海裡。事實上，把酒放到海底的過程有許多技術細節。船上裝有吊車用來垂降箱籠，裡面放著經過特殊封蓋的酒瓶，同時會有一名潛水員監測溫度和水壓。一旦放至海底，它們會留在那邊最多達十八個月。

　　該公司創辦人波爾哈・薩拉丘表示，在這種增壓、陰暗和恆溫的環境中，會生產出特別柔和順滑的酒。他接受英國《衛報》訪問時回想喝到公司首批海底美酒的經驗：「非常驚豔。葡萄酒在海底的變化，與在陸地上處理的同種葡萄酒非常不同。」薩拉丘是在聽聞在波羅的海海底發現美妙的百年香檳報導後，得到啟發而開始了這樣的釀酒計畫。

　　克魯索寶藏的獨特事業已獲得西班牙政府特許使用五百平方公尺的海床。這是因為該公司用來陳酒的混凝土構工也能充當人工海礁，有助於海洋生物的生存。所以看起來這間酒廠在製造美酒的同時，似乎也在做公益。

A　35. 根據本文，地下酒窖為何是藏酒的理想之地？
　　(A) 它們具有理想的溫度和溼度。　　(B) 它們能一次貯藏許多瓶酒。
　　(C) 它們避免酒瓶受到陽光直射。　　(D) 它們容易維護與保持清潔。

[理由]
根據本文第一段第四句，由於涼爽的環境和固定的溼度，洞穴和地下酒窖是理想的藏酒地點，故 (A) 項應為正選。

TEST 10

C 36. 第二段中的 they 指的是什麼？
(A) 船。　　(B) 吊車。　　(C) 酒瓶。　　(D) 潛水員。

理由
根據本文第二段倒數第二句提及，船上裝有吊車用來垂降箱籠，裡面放著經過特殊封蓋的酒瓶，可推知留在海底的是酒瓶，故 (C) 項應為正選。

C 37. 波爾哈・薩拉丘如何會有海底藏酒的想法？
(A) 他讀到《衛報》刊登的一篇文章。
(B) 他曾去波羅的海游泳與潛水。
(C) 他聽到發現香檳的正面報導。
(D) 他被告知在英國有相似的計畫。

理由
根據本文第三段最後一句，薩拉丘是在聽聞在波羅的海海底發現美妙的百年香檳報導後，得到啟發而開始了這樣的釀酒計畫，故 (C) 項應為正選。

B 38. 為何西班牙政府特許克魯索寶藏酒廠使用五百平方公尺的海床？
(A) 這樣有助西班牙償還許多國債。
(B) 這樣有助保護當地的海洋生物。
(C) 這樣會吸引遊客，進而促進當地經濟。
(D) 這樣會保護西班牙免於外國入侵的威脅。

理由
根據本文第四段第二句，這是因為該公司用來陳酒的混凝土構工也能充當人工海礁，有助於海洋生物的生存，故 (B) 項應為正選。

重要字詞片語

1. **winery** [ˈwaɪnərɪ] *n.* 釀酒廠
2. **date back** + 一段時間
   回溯至……（一段時間）前
3. **complex** [ˈkɑmplɛks] *n.* 建築群
4. **cellar** [ˈsɛlɚ] *n.* 地窖，酒窖 & *vt.*
   把……藏入地窖／酒窖
5. **humidity** [hjuˈmɪdətɪ] *n.* 溼度（不可數）
6. **turn to...** 求助於……
7. **age** [edʒ] *vt.* （藉由存放時間）使味道成熟變醇
8. **crane** [kren] *n.* 起重機；吊車
9. **monitor** [ˈmɑnətɚ] *vt.* 監控，監視
10. **firm** [fɝm] *n.* 公司
11. **atmospheric** [ˌætməsˈfɛrɪk] *a.* 大氣的
    atmospheric pressure　大氣壓力
12. **constant** [ˈkɑnstənt] *a.* 穩定的，不變的
13. **reflect** [rɪˈflɛkt] *vi.* 仔細思考
    reflect on...　好好想一想……
14. **evolution** [ˌɛvəˈluʃən] *n.* 演變，演化（不可數）
15. **distinct** [dɪˈstɪŋkt] *a.* 顯然不同的
    be distinct from...　與……顯然不同
16. **champagne** [ʃæmˈpen] *n.* 香檳（不可數）
17. **venture** [ˈvɛntʃɚ] *n.* （有風險的）商業活動
18. **grant** [grænt] *vt.* 准許
19. **concrete** [ˈkɑnkrit] *a.* 混凝土製的；具體的
20. **reef** [rif] *n.* 礁

21. **sustain** [sə'sten] *vt.* 維持（生命）
22. **marine** [mə'rin] *a.* 海洋的
23. **pay off...**　　還清……
24. **debt** [`dɛt] *n.* 債
25. **invasion** [ɪn`veʒən] *n.* 入侵，侵略

第 39 至 42 題為題組

　　猴麵包樹是世界上最重要的樹木之一。在印度、澳洲、非洲大陸、馬達加斯加都可見到猴麵包樹的蹤跡，是地球上最巨大的樹木之一。它們可以生長到五至三十公尺不等。猴麵包樹的樹幹沒有樹枝，直徑可達七至十一公尺，內可蘊含十二萬公升的水。樹頂的寥寥數根樹枝往往沒有樹葉，因此看似樹根，讓樹木的外觀彷彿上下顛倒一般。

　　猴麵包樹為人類與動物提供食物、水以及庇護所。猴麵包樹的果實被稱為「猴子麵包」，富含維生素 C、維生素 B6、鉀、鎂與鈣。猴麵包果在生長的區域被當作食物，而且根據各地傳統料理方式的不同，可添加在湯品、燉菜與甜點當中。在西方國家，新鮮的猴麵包果很稀有，大多數人買的是粉狀物，加在冰沙或果汁裡。猴麵包果富含纖維質，可以讓人維持較長時間的飽足感，所以如果你想要減重，這種水果可能正是你所需要的。另外，猴麵包樹像軟木塞質感的樹皮常被用來製作繩索與衣服，因為它防火。猴麵包樹的樹葉也會被製成調味料與藥物。難怪猴麵包樹被尊稱為生命之樹。

　　猴麵包樹可在嚴苛條件下生存，因此能夠存活數百至數千年。然而情況可能已經改變，因為它們正在神祕地死亡。從二十一世紀初起，一組來自美國、羅馬尼亞以及南非的研究團隊，就在持續探訪非洲南部各地的古老猴麵包樹。他們利用放射性碳定年法來研究並調查這些樹木的年齡和結構。遺憾的是，他們最近的報告表示大多數最古老且最巨大的猴麵包樹已經死亡。這些樹木的年齡都在一千至兩千五百歲之間。研究人員歸咎於氣候變遷，舉出猴麵包樹棲地氣溫升高與乾旱期延長等因素。

A 39. 下列哪一項不是猴麵包樹的特徵？
(A) 樹葉茂密的樹枝。　　　　　　(B) 像儲水槽的樹幹。
(C) 極長的壽命。　　　　　　　　(D) 巨大的體型與形狀。

理由
根據本文第一段第四、五句，猴麵包樹的樹幹沒有樹枝，直徑可達七至十一公尺，……樹頂的寥寥數根樹枝往往沒有樹葉……，故 (A) 項應為正選。

B 40. 第二段中 **just what the doctor ordered** 暗指什麼？
(A) 醫藥專業人員通常會開猴麵包果粉末給病患吃。
(B) 吃猴麵包果可能正是你想變瘦時該做的事。
(C) 猴麵包果的營養價值被誇大了。
(D) 在西方國家，點早午餐時通常會搭配猴麵包樹冰沙。

理由
根據本文第二段第五句，猴麵包果富含纖維質，可以讓人維持較長時間的飽足感，所以如果你想要減重……，可推知粗體字暗指瘦身時，猴麵包果正是所需要的東西，故 (B) 項應為正選。

D 41. 猴麵包樹的哪一個部位可以防火？
(A) 果實。　　　(B) 樹葉。　　　(C) 樹枝。　　　(D) 樹皮。

> 理由

根據本文第二段倒數第三句，另外，猴麵包樹像軟木塞質感的樹皮常被用來製作繩索與衣服，因為它防火，故 (D) 項應為正選。

B 42. 研究人員在本世紀發現了什麼？
(A) 老猴麵包樹比年輕的樹還強壯。
(B) 地球暖化已導致許多猴麵包樹死亡。
(C) 猴麵包樹已在世界的其他角落開始生長。
(D) 放射性碳定年法不適合用來研究樹木。

> 理由

根據本文第三段第五至七句，遺憾的是，他們最近的報告表示大多數最古老且最巨大的猴麵包樹已經死亡。這些樹木的年齡都在一千至兩千五百歲之間。研究人員歸咎於氣候變遷，舉出猴麵包樹棲地氣溫升高與乾旱期延長等因素，故 (B) 項應為正選。

> 重要字詞片語

1. **baobab** [ˈbeəˌbæb] n. 猴麵包樹
2. **trunk** [trʌŋk] n. 樹幹
3. **upside down** 上下顛倒
4. **potassium** [pəˈtæsɪəm] n. 鉀（不可數）
5. **magnesium** [mægˈnɪzɪəm] n. 鎂（不可數）
6. **calcium** [ˈkælsɪəm] n. 鈣（不可數）
7. **scarce** [skɛrs] a. 稀有的，罕見的
   scarce resources　稀有資源
8. **be high in...**　富含有……
9. **fiber** [ˈfaɪbɚ] n. 纖維素（不可數），纖維
10. **just what the doctor ordered**
    正是想要的東西，正是需要的東西
11. **bark** [bɑrk] n. 樹皮（不可數）
12. **resistant** [rɪˈzɪstənt] a. 抵抗的，防禦……的
    be resistant to...　能抗……的
13. **seasoning** [ˈsiznɪŋ] n. 調味料
14. **harsh** [hɑrʃ] a. 嚴苛的，嚴厲的
15. **radiocarbon** [ˌredɪoˈkɑrbən] n. 放射性碳
    radiocarbon dating　放射性碳定年法
16. **investigate** [ɪnˈvɛstəˌget] vt. 調查
17. **blame** [blem] n. 責備，怪罪（不可數）
    pin / put / lay the blame on...
    將罪歸咎於……
18. **drought** [draʊt] n. 乾旱
19. **span** [spæn] n. 一段時間
    a life span　壽命
20. **prescribe** [prɪˈskraɪb] vt. 開藥
21. **nutritional** [nuˈtrɪʃənḷ] a. 營養的
22. **repel** [rɪˈpɛl] vt. 抗禦

第 43 至 46 題為題組

　　威廉‧莫爾頓‧馬斯頓是一位二十世紀前半期的美國心理學家。他特別出名的包括發明初代的測謊測驗，以及創造 DC 漫畫角色「神力女超人」。不過，他所建立關於性格的理論，可能才是他最驚人的成就。

　　馬斯頓在 1928 年出版的著作《普通人的情緒》裡概述了他的理論。他沒有像他的同行那樣調查罪犯或精神病患的行為，反而試圖解釋所謂「一般」大眾的行為。他承認人們在不同的環境中的行為會有不同的理由，因此沒辦法確切地分類，但他仍歸類出四種廣義的性格，與英文字母 DISC 相對應。那些展現出支配特徵的人，會使用魄力來處理事情，而展現誘導特徵的人則會利用魅力。展現服從特徵的人自願接受得要做的事，而展現遵從特徵的人，會以懼怕的方式屈從別人的意志。

　　在馬斯頓首次概述 DISC 理論後的多年間，有多種職場評量以及人格測驗被發展出來，為合適的角色找到合適的人選、改善組織內部溝通，以及用來強化員工的自我認知。最有名的系統之一是由梅里克‧羅森堡所研發出的測驗。他是專辦多項企業訓練課程的起飛學習公司的共同創辦人兼執行長。

　　羅森堡將四種性格與鳥類做聯想，好讓這四種性格更有視覺感、更好記。老鷹代表支配，好鬥、果斷、善於解決問題。鸚鵡代表誘導，樂觀、愛交際、善於說服他人。白鴿代表服從，有耐心、能體諒他人、長於團隊合作。貓頭鷹代表遵從，有禮貌、客觀、善於細節工作。當然，如同前面暗示過的，沒有人會僅符合單一類別。不過許多公司覺得這種評量在改善他們日常的效率與決策過程上很有幫助。

C 43. 根據本文，下列哪一項不是威廉‧莫爾頓‧馬斯頓的事跡？
(A) 他想出一個女性漫畫角色的點子。
(B) 他發明出可以辨別他人是否誠實的測驗。
(C) 他進行對囚犯行為的研究。
(D) 他創建出解釋普通人行為的理論。

> 理由
> 根據本文第二段第二句，他沒有像他的同行那樣調查罪犯或精神病患的行為，反而試圖解釋所謂「一般」大眾的行為，故 (C) 項應為正選。

B 44. 本文第三段的主旨是什麼？
(A) 羅森堡的公司何時成立。　　　　(B) 馬斯頓的理論如何被運用。
(C) DISC 觀點為什麼不再適用。　　(D) 訓練課程通常如何被設計。

> 理由
> 根據本文第三段表示，馬斯頓的理論發展出許多相關的測驗，並運用在認定正確的人選上，或是改善組織內的溝通及強化員工自我認知，故 (B) 項應為正選。

TEST 10

B 45. 瑞秋是個正向開朗的人，她很樂於替同事安排團體活動。根據羅森堡的觀點，下列哪一種鳥與她最相符？

(A)　　　　　　　　　　　　　　(B)

(C)　　　　　　　　　　　　　　(D)

理由
根據本文第四段第三句，鸚鵡代表誘導，樂觀、愛交際、善於說服他人，故 (B) 項應為正選。

A 46. 最後一段中 **alluded to** 最有可能是什麼意思？
(A) 間接提及。　　　　　　　　(B) 仔細挑選。
(C) 在電視上廣為放送。　　　　(D) 近期出版。

理由
根據本文第二段第三句，馬斯頓承認人們在不同的環境中的行為會有不同的理由，因此沒辦法確切地分類，故可推知粗體字最接近表間接提及，故 (A) 項應為正選。

重要字詞片語

1. **psychologist** [saɪˋkɑlədʒɪst] *n.* 心理學家
2. **detector** [dɪˋtɛktɚ] *n.* 偵測器
   lie detector　測謊器
3. **personality** [ˏpɝsnˋælətɪ] *n.* 性格，個性
4. **outline** [ˋaʊtˏlaɪn] *vt.* 概述；畫出……的輪廓
5. **criminal** [ˋkrɪmənḷ] *n.* 罪犯
6. **mentally** [ˋmɛntḷɪ] *adv.* 心理上
7. **peer** [pɪr] *n.* 同輩，同儕，同行
   peer pressure　同儕壓力
8. **acknowledge** [əkˋnɑlɪdʒ] *vt.* 承認
   acknowledge that...　承認……
9. **categorize** [ˋkætəgəˏraɪz] *vt.* 將……分類

10. **broad** [brɔd] *a.* 寬闊的
11. **trait** [tret] *n.* 特質，特點
    a personality / character trait
    人格特質
12. **dominance** [ˈdɑmənəns] *n.* 主導，主要
13. **inducement** [ɪnˈdjusmənt] *n.* 引誘，誘導
14. **submission** [sʌbˈmɪʃən] *n.* 屈服，投降
15. **compliance** [kəmˈplaɪəns] *n.* 遵守（不可數）
    in compliance with...　遵守……
16. **adapt** [əˈdæpt] *vt. & vi.* （使）適應
    adapt to sth　適應某事物
17. **assessment** [əˈsɛsmənt] *n.* 評估
    make an assessment of...
    對……做出評估
18. **run** [rʌn] *vt.* 經營，開辦
19. **competitive** [kəmˈpɛtətɪv] *a.* 競爭的
20. **decisive** [dɪˈsaɪsɪv] *a.* 果決的；決定性的；確定的
21. **optimistic** [ˌɑptəˈmɪstɪk] *a.* 樂觀的
22. **persuade** [pɚˈswed] *vt.* 說服
    persuade sb to + V
    說服某人做……
23. **courteous** [ˈkɝtɪəs] *a.* 有禮貌的
24. **objective** [əbˈdʒɛktɪv] *a.* 客觀的
25. **allude to...**
    間接提到……，暗指……
26. **efficiency** [ɪˈfɪʃənsɪ] *n.* 效率
27. **folk** [fok] *n.* 人們（表此意時，本身即為複數，也可寫成 folks）

TEST 10

第貳部分、混合題（占 10 分）

第 47 至 50 題為題組

當我們睡覺時，身體會經歷兩個明顯階段：非快速動眼期和快速動眼期。前個階段包括進入夢鄉，經由淺眠再過渡到深度睡眠。當我們從淺眠轉換到深度睡眠時，我們的心率和呼吸會變慢，給予身體修復組織、再生細胞和強化免疫系統的機會。一旦我們完全熟睡，就進入了快速動眼期。這時我們的心率和呼吸會再度變快，眼球快速移動。這也是做夢的時候，讓我們的大腦有大好機會來處理我們前一天的經歷和記憶。

在快速動眼期，腦部會傳達訊號關閉身體的肌肉，使人無法動彈。有意思的是，有些人在快速動眼期結束前就會意識到周遭狀況，讓他們處在一種睡眠癱瘓狀態中。許多患者描述自己除了眼睛之外全身都動彈不得，並覺得胸部遭重物壓迫。他們也有可能產生幻覺，或感覺有某人或某物──通常是邪惡的──在自己的房間裡。儘管睡眠癱瘓症十分正常，卻是極少發生的現象。多數人就算是真的經歷，一生也不過一兩回而已。所幸這種現象最多只會持續數秒到數分鐘。

你可以嘗試以下辦法來避免睡眠癱瘓症的發生。首先，試著保持規律的睡眠模式，因為成年人每晚都需要在黑暗、安靜和舒適的狀態下睡眠六至八小時。如果可能的話，每晚在同一時間就寢，然後在早上同一時間起床。另外要避免在激烈運動、抽菸、飲酒或吃完大餐後馬上就寢。藉由遵守這些規則，我們不僅可以避免睡眠癱瘓而且還可以確保我們能有最佳的睡眠品質。

47-49. 請利用本文中的資訊，填入下方的空格。

睡眠階段	身體反應	優點
非快速動眼期	心率和呼吸會變慢。	我們的身體可以修復組織、再生細胞和強化免疫系統。 47. repair tissue, regenerate cells, and strengthen our immune system 理由 本文第一段第四句指出非快速動眼期給予身體修復組織、再生細胞和強化免疫系統的機會，故知空格應置 repair tissue, regenerate cells, and strengthen our immune system（修復組織、再生細胞和強化免疫系統）。

| 快速動眼期 | 心率和呼吸變快而且我們的眼球快速移動。

48. <u>our eyes move rapidly</u>
理由
本文第一段第六句指出快速動眼期的時候，我們的心率和呼吸會再度變快，眼球快速移動，故知空格應置 our eyes move rapidly（我們的眼球快速移動）。 | 我們的大腦可以處理我們前一天的經歷和記憶。

49. <u>process our experiences and memories from the previous day</u>
理由
本文第一段最後一句指出快速動眼期讓我們的大腦有大好機會來處理我們前一天的經歷和記憶，故知空格應置 process our experiences and memories from the previous day（處理我們前一天的經歷和記憶）。 |

B E 50. 關於睡眠癱瘓，下列哪幾項是正確的？
(A) 發生於非快速動眼睡眠階段。
(B) 會伴隨一種旁邊有人的感覺。
(C) 一般每年會發生一到兩次。
(D) 特徵是缺乏眼球運動。
(E) 可能因為夜晚的活動而引發。
(F) 只能透過藥物治療。

理由
根據本文第二段第四句，他們也有可能產生幻覺，或感覺有某人或某物在自己的房間裡，故 (B) 項應為正選。又根據本文第三段第四句，避免在激烈運動、抽菸、飲酒或吃完大餐後馬上就寢，故 (E) 項亦應為正選。

重要字詞片語

1. **rapid** [ˈræpɪd] *a.* 快速的
Strong ocean currents often cause rapid and high waves.
強勁的洋流時常引起又快速又強的波浪。

2. **encompass** [ɪnˈkʌmpəs] *vt.* 包含，包括
This volunteer group encompasses people from all walks of life.
這個志工團包含各種行業的人。

3. **transition** [trænˈzɪʃən] *vi. & n.*
轉換，轉變

4. **shut down(...)** 停止／關閉（……）
It's a pity that this grocery store is shutting down.
很可惜這家雜貨店要歇業了。

5. **surroundings** [səˈraʊndɪŋz] *n.* 四周環境（恆用複數）

6. **paralysis** [pəˈræləsɪs] *n.* 癱瘓；麻痺
sleep paralysis
睡眠癱瘓（俗稱鬼壓床）

7. **hallucination** [həˌlusnˈeʃən] *n.* 幻覺

8. **remedy** [ˈrɛmədɪ] *n.* 解決辦法；療法

9. **strenuous** [ˈstrɛnjʊəs] *a.* 費力的；艱苦的
strenuous exercise　劇烈運動

307

TEST 10

第參部分、非選擇題（占 28 分）

一、中譯英（占 8 分）

1. 有些電玩遊戲的情節會使人焦慮，因而對青少年的心理健康產生負面影響。

   示範譯句
   Some video game plots might be so disturbing that they could have a negative effect on the mental health of teenagers.

   或：Some unnerving video game storylines could adversely shape the thoughts of teenagers.

   翻譯要點

   a. **plot** [plɑt] *n.* （小說、電影）情節，布局
   b. **disturbing** [dɪˋstɝbɪŋ] *a.* 令人焦慮的
   c. **have an effect on…**
   = have an influence on…
      對……有影響/作用
      Any changes in lifestyle will have an effect on your health.
      任何生活方式的改變都會影響你的健康。
   d. **negative** [ˋnɛɡətɪv] *a.* 負面的，不好的
   e. **mental** [ˋmɛntḷ] *a.* 心理的；精神的
   f. **unnerving** [ʌnˋnɝvɪŋ] *a.* 使人緊張不安的
   g. **storyline** [ˋstɔrɪˏlaɪn] *n.* 故事情節
   h. **adversely** [ədˋvɝslɪ] *adv.* 不利地

2. 有些人認為應制定法律限制這類遊戲，但也有人認為不該將每個問題歸咎於遊戲本身。

   示範譯句
   Some people believe that laws should be made to restrict such games, while others don't think they should blame the games for every problem.

   或：Some people believe laws should be enacted to restrict games of this sort, but others don't think the games themselves are entirely to blame.

   翻譯要點

   a. **some… others…** 有些……另一些……（用於非限定的兩個群體）
      Some girls like to wear skirts in the summer, while others prefer shorts.
      有些女生喜歡在夏天穿裙子，而有些則喜歡穿短褲。
   b. **restrict** [rɪˋstrɪkt] *vt.* 限制
   c. **blame A for B** 把 B 歸咎於 A
   = blame B on A
      be to blame 該負責
      Sam blamed the muddy field for the team's loss.
      山姆把球隊輸球歸咎於場地泥濘。
      I am responsible for this incident. However, you are also to blame.
      我要對此事負責。然而，你也有責任。
   d. **enact** [ɪnˋækt] *vt.* 制定（法律）
      The new legislation on abortion will be enacted next year.
      有關墮胎的新法規將於明年制定。
   e. **N + of this sort** 這種……
   f. **entirely** [ɪnˋtaɪrlɪ] *adv.* 完全地，全部地

二、英文作文（占 20 分）

提示：請仔細觀察以下三幅連環圖片的內容，並想像第四幅圖片可能的發展，寫出一個涵蓋連環圖片內容並有完整結局的故事。

示範作文

　　On a Saturday morning around noon, Mary and three of her female friends were going to a fancy Italian restaurant to have lunch. They were all Mary's besties since they often hung out after school and on weekends. When they were seated and were about to order food, Cindy began to snap pictures of everything in the restaurant, including the decorations on the wall and the menu. When the dishes they had ordered were finally served, Mary couldn't wait to dig in because she skipped breakfast that morning.

　　When Mary reached out to pick up a piece of pizza, Cindy stopped her. She said she wanted all of them to delay eating until she finished taking pictures of all the dishes. Although the food on the table made their mouths water, they had to refrain from eating while she was taking pictures. She even took several selfies with the main dish and its garnish. They waited about 30 minutes before they could

TEST 10

enjoy the delicacies. Despite feeling a bit upset, Mary and the other two girls did not complain. They knew Cindy was not only their best friend but also a hopeless narcissist.

在某個接近中午的星期六早上，瑪麗和她的三位女性友人正在前往一間高檔義式餐廳吃午餐。她們都是瑪麗的閨密，因為她們常在放學後和週末一起出去玩。當她們就座並準備點餐時，辛蒂開始猛拍餐廳裡的所有東西，包括牆上的裝飾品和菜單。當她們點的菜終於送上時，瑪麗等不及要大快朵頤，因為她那天早上沒吃早餐。

當瑪麗伸手拿起一塊披薩時，辛蒂阻止了她。她說希望全部人都等她拍完所有餐點後再開始吃。雖然餐桌上的食物令她們垂涎三尺，但她們在辛蒂拍照時必須忍住不吃東西。她甚至和主餐跟配菜拍了好幾張自拍。她們等了大約三十分鐘才得以享用那些美食。儘管覺得有些不悅，瑪麗和另外兩個女孩並沒有抱怨。她們明白辛蒂不只是她們最要好的朋友，還是一個無可救藥的自戀狂。

重要字詞片語

1. **bestie** [ˈbɛsti] *n.* 閨密，最好的朋友
2. **hang out** 閒晃，徘徊
   hang out with... 和……玩在一塊兒
   It's nice to hang out with old friends after we haven't seen each other for years.
   多年未見之後還能和老朋友一同玩樂是件很棒的事。
3. **snap** [snæp] *vt.* 拍攝（照片）
   During our visit to the Eiffel Tower, Lucy snapped over 100 pictures.
   我們去參觀艾菲爾鐵塔時，露西拍了一百多張相片。
4. **decoration** [ˌdɛkəˈreʃən] *n.* 裝飾品（可數）；裝飾，裝潢（不可數）
5. **dig in** 開始吃
   The food's getting cold. Let's dig in!
   食物要涼了。我們開動吧！
6. **delay** [dɪˈle] *vt. & n.* 延遲，延誤
   Due to the storm, our flight was delayed for two hours.
   我們的班機因為暴風雨而延誤了兩個小時。
7. **water** [ˈwɔtɚ] *vi.* 流口水
   My mouth watered when I saw the food.
   我看到那些食物時，便流口水了。
8. **refrain** [rɪˈfren] *vi.* 克制，忍耐
   refrain from N/V-ing 忍住不……
   Please refrain from eating or speaking loudly in the library.
   在圖書館內禁止飲食或大聲喧嘩。
9. **garnish** [ˈgɑrnɪʃ] *n.* （食物上的）裝飾菜
10. **delicacy** [ˈdɛləkəsɪ] *n.* 美食，佳餚
11. **complain** [kəmˈplen] *vi.* 抱怨
    complain about... 抱怨……
    Anna complained about the delay caused by the construction of the new MRT line.
    安娜抱怨新捷運路線施工導致的延誤。
12. **narcissist** [ˈnɑrsɪsɪst] *n.* 自戀者

NOTE

NOTE

NOTE

國家圖書館出版品預行編目（CIP）資料

新制學測英文 10 回決勝模擬試題（試題＋詳解）：
詳解本／賴世雄作. -- 初版. -- 臺北市：常春藤數
位出版股份有限公司, 2025.04　面；　公分. --
（常春藤 108 課綱核心素養・升大學系列；A108-2）
ISBN 978-626-7225-87-5（平裝）

1. CST：英語教學　2. CST：讀本
3. CST：中等教育
524.38　　　　　　　　　　　　　114003071

**填讀者問卷
送熊贈點**

常春藤 108 課綱核心素養・升大學系列【A108-2】
**新制學測英文 10 回決勝模擬試題（試題＋詳解）
－詳解本**

總 編 審	賴世雄
終　　審	梁民康
執行編輯	許嘉華
編輯小組	畢安安・Nick Roden・Brian Foden
設計組長	王玥琦
封面設計	林桂旭
排版設計	林桂旭・王穎緁
法律顧問	北辰著作權事務所蕭雄淋律師
出 版 者	常春藤數位出版股份有限公司
地　　址	臺北市忠孝西路一段 33 號 5 樓
電　　話	(02) 2331-7600
傳　　真	(02) 2381-0918
網　　址	www.ivy.com.tw
電子信箱	service@ivy.com.tw
郵政劃撥	50463568
戶　　名	常春藤數位出版股份有限公司
定　　價	420 元（2 書）

©常春藤數位出版股份有限公司 (2025) All rights reserved.　　Y000041-3577

本書之封面、內文、編排等之著作財產權歸常春藤數位出版股份有限公司所有。未經本公司
書面同意，請勿翻印、轉載或為一切著作權法上利用行為，否則依法追究。

如有缺頁、裝訂錯誤或破損，請寄回本公司更換。　　【版權所有　翻印必究】

新制學測英文
10回決勝

模擬試題 [試題＋詳解]

試題本

序言

　　108 新課綱上路，學測也迎來新題型。綜觀而言，新實施的英語文課綱著重培養學生的「核心素養」，期望學生除了具備英語文的能力之外，更能實際運用在日常生活，進而提升解決問題的能力，對於跨領域的學科，也能透過語言能力獲取新知。

　　我們知道新制學測與以往最大的不同是新增**「混合題」**及**「篇章結構題」**。混合題是以**手寫作答**的方式測驗考生**整合文章資訊及應變的能力**等；而篇章結構則是指考的必考題型，從 **115 學年度**起，更是將原先 4 個空格搭配 4 個選項的測驗方式，**調整為 4 個空格搭配 5 個選項**。

　　為了幫助考生輕鬆掌握新制學測考題方向，我們特地將本公司兩本重點書籍《迎戰 108 新課綱：新制學測英文 5 回必勝模擬試題》、《迎戰 108 新課綱：新制學測英文 5 回搶分模擬試題》合併＋升級；除了修改篇章結構為 4 個空格搭配 5 個選項的題型之外，更深入研究近幾年新制學測的考題方向等等，去調整我們的試題，將本書的擬真度大幅提升！

　　我們的文章選材豐富多元，涉及的領域跨越各個學科，命題方向則參考大考中心所公布的準則，讓考生能充分練習，並熟悉新題型，且為使考生正式考試時能更輕鬆以對，我們特地將本書考題**難度提高、加深混合題的靈活度**，讓考生加倍累積作答經驗，將來必能穩操勝算。

　　祝各位學習成功！

目錄

TEST 01 ……………………………………………………… 3

TEST 02 ……………………………………………………… 17

TEST 03 ……………………………………………………… 31

TEST 04 ……………………………………………………… 45

TEST 05 ……………………………………………………… 59

TEST 06 ……………………………………………………… 73

TEST 07 ……………………………………………………… 87

TEST 08 ……………………………………………………… 101

TEST 09 ……………………………………………………… 115

TEST 10 ……………………………………………………… 129

附錄：測驗用答案紙 …………………………………………… 141

TEST 01

第壹部分、選擇題

一、詞彙題
二、綜合測驗
三、文意選填
四、篇章結構
五、閱讀測驗

第貳部分、混合題

第參部分、非選擇題

一、中譯英
二、英文作文

第壹部分、選擇題（占 62 分）

一、詞彙題（占 10 分）

說明　第 1 題至第 10 題，每題 1 分。

1. At the moment, it is not clear whether Ukraine will _____ triumph in its war with Russia.
   (A) essentially　　(B) eventually　　(C) partly　　(D) namely

2. The company has decided to spend money on developing electric vehicles, as they believe that industry is _____ for investment.
   (A) regretful　　(B) criminal　　(C) ripe　　(D) swift

3. If Sandra passes the driver's test and gets a _____, she will be able to drive to work instead of taking the bus.
   (A) reply　　(B) signal　　(C) contract　　(D) license

4. We should donate some food and money to help prevent the children in Africa from _____ to death.
   (A) starving　　(B) leaking　　(C) interfering　　(D) negotiating

5. Jack is not a very _____ person, so you can hardly ever tell what he's thinking or feeling.
   (A) energetic　　(B) courageous　　(C) expressive　　(D) carefree

6. Shelly fell off her bike yesterday, and the doctor said she has a small _____ in her wrist.
   (A) edge　　(B) fracture　　(C) ritual　　(D) hardship

7. Please turn off your cell phone before the movie starts so that the ringing will not _____ the other audience members.
   (A) divide　　(B) disturb　　(C) reveal　　(D) satisfy

8. The huge earthquake did serious damage to the area and caused a lot of buildings to _____.
   (A) collapse　　(B) evolve　　(C) recover　　(D) arise

9. In front of their families and friends during their wedding ceremony, Carl and his wife promised to stay _____ to each other.
   (A) faithful　　(B) profitable　　(C) intelligent　　(D) outgoing

3

10. Dave didn't know how to clean his wound, so it got dirty and resulted in a(n) _____.
    (A) imagination　　(B) distraction　　(C) attention　　(D) infection

二、綜合測驗（占 10 分）

說明　第 11 題至第 20 題，每題 1 分。

第 11 至 15 題為題組

　　Not all ideal island tourist destinations are in the Pacific and Indian Oceans. Of course, Hawaii, Tahiti, Palau, and the Maldives are internationally __11__ as the "perfect" locations for a leisure vacation. Not so well known but certainly worth the time, expense, and effort of getting there __12__ some of the islands in the Mediterranean Sea. Among these, many people consider the Greek island of Santorini their first choice.

　　Located nearly 200 kilometers south of the Greek mainland, about halfway to Crete, Santorini offers travelers exotic views and historic landmarks. The island is part of the remains of a massive volcanic __13__ that occurred about 3,600 years ago. This event completely changed the shape of Santorini, creating the famous cliffs that the beautiful white-and-blue buildings cling to today. Many tourists visit the island for the stunning __14__ and views of the crystal-clear ocean that these cliffs provide.

　　Santorini also boasts some delicious local cuisine, which uses ingredients that are __15__ to the island. Popular choices include *apochti*, a traditional salted pork dish, and *chlorotyri*, a goat cheese that is unique to Santorini. To wash these down, visitors might like to try one of the locally produced wines, which have won international awards.

11. (A) shattered　　(B) identical　　(C) miserable　　(D) renowned
12. (A) is　　(B) being　　(C) are　　(D) has
13. (A) religion　　(B) routine　　(C) explosion　　(D) tribe
14. (A) photo opportunities　　(B) purchasing experiences
    (C) life necessities　　(D) emergency kits
15. (A) acute　　(B) native　　(C) dreadful　　(D) frank

第 16 至 20 題為題組

　　When we think of the great painters of the 19th and 20th centuries, Pablo Picasso, Vincent van Gogh, and Salvador Dali come to mind. Despite working in different countries at different times, they all had one thing in __16__: they were all men. Women painters were __17__ fewer in number and less well-known. That does not mean their works are not worth appreciating, though. Marie Laurencin is a case in point.

　　The early years of the 20th century were a revolutionary time. In painting, the Cubists, represented by Picasso, Dali, and others, brought about a visual revolution by painting abstract pictures rather than lifelike ones. Joining them, Laurencin depicted women not as they look in real life __18__ as representatives of abstract femininity. However, there were __19__ between Cubist norms and how Laurencin painted. Whereas many of the Cubists used bright, even glaring colors, Laurencin worked in pastels. While the Cubists tended to use straight and sharply angular lines, Laurencin rejoiced in painting women with curves.

　　Nowadays, Laurencin's paintings can be viewed in museums __20__, in cities ranging from her native Paris to New York and London. For a time, there was also a museum in Tokyo that was dedicated to her artworks. However, this museum is permanently closed.

16. (A) advance　　　　(B) common　　　　(C) labor　　　　(D) bulk
17. (A) lot　　　　　　 (B) more　　　　　 (C) far　　　　　(D) farther
18. (A) either　　　　　(B) or　　　　　　 (C) but　　　　　(D) and
19. (A) possible answers　　　　　　(B) ancient relics
　　(C) various supporters　　　　　(D) important differences
20. (A) around the world　　　　　　(B) in the public interest
　　(C) only in imagination　　　　　(D) beyond description

三、文意選填（占 10 分）

說明 第 21 題至第 30 題，每題 1 分。

第 21 至 30 題為題組

　　One of today's most popular articles of clothing is the polo shirt. Despite its name, one doesn't have to be riding around on a horse carrying a long wooden hammer and trying to hit a small ball during a polo match to wear one. Today, the shirt is considered smart casual wear as well as a symbol of a sporty __21__.

　　Though the shirt is commonly associated with polo, it actually got its start with the game of tennis. From the late 1800s to the early 1900s, players typically wore stiff white button-up shirts with the long sleeves rolled up and __22__ them with ties and flannel pants. For some, the clothes felt unsuitable for the fast-moving

TEST 01

and __23__ sport. Fortunately, Frenchman René Lacoste came along. The seven-time Grand Slam tennis champion designed a white, loose-fitting, short-sleeved shirt to __24__ the problem. He first wore this more practical and comfortable shirt at the 1926 US Open championship. Then, to __25__ his press-given nickname "The Crocodile," Lacoste added a green crocodile logo to his creation. After __26__ in the early 1930s, he teamed up with businessman André Gillier to form a company and mass-produce his shirt. It was a big hit, and soon polo players were also __27__ their own heavy and uncomfortable attire with shirts similar to Lacoste's design. Before long, tennis players began to refer to their shirt as a polo shirt in spite of the fact that their sport had __28__ it before polo did. By the 1950s, it was all anyone ever called it. What's more, golf professionals began wearing the exercise-friendly shirt as part of their __29__ attire.

Today, the Lacoste company makes a wide __30__ of sporting goods and clothing. Now, it isn't hard to spot someone, both on and off the court, wearing a white, short-sleeved athletic shirt with a green crocodile on it.

(A) paired　　(B) fix　　(C) standard　　(D) adopted　　(E) attitude
(F) retiring　　(G) range　　(H) replacing　　(I) vigorous　　(J) acknowledge

四、篇章結構（占 8 分）

說明 第 31 題至第 34 題，每題 2 分。

第 31 至 34 題為題組

　　Milina Cunning is a woman from a large town near Glasgow in Scotland. When she was in her 20s, she had a series of health problems and was put into an induced coma by her doctor. After 52 days, Cunning awoke without her eyesight. "When I woke up, I saw completely black," she told the BBC. __31__ Then, a few months later, strange things started to happen. Although she was blind, Cunning often saw colors in her mind. When she told her doctor about this, he put her in touch with Gordon Dutton, a professor of visual science. Dutton decided to conduct an experiment. __32__ On her first attempt, Cunning crashed into the chairs. Then, the professor asked her to try it again at a faster pace. To everyone's amazement, she didn't bump into a single chair.

　　Dutton told her that she had "blindsight," a strange condition that affects a small number of blind people worldwide. __33__ If these are all destroyed, we will go "completely" blind. If only some pathways are damaged, though, blindsight may occur. Although people with blindsight cannot physically see, their unconscious mind retains the ability to sense the environment around them. This mysterious ability seems to work best when the person doesn't focus or try too hard to see. __34__ For example,

Cunning still manages to clean her home despite being blind. Her brain automatically nudges her to move around objects on the floor, even though she can't physically see them. Somehow, she just "knows" they are there. "It's strange the things I can see but I'm not meant to see because I'm blind," Cunning told the BBC. If she tries to focus, though, the task becomes harder. Blindsight has shown scientists that there is still a lot to learn about vision, as well as the human brain.

(A) This allows their subconscious mind to take over and get the job done.
(B) Thankfully, Cunning's vision returned to normal six months after the accident.
(C) He set several chairs in the hallway and asked Cunning to walk towards them.
(D) Doctors informed her that she had gone blind after suffering a stroke.
(E) He explained that we all have different pathways in our brains which help us see and sense objects.

五、閱讀測驗（占 24 分）

說明 第 35 題至第 46 題，每題 2 分。

第 35 至 38 題為題組

The Sydney Opera House is one of the most iconic buildings in the world. Rising above Sydney Harbour like a stack of seashells, the structure is actually a collection of buildings dedicated to the arts.

Ecaterina Sciuchina / Shutterstock.com

The idea for an arts center for Sydney began as early as the late 1940s. As Australia was becoming a more developed and wealthy nation, the city government of Sydney, the country's largest and most rapidly growing city, felt the need for a center that would provide venues for a variety of artistic performances. An international design competition for such a center was held in 1955. Two years later, Jørn Utzon, a Danish architect, was chosen to lead the construction of the complex, which began after another two years. The project was so sophisticated that it was originally divided into three stages.

Many problems were encountered during the construction of the opera house. The novel designs of the buildings caused multiple issues, and much time was spent trying to determine how to produce the "shells" for the roof. Torrential rain and strong winds impacted the construction timetable, which was behind schedule almost from day one. And Jørn Utzon resigned from the project after a few years. This latter factor was due to disagreements between Utzon and successive Australian governments and the varying levels of input and interference from the latter. Utzon finally left the project in 1966 and was replaced by Australian architect Peter Hall. Hall oversaw the remainder of the construction until its completion in 1973, ten years late and a staggering 14 times over budget. Hall is credited with bringing a renewed sense of clarity and purpose to the project. Nevertheless, it is Utzon whose name will forever be associated with the design and construction of this famed masterpiece.

35. What is the main purpose of this article?
    (A) To urge the public to support the arts.
    (B) To inform the public of upcoming artistic events.
    (C) To detail the history of a famous construction.
    (D) To tell the life story of a renowned architect.

36. When did the construction of the Sydney Opera House begin?
    (A) In the late 1940s.   (B) In 1955.
    (C) In 1959.   (D) In 1973.

37. Who was Peter Hall?
    (A) A government minister who supported the opera house.
    (B) An architect who took over from Jørn Utzon.
    (C) An actor who performed at the opera house.
    (D) A designer who inspired the work of Jørn Utzon.

38. Which problem was NOT encountered during the construction of the opera house?
    (A) The departure of the chief architect.
    (B) The lack of public interest in the project.
    (C) The appearance of poor weather conditions.
    (D) The difficulties posed by the unusual designs.

第 39 至 42 題為題組

Imagine a country three times the size of Taiwan with a population of only 366,000. That country is Iceland, one of the most unusual in the world.

Located where the North Atlantic Ocean meets the Arctic Ocean, Iceland is frozen for much of the year. Due to a warm ocean current that comes from the Gulf of Mexico, however, Iceland is blessed with a **temperate** rather than a polar climate. Temperatures are between 10°C and 20°C in the summer and average just below zero from November through March. Not surprisingly, though, Iceland has its fair share of snow and ice. Glaciers cover some 10% of the land. Nearly two-thirds of the land is tundra, which means that trees cannot grow as the soil below the ground is permanently frozen. With more than 100 volcanoes, Iceland is one of the most geologically active places on the planet. Therefore, earthquakes are common but not very severe.

Fishing has always been an important part of the Icelandic economy, and it now still accounts for around 40% of export earnings annually. Not all of the fish are exported, though. Seafood plays an integral role in Icelandic cuisine, with cod and haddock being two common ingredients. Perhaps the most infamous seafood in Iceland is *hákarl*, or fermented shark. This is typically consumed in only small quantities, as it produces a foul smell of ammonia. Stories abound of unsuspecting tourists struggling to eat it or even spitting it out.

Tourism attracts over one million visitors every year, most of them coming to see the glaciers, volcanoes, and many species of whales living near the Icelandic coast. Although island tours that encompass these sights—along with the waterfalls and geysers—are very popular, most tourists choose to base themselves in the capital, Reykjavik. With two-thirds of the island's inhabitants residing in the greater Reykjavik area, it is by far the most developed city. It is also relatively close to another popular tourist site: a geothermal spa called the Blue Lagoon.

39. What is the main purpose of the second paragraph?
    (A) To describe the geology and geography of Iceland.
    (B) To offer a picture of the economy of Iceland.
    (C) To introduce some rare animals living in Iceland.
    (D) To explain why the population of Iceland is so low.

40. Which of the following is closest in meaning to the word "**temperate**" in the second paragraph?
    (A) Particularly hot during summer.
    (B) Neither too hot nor too cold.
    (C) Likely to produce much snowfall.
    (D) Prone to sudden temperature extremes.

41. Based on the passage, how would a visitor to Iceland most likely describe *hákarl*?
    (A) Fragrant.　　(B) Appetizing.　　(C) Disgusting.　　(D) Appealing.

42. How does the author conclude the last paragraph?
    (A) By listing famous tourist locations within Reykjavik.
    (B) By providing further details of a round-island tour.
    (C) By giving a history of the spa culture in Iceland.
    (D) By mentioning another reason to stay in the capital.

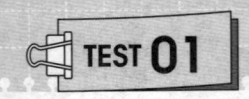

第 43 至 46 題為題組

　　Markhors are large, wild goats that live mainly in Central and Southern Asia. Most of them are found in the mountains of Pakistan, and they are the national animal of that country. The animal features on the logo of Pakistan's intelligence agency and was for a time part of the logo of the national airline.

　　One theory about the name "markhor" is that it comes from the Persian for "snake eater." Local legends tell of markhors using their long, spiral-shaped horns to kill and eat snakes and then spitting a foamy substance on the ground. Locals would then use **this** as a supposed cure for snakebites. Another theory states that their name derives from the snake-like shape of their horns. Still another points to a translation from the Urdu for "screw-horned goat," as their horns also resemble the shape of a corkscrew.

　　Aside from the unique horns, there are other features of their appearance that are remarkable. They are one of the tallest and heaviest of the goat family, standing up to 155 centimeters in height and weighing up to 110 kilograms. In winter, they grow thick, long hair to keep themselves warm. Both males and females have beards, although the male beard is longer, extending down to the chest.

　　This hair keeps them warm in the mountainous terrain, where they employ their incredible climbing skills to compete with domestic goats for grass in the summer and tree leaves in the winter. Winter is also the mating season, during which the males lock horns and fight with each other to win the attention of the females. For much of the year, though, the males head out to scavenge for food, leaving the females with the kids.

　　Regardless of their ability to scale steep mountain cliffs where humans can never go, markhors are facing ongoing threats from humans. Hunters pursue them for their valuable and distinctive horns. Local residents kill them for food. Markhors are thus listed as "Near Threatened" by the International Union for Conservation of Nature. Nevertheless, there are tentative signs that their number might be increasing.

43. Which of the following is NOT a theory about the origin of the name "markhor"?
    (A) It is connected to the eating of a reptile.
    (B) It is linked to the name of a wine opener.
    (C) It is derived from the appearance of an airplane.
    (D) It is connected to the shape of an animal.

44. What does "**this**" refer to in the second paragraph?
    (A) The horns of the markhor.
    (B) The animal the markhor has eaten.
    (C) The area where the markhor lives.
    (D) The liquid the markhor has left on the ground.

45. According to the passage, which of the following pictures most likely resembles the markhor?
    (A)
    (B)
    (C)
    (D)

46. According to the passage, which of the following is a threat to the future of the markhor?
    (A) Their declining ability to ascend mountains.
    (B) The poor hunting methods of the females.
    (C) Their highly prized body parts for hunters.
    (D) The lack of food sources in the colder months.

11

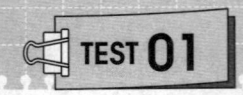

第貳部分、混合題（占 10 分）

說明 本部分共有 1 題組，每一子題配分標於題末。限在標示題號作答區內作答。選擇題使用 2B 鉛筆作答，更正時，應以橡皮擦擦拭，切勿使用修正液（帶）。非選擇題請由左而右橫式書寫。

第 47 至 50 題為題組

The healthcare system in the United Kingdom is called the National Health Service (NHS). Established in 1948, it is funded primarily through general taxation and is based on the idea that treatment is free for everyone at the point of delivery. Here are two people's opinions on the NHS.

Sandra

The NHS holds a special place in my heart. As a former nurse, I have witnessed firsthand how the guiding principle of the NHS—that everyone has access to it regardless of financial circumstances—helps to save lives. The wealthy contribute more in tax, ensuring that the poor and vulnerable receive care when they need it. Furthermore, I believe the NHS provides excellent value for money for taxpayers. Such a large organization is able to negotiate low prices for drugs with pharmaceutical companies. The NHS also performed extremely well during the COVID pandemic, delivering the first and one of the fastest vaccine rollouts in the world. I am not blind to its faults, of course; no system is perfect. For example, waiting lists for certain procedures are far too high. However, I firmly believe that the dedicated and professional workforce of the NHS can successfully bring **these** down.

Chris

The NHS's founding principle of universal health coverage is laudable, and it worked well in practice for many years. Indeed, I myself received excellent, prompt treatment from the NHS in my younger years. However, for far too many people, that is no longer the case. The UK has an aging population, and many of the elderly require increasingly expensive medical treatments. These cost more money and lead to longer hospital stays, thus driving up waiting lists. The waiting lists are sky-high due to the pandemic, during which the NHS focused excessively on COVID patients at the expense of those with other medical issues. This still affects us today. I don't believe that funding is the issue, because no matter how much money is poured into the NHS, waiting lists do not significantly come down. The organization is simply too big and bureaucratic, and in its current state is not fit for purpose. It urgently needs to be reformed.

47. 請根據選文內容，從兩則觀點中各選出一個單詞（word），填入下列句子的空格中，並視語法需要做適當的字形變化，使句子語意完整、語法正確，且符合全文文意。**每格限填一個單詞（word）**。（填充，4分）

    Sandra observes that the (A) _____ of the NHS during the pandemic was very good, citing the rollout of the vaccine as an example, but Chris remarks that the NHS placed too much (B) _____ on treating COVID patients.

48. What does "**these**" in Sandra's passage refer to?（簡答，2分）

    _____

49-50. Do the following statements apply to Sandra, Chris, both of them, or neither of them?（勾選，4分）

49. They were employed by the NHS in the past.
    ☐ Sandra   ☐ Chris   ☐ Both   ☐ Neither

50. They think that all UK citizens need to pay more tax for the NHS.
    ☐ Sandra   ☐ Chris   ☐ Both   ☐ Neither

TEST 01

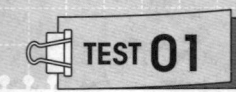

第參部分、非選擇題（占 28 分）

說明 本部分共有二大題，請依各題指示作答，答案必須寫在「答題卷」標示題號之作答區內，作答時不必抄題。

一、中譯英（占 8 分）

說明 1. 請將以下中文句子譯成正確、通順、達意的英文，並將答案寫在「答題卷」上。
2. 請依序作答，並標明子題號。每題 4 分，共 8 分。

1. 最近，臺灣許多關於食品安全的負面新聞讓大家都很害怕吃外食。

2. 因此，許多人選擇自己在家作飯，因為那不但比較健康，也比較安全。

二、英文作文（占 20 分）

說明 1. 依提示在「答題卷」上寫一篇英文作文。
2. 文長至少 120 個單詞（words）。

提示：你認為下面兩張圖中呈現的是什麼景象？你對這個景象有什麼感想？請根據圖片內容，寫一篇英文作文。文分兩段，第一段描述兩張圖片的內容，包括其中人、事、物以及發生的事情；第二段討論你認為未來應該採取什麼具體的措施，以避免相同的情況再次發生。

TEST 02

第壹部分、選擇題

一、詞彙題
二、綜合測驗
三、文意選填
四、篇章結構
五、閱讀測驗

第貳部分、混合題

第參部分、非選擇題

一、中譯英
二、英文作文

第壹部分、選擇題（占 62 分）

一、詞彙題（占 10 分）

說明 第 1 題至第 10 題，每題 1 分。

1. When Geoff made a(n) _____ about the poor service at the restaurant, he was given a discount on his bill.
   (A) crash (B) complaint (C) interruption (D) postponement

2. The scientist described the summer temperatures in recent years as _____, stating that they were far higher than usual.
   (A) abnormal (B) nutritious (C) informative (D) apparent

3. Kathy found that her steak was only _____ cooked when she cut it, so she asked the waiter to have it replaced.
   (A) readily (B) necessarily (C) partially (D) equally

4. After the earthquake hit, many victims were trapped in the mountains and were in _____ need of medical supplies and water.
   (A) superior (B) accidental (C) urgent (D) changeable

5. A huge hawk caught sight of a small rabbit and quickly flew down to catch the _____.
   (A) authority (B) fluency (C) prey (D) threat

6. The shirt you're looking for is not _____ at the moment, but we should have some next week.
   (A) acceptable (B) suitable (C) tolerable (D) available

7. After years of training, I _____ a black belt in karate and got the opportunity to compete in an international tournament.
   (A) ignored (B) calculated (C) delivered (D) achieved

8. The sales of the new product fell short of _____, so the company needed to figure out a new marketing strategy.
   (A) expectations (B) nominations (C) combinations (D) imitations

9. The soldiers refused to _____ to their enemy even though it meant that they might be killed in combat.
   (A) retreat (B) transmit (C) reunite (D) surrender

10. The local government _____ an eco-friendly program, hoping to increase public awareness about environmental protection.
    (A) inhabited   (B) initiated   (C) assaulted   (D) accused

二、綜合測驗（占 10 分）

說明 第 11 題至第 20 題，每題 1 分。

第 11 至 15 題為題組

Ice cream cones seem so important in our culture that it's hard to imagine enjoying ice cream without them. However, the origin of these edible __11__ is shrouded in mystery and disagreement. In the US, there are various stories about the invention of the ice cream cone. The most popular one is about an ice cream salesperson that folded hot wafers and used them to serve his customers their ice cream when he __12__ bowls. It is often claimed that this happened at the 1904 World's Fair, which was held in St. Louis, Missouri. However, an Italian immigrant called Italo Marchiony had already received a patent for an ice cream cone mold one year earlier.

Despite this record of the patent from the turn of the century, there is clear __13__ that ice cream cones had already been in use in Europe much earlier. Several French and British cookbooks refer to edible wafers being used for __14__ during the 19th century. The historian Robert J. Weir has even written about pictorial proof of ice cream cones from 1807. We may never know who __15__ came up with the ice cream cone. Nevertheless, when summer comes, we all truly appreciate its invention.

11. (A) recipes   (B) chiefs   (C) delights   (D) fridges
12. (A) ran out of   (B) got used to   (C) got along with   (D) looked up to
13. (A) passion   (B) evidence   (C) security   (D) adjustment
14. (A) sealing the package   (B) holding the treat
    (C) setting the table   (D) describing the taste
15. (A) relatively   (B) immediately   (C) mutually   (D) initially

第 16 至 20 題為題組

Nearly every culture in the world celebrates New Year. It doesn't matter when it occurs. In most countries, it is celebrated on January 1 of the solar calendar. In __16__, it occurs earlier in December or later in February or even April. What matters is that everyone has a holiday and __17__ for the upcoming year. If people have just experienced a difficult twelve-month period, they may see the approaching new year as an opportunity to reset their lives and their goals. Many like to create resolutions about what they hope to achieve over the next year.

In Spain, a local custom called the Twelve Grapes is held at midnight on December 31. As neighborhood churches and cathedrals begin ringing in the last 12 seconds of the last day of the year, 18 eat one grape for each toll. The celebration is 19 to welcome a year of prosperity and good luck.

This custom was started by vine growers in Spain as early as 1895. By 1909, it 20 the old Spanish Empire, including such countries as Mexico and the Philippines. Today it has become a fun and flavorful way to bring in the new year.

16. (A) other　　　　　(B) others　　　　　(C) the other　　　　(D) the others
17. (A) night shifts　　　　　　　　　　　(B) union members
    (C) new records　　　　　　　　　　　(D) high hopes
18. (A) exporters　　(B) copiers　　(C) locals　　(D) detectives
19. (A) probable　　(B) supposed　　(C) likely　　(D) doomed
20. (A) had spread throughout　　　　　(B) was invented by
    (C) had been offered to　　　　　　(D) had endured for

三、文意選填（占 10 分）

說明　第 21 題至第 30 題，每題 1 分。

第 21 至 30 題為題組

When it comes to desserts, few dishes are as delicious as a slice of Black Forest cake. The cake consists of several 21 of chocolate sponge separated with generous amounts of cherries and whipped cream filling. Then, the cake is decorated with 22 cherries, whipped cream, and tiny pieces of chocolate. Quite often, cherry alcohol is added to the filling and icing for 23 and to kick things up a notch.

Although people have been eating Black Forest cake for centuries, the origins of the treat are somewhat 24 . The dessert is said to 25 to the late 1500s, and historians are convinced that it was first made in Germany's Black Forest region. After that, things get a bit vague. Some historians believe that it got its name because the liquor used in the recipe came from the Black Forest region. Others feel the name was chosen because the cake's appearance 26 the way women in the Black Forest used to dress. In the 16th century, the traditional 27 of these women included a white shirt, a black dress, and large hats topped with fluffy red pompoms.

Over the years, the original recipe for preparing the cake was lost, although it is likely that it continued to be made in southwestern Germany. A pastry chef named Josef Keller claims to have created the modern __28__ of the cake. He says he did so in 1915 while working at a café in the town of Bad Godesberg. Keller later __29__ the cake's recipe to one of his students, August Schaefer. Schaefer kept Keller's recipe a __30__ until he eventually handed it down to his son, Claus. Today, Claus still owns the recipe which was handwritten into an old cookbook, and he continues to bake Black Forest cakes following Keller's instructions.

(A) costume   (B) disputed   (C) secret   (D) flavor   (E) layers
(F) date back (G) resembles   (H) version   (I) additional (J) passed on

四、篇章結構（占 8 分）

說明 第 31 題至第 34 題，每題 2 分。

第 31 至 34 題為題組

There is a famous saying in English that goes, "Dogs are man's best friend." This is especially accurate for an elite group of canines called detection dogs. Quite often, these dogs are required to put their own lives at risk to assist in the prevention and resolution of crimes. In return, all they ask for is an insignificant favor—a squeaky toy. Dogs have powerful noses that are hundreds of times more sensitive than the noses of humans. __31__ Using their extraordinary sense of smell, they sniff out illegal or dangerous substances connected with crimes or smuggling. These include things such as drugs, explosives, and trails of blood.

Detection dogs work alongside members of law enforcement or the military who guide them around various places. __32__ From a distance, they can sniff out the contents of suitcases. If they detect any prohibited items, they will alert their handlers, who can deal with the problem. Earlier this decade, detection dogs were used in some airports, such as Helsinki Airport in Finland and Miami International Airport in the United States, to determine whether travelers were infected with COVID-19. Dogs have also been used to detect mines and other explosive devices in Ukraine during the war there.

Most detection dogs receive specialized training when they are mere puppies. Although several dog breeds, from German shepherds to Labrador retrievers, can become detection dogs, the majority of them are beagles. Compared to other breeds, these small hounds have an exceptional sense of smell. In addition, beagles are known for their cool and calm temperament and are eager to please. __33__ Many of the dogs are trained in Eastern Europe and can cost nearly NT$1 million per dog.

__34__   However, to date, they haven't invented any machines that are as precise as a dog's nose.

(A) The dog retired from the force after nearly ten years of faithful service.
(B) As a result, researchers are trying to develop technologies to replace detection dogs.
(C) Take, for example, detection dogs that patrol the baggage claim areas at international airports.
(D) Thus, they stay focused on the task and don't get aggressive when surrounded by lots of people.
(E) Therefore, they are able to detect even small amounts of substances they are trained to target.

五、閱讀測驗（占 24 分）

說明　第 35 題至第 46 題，每題 2 分。

第 35 至 38 題為題組

　　Nine in ten people are right-handed, which means only 10 percent are left-handed. What are the possible reasons for this disparity, and how has handedness been viewed over the years?

　　One theory about why most people are right- rather than left-handed is that the part of the brain used for talking and handiwork is the left side. Given the **nature** of the brain, this results in right-handedness. Another theory points to simple genetics. As most parents are right-handed, this trait is naturally passed on to their offspring. Even two left-handed parents have only a 26% chance of having a left-handed child, although that is already a much higher percentage than that of the general population. Whatever its cause or causes, handedness is a fact of life.

　　However, left-handedness has not been well received by the right-handed over the centuries. Many superstitions and customs have arisen from left-handedness. Not only tribal groups but also Christians, Jews, and Muslims looked down on left-handedness, even considering it evil. Left-handed European school children used to face physical punishment if they did not use their right hand. Even today, Chinese children are encouraged from an early age to write and use chopsticks with their right hand. Westerners always reach out their right hand to shake when greeting others.

TEST 02

Language reflects this discrimination, too. For example, the English word "right" also refers to "correct" or "proper." Left-handed people can struggle to use daily objects, such as scissors and zippers on clothes. Put simply, the world is built for right-handed people.

Yet, some researchers believe that being left-handed comes with certain advantages. Left-handedness is often linked to creativity. Proponents of this theory often point to such famous artists as Michelangelo and Leonardo da Vinci being "lefties." However, there is little conclusive evidence connecting left-handedness with creativity.

35. What is the main topic of this passage?
    (A) Where left-handedness is most prevalent in the world.
    (B) How left-handedness is an indication of intelligence.
    (C) Where left-handedness comes from and how it is perceived.
    (D) How left-handedness is likely to increase in the future.

36. What is the correct meaning of the word "**nature**" in the second paragraph?
    (A) The essential qualities of something.
    (B) The phenomena of the physical world.
    (C) The characteristics of a person.
    (D) The attitude of a majority.

37. According to the passage, what happened to left-handed students in Europe in the past?
    (A) They were taught to only consume food with their right hands.
    (B) They were beaten or slapped if they used their left hands.
    (C) They were encouraged to use both of their hands to write.
    (D) They were forced to attend schools for left-handed children.

38. Why is Leonardo da Vinci mentioned in the passage?
    (A) He strongly believed that left-handedness was a sin.
    (B) He found a link between left-handedness and creativity.
    (C) He is an example for the argument that left-handers are artistic.
    (D) He led research into the advantages of left-handedness.

第 39 至 42 題為題組

Applying to college can be a stressful time for many students who are making a decision that not only affects the next few years of their lives but could also determine their lifetime career prospects.

Unlike some countries with centralized admissions processing, students in the US can apply to as many schools as they like. This involves more work because each institution requires a separate application. Another difference is the ability to apply using a policy called early decision (ED). This is good for students who are set on going to a particular school. However, you can only use ED to apply to one university, and if accepted, you are required to attend that university. American colleges also employ a different selection process from some other countries. Admissions officers from better universities are looking for students with more than good grades. They are looking for well-rounded individuals who have a multitude of interests and take part in a variety of extracurricular activities. Recommendation letters from outside of the educational world and personal essays are very important in determining which applicants are accepted to higher-quality American schools. In fact, these non-academic elements are often decisive.

Does attending university have such a big impact on students' careers and future earnings? The short answer is yes. Studies consistently show that university graduates earn more than non-graduates. This disparity is more pronounced if the degree earned is higher and the university attended is more prestigious. However, **this generalization masks numerous differences**. For instance, arts graduates tend to earn less over their careers than science graduates. People who choose not to go to college but instead learn a trade, such as plumbing, can end up earning more than many graduates who attend a mid-level university and study a subject that they have little passion for. That is why many careers advisors tell students to pursue their interests whether they are in the academic world or elsewhere.

Nevertheless, attending college—with the complex application process that it entails—is still an overwhelmingly popular choice for today's students.

39. What is the second paragraph mainly about?
    (A) Different college application processes around the world.
    (B) Particular features of the American application procedure.
    (C) The vital importance of high grades to admissions teams.
    (D) A short history of the early decision application policy.

40. According to the passage, who would most likely be accepted to a top university in the US?
    (A) A student with the best test scores in his class.
    (B) A clever student who also has various hobbies.
    (C) A student with letters of praise from his teachers.
    (D) An athletic student who spends all his time on sports.

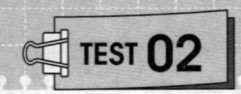

41. What does "**this generalization masks numerous differences**" imply?
    (A) It is wise to consider studying abroad for certain degrees.
    (B) Learning a trade is always more beneficial in the long run.
    (C) Your income isn't necessarily determined by your education level.
    (D) Choosing the right high school careers advisor is essential.

42. How does the author conclude the passage?
    (A) With a suggestion.
    (B) With a prediction.
    (C) With an example.
    (D) With an admission.

第 43 至 46 題為題組

　　Watching television in the comfort of our own homes is a hugely popular activity, and it actually has numerous advantages. It is an easily accessible form of entertainment, which can be enjoyed individually or as part of a collective experience. While many people take pleasure in binge-watching entire seasons of shows in one go, enjoyment can also be found in waiting anxiously to discover what happens to your favorite characters on your most-loved show one week to the next. TV can be educational, too. There is a wealth of high-quality documentaries on all manner of subjects, from history to travel to cooking, on a seemingly never-ending number of TV channels. TV can also provide company, particularly for the elderly who live alone, and it became a source of escapism for people of all ages during COVID-19 lockdowns.

　　Naturally, though, watching TV has its disadvantages. Since the advent of streaming services such as Netflix, it has become remarkably easy to watch too much TV. This can quickly develop into a form of addiction and can push people into acting in an antisocial manner, in which they prefer the stimulation of the TV to the stimulation of interpersonal relationships. This can lead to a **sedentary lifestyle**, which is already a serious problem in a society accustomed to learning or working from desks for eight hours a day. Watching TV positively encourages us to stay seated and move around less and less. Associated health problems include obesity, diabetes, and poor eyesight.

　　There are ways to alleviate at least this latter problem. There is, for instance, an ideal position from which to watch TV, thus reducing the strain on one's eyes. For a 1080p HDTV, this is no closer than 1.5 times the size of the television screen. For instance, if you have a 40-inch 1080p HDTV, you should sit at least 60 inches (about 1.5 m) from the screen. However, if you have a 4K Ultra HD TV, you can sit closer without experiencing eye strain. Additionally, whichever TV you own, you should not need to look more than 15 degrees downward or upward to see the screen.

43. Which of the following is the most suitable title for the passage?
    (A) The Advantages and Disadvantages of Ultra HD TVs
    (B) Why Television Documentaries are an Educational Tool
    (C) The Pros and Cons of Watching the Small Screen
    (D) How Binge-Watching Shows Became a National Hobby

44. Which of the following is NOT mentioned as a supporting argument for watching television?
    (A) It is a readily available hobby.
    (B) It is a pleasurable group activity.
    (C) It stops you from feeling anxious.
    (D) It provides companionship for old people.

45. What does "**sedentary lifestyle**" most likely mean in the third paragraph?
    (A) An existence that lacks a work-life balance.
    (B) A way of living involving little physical activity.
    (C) A life that has too much pleasure and too little education.
    (D) A desire to spend money on products advertised on television.

46. Which of the following illustrates the ideal seating position for someone watching a 50-inch 1080p HDTV?

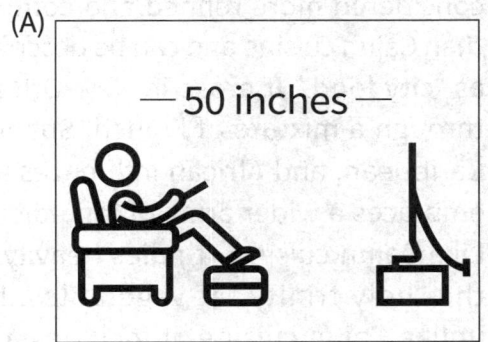

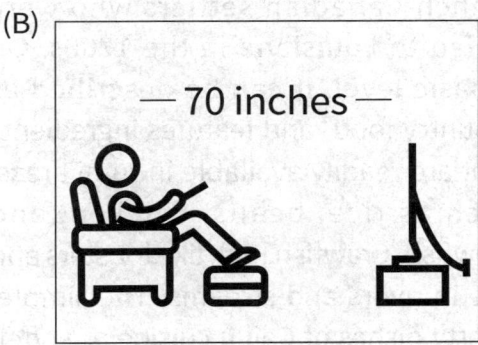

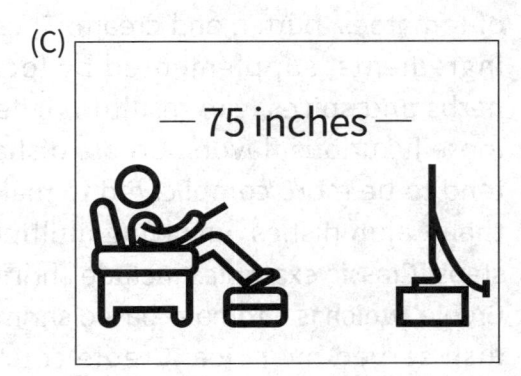

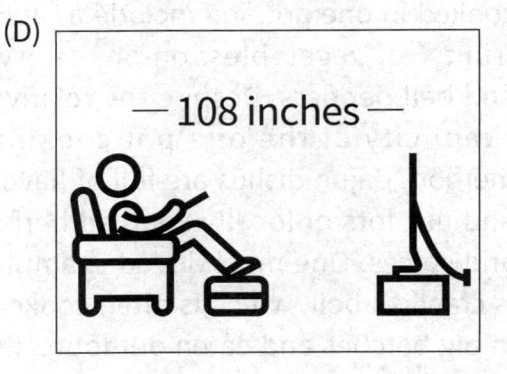

    (A) 50 inches
    (B) 70 inches
    (C) 75 inches
    (D) 108 inches

TEST 02

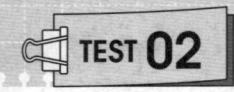

第貳部分、混合題（占 10 分）

說明　本部分共有 1 題組，每一子題配分標於題末。限在標示題號作答區內作答。選擇題使用 2B 鉛筆作答，更正時，應以橡皮擦擦拭，切勿使用修正液（帶）。非選擇題請由左而右橫式書寫。

第 47 至 50 題為題組

　　Cajun and Creole are two cuisines that are fundamentally linked to the southern US state of Louisiana, particularly the area around New Orleans. They share many similarities, but there are also important differences between them.

　　Cajun cuisine has its roots in the French-Canadian settlers who were exiled to Louisiana in the 1700s. On a basic level, it can be described as "country food" and features ingredients that are readily available in rural areas, such as rice, beans, chicken, and crawfish. Crawfish look like lobsters and live in rivers and streams. The simple, hearty dishes of Cajun cuisine are often cooked in one pot and include a "holy trinity" of vegetables: onion, celery, and bell peppers. Despite the relative simplicity of the one-pot cooking method, Cajun dishes are full of flavor and use lots of locally sourced herbs and spices. One much-loved example is crawfish boil, which is often cooked in big batches and eaten outdoors. Its ingredients include corn, potatoes, and spices in addition to crawfish.

　　Creole cuisine is generally considered more refined and complex than Cajun cuisine and can be described as "city food." It arose in New Orleans through a mixture of French, Spanish, Caribbean, and African influences and embraces a wider array of ingredients. Like Cajun cuisine, it relies heavily on the "holy trinity" of vegetables, but unlike Cajun cuisine, it includes a lot of tomatoes, butter, and cream. These ingredients, supplemented by local herbs and spices, can result in richer, more luxurious flavors. Creole dishes tend to be more complicated to make than Cajun dishes, involving multiple steps. Classic examples include shrimp Creole, which is a tomato-based shrimp dish served over rice; Creole court-bouillon, which is a seafood stew; and Pompano en Papillote, which is fish

Étouffée, meanwhile, is a stew made with shellfish or chicken and vegetables and served over rice. It features in both Cajun and Creole cuisine. The Cajun version tends to be spicier and uses a dark roux, which is a mixture of fat and flour, as a base.

baked in paper with vegetables. Many Creole dishes use a medium roux as a base.

47. Which THREE vegetables are commonly used in both Cajun and Creole cuisine? （多選題，4 分）

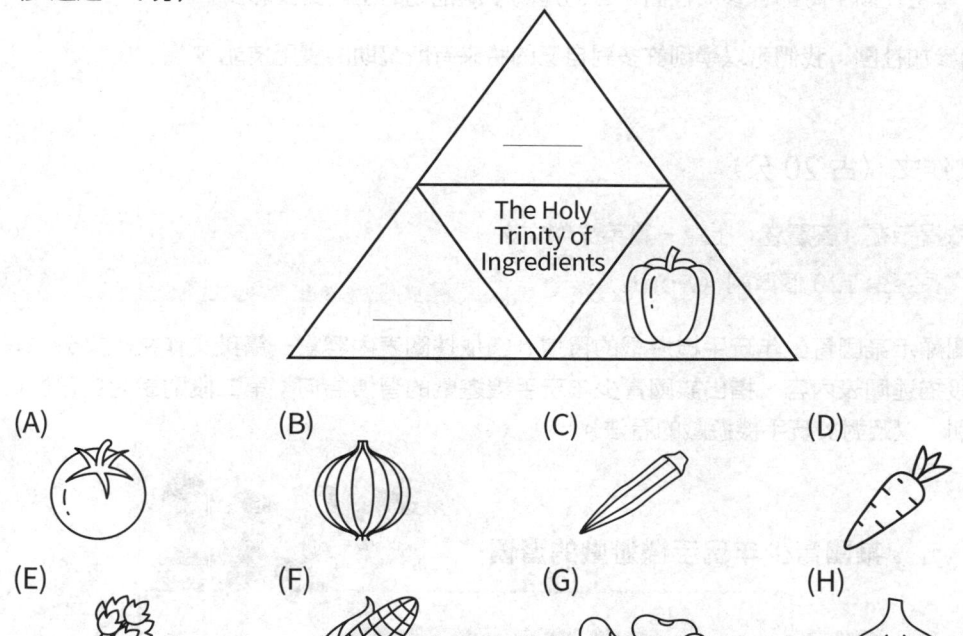

(A) (B) (C) (D)
(E)  (F)  (G) 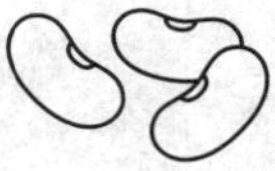 (H)

48-50. Using single words from the article, complete the chart about the similarities and differences between Cajun cuisine and Creole cuisine. （填空，6 分）

- Can be called food that comes from the country
- Dishes are often made in one __(48)__

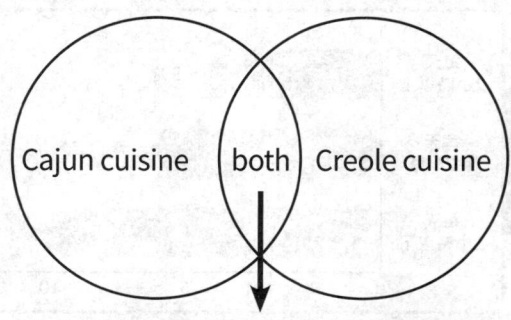

Cajun cuisine | both | Creole cuisine

- Can be called food that comes from the city
- __(49)__ contribute to rich flavors in dishes

- Use spices and herbs from the local area
- Use __(50)__ as a base in some dishes

TEST 02

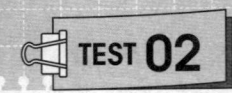

第參部分、非選擇題（占 28 分）

說明 本部分共有二大題，請依各題指示作答，答案必須寫在「答題卷」標示題號之作答區內，作答時不必抄題。

一、中譯英（占 8 分）

說明 1. 請將以下中文句子譯成正確、通順、達意的英文，並將答案寫在「答題卷」上。
2. 請依序作答，並標明子題號。每題 4 分，共 8 分。

1. 許多學生在高中時都會參加社團，目的是為了讓他們的生活更多彩多姿。

2. 藉由參加社團，我們可以學到許多對自己的將來有所幫助的實用技能。

二、英文作文（占 20 分）

說明 1. 依提示在「答題卷」上寫一篇英文作文。
2. 文長至少 120 個單詞（words）。

提示：下圖顯示某國青少年玩手機遊戲的習慣。請依據圖表內容寫一篇英文作文，文分二段，第一段描述圖表內容，指出該國青少年玩手機遊戲的習慣為何；第二段則說明自己屬於哪個類別，以及對於玩手機遊戲的看法。

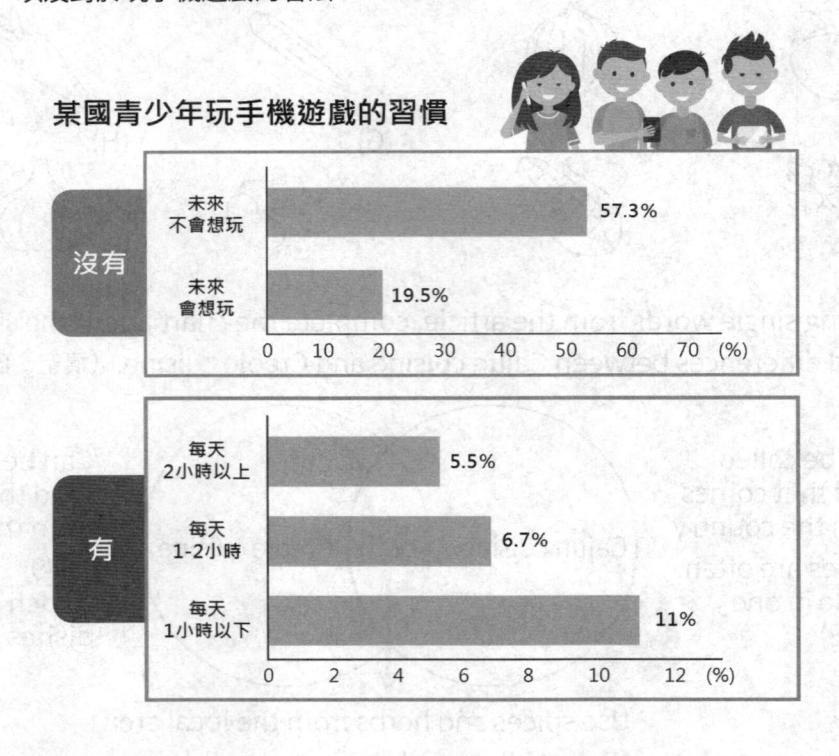

某國青少年玩手機遊戲的習慣

沒有：
- 未來不會想玩：57.3%
- 未來會想玩：19.5%

有：
- 每天 2 小時以上：5.5%
- 每天 1-2 小時：6.7%
- 每天 1 小時以下：11%

TEST 03

第壹部分、選擇題

一、詞彙題
二、綜合測驗
三、文意選填
四、篇章結構
五、閱讀測驗

第貳部分、混合題

第參部分、非選擇題

一、中譯英
二、英文作文

第壹部分、選擇題（占 62 分）

一、詞彙題（占 10 分）

說明 第 1 題至第 10 題，每題 1 分。

1. In order to stay _____ in a fast-changing world, the company decided to expand into artificial intelligence.
   (A) rural   (B) academic   (C) relevant   (D) cooperative

2. Much of the world looked on in _____ when Donald Trump was elected as president for a second time.
   (A) retirement   (B) amazement   (C) announcement   (D) involvement

3. Nick's teacher _____ him for cheating on the English test and she gave him a zero as a consequence.
   (A) advertised   (B) notified   (C) endured   (D) scolded

4. The article has been _____ at the bottom of the last page, so if you don't have time to read the whole thing, just take a look at the last few lines.
   (A) summarized   (B) memorized   (C) motivated   (D) eliminated

5. People tend to treat their pets as members of the family because these animals always keep them _____.
   (A) concrete   (B) contrast   (C) company   (D) commerce

6. According to doctors, people are most _____ when their flu or cold symptoms are at their worst.
   (A) contagious   (B) convincing   (C) dependable   (D) distinguished

7. I had a hard time convincing Vincent to accept my suggestions for the project because he is such an _____ person.
   (A) ambiguous   (B) admirable   (C) occasional   (D) obstinate

8. Ted vacationed on a remote island because he was trying to _____ from all the hustle and bustle of the big city.
   (A) reflect   (B) assure   (C) provide   (D) escape

9. Sean became _____ disabled because of a serious car accident seven years ago. Since then, he has had to use a wheelchair.
   (A) appropriately (B) permanently   (C) consistently   (D) dynamically

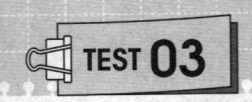

10. The doctor examined the patient's _____ carefully before he had the nurse stitch and bandage it up.
    (A) wound　　　　(B) temperature　　(C) structure　　(D) deadline

二、綜合測驗（占 10 分）

說明　第 11 題至第 20 題，每題 1 分。

第 11 至 15 題為題組

　　The baby shower is a tradition that has spread from North America to many parts of the world. Traditionally, a baby shower is a party thrown to celebrate the birth of a baby. Some baby showers are held a short time before the baby is born, __11__ others are held later. In the past, it was common to have only women at a baby shower, but this is changing. Men __12__ baby showers, particularly those to which work colleagues are invited. Games are usually played, with one of the most popular involving identifying different parts of the baby's anatomy on a sonogram.

　　The point of a baby shower, however, is not just to have a fun party but to have friends and family members __13__ with the cost of having a baby. When a baby arrives, there are a lot of new __14__ that come all at once. Guests bring gifts for the baby, such as clothes, toys, and diapers. A good baby shower helps new parents get some of the things they'll need so they can concentrate on the baby and not have to worry about __15__. In this way, a baby shower is a vital tool to help couples prepare for parenthood.

11. (A) when　　　(B) or　　　　　(C) so　　　　　(D) while
12. (A) aren't interested in　　　　(B) are no longer welcomed to
    (C) now often attend　　　　　(D) still dedicate themselves to
13. (A) help　　　(B) to help　　　(C) helps　　　　(D) helped
14. (A) expenses　(B) savings　　　(C) funds　　　　(D) incomes
15. (A) rushing to the hospital　　　(B) busting their budget
    (C) taking maternity leave　　　(D) consuming efficient nutrients

第 16 至 20 題為題組

　　You're a student on a very tight budget. Or maybe you're too drunk to return home to face the anger of your family. Or maybe you're a self-employed businessman traveling around on a business __16__ and want to save money. Most hotels __17__ around US$100 and up a night. In Japan, many of the above people choose a capsule hotel to spend the night.

Started in Osaka, Japan, in 1979, capsule hotels have become quite popular. For those who demand first-class service, spacious rooms, and all the comforts of home, __18__. Each guest is provided a "room" that is a little bigger than the drawers used to store corpses in a morgue. For this reason, capsule hotels are obviously not suitable for guests who suffer from claustrophobia.

Inside each capsule are a TV, an air-conditioning unit, and a reading light. The hotel also offers __19__ bathrooms. There may be other shared facilities, too, such as a snack bar, a lounge, or even a sauna. Capsule hotels can now be found across the world and typically cost between US$20 and US$40 __20__ night. For those strapped for cash, they're not a bad idea.

16. (A) agency (B) banquet (C) document (D) trip
17. (A) cost (B) take (C) spend (D) pay
18. (A) check in now (B) look elsewhere
    (C) renew your passport (D) call for room service
19. (A) communicated (B) communicable (C) communicative (D) communal
20. (A) via (B) among (C) per (D) since

三、文意選填（占 10 分）

說明 第 21 題至第 30 題，每題 1 分。

第 21 至 30 題為題組

Colors are everywhere, and they affect us in different ways. For instance, black is seen as a grim shade, which is why in the West, dark-colored clothing is often worn at __21__. On the other hand, red is a more vibrant color. White is seen as pure and clean. You might wonder why, then, doctors wear green or blue clothing, not white, when they are __22__ operations on patients. At one time, white clothing was indeed commonly used by surgeons. Starting in the early 20th century, though, this shifted. The cause for the change is related to the fact that various colors __23__ our eyes in differing ways.

According to a 1998 article in a nursing magazine, the reason why surgical clothing — known as scrubs — __24__ to green was due to one influential doctor. Apparently, he thought white was too hard on a surgeon's eyes. That is, along with the __25__ lights in the operating room, the white from the doctors' clothing created a strain on the eyes. Green proved to be the __26__ choice because it is the opposite of red on the color wheel. What that means is that it provides relief to the eyes of a surgeon who has been __27__ at red blood a lot during an operation. In addition,

33

looking at green or blue occasionally makes it easier for doctors to see   28   in hues of red because those colors contrast better with red than white does.

There is yet another reason why green or blue is better for scrubs. If a person sees red too much and then looks at a white   29 , he or she will see green images. These illusions can be distracting, which, clearly, is best   30   in the operating room. Therefore, it's a good thing white isn't used for scrubs anymore.

(A) impact　　　(B) ideal　　　(C) staring　　　(D) bright　　　(E) variations
(F) surface　　　(G) switched　　(H) funerals　　(I) avoided　　(J) performing

四、篇章結構（占 8 分）

說明 第 31 題至第 34 題，每題 2 分。

第 31 至 34 題為題組

Some of the world's poorest and most underprivileged people live in South and Southeast Asia and Africa, where hundreds of millions of citizens never have the chance of even a primary school education.   31   Beginning in 1999, however, many such people began to see another possibility for their lives.

That was the year that a Microsoft marketing executive, John Wood, decided to take a break from his high-pressure world of work.   32   While there, he was appalled at how little locals had to offer their children in terms of education. He found that the children had no books, desks, or lighting other than what came through the one-classroom windows. Wood mentioned the lack of books to one schoolmaster, who simply said, "Perhaps, sir, you will someday come back with books." That was the catalyst which changed Wood's life and those of more than 40 million children.

Soon afterward, Wood, along with Erin Ganju and Dinesh Shrestha, founded Room to Read, a charity that works with people in their own villages to improve or provide equipment and teacher training at the local level. It establishes literacy programs and libraries and helps to improve school infrastructure. It also focuses on improving gender equality by encouraging girls to complete secondary education and develop life skills.   33   The first one was that bold goals attract bold people, and they should try to hang out with people who share the same vision. The second one was to get stuff done.   34   And the third: A hand up, not a hand out. Room to Read expects locals to provide whatever they can to help build their school for their children. Today, 40 million disadvantaged children in multiple developing countries—from Pakistan and Cambodia to Tanzania and Zambia—have their chance at more and better education.

(A) Most of these rural villagers are limited in how much of their innate talent they can develop.
(B) People should stop talking about what to do and do it, no matter what the odds are.
(C) Wood came up with three simple rules to guide his new service.
(D) He opted for a three-week vacation of trekking in the Himalayas.
(E) Room to Read is headquartered in the US and employs over 1,400 people worldwide.

五、閱讀測驗（占 24 分）

說明 第 35 題至第 46 題，每題 2 分。

第 35 至 38 題為題組

In America, people with a Northeastern accent are typically considered intelligent, while those with a Southern twang are often seen as nice but perhaps uneducated. New York accents, meanwhile, are often judged as rude. Across the pond, the British have their own unfounded beliefs, or biases, about their regional accents. People from Birmingham and Liverpool are held in the same light as Americans from the South. Those who speak using Received Pronunciation—that is, in a traditionally southern, middle-class accent—convey the idea that they are educated and worth trusting.

However, these impressions are not rooted in reality. They are stereotypes that have developed over time. We learn to trust certain accents as babies. In the first few months of our time on Earth, we can already tell the difference between languages and dialects. At that age, we also show a preference for people who speak in a manner that's familiar to us. **This** is known as the own-accent bias. It continues as we grow into children, making us less trusting of people with unfamiliar accents. Adding to that doubt and suspicion is the fact that we have become more aware of the social status and stereotypes often attached to those accents.

The good thing is that it doesn't have to stay that way. We can change our trust in accents through the people we associate with on a daily basis. For much of human existence, people primarily mixed with others in the same village or community. Yet, in today's interconnected world, we are exposed to multiple regional, national, and international accents all the time. We have countless opportunities to challenge our prejudices about accents and start to accept people for who they truly are and not for what their accents say about them.

35. What do Americans from the South have in common with Britons from Birmingham?
    (A) They are held in high regard.
    (B) They are anything but nice.
    (C) They are regarded as bad-mannered.
    (D) They are viewed as less educated.

36. What does "**This**" refer to in the second paragraph?
    (A) A desire to hear different tones of voice.
    (B) A need to follow a set daily routine.
    (C) A liking for those who talk like we do.
    (D) A fondness for hearing our parents speak.

37. How can people get rid of their biases toward accents?
    (A) By learning to speak a foreign language as a child.
    (B) By spending time with a multitude of different people.
    (C) By training to speak with a more neutral accent.
    (D) By associating with the locals in their hometowns.

38. What is the author's attitude toward accents?
    (A) They are becoming more similar nowadays.
    (B) They all sound funny and foreign to his ear.
    (C) They can reveal a lot about someone's upbringing.
    (D) They are not truly reflective of a person's character.

第 39 至 42 題為題組

Our Moon is an almost constant presence in the night sky, but its appearance alters on a daily basis. The most obvious change, visible night by night, is that the Moon's sunlit surface either increases or decreases. It takes about two weeks for the new moon—that is, when the Moon is nearest the Sun and is invisible to us on Earth—to reach the stage when its surface is fully lit, or the full moon. This period is called the waxing moon. The transition from the full moon back to the new moon also takes about two weeks. This period is called the waning moon.

Another interesting fact about the Moon relates to its orbit. The Moon circles the Earth, but its orbit is not circular. Rather, it is oval-shaped. This means that sometimes the Moon is closer to the Earth than at other times. When the Moon is closest to the Earth (known as "perigee"), it is some 363,000 kilometers away. When furthest from the Earth (known as "apogee"), it is some 405,000 kilometers away. These differences result in the Moon varying by as much as 14% in size and 30% in brightness. When the full moon is at or close to its perigee, it is called a supermoon.

While all of this terminology is relatively modern, people have been observing the Moon for thousands of years. Many ancient civilizations used the Moon as a marker of time due to its reliability and regularity. It is believed that the ancient Sumerians—a people that lived in southern Mesopotamia between 4500 and 1900 BC—were the first to do this. They created a lunar calendar consisting of twelve lunar months, each with 29 or 30 days and each commencing with the appearance of a new moon. An additional month was added every three years to bring it into line with the solar year. This can be compared to adding an extra day at the end of February every four years, **a practice** that was introduced by the Romans.

39. What is the waxing moon?
    (A) A period when we cannot see the Moon in the sky.
    (B) A phase between a new moon and a full moon.
    (C) A two-week interval when the Moon is completely lit up.
    (D) A time when a full moon becomes a new moon.

40. According to the passage, what can we infer about a supermoon?
    (A) It appears in the sky on an annual basis.
    (B) It sometimes occurs when the moon is at its apogee.
    (C) It looks brighter and larger than a regular moon.
    (D) It appears more often than it used to.

41. According to the passage, what did the ancient Sumerians do?
    (A) They used the Moon to make a calendar.
    (B) They wrote myths and legends about the Moon.
    (C) They based lots of new words on the Moon.
    (D) They introduced the concept of the Moon to the Romans.

42. What does "**a practice**" refer to in the third paragraph?
    (A) The division of the months into 29 or 30 days.
    (B) The addition of another day every few years.
    (C) The introduction of a new month after three years.
    (D) The implementation of lunar and solar calendars.

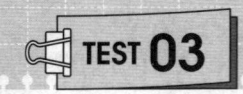

第 43 至 46 題為題組

　　Over the years, Dubai has grabbed the headlines with audacious offshore islands, rotating buildings, a seven-star hotel, and even an air-conditioned beach. However, it is arguably most famous for being the location of the world's tallest building. At nearly 830 meters—incredibly, more than half a mile—in height, the Burj Khalifa easily smashed the previous world record held by Taiwan's 508-meter Taipei 101. Indeed, even buildings constructed after the Burj Khalifa haven't been tall enough to knock the Dubai skyscraper off the top spot. The current second tallest in the world, Shanghai Tower, stands at 632 meters. Meanwhile, Kuala Lumpur's Merdeka 118—due to be completed in late 2022—will stand at nearly 679 meters.

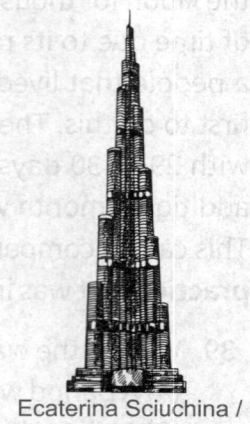

Ecaterina Sciuchina / Shutterstock.com

　　Construction on what was initially called the Burj Dubai started in 2004 and took six years. By then, it had been renamed the Burj Khalifa in honor of the president of the United Arab Emirates, who had lent money to Dubai to facilitate the skyscraper's completion. While the general design of the building mimics Islamic architecture throughout the United Arab Emirates, much of the specifics were determined by safety. For instance, the Y-shape of the floor plan helps to reduce the impact of wind on the structure, while the concrete core and attached wings ensure stability.

　　Safety also plays a role elsewhere in the building. Although there are 57 elevators to transport residents, guests, office workers, shoppers, and diners up and down the structure's 160 habitable floors, there needs to be an alternative for emergencies. Thus, refuge areas are located on multiple floors to provide **sanctuary** in the event of a disaster.

　　For the large number of Muslims residing in the Burj Khalifa, the height of the skyscraper poses different concerns. During Ramadan, Muslims must fast between dawn and dusk. However, the building is so tall that the sun can still be seen on high floors after it has set at ground level. To get around this issue, Muslims on higher floors have been instructed to start to consume food two or three minutes later than those on lower floors.

43. Which of the following shows the correct height order, from the tallest to the shortest, of the buildings?
    (A) Burj Khalifa > Taipei 101 > Shanghai Tower > Merdeka 118
    (B) Taipei 101 > Shanghai Tower > Merdeka 118 > Burj Khalifa
    (C) Burj Khalifa > Merdeka 118 > Shanghai Tower > Taipei 101
    (D) Merdeka 118 > Burj Khalifa > Taipei 101 > Shanghai Tower

44. What is implied about the Burj Khalifa in the passage?
    (A) It changed its name on two occasions while being constructed.
    (B) Its design was influenced by the president of the United Arab Emirates.
    (C) Its construction was brought to a close and it opened in 2010.
    (D) Its design is completely unique in the United Arab Emirates.

45. Which of the following is closest in meaning to the word "**sanctuary**" in the third paragraph?
    (A) Pressure.
    (B) Safety.
    (C) Religion.
    (D) Communication.

46. According to the passage, what have Muslims living on high floors of the Burj Khalifa been asked to do?
    (A) Move to a lower floor during Ramadan.
    (B) Refrain from eating or drinking for slightly longer.
    (C) Protect themselves from the bright sunlight.
    (D) Look for dangers connected to the building's height.

TEST 03

TEST 03

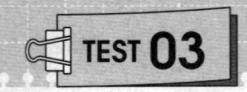

第貳部分、混合題（占 10 分）

說明 本部分共有 1 題組，每一子題配分標於題末。限在標示題號作答區內作答。選擇題使用 2B 鉛筆作答，更正時，應以橡皮擦擦拭，切勿使用修正液（帶）。非選擇題請由左而右橫式書寫。

第 47 至 50 題為題組

For Rent:
One-Bedroom Apartment in Daan District

This compact but stunning one-bedroom apartment in the Daan district of Taipei is available for rent now. With a recently refurbished living room, a contemporary bathroom, and a small balcony overlooking the beautiful Daan Forest Park, the apartment is sure to disappear from the market quickly. It is located close to Daan Park MRT station, which provides easy access to a multitude of popular areas in Taipei. So, if you prize convenience and want to save time, this is the ideal option for you. Although there are no cooking facilities, there is an abundance of affordable eateries in the area. The rest of the rooms come fully furnished, with the exception of a television. High-speed internet access is provided.

- Size: 15 ping
- Rent: NT$30,000 per month
- Management fee: included in rent
- Minimum contract term: two years
- Prospective tenants, please contact: Real Taipei Rentals at 02-1357-2468

Person A
I currently live in an apartment in Taoyuan, but this is less than suitable for me. I work in Taipei, so I have to get up very early to avoid the horrendous traffic jams and get to the office on time. I also arrive home very late every night. This daily commute has really started to take its toll on me. I have little free time to pursue my hobbies, such as going to the gym or socializing with friends. It feels at the moment that my life revolves around my job!

Person B
The contract on my current apartment expires next month, so I need to find somewhere new to rent. With its wealth of greenery and fresh air, the area around Daan Forest Park would be an excellent location for me. Plus, it's close to where my mom and dad live. I need somewhere with a reasonably sized kitchen so that I can prepare meals. Not only is cooking at home healthier, but it also helps to save money. I also enjoy inviting lots of friends over to sample my latest culinary creations and have fun!

47. 請從租屋廣告中選出一個單詞（word）填入下列句子的空格，並視語法需要作適當的字形變化，使句子語意完整、語法正確，且符合租屋廣告的文意。（填空，2 分）
All furnishings __47__ a TV are supplied with the apartment.

48. Why is the apartment appropriate for Person A?（填空，2 分）
He can __48__ going to work.

49. Why is Person B NOT suitable for renting the apartment?（填空，2 分）
The apartment doesn't have a __49__.

50. From (A) to (F) below, choose the statements about Person A and Person B that are true.（多選題，4 分）
(A) Person A is currently employed in Taoyuan.
(B) Person B lives with her parents at present.
(C) Person A wants more leisure time in his life.
(D) Person B enjoys hosting parties at home.
(E) Person A uses the commute to do his work.
(F) Person B prefers to exercise indoors.

TEST 03

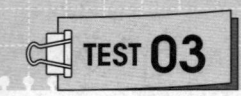

第參部分、非選擇題（占 28 分）

說明 本部分共有二大題，請依各題指示作答，答案必須寫在「答題卷」標示題號之作答區內，作答時不必抄題。

一、中譯英（占 8 分）

說明 1. 請將以下中文句子譯成正確、通順、達意的英文，並將答案寫在「答題卷」上。
2. 請依序作答，並標明子題號。每題 4 分，共 8 分。

1. 眾所周知，許多成功的人往往都很謙虛。
2. 這是因為他們知道自己所擁有的一切得來不易，因此總是心存感激。

二、英文作文（占 20 分）

說明 1. 依提示在「答題卷」上寫一篇英文作文。
2. 文長至少 120 個單詞（words）。

提示：臺灣的夜市文化是全世界數一數二的。除了逛街和玩樂外，夜市內的許多美食更被外國朋友譽為臺灣之光。假如你要向外國友人介紹臺灣的夜市文化，你要如何讓他留下深刻的印象呢？請以此為題，寫一篇英文作文，第一段請介紹臺灣的夜市文化，第二段則說明你會推薦哪一道夜市美食，並說明這道美食的特色及推薦原因。

TEST 04

🌱 第壹部分、選擇題

一、詞彙題
二、綜合測驗
三、文意選填
四、篇章結構
五、閱讀測驗

🌱 第貳部分、混合題

🌱 第參部分、非選擇題

一、中譯英
二、英文作文

第壹部分、選擇題（占 62 分）

一、詞彙題（占 10 分）

說明　第 1 題至第 10 題，每題 1 分。

1. Emma hopes the robot vacuum cleaner will provide _____ to her elderly father, who struggles to bend down these days.
   (A) criticism　　(B) assistance　　(C) exposure　　(D) intelligence

2. The _____ of the sun prompted Grace to put on a hat and wear her new sunglasses.
   (A) clarity　　(B) damp　　(C) scope　　(D) intensity

3. Alice tried to keep pace with the rabbit, but she lost track of it after it _____ from a hole in the ground.
   (A) vanished　　(B) sparkled　　(C) whispered　　(D) collided

4. You could tell from her _____ smile that Linda did feel happy for her cousin when he told her that he was going to get married.
   (A) ignorant　　(B) genuine　　(C) critical　　(D) distinctive

5. As the storm _____, the rain and wind became very strong. Therefore, the principal let the students go home immediately.
   (A) reacted　　(B) shivered　　(C) approached　　(D) wandered

6. You should call the Japanese restaurant _____ to make a reservation. Otherwise, you might have to wait for hours.
   (A) originally　　(B) accordingly　　(C) beforehand　　(D) afterwards

7. The detective was carefully _____ the suspect for any signs of lying as he responded to the questions.
   (A) distributing　　(B) criticizing　　(C) emphasizing　　(D) observing

8. If you continue your _____ spending and buy things you can't afford, you will end up with no savings.
   (A) passive　　(B) singular　　(C) reckless　　(D) moderate

9. Henry's _____ to become the manager of the sales department finally paid off when he was promoted this year.
   (A) endeavors　　(B) reflections　　(C) dilemmas　　(D) qualifications

45

TEST 04

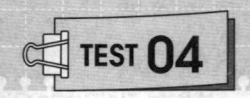

10. Linda's lips are very _____ to dry weather and chap easily, so she always has lip balm in her purse.
    (A) satisfied   (B) attractive   (C) sensitive   (D) pleased

二、綜合測驗（占 10 分）

說明 第 11 題至第 20 題，每題 1 分。

第 11 至 15 題為題組

　　Preparing more food than you or your family can eat at one meal is a common occurrence throughout the developed world. Naturally, people don't want to throw the leftovers out and __11__ perfectly good food. Instead, they just grab a Ziploc bag, open it, set the food inside, and then pinch or use the zipper to close the bag. This way, they won't have to use plastic wrap to cover plates or bowls, which __12__ a lot of room in the refrigerator. Plastic wrap also dries the food, making plates or bowls harder to clean later.

　　Such a simple thing as a plastic bag to hold leftovers is not a new idea. It has a history of over half a century. Ziploc bags did not really become a consumer product, however, until their __13__ improved in the 1980s to make them cheaper. Today, they can be seen in nearly every kitchen or pantry and are available in __14__ and for a variety of uses, from huge bags for the freezer to small bags for snacks. Simple ideas, when they become __15__, can revolutionize an industry. Ziploc bags have now become a household necessity.

11. (A) dominate   (B) assemble   (C) sprinkle   (D) waste
12. (A) hold onto   (B) take up   (C) appeal to   (D) stand for
13. (A) manufacturing (B) volunteering (C) vaporizing (D) seasoning
14. (A) a range of flavors   (B) a list of competitors
    (C) a multitude of sizes   (D) a series of commercials
15. (A) anonymous   (B) practical   (C) diligent   (D) harmful

第 16 至 20 題為題組

　　If you see someone chewing on the ends of their fingers, you might be inclined to think that they are extremely hungry, and suggest that they __16__ a sandwich instead. But hunger probably has nothing to do with it. Many people have the habit of biting their nails. Almost 45% of teenagers bite their nails, and for most it is not an easy habit to __17__.

Aside from the bad __18__ given by chewing on one's fingers, there are other reasons to avoid the habit of nail-biting. One reason, which will be quite obvious to any serious nail-biter, is the pain it causes. The area where the skin meets the nail can be extremely __19__ to pain. Nails are breeding grounds for bacteria, especially when people don't wash their hands thoroughly. Nail-biting can therefore lead to stomach discomfort and illnesses. It can also lead to dental problems and cause pain in the jaw.

The habit is usually related to anxiety, and treatment often involves __20__. Therapy that can help nail-biters to replace the habit with a less harmful one is available. However, a cheaper option is to apply a bitter nail polish to one's nails in order to discourage biting.

16. (A) buy   (B) to buy   (C) buying   (D) bought
17. (A) come up with (B) get rid of   (C) make up for   (D) keep pace with
18. (A) pessimism   (B) recognition   (C) impression   (D) inspection
19. (A) sensitive   (B) allergic   (C) critical   (D) aware
20. (A) paying for health insurance   (B) trimming off the fat
    (C) controlling the outbreak   (D) dealing with stress

三、文意選填（占 10 分）

說明 第 21 題至第 30 題，每題 1 分。

第 21 至 30 題為題組

Nowadays, food delivery services, like Uber Eats, are popular and found everywhere around the globe. They rely on digital databases and drivers to get orders delivered on time. However, in India, *dabbawalas* have been doing this for more than 125 years without __21__ technology.

In Hindi, "dabbawala" literally means "one who carries the box." Dabbawalas are delivery workers who bring lunchboxes to __22__ Indians, using bicycles and the public train system. The tradition of dabbawalas began in 1890 in Mumbai. At that time, fast food didn't __23__ and office workers needed convenient meals. The business started with 100 dabbawalas, but that number quickly __24__. Today, dabbawalas deliver approximately 200,000 meals across India every single day.

Over the years, the methods used by dabbawalas to carry on their daily __25__ became more and more efficient. The process begins when dabbawalas, dressed in white uniforms and traditional Gandhi caps, collect their daily orders from workers' homes by bicycle. Since many dabbawalas don't read well, the lunchboxes are color-coded to __26__ the proper delivery information. The dabbawalas will then transport the lunchboxes to a central __27__, where they are organized into groups. Then, the groups of lunchboxes are loaded onto trains. At each station, the lunchbox groups are picked up by local dabbawalas who deliver them to customers. The __28__ lunchboxes are collected after lunch or the next day and sent back to their respective houses.

Although modern delivery companies have launched their services in India, dabbawalas don't fear the __29__. In fact, the dabbawalas industry continues to expand by 5% to 10% every year. Many Indians __30__ using dabbawalas because they are reliable and the service is cheap. There's also a human element, as many customers become friendly with their dabbawalas after seeing them on a daily basis for years.

(A) convey   (B) prefer   (C) empty   (D) exist   (E) increased
(F) hungry   (G) location   (H) advanced   (I) routine   (J) competition

四、篇章結構（占 8 分）

說明 第 31 題至第 34 題，每題 2 分。

第 31 至 34 題為題組

The famous Sagrada Família is one of Barcelona's most recognizable landmarks, with more than 4.5 million people visiting the structure every year. Located in the Eixample district of the city, the Roman Catholic church is notable for its immense size and majestic, avant-garde architecture. The original blueprints to build the church were drawn up in 1882. __31__ He planned to build a traditional, Gothic-style church, similar to many other churches in Europe at that time. However, Villar resigned in 1883 and a young, 31-year-old architect named Antoni Gaudí took over the project. At that time, Gaudí was best known for designing Casa Vicens, a modernist private building that is now a museum.

__32__ He decided that the church should stand as a monument to Christians, who pray to God for the forgiveness of their sins. As a result, Gaudí wanted to use all of Christianity's key symbols to give visitors a true religious experience. Gaudí's plans for the Sagrada became so grand that he himself estimated it would take centuries to complete. When he was hit by a tram and died in 1926, the temple was only 20% complete. However, future generations have continued his work to this day.

__33__ The Sagrada is not a government-funded project. All of the money raised to support this work has been paid for by donations from visitors and the general population. Until 2019, the Sagrada didn't even have a building permit. Although

Gaudí originally applied for one in 1885, it was never approved. So, by local laws, the Sagrada was built illegally. __34__ It must also pay another US$40 million as a penalty for building without government permission for more than 130 years. It is currently hoped that the Sagrada Família will be finished by 2026, one hundred years after Gaudí's death.

(A) Financing issues have also slowed progress at times.
(B) Gaudí scrapped Villar's plans for the Sagrada completely and came up with his own concept.
(C) As part of the recent permit deal, the Sagrada will pay roughly US$5 million for the new permit.
(D) The refusal of the Sagrada building permit caused panic among the contractors.
(E) Initially, the project was supposed to be under the direction of architect Francisco de Paula del Villar.

五、閱讀測驗（占 24 分）

說明 第 35 題至第 46 題，每題 2 分。

第 35 至 38 題為題組

People have been sleeping with their pets—most often, their dogs—for thousands of years. In modern times, however, the idea of sleeping with one's pet draws mixed reactions.

An online study by Central Queensland University of more than 13,000 people found that many people get a better night's sleep with a pet rather than a partner in their bed. In this study, partners—particularly those who snore—were more likely to be disruptive than pets. According to Roger Valentine, a renowned veterinarian in Santa Monica, California, sleeping with your dog reduces stress and allows more restful sleep. Studies have shown that pet owners have lower blood pressure and better psychological well-being than non-pet owners. Indeed, sleeping with a pet can help to relieve anxiety and depression, as **they act as a kind of security blanket**.

Some physicians and public health authorities, citing the hazards of increased exposure to allergens, ticks, and parasites, are strongly opposed to the idea of sleeping with your pet, and veterinarians generally don't recommend it. Dogs are light sleepers and stay alert for sounds and other signs of danger, which means their presence can be disruptive, particularly in smaller beds. There is also the danger that a frightened pet might harm its owner during the night, or an owner could even injure their pet during a restless night of sleep.

TEST 04

Ultimately, it is up to the individual to weigh the pros and cons and decide for themselves. For those who do choose to slumber with their dog, there are ways to ensure a more harmonious experience. One is to take your pooch for a walk prior to bedtime to tire them out. Another is to be consistent with the rules about exactly where on your bed the dog can sleep. Still another is to change your bedding on a regular basis to guarantee cleanliness.

35. What does "**they act as a kind of security blanket**" mean in the second paragraph?
    (A) Guard dogs can deter thieves from breaking in.
    (B) Pets can be a source of comfort to their owners.
    (C) Dogs and cats are likely to ruin your blankets and sheets.
    (D) Pets can help to keep their owners warm during winter.

36. According to the passage, why could sharing your bed with your pet be a bad idea?
    (A) Because it could make you anxious.
    (B) Because there is a lack of evidence of benefits.
    (C) Because of potential health concerns.
    (D) Because your partner might become jealous.

37. What is the author's opinion of sleeping with pets?
    (A) It is a practice that is not suited to the modern world.
    (B) It is too dangerous due to the risk of harm to the pet.
    (C) It is definitely beneficial to all cat and dog owners.
    (D) It is down to each person to evaluate its suitability.

38. Which of the following advice about sleeping with dogs is NOT mentioned in the passage?
    (A) Make sure your dog knows where it can and can't sleep.
    (B) Make sure your dog has some exercise before bedtime.
    (C) Make sure you regularly replace the sheets on your bed.
    (D) Make sure you remove your dog from the bed if it misbehaves.

第 39 至 42 題為題組

　　Some natural disasters can be so devastating that they earn their place in the world's history books. One example of a truly unforgettable natural disaster is the eruption of Mount Vesuvius in Italy nearly 2,000 years ago.

　　In 79 AD, when the volcano blew its top, there were about 20,000 residents living in the nearby city of Pompeii and the surrounding area. On August 24 of that year—the long-believed date of the disaster—residents were shocked by a tremendous eruption that filled the sky with ash and smoke. By the time the disaster ended, the volcanic eruption had lasted for nearly two days. There was no **relief** effort in the aftermath; no help could get there as Pompeii was covered with the huge amount of ash that had spewed out of Mount Vesuvius. The volume was so great that Pompeii was buried 4-6 meters under it. Pliny the Younger, a famous lawyer and author from the time, wrote that "it was daylight now elsewhere in the world" but in Pompeii, "the darkness was darker and thicker than any night." It is estimated that around 2,000 people died.

　　The buried city remained forgotten for centuries until it was rediscovered in the late 1500s, and archeologists began excavating it in the 1700s. It was concluded that the residents of Pompeii died as a result of the ash and poisonous gases. People had accepted this explanation for a long time before new tests suggested that it was the heat, not the ash and gases, that was the actual killer. The heat that had blasted from the volcano was so intense—with temperatures reaching 300°C—that it killed people instantly. This helps to explain why the remains of many of the victims were found in lifelike poses: They simply did not have time to react before they died.

　　Today, the remains of Pompeii are a UNESCO World Heritage Site and attract many tourists. However, tourism is restricted to certain areas in order to preserve what is left of the devastated town. Regardless of its accessibility, the story of the destruction of Pompeii will never be forgotten.

39. Which of the following is closest in meaning to the word "**relief**" in the second paragraph?
    (A) Reassurance.　　(B) Easing.　　(C) Assistance.　　(D) Interruption.

40. Why is Pliny the Younger mentioned in the passage?
    (A) He was killed in the tragedy at Pompeii.
    (B) He recorded his thoughts of the events.
    (C) He discovered the remains of Pompeii.
    (D) He warned of the dangers of volcanoes.

41. What happened in the 18th century?
    (A) There was another explosion from Mount Vesuvius.
    (B) Pompeii began to attract a large amount of tourism.
    (C) Specialists started to dig up the ruins of Pompeii.
    (D) Dangerous gases were emitted from the volcano.

42. What did the later tests prove about the eruption?
    (A) How people died.
    (B) What caused the eruption.
    (C) When the volcano exploded.
    (D) How many people survived.

第 43 至 46 題為題組

At first glance, spiny lobsters look similar to common lobsters: they have long bodies that are covered with a hard shell. However, look closer and you'll discover that rather than traditional lobster claws, spiny lobsters possess spines on their backs and long antennae on their heads that are used to scare off predators. Different subspecies can be found across the globe, from the Caribbean to the Mediterranean to New Zealand.

Perhaps the most interesting aspect of spiny lobsters is their migratory habits. Unlike birds, many of which famously migrate in a V-shaped pattern, spiny lobsters form long, straight lines of up to 50 lobsters. They then proceed in single file in a non-stop march from their usual habitat—coral reefs and crevices—in search of warmer waters for the winter. Much of this is achieved under cover of darkness, as is their search for food including clams and crabs.

Studies have shown that these abilities to navigate in the dark and seek out new homes in unfamiliar waters are down to a connection with the Earth's magnetic field. Spiny lobsters can detect our planet's magnetic field and use it to **orient** themselves and work out their route. These remarkable navigational skills are supplemented by two smaller antennae, which they use to sense movement and chemical changes in the water.

These navigational abilities don't stop them from landing on our plates, though. If you've ever eaten lobster tails in a restaurant, you are more than likely to have eaten spiny lobsters. Lobster fishing is big business. It accounts for a large proportion of the export economy of the Bahamas, to give just one example. Although many countries have restrictions on the number, age, and size of spiny lobsters that can be caught, some unscrupulous fishermen ignore this.

An additional threat **ironically** comes from the aforementioned migratory patterns of spiny lobsters. As they move around in large groups, disease can quickly spread from one lobster to the next. Moreover, they have become increasingly vulnerable to disease. This is because of changes in their favored coral reef environments, which are suffering due to climate change.

43. Which of the following illustrates the migratory pattern of spiny lobsters?
    (A)
    (B)
    (C)
    (D)

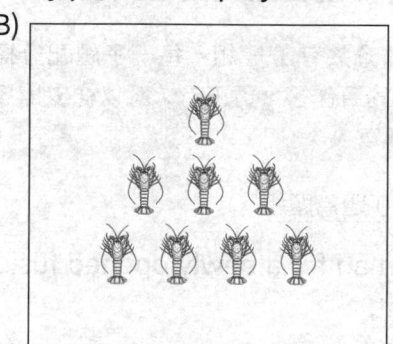

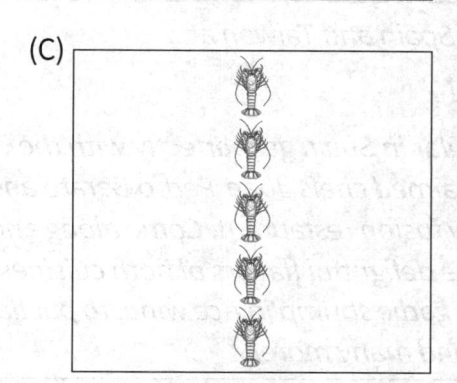

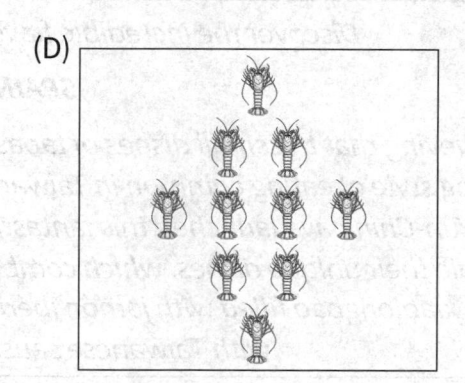

44. Which of the following is closest in meaning to the word "**orient**" in the third paragraph?
    (A) Disguise.　　　(B) Locate.　　　(C) Focus.　　　(D) Protect.

45. According to the passage, which of the following statements about spiny lobsters is true?
    (A) Their outer shells make them different from common lobsters.
    (B) Their numbers are currently worryingly low in the Bahamas.
    (C) Their spines help them to hunt for food in awkward places.
    (D) Their tails are frequently eaten in restaurants around the world.

46. Why is the word "**ironically**" used in the last paragraph?
    (A) Because the way spiny lobsters migrate also causes them harm.
    (B) Because it was unexpected that spiny lobsters would catch a disease.
    (C) Because climate change is a familiar problem in today's world.
    (D) Because it is unusual for lobsters to live in areas with coral reefs.

53

TEST 04

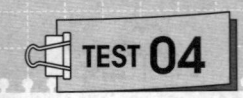

第貳部分、混合題（占 10 分）

說明 本部分共有 1 題組，每一子題配分標於題末。限在標示題號作答區內作答。選擇題使用 2B 鉛筆作答，更正時，應以橡皮擦擦拭，切勿使用修正液（帶）。非選擇題請由左而右橫式書寫。

第 47 至 50 題為題組

Here is an ad for a newly opened fusion restaurant and four people's reviews of that restaurant.

Discover the incredible flavors of Spain and Taiwan at…

SPAINWAN!

Believing that the small dishes of tapas popular in Spain gel perfectly with the sharing style of eating common in Taiwan, acclaimed chefs Juan-Pedro Barato and Liao Yun-Chih have launched this fantastic new fusion restaurant. Come along and sample their unique dishes, which combine the delightful flavors of both cuisines, from xiaolongbao filled with jamón ibérico, to garlic shrimp in rice wine, to paella with Taiwanese sausage, and many more!

(A) Rita

If you're seeking a new culinary adventure, I heartily recommend Spainwan. Having traveled to Spain on numerous occasions, I'm very familiar with Spanish food, so I knew what to expect in that regard. However, I'm less accustomed to Taiwanese cuisine. The combination of the two, though, was a revelation. I particularly loved the xiaolongbao. The way they burst open, exposing the Spanish ham inside, was amazing. Even better, the prices are remarkably competitive!

(B) Terrance

Before I dined at this restaurant, I was concerned that the bold Taiwanese flavors might overpower the subtler Spanish ones. I am pleased to say that my fears were unfounded. Barato and Liao have skillfully combined the elements to ensure that the cuisines from both cultures shine through. As a chef myself, I know that is a challenging task, and I commend them for achieving it so well. The Spanish potatoes with Taiwanese spices were a personal favorite.

54

(C) Abigail

After several disappointments over the years, my opinion of fusion restaurants is quite low. Having dined at Spainwan on opening night, I'm sorry to say that my view hasn't changed. Although the prices were affordable and the atmosphere was pleasant, I felt that the food and flavors were substandard. Neither particularly Spanish nor particularly Taiwanese, the dishes fell into a gray area in between and failed to satisfy me.

(D) Bradley

I was somewhat skeptical about the concept at first: Why risk ruining two excellent cuisines by forcing them together in an unnatural marriage? Spainwan, though, blew me away. All of the dishes were outstanding, but the garlic shrimp in rice wine was the highlight. It was so flavorful and delicious that I ordered a second portion. With food this good at such reasonable prices, I'll certainly recommend Spainwan to all of my friends.

47. Which of the reviewers refer to dishes that are mentioned in the ad? Write the letter(s) of the reviewer(s) below. （多選，4 分）

_____

48-50. Write down the letter of the reviewer that the following sentences relate to. （單選題，6 分）

48. _____ mentions his/her own profession.

49. _____ makes reference to his/her travel history.

50. _____ has had many negative experiences at similar restaurants.

TEST 04

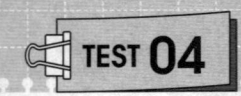

第參部分、非選擇題（占 28 分）

說明 本部分共有二大題，請依各題指示作答，答案必須寫在「答題卷」標示題號之作答區內，作答時不必抄題。

一、中譯英（占 8 分）

說明 1. 請將以下中文句子譯成正確、通順、達意的英文，並將答案寫在「答題卷」上。
2. 請依序作答，並標明子題號。每題 4 分，共 8 分。

1. 隨著外送平臺的興起，越來越多顧客為了節省時間而選擇訂外送。

2. 外送員滿街跑的現象引起許多爭議，其中一個大家最關注的議題就是外送員的安全。

二、英文作文（占 20 分）

說明 1. 依提示在「答題卷」上寫一篇英文作文。
2. 文長至少 120 個單詞（words）。

提示：你最好的朋友 Cindy 的生日即將來臨，因此你想安排一天請她看場電影來為她慶生。請寫一封信給 Cindy，根據以下的電影時刻表，告訴 Cindy 你打算帶她去看哪一部電影及時間，並告知她當天慶生活動的其他安排。文末請以 George 署名。

IVY CINEMA Saturday, December 28	
Star Wars: The Rise of Skywalker Genre | Science Fiction, Action	10:00 | 12:00 | 14:00 16:00 | 18:00 | 20:00 22:00
Beauty and the Beast Genre | Animation, Fantasy	10:30 | 13:30 | 17:00 19:30 | 21:30
The Life of Albert Einstein Genre | Biography, Drama	11:30 | 15:30 | 19:30

TEST 05

第壹部分、選擇題

一、詞彙題
二、綜合測驗
三、文意選填
四、篇章結構
五、閱讀測驗

第貳部分、混合題

第參部分、非選擇題

一、中譯英
二、英文作文

第壹部分、選擇題（占 62 分）

一、詞彙題（占 10 分）

說明 第 1 題至第 10 題，每題 1 分。

1. Before he could travel to India, Corey needed to wait for the _____ of his visa by that nation.
   (A) strength   (B) approval   (C) volume   (D) property

2. Some experts worry that teenagers are watching too many short videos on their smartphones rather than engaging in _____ conversations.
   (A) meaningful   (B) sorrowful   (C) grateful   (D) truthful

3. This candy contains too much _____ sweetener and corn syrup, both of which can lead to weight gain and tooth decay.
   (A) financial   (B) artificial   (C) reliable   (D) honorable

4. My _____ to your proposal is that it sounds too extravagant, and we don't have enough funds to make it work.
   (A) assurance   (B) permission   (C) conscience   (D) objection

5. The trip to New York last year motivated me to work harder and study English much more _____.
   (A) extremely   (B) leisurely   (C) tightly   (D) diligently

6. Mark tried to _____ into his room when he came home last night, but he still woke his parents up.
   (A) freeze   (B) brake   (C) sneak   (D) peep

7. Sharon is a good parent since she always _____ her children with praise and hugs instead of toys or candy.
   (A) assigns   (B) dodges   (C) tortures   (D) rewards

8. Jenny is not a very sociable person, so there wasn't much _____ between her and her date when they went out for the first time.
   (A) recreation   (B) confusion   (C) explosion   (D) interaction

9. We think Jimmy is a _____ person because he's only concerned with money, fame, and social status.
   (A) productive   (B) precise   (C) luxurious   (D) superficial

TEST 05

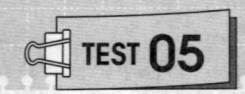

10. Jack didn't _____ to read the contract's fine print before signing it, which resulted in a great deal of trouble for him later.
    (A) imply   (B) suggest   (C) bother   (D) amuse

二、綜合測驗（占 10 分）

說明 第 11 題至第 20 題，每題 1 分。

第 11 至 15 題為題組

There is a big difference between feeling sad for a little while and having what is called major or clinical depression. Major depression is not just a day or two of unhappy feelings. It __11__ people's performance at school or work, the way they eat and sleep, and their ability to function normally. The main __12__ of this disorder are low self-esteem and lack of enjoyment in the things that usually interest the person. However, there are __13__ other signs which can often be confused with different ailments. These include reduced energy levels, difficulty in concentrating, and digestive problems.

While major depression is still not understood completely, it has been connected to abnormal chemical levels in the brain. There may, for instance, be a chemical __14__ in the areas of the brain that control behavior, thoughts, and mood. Drugs are commonly prescribed to adjust the chemical levels and help sufferers __15__. Talking to a trained therapist and learning how to identify other causes of your depression and react to them can also help a great deal. Very often, a combination of medication and therapy is used to help treat major depression.

11. (A) adopts   (B) attains   (C) affects   (D) abandons
12. (A) symptoms   (B) synonyms   (C) symbols   (D) symphonies
13. (A) spare   (B) numerous   (C) obedient   (D) fantastic
14. (A) admission   (B) border   (C) imbalance   (D) meadow
15. (A) become the norm   (B) have mixed emotions
    (C) reach an agreement   (D) live normal lives

第 16 至 20 題為題組

Hummingbirds are tiny, brightly colored birds native to the Americas. One of the smallest of the species weighs just 1.8 grams. Their beaks set them apart from all other birds because they are specially adapted with grooved tongues to suck out nectar from flowers, which they __16__. Their diet is so specialized that they don't need to

17 with insects for nectar because they suck from only red, orange, and pink flowers.

　　Their flying skills are also very impressive. They are the only bird species that can rotate their wings to fly forward, backward, and sideways, or hover in midair. They flap their wings very fast, creating the humming sounds which can be heard by humans and which   18 . The sounds are also used to communicate with other hummingbirds and alert them to the arrival of friend or foe.

　　Despite their tiny size, they can fly incredibly long distances. The ruby-throated hummingbird annually travels distances of 2,000 miles between Canada and Panama, including a 500-mile non-stop   19   over the Gulf of Mexico. Before they set off on their long   20   flight, these hummingbirds usually eat extra food to build up enough fat so they can make it across the ocean.

16. (A) bring up　　(B) live on　　(C) work out　　(D) pass down
17. (A) argue　　(B) bargain　　(C) compete　　(D) quarrel
18. (A) kept them as a pet　　(B) led to their name
　　(C) caused hearing loss　　(D) misled the navigator
19. (A) disaster　　(B) barrier　　(C) anxiety　　(D) stretch
20. (A) arrogant　　(B) ethnic　　(C) migratory　　(D) federal

三、文意選填（占 10 分）

說明 第 21 題至第 30 題，每題 1 分。

第 21 至 30 題為題組

　　Like hamburgers and French fries, pizza has become an international hit. People in restaurants all over the world enjoy consuming this food. Italy is often   21   with its spread and development, as the ancient Romans had eaten a kind of flat bread with added toppings. Besides that, people in Naples invented the more modern   22   using tomatoes.

　　Toppings not only make pizza more attractive but also more delicious. Many places around the world get creative by adding their own local ingredients. For some, pineapples are welcome, while for others, the tropical fruit clearly does not   23   in any Mediterranean dish. Though no one is certain of who   24   tomato sauce onto Neapolitan pizzas, history does record the man who first put pineapples on pizza.

　　That man was Sam Panopoulos, a Greek   25   who moved to Ontario, Canada. In 1962, he wondered how pizza topped with pineapple would taste. To   26   his curiosity, he threw some on one along with bits of ham and bacon. He enjoyed the contrast between the sweet, juicy fruit and the savory meat. He named it a Hawaiian pizza after the name of the   27   pineapples he used, and the rest is history.

When the president of Iceland said he would   28   pineapple as a pizza topping if he could in early 2017, he was immediately challenged by the prime minister of Canada. Fortunately, nothing came of this friendly disagreement. Even so, the idea of using any non-Italian toppings on pizza has long been controversial. Purists insist that food should be prepared in   29   ways that stay true to the original taste. Others feel that everything we eat comes from   30   places, so dishes can be experimented with and improved upon. Perhaps all such controversies can be settled by just accepting the fact that if you don't like something, you don't have to eat it.

(A) belong   (B) different   (C) immigrant   (D) ban   (E) variety
(F) canned   (G) introduced   (H) traditional   (I) credited (J) satisfy

四、篇章結構（占 8 分）

說明 第 31 題至第 34 題，每題 2 分。

第 31 至 34 題為題組

At one time or another, everybody overeats. Perhaps it is the temptation of an all-you-can-eat buffet, with its row upon row of delicious cuisines from countries across the world. Maybe you stuff your face at a holiday meal, helping yourself to seconds and thirds of the succulent Thanksgiving turkey.   31   Within minutes, your belly puffs out and your mind gets foggy and dull. If you're home, you'll likely head to the nearest couch and fall asleep in no time. There's a funny term for this sleepy feeling that you get after a big meal: a food coma.

Here's the science behind why it occurs. Whenever we eat, hormones tell our bodies to produce juices to help our stomachs digest the food.   32   When this occurs, the rest of the body temporarily has less blood. As you eat larger portions of food, more blood is required in the stomach. When our brain and muscles have less blood, they don't function quite as well. So, the body's natural reaction is to make you feel sleepy and subtly encourage you to get some rest. Then, while you're dreaming, the body can concentrate its efforts on processing the huge meal you've just devoured.

  33   Quality also counts. High-protein meals eaten without carbohydrates or too much fat, such as grilled chicken with vegetables or salmon with salad, usually don't cause food comas because they stimulate the release of amino acids.   34   In which case, you should stay away from white rice, oven-ready pizzas, and sugary desserts like donuts. Overeating frequently obviously isn't healthy. It can lead to weight gain and an increased chance of developing a host of chronic diseases, from

high blood pressure to type 2 diabetes. However, there is no evidence suggesting that food comas themselves are dangerous in the long run.

(A) Either way, you end up paying the price for the extra food you've consumed.
(B) On the other hand, eating lots of processed carbohydrates will make insulin levels spike and put you to sleep faster than you can imagine.
(C) It is possible to offset the effects of a food coma by performing certain light exercises.
(D) It's not just the quantity of food you eat that determines if you slip into a food coma or not.
(E) In turn, our stomachs require more blood to transport the nutrients from the food elsewhere.

五、閱讀測驗（占 24 分）

說明 第 35 題至第 46 題，每題 2 分。

第 35 至 38 題為題組

One of the most common elements of a professional presentation is the use of PowerPoint. The reason for this lies in the fact that its slide presentations create impact. They can focus an audience's attention and stress points effectively. In fact, many presenters have difficulty giving a good presentation without the use of PowerPoint. Yet, many people still make serious mistakes when delivering these types of presentations.

Probably the biggest error people make is putting too much information on a single slide. There is strong evidence that suggests people can only remember a limited amount of data. Speakers often compound this problem by using small fonts so that they can cram more statistics and analyses onto a single slide. These presenters are mistaken in their belief that a presentation should be overloaded with facts. Actually, members of the audience have trouble reading and understanding such complicated slides. Those slides take the audience's attention away from the presenters and their message.

Another mistake that people make is relying so much on the PowerPoint images that they neglect their audience. In other words, they turn towards the screen, which is usually behind them, taking their attention away from the audience. While such presenters may be under the impression that they are giving a good presentation, this is not true. When speakers turn their backs on the listeners, they lose the impact they would have when facing the audience.

Fortunately, once a presenter knows what not to do, it is fairly easy to correct these mistakes. Regarding the problem of putting too much information on slides, it should come as no surprise that the answer is to simplify your slides. If you're constantly reading from your slides and ignoring the audience, the solution is also staring you in the face.

35. What is this passage mainly about?
    (A) The reasons why PowerPoint presentations are good to use.
    (B) The things you shouldn't do when giving PowerPoint presentations.
    (C) The reasons why many presenters have stopped using PowerPoint.
    (D) The various types of PowerPoint presentations that are available.

36. Which of the following is NOT mentioned as a reason you shouldn't include too much information on a slide?
    (A) Doing so can detract from you and your presentation.
    (B) The audience can only retain a certain number of details at once.
    (C) Doing so entails using fonts that are too small.
    (D) The slides are much more time-consuming to produce.

37. According to the passage, what will a presenter who relies too much on PowerPoint do?
    (A) Use slides that are difficult to read.
    (B) Give a memorable presentation.
    (C) Make less eye contact with listeners.
    (D) Focus strongly on the audience.

38. What is the purpose of the last paragraph?
    (A) To identify an additional PowerPoint error.
    (B) To give advice on how to fix presentation problems.
    (C) To discuss ways to make your slides eye-catching.
    (D) To outline why audience participation is required.

第 39 至 42 題為題組

Experts say that most adults need about eight hours of sleep per night, although the exact number varies among individuals. However, getting this much shut-eye is difficult to achieve for some people due to a condition known as insomnia. This is a disorder where people have trouble falling or staying asleep. The telltale signs that a person has this condition include dark, unsightly circles and bags under the eyes and an overall drowsy appearance. **They** may exhibit grumpiness, struggle to remember things, and have difficulty concentrating. Insomnia can also lead to more serious health problems. In addition to increasing people's risk of heart disease, it can heighten their chance of suffering from a stroke or diabetes.

What causes insomnia? Major life events, such as losing a loved one or changing career, can lead to nights of sleeplessness, as can anxiety, depression, and other mental health issues. Certain prescription medications, the abuse of alcohol, and the use of illegal drugs can also be culprits. Some of these causes may lead to insomnia that is only transitory. For example, feeling stressed about a career change may not last for more than a few days. Thus, the insomnia may resolve itself without intervention. However, insomnia caused by long-standing mental health issues might linger and require treatment. This can range from sleeping pills to cognitive behavioral therapy with a trained professional.

Insomnia can affect animals, too. Studies have shown that rats experience insomnia when placed in a stressful environment. Horses that have to nap standing up—during which time they are unable to enter a deep sleep—exhibit signs of sleep deprivation and sometimes collapse. Scientists also believe that zebrafish can suffer from disrupted sleep patterns. These kinds of findings could help to shed light on the mysteries of sleep and potentially lead to new treatments for people with insomnia. Sleep is vital to the health and well-being of humans and animals, and we need to ensure that we all get enough of it.

39. What is the first paragraph mainly about?
    (A) The treatment options for sleep disorders.
    (B) The prevalence of insomnia in the population.
    (C) The signs and consequences of insomnia.
    (D) The recommended amount of sleep per night.

40. What does **They** refer to in the first paragraph?
    (A) Major symptoms of insomnia.
    (B) People suffering from insomnia.
    (C) Health issues caused by insomnia.
    (D) Experts researching insomnia.

41. Which cause of insomnia is NOT mentioned in the passage?
    (A) Feelings of nervousness and worry.
    (B) Disruptions in employment.
    (C) Long-term physical health issues.
    (D) Consumption of banned substances.

42. What can be inferred about horses from the passage?
    (A) They require more sleep than other animals.
    (B) They sleep more deeply when lying down.
    (C) They rarely suffer from serious insomnia.
    (D) They fall over when they sleep for too long.

TEST 05

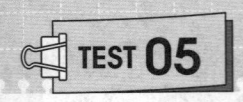

第 43 至 46 題為題組

The French Revolution of 1789 was one of the most pivotal events in European and world history. Although some historians disagree about its causes, no one is in any doubt about its far-reaching consequences.

For several decades prior to 1789, France had been engaged in many wars. These military engagements piled up a huge amount of debt that the country—under the reign of the extravagant and ineffective King Louis XVI—could not pay back. Compounding this was the fact that the commoners, not the nobility nor the clergy, paid all of the taxes. Frustration with this situation, along with high levels of unemployment and widespread famine, boiled over in mid-1789. The commoners were fighting back. They wanted a more just system for paying taxes, a society where everyone was treated the same, and freedom from control by the monarchy. In short, they wanted democracy.

The revolutionaries did achieve some success: the monarchy was abolished, France became a republic with a new constitution and a new system of taxation, and Louis XVI was executed on the grounds of treason. However, not everything went as smoothly as this simplified version of events might suggest. Maximilien Robespierre, one of the leaders of the revolution, began the Reign of Terror, which saw the deaths of at least 18,000 "counter-revolutionaries." The political chaos ultimately led to the rise of the infamous Napoleon Bonaparte, who imposed a period of military rule on France.

The effects of the French Revolution could be felt around Europe for decades, if not centuries, afterwards. The idea that people were citizens of a state and not simply subjects of a king grew into a belief in nationalism that took root in much of Europe. The execution of Louis XVI put pressure on other European monarchies to adapt to a changing world and give more rights to their people. The aims and tactics of the revolutionaries became a model for others seeking change in their own countries. Indeed, it is possible to see a direct link between the French Revolution of 1789 and the Russian Revolution of 1917.

43. Which word would the author probably use to describe Louis XVI?
    (A) Helpful.　　(B) Humorless.　　(C) Heroic.　　(D) Hopeless.

44. Which of the following would most likely be a slogan of the French revolutionaries?
    (A) "A new king or queen for France!"
    (B) "Fair taxation and an equal society!"
    (C) "More opportunities for the nobility!"
    (D) "Down with democracy; long live monarchy!"

45. According to the passage, what did Maximilien Robespierre do?
    (A) Kill the former king of France.
    (B) Murder thousands of his enemies.
    (C) Get rid of the hated Napoleon Bonaparte.
    (D) Take over from Louis XVI as monarch.

46. Which of the following consequences of the French Revolution is NOT mentioned in the passage?
    (A) Increasing feelings of connection to one's own country.
    (B) Changing attitudes among royals to their subjects.
    (C) Decreasing ties to worldwide religious institutions.
    (D) Growing desires for similar changes in other nations.

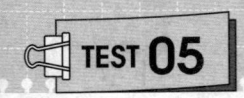

第貳部分、混合題（占 10 分）

說明 本部分共有 1 題組，每一子題配分標於題末。限在標示題號作答區內作答。選擇題使用 2B 鉛筆作答，更正時，應以橡皮擦擦拭，切勿使用修正液（帶）。非選擇題請由左而右橫式書寫。

第 47 至 51 題為題組

Potato chips are very thin slices of potato that have been fried and flavored. Depending on which story you believe, they were either created in the UK in 1817 or the US in 1853. Regardless of the real truth, potato chips have developed into one of the world's best-loved snacks, and their production method has been perfected over time.

Potatoes are delivered from farms to manufacturing plants on a daily basis. Once there, they must be examined for flaws, which could include black spots, green edges, or a soft texture. After poor-quality potatoes have been weeded out, peeling must take place. This is done automatically by a peeling machine, which separates out the peel for transportation back to farms as animal feed.

Slicing is the next essential step in the process. This can either be done with a straight blade, which produces regular potato chips, or a ridged blade, which unsurprisingly produces ridged chips. During this part of the process, the sliced potatoes are washed to get rid of excess starch. Frying in vats of oil at temperatures of up to 190°C is the next vital step—although some manufacturers now choose baking in order to produce a healthier product.

Another stage is cooling, which takes place on a wire mesh that also allows the oil to drain away. However, before this is the seasoning stage, in which salt—or a multitude of other powdered flavorings from cheese to sour cream and onion—is added to the potato chips. And, of course, the final stage is packaging. A pre-determined amount of potato chips is delicately placed into each bag to reduce the chance of breakage. Also added is nitrogen gas, which, unlike oxygen, helps to keep the contents fresh.

Quality control is of paramount importance throughout this process. Potato chip manufacturers build their reputations on producing reliable, consistent, tasty products. Thus, random samples are regularly checked for overall taste, levels of seasoning, and even appropriate color. It certainly seems as though a lot of time, effort, and dedication go into producing the humble potato chip.

47-49. Based on the passage, fill in the missing steps in the potato chip production process.（填空，6 分）

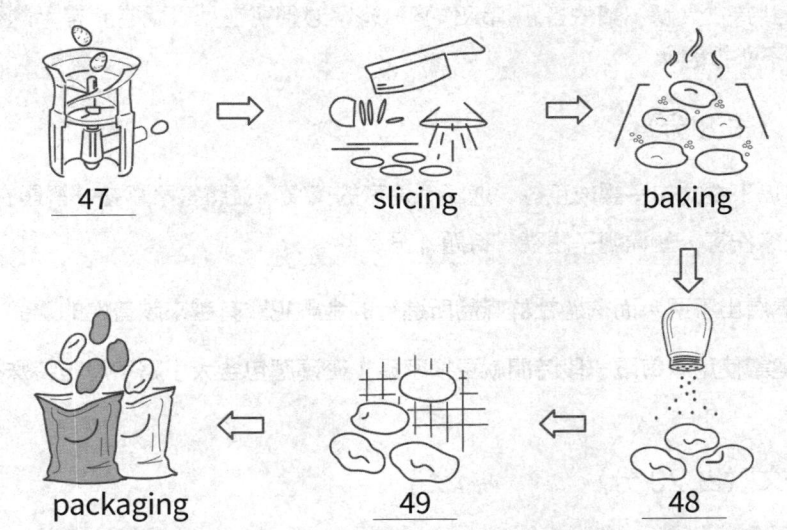

47	slicing	baking

packaging	49	48

50. Choose the correct word(s) from the passage to complete the following sentence: （填空，2 分）

Bags of potato chips are filled with ___50___ to ensure the chips stay fresh.

51. Choose the correct synonym for the blank in this sentence from the passage: "Quality control is of _____ importance throughout this process."（單選題，2 分）
(A) Trivial.
(B) Supreme.
(C) Costly.
(D) Secondary.

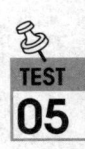

TEST 05

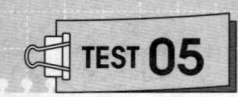

第參部分、非選擇題（占 28 分）

說明　本部分共有二大題，請依各題指示作答，答案必須寫在「答題卷」標示題號之作答區內，作答時不必抄題。

一、中譯英（占 8 分）

說明　1. 請將以下中文句子譯成正確、通順、達意的英文，並將答案寫在「答題卷」上。
　　　2. 請依序作答，並標明子題號。每題 4 分，共 8 分。

1. 網路詐騙層出不窮，而透過社群媒體所進行的金融犯罪有越來越普遍的趨勢。

2. 因此，建議使用者每隔一段時間就更換密碼，密碼應包含大小寫字母、特殊符號和數字。

二、英文作文（占 20 分）

說明　1. 依提示在「答題卷」上寫一篇英文作文。
　　　2. 文長至少 120 個單詞（words）。

提示：請仔細觀察以下三幅連環圖片的內容，並想像第四幅圖片可能的發展，然後寫出一篇涵蓋每張圖片內容且結局完整的故事。

TEST 06

🌱 第壹部分、選擇題

一、詞彙題
二、綜合測驗
三、文意選填
四、篇章結構
五、閱讀測驗

🌱 第貳部分、混合題

🌱 第參部分、非選擇題

一、中譯英
二、英文作文

第壹部分、選擇題（占 62 分）

一、詞彙題（占 10 分）

說明 第 1 題至第 10 題，每題 1 分。

1. This toy store usually employs additional _____ workers to help the permanent staff during the busy Christmas period.
   (A) infinite　　(B) authentic　　(C) primitive　　(D) temporary

2. Wilma was making spaghetti in the kitchen; _____, her husband Fred was watching a documentary in the living room.
   (A) likewise　　(B) besides　　(C) meanwhile　　(D) thereby

3. Everyone's fingerprints are _____, so they are often used to establish a person's identity or solve crimes.
   (A) unique　　(B) organic　　(C) reluctant　　(D) brilliant

4. The company _____ under the new CEO's leadership. It was even rated as one of the best companies in Asia.
   (A) prospered　　(B) persisted　　(C) raged　　(D) behaved

5. We _____ that it was John who stole the confidential document because he was the only other person who had the key to the safe.
   (A) defined　　(B) suspected　　(C) pledged　　(D) commanded

6. It was Irene's dedication to writing that allowed her career to _____ over the past few years.
   (A) browse　　(B) flourish　　(C) vibrate　　(D) stutter

7. Due to an injured ankle, Walter had no alternative but to drop out of the bike _____ last month.
   (A) attraction　　(B) realization　　(C) decoration　　(D) competition

8. Mom _____ the bottle of cough syrup so that we could easily distinguish it from the other bottles in the cabinet.
   (A) constituted　　(B) labeled　　(C) plotted　　(D) invested

9. After the tragic accident on the high-speed rail, government officials expressed their sorrow and _____ to the victims' family.
   (A) regret　　(B) motivation　　(C) bargain　　(D) presentation

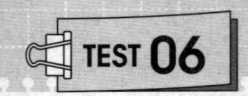

10. The patient is waiting for her health _____ to see if she needs to have heart surgery.
    (A) evolution　　(B) regulation　　(C) evaluation　　(D) revolution

二、綜合測驗（占 10 分）

說明 第 11 題至第 20 題，每題 1 分。

第 11 至 15 題為題組

　　Thailand, a country famous for its elephants, was formerly known as the Kingdom of Siam. While it is still a monarchy today, its kings used to wield much greater power and had enormous wealth. As with most royal families, tensions would arise between the king and those trying to take advantage of him or have him __11__. Such conflicts resulted in an English idiom: a white elephant.

　　According to legend, a Thai king would give a white elephant as a gift to a courtier he __12__. Everyone thought the king had given the courtier a valuable and expensive gift. In __13__, however, white elephants are extremely difficult to raise and care. The financial burden of providing around 130 kilograms of food per day for the enormous animal to consume __14__ to propel anyone into bankruptcy. In other words, it was a troublesome gift and ruined the courtier. That is __15__ today, "a white elephant" is a disapproving term that refers to any present or item that may have cost a lot of money but is considered useless.

11. (A) for replacing　　(B) to replace　　(C) replaced　　(D) replace
12. (A) disliked　　(B) discounted　　(C) discomforted　　(D) distinguished
13. (A) decision　　(B) fortune　　(C) reality　　(D) request
14. (A) is next to impossible　　　　(B) would be enough
    (C) is more convenient than　　　(D) could still be inefficient
15. (A) who　　(B) where　　(C) what　　(D) why

第 16 至 20 題為題組

　　For many people, umbrellas are a dime a dozen. The smallest gust of wind can cause them to turn inside out and collapse, making them ineffective. Often they are not worth investing in __16__ most are cheaply made. That's not the case with umbrellas from the Maglia Umbrella Company.

　　Founded in 1854, the company is __17__ and run by Francesco Maglia, the sixth-generation descendant of the company's namesake. He is one of Italy's most exclusive umbrella makers and still employs traditional production methods. His masterpieces of form and function are all handmade using an 80-step __18__ . They are worth every penny of the US$300 or more that each one sells for.

  Extremely practical, rain or shine, each Maglia umbrella __19__ around 25 high-quality parts. Local wood is used to produce the shafts, while tough yet stylish fabrics are employed for the canopies. A customized service is also available, allowing each customer to personally select every detail of their umbrella. The company, whose best-known umbrellas look like walking sticks when closed, makes a product meant to last. They are solid enough to __20__ of the street and almost anything Mother Nature blows their way.

16. (A) that   (B) unless   (C) although   (D) because
17. (A) dramatically declined   (B) currently owned
  (C) heavily criticized   (D) previously auctioned
18. (A) process   (B) structure   (C) display   (D) workload
19. (A) accounts for   (B) results from   (C) engages in   (D) consists of
20. (A) act as a weapon   (B) provide political asylum
  (C) withstand the pounding   (D) assist the needy

三、文意選填（占 10 分）

說明 第 21 題至第 30 題，每題 1 分。

第 21 至 30 題為題組

  The South Asian country of India is the seventh largest in the world, and its education system is one of the most competitive. In a nation with a population of over one billion people, only the best of the best are __21__ for higher education. Quite often, top universities require students to score over 98% on national exams to gain __22__ . Although this system has developed many brilliant minds and provided the world with talented workers, it also has a dark side. To achieve better scores, many students resort to cheating on exams or paying large __23__ to professors. What's worse is that studies indicate that 25% of Indian children between the ages of 13 and 15 suffer from depression.

  In an effort to improve students' mental and __24__ health, the Indian government has devised a special class that teaches students happiness. The course doesn't require any books and there are no homework __25__ . There are also no tests to ensure that students have understood the material taught in class. Instead, students are allowed to relax, listen to stories, and practice __26__ . The main goal is to instruct students on how to effectively __27__ the pressures of life. They do this by giving students tips and techniques on how they can manage their stress levels.

In one exercise, students are told to shut their eyes and 28 the sound of their breath. This technique may sound simple, but it helps students to pause their 29 and return to the present moment. Although it's still too early to measure the program's success, the early feedback is 30 . It appears that the concept of happiness classes is catching on elsewhere. Several countries, including Mexico and Peru, have plans to launch similar programs that are designed to elevate students' moods and address their well-being.

(A) focus on   (B) bribes   (C) thinking   (D) selected   (E) meditation
(F) emotional   (G) promising (H) admittance (I) cope with (J) assignments

四、篇章結構（占 8 分）

說明 第 31 題至第 34 題，每題 2 分。

第 31 至 34 題為題組

　　Technically, she is known as AL 288-1 and consists of several hundred bone fossils. 31 Discovered in Ethiopia by American researcher Donald Johanson, Lucy, a fossil of a hominin (early and modern human) species, was an instant hit with the public. She was believed to be the earliest example of a human ancestor ever discovered. She was given the name Lucy because Johanson and his team listened to the song "Lucy in the Sky With Diamonds," by the 1960s British band The Beatles, on the night of the discovery and considered the name to be both attractive and relatable.

　　Johanson first found part of a shinbone, which was determined to be more than three million years old, in 1974. The next year, he and his team returned to the area and found a jaw, a piece of an arm bone, and a portion of the back of a small skull. They kept looking and found more, including bits of a pelvis and ribs. 32 They determined she was 110 centimeters in height, weighed 29 kilograms, had an appearance that resembled a chimpanzee, and consumed a plant-based diet. Through examination of her leg bones and pelvis, the researchers concluded Lucy had walked upright. This finding supports the theory that early humans began using their legs to walk before their brains increased in size.

　　In 2016, other researchers made another amazing find in Ethiopia. 33 The fossil has been described as an extremely rare treasure, one that sheds more light on the evolution of humans. The newly found skull was determined to be roughly 3.8 million years old, which predates Lucy's remains. 34 While this presents complications to scientists who struggle to piece together an accurate picture of man's evolutionary history, it also represents an exciting new chapter in the study of human development.

(A) In total, they found about 40% of Lucy, enough to get a good idea of what she probably looked like.
(B) Nevertheless, scientists believe the two species lived at the same time for a period of about 100,000 years.
(C) Despite these fascinating findings in Ethiopia, Lucy's appearance remains largely a mystery.
(D) To those outside the scientific community, though, this collection of ancient bone pieces is more affectionately known as "Lucy."
(E) They discovered an almost complete skull of a human ancestor that dated back even further than Lucy.

五、閱讀測驗（占 24 分）

說明 第 35 題至第 46 題，每題 2 分。

第 35 至 38 題為題組

It is such an irony that the planet we live on is called Earth. Perhaps Aqua or Oceana might be a more appropriate name. Why? That is because more than 70% of the surface of this planet is covered by water, not land. Of that water, some 97% is salt water. Geographers over the centuries have named the largest of these vast bodies of salt water oceans: the Pacific, the Atlantic, the Indian, and the Arctic. Though for centuries these four oceans have been the only ones drawn on world maps, a fifth one called the Southern Ocean is increasingly being recognized by the geographic community.

The borders of **this newly defined body** are around our planet's southernmost continent, Antarctica. They are determined by the presence of the Antarctic Circumpolar Current (ACC), which flows from west to east. Waters within the ACC are colder and less salty than one would find in other oceans. They are home to an array of unique species, such as the Antarctic icefish and the Hoff crab. The Southern Ocean also plays a role in limiting the damage caused by climate change, as its deep waters store huge carbon deposits. However, this fifth ocean is not universally acknowledged. For instance, it is recognized by the National Geographic Society but not by the International Hydrographic Organization.

Names aside, what we should remember from all this is to respect our oceans. Though there is much more ocean water than land, this water is not beyond the harmful effects of mankind. Whether we regard the Earth's ocean waters as separate identities or not, their temperature, composition, and marine life are subject to environmental pollution. Biologists say that life began in the oceans. It would be a tragedy if all life on our planet died with them.

35. Why does the author suggest giving a new name to our planet?
    (A) Because most of our planet is covered in water.
    (B) Because ancient geographers did not understand our planet.
    (C) Because we now know how many oceans there are.
    (D) Because fresh water is more useful than salt water.

36. What does "**this newly defined body**" refer to in the second paragraph?
    (A) The Antarctic Circumpolar Current.
    (B) The scientific community.
    (C) The continent of Antarctica.
    (D) The Southern Ocean.

37. According to the passage, which of the following statements is true?
    (A) The National Geographic Society gave the Southern Ocean its name.
    (B) The Hoff crab can be found in a number of the world's oceans.
    (C) The Antarctic Circumpolar Current's waters are not as warm as others.
    (D) The Southern Ocean's carbon deposits may speed up climate change.

38. What is the purpose of the last paragraph?
    (A) To introduce further details about the Southern Ocean.
    (B) To claim that the number of oceans has changed.
    (C) To highlight the importance of environmental protection.
    (D) To disagree with the idea that life started in the oceans.

第 39 至 42 題為題組

　　Ludwig van Beethoven is among the most famous and beloved composers the world has ever known. His compositions, some of which combined vocals and instruments in groundbreaking ways, are regarded as works of genius. However, he faced numerous struggles during his life.

　　Beethoven was born in 1770 in Bonn, Germany. Both his father and grandfather were singers, while his father also taught piano and violin. However, his father was an abusive alcoholic. He would beat his young son for any slight error during piano lessons and would frequently deprive him of sleep in order to practice. Despite—or perhaps because of—his father's **abhorrent** behavior, the young Beethoven quickly developed a prodigious musical talent. By the age at which most children today enter primary school, he had given his first public concert. At the age of 12, he published his first composition, and two years later he was appointed assistant court organist. Like his contemporary Wolfgang Amadeus Mozart, Beethoven was truly a child prodigy.

　　Thankfully, Beethoven was influenced by people other than his violent father. While it is debatable whether he actually spent time with Mozart, he definitely studied under another distinguished contemporary, Joseph Haydn. This Austrian composer helped Beethoven to further refine his already considerable talents. It was in Haydn's hometown of Vienna that Beethoven solidified his reputation for flawless performance and inspired improvisation. Even though Beethoven's fame soon eclipsed that of Haydn, the pair remained good friends until the latter's passing.

　　Having never married, though, Beethoven spent much of his adult life alone. He even withdrew from most social events. This was to conceal the heartbreaking fact that he was going deaf. Letters he wrote show that this was happening as early as 1801, and the condition got progressively worse until his death in 1827. Yet, this period was the most astonishingly productive of his life, witnessing the composition of stunning symphonies, piano sonatas, overtures, songs, and even an opera. It verges on the unbelievable that he was able to produce all of these universally celebrated works while barely being able to hear.

39. What would be the most suitable title for this passage?
    (A) How Musical Traditions Developed in Germany
    (B) The Most Recognized Works of Ludwig van Beethoven
    (C) How Alcoholism Destroyed a Promising Musical Career
    (D) The Trials and Triumphs of Ludwig van Beethoven

40. Which of the following is closest in meaning to the word "**abhorrent**" in the second paragraph?
    (A) Defensive.　　(B) Cooperative.　　(C) Disgusting.　　(D) Cautious.

41. According to the passage, which of the following statements is accurate?
    (A) There is much evidence that Mozart and Beethoven studied together.
    (B) Ludwig van Beethoven came to be more admired than Joseph Haydn.
    (C) Mozart and Haydn shared an intense rivalry that affected their music.
    (D) Haydn bonded with Beethoven as they both had father issues.

42. What does the author imply about Beethoven in the final paragraph?
    (A) He actually composed many operas during his life.
    (B) His deafness has not been confirmed by historians.
    (C) He most likely got married in a secret ceremony.
    (D) His deafness makes his achievements even greater.

TEST 06

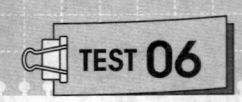

第 43 至 46 題為題組

　　Tropical storms—variously called hurricanes, cyclones, and typhoons in different parts of the world—are violent storms in which the wind moves very fast in a circular direction. They are formed when warm, moist air over the ocean begins to rise, creating storms and clouds which then rotate. In the Northern Hemisphere, they rotate in a counterclockwise direction, whereas in the Southern Hemisphere, they rotate clockwise. Sometimes, two storms form near each other at the same time and are drawn together. This is known as the Fujiwhara Effect.

　　Named after Japanese meteorologist Sakuhei Fujiwhara, the phenomenon has been described as two storms "dancing" around each other. This "dance" proceeds in the same direction as the rotation of the storms, depending on the hemisphere. Essentially, they both move around a common center of mass. Although various factors can affect when this happens, it typically occurs when the storms are within 1,400 kilometers of each other. If the storms are of roughly the same size and intensity, they will move around the common center point. One of them might move away in a direction different from its initial **trajectory**, which could be a good thing if it was originally going to hit land. If the storms are of different sizes and intensities, they will move around each other and then possibly begin to merge. This does not create a super-sized storm; rather, the smaller storm is absorbed by the more dominant one.

　　There are numerous examples of the Fujiwhara Effect from the last two decades. In 2005, Hurricane Wilma caused immense damage when it hit southwest Florida but weakened as it reached the Atlantic. However, once there, it absorbed Tropical Storm Alpha and regained strength. In 2008, Cyclones Fame and Gula interacted for a short time in the South-West Indian Ocean but remained as two separate entities. Four years later, Hurricane Sandy merged with a winter storm to create what was dubbed a "superstorm." It went on to kill 233 people across the US, Caribbean, and Canada and cause nearly US$70 billion worth of damage.

43. Which of the following conditions is most likely to cause a hurricane to develop?
    (A) Warm and wet air over land.
    (B) Cool air rising over the ocean.
    (C) Hot and humid air over the sea.
    (D) Low temperatures and rain over land.

44. Based on the passage, if Typhoon A (with a diameter of 110 kilometers) and Tropical Storm B (with a diameter of 65 kilometers) exhibit the Fujiwhara Effect over the Northern Pacific, which picture shows what will most likely happen?

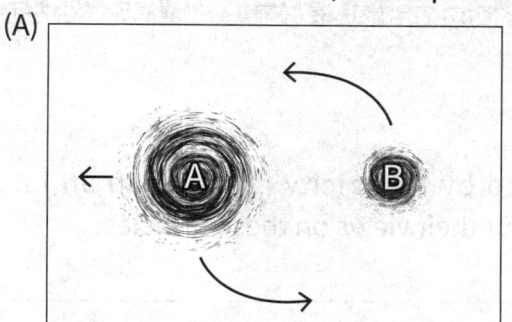

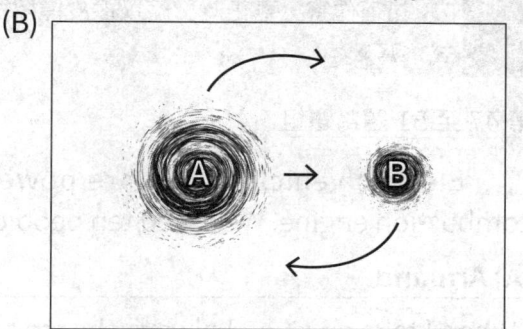

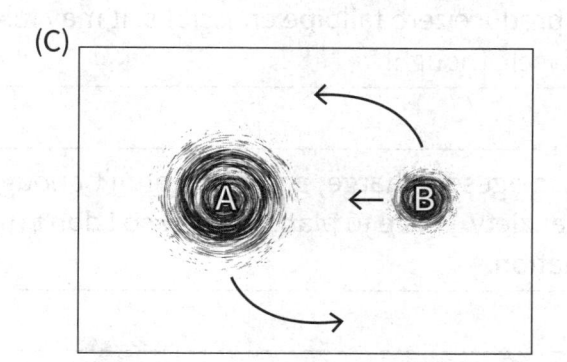

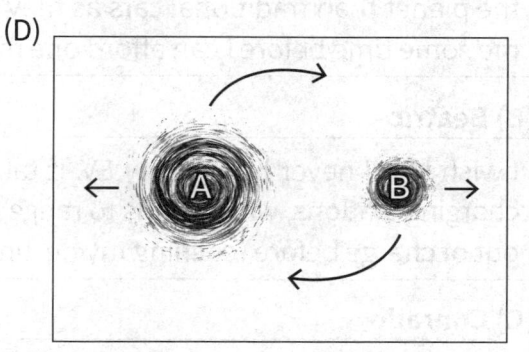

(A)　　(B)　　(C)　　(D)

45. Which of the following is closest in meaning to the word "**trajectory**" in the second paragraph?
    (A) Power.　　(B) Result.　　(C) Aftermath.　　(D) Course.

46. According to the passage, which of the following is true?
    (A) Hurricane Sandy caused destruction in 2008.
    (B) Tropical Storm Alpha absorbed Hurricane Wilma.
    (C) Fame and Gula merged into one cyclone in 2008.
    (D) Hurricane Wilma became stronger when it met Alpha.

TEST 06

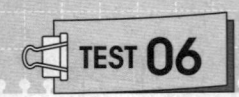

第貳部分、混合題（占 10 分）

說明：本部分共有 1 題組，每一子題配分標於題末。限在標示題號作答區內作答。選擇題使用 2B 鉛筆作答，更正時，應以橡皮擦擦拭，切勿使用修正液（帶）。非選擇題請由左而右橫式書寫。

第 47 至 51 題為題組

Electric vehicles (EVs) are powered by electricity rather than an internal combustion engine. We asked ten people for their views on these vehicles.

(A) Armand

When I take an Uber, I always choose an electric vehicle. EVs are so much better for the planet than traditional cars as they produce zero tailpipe emissions. It may take me some time before I can afford one myself, though!

(B) Beatrice

I wish I had never bought my EV. It takes ages to charge, and there aren't enough charging stations, which leads to range anxiety. I have to plan carefully so I don't run out of charge before reaching my destination.

(C) Conrado

People claim that electric vehicles are wonderful for the planet, but that isn't true. Manufacturing them emits harmful gases, their batteries are difficult to recycle, and they need to be charged from a power grid that uses fossil fuels!

(D) Debra

I recently purchased an EV, and I think it's great. I can charge it overnight in my garage, and the cost per mile is significantly lower than a gas-powered car. Plus, it's very responsive, making it a pleasure to drive.

(E) Enoch

I suffer from range anxiety regarding my EV, as long-distance driving requires a lot of planning. But this is made up for by the money I save on fuel and the enjoyment I get from driving such an energy-efficient vehicle.

(F) Frankie

Walking in the city is more dangerous thanks to electric vehicles. I can always hear a gas-powered car coming, but EVs are so silent that you can't hear them approaching. I suppose they're great for the environment, though.

(G) Gordon

I can't argue with the principle of electric cars. As a mechanic, though, I worry about the impact on my industry. EVs have fewer moving parts than regular cars, so they require less maintenance.

(H) Henrietta

My friend drives an EV and complains about the slow speed of charging. However, I'm a little jealous of his car. From what I've been told, EVs are easy to drive: They accelerate immediately, and you can't stall them!

(I) Iain

Electric vehicles make me so angry! Why are we being encouraged to buy cars that cost a fortune, take an eternity to charge, and have batteries vulnerable to cold weather? I will never buy one!

(J) Juliet

I absolutely adore my EV! It's wonderful for the environment and thrilling to drive; it's inexpensive and convenient to charge; it never requires maintenance; and it comes with tons of smart features. I could go on and on!

47-48. 請根據選文內容，從文章中選出兩個單詞，分別填入下列句子空格，並視句型結構需要作適當的字形變化，使句子語意完整、語法正確，且符合全文文意。**空格限填一個單詞 (word)**。(填充，4分)

More than one person mentions that planning a journey in an electric vehicle makes them feel __47__. Another person, meanwhile, makes reference to the __48__ EVs can pose on city streets.

49-51. From most positive to most negative in terms of the content of their responses, put the missing names into the following list. (填充，6分)

Juliet > Debra > __49__ > Henrietta > Enoch > __50__ > Frankie > Beatrice > __51__ > Iain

TEST 06

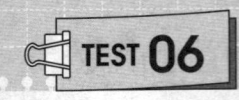

第參部分、非選擇題（占 28 分）

說明 本部分共有二大題，請依各題指示作答，答案必須寫在「答題卷」標示題號之作答區內，作答時不必抄題。

一、中譯英（占 8 分）

說明 1. 請將以下中文句子譯成正確、通順、達意的英文，並將答案寫在「答題卷」上。
2. 請依序作答，並標明子題號。每題 4 分，共 8 分。

1. 從小，父母便教導我們要養成準時的好習慣。

2. 準時不僅可以表示尊重，同時也能給別人留下好印象。

二、英文作文（占 20 分）

說明 1. 依提示在「答題卷」上寫一篇英文作文。
2. 文長至少 120 個單詞（words）。

提示：不同的游泳場所，可能樣貌不同，特色也不同。請以此為主題，並依據下列兩張圖片的內容，寫一篇英文作文，文分兩段。第一段描述圖 A 和圖 B 中的游泳場所各有何特色，第二段則說明你心目中理想游泳場所的樣貌與特色，並解釋你的理由。

A   B

TEST 07

🌱 第壹部分、選擇題

一、詞彙題
二、綜合測驗
三、文意選填
四、篇章結構
五、閱讀測驗

🌱 第貳部分、混合題

🌱 第參部分、非選擇題

一、中譯英
二、英文作文

第壹部分、選擇題（占 62 分）

一、詞彙題（占 10 分）

說明 第 1 題至第 10 題，每題 1 分。

1. Studying penguins in a remote area of the Antarctic, the scientist felt a strong sense of _____.
   (A) modesty　　(B) isolation　　(C) tolerance　　(D) philosophy

2. Being paid in a digital currency such as Bitcoin is increasingly _____ to employees in the tech industry.
   (A) professional　　(B) economic　　(C) abrupt　　(D) desirable

3. Lucy was so scared of being in the water that she couldn't relax and _____ in the pool.
   (A) sweat　　(B) float　　(C) tremble　　(D) drown

4. Olivia is so addicted to social networking websites that she is _____ checking her Facebook and Twitter pages every 20 minutes.
   (A) adequately　　(B) spiritually　　(C) constantly　　(D) mysteriously

5. Food, air, and water are all _____ to living creatures, which means that life on many other planets is impossible.
   (A) favorable　　(B) accurate　　(C) essential　　(D) immense

6. Vincent found that he couldn't _____ Jennifer's bad temper anymore, so he decided to file for a divorce.
   (A) discard　　(B) allege　　(C) tolerate　　(D) compile

7. Alan's _____ with Japan made it easy for him to travel from city to city with his friends.
   (A) familiarity　　(B) necessity　　(C) possibility　　(D) quantity

8. One of our colleagues is going to retire at the end of this month, so we are planning a _____ party for him.
   (A) potential　　(B) plentiful　　(C) farewell　　(D) furious

9. A study found that bees stopped flying during the total solar _____ because they thought it was nighttime.
   (A) eclipse　　(B) impact　　(C) horizon　　(D) vacancy

TEST 07

10. There are _____ sections at the book fair, including comics, magazines, novels, and even electronic material.
    (A) skillful   (B) influential   (C) various   (D) flexible

二、綜合測驗（占 10 分）

說明 第 11 題至第 20 題，每題 1 分。

第 11 至 15 題為題組

It is said that the eyes are the windows to the soul. That is especially true when it comes to felines. Their eyes can reveal moods, emotions, and more. The color also holds a lot of information.

All cats' eyes change color. The color is __11__ by the amount of melanocytes, the cells that produce the pigment melanin, in the eyes. The more cells the eyes have, the darker they are. Blue-eyed cats have none, while green-eyed cats have some, gold-eyed cats have more, and copper-eyed cats have __12__. As kittens, all cats have blue eyes because the melanocytes haven't __13__ yet. They start working anywhere from four to six weeks after birth. By four months of age, cats will have their true adult eye color. The eyes of some cats stay blue, but most turn green, gold, copper, and every __14__ in between.

It's also normal for cats to have two different colored eyes. However, sudden color changes aren't normal. They're signs of __15__. Healthy eyes turning orange or red means they are inflamed, while dark yellow or brown can indicate feline leukemia or feline AIDS. There's truly more to cat eye color than meets the eye.

11. (A) preserved   (B) determined   (C) promoted   (D) released
12. (A) most often   (B) the longest   (C) far inferior   (D) the most
13. (A) checked in   (B) signed in   (C) kicked in   (D) faded in
14. (A) shade   (B) paint   (C) term   (D) light
15. (A) happiness and joy   (B) sickness and disease
    (C) function and operation   (D) instinct and intention

第 16 至 20 題為題組

Anyone who has spent time in Taiwan has undoubtedly noticed that the island has a vast number of convenience stores. With 7-Elevens and FamilyMarts seemingly on every street corner, convenience stores are a way of life for Taiwan's locals. But what is the   16   of these ever-present shops? And what makes them unique, compared to "regular" stores?

  The first "true" convenience store   17   in Dallas, Texas, in 1927. It was opened by Southland Ice Company employee John Jefferson Green. He realized that people often needed to buy goods like bread, eggs, and milk after grocery stores   18 . Green's first store had a Native American totem pole out front. This attracted a lot of attention, eventually leading to a chain of Tote'm Stores across Dallas. These stores were later bought by a Dallas banker,   19   changed the name to 7-Eleven to reflect the stores' new opening hours of 7:00 a.m. to 11:00 p.m.

  Nowadays, there are more than 70,000 7-Elevens around the world, and the majority of the stores are open 24/7. Some have gas stations, ATMs, and donut shops, while others sell   20   anything one can imagine. Without a doubt, modern convenience stores certainly live up to their name.

16. (A) accent   (B) origin   (C) charity   (D) ground
17. (A) sprang up   (B) passed out   (C) took part   (D) gave birth
18. (A) held an annual sale   (B) had a grand reopening
    (C) had closed   (D) carried little stock
19. (A) where   (B) what   (C) who   (D) that
20. (A) barely   (B) namely   (C) specifically   (D) practically

三、文意選填（占 10 分）

說明 第 21 題至第 30 題，每題 1 分。

第 21 至 30 題為題組

  There are lots of things that airline passengers grumble about. It almost goes without saying, though, that the one thing they unanimously complain about is the food served during their flight. Indeed, there are websites full of criticisms about the quality of in-flight meals. In   21   to these nearly universal complaints, many airlines have conducted a great deal of research, and the results are quite helpful and interesting.

  It turns out that our senses, which give us information about our   22   environment, are altered when cruising at a typical altitude of over 30,000 feet. Height is not the only factor, however. Inside a pressurized aircraft cabin, the   23   of humidity is greatly reduced, which dries out our nasal passages. Since we   24   taste with our nose, not just our mouth, our taste is necessarily affected. The two taste   25   that are impacted the most in this environment are sweet and salty. Accordingly, airline chefs add more sweet and salty 26 when preparing airline meals to make up for the high-altitude dining experience. Bitter, sour, and spicy tastes seem not to be affected much.

Surprisingly, researchers also found a 27 between the consistently loud noise made by jet engines and our perception of the food and drink we consume on board. Essentially, loud noise can distract us from what we are eating. However, wearing headphones tuned to different kinds of music could 28 the loss of our normal senses of taste and smell. Researchers are also looking at 29 ways to cook or reheat the food. Since gas-fired and even microwave ovens are not allowed on planes for safety reasons, new 30 of heating food slowly in plastic bags before serving are being tried to improve the taste of in-flight meals. Hopefully, airline passengers will soon start to taste the difference in the food they're consuming in the sky.

(A) perceive   (B) reduce   (C) alternative   (D) response   (E) methods
(F) level   (G) ingredients (H) immediate   (I) connection   (J) sensations

四、篇章結構（占 8 分）

說明 第 31 題至第 34 題，每題 2 分。

第 31 至 34 題為題組

You probably know a little about what gymnastics involves. You may have even practiced some combination of the physical strength, acrobatic skills, and artistry of gymnastics during sports classes at school. 31

The word "gymnastics" comes from the ancient Greek for "disciplinary exercises." Physical fitness was highly prized by the early Greeks, so vigorous exercise in *gymnazein* (gymnasiums) was strongly encouraged. They believed, correctly, that taking care of one's physical health was essential for improving one's mental and spiritual health and that physical fitness helped ward off many diseases. 32 When the Roman Empire faded into history, though, so did gymnastics. This was partly because some Christians at the time considered physical improvement to be less important than spiritual improvement.

We can credit another European country—this time Germany—with resurrecting gymnastics for the modern era. 33 His inventions included the balance beam, the horizontal bar, and the parallel bars, which became standard equipment for modern gymnastics. Interest in the sport quickly spread throughout the continent, before traveling to the US via a wave of immigration in the 1880s. And, just before the end of the 19th century, men's gymnastics was featured as part of the first modern Olympic Games.

Gymnastics remains a popular and integral part of the Olympics today. Artistic gymnastics is performed separately by men and women and involves short routines on a variety of equipment. __34__ In this women's competition, the gymnast must perform a routine of leaps and turns on a padded spring beam to show off balance and strength. A unique element of the men's artistic event is the pommel horse, on which the gymnast demonstrates complicated leg work. Rhythmic gymnastics, meanwhile, is for female gymnasts only. This branch of the sport involves the use of equipment—such as a ball, hoop, clubs, or ribbon—to showcase flexibility and musicality.

(A) That is why gymnastics is a popular element of physical education in schools in both Germany and Greece.
(B) One piece of equipment that is unique to the women's artistic event is the balance beam.
(C) What you may not know is that the origins of this sport can be traced back to ancient Greece.
(D) In the late 1700s, Friedrich Ludwig Jahn of Germany developed much of the equipment we still use today.
(E) When the Romans conquered Greece, they formalized the sport and used the training venues to prepare their warriors for battle.

五、閱讀測驗（占 24 分）

說明　第 35 題至第 46 題，每題 2 分。

第 35 至 38 題為題組

The dangers of cigarette smoking are well known. The World Health Organization (WHO) estimates that there are some 1.3 billion smokers in the world today. Of these, about eight million people die annually, six times the number of people that die from malaria and AIDS combined. Since tobacco and smoking are necessarily linked, reducing the amount of tobacco consumed and the number of smokers could save trillions of dollars in healthcare and lost production annually, not to mention countless lives around the world.

Russia has joined most of the other wealthy nations in taking steps to do just that. In 2014, the government banned sales of tobacco products at sidewalk kiosks, where most people buy their cigarettes. Banning smoking in public places like schools and restaurants was the next step, keeping Russia in line with many other nations. By 2025, Russia hoped to have reduced the smoking rate from 31% to 25%. Last but not least, the government wants to prohibit smoking in all forms and at all ages from 2033.

These steps will ensure that Russia can begin to address the problem of its shrinking population, which has fallen from 148 million in 1991 to 144 million today. With the deaths of 330,000 smokers per year, cigarette smoking is responsible for a large part of that decrease. The average life expectancy in Russia today is only 73 years, compared to 79 to 82 for other developed countries.

Foreign tobacco companies in the UK, Japan, and the US are predictably against the new legislation. They account for about 90% of cigarette sales, which are worth an estimated US$19 billion a year in Russia. Of course, it is no surprise that smokers are upset with the new laws, which are expected to be hard to enforce. But laws that protect public health can only work when all citizens are required to follow them.

35. What is the main topic of the passage?
    (A) The different rates of smoking throughout the world.
    (B) A study of smoking habits conducted by the WHO.
    (C) The challenge posed by infectious diseases in Russia.
    (D) One country's attempts to make its population healthier.

36. What could we say about how Russia's government is dealing with the tobacco problem?
    (A) It is gradually introducing steps to counter cigarette smoking.
    (B) It has closed down almost all sidewalk kiosks.
    (C) It has increased the cost of cigarettes to discourage purchases.
    (D) It is prohibiting the sale of foreign cigarettes.

37. According to the passage, what can be inferred about Russia's population?
    (A) It will decrease even faster after tobacco is outlawed.
    (B) It will stop declining when fewer people smoke.
    (C) It will rise sharply due to improved healthcare facilities.
    (D) It will continue to go down due to other illnesses.

38. What does the writer think about anti-tobacco policies?
    (A) They will only work if they are applied internationally.
    (B) They will increase rather than decrease cigarette consumption.
    (C) They can cause problems that are difficult to predict.
    (D) They can be successful if the public must obey them.

第 39 至 42 題為題組

During the Japanese occupation of Taiwan from 1895 to 1945, the Taiwanese yen was used as the currency. When World War II came to its conclusion and the Empire of Japan was defeated, Taiwan came under the control of the Republic of China. One year later, the Taiwan dollar was introduced as the island's currency. However, due to the effects of the Chinese Civil War, both Taiwan and China experienced hyperinflation, which is when prices rise rapidly. To combat this problem, the government had to issue banknotes in increasingly higher denominations, up to and including a one million dollar note. Finally, on June 15, 1949, the Taiwan dollar was replaced with the New Taiwan dollar at an exchange rate of one new to 40,000 old. Thus, the original Taiwan dollar is often referred to as the Old Taiwan dollar to distinguish it from its present incarnation.

Taiwan is not alone in having replaced its currency to deal with hyperinflation. In fact, Taiwan's experience pales in comparison to that of Hungary. This Central European country experienced the worst case of hyperinflation in history after its transportation network and industrial capacity were decimated by World War II. In order to stimulate the economy, the government printed reams and reams of money, **doling it out** to banks, companies, and consumers alike. Incredibly, prices were doubling every fifteen hours! The policy actually proved to be a success, and by August 1946—only a year after the end of the war—industrial production had recovered and the government was able to replace the Hungarian pengö with a new currency, the Hungarian forint.

A current example of hyperinflation comes from Venezuela. Colossal mismanagement of the South American nation's economy by its socialist government has led to a situation where three-quarters of the population live in extreme poverty and, as of 2021, a loaf of bread costs seven million bolívares. While the currency has yet to be replaced by a completely new one, it has had fourteen zeros removed from it since 2008. Many experts predict this will not help: "the zeros that are being removed […] will soon return," said economist Jose Manuel Puente.

39. What is this passage mainly about?
    (A) Famous currencies in Europe and Asia.
    (B) Different experiences of hyperinflation.
    (C) Taiwan's currencies over the centuries.
    (D) Terminology connected to inflation.

40. Which of the following is NOT true about Taiwan and Hungary with regard to hyperinflation?
    (A) They both went through it because of war.
    (B) They both dealt with it by replacing their currency.
    (C) They both experienced it to the same severity.
    (D) They both endured it at roughly the same time.

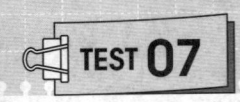

41. What does "**doling it out**" refer to in the second paragraph?
    (A) Creating jobs.   (B) Giving money.   (C) Providing food.   (D) Reducing prices.

42. According to the passage, what is likely to happen in Venezuela in the future?
    (A) Hyperinflation will continue to worsen.
    (B) The economic situation will improve.
    (C) Levels of poverty will start to decline.
    (D) The price of bread will slowly stabilize.

第 43 至 46 題為題組

Archerfish live in freshwater rivers and salty mangrove rivers in Northern Australia and South Asia. They range from 12 to 40 centimeters in length, and their bodies are almost flat. This makes them difficult to be seen when they are approaching their prey, which typically consists of insects such as flies and crickets that live above the surface of the water. However, it is the method they use to actually catch their prey that is most fascinating.

While their body remains submerged, archerfish poke their mouth out of the water. They put their tongue against the roof of their mouth to create a channel, out of which they shoot a jet of water up to 3 meters in the air. This perfectly controlled jet travels slower at the front than at the back, meaning that once **it** reaches its target, it has formed into a blob. This ball of spit then knocks the intended insect into the river, where it can be devoured by the waiting archerfish. It should therefore come as no surprise that they have been compared to water pistols.

Another element of their hunting ability is equally impressive. Archerfish have to learn how to adjust their aim to compensate for refraction. That is, they have to be aware of the fact that light changes direction when it moves from one medium, such as water, to another, such as air. They do this by observing older members of the species alter their positions and adjust their shooting angles to successfully hit their targets. Research has shown that their preferred position is not directly below their prey, where refraction would be less of an issue, but at an angle to the side, in front of or behind it.

A recent study, published in the journal *Animal Behaviour* and reported in *National Geographic*, revealed further interesting details about archerfish. Scientists used food to train archerfish to distinguish between three-dimensional images of different human faces. The fish shot water at the correct facial image even when the images were rotated. This is yet more evidence of the extraordinary skills possessed by archerfish.

43. Which of the following is a true statement about archerfish?
    (A) They can only be found in water that is salty.
    (B) They have tongues that can extend to three meters.
    (C) They move faster than water from a typical water pistol.
    (D) They cannot be easily noticed by those they are hunting.

44. What does "**it**" most likely refer to in the second paragraph?
    (A) The archerfish itself.
    (B) The mouth of the archerfish.
    (C) The water spit out by the archerfish.
    (D) The prey that is hunted by the archerfish.

45. Which picture correctly shows the preferred position of archerfish when they are seeking their prey?
    (A)
    (B)
    (C)
    (D)

46. What is implied about archerfish in the last paragraph?
    (A) Their diets are starting to change.
    (B) They can recognize people's faces.
    (C) Their shooting abilities are worsening.
    (D) They cannot be trained in a laboratory.

TEST 07

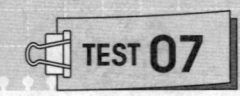

第貳部分、混合題（占 10 分）

說明 本部分共有 1 題組，每一子題配分標於題末。限在標示題號作答區內作答。選擇題使用 2B 鉛筆作答，更正時，應以橡皮擦擦拭，切勿使用修正液（帶）。非選擇題請由左而右橫式書寫。

第 47 至 51 題為題組

　　Japan has been named as the host country for the Summer Olympic Games on three occasions. In 1936, the International Olympic Committee (IOC) announced that Tokyo would host the 1940 Summer Olympics, becoming the first non-Western city to achieve this honor. Preparations were immediately underway, with plans drawn up for new stadiums and an Olympic Village. However, in 1937, Japan launched a full-scale invasion of China, leading to the Second Sino-Japanese War. –[1]– Amid criticism of Japanese aggression abroad and rising military expenditure at home, the Japanese government said that it would be unable to host the Games. The IOC proceeded to award the Games to Helsinki, Finland, but these were ultimately canceled due to the outbreak of World War II. –[2]–

　　Global conflicts, though, did not get in the way of Japan hosting the 1964 Summer Olympics. By this time, the country had re-emerged on the world stage as a modern, peaceful, industrialized nation, and the Games served to symbolize this fact. In the lead-up to the sporting event—which was held in the fall to avoid the muggy summer months—the host city of Tokyo was transformed. –[3]– Cheered on by an enthusiastic crowd, the home nation went on to win 29 medals, which at that time was its best performance in Olympic history. The world witnessed this, too, as these Olympic Games were the first to be televised internationally via satellite.

　　When Tokyo again hosted the Olympics more than half a century later, the Japanese team doubled this medal tally. –[4]– However, Tokyo 2020 is usually remembered less for its sporting achievements than for the circumstances in which it was held. Originally scheduled to commence in July 2020, the Games were postponed until July 2021 due to the COVID-19 pandemic. When they did take place, most events were held behind closed doors for fear that the virus would spread like wildfire. The lack of spectators in the stadiums inevitably had an effect on the atmosphere and potentially had an impact on the performance of the athletes. Nevertheless, these Olympics showed that both Japan and the global sporting community could be resilient in the face of exceptionally challenging conditions.

47. Which phrase in the article means "without the public being allowed in the venues to watch"?（簡答，2 分）

_____

48-50. 請根據選文內容，從文章中選出三個單詞，分別填入下列時間表內的空格，並視句型結構需要作適當的字形變化，使句子語意完整、語法正確，且符合全文文意。<u>每格限填一個單詞</u> (word)。（填空，6 分）

1936	• The IOC made the announcement that Tokyo would host the Olympics in four years' time.
1937	• Japan __48__ China, sparking the Second Sino-Japanese War.
1940	• The Second World War led to the __49__ of the Olympic Games.
1964	• The Olympic Games were a symbol that Japan was back on the international stage.
2020	• The COVID-19 pandemic prompted the __50__ of that year's Olympics.
2021	• Tokyo 2020 showed that Japan could cope with challenging situations.

51. In which of the positions marked [1], [2], [3], and [4] does the following sentence best belong?（單選，2 分）
"Highways were widened, new subway lines were completed, and the bullet train between Tokyo and Osaka began operation."
(A) [1]
(B) [2]
(C) [3]
(D) [4]

TEST 07

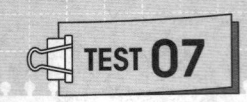

第參部分、非選擇題（占 28 分）

說明 本部分共有二大題，請依各題指示作答，答案必須寫在「答題卷」標示題號之作答區內，作答時不必抄題。

一、中譯英（占 8 分）

說明 1. 請將以下中文句子譯成正確、通順、達意的英文，並將答案寫在「答題卷」上。
2. 請依序作答，並標明子題號。每題 4 分，共 8 分。

1. 按摩是一種減緩壓力、疼痛與肌肉緊繃的有效療法。

2. 近年來，車站、醫院，甚至機場都有提供按摩的服務。

二、英文作文（占 20 分）

說明 1. 依提示在「答題卷」上寫一篇英文作文。
2. 文長至少 120 個單詞（words）。

提示：下圖顯示某個國家資源回收成果的狀況。請依據圖表內容寫一篇英文作文，文長至少 120 個單詞。文分二段，第一段描述圖表內容，指出該國垃圾回收的情形如何，第二段則說明你自家垃圾回收分類的比例與圖表上的異同，並解釋背後可能的原因。

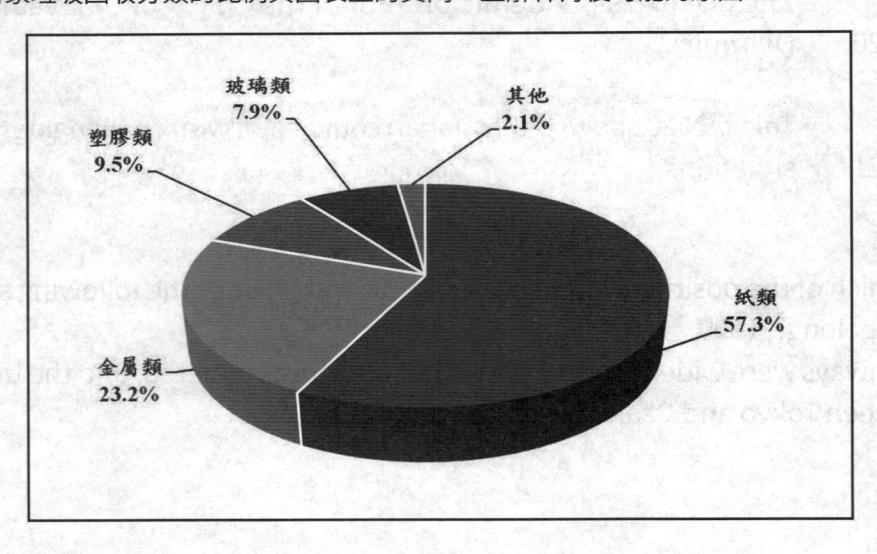

一張圓餅圖，顯示資源回收比例：
- 紙類 57.3%
- 金屬類 23.2%
- 塑膠類 9.5%
- 玻璃類 7.9%
- 其他 2.1%

TEST 08

🌱 第壹部分、選擇題

一、詞彙題
二、綜合測驗
三、文意選填
四、篇章結構
五、閱讀測驗

🌱 第貳部分、混合題

🌱 第參部分、非選擇題

一、中譯英
二、英文作文

第壹部分、選擇題（占 62 分）

一、詞彙題（占 10 分）

說明 第 1 題至第 10 題，每題 1 分。

1. Tammy's _____ was longer than usual because it took place when thousands of people were leaving a concert at Taipei Dome.
   (A) district   (B) council   (C) budget   (D) journey

2. The newly built hotel is in a _____ location, close to the best shops, bars, and restaurants in the city.
   (A) guilty   (B) fragile   (C) prime   (D) peculiar

3. Steve Jobs' success in the computer industry has _____ many young students around the world to pursue their dreams.
   (A) entertained   (B) endangered   (C) witnessed   (D) inspired

4. I felt really _____ when I didn't finish all the questions on my exam in two hours.
   (A) touched   (B) frustrated   (C) advanced   (D) delighted

5. _____, my sister crashed into a fence and damaged the family car the first time she took it out for a drive.
   (A) Accordingly   (B) Unfortunately (C) Undoubtedly   (D) Genetically

6. Wendy and her family had to _____ their home in the mountains as a result of the typhoon.
   (A) abandon   (B) revise   (C) violate   (D) console

7. The Golden Gate Bridge is the most distinct icon in California and one of the most recognizable _____ in the world.
   (A) landlords   (B) landmarks   (C) landscapes   (D) landslides

8. While the man's voice sounded quite calm, his facial _____ indicated that he was very worried.
   (A) discussions   (B) formations   (C) expressions   (D) intonations

9. This writer has a talent for describing common events in a _____ way. Her books never fail to make readers laugh out loud.
   (A) humorous   (B) defensive   (C) considerate   (D) pessimistic

TEST 08

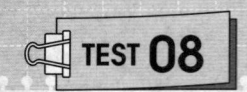

10. The _____ light at the restaurant added to its romantic atmosphere, but Johnny could barely read the menu.
    (A) tame　　　(B) frigid　　　(C) dim　　　(D) vivid

二、綜合測驗（占 10 分）

說明 第 11 題至第 20 題，每題 1 分。

第 11 至 15 題為題組

Just like bald eagles in the United States and kangaroos in Australia, elephants are symbolic of Thailand. The animals have long been valued by the country's population. However, in recent years, elephants have been pressed into service to help with industrial development and the __11__ of valuable timber from the country's tropical forests. Unfortunately, many go blind __12__ the work that they are forced to do. What's worse, when the work is done, the elephants are discarded. Basically, they are left to fend for themselves.

Elephants World was __13__ established to provide a home for these abused animals. Tourists can visit the elephants and help to feed and bathe them in a caring and controlled environment. British-born pianist Paul Barton was moved by the stories of the disabled beasts when he discovered the shelter online. He arranged to have his piano hauled to the park. There, he plays __14__. Amazingly, the elephants react by standing still and listening intently.

Elephants and humans have a lot __15__. They have long memories, communicate in complex ways, and are very social. They are also emotional. Elephants seem to be moved by music just as much as people are.

11. (A) harvesting　　(B) releasing　　(C) withdrawing　　(D) capturing
12. (A) in keeping with　(B) by means of　(C) apart from　(D) due to
13. (A) yet　　(B) instead　　(C) thus　　(D) otherwise
14. (A) sports with his friends　　(B) slow classical music
    (C) first chair in the band　　(D) in the entertainment business
15. (A) on demand　(B) in common　(C) within reach　(D) under control

第 16 至 20 題為題組

You probably haven't given too much thought to the knives used to prepare meals. Of course, some cut better than others, and for most people, that's probably as much as they would bother to think about these cutting tools. However, there are people like Bob Kramer, an American who has given a lot of __16__ to knives.

　　Kramer is one of the most famous knife makers in the world. In the early 1990s, he took a course on constructing knives and later __17__. After becoming a master bladesmith, he decided to sell his own products. He uses a special, time-consuming method of production that __18__ knives of outstanding quality. His philosophy, based on the Japanese idea of *kaizen*, is to constantly improve his skills.

　　Originally, his knives sold for about US$150 each. But after a cooking magazine reported that Kramer's knives were the best it had ever tested, the demand—and price—for his knives __19__. Soon, a waiting list for his knives formed. These days, his knives are sold at auctions at incredibly __20__ prices. To give just one example, a handmade knife from Kramer sold for US$30,000 in 2015. Now that is an expensive cutting tool to have in your kitchen!

16. (A) distribution　　(B) motivation　　(C) consideration　　(D) prediction
17. (A) hired a kitchen hand　　　　(B) polished the silverware
　　(C) struck the heated iron　　　　(D) made that his career
18. (A) convinces　　(B) forbids　　(C) forges　　(D) affords
19. (A) surprisingly plunged　　　　(B) greatly increased
　　(C) mistakenly overcharged　　　(D) unwillingly shrank
20. (A) steep　　(B) violent　　(C) chilly　　(D) massive

三、文意選填（占 10 分）

說明　第 21 題至第 30 題，每題 1 分。

第 21 至 30 題為題組

　　Glaciers are far more than just extremely huge, slow-moving rivers of ice. As they melt, they produce enormous __21__ of water, which eventually create lakes and rivers on land and icebergs in the ocean. Most glaciers form in mountains located in far northern __22__. One such location is the Yukon Territory in Canada, __23__ between the US state of Alaska and the great, desolate expanse of the Canadian Northwest Territories. The Kaskawulsh glacier originally fed two medium-sized rivers, the Slims and the Alsek. After a few months of the glacier melting in 2016, the Slims River all but dried up, while the Alsek became a __24__ river. How could this happen?

　　Geologists have long known that a lake- or river-feeding glacier can change course or meet __25__ on its slow flow down a mountain. As the glacier and its flow of water change course, the redirected water can __26__ a formerly dry land surface

103

like a plain or meadow, or it can add to already established sources of water like lakes or rivers. Scientists refer to this phenomenon as "river piracy" or "stream capture." Normally, this 27 may take hundreds of years. Indeed, no instance of river piracy had been recorded in 28 times. When this case of river piracy happened over the course of only a few days, it gave geologists a new puzzle to 29 .

In the case of the Kaskawulsh glacier, its leading edge was blocked by huge ice and rock boulders at the end of a canyon. This 30 runoff water to enter the Alsek River source instead of feeding both rivers. Basically, the Slims River was cut off from its source of water and rapidly disappeared. This is another example of the role glaciers play in shaping the landscape. It will be fascinating to see whether there are more instances like this in the near future.

(A) obstructions (B) process   (C) caused   (D) sandwiched (E) modern
(F) solve   (G) latitudes   (H) raging   (I) flood   (J) quantities

四、篇章結構（占 8 分）

說明 第 31 題至第 34 題，每題 2 分。

第 31 至 34 題為題組

Over the past couple of decades, there has been a growing phenomenon known as "nail art culture." 31 Not long ago, nail polish was viewed as a sophisticated type of makeup for women of means. Back then, mostly red and pink colored polishes were available. However, there have actually been numerous changes in the development and perception of nail polish over the centuries.

The history of nail polish is surprisingly long. By the time of what is accepted as the beginning of Chinese culture in 3000 B.C., some upper-class women were applying colors to their nails. 32 Hues of red or black were preferred in the Ming Dynasty, 2,000 years later. In addition, people from different social classes and in different countries preferred different colors. In Egypt, for example, the royalty and the elite painted their nails red while the lower class used subtler, paler shades.

With the rise of the middle class due to the Industrial Revolution, more women could afford to color their nails. However, the traditional look was the use of a single color for either or both the fingernails or toenails. This reflected the desired beauty standards of the time, with simplicity and cleanliness being preferred. Having one's nails painted was a sign of sophistication and elegance, traits which became highly regarded during those changing times.

Today, it seems that anything goes, and there is a rainbow assortment of colors and styles available. __33__ One such nail artist is Jenny Bui. Known as the "Queen of Bling," Bui fled from her native Cambodia in her teenage years and now owns two salons in New York that employ 20 people. __34__ Helped by this musical association, as well as a successful Instagram account which boasts over one million followers, Bui's position in the industry looks set to grow and grow.

(A) Many talented nail artists have emerged in the blossoming industry, and some have even become internationally famous.
(B) This refers to the creative application of nail polish on the fingernails or toenails, or both.
(C) Her signature designs are studded with crystals and are the favorite of the American rapper Cardi B.
(D) However, it is essential that all nail salons follow strict hygiene practices.
(E) By 600 B.C., Chou Dynasty royalty favored gold- and silver-colored nail polishes.

五、閱讀測驗（占 24 分）

說明 第 35 題至第 46 題，每題 2 分。

第 35 至 38 題為題組

Airlines are frequently criticized for hurting the environment. Critics generally point out that flying requires the burning of lots of fuel, which pollutes the air. However, people often overlook the enormous amount of trash that's produced by passengers inside the planes.

The garbage comes from the large amount of plastic that is left behind as a result of meals and drinks served during flights. Consider the sheer number of items you use, particularly on long-haul flights, that are either made of plastic or wrapped in plastic: meal containers, cutlery, snack wrappers, cups, and drink bottles, not to mention items such as headphones that come in plastic bags. According to the International Air Transport Association (IATA), airlines produced 6.7 million tons of cabin waste—comprising plastic, food, and other trash—in 2018. This figure is sure to grow. Although people are told that plastic is recyclable, it isn't really the case. Most of the plastic garbage produced on airplanes winds up in landfills because it's too expensive and time-consuming to process.

Some airlines have reacted to this worrying and unsustainable situation by taking steps to reduce the amount of plastic they use. On World Earth Day in 2019, Etihad

Airways operated a long-haul flight that didn't use any single-use plastics. That same year, Iberia Airlines brought in new trolleys that facilitate the collection and separation of waste for recycling. Ryanair has vowed to ditch all single-use plastics by 2023. However, there is no industry-wide strategy to reduce or eliminate the use of plastic on board planes. While the aforementioned airlines should be **lauded** for their specific efforts, there is still a long way to go. Plastic is light and cheap, and as yet there is no one material that can replace it. Until science produces such a material, it seems likely that you will continue to handle some form of plastic at 35,000 feet.

35. What is the second paragraph mainly about?
    (A) How airlines are using too much gasoline.
    (B) An airline that aims to save the environment.
    (C) How to reduce the cost of long-haul flights.
    (D) A way that airlines and passengers cause pollution.

36. According to the passage, what do most airlines do with their plastic trash?
    (A) They spend time sorting it out.
    (B) They send it to a recycling factory.
    (C) They toss it away into the trash.
    (D) They give it to the IATA to deal with.

37. What does "**lauded**" in the third paragraph most likely mean?
    (A) Criticized.　　(B) Praised.　　(C) Banned.　　(D) Punished.

38. How does the author feel about the chances of eliminating plastic on board planes?
    (A) It is certain to happen by the mid-2020s.
    (B) It can be achieved by specific airlines.
    (C) It is unlikely without a better alternative.
    (D) It will not happen on long-haul flights.

第 39 至 42 題為題組

As anyone who has ever dreamed, talked, or walked while sleeping will tell you, our brains are most certainly active during non-waking hours. There is in fact a study that proves that the brain can perform complex tasks—like classifying words—while we are asleep.

Researchers from France and the UK conducted the study—published in the journal *Current Biology*—which asked a group of male and female participants to complete a word classification task in a dark room. The task involved listening to spoken words and then either pressing a button with their right hand to classify the word as an animal or using their left hand to classify the word as an object. After the subjects had drifted off, they were still able to identify the words as accurately as when they were awake. The subjects didn't actually **respond physically** while asleep, but they exhibited the same activity in the right and left hemispheres of their brains that would normally cause their hands to push the buttons. The only differences were that it took them three times longer to classify the words, and they couldn't remember the words they had heard during sleep when they awoke.

Sid Kouider, one of the researchers, explained that this study may offer insight into why humans are responsive to their name or the specific sound of their alarm clock when sleeping, but can block out outside noises. It may also shed light on our ability to learn while asleep. We have known for a long time that sleep helps us consolidate what we have learned, but could it also help us to learn new things? This latter question raises an important issue: whether we should risk disrupting our regenerative slumber time by forcing our brain to learn. Kouider shares this concern: "Research focusing on how to take advantage of our sleeping time must consider what is the associated cost, if any, and whether it is worth it."

39. What is the main purpose of the second paragraph?
    (A) To identify the problems in a study.
    (B) To discuss the background of a journal.
    (C) To outline the details of an experiment.
    (D) To recognize the importance of sleep.

40. What does "**respond physically**" in the second paragraph refer to?
    (A) Turning on lights.
    (B) Pressing buttons.
    (C) Talking to researchers.
    (D) Blinking eyes.

41. What did it take participants triple the amount of time to do?
    (A) Wake up after a long sleep.
    (B) React to words while sleeping.
    (C) Push buttons during sleep.
    (D) Recite what they had learned.

42. What is implied in the last paragraph?
    (A) Disturbing our sleep to learn may not be worthwhile.
    (B) Sounds from outside are becoming harder to block.
    (C) Researching sleep learning is currently too expensive.
    (D) The right amount of light in a bedroom is important.

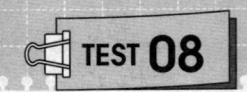

第 43 至 46 題為題組

Our ancestors long ago noticed that flowers and plants had a calming effect on them. Over time, they were able to extract the fragrances from these plants to make essential oils and create a medicinal practice known today as aromatherapy.

The ancient Egyptians used essential oils for cooking and bathing, but their primary use of them was for religious rituals. For instance, kyphi was burned in temples during the evenings in an offering to the gods. The ancient Chinese utilized the oils from aromatic plants and trees in both religious rituals and medicine. Sandalwood is one that was used medicinally, as it was believed that it could alleviate respiratory problems and treat skin conditions. The ancient Indians, meanwhile, employed essential oils in massage, using geranium and others to promote deep relaxation.

Nowadays, essential oils can be used in a variety of similar ways. They can be placed a few drops at a time into a hot bath, mixed with water and heated in an incense burner, or added to massage oil for a soothing and relaxing way to end the day. However, essential oils should never be applied directly to the skin without the use of a carrier oil to dilute them. It is also important to note that **they** can produce side effects in some people, so professional advice should be sought before using them.

There are many common essential oils, each with their own functions. Calming essential oils, which tend to be floral and sweet, include lavender and chamomile. Breathing in the former can help alleviate headaches, while rubbing its diluted oil on the skin can ease swelling and itching from bites. The latter can be inhaled through steam to reduce anxiety and calm a racing mind.

Invigorating essential oils, which are often fresh and fruity, include lemongrass and peppermint. Applying a diluted amount of the former can help to heal wounds and prevent infection, while inhaling the latter can promote digestive health and even reduce symptoms of irritable bowel syndrome. Rubbing diluted peppermint oil on the skin can also help to ease sunburn and muscle pain.

43. What is the main purpose of the second paragraph?
    (A) To argue that ancient cultures used aromatherapy for the same purpose.
    (B) To detail how aromatherapy has been used by various civilizations.
    (C) To probe the disputed origins of aromatherapy and essential oils.
    (D) To discuss the advantages and disadvantages of massage techniques.

44. What does "**they**" refer to in the third paragraph?
    (A) Carrier oils.
    (B) Massage oils.
    (C) Essential oils.
    (D) Incense burners.

45. Which use of essential oils is NOT mentioned in the passage?
    (A) Making them an element of your daily massage.
    (B) Incorporating them into your bathing routine.
    (C) Diluting them in a drink to cure feelings of nausea.
    (D) Inhaling them after they are burned along with water.

46. Jake can't sleep because he just ate a huge meal and he is worrying about work. Which two essential oils should he use?
    (A) Geranium and lavender.
    (B) Kyphi and chamomile.
    (C) Sandalwood and lemongrass.
    (D) Chamomile and peppermint.

TEST 08

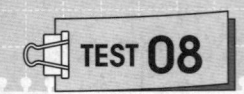

第貳部分、混合題（占 10 分）

說明　本部分共有 1 題組，每一子題配分標於題末。限在標示題號作答區內作答。選擇題使用 2B 鉛筆作答，更正時，應以橡皮擦擦拭，切勿使用修正液（帶）。非選擇題請由左而右橫式書寫。

第 47 至 50 題為題組

Not only are fossil fuels a finite resource, but the burning of them pollutes our planet and threatens an environmental catastrophe. That is why countries are investing in alternative sources of power. Here are four of them:

Solar

This is where we harness the Sun's power to create energy here on Earth. On a small scale, it involves solar panels attached to the roofs of buildings providing heat and light for those buildings. Installing these panels is expensive, but they can quickly result in significantly lower utility bills. On a large scale, it involves solar farms, which can provide power for whole communities. Solar energy is obviously very reliant on the weather, so places that tend to be cloudy—such as some coastal areas—are less suitable.

Wind

Like solar power, wind can provide energy to both individual homes (via small turbines) and large areas (via wind farms). However, wind power is unreliable, as both too little wind and too much wind can cause problems for turbines, and some people complain that these turbines are unsightly and noisy. Nevertheless, once up and running, their maintenance and operating costs are low, and the land they are on can also be used for agriculture.

Water

Water can generate power in multiple ways. For instance, flowing water over a waterfall or behind a dam can cause the blades of turbines to spin, which in turn powers generators. The movement of waves on the ocean can power generators that sit on the surface of the water. The predictable movement of the tides can do likewise. However, each of these uses is location-specific.

Nuclear

Nuclear plants use fission—the splitting of the nucleus of an atom—to produce energy. Proponents of nuclear power argue that it is low-cost and reliable, while the energy it creates can be used to remove the salt from sea water. Detractors point to the risks of nuclear accidents and the difficulty of disposing of the nuclear waste. Furthermore, nuclear power is not a renewable energy resource, as uranium—the fuel it uses—will not last forever. That is to say, it is finite.

47. Both wind and water power involve the use of ___47___ to generate energy.（填充，2 分）

48. Unlike solar power, which is unlimited, nuclear power depends on uranium, which is ___48___.（填充，2 分）

49. Some people are protesting against the proposed establishment of a wind farm near their homes. According to the passage, which TWO of the following slogans might they use?（多選題，4 分）
    (A) "No radiation near our homes!"
    (B) "They're too costly to repair!"
    (C) "An eyesore in our community!"
    (D) "The sound will be deafening!"
    (E) "Our utility bills will increase!"
    (F) "They're dangerous to install!"

50. Seaton is a large town that overlooks the sea. According to the passage, which form of alternative energy would be LEAST appropriate?（單選題，2 分）
    (A) Solar power.
    (B) Wind power.
    (C) Water power.
    (D) Nuclear power.

111

TEST 08

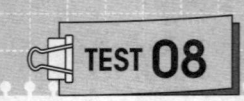

第參部分、非選擇題（占 28 分）

說明 本部分共有二大題，請依各題指示作答，答案必須寫在「答題卷」標示題號之作答區內，作答時不必抄題。

一、中譯英（占 8 分）

說明 1. 請將以下中文句子譯成正確、通順、達意的英文，並將答案寫在「答題卷」上。
2. 請依序作答，並標明子題號。每題 4 分，共 8 分。

1. 為了增加自己的競爭力，許多人會利用空閒時間學習第二語言。

2. 他們深信擁有良好的外語能力是脫穎而出的方式之一。

二、英文作文（占 20 分）

說明 1. 依提示在「答題卷」上寫一篇英文作文。
2. 文長至少 120 個單詞（words）。

提示：近來不知為何，你們教室突然開始出現很多垃圾，造成環境髒亂。請以衛生股長的身分（英文名字必須假設為 Paul 或 Rachel），寫一封信勸告亂丟垃圾的同學，請他們共同努力維持學習環境的舒適與整潔。

TEST 09

🌱 第壹部分、選擇題
- 一、詞彙題
- 二、綜合測驗
- 三、文意選填
- 四、篇章結構
- 五、閱讀測驗

🌱 第貳部分、混合題

🌱 第參部分、非選擇題
- 一、中譯英
- 二、英文作文

第壹部分、選擇題（占 62 分）

一、詞彙題（占 10 分）

說明 第 1 題至第 10 題，每題 1 分。

1. It is highly _____ that the trade war between the two countries will result in anything positive for either side.
   (A) racial (B) prior (C) vain (D) doubtful

2. If the world continues to get warmer, the _____ conclusion is that more ice will melt and sea levels will rise.
   (A) visual (B) logical (C) multiple (D) messy

3. Sometimes famous movie stars and big-name directors are no _____ that their movie will be a blockbuster.
   (A) guarantee (B) chemistry (C) insurance (D) blossom

4. When you travel to a foreign country, you should _____ of pickpockets. You could get your money and passports stolen if you're not careful.
   (A) gesture (B) frown (C) beware (D) inquire

5. Vanessa _____ a horrific knee injury and will be back playing tennis again by the time this year's tournament rolls around.
   (A) overcame (B) controlled (C) pursued (D) awaited

6. The flight attendants politely _____ everyone to fasten their seat belts and listen to the safety announcement before take-off.
   (A) calculated (B) withdrew (C) instructed (D) assigned

7. Janice was suffering from a bad cold, but after a few days of rest, she _____ got better and returned to work.
   (A) precisely (B) gradually (C) regularly (D) practically

8. Most college students prefer to wear _____ clothing, such as jeans, graphic T-shirts, and hoodies.
   (A) formal (B) splendid (C) casual (D) naughty

9. Anna presented her teacher with a bunch of flowers at the graduation ceremony as an expression of _____.
   (A) privilege (B) dominance (C) curiosity (D) gratitude

115

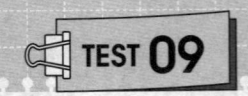

10. All songs on this website are protected by _____. It's illegal to download and share them without permission.
    (A) privacy   (B) discipline   (C) copyright   (D) moral

二、綜合測驗（占 10 分）

說明 第 11 題至第 20 題，每題 1 分。

第 11 至 15 題為題組

When you mention wine, you'll often hear words like "aroma" and "bouquet" being tossed around. Both terms are used to describe the smell of wine.   11 , they refer to the origins of the smells.

There are three categories of wine smells. The first, or primary, aromas come from the type of grape   12   to make the wine. These are often fruit, floral, and herbal flavors like peach, rose, and mint, respectively. The secondary ones are the results of the fermentation process. Due to the yeast added   13   in winemaking, the smell can be reminiscent of beer or old cheese. The third, or tertiary, aromas develop when the wine   14   the process of aging. This is often done in oak barrels, which infuse the wine with wood and nutty flavors. Sweet smells, such as those of caramel and tobacco, are common in this category.

When it comes to a wine's aroma and bouquet, the difference is simple. Aroma refers to its primary scents, while bouquet includes all of its secondary and tertiary smells. Although smelling wine is not exactly scientific, it does provide an interesting   15   into the process used to create the well-loved alcoholic beverage.

11. (A) Scarcely   (B) Specifically   (C) Relatively   (D) Accordingly
12. (A) usage   (B) uses   (C) using   (D) used
13. (A) across the vineyard   (B) during this stage
    (C) on the shelves   (D) beside the storage
14. (A) brings along   (B) comes across   (C) goes through   (D) takes over
15. (A) insight   (B) agency   (C) emission   (D) legend

第 16 至 20 題為題組

Just a stone's throw away from Vladivostok, the largest city in the far east of Russia, is a quiet little area called Ussuri Bay. It has recently caught the attention of people all over the world, not for its black sand beach, but for the unusual   16   on its shores.

As the story goes, back when Russia was still part of the Soviet Union, truck after truck would dump their loads in the bay. The waste they carried was __17__ broken jars, cracked pieces from a local porcelain factory, and empty beer, wine, and vodka bottles. Rather than simply turning into an __18__ garbage dump, though, something extraordinary happened. Over time, the pounding of the waves in and out of the bay __19__ the sharp edges of the broken glass and ceramics. What's more, it polished them into colorful pebbles that now look more like jewels than stones.

Known locally as Glass Beach, it has drawn crowds of tourists to its rainbow shores for decades. However, due to a combination of visitors pocketing the pebbles and the continual erosion by the sea, the beach might not be around in its current state __20__.

16. (A) lifeguard   (B) perfume   (C) reptile   (D) garbage
17. (A) fed up with   (B) used as   (C) made up of   (D) worn out by
18. (A) edible   (B) innocent   (C) optimistic   (D) unsightly
19. (A) smoothed   (B) squeezed   (C) teased   (D) delivered
20. (A) on a daily basis   (B) for much longer
    (C) in the peak season   (D) from time to time

三、文意選填（占 10 分）

說明 第 21 題至第 30 題，每題 1 分。

第 21 至 30 題為題組

The late British theoretical physicist Stephen Hawking has at times been called the modern-day Einstein. His work in the theory and mathematics of black holes and other astronomical phenomena __21__ him this recognition. He was the director of research at the Centre for Theoretical Cosmology, he received the Presidential Medal of Freedom, and he was the best-selling author of *A Brief History of Time*. Put simply, when Hawking talked, not only the entire scientific community but the entire world listened. His comments about the future of mankind still deserve careful attention.

Hawking __22__ the many problems facing the human race today. Social problems such as war, famine, and economic depression, as well as environmental threats, including the hole in the ozone layer, acid rain, and global warming, __23__ Hawking to suggest that the only solution is a future based off planet Earth. In other words, human __24__ may well depend on our ability to live on the moon, Mars, or other astronomical bodies. The human population is now over seven billion and __25__ reach nine billion by the middle of the 21st century. There simply aren't enough

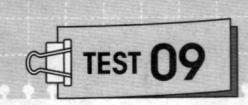

26   for everyone to live a secure and prosperous life. Only by   27   at least part of the globe's population to other worlds in space will the human species be able to survive.

Of course, Hawking was aware of the expense and technical difficulties of living outside of the Earth when he suggested this idea. He also warned that should we meet aliens in space, we should be   28   of them since they are unlikely to be friendly. This picture of man's   29   fate is quite dark, yet not totally unreasonable. Perhaps by   30   a worst-case scenario, Hawking was encouraging us all to pay more attention to our common problems and work together to solve them.

(A) wary (B) is expected to (C) was concerned about (D) survival
(E) resources (F) removing (G) earned (H) painting (I) led
(J) ultimate

四、篇章結構（占 8 分）

說明 第 31 題至第 34 題，每題 2 分。

第 31 至 34 題為題組

The Maya were a relatively advanced civilization that occupied territory in present-day Mexico and Central America for over 3,000 years. Dating back to around 900 BC, Tikal was once the heart of this civilization. Initially a small village, Tikal grew into a huge city with an estimated population of just under 100,000. By the 10th century AD, it had been abandoned, but in its prime it was an important center for trade and commerce.

Located in the jungle of what is now northern Guatemala, Tikal is best known for its grand architecture.   31   Also impressive were the three large complexes called acropoles, which were made up of temples and palaces presumably for the upper class. However, the most imposing structures were the six major temples, where respects could be paid to former kings.   32

Two of these star-gazing temples stood out in particular. The Temple of the Great Jaguar rose 45 meters from the ground and consisted of nine tiers.   33   At 42 meters, the Temple of the Masks stood west of it. Together, they marked the ends of the Great Plaza. This was a vast public space that was surrounded by palaces, terraces, and ball courts.

The ruins of those grand structures are the main attraction at Tikal National Park. Established in the 1950s, it was declared a UNESCO World Heritage Site in 1979 and now receives around 200,000 visitors every year. The park comprises nearly 60,000 hectares of wetlands, savannah, and rainforest. 34 Five big cat species, several types of monkeys and anteaters, and more than 300 bird species are among some of the more notable wildlife. Over 200 different types of trees and 2,000 recorded plants make up the forests. The park and Tikal have become a source of pride as well as a national symbol for Guatemala.

(A) It was this natural disaster that caused many of the temples to collapse.
(B) It is home to a wide variety of plants and animals.
(C) More than 3,000 buildings occupied the city center alone, covering around 16 square kilometers.
(D) It was from these places of worship that the Maya also tracked the movements of the planets and stars.
(E) Each of these corresponded to one of the nine levels of the Maya underworld.

五、閱讀測驗（占 24 分）

說明 第 35 題至第 46 題，每題 2 分。

第 35 至 38 題為題組

The *Victoria amazonica* is a water lily that grows in the calm, shallow waters of South America's Amazon River basin. Almost like something out of a science-fiction movie, this plant is the largest water lily on the planet. It was first identified in 1801 by Thaddäus Haenke, a botanist and explorer from what is now the Czech Republic. It was introduced to Europe in the mid-19th century, but its natural habitat will always be in and around the Amazon.

The defining characteristics of the *Victoria amazonica* are its enormous leaves and special flowers. The circular, green leaves can grow up to three meters in diameter, and it is said they are strong enough to hold a person or animal that weighs up to 30 kilograms. They have a lip around the edge that is notched to facilitate the drainage of water, and they have a ribbed underside that traps air and helps to keep them afloat. The plant also produces delicate-looking white flowers that grow to a diameter of up to 40 centimeters, but they only last for 48 hours. During that time, they use their sweet, pineapple-like scent to attract flying beetles to pollinate them. After a beetle lands on the flower, it closes up temporarily and loses its scent. The flowers don't eat the insects, though, releasing them the next evening to fly away and carry pollen to other water lilies. By this time, the flowers have changed from white to pink, and from female to male.

Also notable about the *Victoria amazonica* is **its unseen portion**. Under the surface of the water, the plant's stalks extend eight meters downward and embed themselves in the river bed. They feature sharp spikes that protect them from fish that might otherwise want to feed on the plant. Truly, the *Victoria amazonica* is a wonder to behold.

35. What is this passage mainly about?
    (A) The variety of plant life in South America.
    (B) Research conducted on special vegetation.
    (C) The fascinating features of a unique plant.
    (D) Different water lilies found across the globe.

36. Why is the Czech Republic mentioned in the passage?
    (A) It is where the plant was first discovered.
    (B) It is where the scientist who found the plant was from.
    (C) It is where most of the plants are currently grown.
    (D) It is where the plant was studied in great detail.

37. Which of the following statements about the flowers of the *Victoria amazonica* is true?
    (A) They switch color on the second day.
    (B) They attract beetles in order to eat them.
    (C) They change sex from male to female.
    (D) They are large enough to support a person.

38. What does "**its unseen portion**" in the last paragraph refer to?
    (A) The bottom of the leaves.   (B) The stalks of the plant.
    (C) The bed of the river.   (D) The pollen of the flowers.

第 39 至 42 題為題組

The magnificent song called "Silent Night" has long been adored by people celebrating the Christmas season. In fact, it is the most beloved Christmas song ever, having been translated into more than 300 languages.

In 2018, Austria celebrated the 200th anniversary of the creation of "Silent Night," owing to the fact that the songwriters were

Austrian. "Silent Night" was first performed by the two men who penned the music and lyrics: a music teacher named Franz Xaver Gruber and a **clergyman** named Joseph Mohr. They sang the song on Christmas Eve of 1818, although Mohr had written it as a poem while working as an assistant priest two years earlier. It is believed that Gruber wrote the music for the guitar and played it on that instrument because the organ in the church where they sang wasn't operational. In fact, the church—St. Nicholas Church in Oberndorf bei Salzburg—was later damaged beyond repair by several floods. It was ultimately replaced by the Silent Night Chapel, which now stands as a monument to the song.

Before long, others perceived the beauty of "Silent Night," and it started to be played in other regions. Two families of singers, the Rainer Family and the Strasser Siblings, loved it so much that they included it in their performances as they traveled around. Through them, it was performed in England, Germany, and Sweden, eventually gaining the slightly different melody that we are familiar with today. It became extensively known in Europe when the song was published in a book. However, it was not until American singer Bing Crosby recorded his version of "Silent Night" in 1935 that the song became popular all over the globe.

By that time, Mohr had been forgotten as one of the writers of the song. It was widely assumed that a well-known figure such as Mozart or Beethoven had been responsible for it. However, Mohr's handwritten copy of the poem was found in 1995, which proved he was one of the songwriters of "Silent Night." Thus, he regained his place as the co-creator of one of the most-cherished Christmas tunes in the world.

39. What would be the most suitable title for the passage?
    (A) The Most Popular Austrian Christmas Songs
    (B) A Very Brief History of Song Translation
    (C) The Origins and Evolution of a Famous Tune
    (D) An Introduction to the Silent Night Chapel

40. What does "**clergyman**" in the second paragraph most likely mean?
    (A) School principal.   (B) Tour guide.
    (C) Organ player.   (D) Religious leader.

41. What made the song "Silent Night" popular worldwide?
    (A) A German traveler wrote a new version of it.
    (B) An English singer introduced it to his family.
    (C) A Swedish author wrote a book about it.
    (D) An American singer released a version of it.

42. What does the last paragraph imply about Joseph Mohr and "Silent Night"?
    (A) His involvement in the song was unfairly overlooked for years.
    (B) His idea for the song was stolen from a famous composer.
    (C) His contribution to the song has long been overstated.
    (D) His terrible handwriting caused the lyrics to be misread.

第 43 至 46 題為題組

A boutonnière is a flower that is worn on the lapel of a suit jacket or tuxedo. Lapels are the folded strips of cloth on the front of jackets. Although you may see boutonnières being worn in various positions—for instance, on the right side of the jacket or in the breast pocket—there is actually only one suitable position, and that is in the lapel buttonhole, on the wearer's left side of the jacket. The stem of the flower is usually kept in place by a small loop at the back of the buttonhole. If there is no loop present, the flower may be pinned to the jacket to keep it secure.

Opinions differ as to the origins of boutonnières. Some claim that they can be traced back to ancient Egypt, while others point to the decorations first being worn during the English Civil War to identify the opposing sides. However, it is in the 18th and 19th centuries that boutonnières as we would recognize them became popular. It was thought that wearing a flower as part of one's attire warded off not only bad smells but also evil spirits. Furthermore, these accessories became daily fashion statements and were viewed as a sign of refinement and sophistication. This idea persisted well into the 20th century.

These days, boutonnières are reserved for formal occasions, such as weddings and proms. At weddings, the color of the boutonnière will likely match the color of the bride's bouquet. It is standard practice for the men in the wedding party—that is, the groom, best man, and fathers of the bride and groom—to all wear a boutonnière. The groom's, though, will probably be bigger or special in some way. Tradition also dictates the type of flowers to use, with red or white carnations, blue cornflowers, or white gardenias being the most familiar. However, other flowers are increasingly being chosen, and it is most often the wishes of the bride and groom and the color scheme of the wedding that determine the choice of this important finishing touch.

43. According to the passage, where is the correct position for the boutonnière?
    (A) Position A.
    (B) Position B.
    (C) Position C.
    (D) Position D.

44. Which of the following words are used in the passage to refer to the boutonnière?
    a. decoration   b. wish   c. accessory   d. flower   e. bouquet   f. touch
    (A) a, b, d, f
    (B) b, c, d, e
    (C) a, b, c, d
    (D) a, c, d, f

45. Which potential origin of boutonnières is NOT mentioned in the passage?
    (A) They were worn by people in an old civilization.
    (B) They were adopted as everyday wear in the 1800s.
    (C) They were created to identify different families.
    (D) They were used to distinguish people on a battlefield.

46. According to the passage, what most likely dictates the choice of boutonnières at a modern wedding?
    (A) The height and build of the bridegroom.
    (B) The availability of flowers at the florist.
    (C) The desires of the couple getting married.
    (D) The size of the accompanying bouquet.

TEST 09

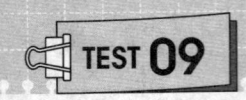

第貳部分、混合題（占 10 分）

> **說明** 本部分共有 1 題組，每一子題配分標於題末。限在標示題號作答區內作答。選擇題使用 2B 鉛筆作答，更正時，應以橡皮擦擦拭，切勿使用修正液（帶）。非選擇題請由左而右橫式書寫。

第 47 至 51 題為題組

Here is a news report and four people's opinions on the issue it raises.

Don't Forget Your Toothbrush!
By Adam Denehy
Staff Reporter

Hotels in Taiwan are now prohibited from providing single-use toiletries to their guests. The new regulations, which came into effect January 1, state that hotels cannot supply items such as shower gel and shampoo in containers less than 180 ml. In addition, they are not allowed to provide personal hygiene products such as combs, razors, and toothbrushes in the rooms. Guests can bring their own, or they can acquire or buy such items from reception. The policy is designed to reduce plastic waste and promote sustainability.

(A) Eleanor

It is clear to me that this policy is good for the environment. When I was cleaning rooms in the past, I frequently had to throw away half-used bottles of shampoo and conditioner. Now, I just refill the big bottles that we keep in the rooms. I'm sure some guests moan to reception about no longer being provided with tiny tubes of toothpaste, but it's a small price to pay for a cleaner planet.

(B) Rhett

Complimentary toiletries are one of the advantages of staying in a hotel. I travel to Taiwan regularly for business, and I used to like the fact that I would be presented with my own little set of toiletries in my hotel room. That way, I could freshen up properly before meeting clients without worrying about whether I'd forgotten to pack anything. These days, I have to bring everything from a razor to a comb with me.

(C) Sylvia

I can appreciate the need to reduce plastic waste, but those in the government who come up with these ideas don't have to deal with annoyed hotel guests. Even though we have published the new rules on our website, people are still shocked when I remind them about the policy at check-in. Then, they complain about paying for a toothbrush or a razor that they didn't realize they needed to bring.

(D) Chad

Aside from slashing plastic waste, this policy has a myriad of other benefits. These include: reducing carbon emissions by an estimated 2,500 metric tons annually, encouraging people to adopt more sustainable habits in other areas of their lives, showing that Taiwan is a responsible player on the global stage, and many more. I, for one, am proud of the role I played in implementing this policy.

47-49. Write the letter of the people above next to their most likely job title.（填空，6分）

Hotel desk clerk: _____47_____

Hotel housekeeper: _____48_____

Traveling salesman: _____49_____

50. Which single-use item is mentioned in the news article AND at least TWO of the RESPONSES?（單選，2分）

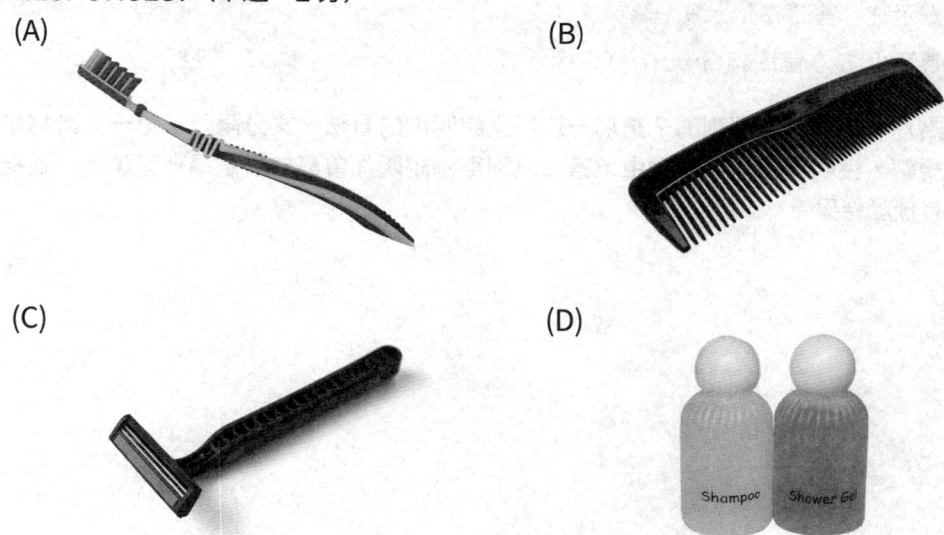

(A)　　　　　　　　　　　(B)

(C)　　　　　　　　　　　(D)

51. Which word in the responses means "a very large number of something"? （簡答，2分）

TEST 09

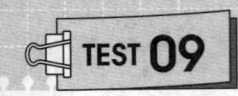

第參部分、非選擇題（占 28 分）

說明 本部分共有二大題，請依各題指示作答，答案必須寫在「答題卷」標示題號之作答區內，作答時不必抄題。

一、中譯英（占 8 分）

說明 1. 請將以下中文句子譯成正確、通順、達意的英文，並將答案寫在「答題卷」上。
2. 請依序作答，並標明子題號。每題 4 分，共 8 分。

1. 行動支付結合了消費者的錢包與手機而成為新的消費趨勢。

2. 這讓人們就算沒有攜帶任何現金也可以在店家購物。

二、英文作文（占 20 分）

說明 1. 依提示在「答題卷」上寫一篇英文作文。
2. 文長至少 120 個單詞（words）。

提示：你認為凡事都要事前規劃嗎？請寫一篇短文說明你的看法。文分兩段，第一段針對是否要事前規劃，說明你的看法及理由，第二段則舉例說明你曾事前規劃過什麼事情，並描述規劃後有什麼結果。

TEST 10

第壹部分、選擇題
一、詞彙題
二、綜合測驗
三、文意選填
四、篇章結構
五、閱讀測驗

第貳部分、混合題

第參部分、非選擇題
一、中譯英
二、英文作文

第壹部分、選擇題（占 62 分）

一、詞彙題（占 10 分）

說明　第 1 題至第 10 題，每題 1 分。

1. The two celebrities posted a _____ statement on Instagram, announcing that they were going to get married in the summer.
   (A) cunning　　　(B) steady　　　(C) satisfactory　　　(D) joint

2. Amelia was disappointed that she was unable to _____ tickets to see Taylor Swift because they sold out too quickly.
   (A) purchase　　　(B) cite　　　(C) compromise　　　(D) sue

3. The annual safety _____ at the factory will be focused on fire prevention, emergency lighting, and backup power.
   (A) limitation　　　(B) association　　　(C) inspection　　　(D) composition

4. This swimming pool is so _____ that even my three-year-old sister can easily stand up in it.
   (A) dense　　　(B) shallow　　　(C) narrow　　　(D) gigantic

5. The ballet dancer danced so gracefully that everyone in the audience was amazed by her _____ moves.
   (A) awkward　　　(B) tricky　　　(C) elegant　　　(D) solemn

6. Make sure to _____ anti-virus software programs before connecting your new computer to the internet.
   (A) adapt　　　(B) equip　　　(C) install　　　(D) relate

7. The experienced teacher employs a variety of teaching _____ to meet the learning needs of different students.
   (A) bulletins　　　(B) techniques　　　(C) souvenirs　　　(D) invitations

8. On Halloween night, many children dress up in scary _____ and try to frighten their neighbors into giving them treats.
   (A) costumes　　　(B) remarks　　　(C) fabrics　　　(D) wagons

9. The fish dishes at that restaurant are some of the best I've ever had. _____, they are fresh and inexpensive.
   (A) Perhaps　　　(B) Somehow　　　(C) Nevertheless　　　(D) Furthermore

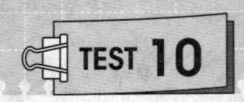

10. Jeffery's factory _____ zippers in all sizes and colors and exports them to countries all over the globe.
    (A) manufactures   (B) demonstrates   (C) constructs   (D) harvests

二、綜合測驗（占 10 分）

說明 第 11 題至第 20 題，每題 1 分。

第 11 至 15 題為題組

　　The Book Café in Shimla, India, was in many ways just a simple coffeehouse. It had enough seats for 40 customers, a(n) __11__ of delicious snacks and tasty drinks, and over 450 books for the customers to enjoy. Visitors could also relax and take in the breathtaking view of the mountains.

　　__12__ made the Book Café different from all other cafés, though, was its staff. It was run by four convicted criminals who were __13__ life sentences at the nearby Kaithu Jail. Away from the watchful eyes of prison officers, they worked from 10:00 a.m. to 9:00 p.m. every day. After that, they strolled back to the prison for the night.

　　The first of its kind, the Book Café was created by the Himachal Pradesh prison department to help convicts change their ways. It gave them the opportunity to be a __14__ part of society while also earning money for their families. After opening in April 2017, the Book Café gave the prisoners new skills and a chance to connect with __15__. More importantly, it allowed them to live with dignity and feel like they really mattered. Unfortunately, in 2019, the Book Café was taken over by a businessman and has since permanently closed.

11. (A) abortion   (B) selection   (C) possession   (D) description
12. (A) That   (B) All   (C) Where   (D) What
13. (A) serving   (B) appointing   (C) deceiving   (D) exhibiting
14. (A) fluent   (B) delicate   (C) negative   (D) productive
15. (A) the annual coffee trade fair   (B) the information center there
    (C) the outside world again   (D) the security guard now

第 16 至 20 題為題組

　　A new study is making contact lens wearers see the error of their ways. __16__ by researchers at Arizona State University, it reveals that many of these consumers are unknowingly polluting the environment. The deed is done when they flush their contacts down the drain or the toilet.

Just like single-use straws, grocery bags, and eating __17__, contact lenses are made of plastic and readily disposable. They are also very common. In fact, in the US alone, 45 million people use them to see clearly. That amounts to roughly 15 billion lenses worn a year. Sadly, 20% of them end up in the sewer.

The tiny bits of plastic are then further broken down into microplastics at water treatment plants. As they are __18__ impossible to filter out, they make it into the ground with the wastewater. What's more, they flow into rivers and __19__. By then, the harm is already done because birds, fish, and other animals will mistakenly consume microplastics that look like tasty food to them. That, in turn, introduces the __20__ into the larger food chain.

Rather than flushing their contacts down the toilet, contact lens wearers should place them in the trash alongside other household garbage.

16. (A) Reserved   (B) Conducted   (C) Suspended   (D) Maintained
17. (A) utensils   (B) outfits   (C) facilities   (D) appliances
18. (A) other than   (B) as far as   (C) next to   (D) by no means
19. (A) later have been recycled   (B) then create huge waves
    (C) eventually out to sea   (D) finally improve the ecosystem
20. (A) cargoes   (B) diplomas   (C) faucets   (D) pollutants

三、文意選填（占 10 分）

說明 第 21 題至第 30 題，每題 1 分。

第 21 至 30 題為題組

Many tourists who travel to Taiwan visit only Taipei City and its surrounding areas, such as Tamsui, Keelung, and Ruifang. There is so much more to see in Taiwan, though. Too many tourists __21__ the splendors of Taiwan's east coast, Kenting National Park, and the offshore islands of Penghu and Lanyu. Another site unknown to many travelers is the Alishan Forest Railway, located in the county of Chiayi.

This railway system was built in 1912 during the Japanese __22__. Its original purpose was for logging. By 1918, however, passenger cars were added to the 86-kilometer network for tourists to take advantage of the __23__ views of Taiwan's Central Mountain Range, culminating at the top of Alishan. Where else can you travel from an __24__ of 30 to 2,216 meters by rail? As the altitude increases, the vegetation changes from tropical to temperate to alpine. After Taiwan's liberation in 1945, the Alishan Forest Railway continued to be used for commercial purposes. When the Alishan Highway was opened in the 1980s, the railway became __25__ a tourist attraction.

TEST 10

Unfortunately, the Alishan district __26__ earthquakes and sometimes typhoons. Over the years, these have damaged the railway lines and __27__ the network's usage. These problems, __28__ man-made faults such as derailments, have reduced the appeal of the Alishan Forest Railway. This is a pity because such a network is now __29__ used anywhere else in the world. Interestingly, the network lines are anything but straight. The whole network includes 50 tunnels, 77 wooden bridges, and Z-shaped switchbacks, guaranteeing an exciting ride. However, this also means that fixing the lines can be a complex and time-consuming task. Hopefully, they won't need to be __30__ too many times in the future, and the Alishan Forest Railway can continue to serve tourists at home and from abroad.

(A) breathtaking (B) is prone to   (C) miss out on   (D) rarely   (E) primarily
(F) occupation   (G) along with   (H) elevation   (I) repaired   (J) restricted

四、篇章結構（占 8 分）

說明 第 31 題至第 34 題，每題 2 分。

第 31 至 34 題為題組

It was a long time coming, but the National Taichung Theater finally opened for business in 2016. __31__ This futuristic, multi-media-capable structure has put the central Taiwanese city of Taichung on the map.

As early as 1992, Taiwan's central government proposed a National Musical House. Ten years later, due to the efforts of Jason Hu, the then mayor of Taichung, the government decided to locate the building in his city. Toyo Ito and 32 other architects from 12 countries contributed their design plans. __32__ This is the same year that the National Stadium in Kaohsiung, also designed by Ito, opened.

The structure of the National Taichung Theater is nothing short of eye-popping. The theater is situated in a huge park surrounded by high-tech skyscrapers. The building is basically rectangular but is covered by wavy designs, breaking the straight-line edges of so many tedious, modern buildings. The walls inside the theater are curved, lending an air of fluidity to both the rooms and the performances. Ito also included eco-friendly features in the design. __33__ The materials used in the building are recyclable. Even the building's shape reduces energy consumption.

The inside of the theater is even more exciting. The Grand Theater is the crown jewel of the building, seating 2,007 art lovers for each performance. Additionally, a 794-seat Playhouse and 200-seat Black Box can accommodate other, mostly nonmusical artistic presentations. Across these spaces, the theater holds many annual festivals, including the Taiwan International Festival of Arts, Summer Fun Time, and Fall for Great Souls.

　　Taichung is the perfect destination for it. __34__ Now, with the popularity of the National Taichung Theater, the city has also marked itself out as a center for the arts. And even when there are no performances taking place, a walk through the theater is a feast for the eyes.

(A) Rainwater is collected from the roof to be used to water the surrounding park and gardens, as well as in restroom toilets.
(B) Designed by world-famous Japanese architect Toyo Ito, it actually looks as though it were designed by aliens.
(C) Ito won the competition and was contracted in 2009 to design the National Taichung Theater.
(D) Clean, efficient, and vibrant, the city has all the makings of a sustainable 21st century metropolis.
(E) The musician's performance at the venue on opening night received largely positive reviews from critics.

五、閱讀測驗（占 24 分）

說明　第 35 題至第 46 題，每題 2 分。

第 35 至 38 題為題組

　　Wine has been around for thousands of years. The earliest known winery dates back more than 6,000 years. Located in Armenia, it was found in a cave complex. Caves and underground cellars are ideal locations for storing wine owing to their cool environments and regular humidity levels. But now there is a new trend for cellaring wine: underwater storage.

　　Crusoe Treasure in Spain is one such winery that is turning to the sea to age its wine. Once their wine is bottled, instead of putting the bottles on shelves or keeping them in a temperature-controlled room, they drop them into the ocean. Actually, the process of getting the wine to the sea floor is quite technical. Cranes aboard boats are used to lower cages filled with specially sealed wine bottles, while a diver monitors temperature and water pressure. Once underwater, **they** are left there for up to 18 months.

133

TEST 10

The firm's founder, Borja Saracho, says that this environment—increased atmospheric pressure, darkness, and a constant temperature—produces wines that are unusually soft and silky. Reflecting on his experience of drinking the company's first underwater wines, he told the British newspaper *The Guardian* that they were "astounding. The wines' evolution underwater was very distinct from what would happen with the same grape on land." Saracho was inspired to start the project after hearing reports of superb century-old champagne that had been discovered on the bed of the Baltic Sea.

For their unusual venture, Crusoe Treasure has been granted the use of 500 square meters of seabed by the Spanish government. This is because the concrete structures the company uses to age their wine can act as an artificial reef, which helps to sustain marine wildlife. So, it seems the winery is doing good while making some enjoyable wine.

35. According to the passage, why are underground cellars perfect for wine storage?
    (A) They have ideal temperature and humidity levels.
    (B) They can store many bottles of wine at a time.
    (C) They keep bottles out of direct sunlight.
    (D) They are easy to maintain and keep clean.

36. What does "**they**" in the second paragraph refer to?
    (A) The boats.　　(B) The cranes.　　(C) The bottles.　　(D) The divers.

37. How did Borja Saracho get the idea for underwater wine storage?
    (A) He read an article that was published in *The Guardian*.
    (B) He went swimming and diving in the Baltic Sea.
    (C) He heard positive things about a discovery of champagne.
    (D) He was told about a similar project in the UK.

38. Why did the Spanish government grant Crusoe Treasure the use of 500 square meters of sea bed?
    (A) It will help Spain pay off its many national debts.
    (B) It will assist in the preservation of local marine life.
    (C) It will attract tourists and thus boost the local economy.
    (D) It will protect Spain from the threat of foreign invasions.

第 39 至 42 題為題組

One of the most important trees in the world is the baobab. Found in India, Australia, mainland Africa, and Madagascar, baobabs are one of the largest trees on Earth. They can grow anywhere from 5 to 30 meters in height. They also have branchless trunks that reach 7 to 11 meters in diameter and can hold up to 120,000 liters of water. The few branches they have on top are often without leaves, making them look like roots and giving the trees the appearance of being upside down.

    Baobabs provide food, water, and shelter for both humans and animals. Called monkey bread, baobab fruit is full of vitamin C, vitamin B6, potassium, magnesium, and calcium. It is eaten everywhere the tree is found, and depending on the traditional recipes of each area, can be added to soups, stews, and desserts. In the West, where fresh baobab fruit is scarce, most people buy it in powdered form and add it to smoothies and juices. Baobab fruit is high in fiber, which can help you to feel fuller for longer, so if you're looking to lose weight, this fruit might be **just what the doctor ordered**. The trees' cork-like bark, meanwhile, is often used to make rope and clothing, as it is resistant to fire. Also, their leaves are turned into seasoning and medicine. No wonder baobabs are respectfully called the tree of life.

    With the ability to survive harsh conditions, baobabs live hundreds to thousands of years. However, that may no longer be the case, because they are mysteriously dying. A team of researchers from the US, Romania, and South Africa have been visiting ancient baobabs across southern Africa since the early 2000s. Using radiocarbon dating, they study and investigate the age and structure of the trees. Sadly, they have recently reported that the majority of the oldest and largest baobabs have died. They were all between 1,000 and 2,500 years old. The researchers pin the blame on climate change, citing increased temperatures and prolonged droughts in the baobabs' habitats.

39. Which of the following is NOT a feature of baobabs?
    (A) Densely packed branches.
    (B) Trunks like storage tanks.
    (C) Extremely long life spans.
    (D) Enormous size and shape.

40. What does "**just what the doctor ordered**" in the second paragraph imply?
    (A) Medical professionals often prescribe baobab powder to patients.
    (B) Eating baobab fruit could be exactly what you need to do to become slimmer.
    (C) The nutritional benefits of the baobab fruit have been overstated.
    (D) Baobab smoothies are often ordered with brunch in western countries.

41. Which part of the baobab can repel flames?
    (A) Their fruit.　　(B) Their leaves.　　(C) Their branches.　　(D) Their bark.

42. What did researchers discover this century?
    (A) Older baobab trees are stronger than younger ones.
    (B) The warming planet has caused many baobabs to die.
    (C) Baobabs have started to grow elsewhere in the world.
    (D) Radiocarbon dating is not a suitable way to study trees.

第 43 至 46 題為題組

William Moulton Marston was an American psychologist who lived during the first half of the 20th century. He is particularly famous for inventing an early version of the lie detector test and for creating the DC Comics character Wonder Woman. However, it is his development of a theory about personalities that is arguably his most fascinating achievement.

Marston outlined his theory in *Emotions of Normal People*, published in 1928. Rather than investigate the actions of criminals or the mentally ill, as many of his peers did, Marston sought to explain the behavior of "normal" everyday people. While acknowledging that people act for different reasons in different environments and therefore cannot be definitively categorized, he created four broad personality types that correspond to the letters DISC. Those who exhibit traits of Dominance use force to deal with situations, while those who show traits of Inducement use charm. People who display qualities of Submission voluntarily accept the need to do things, while people who show signs of Compliance adapt to the will of others in a more fearful way.

In the years since Marston first outlined the DISC theory, numerous workplace assessments and personality tests have been established to identify the right people for the right roles, improve communication within organizations, and facilitate greater self-awareness among employees. One of the most notable was developed by Merrick Rosenberg, the co-founder and CEO of Take Flight Learning, a company that runs corporate training programs.

Rosenberg linked the four personality types to birds in order to make them more visual and memorable. Eagles represent Dominance and are competitive, decisive, and good at solving problems. Parrots represent Inducement and are optimistic, sociable, and good at persuading people. Doves represent Submission and are patient, understanding, and good team players. Owls represent Compliance and are courteous, objective, and good at detailed work. Of course, as **alluded to** above, no one fits neatly into a single category. But many companies find this kind of assessment useful in improving their day-to-day efficiency and decision-making processes.

43. According to the passage, which of the following did William Moulton Marston NOT do?
    (A) He thought up the idea of a female comic book character.
    (B) He invented a test to tell if a person is being truthful.
    (C) He conducted a study into the behavior of prisoners.
    (D) He created a theory to explain the actions of regular folk.

44. What is the main topic of the third paragraph?
    (A) When Rosenberg's company was established.
    (B) How Marston's theory has been applied.
    (C) Why the DISC ideas are no longer suitable.
    (D) How training programs are typically designed.

45. Rachel is a positive and cheerful person who is happiest when organizing group events for her work colleagues. Based on Rosenberg's ideas, which bird does she most closely match?
    (A)
    (B)
    (C)
    (D)

46. What does "**alluded to**" most likely mean in the final paragraph?
    (A) Mentioned indirectly.
    (B) Selected carefully.
    (C) Televised widely.
    (D) Published recently.

137

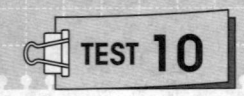

第貳部分、混合題（占 10 分）

說明：本部分共有 1 題組，每一子題配分標於題末。限在標示題號作答區內作答。選擇題使用 2B 鉛筆作答，更正時，應以橡皮擦擦拭，切勿使用修正液（帶）。非選擇題請由左而右橫式書寫。

第 47 至 50 題為題組

　　When we sleep, our bodies go through two distinct stages: non-REM (rapid eye movement) sleep and REM sleep. The former stage encompasses the period from falling asleep through light sleep and into deep sleep. As we transition from light to deep sleep, our heart rate and breathing rate slow down. This gives our body the opportunity to repair tissue, regenerate cells, and strengthen our immune system. Once we are in full deep sleep, we enter REM sleep. This is when our heart rate and breathing rate increase again and our eyes move rapidly. It is also the time when dreams occur and when our brain has the important opportunity to process our experiences and memories from the previous day.

　　During REM sleep, the brain sends signals to the body's muscles to shut down, making it impossible for the person to move. Interestingly, some people become aware of their surroundings before the REM cycle has finished, putting them in a state of sleep paralysis. Many sufferers report being unable to move anything except their eyes and feeling a great weight pressing down on their chests. They may also experience hallucinations or feel as if someone or something—usually evil—is in the room with them. Even though sleep paralysis is completely normal, it is rare. Most people experience it only once or twice in their lives, if ever. Fortunately, it usually lasts a few seconds to a few minutes at most.

　　There are remedies you can try to prevent sleep paralysis from happening. First, try to have a regular sleep pattern because adults need six to eight hours of rest a night in dark, quiet, and comfortable conditions. If possible, go to sleep at the same time each night and wake up at the same time each morning. Also, avoid going to sleep soon after strenuous exercise, smoking, drinking, or having a large meal. By following these rules, we can not only avoid sleep paralysis but also ensure we get the best quality sleep possible.

47-49. Using the information in the passage, fill in the blanks below. (填空，6分)

Sleep Stage	Body's Reaction	Benefits
Non-REM	Heart rate and breathing rate slow down.	Our body can 47._____.
REM	Heart rate and breathing rate increase and 48._____.	Our brain can 49._____.

50. Which of the following are true about sleep paralysis? (多選題，4分)
    (A) It occurs during the non-REM stage of sleep.
    (B) It is accompanied by the feeling of not being alone.
    (C) It typically happens once or twice every year.
    (D) It is characterized by a lack of eye movement.
    (E) It can be brought on by activity late at night.
    (F) It can only be cured by taking medication.

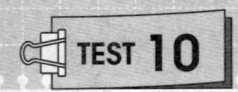

第參部分、非選擇題（占 28 分）

說明：本部分共有二大題，請依各題指示作答，答案必須寫在「答題卷」標示題號之作答區內，作答時不必抄題。

一、中譯英（占 8 分）

說明：1. 請將以下中文句子譯成正確、通順、達意的英文，並將答案寫在「答題卷」上。
2. 請依序作答，並標明子題號。每題 4 分，共 8 分。

1. 有些電玩遊戲的情節會使人焦慮，因而對青少年的心理健康產生負面影響。

2. 有些人認為應制定法律限制這類遊戲，但也有人認為不該將每個問題歸咎於遊戲本身。

二、英文作文（占 20 分）

說明：1. 依提示在「答題卷」上寫一篇英文作文。
2. 文長至少 120 個單詞（words）。

提示：請仔細觀察以下三幅連環圖片的內容，並想像第四幅圖片可能的發展，寫出一個涵蓋連環圖片內容並有完整結局的故事。

附錄 測驗用答案紙

常春藤 大學學測模擬試題　第❶回

（適用於 108 課綱）
英文考科
答題卷

應試號碼、條碼、姓名（不得污損、塗改或破壞）

☐　確認答題卷應試號碼正確無誤

確認後考生簽名

請用正楷簽名

※ 考試開始鈴響後，經確認確為本人之應試號碼與姓名後，於右方之方格內劃記，並於「確認後考生簽名」欄以正楷簽名。
※ 請詳閱試題本上作答注意事項與答題卷劃記及書寫注意事項。
※ 選擇題正確作答樣例：A̲　B̲　**C̲**　D̲

第壹部分、選擇題（占 62 分）

注意：考生如未能劃滿方格，或不依試題本之作答注意事項劃記致機器無法正確辨識答案時，恐將影響成績並損及權益。

第貳部分、混合題（占 10 分）

題號	作 答 區
	注意：1. 應依據題號順序，於作答區內作答。2. 除另有規定外，書寫時應由左至右橫式書寫。3. 作答須清晰，若未依規定而導致答案難以辨識或評閱時，恐將影響成績並損及權益。4. 不得於作答區書寫姓名、應試號碼或無關之文字、圖案符號等。
47	【請用黑色墨水的筆作答】 (A) _____ (B) _____
48	【請用黑色墨水的筆作答】
49	☐ Sandra　☐ Chris　☐ Both　☐ Neither　【請用黑色墨水的筆作答】
50	☐ Sandra　☐ Chris　☐ Both　☐ Neither　【請用黑色墨水的筆作答】

第參部分、非選擇題（占 28 分）

題號	作 答 區
	注意：1. 應依據題號順序，於作答區內作答。2. 除另有規定外，書寫時應由左至右橫式書寫。3. 作答須清晰，若未依規定而導致答案難以辨識或評閱時，恐將影響成績並損及權益。4. 不得於作答區書寫姓名、應試號碼或無關之文字、圖案符號等。

一、中譯英　【請用黑色墨水的筆作答】

1.

2.

題號	作　　答　　區
	注意：1. 應依據題號順序，於作答區內作答。2. 除另有規定外，書寫時應由左至右橫式書寫。3. 作答須清晰，若未依規定而導致答案難以辨識或評閱時，恐將影響成績並損及權益。4. 不得於作答區書寫姓名、應試號碼或無關之文字、圖案符號等。

二、英文作文　【請用黑色墨水的筆作答】

常春藤 大學學測模擬試題　第❷回

應試號碼、條碼、姓名（不得污損、塗改或破壞）

（適用於 108 課綱）
英文考科
答題卷

※ 考試開始鈴響後，經確認確為本人之應試號碼與姓名後，於右方之方格內劃記，並於「確認後考生簽名」欄以正楷簽名。

※ 請詳閱試題本上作答注意事項與答題卷劃記及書寫注意事項。

※ 選擇題正確作答樣例：A B C D

▭	確認答題卷應試號碼正確無誤
確認後 考生簽名	請用正楷簽名

第壹部分、選擇題（占 62 分）

注意：考生如未能劃滿方格，或不依試題本之作答注意事項劃記致機器無法正確辨識答案時，恐將影響成績並損及權益。

題號												
1	A	B	C	D	E	F	G	H	I	J	K	L
2	A	B	C	D	E	F	G	H	I	J	K	L
3	A	B	C	D	E	F	G	H	I	J	K	L
4	A	B	C	D	E	F	G	H	I	J	K	L
5	A	B	C	D	E	F	G	H	I	J	K	L
6	A	B	C	D	E	F	G	H	I	J	K	L
7	A	B	C	D	E	F	G	H	I	J	K	L
8	A	B	C	D	E	F	G	H	I	J	K	L
9	A	B	C	D	E	F	G	H	I	J	K	L
10	A	B	C	D	E	F	G	H	I	J	K	L
11	A	B	C	D	E	F	G	H	I	J	K	L
12	A	B	C	D	E	F	G	H	I	J	K	L
13	A	B	C	D	E	F	G	H	I	J	K	L
14	A	B	C	D	E	F	G	H	I	J	K	L
15	A	B	C	D	E	F	G	H	I	J	K	L
16	A	B	C	D	E	F	G	H	I	J	K	L
17	A	B	C	D	E	F	G	H	I	J	K	L
18	A	B	C	D	E	F	G	H	I	J	K	L
19	A	B	C	D	E	F	G	H	I	J	K	L
20	A	B	C	D	E	F	G	H	I	J	K	L
21	A	B	C	D	E	F	G	H	I	J	K	L
22	A	B	C	D	E	F	G	H	I	J	K	L
23	A	B	C	D	E	F	G	H	I	J	K	L
24	A	B	C	D	E	F	G	H	I	J	K	L
25	A	B	C	D	E	F	G	H	I	J	K	L
26	A	B	C	D	E	F	G	H	I	J	K	L
27	A	B	C	D	E	F	G	H	I	J	K	L
28	A	B	C	D	E	F	G	H	I	J	K	L
29	A	B	C	D	E	F	G	H	I	J	K	L
30	A	B	C	D	E	F	G	H	I	J	K	L
31	A	B	C	D	E	F	G	H	I	J	K	L
32	A	B	C	D	E	F	G	H	I	J	K	L
33	A	B	C	D	E	F	G	H	I	J	K	L
34	A	B	C	D	E	F	G	H	I	J	K	L
35	A	B	C	D	E	F	G	H	I	J	K	L
36	A	B	C	D	E	F	G	H	I	J	K	L
37	A	B	C	D	E	F	G	H	I	J	K	L
38	A	B	C	D	E	F	G	H	I	J	K	L
39	A	B	C	D	E	F	G	H	I	J	K	L
40	A	B	C	D	E	F	G	H	I	J	K	L
41	A	B	C	D	E	F	G	H	I	J	K	L
42	A	B	C	D	E	F	G	H	I	J	K	L
43	A	B	C	D	E	F	G	H	I	J	K	L
44	A	B	C	D	E	F	G	H	I	J	K	L
45	A	B	C	D	E	F	G	H	I	J	K	L
46	A	B	C	D	E	F	G	H	I	J	K	L

第貳部分、混合題（占 10 分）

題號	作答區
	注意：1. 應依據題號順序，於作答區內作答。2. 除另有規定外，書寫時應由左至右橫式書寫。3. 作答須清晰，若未依規定而導致答案難以辨識或評閱時，恐將影響成績並損及權益。4. 不得於作答區書寫姓名、應試號碼或無關之文字、圖案符號等。
47	A B C D E F G H 　　　　　　　【請用 2B 鉛筆作答】
48	【請用黑色墨水的筆作答】
49	【請用黑色墨水的筆作答】
50	【請用黑色墨水的筆作答】

第參部分、非選擇題（占 28 分）

題號	作答區
	注意：1. 應依據題號順序，於作答區內作答。2. 除另有規定外，書寫時應由左至右橫式書寫。3. 作答須清晰，若未依規定而導致答案難以辨識或評閱時，恐將影響成績並損及權益。4. 不得於作答區書寫姓名、應試號碼或無關之文字、圖案符號等。

一、中譯英　【請用黑色墨水的筆作答】

1.

2.

作 答 區

題號 注意：1. 應依據題號順序，於作答區內作答。2. 除另有規定外，書寫時應由左至右橫式書寫。3. 作答須清晰，若未依規定而導致答案難以辨識或評閱時，恐將影響成績並及損及權益。4. 不得於作答區書寫姓名、應試號碼或無關之文字、圖案符號等。

二、英文作文 【請用黑色墨水的筆作答】

常春藤 大學學測模擬試題　第❸回

（適用於108課綱）
英文考科
答題卷

第壹部分、選擇題（占62分）

第貳部分、混合題（占 10 分）

題號	作答區
	注意：1. 應依據題號順序，於作答區內作答。2. 除另有規定外，書寫時應由左至右橫式書寫。3. 作答須清晰，若未依規定而導致答案難以辨識或評閱時，恐將影響成績並損及權益。4. 不得於作答區書寫姓名、應試號碼或無關之文字、圖案符號等。
47	【請用黑色墨水的筆作答】
48	【請用黑色墨水的筆作答】
49	【請用黑色墨水的筆作答】
50	A B C D E F　　【請用 2B 鉛筆作答】

第參部分、非選擇題（占 28 分）

題號	作答區
	注意：1. 應依據題號順序，於作答區內作答。2. 除另有規定外，書寫時應由左至右橫式書寫。3. 作答須清晰，若未依規定而導致答案難以辨識或評閱時，恐將影響成績並損及權益。4. 不得於作答區書寫姓名、應試號碼或無關之文字、圖案符號等。

一、中譯英　【請用黑色墨水的筆作答】

1.

2.

二、英文作文 【請用黑色墨水的筆作答】

常春藤 大學學測模擬試題　第❹回

（適用於 108 課綱）
英文考科
答題卷

應試號碼、條碼、姓名（不得污損、塗改或破壞）

※ 考試開始鈴響後，經確認確為本人之應試號碼與姓名後，於右方之方格內劃記，並於「確認後考生簽名」欄以正楷簽名。
※ 請詳閱試題本上作答注意事項與答題卷劃記及書寫注意事項。
※ 選擇題正確作答樣例： A　B　**C**　D

確認後考生簽名　｜　確認答題卷應試號碼正確無誤

請用正楷簽名

第壹部分、選擇題（占 62 分）

注意：考生如未能劃滿方格，或不依試題本之作答注意事項劃記致機器無法正確辨識答案時，恐將影響成績並損及權益。

第貳部分、混合題（占 10 分）

題號	作答區
	注意：1. 應依據題號順序，於作答區內作答。2. 除另有規定外，書寫時應由左至右橫式書寫。3. 作答須清晰，若未依規定而導致答案難以辨識或評閱時，恐將影響成績並損及權益。4. 不得於作答區書寫姓名、應試號碼或無關之文字、圖案符號等。
47	【請用黑色墨水的筆作答】
48	Ⓐ Ⓑ Ⓒ Ⓓ　【請用 2B 鉛筆作答】
49	Ⓐ Ⓑ Ⓒ Ⓓ　【請用 2B 鉛筆作答】
50	Ⓐ Ⓑ Ⓒ Ⓓ　【請用 2B 鉛筆作答】

第參部分、非選擇題（占 28 分）

題號	作答區
	注意：1. 應依據題號順序，於作答區內作答。2. 除另有規定外，書寫時應由左至右橫式書寫。3. 作答須清晰，若未依規定而導致答案難以辨識或評閱時，恐將影響成績並損及權益。4. 不得於作答區書寫姓名、應試號碼或無關之文字、圖案符號等。

一、中譯英　【請用黑色墨水的筆作答】

1.

2.

二、英文作文 【請用黑色墨水的筆作答】

常春藤 大學學測模擬試題　第❺回

（適用於108課綱）
英文考科
答題卷

應試號碼、條碼、姓名（不得污損、塗改或破壞）

※ 考試開始鈴響後，經確認確為本人之應試號碼與姓名後，於右方之方格內劃記，並於「確認後考生簽名」欄以正楷簽名。
※ 請詳閱試題本上作答注意事項與答題卷劃記及書寫注意事項。
※ 選擇題正確作答樣例：A̲　B̲　**C**　D̲

☐　確認答題卷應試號碼正確無誤

確認後考生簽名

請用正楷簽名

第壹部分、選擇題（占62分）

注意：考生如未能劃滿方格，或不依試題本之作答注意事項劃記致機器無法正確辨識答案時，恐將影響成績並損及權益。

第貳部分、混合題（占 10 分）

題號	作答區
	注意：1. 應依據題號順序，於作答區內作答。2. 除另有規定外，書寫時應由左至右橫式書寫。3. 作答須清晰，若未依規定而導致答案難以辨識或評閱時，恐將影響成績並損及權益。4. 不得於作答區書寫姓名、應試號碼或無關之文字、圖案符號等。
47	【請用黑色墨水的筆作答】
48	【請用黑色墨水的筆作答】
49	【請用黑色墨水的筆作答】
50	【請用黑色墨水的筆作答】
51	A B C D　　　　　　　　　　　　　　　　　　　　　【請用 2B 鉛筆作答】

第參部分、非選擇題（占 28 分）

題號	作答區
	注意：1. 應依據題號順序，於作答區內作答。2. 除另有規定外，書寫時應由左至右橫式書寫。3. 作答須清晰，若未依規定而導致答案難以辨識或評閱時，恐將影響成績並損及權益。4. 不得於作答區書寫姓名、應試號碼或無關之文字、圖案符號等。

一、中譯英　【請用黑色墨水的筆作答】

1.

2.

題號 作 答 區

注意：1. 應依據題號順序，於作答區內作答。2. 除另有規定外，書寫時應由左至右橫式書寫。3. 作答須清晰，若未依規定而導致答案難以辨識或評閱時，恐將影響成績並損及權益。4. 不得於作答區書寫姓名、應試號碼或無關之文字、圖案符號等。

二、英文作文　【請用黑色墨水的筆作答】

常春藤 大學學測模擬試題　第 ❻ 回

（適用於 108 課綱）
英文考科
答題卷

應試號碼、條碼、姓名（不得污損、塗改或破壞）

※ 考試開始鈴響後，經確認確為本人之應試號碼與姓名後，於右方之方格內劃記，並於「確認後考生簽名」欄以正楷簽名。
※ 請詳閱試題本上作答注意事項與答題卷劃記及書寫注意事項。
※ 選擇題正確作答樣例：A̲ B̲ **C** D̲

□　確認答題卷應試號碼正確無誤

確認後考生簽名

請用正楷簽名

第壹部分、選擇題（占 62 分）

注意：考生如未能劃滿方格，或不依試題本之作答注意事項劃記致機器無法正確辨識答案時，恐將影響成績並損及權益。

第貳部分、混合題（占 10 分）

題號	作答區
	注意：1. 應依據題號順序，於作答區內作答。2. 除另有規定外，書寫時應由左至右橫式書寫。3. 作答須清晰，若未依規定而導致答案難以辨識或評閱時，恐將影響成績並損及權益。4. 不得於作答區書寫姓名、應試號碼或無關之文字、圖案符號等。
47	【請用黑色墨水的筆作答】
48	【請用黑色墨水的筆作答】
49	【請用黑色墨水的筆作答】
50	【請用黑色墨水的筆作答】
51	【請用黑色墨水的筆作答】

第參部分、非選擇題（占 28 分）

題號	作答區
	注意：1. 應依據題號順序，於作答區內作答。2. 除另有規定外，書寫時應由左至右橫式書寫。3. 作答須清晰，若未依規定而導致答案難以辨識或評閱時，恐將影響成績並損及權益。4. 不得於作答區書寫姓名、應試號碼或無關之文字、圖案符號等。

一、中譯英　【請用黑色墨水的筆作答】

1.

2.

二、英文作文 【請用黑色墨水的筆作答】

常春藤 大學學測模擬試題　第❼回

（適用於 108 課綱）
**英文考科
答題卷**

第壹部分、選擇題（占 62 分）

第貳部分、混合題（占 10 分）

題號	作答區
	注意：1. 應依據題號順序，於作答區內作答。2. 除另有規定外，書寫時應由左至右橫式書寫。3. 作答須清晰，若未依規定而導致答案難以辨識或評閱時，恐將影響成績並損及權益。4. 不得於作答區書寫姓名、應試號碼或無關之文字、圖案符號等。
47	【請用黑色墨水的筆作答】
48	【請用黑色墨水的筆作答】
49	【請用黑色墨水的筆作答】
50	【請用黑色墨水的筆作答】
51	A B C D　　　　　　　　　　　　　　　　【請用 2B 鉛筆作答】

第參部分、非選擇題（占 28 分）

題號	作答區
	注意：1. 應依據題號順序，於作答區內作答。2. 除另有規定外，書寫時應由左至右橫式書寫。3. 作答須清晰，若未依規定而導致答案難以辨識或評閱時，恐將影響成績並損及權益。4. 不得於作答區書寫姓名、應試號碼或無關之文字、圖案符號等。

一、中譯英　【請用黑色墨水的筆作答】

1.

2.

二、英文作文 【請用黑色墨水的筆作答】

常春藤 大學學測模擬試題　第 8 回

應試號碼、條碼、姓名（不得污損、塗改或破壞）

（適用於 108 課綱）
英文考科
答題卷

※ 考試開始鈴響後，經確認確為本人之應試號碼與姓名後，於右方之方格內劃記，並於「確認後考生簽名」欄以正楷簽名。

※ 請詳閱試題本上作答注意事項與答題卷劃記及書寫注意事項。

※ 選擇題正確作答樣例：A　B　C　D

□ 確認答題卷應試號碼正確無誤	
確認後考生簽名	請用正楷簽名

第壹部分、選擇題（占 62 分）

注意：考生如未能劃滿方格，或不依試題本之作答注意事項劃記致機器無法正確辨識答案時，恐將影響成績並損及權益。

題號												
1	A	B	C	D	E	F	G	H	I	J	K	L
2	A	B	C	D	E	F	G	H	I	J	K	L
3	A	B	C	D	E	F	G	H	I	J	K	L
4	A	B	C	D	E	F	G	H	I	J	K	L
5	A	B	C	D	E	F	G	H	I	J	K	L
6	A	B	C	D	E	F	G	H	I	J	K	L
7	A	B	C	D	E	F	G	H	I	J	K	L
8	A	B	C	D	E	F	G	H	I	J	K	L
9	A	B	C	D	E	F	G	H	I	J	K	L
10	A	B	C	D	E	F	G	H	I	J	K	L
11	A	B	C	D	E	F	G	H	I	J	K	L
12	A	B	C	D	E	F	G	H	I	J	K	L
13	A	B	C	D	E	F	G	H	I	J	K	L
14	A	B	C	D	E	F	G	H	I	J	K	L
15	A	B	C	D	E	F	G	H	I	J	K	L
16	A	B	C	D	E	F	G	H	I	J	K	L
17	A	B	C	D	E	F	G	H	I	J	K	L
18	A	B	C	D	E	F	G	H	I	J	K	L
19	A	B	C	D	E	F	G	H	I	J	K	L
20	A	B	C	D	E	F	G	H	I	J	K	L
21	A	B	C	D	E	F	G	H	I	J	K	L
22	A	B	C	D	E	F	G	H	I	J	K	L
23	A	B	C	D	E	F	G	H	I	J	K	L
24	A	B	C	D	E	F	G	H	I	J	K	L
25	A	B	C	D	E	F	G	H	I	J	K	L
26	A	B	C	D	E	F	G	H	I	J	K	L
27	A	B	C	D	E	F	G	H	I	J	K	L
28	A	B	C	D	E	F	G	H	I	J	K	L
29	A	B	C	D	E	F	G	H	I	J	K	L
30	A	B	C	D	E	F	G	H	I	J	K	L
31	A	B	C	D	E	F	G	H	I	J	K	L
32	A	B	C	D	E	F	G	H	I	J	K	L
33	A	B	C	D	E	F	G	H	I	J	K	L
34	A	B	C	D	E	F	G	H	I	J	K	L
35	A	B	C	D	E	F	G	H	I	J	K	L
36	A	B	C	D	E	F	G	H	I	J	K	L
37	A	B	C	D	E	F	G	H	I	J	K	L
38	A	B	C	D	E	F	G	H	I	J	K	L
39	A	B	C	D	E	F	G	H	I	J	K	L
40	A	B	C	D	E	F	G	H	I	J	K	L
41	A	B	C	D	E	F	G	H	I	J	K	L
42	A	B	C	D	E	F	G	H	I	J	K	L
43	A	B	C	D	E	F	G	H	I	J	K	L
44	A	B	C	D	E	F	G	H	I	J	K	L
45	A	B	C	D	E	F	G	H	I	J	K	L
46	A	B	C	D	E	F	G	H	I	J	K	L

第貳部分、混合題（占 10 分）

題號	作 答 區
	注意：1. 應依據題號順序，於作答區內作答。2. 除另有規定外，書寫時應由左至右橫式書寫。3. 作答須清晰，若未依規定而導致答案難以辨識或評閱時，恐將影響成績並損及權益。4. 不得於作答區書寫姓名、應試號碼或無關之文字、圖案符號等。
47	【請用黑色墨水的筆作答】
48	【請用黑色墨水的筆作答】
49	A B C D E F　　　　　　　　　　　　　　　　　　　　　　　　【請用 2B 鉛筆作答】
50	A B C D　　　　　　　　　　　　　　　　　　　　　　　　　　【請用 2B 鉛筆作答】

第參部分、非選擇題（占 28 分）

題號	作 答 區
	注意：1. 應依據題號順序，於作答區內作答。2. 除另有規定外，書寫時應由左至右橫式書寫。3. 作答須清晰，若未依規定而導致答案難以辨識或評閱時，恐將影響成績並損及權益。4. 不得於作答區書寫姓名、應試號碼或無關之文字、圖案符號等。

一、中譯英　【請用黑色墨水的筆作答】

1.

2.

二、英文作文 【請用黑色墨水的筆作答】

常春藤 大學學測模擬試題　第 ❾ 回

（適用於 108 課綱）
英文考科
答題卷

第壹部分、選擇題（占 62 分）

第貳部分、混合題（占 10 分）

題號	作答區
	注意：1. 應依據題號順序，於作答區內作答。2. 除另有規定外，書寫時應由左至右橫式書寫。3. 作答須清晰，若未依規定而導致答案難以辨識或評閱時，恐將影響成績並損及權益。4. 不得於作答區書寫姓名、應試號碼或無關之文字、圖案符號等。
47	【請用黑色墨水的筆作答】
48	【請用黑色墨水的筆作答】
49	【請用黑色墨水的筆作答】
50	A B C D　　　　　　　　　　　　　　　　　　【請用 2B 鉛筆作答】
51	【請用黑色墨水的筆作答】

第參部分、非選擇題（占 28 分）

題號	作答區
	注意：1. 應依據題號順序，於作答區內作答。2. 除另有規定外，書寫時應由左至右橫式書寫。3. 作答須清晰，若未依規定而導致答案難以辨識或評閱時，恐將影響成績並損及權益。4. 不得於作答區書寫姓名、應試號碼或無關之文字、圖案符號等。

一、中譯英　【請用黑色墨水的筆作答】

1.

2.

二、英文作文　【請用黑色墨水的筆作答】

常春藤 大學學測模擬試題　第❿回

（適用於108課綱）
英文考科
答題卷

第壹部分、選擇題（占62分）

第貳部分、混合題（占 10 分）

題號	作答區
47	【請用黑色墨水的筆作答】
48	【請用黑色墨水的筆作答】
49	【請用黑色墨水的筆作答】
50	A B C D E F 【請用 2B 鉛筆作答】

第參部分、非選擇題（占 28 分）

注意：1. 應依據題號順序，於作答區內作答。2. 除另有規定外，書寫時應由左至右橫式書寫。3. 作答須清晰，若未依規定而導致答案難以辨識或評閱時，恐將影響成績並損及權益。4. 不得於作答區書寫姓名、應試號碼或無關之文字、圖案符號等。

一、中譯英　【請用黑色墨水的筆作答】

1.

2.

二、英文作文 【請用黑色墨水的筆作答】

NOTE

常春藤 108 課綱核心素養．升大學系列【A108-1】
新制學測英文 10 回決勝模擬試題（試題＋詳解）
－試題本

總 編 審	賴世雄
終 審	梁民康
執行編輯	許嘉華
編輯小組	畢安安・Nick Roden・Brian Foden
設計組長	王玥琦
封面設計	林桂旭
排版設計	林桂旭・王穎緁
法律顧問	北辰著作權事務所蕭雄淋律師
出 版 者	常春藤數位出版股份有限公司
地 址	臺北市忠孝西路一段 33 號 5 樓
電 話	(02) 2331-7600
傳 真	(02) 2381-0918
網 址	www.ivy.com.tw
電子信箱	service@ivy.com.tw
郵政劃撥	50463568
戶 名	常春藤數位出版股份有限公司
定 價	420 元（2 書）

©常春藤數位出版股份有限公司 (2025) All rights reserved.　　Y000041-3577
本書之封面、內文、編排等之著作財產權歸常春藤數位出版股份有限公司所有。未經本公司書面同意，請勿翻印、轉載或為一切著作權法上利用行為，否則依法追究。

如有缺頁、裝訂錯誤或破損，請寄回本公司更換。　　【版權所有　翻印必究】